MODERN RETAILING

Management Principles and Practices

Third Edition

Melvin Morgenstein
*Emeritus, Teachers College, Columbia University
and Nassau Community College*

Harriet Strongin
Nassau Community College

REGENTS/PRENTICE HALL, Englewood Cliffs, New Jersey 07632

Library of Congress Cataloging-in-Publication Data

Morgenstein, Melvin.
    Modern retailing : management principles and practices / Melvin
Morgenstein. Harriet Strongin. —3rd ed.
        p.   cm.
    Includes index.
    ISBN 0-13-588120-X
    1. Retail trade.   I. Strongin, Harriet.   II. Title.
HF5429.M598   1992
658.8'7—dc20   91-32007
                                                   CIP

Editorial/production supervision and
   interior design: **Janet M. DiBlasi**
Cover design: **Patricia Kelly**
Manufacturing buyer: **Ed O'Dougherty**
Prepress buyer: **Ilene Levy**
Acquisition editor: **Maureen Hull**
Marketing manager: **Robert Kern**
Cover photo: **SuperStock**

© 1992 by REGENTS/PRENTICE HALL
A Simon & Schuster Company
Englewood Cliffs, New Jersey 07632

Printed in the United States of America
10 9 8 7 6 5 4 3 2 1   JUN 1 0 1994

ISBN   0-13-588120-X

Prentice-Hall International (UK) Limited, *London*
Prentice-Hall of Australia Pty. Limited, *Sydney*
Prentice-Hall Canada, Inc., *Toronto*
Prentice-Hall Hispanoamericana, S.A., *Mexico*
Prentice-Hall of India Private Limited, *New Delhi*
Prentice-Hall of Japan, Inc., *Tokyo*
Simon & Schuster Asia Pte. Ltd., *Singapore*
Editora Prentice-Hall do Brasil, Ltda., *Rio de Janeiro*

CONTENTS

3 Merchandising

4   Promotion: Communicating with the Customer

5   Controls

Chapter 18   Credit   578

6 Making Decisions

Chapter 19   Research for Retailers   608

Chapter 20   Entrepreneurship and Franchising   641

PREFACE

The hectic pace of acquisitions and mergers during the past few years has added an additional dimension to the dynamics of retailing. Even vendors and merchants are confused at times by the frequent changes in retail ownership. In writing this third edition, therefore, the authors have been mindful of the difficulty of maintaining currency in the identification of retail owners. Nevertheless, we have done our best to update the facts.

Changes in retailing are not restricted to ownership, of course. As we wrote in the preface to the second edition of this text, "With innovations ranging from new types of retail outlets to state-of-the-art technology, we continue to witness remarkable movement in the field of retailing." If anything, the pace of change has quickened as new forms of retailing are developed and technology is designed to meet enhanced consumer demand. Our goal is to introduce the student to a fascinating business area, retailing, and to make that area as "real" as a textbook can. We do this by describing actual retail practices within the context of a management approach.

Keeping current with the ever-changing and very progressive field of retailing, this comprehensive, introductory book is written for students who intend to specialize in retailing as well as those who want to understand and appreciate the dynamics of one of today's most exciting industries. Stressing the uses and significance of computers in retailing, the book is divided into these major areas:

Overview
Retailing Structure
Merchandising
Promotion—Communicating with the Customer
Controls
Making Decisions

In addition to the in-depth, easy-to-read subject matter, each chapter contains the following features:

- A set of learning objectives
- A list of new terms
- Highlights that summarize the chapter
- An illustration of successful retail strategy
- Review and discussion questions
- Cases that test an understanding of retail principles
- References

Each Part starts with an identification of the material in that Part. The book also contains a complete Glossary, with each term identified by the chapter in which it is defined. Appropriate appendixes supplement the material.

New features in this edition include:

- Interviews with successful retail practitioners
- New terms listed at the end of each chapter.
- Striking changes in the retail catalog business
- Expansion of the section on American retailers in foreign countries
- Wal-Mart's challenge to Sears Roebuck and K mart as the nation's foremost retailer
- Popularity of hypermarkets, warehouse clubs, and off-price retailing
- Updated demographics for the 1990s
- Acquisitions, mergers, and leveraged buyouts
- Increasing importance of specialty retailing
- Fresh examination of store location
- Trends in shopping center construction
- Emphasis on customer services
- Opening of Eastern European markets
- Description and implications of the Quick Response system
- Civil recovery laws
- Importance of cash flow
- Proliferation of credit cards
- Outlook for franchising

As with the second edition, the comprehensiveness of this volume enables the instructor to adapt it to the students' needs. For institutions requiring full treatment of retailing principles, the material is of sufficient depth for that purpose. For those with other objectives, the chapters are arranged for a flexible selection to meet specific course requirements.

An Instructor's Manual containing the following items is provided to adopters:

Section I—For each chapter,

- A brief overview that presents the main points of the subject matter
- An outline for use in lesson planning and classroom coverage
- Teaching suggestions to enrich classroom activities
- Answers to the end-of-chapter review and discussion questions
- Answers to the end-of-chapter cases
- A field project that may be assigned for application of retail theory
- Suggestions to students for carrying out the end-of-chapter projects

Section II—For each chapter, a comprehensive test bank consisting of

- True-false questions
- Multiple-choice questions
- Matching questions
- Essay questions

Section III

- Figures and illustrations from the textbook for easy conversion into transparencies. Their inclusion is designed to augment classroom lectures and discussions.

Section IV

- Mini-Internships that enable students to experience the excitement and problems faced by retail executives. One Internship deals with the responsibilities of a Branch Store Manager and other department store executives; the other involves the myriad facets of sales promotion in a department store.

Section V

- Solutions to the Mini-Internships

Acknowledgments

A note of thanks is due the following people who reviewed the first edition: Dr. Jerry Boles, Western Kentucky University; Dr. Jack Crespin, Bergen Community College; Professor Albert T. Fragala, Warrant County Junior College District; Professor Myron Gable, Shippensburg State College; Professor John W. Lloyd, Monroe Community College; Professor Robert L. Walker, Thomas Nelson Community College; Ms. Pam Phillips, Retailing and Marketing Consultant.

We are also grateful to the following for their reviews of the second edition: Dr. William F. Ashford, Marshall University, Huntington, West Virginia; Dr. Jerry Boles, Western Kentucky University, Bowling Green, Kentucky; Dr. Louis Cohen, Laines, Inc., Troy, New York; Ms. Ann Keenes, Neiman-Marcus, Dallas, Texas; Professor Jacqueline Z. Nicholson, Eckerd College, St. Petersburg, Florida; Professor Therese M. Riordan, St. John Fisher College, Rochester, New York; Professor Duane Schecter, Muskegon Community College, Muskegon, Michigan; Dr. Brenda Witter, Michigan State University, East Lansing, Michigan.

And, of course, we thank the following for their reviews of this third edition: Ardyce S. Lightner, D'Youville College; Cynthia Baker, Berkeley College of Business; Julius Kantor, Bauder College; Nancy Bailey, Middlesex County College; and Kathleen Conway.

We thank the following faculty members at Nassau Community College for their helpful comments and suggestions with the Instructor's Manual and Retail Projects Manual: Marguerite Ehlen; Patricia O'Beirne; Angela Bruno; Tanya Lowenstein; and Eleanor Smiley.

A thank-you, too, to the following companies that contributed material to the third edition: A&P Food Stores; Abraham & Straus; Albertson's Inc.; Best Products, Inc.; Certified Fashion Guild; David Hocker & Associates, Inc.; Edison Brothers Stores, Inc.; Giant Food, Inc.; Grand Union Company; Great Northern Video Wall; Hampton Inn; Henry Doneger Associates, Inc; IBM Corporation; J.C. Penney; Judith Ann Creations; Julius Blumberg, Inc.; Lowe's Companies, Inc.; Marks & Spencer; Metrologic Instrument, Inc.; Montgomery Ward; Neiman Marcus; Photographic Sciences Corp.; Sears, Roebuck & Co.; Sensormatic Electronics Corp.; Southland Corp.; Strawbridge and Clothier; Telisman Sales; The Dallas Apparel Mart; The Limited, Inc.; Thrifty Rent-A-Car; Walgreens.

The following people gave their time graciously in the development of this third edition: Carolina Amato, Carolina Amato & Co.; Terry Chlan, Sears, Roebuck & Co.; Judith Ann Eigen, Judith Ann Creations; Joan Gosnell, Historian Archivist, J.C. Penney; Henry Hintermeister, Coastal Management; Linda Johannsen, Sensormatic Electronics Corp.; Neal Kaplan Esq., Kabro Associates; Gil Kunikopf, Certified Fashion Guild; Akira Maki, Akira; Gae Marino, Henry Doneger Associates, Inc.; Frank Nieves, Abraham & Straus; James O'Beirne, Abraham & Straus; Laurie Paguette, David Hocker & Associates, Inc.; Judy Smith, Edison Brothers Stores, Inc.; Rita Steffie, Abraham & Straus; Shirley Telisman, Telisman Sales; Charles H. Thorne, Montgomery Ward; Gilda Tosca, Strawbridge & Clothier; William J. Vitulli, A&P Food Stores; and Robin Wilson Wells, Dallas Apparel Market.

A special thanks to Maureen Hull, acquisition editor and Janet DiBlasi, production editor, for their professional assistance in preparing this edition.

As with our first and second editions, we hope that those who read this book will benefit from it as professionals and consumers.

Melvin Morgenstein
Harriet Strongin

Part 1

Overview

Retailing touches the lives of many people—consumers, workers, entrepreneurs. The myriad activities in which we engage bring us into almost daily contact with a variety of retail functions: shopping, buying, selling, returning, or paying for goods; working in a retail store; checking the latest fashions; dealing with door-to-door vendors; using a department store's catalog; and so on.

This book consists of six parts. In Chapter 1 of Part One we view the development and growth of American retailing. We also see how retail outlets emerged to meet the demands of a changing society. Next we study the status of international retailing. Finally we learn about the economic importance of retailing and the diverse career opportunities it generates.

After the introduction of the wheel of retailing concept, Chapter 2 deals with some major factors that influence retailing: computers, fashion, and consumerism. We see how each of these maintains retailing as a dynamic force in our economic and social lives.

Chapter 3 analyzes several aspects of consumer behavior. We look at consumer behavior in terms of buying motives based on emotion, rational thinking, biogenic and psychogenic factors, and patronage appeal. Next we examine consumer behavior with regard to how consumers satisfy their needs. We then see how consumer learning takes place, and identify the concepts that are used to understand personality. After studying the steps in the buying process, we analyze demographics and lifestyles and identify their implications for retailers.

Chapter 1

The Development and Growth of Retailing

After completing this chapter, you should be able to:

- Identify the differences among manufacturing, wholesaling, and retailing.
- Recount the history of American retailing.
- Discuss the status of international retailing.
- Discuss the economic importance of retailing.
- Identify career opportunities in retailing.

This book is about people who buy goods and services. It concerns students who purchase books and supplies; homemakers who buy food and other household items; workers who pay to get to and from their jobs; and sports fans who purchase tickets to games.

This book is also about the businesses that sell goods and services to people. It deals with large companies like Sears, Roebuck and F. W. Woolworth, and with small neighborhood stores like your local grocer and jewelry shop; with supermarkets like Kroger, A&P, and Safeway; and with businesses that sell services, such as health clubs and auto body shops.

In one way or another we all play a part in this business of goods and services, the business called retailing. It provides some people's livelihood, while others depend on it for the things they need. Let's take a closer look at the retailing field.

THE NATURE OF RETAILING

Definition of retailing

Retailing consists of the selling of goods and services to their ultimate consumers, that is, individuals who buy something for personal or household use. Someone who purchases a toaster or chair for use in the home, for example, is an ultimate consumer; so are you when you buy a compact disc.

Three main types of businesses are usually involved in getting goods and services to consumers: *manufacturers, wholesalers,* and *retailers*. **Manufacturers,** such as General Motors and Guess, make the products that people buy. **Wholesalers,** or **middlemen,** purchase and distribute manufactured products to retailers. **Retailers** sell goods and services directly to the ultimate consumer.

How goods and services reach the consumer

The path that a product takes to reach the consumer is called a **channel of distribution.** Figure 1-1 indicates that manufacturers may sell directly to consumers. The Avon Products Company, which sells cosmetic products from door to door, is an example of this type of manufacturer. So is Electrolux, a company that manufactures vacuum cleaners. Companies like the Thom McAn Shoe Company manufacture goods and sell them directly to consumers in their own retail stores.

Manufacturers often sell their goods to retail operations like R. H. Macy & Company and J. C. Penney Company. The retailer then sells the product to the consumer. Manufacturers often sell their goods to wholesalers in large quantities. The wholesalers, in turn, sell the goods to retailers in smaller quantities. For example, General Electric sells one of its products, light bulbs, to various wholesalers. The wholesalers then sell the bulbs to a variety of retailers, such as hardware stores and supermarkets, for final sale to consumers. In some cases, there may be more than one wholesaler in a channel of distribution.

Although the role of wholesaling in the merchandise distribution cycle is still

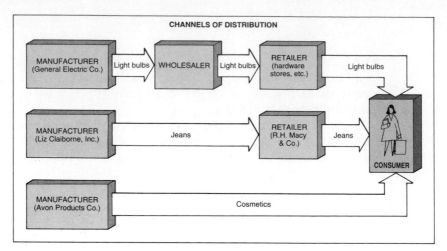

Figure 1-1 Channels of distribution.

significant, there are indications that manufacturers and retailers are developing relationships that diminish the role of wholesalers. For example, the increasing versatility of computers as well as the nature of the product enables many retailers to purchase goods without wholesaler involvement.

THE DEVELOPMENT OF AMERICAN RETAILING

To appreciate the present state of retailing, it is helpful to know how it evolved. In the following pages we will show how modern retailing institutions emerged from early American practices.

Trading Posts

One of the earliest forms of retailing in this country was the **trading post,** where **bartering** (trading goods for goods) was the accepted mode of exchange. At the post such items as trinkets and knives were sold to Indians in exchange for hides and furs. Farmers visiting the post traded farm products for European manufactured goods. To this day trading posts can be found in the southwestern United States. Today, of course, cash, rather than barter, is the usual method of exchange at these posts.

Itinerant Peddlers

In less settled areas, itinerant **peddlers,** on foot or with horse and wagon, carried a variety of merchandise. They sold knives, pans, scissors, sewing needles, tea, and coffee. Some specialized in particular types of merchandise, such as housewares or spices, or even carried a line of bulkier items, including sewing machines and furniture.

Much of a peddler's trade was conducted through barter because customers frequently had no other means of exchange. As a result, the peddler returned home laden with farm products and handmade furniture for sale to merchants.

In this country, as in Europe, peddlers were a mixed blessing to their customers, for while they satisfied the customers' material needs, they were not always honest. Because the settlers hungered for material items and were unsophisticated about retail practices, they were frequently overcharged. It was not uncommon, for example, for peddlers to make profits in excess of 100 percent.

Peddlers served a positive social function by bringing much-welcomed news to people living on the frontiers. They were also one of the few links between frontier families and suppliers seeking outlets for their products. The founders of two well-known department stores, Morris Rich (Rich's) and Joseph Goldwater (Goldwater's), began their careers as peddlers.

General Stores

The emergence of the general store

The first authentically American retailing institution was the **general store**. In it the storekeeper maintained a limited but varied stock of merchandise ranging from foodstuffs to manufactured goods. Catering to both townspeople and rural customers, the general store sold for credit as well as for cash and functioned as a social gathering place.

The merchant was largely ignorant of the changes that were taking place in the development and manufacture of merchandise. Relying on information from traveling salespeople, storekeepers learned little beyond what the salespeople themselves knew or cared to tell them. Consequently, their customers also had little knowledge about the merchandise.

One of the reasons that general stores succeeded was the lack of competition. Restricted as they were by the difficulty of transportation, people relied heavily on the general store for basic as well as luxury goods. Without any competition beyond that provided by peddlers, the store could charge whatever prices it liked.

The helter-skelter arrangement of merchandise in general stores made for inefficiency and waste. By paying little attention to store organization, storekeepers were unknowingly slowing their own progress and stimulating others to develop more efficient forms of retailing.

Mail Order Retailing

Mail order retailing encroaches on the general store

Another factor that made general stores vulnerable to more sophisticated retailing methods was the advent of the railroad. Freed from the hazards, slowness, and unreliability of wagon-drawn transportation, a new type of retail institution, the **mail order house,** entered the retailing scene. Pioneered by Aaron Montgomery Ward in 1872 mainly as a means of selling to farmers, buying by mail

An early itinerant peddler selling goods to frontier customers. Bettman Archive.

started modestly with merchandise featured in a one-page catalog. The idea caught on quickly as customers found that they could rely on Ward for honesty and low prices. In 1886 Richard W. Sears started a mail order business that sold watches, and was immediately successful. In 1887 he hired Alvah Curtis Roebuck to service and repair watches, and the association of these two men resulted in the establishment of Sears, Roebuck and Company in 1893. At that time the firm's catalog contained almost 200 pages; by 1895 it contained more than 500. Despite Richard Sears's occasional hucksterism, by 1900 the company had surpassed Montgomery Ward as the nation's leading mail order house. Interestingly, both firms' catalog divisions fared poorly during the mid- to-late 1980s. So much so, in fact, that Montgomery Ward dropped its catalog business in 1985, while Sears, Roebuck was considering selling or terminating its catalog operation in the early 1990s.

Both Montgomery Ward and Sears profited tremendously, as did other mail order houses, from the start of rural free delivery at the end of the nineteenth century and the introduction of parcel post mailing just prior to World War I. By this time mail order catalogs routinely ran to hundreds of pages and displayed a wide variety of merchandise.

The original concept of a wide, varied catalog offering has been augmented by mail order companies that specialize in certain types of merchandise, such as outdoor sporting wear (e.g., L. L. Bean of Maine), retail stores that sell by mail

In the early 1920s, individual J. C. Penney stores would distribute small catalogs called *Pictorial Particulars*. These flyers were then called *The Store News*. The page shown (1926) is an example. *Courtesy:* J. C. Penney Co., Inc.

(e.g., Neiman Marcus), and manufacturing concerns that mail goods directly to customers (e.g., Roots of Toronto, Canada, which makes and sells shoes).

Speciality (Limited-Line) Stores

The specialty store carries a particular type of merchandise

Along with the development of the general store and the mail order house came the **specialty** or **limited-line store.** As the industrial revolution of the 1800s gathered momentum, the variety of goods manufactured for retail sale increased enormously. The general store, with its limited outlook, stocked only a small amount of the available merchandise. The mail order house, successful though it was, could not satisfy consumers who wanted immediate contact with and delivery of new products. Since the specialty store carried a particular line of merchandise, such as hardware, shoes, or food, it stocked that product fully. It also offered a greater variety of items within the same line. And unlike the owners of general stores, who knew little about the goods they carried, the owners of specialty stores had a thorough knowledge of a limited line of products.

The J. C. Penney Company started as a specialty store in Kemmerer, Wyoming, in 1902. Known as the Golden Rule to symbolize James Cash Penney's belief that an ethical yardstick should apply in business as well as personal life, the store carried apparel and novelty goods for men, women and children.

Chains

Chain Stores (Food)

Food chains emerge

In the late 1800s some of the more aggressive specialty store owners opened additional outlets. This was the start of the phenomenal growth of the modern food **chain store,** exemplified by such companies as Safeway, A&P, and Winn-Dixie Stores. A chain store consists of multiple retail outlets under common, centralized ownership which sell similar lines of merchandise. However, the Bureau of the Census defines a chain as having at least eleven outlets.

Although retail chains had existed in the Orient and Europe for many years, it was not until 1859 that the first well-known food chain in this country had its start. George F. Gilman and George Huntington Hartford opened a tea business in New York City that eventually became the Great Atlantic & Pacific Tea Company (A&P). Other food merchants joined the chain phenomenon; among them were the Jewel Tea Company, Grand Union Company, Lucky Stores, and Kroger's. The westward movement of the frontier and an expanding population gave impetus to the opening of large numbers of chain units, with some of the chains opening as many as 200 new stores per week.

The supermarket dominates the retail food business

At the beginning of this century, but particularly from 1930 to 1940, the **supermarket** became the dominant type of retail food outlet. Stressing low prices and self-service, supermarkets like A&P and Safeway quickly overtook local grocers in sales volume. Since their emergence as a major force in retailing,

The A&P food chain opened
thousands of stores such as
the ones shown here.
Courtesy: A&P.

supermarkets have expanded their product lines to include housewares, drugs, and other nonfood items.

To understand the phenomenal success of the supermarket, one has to appreciate the limitations of the small food stores operated by A&P and other food merchants in earlier days. Their stores were generally cramped, with few eye-catching displays to attract customers. Catering to consumers who lived within walking distance of their stores, they saw little need to do much more than provide food products and personalized services.

Self-service; cash-and-carry

In 1916 Clarence Saunders opened a store in Memphis called Piggly Wiggly that brought new selling techniques to the retailing of food. He introduced the self-service concept to the retail food business and augmented it with a cash-and-carry policy and low prices. Though it took time for these radical changes to be accepted, by the 1920s they were well entrenched in food merchandising. In fact, Saunders's ideas were so sound that large food chain organizations like A&P eventually adopted them.

Supermarkets began to sprout across the country. Opening stores in low-rent areas, people in the East and Midwest like Michael Cullen (King Kullen) and B. H. Kroger (Kroger Company) pushed the cash-and-carry and self-service principles vigorously. In California, enterprising individuals based their new stores on Saunders's methods and found a responsive public.

Perhaps the two most significant reasons for the explosive growth of supermarkets in the 1930s were the mobility provided by the automobile and the severe economic depression that prevailed in the early years of the decade. No longer relying on local food stores, consumers traveled to more distant supermarkets where they could sample a wider selection of merchandise at lower prices. No longer were they confined to small, dingy stores for their grocery needs. Instead, they had access to bright, modern establishments that carried produce and meat items as well as groceries.

One of the chief outcomes of the supermarket concept has been the elimination by chain organizations of their small stores. Recognizing that they can make more money in larger outlets, the companies now operate in quarters that can accommodate a variety of food and nonfood products in large quantities. In fact, many supermarkets present so diversified an assortment of merchandise that they bear a strong resemblance to a set of specialty store organizations under one roof. For example, Jewel's, originally a food-based company, now maintains drug-food combination stores as well.

Chain Stores (Variety)

Variety chains emerge

Another type of chain store that developed in the late 1800s was the **variety store,** which sold novelty items at low prices. This type of outlet was popularized by Frank W. Woolworth, who sold such goods as combs, pins, pencils, and thread for five or ten cents. Capitalizing on the theory that cut-rate (but still profitable) prices would attract customers, Woolworth opened so-called Five and Dime stores in large numbers. Within a short period he had established a giant nationwide chain whose name was known by all.

Woolworth's wasn't the only variety chain that prospered. Others included H. Kress & Company, a Tennessee-based store; S. S. Kresge, today's K mart; and McCrory's. However, the chains' low-price policy caused them to compete aggressively for customers, and frequent price wars resulted. In addition, the chains had to expand their merchandise lines constantly as well as change their prices in order to keep pace with their competitors.

Department Stores

The great department stores develop

Along with the development of chain stores, the last half of the nineteenth century witnessed the emergence of the **department store.** This form of retailing was totally different from the general store. Instead of a hodge-podge arrangement of stock, the department store offered carefully selected merchandise in specific departments. As a result, customers could make quick purchases of a variety of goods and services under one roof (**one-stop shopping**). Thus, the department store also differed from the specialty store by selling several types of goods: clothing, hardware, furniture, and so forth.

RETAIL STRATEGY
Expanding Through New Types of Outlets

Lucky Stores, based in California, is one of the nation's largest supermarket chains. In addition to its food stores, however, Lucky Stores also owns several different kinds of specialty stores (e.g., apparel, automotive, fabric). Even though its specialty store sales are only a fraction of its supermarket sales, the specialty stores account for a better profit percent than do the supermarkets. This situation is not unique to Lucky Stores; other retailers have discovered the same thing. Consequently, more and more large retailers are acquiring specialty stores as a means of increasing their overall percents of profit.

One-price policy

    The first American department store was probably opened in New York City by Alexander Stewart in 1848. Unlike most retailers of the period, who haggled over prices, Stewart instituted a **one-price policy.** In other words, he charged all customers the same price for a particular product. The success of this policy made it possible for him to build a far larger store in another part of the city.

    Stewart's experience led to the entrance of other people into the department store business. Rich's, which operates stores in Georgia, got its start in Atlanta shortly after Stewart's second store was opened. Out west, Brigham Young opened a store in Salt Lake City. Simon Lazarus started a business in Columbus, Ohio, that today is the well-known F&R Lazarus. Rowland Macy's early success with competitive pricing policies resulted in the establishment of the famous R. H. Macy's stores. In Philadelphia, John Wanamaker advertised extensively and offered refunds to dissatisfied customers. His innovations were so successful that he is often referred to as the father of retailing. Adam Gimbel's original store in Vincennes, Indiana, grew from an early trading post into a large business with stores in New York, Milwaukee, and Philadelphia. (Gimbel's closed in 1986.) Others who pioneered successful enterprises were William Filene (Filene's of Boston), Marshall Field of Chicago, Joseph Hudson (J. L. Hudson Company in Detroit), Mary Ann and John Magnin (I. Magnin & Company of San Francisco), and A. L. Neiman and Herbert Marcus (Neiman Marcus in Dallas).

    By and large, department stores are credited with raising the level of retailing practices. Abandoning the old ways of bargaining, the stores instituted a one-price system. Offering their customers quality merchandise, attractive surroundings, and personal services, they captured the loyalty of a large part of the public. Today, department stores are under increasing pressure from specialty stores and other retail forms such as buying through television.

Discount Stores

To complete our brief history of the development of American retailing, mention should be made of the **discount store.** This form of retailing started after World War II as a way of meeting consumer demand for such **hard goods** as home appliances, cameras, and jewelry. Discount stores offered few services, but their low-price policy quickly gained favor with the public. Early discounters like Korvette's (now defunct) and Masters were joined by other chain discount companies like K mart. All offered a wide variety of merchandise at highly competitive prices.

The first discount houses were small, threadbare stores that cut costs—and also prices—to a minimum. They offered few, if any, customer services, concentrated on selling well-known brands, and appealed to price-conscious consumers. Their stores were open long hours to accommodate working people, and were

How the stores operated by today's giant chains looked years ago.

located close to large population clusters. From a profit point of view, every attempt was made to sell stock quickly.

Though discount stores started with the sale of hard goods, they quickly extended their product lines to include **soft goods** (apparel). As the discount concept took hold, department and specialty stores adopted discount policies of their own. Today few people speak of a "discount store" as such. Instead, we find discounting in virtually every aspect of retailing: There are discount department stores, discount chains, and so forth. So popular have discount operations become that sales from these units crossed the $140 billion mark in 1988. An indication of the importance of discounting is the publication of a biweekly newspaper, *Discount Store News,* which is devoted exclusively to discount retailing. Because of the wide variety of goods they stock and the considerable volume they sell, large discounters such as K mart and Sears, Roebuck are also known as **mass merchandisers.**

AN EARLY INNOVATOR IN RETAILING

Aristede Bouçicaut

Although no one knows for sure when the world's first department store was established, it is generally agreed that today's department stores stem from Bon Marché, the Paris emporium started by Aristede Bouçicaut in the first half of the nineteenth century. At first Bouçicaut sold only piece goods, but he subsequently extended his product line to include clothing, shoes, and hardware.

Bouçicaut introduced a number of novel retailing practices, including money-back guarantees, a one-price policy, and relatively low profits on sales. Depending on large sales volume for success, he encouraged consumers to shop at Bon Marché by forbidding sales clerks to harass customers over prices, a common procedure in those days.

Bouçicaut was disliked by many contemporary retailers because of his departure from conventional practices. However, his persistence in developing innovative policies eventually proved the wisdom of his ideas and caused competitors to adopt the same policies.

The early American department store retailers—Marshall Field, John Wanamaker, Rowland Macy, A. T. Stewart, and others—were greatly influenced by Bouçicaut. As these merchants transformed their stores from specialty shops to department stores, they borrowed liberally from Bouçicaut's ideas. The end result was the impressive department stores that are so familiar to us today.

INTERNATIONAL RETAILING

American and European retailing are similar

Up to this point our discussion has centered on retailing in the United States. Yet European countries have pioneered some interesting innovations, some of which have been copied by American retailers. In addition, retailing has become truly international, with famous-name retailers functioning both here and abroad.

Inasmuch as living styles in Western Europe are fairly similar to those in the United States, we would expect retail practices and experiences to be similar, too. In fact, this is so. Let's examine two of these similarities.

First of all, individual retailers in Europe are just as vulnerable to changing business conditions as their counterparts in this country. Owing to economic pressures and new forms of retailing, many of them have been forced out of business. Others have joined voluntary chains or buying groups (see Chapters 4 and 9). In other cases they have had to develop creative retail strategies in order to compete with the larger firms. For example, small retailers have jointly designed pedestrian malls that are actually collections of small stores (boutiques), with ownership in the hands of the merchants.

Second, like those in the United States, mass retailers in European countries rely on self-service, price appeal, and advertising. With both food and nonfood products in stock, such stores carry between 20,000 and 50,000 brand name items. Operating in a similar fashion to U.S. discounters, they offer low prices and little service.

Marks & Spencer store in London. *Courtesy:* Marks & Spencer, Canada Inc.

A distinctive feature of European retailing is the food discount practice followed by many small stores. These outlets carry a small number of the popular items featured in supermarkets, concentrating on high turnover and high volume.

The most recent type of European retailing to penetrate the United States is the **hypermarket.** This type of store, with an area exceeding 100,000 square feet, features discount shopping for food, general merchandise, and soft goods. In 1988 Carrefour, the owner of the largest chain of hypermarkets in France, opened its first store (170,000 square feet) near Philadelphia. (A further discussion of hypermarkets is contained in Chapter 5.)

Retailers in Foreign Markets

Many large American, European, and Asian retailers have extended their operations to other countries in search of new markets. They view expansion overseas as an opportunity to increase their number of outlets and to enhance profits.

U.S. Retailers in Foreign Markets

Toys "Я" Us, this nation's most powerful toy retailer, has developed a plan of global expansion through its own divisions abroad and through **joint ventures** (a partnership or cooperative agreement) with foreign firms. The chain's first international store in Kuwait (a joint venture) was so successful that additional stores were opened in the Middle East and Singapore. As part of the agreement, the toy chain provides assistance in merchandising, purchasing, marketing, and promotion. The strategy for new stores in Toronto and Great Britain follows the same lines as those in its domestic market: wide selection of goods, aggressive pricing, liberal return policy, and a high-image advertising posture. The units are wholly owned by the chain and are operated through its foreign division. Today, Toys "Я" Us operates 74 stores in foreign countries, with an eye to continued expansion. In fact, its global strategy calls for the opening of Kids "Я" Us units as well.

Pizza Hut and Burger King have also planned international expansions. The former plans to open 15 outlets in Hungary by 1998, while Burger King has targeted 60 new restaurants in Spain by 1996.

Woolworth's Worldwide Specialty Stores account for about one quarter of Woolworth's total sales volume and more than half of its total operating profits. In fact, Woolworth is one of the few American retailers that has solid representation on three continents—North America, Europe, and Australia.

Jewel, the food and drug conglomerate, has expanded its activities to include Mexico's largest food chain, Aurrera. Jewel owns 41 percent of the Mexican supermarket chain as a joint venture and supplies Aurrera with computerized management controls and professional expertise.

Because of the availability of large markets overseas, more than 200 American businesses operate some 20,000 outlets in other countries. For example,

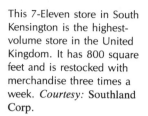

This 7-Eleven store in South Kensington is the highest-volume store in the United Kingdom. It has 800 square feet and is restocked with merchandise three times a week. *Courtesy:* Southland Corp.

McDonald's and 7-Eleven are involved in more than 2,000 units overseas. Although the McDonald's network extends to 25 countries, 7-Eleven has transported its store image to much of Japan. As a joint venture, 7-Eleven provides the use of its name, inventory, financing, and technical assistance.

In an unusual international agreement, Barneys New York, an apparel chain, and the Isetan Company, Japan's sixth largest retailer, have entered into a joint venture to open stores in the United States, Japan, and other Asian countries under the Barneys name. The first Barneys store opened in Tokyo in 1990.

Tiffany & Company has exported its upscale jewelry business to Europe and the Orient. The chain's operation in Japan consists of boutiques in the Mitsukoshi department stores. In Hong Kong, the Tiffany store is located in the prestigious Peninsula Hotel, with other famous designer stores nearby. In London and Munich, the stores are owned partially by other investors. The company plans a worldwide store expansion in Europe, Taiwan, and Canada.

Other American retailers that have extended their operations overseas include Sears, K mart, Woolworth, and Jewel, the supermarket chain. K mart's foreign investments include outlets as well as an arrangement to sell merchandise to foreign retailers. In addition to this involvement, K mart provides a counseling service to Japanese retailers consisting of technical know-how in all phases of merchandising.

Foreign Retailers in U.S. Markets

Well-known European firms have established successful retail operations in this country through conventional stores and ownership of American firms. Of particular note are stores such as Gucci, known for its leather goods, Liberty of London (silks and cottons), Cartier (fine jewelry), Burberry's (clothing), and Ferragamo (clothing and leather goods). Aquascutum, the London-based raincoat manufacturer, opened its first U.S. store in New York City in 1984.

One of the great manufacturing-retailing success stories, the Benetton Group, has more than 700 independently owned stores in the United States. This family-owned Italian sweater-knitting business is one of the largest manufacturers of knitwear in the world.

In other cases, foreign companies have purchased major interests in American retail firms. For example, in food retailing the A&P Company is owned by Tengelman of Germany, while Brooks Brothers was acquired by the British retailer, Marks & Spencer.

Risks in Foreign Expansion

Although growth opportunities for retailers exist in overseas markets, foreign expansion is not without risk. The fluctuation of foreign currency, for example, can present problems when the exchange rate is translated into American dollars. In many foreign markets, changes in the political environment can bring rapid changes that alter a nation's laws and outlook toward foreign investors. Differences in culture and social customs, too, are factors that retailers must consider before attempting to penetrate other markets.

THE ECONOMIC IMPORTANCE OF RETAILING

Sales

Since retail sales account for about one-third of economic activity in the United States, we should note some statistics about those sales. Table 1-1 indicates that retail sales rose from approximately $957 billion in 1980 to $1,799 billion

TABLE 1-1   Retail Sales and Gross National Product in the United States—Summary, 1980–1990

Year	Retail Sales (billions of dollars)	Gross National Product (trillions of dollars)	Retail Sales as a Percentage of Gross National Product
1980	$ 957	$2.7	35%
1981	1,039	3.1	34
1982	1,069	3.2	33
1983	1,168	3.4	34
1984	1,282	3.8	34
1985	1,366	4.0	34
1986	1,436	4.2	34
1987	1,521	4.5	34
1988	1,629	4.9	33
1989	1,734	5.2	33
1990	1,799	5.5	33

Sources: U.S. Department of Commerce, Bureau of Economic Analysis, *Business Statistics, 1961–88* (Washington, D.C.: U.S. Government Printing Office, December 1989), and *Survey of Current Business*, January 1981–1991).

TABLE 1-2   Retail Sales by Stores and Products Sold, 1988

Store	Sales (billions of dollars)
Apparel and accessory	$ 82.0
Automotive dealer	369.0
Building materials, supplies, hardware, mobile homes	88.9
Drug and proprietary	58.7
Eating and drinking	157.5
Food	331.9
Furniture, home furnishings, equipment	93.0
Gasoline service stations	101.9
General merchandise	183.8

Source: U.S. Bureau of the Census, *Statistical Abstract of the United States: 1990* 110th edition (Washington, D.C., 1990) p. 772.

(about $1.8 trillion!) in 1990, an increase of 88 percent. This was somewhat more than the inflation rate over those years.

The gross national product (GNP) is the total market value of all the goods and services produced in the United States. Table 1-1 shows that the relationship between annual retail sales and the GNP from 1980 to 1990 was significant, ranging from 35 percent in 1980 to 33 percent in 1990.

Table 1-2 contains a partial breakdown of 1988 retail sales by stores and products sold. Automotive dealers led the group, with sales of $369.0 billion. They were followed by food stores (supermarkets, etc.), with sales of $331.9 billion.

Employment

Another indication of the crucial place retailing occupies in our economy is the number of people it employs. Table 1-3 shows that employment in the retail trade went from 15,035,000 in 1980 to 19,791,000 in 1990, an increase of 32 percent. Of the total civilian *working* labor force of approximately 117.3 million people at the end of 1990, about 17 percent, or one out of every six workers, was gainfully employed by a retailing institution.

Large Retail Companies

To appreciate the dimensions of retailing in the United States, it helps to examine statistics about leading retail companies. Table 1-4 lists the 1990 sales, profits, and assets (the things a business owns) of the ten largest American retailers. Sears, Roebuck was the leader in sales and assets, while Wal-Mart registered the highest profits. K mart was second in assets, and McDonald's, the fast food operator (not listed in Table 1-4), was third in profits.

Early in 1991 Wal-Mart, which had not been among the top ten sales leaders

TABLE 1-3 Employment in Retail Trade in the United States, 1980–1990

Year	Employment
1980	15,035,000
1981	15,189,000
1982	15,179,000
1983	15,613,000
1984	16,584,000
1985	17,415,000
1986	17,930,000
1987	18,509,000
1988	19,203,000
1989	19,580,000
1990	19,791,000

Source: U.S. Department of Commerce, Bureau of Economic Analysis, *Survey of Current Business*, January 1981–1991.

TABLE 1-4 The Ten Largest Retailing Companies in the United States, Fiscal Year Ending January 31, 1991

Rank by Sales 1990	1989	Company	Sales $ Millions	Sales % change from 1989	Profits $ Millions	Profits Rank	Profits % change from 1989	Assets $ Millions	Assets Rank
1	1	Sears Roebuck Chicago	55,971.7	3.8	902.2	2	(40.2)	96,252.8	1
2	3	Wal-Mart Stores Bentonville, Ark.	32,601.6	25.8	1,291.0	1	20.0	11,388.9	4
3	2	K mart Troy, Mich.	32,080.0	8.5	756.0	4	134.1	13,899.0	2
4	4	American Stores Salt Lake City	22,155.5	0.6	182.4	15	54.4	7,244.7	8
5	5	Kroger Cincinnati	20,261.0	6.1	82.4	28	-	4,118.5	13
6	6	J.C. Penney Dallas	17,410.0	6.1	577.0	5	(28.1)	12,325.0	3
7	7	Safeway Oakland	14,873.6	3.8	87.1	27	3,384.0	4,739.1	11
8	8	Dayton Hudson Minneapolis	14,739.0	8.0	412.0	7	0.4	8,524.0	6
9	10	Great Atlantic & Pacific Tea Montvale, N.J.	11,164.2	10.8	146.7	21	15.0	2,831.6	22
10	9	May Department Stores St. Louis	11,027.0	(8.4)	500.0	6	0.4	8,295.0	7

Source: Courtesy of *Fortune* magazine, Copyright© June 3, 1991, Time, Inc.

as late as 1985, moved ahead of Sears, Roebuck as the nation's leading retailer. K mart continued to rank third in sales.

All ten of the firms in Table 1-4 had sales above $11 billion. Although four of the companies—American Stores, Kroger, Safeway, and A & P—are food retailers, their profits were significantly lower than the nonfood chains in the group. This is not surprising because food retailers are traditionally high-volume, low-profit companies.

With regard to comparative 1989–90 sales rankings among the top ten retailers, the only change involved the switch of A & P with May Department Stores, A & P having moved into ninth place.

CAREERS IN RETAILING

A number of retail consultants feel that one of the biggest problems retailers face today is the lack of competent people in middle and upper management levels. This shortage has increased the tendency to hire executives who have already had significant success in retailing. Because of this scramble for people, companies such as Bloomingdale's, Macy's, and Nordstrom have started training programs to "grow" their own people, whereas other stores are stepping up their efforts to recruit college graduates from two- and four-year schools.

Retailing Opportunities

Demand for retailing personnel remains high

Continued growth and opportunities in the retail trade are expected to provide more job openings than almost any other occupation through the mid-1990s. Stores (and alternative methods of acquiring goods and services) are always in demand because people need merchandise to satisfy their needs. Therefore, it is likely that demand for retailing personnel will continue. As the population grows and rising incomes enable people to buy more goods, retail trade employment increases.

For many people, however, a job as a retail worker serves as a source of temporary income rather than as a career. For example, more than half of all retail sales workers have part-time jobs. Many students and homeworkers looking for part-time work are employed in local stores all over the country. The types of retail firms expected to show large employment increases are specialty store chains, department stores, grocery stores, new car dealerships, and eating and drinking places. The growth of specialty store chains at this time has created a greater demand for retail executives than in other retail institutions.

Although the United States population is expected to grow more slowly the next 12 years than it did the previous 12 years, the demand for goods and services will increase, too. This should cause a greater demand for workers in many occupational areas, including retailing.

Some 3.8 million additional jobs will be available in the retail trade, bringing the total number of retail workers to 22.9 million by the year 2,000, up 20 percent from the 1988 level (Figure 1-2). Substantial increases in retail employment are anticipated in grocery stores, department stores, and a variety of shopping goods stores.

Technology aids retailing careers

Despite the use of labor-saving innovations such as self-service merchandising and computerized inventory systems, career areas in large retailing firms have expanded. Computer-generated information provides a wide spectrum of merchandise information upon which department and major specialty stores depend. The computer has also been a direct cause of the tremendous growth in direct-mail and catalog retailing. The increase in **armchair shopping** or **in-home shopping,**

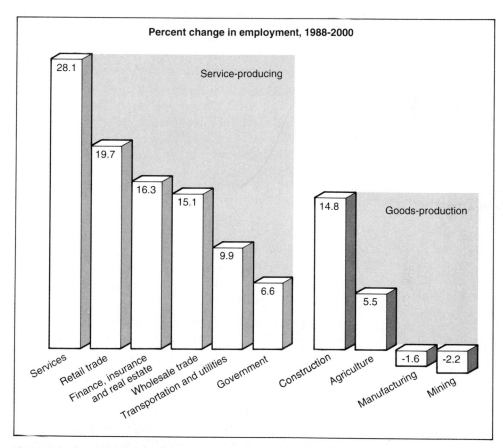

Figure 1-2   Some industries will grow more rapidly than others. *Source: Occupational Outlook Handbook,* 1990–1991 edition (Washington D.C.: U.S. Department of Labor, Bureau of Labor Statistics, 1990, p. 10).

which was made possible by computers, has increased the number of letters, brochures, fliers, and catalogs being mailed to consumers. These publications offer all types of merchandise, from clothes to home furnishings. Consequently, the need for people to prepare this material has increased the job opportunities for those with ability and skills in art, writing, and computers.

The increase in consumer awareness has expanded customer relations departments in many large retail stores. Training in marketing, human relations, and psychology is an asset in this area, and public relations trainees are often hired to fill these jobs.

Advantages and Limitations of Retailing Careers

Advantages

A Broad Selection of Retail Institutions in Which to Work. Basically, there are two main categories of employment in retailing: going into one's own business and working for a retail employer.

The dream of starting a business

Going into One's Own Business. Many people dream of owning their own business. Virtually all large retailers started out as small retailers. Among them were J. C. Penney, Abraham Abraham (of Abraham & Straus), Richard Sears, and R. H. Macy. Today approximately 80 percent of all small retailing establishments are owned by individuals. Although the dream is not impossible to fulfill, a great deal of knowledge and planning is essential in order to diminish the risks. Starting one's own business is treated in detail in Chapter 20.

Working for a Retail Employer. The diversity of retail institutions results in attractive and varied job opportunities in large, medium, and small businesses. More than 80 different types of retail institutions are listed by the U.S. Census of Business. Department stores, mail order houses, food stores, apparel stores, home furnishings stores, and eating and drinking places are only part of the selection.

Employee Mobility. Retailing experience and knowledge can be transferred easily. Because retail shops exist in all communities, people who want to relocate can usually find employment in their new surroundings.

Opportunities for Advancement. The size and variety of retail establishments provide a diversity of managerial levels in a typical retail organization.

People-Oriented Industry. Retailing affords the opportunity to work with and meet interesting people. Some positions also provide the opportunity to travel.

Reasonable Security. Despite periods of slowdown in the economy, retailing employment usually declines less than employment in other industries. Continued growth and opportunities are predicted for the future.

Limitations

Starting Salaries. These are lower in retailing than in many other fields, but one can climb rapidly.

Nonstandard Working Hours. This is commonly cited as a negative factor. Most stores include evening, Saturday, Sunday, and holiday working time. However, hours are comparable with lower managerial positions in other industries.

Relocation. Many chain stores require personnel to relocate as part of career advancement. This proves to be a hardship for some.

Competition. Certain positions involve excessive pressure because of the competitive nature of retailing.

High Rate of Turnover. The relatively high rate of employee turnover is partially attributed to the large number of part-time noncareer workers.

Areas of Retail Employment in Large Stores

Most job opportunities in large firms are in the areas of merchandising, operations, personnel, control, and sales promotion.

Merchandising consists of buying and selling goods. People in merchandising management are responsible for stocking the store with goods that meet customer needs. Department store buyers, for example, act as merchants who buy merchandise and plan promotional selling activities. Trainees handle goods and records, supervise salespeople, and help with displays. They are in contact with vendors and analyze computer records, do fashion forecasting (predicting), and assist in administering store policies. Although training programs vary with different types of retail firms, they are usually structured so that trainees go through a progression of assignments (see Figure 1-3). Training leads to an initial job as **assistant buyer** or **assistant department manager.** Those with special talents have the opportunity to attain top-level positions, as indicated in the figure. For example, an assistant buyer may be promoted to **department manager,** then to **buyer,** and on upward. The length of training differs from organization to organization and varies from three weeks to four years.

Operations (store management) maintains the store's physical plant and directs sales-supporting activities and customer service. Responsibilities include receiving, protection, and physical distribution of merchandise. Executives in this area must be skilled in organization and supervision. Trainees begin the job in a sales-supporting function or in selling. They then become involved in supervisory store functions on a rotation basis. These positions include acting as a service manager on the selling floor, supervising the receiving of merchandise, handling store security, and participating in warehouse management.

Jobs in operations include those of warehouse manager, customer service manager, store superintendent, security manager, and receiving manager. Execu-

A buyer's activities include managerial as well as merchandising activities. Joel Gordon/P.R.

tive job titles include group sales manager, assistant store manager, and vice-president of stores. Figure 1-4 illustrates a training program that enables a department store trainee to select a career path in merchandising or store management.

The **personnel department (human resource department)** is responsible for effective staffing of the store. It is involved in employee selection, training, advancement, and employee welfare. Training takes place within the personnel department under the supervision of its director and staff. The trainee learns the techniques of employment and recruitment, the process of evaluating employees, and the store's training methods. Advanced training involves the study of labor laws, union negotiations, and management of employee benefits (e.g., hospitalization). Jobs in this division include those of recruiter, interviewer, and training director. Retail personnel executives must acquire experience in both operations and personnel. Executive job titles include manager of compensation and employee relations, manager of executive recruitment, manager of executive development and placement, and vice-president of human relations.

The **control department** is responsible for protecting the store's finances.

Job Title	**Major Responsibilities**

Step 1   Assistant Buyer
(Assistant Department
Manager)

1. Works with buyer; operates a merchandise department in buyer's absence.
2. Learns merchandise planning, pricing, and presentation
3. Provides buyer with information

Step 2   Department Manager

1. Supervises a merchandise department
2. Supervises service and merchandising activities
3. Accountable for operating a profitable area
4. Supervises sales help

Step 3   Buyer

1. Buys merchandise and plans for distribution of goods:
    Pricing
    Sales promotion
    General presentation
2. Develops good vendor and public relations
3. Develops overall plan for department
4. Operates a profitable department

Step 4   Assistant Branch
Store Manager

1. Assists branch store general manager
2. Supervises department managers
3. Helps develop sales goals

Step 5   Divisional Store
Manager

1. Directs buyers with merchandise programs and sales goals
2. Plans storewide promotions
3. Plans advertising for division and sometimes whole store.

Step 6   Branch Store
General Manager

1. Total operation of branch store; accountable for growth, sales, and profits
2. Involved with establishing good relations with the community

Step 7   Divisional
Merchandise Manager

1. Controls the activities of several buyers
2. Coordinates the plans to increase profits and maintain store image

Step 8   General
Merchandise
Manager

1. Interprets and executes management policies
2. Supervises and coordinates the planning, buying, and selling activities of the firm
3. Supervises and directs divisional merchandise managers and buyers

Step 9   Vice-President of
Merchandising

1. Develops objectives and policies
2. Controls specific operations and resources

Figure 1-3   Career pattern in merchandising (traditional department store).

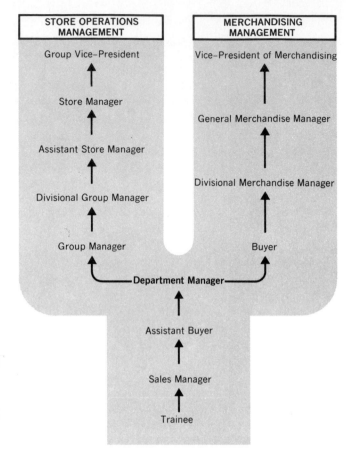

Figure 1-4 Example of an executive training program leading to store operations management and merchandising management.

Trainees must have a knowledge of accounting principles. They are concerned with all the financial aspects of the business, including accounting procedures, sales tallies, customer and supplier bills, credit, and the processing of information. Top executive jobs in this area are generally filled by people with management experience. Computerization has created additional job opportunities in the control division and provides positions for people with training in electronic data processing. Executive job titles include data processing manager, accounts payable manager, credit manager, controller, and treasurer.

Sales promotion is concerned with communicating the store's message to the public through advertising, displays, special events, and public relations. Planning and implementing a store's efforts in this area require specialists. These include copywriters, artists, window and interior display people, special-events and fashion coordinators, and mail order experts.

The career ladders for sales promotion are varied. For example, an artist or layout specialist might begin his or her training by preparing rough advertising layouts. A copywriter might start by assisting a copywriter. A display specialist might begin training as a display assistant or window trimmer.

Public relations is concerned with promoting goodwill through community activities, such as supporting local causes and groups (e.g., civic associations) and making the store's premises available for fashion shows and meetings. Trainees who understand advertising and other techniques for reaching the public often climb the success ladder in this area. The prestigious jobs of advertising manager and sales promotion director, however, are reached only after years of participation in successful programs.

In large specialty chains, training is an important element in the development of effective store managers. Even though the individual stores are generally smaller than large department stores, the retailing functions are similar. Consequently, management training includes on-the-job experience in merchandising, sales promotion, operations, and control. Table 1-5 illustrates the job titles, functions, and training periods leading to the position of store manager in a specialty chain.

Areas of Retail Employment in Medium and Small-Sized Stores

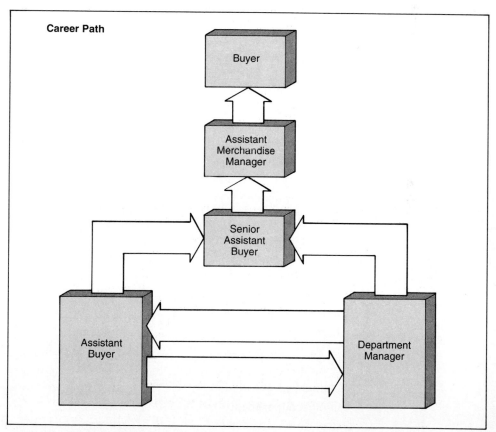

Figure 1-5   *Courtesy:* Strawbridge & Clothier.

TABLE 1-5 Sample four-year executive management program—specialty store

Job Title	Functions	Training Period
Sales Assistant	Basic operations: sales and stock	6 months
Junior Assistant Manager	Merchandising, promotion, customer service	12 months
Assistant Manager	Buying, merchandising, control, personnel	12 months
Senior Assistant Manager	Overall store operations—emphasis on planning	12 months
Store Manager (trial period)	Complete operation of store—under supervision	6 months

Small retail stores offer varied job experiences

More than 2 million retailers are classified as medium (fewer than 100 employees) or small (fewer than 10 employees). In contrast to the formal programs found in large retail organizations, medium and small-sized stores offer informal training. For the employee who eventually wishes to own his or her own store, this kind of training often provides comprehensive experience in a short period. The intimacy of a small firm can help the individual learn how to deal with customers on a personal level. All facets of buying, selling, display, and store operations are readily apparent because they are all conducted within a comparatively small area. However, advancement is limited unless one becomes a part owner of the firm.

Recent graduates and others in search of jobs can improve their chances for challenging employment by careful career planning. What to expect at the job interview, preparing a résumé, and techniques of the job search are treated in Chapter 6.

NEW TERMS

armchair shopping	mail order house
asset	manufacturer
assistant buyer	mass merchandiser
assistant department manager	merchandising
barter	middleman
buyer	one-price policy
chain store	one-stop shopping
channel of distribution	operations
control department	peddler
department manager	personnel department
department store	retailer

discount store

general store

hard goods

human resource department

hypermarket

in-home shopping

joint venture

limited-line store

retailing

sales promotion

soft goods

specialty store

supermarket

trading post

variety store

wholesaler

CHAPTER HIGHLIGHTS

1. Retailing consists of the selling of goods and services to their ultimate consumer.
2. Manufacturing, wholesaling, and retailing are the main types of businesses involved in getting goods and services to consumers.
3. Early American retailing developed through the trading post, the itinerant peddler, and the general store. As the country grew, new retailing institutions emerged: mail order houses, specialty stores, chain stores (food and variety), department stores, and discount stores.
4. International retailing reveals well-known American firms functioning in European countries, and vice versa. Some European retailing practices have been copied in this country.
5. In 1990 retail sales volume stood at $1,799 billion, and the number of people employed in retailing was 19,791,00. In that year Sears, Roebuck had the highest sales and assets of all retailers, while Wal-Mart had the highest profits. By early 1991 Wal-Mart was first in sales volume.
6. The field of retailing offers expanding job opportunities, employee mobility, and a broad selection of institutions in which to work. Self-service and computerized retailing systems have spawned new career patterns for aspiring workers.
7. The diversity of retail institutions offers attractive and varied job opportunities. Most job areas are in merchandising, operations, personnel, control, and sales promotion.

REVIEW QUESTIONS

1. What role do wholesalers play in the merchandise distribution process?
2. Why do we sometimes speak of the itinerant American peddler as having served two purposes?

3. What features popularized the department store as a major type of retail institution?
4. Why have department and specialty stores adopted discount policies?
5. In what ways is European retailing similar to retailing in this country?
6. How do the data in Table 1-3 of this chapter support the statement that "It is likely that demand for retail personnel will continue"?
7. What are the differences between the merchandising and operations functions in a large retail organization?

DISCUSSION QUESTIONS

1. In what ways does a specialty store differ from a department store? Which store type lends itself to one-stop shopping? Why?
2. What changes do you think will occur in supermarkets in the next ten years? Why?
3. What are the implications for retailers in this country arising out of the increasing purchase of American retail institutions by foreign businesses?
4. How might the trend toward a service-oriented economy affect the field of retailing?
5. How do you think the existence of a large part-time work force affects a store's image?

CASE 1

Time for Mail Order?

Gage and Roth, partners in a shoe and clothing mail order business, recently became aware of a national survey showing that the potential mail order market for shoes and clothing is close to saturation. The findings indicated that though these two areas are among the top five product categories in mail order selling, the opportunities for significant increases in their sales levels are limited. As further evidence of this limitation, the survey found that more than 10 percent of the people who buy shoes and clothing by mail do so only because these items are unavailable in their communities in sufficient variety and quality.

In examining the survey statistics, Gage and Roth noted that the total estimated market for direct-mail selling of shoes and clothing is a little less than 30 percent of the total national population. They were disturbed by the fact that this percentage has almost been reached already.

In planning their future, the owners were impressed by the survey's discovery of a large potential market for the sale of sports equipment through mail orders, and by the fact that high-income families are much more likely to buy sports equipment by mail than low-income consumers. With regard to other product categories, however, such as home furnishings, cosmetics, toiletries, and hi-fi equipment, Gage and Roth learned that the potential market is close to being fully tapped.

As aggressive retailers, the two merchants were anxious to develop a strategy for the expansion of their business. They considered both enlargement of their product lines and movement into other forms of retailing.

a. What are the arguments for and against the owners' adoption of a mail order sports equipment line?
b. What other types of retail outlets should Gage and Roth consider in order to expand their sales of shoes and clothing?

CASE 2

Turnaround for A&P?

For generations of Americans, the Great Atlantic & Pacific Tea Company was synonymous with the word *supermarket*. From its origin in 1859 as a tea business, the company grew and opened stores throughout the country. At one point in its history, the number of stores in the A&P chain was 15,000. Through its growth and nationwide presence, A&P became the first well-known chain of food stores. Initially, its stores were small but well-staffed with service personnel, like most stores of the time. But after the concept of the self-service store was successfully introduced in the 1920s, A&P followed suit and changed over to the format that is so familiar today: cash-and-carry, self-service stores with limited personnel. Simultaneously, it began to expand the product lines. By the 1930s, A&P offered its customers a wide variety of food and nonfood products. The company opened larger and larger stores to accommodate the expanded variety of goods. These stores proved more profitable and eventually led the company to close many of the small ones.

By 1950, A&P was probably the best-known chain in the country. Data available suggest that A&P sold 1 out of every 14 pounds of butter and enough coffee to account for 1 out of every 7 cups brewed in this country. Ten cents of every food dollar was spent at A&P.

By the 1970s, however, the chain had slipped badly. Although the company had opened larger stores that were adequate for an earlier era, the chain as a whole had not kept pace with other supermarket chains. Its units generally were small, cramped, and old. They were not well located and were often in areas that offered limited parking. Nor were they competitive in price with other giant chains such as Safeway and Kroger. In addition, A&P, the first chain to unionize, had labor costs that were 2 percent above the national average and the highest in the industry. In a business where supermarket chains operate on margins as low as 1 percent, such costs clearly spelled trouble.

In an effort to become more competitive and improve its financial condition, A&P tried to introduce techniques that were successful in Europe (no-frills stores where customers bagged their own purchases and paid a few cents for each bag used). The effort was a failure.

Moreover, for 20 years the company management had invested relatively little in improvement of its stores, opting instead to use such funds to pay dividends to stockholders.

By 1980, A&P had lost both customers and investors. The stock had dropped to $3.50 per share, down from $70 per share in 1961. The company was seen as one with little future and a poor investment. A&P, once the foremost chain in the country, was "slipping into oblivion," according to James A. Wood, who was hired as chairman in 1980 to turn the company around. His strategy was simple: Cut the chain down in size and increase profit. Under Wood's direction, A&P closed 500 stores over a two-year period and reduced the number of employees by 20,000. The company also closed down its food manufacturing business.

In so doing, the company pulled back from a nationwide stance and announced that henceforth it would no longer be a national chain. A&P even shut down in some areas that were still profitable on the grounds that the company's reputation was too badly damaged to restore in those locations.

The company terminated its existing pension plan and replaced it with another, thus freeing the surplus funds for use. A&P also gained concessions from labor, so that two-thirds of its 53,000 workers became part-timers who were paid less than full-time workers and received fewer fringe benefits. And in the Philadelphia area, A&P took the innovative step of setting up a separate subsidiary, Super Fresh Markets, where employees themselves were responsible for keeping labor costs down to a preset level. If they succeeded, they received 1 percent of the sales generated in their stores as profit sharing.

A&P also began to either remodel its existing stores or replace them with new units characterized by wide aisles, low shelves, and a thoroughly modern look. And in its new stores, the chain began to upgrade product lines. Although still stocking generic goods and its own name products, A&P now carried upscale goods like gourmet foods to attract the higher-income customer. This reflected Wood's belief that although consumers want value, they are not settling for cheaper goods nor are they likely to in the future.

In 1983, A&P, successful in trimming its size and its costs, began to expand again. The chain acquired two smaller chains, Kohl Food Stores in the United States and the Dominion Stores in Canada.

By the end of 1984, A&P had accomplished its immediate goals: It had reversed its declining fortunes and was moderately profitable. But the company's long-term goals remained to be accomplished. These included making A&P a $15 billion supermarket chain and one of the top three in profitability by 1990.

a. If A&P was able to reverse its decline by trimming down its operation, what problems could you foresee in its policy of acquisition and expansion?

b. What factors do you think shaped Mr. Wood's belief that consumers are not interested in trading down to cheaper goods? Do you agree? Do you think this will be so in the future? Why?

c. How important in your view are labor costs in running a supermarket chain like A&P?

d. Do you think the concept of profit sharing with employees is a viable one? Should A&P have tried to implement this strategy throughout all its stores?

REFERENCES

BASS, S. "Japan Eyeing New Areas." *Stores* (August 1990), pp. 66–67.

HARRIS, L. A. *Merchant Princes*. New York: Harper & Row, 1979.

HENDRICKSON, R. *The Great Emporiums*. New York: Stein & Day, 1979.

"Is U.S. Hypermarket-Ready? Carrefour Is Not Sure." *Chain Store Age Executive* (January 1989), pp. 49–50.

PEPPER, C. B. "Fast Forward." *Business Month* (February 1989), pp. 25–30.

Chapter 2

Factors Influencing Retailing

After completing this chapter you should be able to:

- Define the "wheel of retailing" concept and indicate how innovators affect traditional retail institutions.
- Indicate how computers and the new technology have influenced retailing.
- Identify and define the following fashion theories: fashion cycle, trickle-down, trickle-across, trickle-up.
- Recount the background of the consumer movement and describe its effects on retailing.
- Identify consumer laws dealing with products, advertising, and credit.

In Chapter 1 we studied the impact of retailing on the economy and the varied opportunities available to people seeking careers in retailing.

We now turn our attention to some factors that influence retailing. First, we examine the wheel of retailing. Next, we explore the application of computer techniques to retail operations and list the ways in which computers influence retailing. Then, we look at the fashion area and the dynamic ways in which it shapes retail strategy. Finally, we trace the history of consumerism and examine the effects of consumer legislation on various aspects of retailing.

THE WHEEL OF RETAILING

The retailer's continued success and, at times, survival depend on the ability to adjust to consumer behavior, legal developments, technology, competition, and the changing demands of the consumer. A retailer must accommodate to changes that take place in the social, political, and economic environment.

Retailers must adapt

Retailing involves unlimited competition, an endless consumer demand for new products and services, and a constant state of change. Some of the changes can be explained by the **wheel of retailing** concept.

Malcolm P. McNair of Harvard University has attempted to explain the institutional changes that take place in retailing by his "wheel of retailing" theory. In this theory a symbolic wheel turns with every retail innovation. New retailers start as low-priced, low-status, **low-margin** (low-profit) **operators.** They offer little in the way of services or glamour and compete with higher-priced traditional retailers. Because of their price appeal, they gain consumer acceptance and have a significant impact on the retailing scene. As they become popular, other retailers enter the field and imitate them. Faced with growing competition, the innovators gradually upgrade their services, merchandise, facilities, and so forth. Owing to increased operating costs, they show lower profit margins and their growth slows. This cycle comes to an end when the innovators reach maturity and become higher-priced operations open to the challenge of newer, low-priced innovators. A new cycle begins and the wheel is ready for another turn.

This concept can be illustrated by the now defunct discounter Korvette's (Figure 2-1). When this company entered the retailing scene after World War II, it was a low-margin, low-price discount store. It drew customers from traditional department stores that maintained higher prices but offered many services. As discounting made an impact, other discounters entered the field. To meet the competition, Korvette's upgraded its operations and expanded its services. Consequently, its overhead increased, rendering it vulnerable to the emergence of a new class of innovators. Because Korvette's was unable to operate successfully as a traditional retailer, it was forced to close all 55 of its stores.

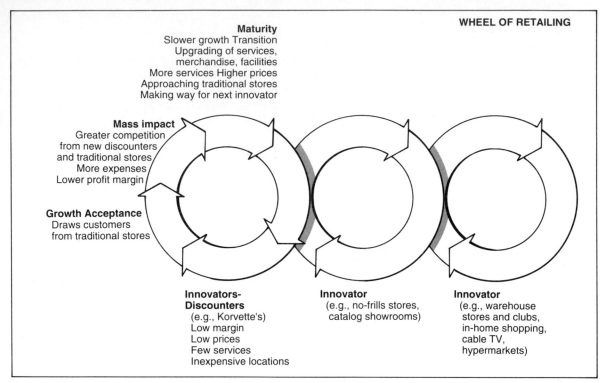

Maturity
Slower growth Transition
Upgrading of services,
merchandise, facilities
More services Higher prices
Approaching traditional stores
Making way for next innovator

Mass impact
Greater competition
from new discounters
and traditional stores
More expenses
Lower profit margin

Growth Acceptance
Draws customers
from traditional stores

WHEEL OF RETAILING

**Innovators-
Discounters**
(e.g., Korvette's)
Low margin
Low prices
Few services
Inexpensive locations

Innovator
(e.g., no-frills stores,
catalog showrooms)

Innovator
(e.g., warehouse
stores and clubs,
in-home shopping,
cable TV,
hypermarkets)

Figure 2-1   The wheel of retailing.

Although the Korvette experience shocked many retailers, discounting continued to flourish and evolve. In fact, discounters such as Target, K mart, and Caldor are performing more profitably than many department stores.

Retail life cycle   As depicted by Tom Heffner of *Management Horizons* magazine, another way to view changes in the retail environment is through the **retail life cycle** (see Figure 2-2). According to Heffner, the time span for changes in the retail life cycle is moving faster. Consequently, what was successful yesterday may not have the magic today. Conventional approaches to retailing are constantly being challenged, for example, specialty stores "feeding off" department stores, manufacturers opening their own retail outlets, and foreign retailers invading the U.S. market.

Major stores are forced to review their strategy more often because the retail environment seems to change more quickly. In an attempt to keep pace, stores like Sears, Woolworth, K mart, and Wal-Mart are playing with different formats, store sizes, and merchandise mixes. For example, Sears has purchased a chain of specialty stores, Woolworth has acquired the Champs sports shop, K mart has added a group of home centers, fashion shops, and Pay Less Stores, and Wal-Mart has ventured into hypermarkets.

According to Heffner, the changes in the retail life cycle depend on the

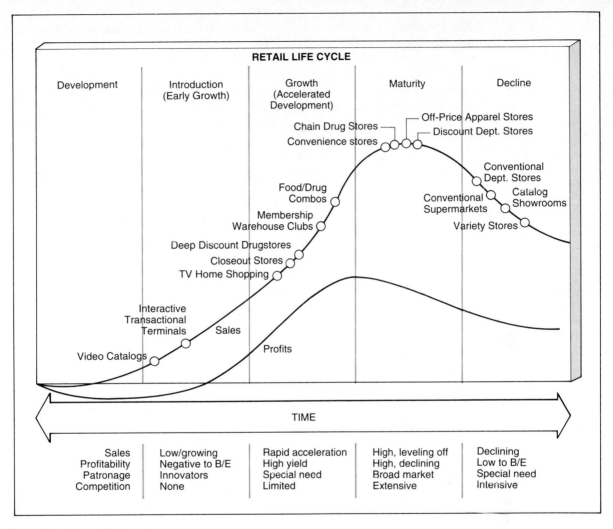

Figure 2-2 The retail life cycle.

"shifts in customer lifestyles." The retailer must observe not only what the consumer buys, but must understand why he buys it.

Current Retail Innovators

Off-Price Retailers

Considered the single fastest-growing segment of the retail industry, **off-price retailing** involves the sale of name brands at discounted prices targeted to the price-conscious consumer. Once seen mainly in warehouse settings, these **no-**

frills operators (surroundings, decor, and services are minimal) have spread to more traditional shopping areas. Examples of off-price stores are K mart's Designer Depots and Dayton Hudson's Plum Shops.

An interesting aspect of the development of off-price shopping centers is the adoption of new names to reflect upgraded images. For example, Outlet Square located in Center Square, Pennsylvania, has been renamed New Woman Marketplace. Similarly, Washington Outlet Center in Virginia is now called Potomac Mills.

An unusual combination of off-price and no-discount retailers exists in Freeport, Maine. Catering primarily to tourists and vacationers, the village boasts such nationally known retailers as L. L. Bean, Ralph Lauren, Cole Hahn, Calvin Klein, Laura Ashley, and Post Horn. This mix of retail outlets with different price levels (price points) continues to be extremely successful.

Factory Outlets

Manufacturer-owned outlets

Factory outlets are owned and operated by manufacturers. They sell their own merchandise, which consists of irregulars, discontinued lines, closeouts, odd lots, and such. Located originally in areas away from metropolitan centers to avoid competition with retailers selling their (the manufacturers') products, these outlets are being grouped increasingly in factory outlet malls. Examples of such malls are located in Murfreesboro, Tennessee, and Jacksonville, Florida. As witnessed by the experience of famous designers like Calvin Klein, Ralph Lauren, and Anne Klein, factory outlets have grown in popularity.

Warehouse-Style Home Centers

Warehouse-style home centers are very large stores (approximately 100,000 square feet) that undersell home-building merchandise to "do-it-yourselfers" and contractors. Shipments are purchased directly from manufacturers and are unloaded onto the sales floor. The Marcus Home Depot chain is an example of a home center whose success is credited to a sales staff trained to offer professional advice. Another example is the Home Depot in Atlanta.

Warehouse Clubs

Also known as **buying clubs, warehouse clubs** are no-frills stores offering sizable discounts to member groups like businesses, unions, and retailers. Individual consumers may also purchase at slightly higher prices; however, special shopping hours are usually set aside for individuals. Wal-Mart operates several warehouse clubs, as does the Price Savers Wholesale Club, located primarily in western states but opening new units in other parts of the country. The popularity of warehouse clubs has increased significantly the last few years. Figure 2-3 shows

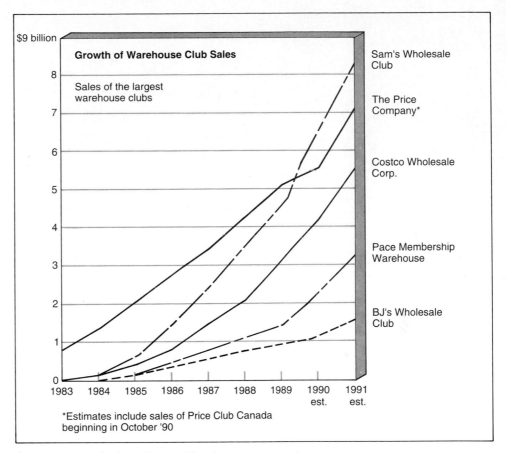

Figure 2-3   Growth of Warehouse Club Sales, 1983–1991. *Source:* Salomon Brothers, as shown in M. Lev, "Hard Times? Not for These Stores," The New York Times, December 10, 1990, pp. D1 and D6.

the growth of warehouse club sales from 1983 to 1989, with estimated sales for 1990 and 1991.

Warehouse Stores

Warehouse stores are large stores, essentially low-price and no-frills, that appeal to the consumer in search of bargains. Stocking mainly food products, and much larger than supermarkets, warehouse stores are very competitive and sometimes force a number of conventional stores out of business. Examples of warehouse stores are Heartland in Boston, Cub Stores in Minneapolis, and Associated Grocers in Kansas City.

A&P's Sav-a-centers feature superstore size and variety. These spacious,
promotional superstores communicate value to consumers who demand low
prices and extensive assortment.

In-Home Shopping

Another innovative approach to retailing involves in-home shopping. In-home purchasing goes back to the chicken farmer with an egg route and the local grocer who took—and delivered—telephone orders. Of course, these merchants largely disappeared after low-cost supermarkets came on the scene in the 1930s. Today in-home shopping on a large scale is possible utilizing closed-circuit television, in-home computer equipment, and automated warehouses. Changes in consumer life-styles, the increased number of dual-career families, a dearth of free time, and the desire for convenience may very well make this approach to shopping commonplace. This suggests that traditional food and nonfood retailers may be vulnerable to a new system of retailing.

RETAIL STRATEGY
J. C. Penney's Fashion Plunge

In an effort to reassert itself as one of this country's top retailers, J. C. Penney Company, based in Dallas, underwent major changes in the mid-1980s to attract large numbers of middle-class shoppers. Some of the latter had been lost because of Penney's muddled image. By 1989, the effort had begun to pay dividends.

After deciding to target a fashion-conscious consumer segment—particularly women—the company restructured its image to become a fashion-oriented department store chain. Its attempt to appear upscale has caused some consumers to view it in the same category as such stores as Dayton Hudson and Bloomingdale's. However, Penney still has a way to go to achieve an upscale image.

With its increased emphasis on men's and women's apparel, management decided to deemphasize hard goods by eliminating such items as electronic equipment. In fact, Penney's apparel stock comprised about 82 percent of its total merchandise mix in 1988.

THE INFLUENCE OF COMPUTERS AND THE NEW TECHNOLOGY

No discussion of the factors that influence retailing would be complete without reference to computers. These remarkable machines, which have been with us for some 30 years, enable retailers to conduct a variety of operations quickly and accurately. They are used in sales, purchasing, inventory control, advertising, payroll, and other operations.

The features of computers that make them such powerful tools are their ability to amass large quantities of information at different locations simultaneously, process the data at electronic speeds, make instantaneous decisions, and turn out useful reports quickly. As you can see, the common element in all of these features is speed. The use of computers is often referred to as **electronic data**

Consumers can now shop from their own homes using closed-circuit television. *Courtesy:* Home Shopping Network.

processing (EDP). Now we'll examine computer techniques commonly used by retail institutions.

Computer Techniques in Retailing

Point-of-Sales (POS)

Many stores, including such successful operations as Mervyn's and Wal-Mart, are equipped with specially designed cash registers that do much more than merely ring up sales. Called **point-of-sales (POS)** or **electronic point-of-sales (EPOS),** this system provides store executives with a wide range of reports on products sold, cash and charge sales, current stock levels, and other vital statistical needs. Because the registers are connected electronically to computers, the information is processed and made available quickly.

Point-of-sale cash registers in action. Notice the scanners amd screens on the top of the registers. *Courtesy:* International Business Machines.

However, constant vigilance by management is essential if POS systems are to remain competitive. For example, Today's Man, a men's wear retailer with some 20 stores, decided in 1988 to update its POS system because pricing mistakes were frequent and unnecessary data were being generated. The new system resulted in reduced labor and equipment costs.

Optical Scanning

Optical scanners use the universal product code

Another version of point-of-sale cash registers, and of particular value to supermarkets, are devices known as optical scanners. This equipment is located at checkout counters and is part of a computerized cash register system. The scanner may be a stationary device or a wand handled by a cashier. Hand-held scanners are more flexible than stationary ones (slot scanners), and are particularly valuable during seasons when sales volume is high, for example, Christmas and Mother's Day. Here is how scanners work.

1. Every package in the store is labeled with sensitized lines (Figure 2-4) that represent the manufacturer, type of product, weight, and size. The lines are symbols for numbers that can be "read" by a scanner. The symbols are part of a standard **universal product code (UPC)** or **bar code** that was introduced in the early 1970s.
2. The cashier runs the package across the scanner, which recognizes the UPC symbols.
3. The scanner transmits the symbol information to an in-store computer in which the price of the product has been stored. At the same time, the information is shown on a screen for the customer's benefit.
4. The computer calculates the sale (including the tax, if any) and the register prints a sales receipt for the customer.

The use of optical scanning equipment reduces checkout time, gives the store better control over inventory, and reduces checkout errors. Although the system encountered some consumer resistance at first, it has gained wide acceptance across the country. For example, the very successful retailer, Toys "Я" Us, adopted a checkout system in 1987 that was an immediate success. In fact, the company's chief executive officer, Charles Lazarus, estimated that Christmas sales that year jumped 30 percent, fueled primarily by the speedup of checkout counter transactions. Another example is Walgreen, a large drug chain, which has installed scanners in its stores.

Figure 2-4   Examples of UPC symbols. *Courtesy:* 1985 Monarch Marking
Systems, Inc. All rights reserved.

Some retailers feature scanning equipment that enables consumers to check out their own purchases. After the self-scanning process is completed, customers receive a bill that is paid for at a cashier's window. The system includes an electronic check of the items to make sure they have been scanned. The retailer benefits from the installation because of the reduced number of checkout clerks needed. Although it is used by a number of supermarkets, including the Pic n' Save chain, the Check Robot system, as it is called, has not yet been adopted widely. This is due to the difficulties many shoppers experience with the system.

Automated price lookup systems (PLU) are also available to speed checkout counter transactions. Acting in conjunction with UPC markings, PLU provides salespeople with instant price information. In addition, **electronic data interchange (EDI)** programs enable retailers to integrate their purchasing activities within their stores and with vendors.

As with all retail technology, the success of PLU and EDI depends on the degree to which personnel is comfortable with the procedures. In fact, Tom Rittenhouse, vice-president and controller of Strawbridge & Clothier, a department store and mass merchandise chain, maintains that a price lookup system is unworkable without the complete cooperation of personnel.[1]

Although many manufacturers have already adopted bar coding, others have been nudged along by their retail customers. For example, F. W. Woolworth Company has pressured its suppliers to package their products with UPC symbols. Since Woolworth is large and powerful, its suppliers have generally fallen into line.

Electronic Funds Transfer

Associated with point-of-sale transactions is a system called **electronic funds transfer** or **EFT.** Its purpose is to eliminate most of the paperwork involved in sales and banking transactions. Here is an example of how it works.

1. An employee's pay is deposited electronically by the employer in the employee's bank account.
2. When the employee purchases merchandise in a store with an EFT installation, he or she uses a bank card (much like a credit card) to record the purchase.
3. After the salesperson has keyed in appropriate sales information, the bank card triggers a computer to automatically deduct the sales price from the customer's bank balance and add it to the store's balance.

This attempt to create a cashless retail society has its drawbacks. For example, the government has to design careful regulations for everyone's protection. Also, a customer can make a purchase through EFT *only* when his or her bank balance is sufficient to cover the purchase.

[1] "Beyond the Challenge," *Chain Store Age Executive,* December 1990, pp. 86, 88.

Automated Teller Machines

Many supermarkets have installed equipment that permits customers to conduct a limited number of banking activities. Coordinated with banks in their areas, these **automated teller machines (ATMs)** reduce the stores' check-cashing transactions, attract additional customers, and provide the stores with rent from the banks. Supermarket chains such as Pathmark, Winn-Dixie, Albertson's, and Pantry Pride are a few of the increasing number of retailers that boast ATMs. A more sophisticated use of the machines ties the equipment to electronic funds transfer systems to produce a consumer-retailer-bank coordinated system.

Rich's department store chain has installed retail transaction terminals for the convenience of its customers. Shoppers can withdraw cash through the terminals, obviating the need to wait in line for a credit or cash transaction. The terminals also enable customers to check their bank balances.

Electronic Spreadsheets

In an attempt to replace the tedious method of updating information by hand, software developers have designed programs called **electronic spreadsheets.** Here is how they are used:

Suppose a retailer tallies the sales of his or her departments daily. Let's assume that this retailer also breaks down the sales within each department by product. If, after computing the total store sales, this retailer discovers an error in a department product category, he or she must recalculate

1. Total sales of that product
2. Total sales of the department
3. Total store sales

These changes involve a great deal of time and effort.

Using an electronic spreadsheet, however, all the retailer has to do is correct the individual department product error. The computer recalculates the various totals automatically, with the updated amounts available on the computer screen and, if desired, in printed form. Thus, the spreadsheet eliminates clerical drudgery and saves precious time.

Companies like Carter Hawley Hale, Dylex, and Sears, Roebuck have computer systems that allow personnel to tap their computers for an endless variety of spreadsheet formats. One of the chief benefits of this capability is that even those with little computer knowledge can develop the reports they need.

Computer Terminals

Salespeople can communicate with computers

Soon to be seen in retail stores are computer terminals, devices that will allow salespeople to communicate with a computer. By keying in certain information, the salesperson will be able to supply immediate answers for such customer questions as Why is this product better than competitive models? How soon can the merchandise be delivered? How does this product differ from similar but differently priced in-store products?

Computer Applications in Retailing

The list that follows contains a sample of computer uses in retailing. Additional applications are contained in succeeding chapters.

Sales Forecasting

Computers can "predict" sales

On the basis of current sales figures and information from other sources, such as manufacturers, wholesalers, accountants, economists, and bankers, retail firms use computers to estimate future sales volume. This is known as **sales forecasting.** The aids to decision making provided by computers enable retailers to plan both short- and long-term sales policies.

Consumer Services

Airlines, hotels, and motels have been using computers for some time to provide customers with instant reservations long in advance of actual use of the accommodations. For example, airlines can provide customers with immediate information about available seats on scheduled flights that are months away. Hotel chains like Hilton can do the same with regard to rooms anywhere in their far-flung network of hotels.

Advertising

With a computer, retailers can select potential customers for special sales. For example, if a store wants to conduct mail advertising directly to people in a certain income category, a computer will compile the list quickly from stored data. It will do the same for other customer characteristics, such as frequency and volume of previous purchases, family or marital status, and education level.

Accounting

Accounting consists of the classification, recording, analysis, and interpretation of financial data. It is of great importance to merchants because of the large quantity of financial information involved in retail operations. Following are several common accounting functions handled by computers.

Computers help in collections

Accounts Receivable.   The term *accounts receivable* refers to the amounts owed by customers to a business. Since selling on credit is such a large part of retail sales, it follows that credit sales records should be computerized.

In a typical accounts receivable system, customers are issued credit (charge) cards for use in making purchases. When making a purchase, the customer presents the credit card to the cashier, who inserts it into the cash register or some other piece of equipment for processing. The customer's credit card number is recorded, along with details of the purchase.

A central computer that contains information about the customer's account receives the data and updates the balance. The computer prints customer charge statements at required intervals, daily and monthly sales totals, sales by departments, and similar reports. It also handles sales returns and customer payments.

The advantages of computerized accounts receivable systems are the timeliness of customer accounts, the ready availability of sales figures, and the reduction of delinquent customer accounts.

Purchasing.   For large retailers, such as department stores and chains, buying merchandise in the right quantity at the right time is essential to efficient management. Nothing so irks a customer as to have a store clerk say, "Sorry, we're out of it!" In order to avoid such embarrassments, computers are used to maintain up-to-the-moment information about inventory.

Many stores have checkout equipment with electronic ties to a computer (POS). The computer uses sales details to keep current records of inventory, and prints out purchase orders when stock gets low. In this way every item in inventory can be maintained at a desired level and customers can be assured of delivery.

Additional Accounting Applications.   Other accounting applications of the computer include payroll and accounts payable. For payroll, the computer prepares payroll records, prints checks, computes taxes, and records payroll entries. For accounts payable, which refers to a retailer's unpaid bills, the computer maintains records of suppliers' invoices and purchase returns, prints checks in time for the retailer to take advantage of suppliers' discounts, and updates amounts owed to suppliers.

Additional Applications

Maintenance and Construction.   Even maintenance procedures in retail areas have been affected by the computer. For example, the Compu-Blend Computerized Cleaning Chemical System developed by the 3M Company enables users to produce cleaning solutions automatically and quickly. As a result, costs are reduced, worker safety is enhanced, and time is saved.

Available to retailers that are planning new outlets is a computer-assisted program (CAD) that provides data about construction and maintenance costs, design and drafting scheduling, and project status. The program enables companies to analyze construction bids accurately and quickly.

Customer Reminder.   Another innovative computer application utilized by retailers—in this case, pharmacies—is the Med-Minder, developed by the General

Computer Corporation. Through recorded messages, the system automatically tells customers by phone that their prescription drugs need to be refilled. These reminders are particularly helpful to the elderly and those suffering from disease. The retailer, of course, benefits from increased sales.

Check Cashing.   The Telecredit Check Guarantee Service is a computer-driven system that enables retailers to verify customers' checks at checkout counters in about 5 seconds. Transactions are handled speedily, customers are grateful, and sales are increased. The system detects bad (unacceptable) checks, saving the retailer collection costs.

Sharing of Tasks.   Mrs. Fields Cookies, an international retailer with some 8,000 employees, uses its complex computer system to relieve personnel of cost-control responsibilities. For example, inventory levels are recorded by the computer. Instead, its staff concentrates on sales programs and selling techniques. This human-computer sharing of tasks has helped catapult the company into a food chain with more than 700 stores.

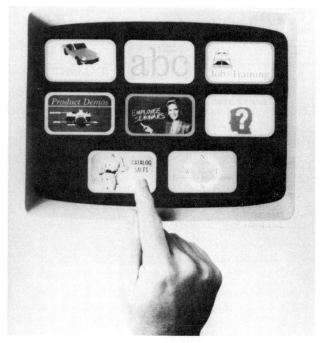

Computerized video systems. *Courtesy:* International Business Machines.

Computerized Video Systems.   Stores are now installing equipment that enables customers independently to decide what merchandise to purchase and to locate goods by themselves.

Book Orders.   The Pubnet computerized ordering system, developed by the General Electric Information Services Corporation, helps bookstores reduce warehouse costs, maintain current price information, and pinpoint out-of-stock books. In effect, it takes the guesswork out of book ordering.

Touch-Screen Systems.   Shoppers seeking information about medications and health aids appear delighted with a new touch-screen system found at many Wal-Mart stores. Called the Pharmacy Information Center (PIC), customers interact with a computer located near the pharmacy area of the store, securing data about health concerns, generic drugs, and specific medications.

Promotional Signs.   The Sears, Roebuck Company prints and distributes signs for its stores through the use of computers. This process overcomes the problem of some stores receiving signs late.

Emerging technological advances in retailing include interactive home shopping devices (between sellers and customers), electronic shelf tags, electronic aisle billboards, self-service merchandise dispensing systems, wireless POS devices, and interactive voice response systems in stores.

Converting to a Computerized System

Before retailers purchase computer hardware, they study their present systems (accounting, inventory, etc.), seek advice from internal and external experts, for example, their accounting firms, and often solicit recommendations from computer manufacturers like the Digital Equipment Company (DEC) and the International Business Machines Company (IBM). They then consider such matters as

1. Cost
2. Availability of software
3. Experience of other retailers
4. Quality and reliability of support from computer manufacturers
5. Security of the system
6. Flexibility of the system

Once these matters have been resolved, merchants involve their staffs in decision making and applications. They attempt to reduce or eliminate employee fears through education and reassurance. With this approach, they make the staff aware of the enormous benefits of computerized systems to themselves and the business. In some cases, computer companies develop software for particular businesses and train salespeople in its use.

A good example of successful retailers that recently installed computer systems are Benetton stores, a large group of apparel outlets. Until recently, most

Courtesy: International Business Machines.

of the stores were still using manual methods for purchase and sales transactions. Because they were losing a competitive edge, many of the stores adopted what is known as the Kliger-Weiss Info System, which generates purchase, sales, inventory, and credit information on a POS basis for timely decision making.

While large retailers have pioneered computer use in the industry, smaller merchants are profiting from that experience. As long as the latter understand their needs, they can adopt any of a number of computer systems for soft or hard goods operations.

Computer Service Companies

Retailers without computer systems and those only partially automated often pay for data processing applications at computer service companies. The merchants reason that either their operations do not merit computer processing or that it is less expensive or more efficient to work with a service company. For example, Modell's, a New York menswear discount specialty chain, has its accounts payable and payroll processed by service companies. At this writing, however, the company is exploring the advisability of automating its operations.

When some or all of the computer applications available to retailers are integrated to form a cohesive process within an organization, the result is called a **retailing information system (RIS).** Put another way, RIS is an ongoing computer-based process for collecting both internal and external data. Internal data are collected from company records, files, and computerized cash registers, while external data are collected from such sources as customers, competitors, and publications. The entire system is designed to prevent as well as solve problems, and it aids management in making profitable decisions and plans. Retailers with RIS are able to conduct useful research regarding customers, merchandise selection, and advertising.

Courtesy: Carolina Amato.

THE INFLUENCE OF FASHION

Communication of fashion news

Fashion expressions and ideas are beamed all over the world via satellites, television, radio, and the press. New ideas and trends move so quickly that it is increasingly difficult for the retailer to keep up with the constantly shifting moods and movements of fashion. Designers are influenced by the nostalgia of bygone days, the excitement of the present, and the challenge of the future. New thinking, new music, new interiors, new lifestyles, and new garments are continually transmitted to us by mass communication techniques. Modern dissemination of fashion news has been the impetus for rapid acceptance or rejection of new ideas, making it more difficult for the retailer to gauge the fashion picture correctly.

It is critical for the retailer to understand the why, how, and when of fashion changes because the salability of most merchandise is affected by fashion. In an attempt to meet the needs of consumers, retailers study fashion terminology, trends, and theories.

Fashion Terms

Fashion is how people live, dress, work, and "play" at a given time and place. What is fashionable today might not be accepted in the next decade. Although many people confuse the terms *fashion* and *style,* and even use the words synonymously, they mean different things.

A **style** of a product has a distinct feature or concept that makes it different from others within a particular category. For example, a double-breasted jacket is a style of jacket. A ranch house is the style of house. When a style is accepted or adopted, it becomes a fashion, or fashionable. Therefore, the fashions at any given time include consumer acceptance of certain styles in clothing, houses, lifestyles, and recreation.

Fashion and style are different

A style that remains in fashion for a long period is considered a **classic.** It is generally simple in design and remains in demand for years. Examples of classics are blazer jackets, shirtwaist dresses, and loafer shoes. A fashion that is adopted and discarded in a short period is known as a **fad.** Fads are generally accepted by small segments of the consumer market. For example, among the fads for teens in the 1980s were punk rock items, neon colors, and snap bracelets. The Persian Gulf War in 1991 gave rise to a show of patriotism and the "wearing" of the American flag on jackets, shirts, etcetera. In addition, a host of special Desert Shield items were produced, such as sun/wind/dust goggles and field jackets.

A **fashion trend** is the direction in which different styles move in response to consumer demand. Trends can be observed in both hard and soft goods. Many trends may exist at the same time. Trends are defined as either incoming or outgoing. **Incoming trends** are on the upward curve of popularity, whereas **outgoing trends** are on the downgrade curve of consumer demand.

Among the theories used to explain the mystery and flow of fashion acceptance are the fashion cycle, the trickle-down theory, the trickle-across theory, and the trickle-up theory. In order for retailers to sell fashion at a profit, they must understand and study the fashion adoption process. By doing so, they can develop greater insight, which can be used in planning merchandise strategy; that is, to buy merchandise that consumers want, at a time they want it, and for how long they want it.

Fashion Theories

The fashion cycle and fashion adoption process

A **fashion cycle** is the movement of a style from introduction to acceptance, peak of popularity, and then decline. In other words, it is the life cycle of an item. In the early stages of the fashion cycle, the style attracts individuals who buy because it is something new. These people are referred to as the avant-garde, pacesetters, or early adopters. They are usually found in the higher socioeconomic groups and are confident enough to risk being different. At the introductory stage of the cycle, expensive, exclusive stores carry the style for a wealthy clientele. As the style is accepted, other fine shops and department stores begin to stock the

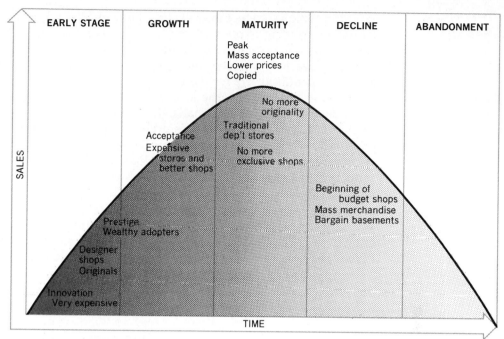

Figure 2-5   The fashion cycle.

item. Although the style is still expensive, it is less costly than the original models. As the style moves to the peak of popularity, it is more widely accepted and is copied by the mass merchandisers and budget shops. As the item is sold to customers in lower socioeconomic groups and featured in low-end stores, the style is considered to be in the decline stage. At this point the original buyers have already discarded the style and started on something new (Figure 2-5).

It should be noted that the fashion cycle has no definite time period because it is consumer demand that keeps the cycle going. For example, the fashion cycle for menswear historically has been longer than that for women's wear. Also, the fashion cycle for infants' clothing is longer than that for teens' clothing. Just as changes in the retail life cycle (Figure 2-2) depend on the consumer, so do changes in the fashion cycle.

The trickle-down theory begins with the upper class

The **trickle-down theory** begins with the higher socioeconomic levels. Once again, a style is introduced with the upper class and passed down to the masses. In the first phase it is adopted by the pacesetters, people with enough money and daring to try it. As it gains impetus, it is taken up by other consumers, those who follow the innovators, and finally by the masses. When the style is generally adopted, it is considered to be in fashion. Both the fashion cycle and the trickle-down theory were widely accepted prior to World War I. At that time Paris was considered the fashion capital of the world, and everyone followed its lead.

Adoration of high society, especially European royalty, was and still is the inspiration for the copying of original creations. For example, the popular Princess of Wales (Diana) has sparked a great deal of demand for copies of the clothes she wears. In America it was the wealthy who adopted the styles that in time were copied by manufacturers for the lower classes.

Today's fashion innovators

After World War II, America started to create its own designs rather than imitate Paris. The social scene changed. Hollywood, theater, politics, royalty, and the middle class found themselves drawn together. Money, rather than family background, became all-important in celebrity status. The inspiration for styles was now drawn from various groups. Changes in society, the media, and mass production challenged the accepted theories that held that style innovations begin only with the upper class.

Successful businesspeople, designers, actors, and people in the news developed into the new fashion leaders. The media helped create celebrities, who became very important to retailers. Merchants who promoted celebrities such as Gloria Vanderbilt, Johnny Carson, and Diane Von Furstenberg, honed a competitive edge by selling "exclusive" merchandise at affordable prices. Johnny Carson licensed his name to Hart, Schaffner and Marx to be used in menswear. Diane Von Furstenberg married a prince and became a royal celebrity overnight; as a result, her name in clothing and accessories made millions of dollars for manufacturers and retailers. The marketing of Gloria Vanderbilt was one of the most dramatic of business success stories. With the popularity of "name labels" established in the public mind, this well-known society name on jeans gave retailers a strong product to sell. The scene was now set for a new concept of fashion adoption.

A current fashion theory

The **trickle-across theory** maintains that innovation can begin with any social class. According to this theory (Figure 2-6), each class has opinion leaders who can influence others to buy and accept new styles. In other words, in every class or walk of life there are people who are emulated and followed by others

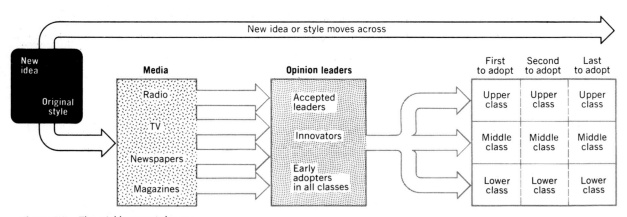

Figure 2-6 The trickle-across theory.

within that class. Furthermore, within a class there are different groups with their own leaders. For example, on a college campus one group might emulate a sports figure, another a scholar, and still another an artist. It is likely then, that the style adopted by a leader will be adopted by others in the group. Thus, the style moves across, rather than down, to another class.

It is also possible to have the same style in different price ranges adopted by more than one class at the same time. For example, when "designer jeans" (e.g., Calvin Klein, Guess, Jordache) were introduced, the "label" concept was adopted by members of more than one class. However, jeans were manufactured in different price lines for different groups.

Fashion works its way up

The **trickle-up theory** states that fashion innovation may start at the bottom of the price range and work its way up to higher prices. For example, punk rock merchandise started at the bottom price range and was adopted at higher prices.

Creating a Fashion Image

The media create fashion awareness

Media coverage, extensive advertising, and customer mobility have created fashion awareness in all classes and market segments at the same time. Because of media coverage, consumers in the most remote areas are aware of the latest fashions. Suburban and urban, rich and poor are all alert to fashion. Under these conditions the fashion cycle has become somewhat shorter, causing changes in the adoption process. Planning was different in the days when merchants were familiar with a style that was passing from one group to another. Today, however, style acceptance by all types of customers at essentially the same time has made merchandise planning more difficult for the retailer.

Customers and the fashion adoption process

The retailer needs a clear picture of how the store's customers fit into the fashion adoption process. Is the store's clientele made up of innovators, the avant-garde who buy only in the early stages? Or are its customers the latecomers who wait for the style to become established? A retailer who buys too soon or too late for the store's customer base will have difficulty selling the merchandise. Since the salability of merchandise is dependent on the extent to which it meets the customer's desires, a vital aspect of the merchant's job is assessing the customer's "taste" requirements.

By understanding fashion theories, the retailer is in a better position to relate fashion innovation to store image and competition. Through merchandising strategy and product assortment, the retailer can choose to be a known leader in fashion, that is, the first to carry a new item or develop a more conservative fashion stance.

The importance of creating a fashion image

A firm fashion image means that the consumer recognizes what the store stands for and to whom it appeals. When the image is clearly established in the public mind, the store attracts customers who respond to that image. For example, Loehmann's, Inc., an off-price specialty chain founded by Frieda Loehmann in 1921, received high marks for creating a quality fashion image at reduced prices.

Shoppers respond to a store's fashion image. (Left) Loehmann's (Right) Macy's.

Loehmann developed an unusual atmosphere for shoppers by transforming a former automobile showroom into an artistic "happening." The furnishings were beautiful, and the store boasted many valuable antiques and works of art. The store's image became firmly established: quality merchandise at low prices.

The Bloomingdale's chain is another example of a store that has established a distinct fashion image. "Bloomie's" is known for fashion excitement and has developed strong customer loyalty. The chain brought its special brand of showmanship to Chicago in 1988, with a sales strategy that included a concentration of high fashion and international designer names. Bloomingdale's chairman, Marvin S. Traub, asserted that "We brought what we believe in and we'll let Chicago tell us."

It is apparent that a store's success is directly linked to its understanding of customers and their fashion appetites. Retailers must decide whom the store will represent in terms of fashion, and then develop the appropriate merchandise strategy.

Because of its favorable fashion image, Dayton's, an upscale department store chain, was the first choice by far in a study of 35- to 44-year-old Minneapolis shoppers. Figure 2-7 indicates that 32.1 percent of those surveyed preferred to shop at Dayton's, while its nearest competitor, Target Stores[2], was the choice of only 9.6 percent.

Another case involves the opening of the Bergdorf Goodman men's store in New York City. Despite the array of designer fashions carried, it will be the store's personality and unique ambiance that make it a preferred destination for those who can afford to shop there. Ira Neimark, the store's president, said that "The men's store, a monument to opulence, is geared to those people who go to the best hotels, the best restaurants, the best clubs, and the best resorts."[3]

[2] Owned by Dayton's.

[3] R. La Ferla, "A Store Is Born," *The New York Times Magazine*, August 26, 1990, pp. 67–69.

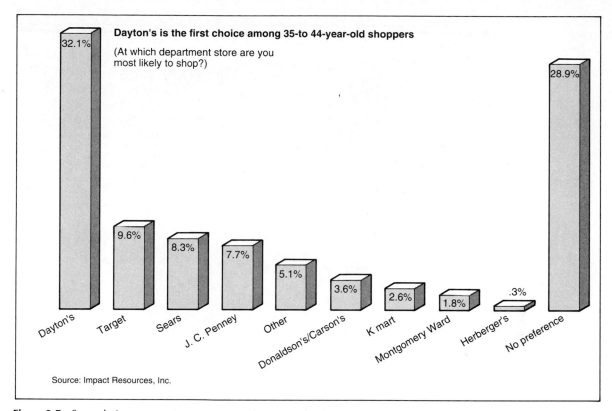

Figure 2-7   Store choices among 35- to 44-year-old Minneapolis shoppers.

THE INFLUENCE OF CONSUMERISM

Consumers exert pressure on business

Today's retailer must deal with a better-educated and more sophisticated customer than was the case in earlier times. Consumers are wiser in their buying decisions and more vocal in fighting for their interests. They are more concerned about inflation, pollution, and the quality of life. They have filed lawsuits against manufacturers, boycotted firms, picketed stores to protest certain business practices, and exerted numerous pressures on business. This increased activism may have come about because of social and economic changes in consumers' lives. Consumers are more affluent, more mobile, and less loyal to local and neighborhood stores. These changes pose additional difficulties for the merchant.

The progressive retailer, who acts as the consumer's buying agent, must be responsive to this consumer activity. Not only are merchants expected to sell goods and services, but it is assumed that they will do business in a legal, responsible manner. This section deals with the consumer protection movement,

PRACTITIONER'S CORNER

What follows is a summary of an interview with Akira Maki, a Japanese-American designer-manufacturer of upscale women's clothing.

1. Located in the heart of New York City's garment center, and known professionally as Akira, Mr. Maki prepares all his designs in the New York area.

2. He deals more and more with specialty stores because department stores are short of knowledgeable fashion personnel. Moreover, many of these personnel leave the department stores, taking customers with them to specialty shops.

3. American retailers pirate fashion personnel from one another, a practice not found in other countries. They also "steal" (copy) others' designs and farm their orders to cheap foreign manufacturers.

4. By and large, department stores are getting weaker in the fashion field, with chains like Saks Fifth Avenue and Bloomingdale's having already lost their strong fashion images. The personal touch and service have diminished at department stores, with unfortunate results.

5. Mr. Maki's firm communicates regularly with stores by telephone and mail and uses such items as humorous cards to cement relationships.

6. Akira pays for and conducts fashion shows at charities, stores, the United Nations, and so on.

7. Since there is insufficient profit in the fashion business, Japanese firms have generally ignored this field. Besides, he maintains that retailers make most of the money in the fashion industry.

8. Since most older people want to look younger, fashion magazines feature young models in clothing designed for older consumers.

9. Akira's firm licenses wedding dresses, evening dresses, suits, and accessories, with their manufacture taking place overseas, mainly in Japan and partially in Italy.

10. He laments the merging of resident buying houses because the resulting large ones handle large accounts only, while smaller ones go unrepresented.

11. American schools do not spend sufficient time on fashion education. If changes aren't made soon, the American fashion business will falter.

12. Akira tries to persuade Japanese women in this country, the wives of Japanese businessmen and diplomats, to be more daring in their choice of clothing. His emphasis is on more colorful outfits—green, orange, and turquoise rather than black, brown, and ash—and he has had modest success with this population. The Japanese consumer is quality, rather than quantity, oriented. Consequently, Akira's prices are significantly higher in Japan than in the United States. His fashions appeal to the upscale Japanese shopper.

---

legislation to protect consumers, the agencies involved, and the influences of this movement on the retailer.

Background

The relationship between the consumer and the retailer has become much more complex than it used to be. The change from small neighborhood shops to large chains has taken away some of the consumer's ability to communicate directly with the producer or seller. For example, in the past, if a customer had a problem with clothing made by a local tailor, he or she knew exactly where to go for satisfaction. At that time the ethics of the merchant were regulated by the marketplace. If a seller wronged a buyer, he or she risked losing a customer and acquiring a bad reputation. Small merchants could not afford a loss of goodwill or customers, so they generally attempted to settle complaints without interference from others.

Consumer dissatisfaction   Today buyers are confronted with a more complicated situation. With changing markets and technology, consumers seldom meet the actual producer of a product. Manufacturers are not always visible, and furthermore, their distributors are not always willing to assume responsibility for complaints. The consumers' difficulties become apparent when they are faced with shoddy products, inadequate warranties, late deliveries, unsafe products, and the like.

Consumer complaints and dissatisfaction in the marketplace prompted the **consumer movement.** This led to a demand for laws protecting the public from unfair trade practices. The term **consumerism** refers to all the activities and organized efforts involved in safeguarding the buyer from mistreatment and exploitation.

In 1962 President John F. Kennedy's consumer address listed the following four rights of consumers that laid the foundation for later legislation.

1. The right to safety, for example, protection against hazardous goods
2. The right to be informed, for example, protection against misleading information
3. The right to choose, for example, a free marketplace that ensures the consumer a variety of offerings
4. The right to be heard, for example, right to complain and seek legal remedies

Many federal laws have been enacted to protect consumers against fraud and other unfair practices. Basically, the legislation falls into two categories: (1) laws that regulate business to promote competition and (2) laws that protect consumers.

Laws that Regulate Business to Promote Competition

These laws were enacted to ensure choice in the marketplace.

Philosophy

The assumption that competition is the natural regulator of the marketplace—and that it results in fair practices and pricing—is what prompted the laws that guard against monopolistic practices. Basically, they curb the abuse of power by business by preventing large companies from smothering smaller firms in the same industry. Without these restrictions, large firms could stifle smaller competitors and bilk the consumer by charging unfair prices. The major consumer laws are listed in the appendix at the end of this chapter.

How Laws to Promote Competition Affect Retailers

Retailers cannot join in a conspiracy to control prices. The Clayton and Robinson-Patman acts make it unlawful for any person knowingly to induce or receive a discriminatory price. It is vital, therefore, for the retailer to exercise caution in negotiating prices. If a supplier indicates that a requested price or special service is discriminatory, it violates the act if the vendor agrees to the merchant's request.

When a retailer undertakes to buy and price merchandise, it is important that he or she have a broad knowledge of the laws that affect buying and pricing. However, these laws change from time to time. For example, the Miller-Tydings Act, also known as the Fair Trades Act, allowed manufacturers to obtain agreements from distributors not to sell certain products below a minimum stated price.

A shopper about to make a decision. *Courtesy:* International Business Machines.

These laws have since been repealed because consumers and dealers were prohibited from offering and receiving better prices in the marketplace. The laws were designed to protect the manufacturer's brand against price cutting by retailers. They were also intended to shield the small merchant from unfair competition by large chains. In effect, however, they served to prevent consumers from buying at lower prices.

Other ways in which laws that promote competition affect retailers are the following.

1. Retailers cannot force suppliers not to sell to competitors.
2. Retailers cannot cut prices with the intent of forcing small merchants out of business.
3. Retailers must be able to substantiate their advertising claims or else advertise a correction.

Laws to Protect Consumers

These laws were enacted to safeguard consumer interests with regard to products, advertising, and credit.

Philosophy

The consumer protection laws were designed to protect the consumer against unfair selling practices, unsafe merchandise, and deceptive information. Although buyers have the right not to buy, consumerists claim that buyers cannot make intelligent decisions when they are influenced by promotion and advertising. The laws in this category are of the following types.

1. Laws that require minimum standards for product safety and performance, for example, standards for food, drug, and cosmetic products. Safety standards for automobiles are also in this group.
2. Laws that require the consumer to be provided with necessary information concerning a purchase, for example, information about credit and warranties.
3. Laws that strengthen communications between manufacturers/retailers and consumers, for example, laws requiring honesty in labeling and advertising.

How Laws Related to Products, Advertising, and Credit Affect Retailers

Caveat venditor   Because retailers act as buying agents for consumers, they are responsible by law for selling safe products and can be sued for selling defective ones. The Latin expression **caveat venditor,** "let the seller beware," sets the tone for all consumer legislation. So in the case of unsafe or faulty products the laws make the retailer, rather than the consumer, responsible for notifying the producer.

The various food, drug, and cosmetic acts require accurate labeling and truthful advertising. Labels should indicate exact weight, ingredients, preservatives, and other chemicals. Because the law requires that drugs and cosmetics be proven safe before they are sold, the retailer must remove a product from the selling floor when its safety is questioned by a responsible agency. After the incidents of the Tylenol poisonings in 1982, for example, the packaging of over-the-counter drugs in "tamper-resistant" containers became law in 1983. Furthermore, the recurrence of Tylenol poisonings in 1986 caused Johnson & Johnson to cease production of Tylenol in capsule form. Retailers selling **store brands**—that is, merchandise sold only in their stores—must abide by the same requirements as manufacturers with regard to labeling, packaging, and pricing.

Retailers should be concerned with quality specifications and guard against selling unsafe and unsanitary products. The law requires that **warranties** (written guarantees of a manufacturer's or retailer's responsibility) be made available to the consumer *before* the purchase. This involves prominent display of warranties at the point of sale.

In the case of a credit transaction, the Truth-in-Lending Law requires the retailer to inform the customer fully regarding credit terms and charges. The Fair Credit Billing Act cautions and regulates the retailer with regard to billing disputes. The Equal Credit Opportunity Act further cautions the retailer in extending credit fairly to all groups.

Finally, in order to advertise a special price, the retailer must have sufficient stock to sell or else must give the customer a "rain check."

Federal Regulatory Agencies

Listed here are the federal "watchdog" agencies that monitor legislation regarding consumer needs and rights.

The Federal Trade Commission (FTC)

Federal watchdogs

This agency was established by the Federal Trade Commission Act of 1914 to prevent practices that are in restraint of trade and to promote competition. The Commission's jurisdiction has been increased by subsequent laws to include advertising, labeling, and unfair practices in commerce. It investigates complaints about unfair practices from consumers, business, and other government agencies. In addition, it identifies and investigates situations that are in need of study.

The Consumer Products Safety Commission

This commission is empowered by the Consumer Products Safety Act to set safety standards for products that could be hazardous to consumers. It handles drugs, cosmetics, and some other products that were originally under the jurisdiction of the Food and Drug Administration.

Office of Consumer Affairs

This office advises the Department of Health and Human Services and the President on consumer matters and coordinates federal activities for consumer protection.

The Department of Agriculture

This agency works with the FTC to enforce various laws. For example, one controversy involved "junk food" sold in school vending machines. The Department subsequently changed its regulations to ensure that food sold in schools makes a nutritional contribution to the student's diet.

The Department of Health and Human Services
(Food and Drug Administration)

The agency was established by the Food and Drug Act to protect consumers against impure and unsafe foods, drugs, cosmetics, and other potential hazards.

Business Regulators

In addition to the federal regulators, there are other institutions and organizations that are literally looking over the shoulders of retailers.

The Better Business Bureau

This nonprofit association has offices in approximately 170 markets around the country and is financed and supported by private businesses. The purpose of the Bureau is to promote truth in advertising and ethical selling practices, and to protect the public against fraud. Its offices investigate complaints, warn merchants, and, if necessary, turn records over to authorities. In one case, the Bureau reported that problems with deliveries by mail order businesses topped the list of consumer complaints. As a result, the Federal Trade Commission developed regulations to deal with this problem. Consumers now have the right to know when an order will be shipped, and if there is no time limit the goods must be mailed within 30 days.

Consumers Union and Consumer Reports Magazine

These publications are noted for their testing of consumer products and their furthering of consumer interests.

Consumerism at the State and Municipal Levels

Regulations for municipalities

In addition to the federal laws, many states and municipalities have enacted their own consumer protection laws and have organized consumer bureaus and agencies. State statutes generally cover misleading advertising, deceptive sales techniques, unfair credit policies, and unethical door-to-door selling practices. Some states have regulations regarding product performance and safety. For example, they have passed "lemon laws" with regard to defective cars.

In order to protect the consumer against defective or faulty cars, "lemon laws" have been enacted in all but four states. In New York State, for example, a new car is protected under the law for the first 18,000 miles of use or the first two years of ownership, whichever comes first. If, during that time, the owner has brought the car in for repairs four or more times, or has had the vehicle in a repair shop for a cumulative total of 30 or more calendar days, without remedying the problem, then the consumer is eligible for "lemon law" relief.

Many municipalities have regulations to protect consumers against dishonest weights and measures, contests that do not offer equal opportunities to win, and **bait-and-switch advertising** (luring a customer into the store with the intention of selling something else). There are also laws requiring food dating and a cooling-off period for door-to-door sales. (This allows the customer to cancel a contract within a certain length of time, such as one to three days.)

At all levels of government, a great deal of literature has been published by various agencies in an attempt to educate the public regarding their rights and how to guard themselves against being cheated. Since the laws act as a warning to business, many producers and retailers have attempted to avoid additional regulations by improving or correcting any irregularities in their practices.

Self-Regulation by Retailers

Three out of four of the nation's major corporations now have a written code of ethics. Large retailers like Sears and J. C. Penney have programs that pretest merchandise before it reaches the selling floor. Other merchants have developed their own consumer relations departments to answer customer questions and complaints. Stores have developed training programs to inform their salespeople regarding product information, thereby preparing them to answer customer questions. Food processors have joined the Food and Drug Administration's Cooperative Quality Assurance Program to ensure the adequacy of their quality standards. In fact, communicating with the various agencies has become so important that some large retailers, such as Penney, have government relations departments in Washington.

Some fast-food restaurants have begun to respond to consumer demand for nutritional data by making information available in a way that resembles the nutritional information on supermarket packages. For example, Pizza Hut distributes cards at its outlets with the complete nutrient breakdown of each of its pizzas, while Arby's offers booklets containing a nutrient analysis of its sandwich combinations.

Today retailers are under constant surveillance. Daily advertisements are checked, special offers are investigated, and most consumer transactions are eligible for public hearings or lawsuits. Class action suits (in which an attorney general sues on behalf of a large group) have become quite common, and many retailers have received negative publicity or been fined.

Private right of action laws allow consumers to sue businesses for false ads and misleading practices without the aid of the attorney general.

Retailers who respond positively to the consumer movement will undoubtedly increase goodwill and fare better than their competitors. The better-educated consumers of the next decade will be willing to pay for long-term quality and have

J. C. Penney's Mechandise Center pretests products before they are offered for sale. *Courtesy:* J. C. Penney & Co.

less interest in short-term bargains. The retailer that provides quality and responsibility and advertises intelligently will be ahead of the competition.

NEW TERMS

automated price look-up system (PLU)   low-margin operator
automated teller machine (ATM)   no-frills operator
bait-and-switch advertising   off-price retailing
bar code   outgoing trend

buying club
caveat venditor
classic
consumer movement
consumerism
electronic data interchange (EDI)
electronic data processing (EDP)
electronic funds transfer (EFT)
electronic point-of-sales (EPOS)
electronic spreadsheet
factory outlet
fad
fashion
fashion cycle
fashion trend
incoming trend

point-of-sales (POS)
retail life cycle
retailing information system (RIS)
sales forecasting
store brand
style
trickle-across theory
trickle-down theory
trickle-up theory
universal product code (UPC)
warehouse club
warehouse store
warehouse-style home center
warranty
wheel of retailing

CHAPTER HIGHLIGHTS

1. If they are to thrive, retailing institutions must adapt to social, political, and economic changes.
2. The wheel of retailing demonstrates the institutional changes that take place when innovators enter the retail arena.
3. The retail life cycle is a way of viewing changes in the retail environment.
4. Current retail innovators that are turning the "wheel" include off-price retailers, factory outlets, warehouse-style home centers, warehouse clubs, and warehouse stores.
5. Changes in consumer lifestyles make in-home shopping a challenge to traditional food retailers.
6. Computers enable retailers to conduct a variety of operations quickly and accurately.
7. Computer techniques in retailing include POS, UPC, PLU, EDI, EFT, ATM, and electronic spreadsheets.
8. New ideas and trends in fashion appear so quickly today that it is difficult for the retailer to keep pace with the changes.
9. In order to meet the challenges of fashion change, the retailer should study fashion trends and theories.

10. The process of fashion adoption is explained by the fashion cycle, the trickle-down theory, the trickle-across theory, and the trickle-up theory.

11. Because of the media explosion, fashion awareness reaches all segments and classes at the same time.

12. Retail success is dependent on establishing and communicating a store's fashion image.

13. Because retailers must deal with better-educated and more sophisticated consumers, they must be responsive to pressures for a "fair deal."

14. Aside from regulating business to promote competition, the federal government has enacted legislation to protect consumers in several areas: foods, drugs, cosmetics, safety, credit, warranties, and labeling.

15. Federal and business regulators are among "watchdogs" that monitor consumer legislation.

REVIEW QUESTIONS

1. Why have no-frills operations become popular?
2. List some of the functions for which retailers utilize computers.
3. What is the difference between POS and EFT?
4. Why is the fashion cycle becoming shorter? How does this affect retailers?
5. How does an understanding of the fashion adoption sequence aid the retailer in developing a fashion image?
6. What is the background of the consumer movement? How have consumer laws affected retailers in everyday practice?
7. What are some of the measures to which retailers have resorted in order to avoid additional regulation?
8. How have minorities been protected by the consumer credit laws?

DISCUSSION QUESTIONS

1. What indications are there that traditional retailers may lose some of their patronage to in-home shopping systems?
2. What are the implications for traditional retailers as more manufacturers sell directly to consumers, as in factory outlets?
3. What are some questions a retailer should ask before deciding between the purchase of a computer system and involvement with a computer service company?

4. Will the use of UPC markings increase or decrease in the near future? Why?

5. Explain how the concept of caveat venditor affects a retailer's responsibilities to consumers.

CASE 1

Railroad Cars in Shopping Centers?

Dining out in redesigned and refurbished railroad cars has been on the scene for some time. With pleasant decors and cozy furnishings, the cars are patronized for their ambience as well as their service. Other cars serve as sleeping accommodations in motels.

Now we are witnessing an extension of the railroad car conversion idea to other retail outlets. Boxcar Industries USA, owners of Boxcar Burger Restaurants and Boxcar Motor Inns, intends to install the cars in shopping centers throughout the United States. Designed as "quick shopping" units, the stores will not replace regular shopping center tenants like department stores and supermarkets. Instead, they will cater to consumers who want to make fast purchases. Merchandise and services will consist of such items as hardware, novelties, and dry cleaning. Shopping itself will be made as simple as possible.

To be called Boxcar Centers, the stores will occupy approximately 30,000 square feet. Each store will have its own store front, and customers will be able to walk through from one car to another. The intention is to develop a complex of small-item one-stop stores.

a. Do you think consumers will respond positively to the Boxcar concept? Why?

b. If you were the owner of a store selling competing items, what would be your reaction to the entrance of Boxcar stores in your shopping center or in one nearby?

CASE 2

Another Turn of the Wheel?

Warehouse club retailing is a fairly new entrant in the retailing industry. Basically, it involves setting up warehouse stores that typically stock a variety of items at wholesale prices to qualified customers who pay a small membership fee, for example, $25 to $30. To maintain their wholesale selling approach, the stores try to ensure that 60 to 65 percent of their customers are businesses. The warehouses act primarily as wholesalers, selling food, office supplies, and other necessities to businesses at prices 8 to 10 percent above cost.

The Price Club of California, the first and most successful of the warehouse clubs, opened in 1976. The club was initially directed toward a fairly small group of bona fide wholesale customers, such as institutions (schools, nursing homes, etc.) and small businesses (lawyers, accountants, real estate and insurance agencies). The store carried limited merchandise to satisfy the basic needs of these business enterprises. The central idea was that, for an annual fee, these customers could buy basic business goods on a cash-and-carry basis at wholesale prices. Employees of the suppliers to the store were also permitted to shop, but purchases for personal use cost more, generally 8 percent above the wholesale price. As the venture grew, membership was expanded to a wider range of employee groups, such as banks, credit unions, and government agencies.

Over a ten-year period, other entrepreneurs like Costco followed the lead of the Price Club and opened their own warehouse clubs.

A typical warehouse club store covers approximately 100,000 square feet in an out-of-the-way location, is not air conditioned, and has only the bare minimum in terms of fixtures. This helps keep plant and building costs down to about 8 percent of sales. Only 3,000 to 4,000 items are stocked, compared with about 60,000 items in a traditional discount store such as K mart. Club members spend an average of $125 each time they shop.

Stock includes general merchandise such as appliances and office supplies and, in some stores, other nonfood and grocery products. Merchandise is shipped to the stores and stocked in a day; thus data processing procedures are very sophisticated to permit continual monitoring of inventory (stock on hand). Warehouse stores are heavily staffed, which helps keep merchandise loss due to shoplifting and theft low. A single entrance/exit door in the store also contributes to a low rate of merchandise loss.

The location of a typical store is at an out-of-the-way industrial site that has very low rent. Operators negotiate long-term leases with options to renew at favorable rates. Large parking areas and loading areas are absolutely essential, because these membership retailing operations are strictly cash-and-carry.

The advertising budget is minimal: After a campaign to advertise the opening, the store relies on limited, tightly targeted direct mailing and on word of mouth. Sales per square foot of selling space, a key indicator to retailers of productivity, can run as high as $1,000 per square foot.

Consistent selection and availability of basic merchandise are critical to profitable warehouse club operation. The institutions and small businesses that form the primary customer base must be able to rely on the warehouse store for the supplies they need at all times.

These factors, coupled with highly automated inventory procedures and controls, limited but appropriate mix of merchandise tailored to the customer base, and low costs of operation have led to the establishment of many successful membership retailing businesses.

Impact on other retailers in areas where warehouse club stores have opened has not been serious thus far, due in part to the narrow selection of merchandise offered. Some experts believe that the more pronounced effect has been on other wholesalers.

However, retail discounters such as Wal-Mart and K mart have already opened warehouse club outlets. Obviously, success moves the wheel of retailing.

The industry is still in a period of growth and has not yet reached what experts term "market saturation." Analysts expect membership retailing as a whole to grow to be a $25 billion business by 1992.

a. Do you think that the warehouse club poses a serious threat to the discount retailer? If so, in what areas?

b. Would you expect more discount retailers to open warehouse club stores, as K mart has done? What problems do you think they may encounter?

c. What factors do you think would tend to limit the growth of membership retailing?

d. As warehouse clubs become more numerous, will independent operations like the Price Club continue to prosper? Explain.

e. Overall, what kind of impact do you think membership retailing will have on the industry?

REFERENCES

BROWN, S. "The Wheel of Retailing: Past and Future." *Journal of Retailing*, **66** (Summer 1990), pp. 143–147.

KIRBY, G. H., AND R. DARDIS. "A Pricing Study of Women's Apparel in Off-price and Department Stores." *Journal of Retailing*, **62** (Fall 1986), pp. 321–330.

LASHINSKY, P. "Dayton's No Longer Stands Alone." *Apparel Merchandising* (September 1988), pp. 62–66.

RAZZANO, R. "Bloomingdale's in Chicago: Reality Sets In." *Chain Store Age Executive*, **65** (January 1989), pp. 22–29.

ROBINS, G. "Integrating Systems." *Stores* (October 1988), pp. 129–132.

APPENDIX

Major Consumer Laws

LAWS THAT REGULATE BUSINESS TO PROMOTE COMPETITION

Sherman Antitrust Act (1890)

Clayton Act (1914)

Federal Trade Commission Act (1914)

Robinson-Patman Act (1936)

Miller-Tydings Act (1937)

Consumer Goods Pricing Act (1957)

LAWS RELATED TO PRODUCTS

Federal Meat Inspection Act (1907)

Federal Food, Drug, and Cosmetic Act (1938)

Wool Products Labeling Act (1939)

Fur Products Labeling Act (1951)

Flammable Fabrics Act (1953—amended 1969)

Textile Fiber Products Identification Act (1959)

Hazardous Substance Act (1961—amended 1968)

Child Protection Act (1966)

Fair Packaging and Labeling Act (1966)

Consumer Products Safety Act (1967—amended 1972)

Toy Safety Act (1968)

Poison Prevention Packaging Act (1970)

Public Health Smoking Act (1970)

PURPOSE

- Ensures the consumer's choice in the marketplace
- Maintains competition

- Antitrust laws

- Ensures the consumer's right to safety
- Ensures safe and healthy food products
- Bans hazardous products sold in stores
- Protects children's toys
- Bans sale of hazardous toys

LAWS RELATED TO PRODUCTS

Magnuson-Moss warranty section of
   the Improvements Act (1974)
Auto recall/repair laws (1975)
"Tamper-resistant" container laws
   (1983)

LAWS RELATED TO ADVERTISING

Federal Trade Commission Act
   (1914)
Federal Communications Act
   (1936)
Wheeler-Lea Act (1938)
Cigarette Labeling and
   Advertising Act (1961)

LAWS RELATED TO CREDIT

Consumer Protection Act—Truth-
   in-Lending (1968—amended
   1980)
Fair Credit Reporting Act (1970)
Fair Credit Billing Act (1974)

Equal Credit Opportunity Act
   (1975)
Electronic Fund Transfer Act
   (1978)

Fair Debt Collection Practices Act
   (1978)

PURPOSE

- Ensures the consumer's right to
  be informed without deception
  or distortion

- Ensures full disclosure and
  conditions of credit transactions
  and charges
- Ensures equal opportunity to
  establish credit
- Provides protection for
  correcting mistakes on credit
  records
- Protects consumers from abuse
  by creditors

Chapter 3

The Consumer

After completing this chapter, you should be able to:

- Identify the influences and factors that affect consumer behavior.
- List and illustrate the five levels of needs in Maslow's hierarchy of needs.
- Identify the ways in which consumer learning takes place and the concepts used to understand personality.
- Identify the demographic categories and explain their impact on consumer behavior.
- Identify the factors that influence lifestyles.

Even more than in prior years, retailers in the 1990s must know who their customers are as well as their changing needs, and most retailers will succeed or fail according to their ability to attract and satisfy customers. To do this, they must have a clear-cut understanding of how, where, what, and when consumers buy. Merchants must be concerned with all the factors that influence the customers, such as merchandise, prices, salespeople, store atmosphere, and customer services. In addition, they must understand the customer's psyche, emotional needs, habits, and motives for buying.

Understanding why one store is "comfortable" for a shopper—that is, makes him or her feel at home—while another makes the shopper feel ill at ease is part of the difficulty of analyzing the customer. For example, a store that encourages the "just looking" customer to examine merchandise without feeling pressured indirectly invites that customer back to the store.

Images are communicated to the customer by the store's atmosphere, location, displays, and salespeople. Customers make decisions about stores on the basis of the services offered, the merchandise and price lines carried, customer conveniences, and their general feelings about the store personnel, decor, and so forth.

Retailers must appeal to the customer in many ways because buying behavior is complicated by psychological, social, and economic factors. Buying behavior and spending patterns are influenced by income, age, location, social situations, and the like. A merchant's ability to develop a sound strategy for pleasing the customer therefore requires constant study of the consumer and the influences on consumer behavior.

ANALYZING AND UNDERSTANDING THE CONSUMER

The process whereby consumers decide whether, what, where, when, and how to buy goods and services is known as **consumer behavior.** Outside influences complicate this behavior before as well as during the buying process. A study of consumers' needs and motives helps us understand *why* they buy.

Consumers' needs and motives determine their buying behavior

The study of consumer behavior involves an understanding of **motivation,** the force that causes people to behave the way they do. Motivation is defined as an inner drive resulting from some stimulus that causes a person to act in some fashion. The stimulus may be a psychological or physical need that drives (motivates) a person to satisfy (act) the need. Motives that cause consumers to act or buy have been classified in several ways; there are emotional, rational, biogenic, psychogenic, and patronage motives. These motives are the reasons that people buy, and are called **buying motives.**

Emotional and Rational Motives

Buying motives

Emotional motives are those that are developed through feelings, such as love and vanity, while **rational motives,** such as security and durability, involve judgment and logical thinking. Retailers generally base their advertising and promotional appeals on these motives when communicating with their customers. While the product benefits of economy, quality, durability, and performance appeal to the customer's sense of reason, products that touch their inner feelings, such as pride, vanity, and desire for romance, are appealed to on the basis of emotion. The following list of products contains examples of both types of motives.

Consumer purchases can be based on emotional (shoes) or rational (appliances) motives. *Courtesy:* Sears, Roebuck, and Company and International Business Machines.

EMOTIONAL	RATIONAL
cosmetics (vanity, enhancement)	insurance (security)
jewelry (prestige)	fine woven fabrics (durability)
furs (status)	compact car (economy)
trip (romance)	alarms (protection)
social club (keeping up with neighbors)	vitamins (health)

In recent years the classification of rational and emotional buying motives has been criticized as too simple. Those who have voiced such criticism claim that many products sold through emotional appeals can also be marketed in rational ways. Consider the following products that can be handled both rationally and emotionally.

PRODUCT	APPEAL	MOTIVE
cosmetics	vanity, romance	emotional
	improved personal appearance; better job	rational
expensive jewelry	impressing others; sign of success	emotional
	good investment	rational
furs	social status; look successful	emotional
	durability; warmth	rational
health club	status, fitness,	emotional
	being fit	rational

Biogenic and Psychogenic Motives

A person's ego must be satisfied, protected, and enhanced

Biogenic motives are related to physical needs, such as the need for food, sex, drink, and comfort. **Psychogenic motives** stem from psychological needs, such as the need to satisfy, protect, or enhance the ego. To satisfy the ego, individuals are motivated to become involved with experiences and relationships that make them feel wanted and accepted. For example, they may join a club for these reasons. To protect the ego, people avoid experiences that may embarrass them, make them lose face, prestige, or status, or expose them to ridicule. This is why many people avoid entering contests. To enhance the ego, people are motivated to achieve, gain recognition, and work hard. For example, they may work long hours or attend school at night.

An understanding of biogenic and psychogenic motives provides useful insights for retailers because these motives affect consumer selection of products, brands, and stores.

Patronage Motives

Understanding specific buying motives helps the retailer appeal to consumers for their patronage. **Patronage motives** are the reasons that consumers choose one place to shop rather than another and include special brands, attractive facilities, personal services, convenience, good values, attentive salespeople, and a good store image.

MASLOW'S HIERARCHY OF NEEDS

A well-known theory that is used to explain why consumers are motivated to satisfy their needs and desires is **Maslow's hierarchy of needs** (Figure 3-1). According to Dr. Abraham Maslow, there are several levels of needs.[1] At each level the individual is motivated to act in order to satisfy his or her needs before going on to the next level. The specific need levels are listed here, beginning with the most important at Level I. The number of consumers decreases as we move from Level I to Level V.

People's basic needs

Level I. Physiological Needs. The basic needs, such as water, food, and shelter, must be satisfied first, and they have the highest priority. Consumers satisfying these needs are motivated rationally.

Level II. The Need for Security. The need to feel safe and secure stimulates rational motives and leads to such purchases as insurance, brand name products, and safety and health devices. At this level there is little experimentation with new products or stores.

Level III. Social Needs, Recognition, and Acceptance. At this level the urge for emotional security and acceptance is so strong that many purchases are made to impress others. There is also a great deal of emotional purchasing. Romance, love, and family stimulate purchases of jewelry, cosmetics, and the like.

Level IV. The Need for Self-esteem and Status. Many products are purchased to enhance the individual's self-image and satisfy his or her need for distinction. The purchase of status symbols like expensive cars is emotionally motivated.

Level V. The Need for Self-actualization. The need to be independent is the last and highest level of needs. People who reach this level are generally affluent, successful in their careers, and concerned with aesthetics. Egoistic (emotional) motives are evident in purchases of designer fashions, hobbies, travel, and the like.

[1] Abraham H. Maslow, *Motivation and Personality* (New York: Harper & Row, 1954), pp. 80–98.

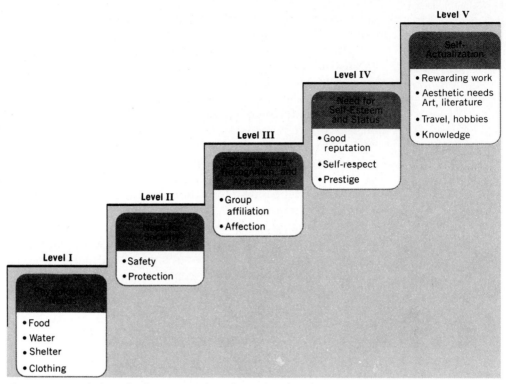

Figure 3-1   Psychological influences: Maslow's hierarchy of needs.

LEARNING

	Motivation studies on consumer behavior have helped retailers select appropriate means of appealing to consumers. *Learning theories* involving consumer behavior, on the other hand, have aided merchants in the development of store services, product assortments, pricing, and advertising campaigns.
Learning defined	**Learning** is generally considered to be any change in an individual's response or behavior resulting from practice or experience.[2] While we cannot observe the learning process in action, changes in consumer attitudes and behavior are observable in purchasing habits. According to James A. Bayton, learning

- Is goal oriented.
- Involves associations that may lead to habitual responses.
- Requires reinforcement of responses.[3]

[2]C. Glenn Walters, *Consumer Behavior: Theory and Practice*, 3rd ed. (Homewood, Ill.: Richard D. Irwin, 1974).

[3]James A. Bayton, "Motivation, Cognition, Learning—Basic Factors in Consumer Behavior," *Journal of Marketing*, 22 (January 1958), pp. 282–287.

The goal might be to acquire some object or to satisfy some physical or mental need. The object is the stimulus that arouses desire in the consumer.

The response is the action the consumer takes to obtain the object. When the response involves pleasant associations with the stimulus (object), it may lead to repeated action (habit).

To be learned, responses must be repeated; consequently, reinforcement is necessary. Reinforcement involves some reward, pleasant association, or satisfaction for correct responses. Table 3-1 shows the relationship of the stimulus-response-reward combination to a consumer's learning pattern.

All consumer behavior is learned through repeated purchase performance. Therefore, retailers attempt to reinforce these purchase patterns through their advertising by repeating information about the store's services, product offerings, and special promotions. In fact, consumers tend to forget information unless retailers and manufacturers use "reminder" strategies in their displays, advertising, and other means of communications. Because a consumer might forget, there is always an opportunity for competition and for change in consumer purchasing patterns. This accounts for the constant reinforcement found in slogans, store logos, brands, and commercials.

Consumer learning occurs on either a physical or a mental level. Physical behavior involves learned attitudes that result in an action or reaction to a stimulus in order to satisfy a desire. For example, a consumer learns

- That one store is easier to travel to than another.
- That one store provides special services and comfort.
- That one store makes the shopping experience pleasant.

On the mental level, consumer learning involves feelings, opinions, beliefs, and mental associations. For example, a consumer learns

- To prefer the service at one store over that at another.
- To associate a desired look with particular brands.
- To associate economy with a compact car.
- To associate crowded stores with holidays.

TABLE 3-1 The Stimulus-Response-Reward learning pattern

Consumer	↔	Stimulus	→	Response	=	Reward
Associates stimulus with benefit or reward		Physical or mental thing desired by the consumer		Action on part of consumer to obtain the physical or mental goal; response based on positive associations		Given for correct action; constant reinforcement or rewards lead to "learned" behavior

Consumer behavior involves both levels of learning. Moreover, individuals seek pleasurable experiences and relationships while avoiding those that involve discomfort. By association, individuals learn to distinguish between pleasant and unpleasant buying activities. It is basically a matter of conditioning. Consumers may avoid the "pain" of inconvenience and poor service by shopping at certain stores despite their higher prices.

Retailers rely on consumers' conditioned responses to communicate their messages. By the association of some benefit or reward with patronage, the merchant can get the consumer into the habit of buying a particular product or shopping at a particular store. For example, one food merchant reduces all perishables by 50 percent one hour before closing the store for the weekend, because this is a slow time for shopping. He finds not only that he stimulates business but that some customers wait to shop at that particular hour.

Perception and Personality

Perception, which is a personal interpretation of information, is how an individual perceives an event or situation. In retail terms, a consumer's perceptions of a product, a store's advertising, and its displays influence the buying action. Because perception is directly related to a consumer's background, a single stimulus or appeal will be perceived differently by different consumers. For example, the Sears Stores of the Future are not the Sears operations the customer expects to find. The new stores are dramatically different in appearance and merchandise arrangement. The customer, then, must reorient his or her perception of Sears.

The elements that contribute to an individual's perception are the type of stimulus, the individual's background, and his or her personality. **Personality** has been used by retailers as another factor in understanding consumer behavior. It is the totality of an individual's characteristics, that is, the sum of attributes that causes an individual to behave in a distinctive manner. In short, it makes a person what he or she is.

Self-Concept Theory

The **self-concept theory** involves individuals' perceptions of themselves. Its elements are the real self, the ideal self, the self-image, and the apparent self.

The **real self** is what the consumer is as a person, that is, the individual's physical, mental, and emotional characteristics (Figure 3-2). The **ideal self** is what the individual would like to be. Contained in the ideal self is a consumer's desire to improve. The **self-image** is how the consumer views himself or herself. The individual's perception includes the real self and the ideal self, that is, the person's understanding of what he or she is and would like to be. The **apparent self** is how others see the individual. Generally, what others see is a combination of the real self, the ideal self, and the self-image.

```
┌─────────────────────────────────────────────┐
│ Real Self                                     │
│     What the consumer is                      │
│ Ideal Self                                    │
│     What the consumer would like to be        │
│ Self-Image                                    │
│     How the consumer views himself or herself │
│ Apparent Self                                 │
│     How others see us                         │
└─────────────────────────────────────────────┘
```

Figure 3-2   Self-concept theory.

The application of the self-concept theory has been helpful to retailers. For example, consumers act to protect or improve their self-image by purchasing goods that meet those needs. In addition, consumers tend to avoid products and services that are not compatible with their self-image or that of the group to which they belong.

Astute retailers are aware of consumers' self-images through the latter's actions, for example, the brands they buy or the price ranges they prefer.

THE BUYING PROCESS—DECISION MAKING

Another way of understanding the consumer is through the buying process. This process consists of the steps the consumer goes through when deciding what, when, where, and how to buy. Understanding this process can provide the retailer with the tools for developing an appropriate strategy for attracting customers. The steps in the buying process are as follows.

Steps in the buying process

1. **Recognition of a need** An advertisement, a suggestion, or some other stimulus makes the consumer aware of a need. For example, an invitation to a costume party might stimulate the need to buy a costume.

2. **Search for information** Once a need has been recognized, the consumer gathers information to satisfy the need. In the case of the costume, the consumer can check the Yellow Pages, ask a friend, or search his or her memory for past shopping experiences.

3. **Evaluation** The consumer makes selections or choices at this stage. The criteria measured are (among others) price, quality, and service.

4. **Decision making** On the basis of the evaluation, the consumer makes a buying decision. The product is purchased or rejected. From the retailer's point of view, this is the most important stage.

5. **Postdecision making** After purchasing a product an individual thinks about the decision. At times the consumer is not convinced that the purchase was a

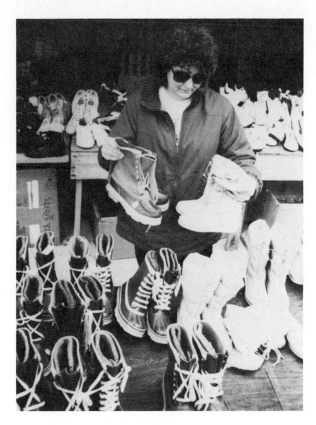

Consumer decision making is a crucial stage in the buying process. Photo by Laima Druskis.

wise one. In trying to justify the purchase, the consumer searches for additional facts or ads to prove to himself or herself that the purchase was correct. On the other hand, the consumer may experience continued satisfaction after the purchase.

DEMOGRAPHICS

Having examined the way retailers attempt to interpret and act on consumer behavior, we now extend our study to the buying habits of consumer groups: the elderly, working women, ethnic groups, and so forth. With our understanding of motivation, learning theories, and personality, we are in a better position to appreciate the complexity of consumer-retailer relationships and the dynamics of retail strategy. In addition, we will examine the forces affecting the decision-making process. This involves the study of consumer segments, which are based on demographic characteristics and lifestyles.

Population characteristics are important to retailers

Demographics is the breakdown of the population into statistical categories: age, education, sex, occupations, income, households, and marital status. This information is particularly helpful for the retailer who wants to reach a special segment of the market. For example, in developing its merchandise offerings a store might be interested in the fact that many senior citizens frequent its premises. Or perhaps a store might want to develop a program to attract the singles group. Information regarding age groups and their spending patterns helps the retailer devise an appropriate retail strategy.

A great deal of demographic information is available from the Department of Commerce, the U.S. Bureau of the Census, and the Bureau of Labor Statistics. In addition, data may be secured from trade associations, professional organizations, and research groups.

RETAIL STRATEGY

Speed—The Most Competitive Weapon

The Limited, a fashion apparel chain, tracks consumer preferences each day through its point-of-sale computers. While most competitors still order their Christmas apparel the previous May, the Limited rushes new fashions off the design board and into the 3,200 stores in fewer than 60 days.

Keeping a daily watch on consumer feedback, facsimile illustrations are sent by satellite to suppliers in the United States, Hong Kong, South Korea, Singapore, and Sri Lanka. Within days, clothing from those distant points begins to collect in Hong Kong. About four times a week, a chartered 747 airplane brings it to the company's distribution center in Ohio, where goods are priced and shipped to stores within 48 hours. Says Chairman Leslie Wexner, "Although we're doing well, that's not fast enough for the Nineties."

For the first time, the Census Bureau projected that the U.S. population is expected to decline in the twenty-first century after peaking at slightly more than 300 million. Despite the predicted slow growth of the population, however, goods and services will still be in demand. In order to plan effectively, therefore, retailers need to know how the composition of that population will change. Let's analyze some of the projected changes and indicate their probable implications for retailers.

Age

Seniors

The 1990s will continue to see a demographic shift to an older America. We are already witnessing this change in the myriad retirement communities in various parts of the country.

Senior-Seniors (75 and older)

The fastest-growing group will be those over age 85. This very senior group will account for 1.8 percent, or 4.9 million, by the year 2000.

The number of 75-and-older groups will increase 26.7 percent during the 1990s. Growth in the number of older people is attributable to research and advances in medical science.

Of those aged 75 and older, whites will decrease from 88 to 86 percent, blacks will remain at 8 percent, while Hispanics and Asians will increase slightly by one percentage point each, to 4 and 2 percent, respectively.

Seniors (65–74)

In 1988 there were more than 29 million people aged 65 and older. The number of 65- to 74-year-olds will decrease 1.4 percent during the 1990s. Regarding racial changes, whites will decrease during that decade from 86 to 82 percent of all 65- to 74-year-olds, whereas Hispanics and Asians will grow by more than 50 percent during that period. Blacks will increase from 8 to 9 percent of this age group, Hispanics from 4 to 6 percent, and Asians from 2 to 3 percent.

Young Seniors (55–64)

The number of 55 to 64-year-olds will increase 13.6 percent during the 1990s. As for racial changes, whites in this group will slide from 82 percent to 80 percent, while blacks will increase their ranks from 9 to 10 percent, Hispanics from 6 to 7 percent, and Asians from 3 to 4 percent.

Implications for Retailers.   This growing population will probably have larger incomes and more education than similar groups in the past. Already reflecting the trend, we find communities containing golf, tennis, swimming, cultural, and spa facilities. The need for more health care services will increase, too. In fact, large hotel chains have entered the retirement development field, targeting the expanding 65-plus market. The Marriott Hotel Chain and Hyatt International, for example, have moved aggressively into the so-called congregate life care industry to provide services such as rental catered-living, assisted-living, and personal care apartments, including medical and nursing facilities. Marriott has directed its efforts at both the affluent senior and the moderate- to low-income group. Plans include modest facilities for couples 70 and older with annual incomes as low as $25,000 and high-rise luxury communities for those with retirement incomes of $50,000 or more. Their complexes offer such services as meals, transportation, and help with the home itself.

Because most seniors see themselves as 10 to 15 years younger than their chronological years, the key to the older market is to forget age and, instead, focus on consumer wants and needs. Businesses are beginning to encounter elderly people who act much younger in the marketplace than past marketing experiences would suggest. Retailers, of course, must evaluate merchandise assortments in departments that cater to senior citizens. The merchandise mix is crucial because this group is still fashion conscious and fairly sound financially. In fact, older Americans spend as much or more than those in other age categories.

Retailers who cater to in-home shoppers will find additional opportunities with seniors because many of the latter are well educated and convenience oriented. In fact, Sears Mature Outlook program is geared to enticing these groups to Sears. The program provides a magazine quarterly, eight newsletters a year, and discounts to seniors. Many other retailers offer special shopping services and promotions to attract this population.

Middle-Year Adults

Into the twenty-first century, the population will consist of relatively fewer children and young people and a considerably greater proportion of middle-aged and older people. The middle-aged population reflects the maturing of the large "baby boom" generation born after World War II (birthdates from 1946 to 1964). "Boomers" make up a third of the U.S. population, America's largest demographic group.

In the year 2000 "boomers" will be 35 to 54-years-old, comprising 43.5 percent of all households. Those households will include 145 million men, women, and children.

Middle-Year Adults (45–54 years old)
The number of 45- to 54-year-olds will climb almost 50 percent during the 1990s. Blacks will increase from 7 to 8 percent, Asians from 3 to 4 percent, and whites will decrease from 80 to 77 percent.

Middle-Year Adults (35–44 years old)
Overall, the number of Americans aged 35–44 will jump 18 percent during the decade. Whites aged 45 to 54 will decrease from 78 to 73 percent, while blacks will increase from 11 to 13 percent, Hispanics from 8 to 10 percent, and Asians from 3 to 4 percent.

Adults (25–34 years old)

Between 1990 and 2000, the number of Americans aged 25 to 34 will fall 15 percent. During the decade, the proportion of white 25 to 34-year-olds will drop from 74 percent to 68 percent, while blacks will increase from 13 to 14 percent, Hispanics from 10 to 14 percent, and Asians from 3 to 5 percent.

Implications for Retailers.   "Boomers" will continue to account for 56 to 58 percent of consumer purchases in most merchandise categories. It is expected that their tastes will change with age and that they will upgrade their purchases to more expensive and status products.

Since this group will head such a large percentage of households, its demands for housing, furniture, and high-tech goods will be strong. Retailers who cater to these consumers can reap the rewards of higher sales because they are the "spenders" and high-wage earners. Retailers should also recognize that many career women are having children later in life.

Teens and Young Adults (16–24 years old)

The population will consist of relatively fewer children and youths. The 16- to 24-year-old population is declining. The number of children under age 18 will drop in 33 of the 50 states between 1990 and 2010. Nationally, the number of people in this group will drop from 64 million in 1990 to 62.6 million by 2010. According to the Census Bureau projection series, by the year 2010, 38 percent of Americans under the age of 18 will belong to minority groups.

Although the total teen population has been declining since the 1950s, this group has been increasing its spending totals. The group not only has money to spend freely, but it has an important influence in family household purchases.

Implications for Retailers.   It is important for retailers to pay attention to this group because a significant number of teenagers work, and most of their income is discretionary. In addition, teenagers help determine what their families buy. Moreover, because a larger proportion of young adults is waiting longer to marry and still lives with mom and dad, this group helps determine what families buy.

Young—"Baby Bust"

Overall, the number of births is expected to fall to 3.4 million in the year 2000 from 3.7 million in 1990, a 9.2 percent decline. These figures are based on the expected decline in the number of women in the prime childbearing ages of 18 to 34. It is interesting to note that from those under age 5 and up to the 75-and-older groups, there will be declines in the proportion of whites and gains among nonwhites and Hispanics since higher birth rates are expected with the latter groups.

Implications for Retailers.   Over the next 20 years, children will lead the way toward an even more diverse future. Schools will have to adjust to this different student body. Businesses that sell to children will have to adapt to a rainbow coalition of parents. Fast-food companies, toy manufacturers, and other businesses that sell to the young will ignore these demographic changes at their peril.

Some interesting projections of the age, sex, and race segments in the years 1988 to 2010 are illustrated in Table 3-2.

Education

The educational level of the labor force has risen dramatically. Between 1976 and 1988, for example, the proportion of workers aged 18 to 64 with at least one year of college increased from 32 to 42 percent, while the proportion with at least

TABLE 3-2 Population Projections
No. 17. PROJECTIONS OF THE TOTAL POPULATION BY AGE, SEX, AND RACE: 1988 TO 2010
[As of July 1. Includes Armed Forces overseas. Data are for middle series. Minus sign ($-$) indicates decrease]

Age, Sex, and Race	Population (1,000)						Percent Distribution			Percent Change		
	1988	1989	1990	1995	2000	2010	1990	2000	2010	1980–1990	1990–2000	2000–2010
Total	**246,048**	**248,251**	**250,410**	**260,138**	**268,266**	**282,575**	**100.0**	**100.0**	**100.0**	**9.9**	**7.1**	**5.3**
Under 5 years old	18,269	18,413	18,408	17,799	16,898	16,899	7.4	6.3	6.0	11.8	-8.2	(Z)
5–17 years old	45,344	45,269	45,630	48,374	48,815	45,747	18.2	18.2	16.2	-3.4	7.0	-6.3
18–24 years old	26,904	26,591	26,140	24,281	25,231	27,155	10.4	9.4	9.6	-13.9	-3.5	7.6
25–34 years old	43,861	44,024	43,925	40,962	37,149	37,572	17.5	13.8	13.3	16.7	-15.4	1.1
35–44 years old	35,321	36,548	37,897	42,336	43,911	37,202	15.1	16.4	13.2	46.5	15.9	-15.3
45–54 years old	24,151	24,872	25,487	31,297	37,223	43,207	10.2	13.9	15.0	12.0	46.0	16.1
55–64 years old	21,799	21,544	21,364	21,325	24,158	35,430	8.5	9.0	12.5	-1.8	13.1	46.7
65–74 years old	17,873	18,129	18,373	18,930	18,243	21,039	7.3	6.8	7.4	17.4	$-.7$	15.3
75 years old and over	12,527	12,863	13,187	14,834	16,639	18,323	5.3	6.2	6.5	31.2	26.2	10.1
16 years old and over	189,810	191,451	192,989	201,018	210,134	227,390	77.1	78.3	80.5	11.9	8.9	8.2
Male, total	**120,054**	**121,159**	**122,243**	**127,123**	**131,191**	**138,333**	**100.0**	**100.0**	**100.0**	**10.2**	**7.3**	**5.4**
Under 5 years old	9,351	9,426	9,426	9,118	8,661	8,668	7.7	6.6	6.3	12.0	-8.1	.1
5–17 years old	23,228	23,190	23,377	24,787	25,027	23,473	19.1	19.1	17.0	-3.2	7.1	-6.2
18–24 years old	13,598	13,440	13,216	12,290	12,770	13,752	10.8	9.7	9.9	-13.8	-3.4	7.7
25–34 years old	22,032	22,126	22,078	20,579	18,662	18,878	18.1	14.2	13.6	17.8	-15.5	1.2
35–44 years old	17,466	18,094	18,785	21,104	21,945	18,586	15.4	16.7	13.4	47.7	16.8	-15.3
45–54 years old	11,750	12,104	12,406	15,292	18,296	21,432	10.1	13.9	15.5	12.8	47.5	17.1
55–64 years old	10,273	10,170	10,103	10,149	11,557	17,173	8.3	8.8	12.4	$-.8$	14.4	48.6
65–74 years old	7,923	8,052	8,171	8,476	8,242	9,691	6.7	6.3	7.0	20.3	.9	17.6
75 years old and over	4,432	4,559	4,681	5,326	6,032	6,681	3.8	4.6	4.8	30.9	28.9	10.8
16 years old and over	91,255	92,070	92,834	96,834	101,392	110,024	75.9	77.3	79.5	12.4	9.2	8.5
Female, total	**125,995**	**127,092**	**128,167**	**133,016**	**137,076**	**144,241**	**100.0**	**100.0**	**100.0**	**9.7**	**7.0**	**5.2**
Under 5 years old	8,918	8,987	8,982	8,681	8,237	8,231	7.0	6.0	5.7	11.7	-8.3	$-.1$
5–17 years old	22,115	22,079	22,253	23,587	23,788	22,274	17.4	17.4	15.4	-3.7	6.9	-6.4
18–24 years old	13,307	13,150	12,924	11,991	12,461	13,402	10.1	9.1	9.3	-14.0	-3.6	7.6
25–34 years old	21,829	21,897	21,848	20,384	18,487	18,694	17.0	13.5	13.0	15.7	-15.4	1.1
35–44 years old	17,854	18,455	19,112	21,233	21,966	18,616	14.9	16.0	12.9	45.4	14.9	-15.3
45–54 years old	12,401	12,768	13,081	16,005	18,927	21,775	10.2	13.8	15.1	11.3	44.7	15.0
55–64 years old	11,527	11,375	11,260	11,175	12,601	18,257	8.8	9.2	12.7	-2.8	11.9	44.9
65–74 years old	9,949	10,077	10,201	10,454	10,001	11,348	8.0	7.3	7.9	15.1	-2.0	13.5
75 years old and over	8,094	8,304	8,505	9,507	10,607	11,642	6.6	7.7	8.1	31.3	24.7	9.8
16 years old and over	98,554	99,381	100,155	104,184	108,742	117,366	78.1	79.3	81.4	11.5	8.6	7.9
White, total	**207,696**	**209,178**	**210,616**	**216,820**	**221,514**	**228,978**	**100.0**	**100.0**	**100.0**	**7.7**	**5.2**	**3.4**
Under 5 years old	14,787	14,899	14,893	14,251	13,324	13,084	7.1	6.0	5.7	10.4	-10.5	-1.8
5–17 years old	36,469	36,317	36,537	38,493	38,569	35,258	17.3	17.4	15.4	-6.3	5.6	-8.6
18–24 years old	22,105	21,775	21,330	19,452	19,998	21,298	10.1	9.0	9.3	-16.7	-6.2	6.5
25–34 years old	36,749	36,798	36,620	33,680	29,988	29,585	17.4	13.5	12.9	13.6	-18.1	-1.3
35–44 years old	30,251	31,223	32,306	35,635	36,574	29,997	15.3	16.5	13.1	44.1	13.2	-18.0
45–54 years old	20,838	21,450	21,950	26,879	31,618	35,860	10.4	14.3	15.7	9.8	44.0	13.4
55–64 years old	19,138	18,852	18,637	18,327	20,667	29,913	8.8	9.3	13.1	-4.5	10.9	44.7
65–74 years old	15,983	16,188	16,380	16,681	15,811	17,875	7.8	7.1	7.8	16.1	-3.5	13.1
75 years old and over	11,375	11,675	11,965	13,421	14,965	16,108	5.7	6.8	7.0	30.2	25.1	7.6

Age, Sex, and Race	Population (1,000)						Percent Distribution			Percent Change		
	1988	1989	1990	1995	2000	2010	1990	2000	2010	1980–1990	1990–2000	2000–2010
16 years old and over	162,390	163,468	164,465	169,665	175,579	186,417	78.1	79.3	81.4	9.6	6.8	6.2
Male	101,689	102,448	103,184	106,365	108,774	112,610	49.0	49.1	49.2	8.0	5.4	3.5
Female	106,007	106,730	107,432	110,455	112,739	116,368	51.0	50.9	50.8	7.4	4.9	3.2
Black, total	**30,287**	**30,719**	**31,148**	**33,199**	**35,129**	**38,833**	**100.0**	**100.0**	**100.0**	**15.8**	**12.8**	**10.6**
Under 5 years old	2,769	2,806	2,814	2,790	2,748	2,820	9.0	7.8	7.3	13.7	−2.3	2.6
5–17 years old	7,062	7,095	7,170	7,697	7,895	7,809	23.0	22.5	20.1	2.5	10.1	−1.1
18–24 years old	3,853	3,845	3,813	3,703	3,924	4,314	12.2	11.2	11.1	−5.4	2.9	9.9
25–34 years old	5,562	5,639	5,685	5,534	5,264	5,590	18.3	15.0	14.4	31.2	−7.4	6.2
35–44 years old	3,826	4,010	4,210	5,041	5,481	5,076	13.5	15.6	13.1	52.9	30.2	−7.4
45–54 years old	2,558	2,620	2,686	3,261	4,106	5,369	8.6	11.7	13.8	17.4	52.9	30.8
55–64 years old	2,135	2,145	2,156	2,288	2,578	3,995	6.9	7.3	10.3	12.1	19.6	55.0
65–74 years old	1,545	1,576	1,608	1,762	1,848	2,277	5.2	5.3	5.9	19.0	14.9	23.2
75 years old and over	956	981	1,005	1,122	1,283	1,584	3.2	3.7	4.1	33.1	27.7	23.5
16 years old and over	21,592	21,920	22,226	23,860	25,708	29,467	71.4	73.2	75.9	19.2	15.7	14.6
Male	14,414	14,625	14,835	15,840	16,787	18,602	47.6	47.8	47.9	16.2	13.2	10.8
Female	15,874	16,094	16,313	17,359	18,342	20,231	52.4	52.2	52.1	15.4	12.4	10.3

Z Less than .05 percent. Includes other races not shown separately.
Source: U.S. Bureau of the Census, *Current Population Reports*, series P-25, No. 1018.

four years of college increased from 16 to 22 percent. See Figure 3-3. The emphasis on education is still considered an important factor in determining the success of young Americans. According to the National Association of College Stores, college students in 1989 had a discretionary income of $20 billion a year. The median income of family heads under age 30 with a college degree was four times greater than that of high school dropouts ($24,000 versus $6,240) in 1986.

Education and income are key factors in buying behavior

Implications for Retailers. The college-educated segment differs in its buying behavior from other workers with similar incomes. While the better educated tend to be more independent in their search for merchandise information, the less educated are more likely to seek information from friends. Because the former group responds positively to ethical, informative advertising, retailers who are interested in selling to this group are wise to stress quality, performance, and other rational buying motives.

Sex

It is obvious that information regarding the number of men and women in the market is crucial for retailers who are targeting (i.e., aiming at) certain populations. For example, a buyer in a men's and boy's department is certainly interested in the size of the potential men's market. In fact, there is currently a trend toward

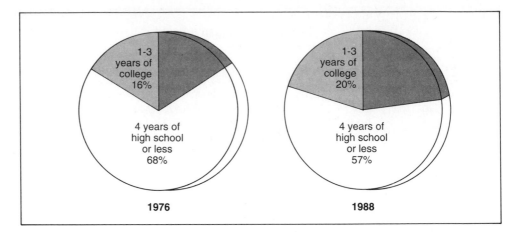

Figure 3-3   The proportion of workers with a college background has increased substantially since the mid-1970's. *Source:* U.S. Department of Labor, Bureau of Labor Statistics, *Occupational Outlook Handbook,* 1990–1991 edition (Washington, D.C.: U.S. DoI, 1990).

stores catering to specific male and female markets, such as the Ladies Foot Locker.

Men and women exhibit different buying patterns. For example, women are more likely than men to shop for food and most small household items. In addition, they do much of the shopping for men. On the other hand, today's couples make many joint decisions regarding high-priced items, and shop together more often.

Implications for Retailers.   Communication to a defined group of consumers whom the retailer tries to satisfy (**target market**) is important. Since women often select and purchase articles of clothing for men, retailers must be careful where they advertise and how their products are displayed. And because more couples are shopping together, store hours should provide the time they need.

Retailers should cater to people who enjoy shopping. The more enjoyable a shopping spree is, the more often they will shop.

Occupations

Changes in the work force

How people earn a living influences the size of their income as well as their purchasing behavior. Workers are classified as either **white-collar** or **blue-collar.** White-collar jobs are found among professionals, in offices, and in service occupations. Blue-collar jobs include those of factory workers and laborers. Growth rates among these groups have differed markedly. Once a small proportion of the total labor force, white-collar workers now represent about half of the total. The number of service workers also has risen rapidly, while the blue-collar work force has grown slowly and the number of farm workers has declined. Technological advances have so changed employment needs that since 1970 an increasing percentage of the work force has been employed in white-collar jobs while the percentage of blue-collar workers has decreased.

According to the Bureau of Labor Statistics, the number of jobs will grow a bit faster than the labor force. As shown in Figure 3-4, growth of the work force will slow from 2.4 percent a year in the 1980s to 1.2 percent in the 1990s. As the baby boomers reach a higher age bracket, therefore, fewer and fewer young people will be available for jobs.

Implications for Retailers. An understanding of occupational types provides insights into consumers' needs. White-collar consumers have a better understanding of buying sources. They are also more information minded than blue-collar workers, who rely to a greater extent on advice from others.

Occupational shifts cause changes in purchasing behavior, and as workers change jobs they present new challenges to retailers. Better-educated white-collar workers have different product preferences and tastes from those of factory workers.

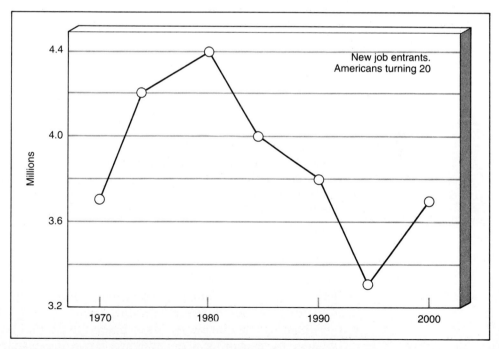

Figure 3-4 Fewer young people to fill jobs. *Source: Fortune* magazine, January 30, 1989.

The changing population of youths (16–24 years of age) will directly affect tomorrow's labor force. According to the Bureau of Labor Statistics, this group will account for only 16 percent of the entire labor force by the year 2000, compared to 19 percent in 1988 and 24 percent in 1976.

Implications for Retailers.   Eating and drinking places will see a decrease in the population from which they draw workers and trade.

Income

Incomes and the cost of living are on the rise again, and it's important for retailers to recognize distinctive income groups in order to sell their particular products. The reason for this expected growth is the number of households with more than one wage earner. Dual incomes will lift more families to affluent-household status, so that by 1993 they could account for one of every three households.

Implications for Retailers.   More people moving into higher income brackets means an increase in buyers for luxury goods and services. Retailers who deal in high-fashion items like jewelry and furs will have added opportunities for sales.

Analysis of Income

The analysis of income and how it is spent has great meaning for retailers. Income is best understood by breaking it down into the following divisions: personal, disposable, discretionary, and real.

- **Personal income** includes all moneys that an individual receives from wages, salaries, investments, interest, and dividends.
- **Disposable income** is the amount of money a person has to spend after taxes have been deducted. It is the portion of income that is available for *essential* household and personal use (rent, mortgage payments, insurance, utilities, health care, etc.).
- **Discretionary income** is money that a person or household has available to spend or save freely after payments for fixed commitments have been deducted. It is the portion of income that an individual is free to spend after paying for essential items.
- **Real income** is the figure that determines the actual dollars available in measuring an individual's purchasing power. Basically, it measures what one dollar will buy in one year as compared to another time. Real income is obtained by measuring all dollar figures according to an index that has been adjusted for the shrinking value of the dollar (inflation). Real income figures are sometimes called **constant dollars** because they refer to a base year. For example, a 1995 income might be restated in "1987 dollars."

As household income increases, there are decided shifts in the way a family spends its money. In 1857 Ernst Engel, a German economist, made some generalizations about consumer expenditures that are known as **Engel's laws.** Engel observed that as a family's income increases,

- Percentage spent for food decreases.
- Percentage spent for clothing tends to increase.
- Percentage spent on housing and household operations remains constant.
- Percentage spent on discretionary products and services increases.

Although Engel developed his generalizations about income expenditures more than a century ago, they are still valid today.

Household and Marital Status

According to the Census Bureau's projections, there will be 19 million more U.S. households in the year 2000 than there are today. The number of middle-aged people in their peak earning years will account for 71 percent of that growth.

A household may be a family unit, a single person, or a nonfamily unit (unrelated people living together). It is expected that in the next decade the number of nonfamily households will grow faster than that of family units. Within the family structure, the number of one-spouse homes will grow more than three times as fast as that of traditional husband-wife units, increasing to one out of five family units.

Despite the increase in nonfamily households, it is expected that the family will remain the dominant market in the United States. However, government projections see a smaller average family size because married couples prefer to have fewer children than previously and more young adults are postponing marriage.

Implications for Retailers.   The trend toward individually run households indicates that consumer shopping patterns may undergo changes. Store hours may require adjustment to conform to the needs of nonfamily household wage earners as well as single people. The anticipated smaller family size will probably shift merchandise strategies toward young and older adult groups. However, despite the projected decrease in the percentage of family units, the purchasing done by married couples for such expensive items as home furnishings, equipment, and appliances will still be based on joint decisions by the spouses, requiring more information from retailers.

Demographics and Special Consumer Markets

Retailers who are interested in reaching special populations are concerned with **market segmentation** (the process of dividing the total market into smaller sections, each having a community, e.g., teenagers, veterans). The more important segments consist of

Married couples frequently make joint shopping decisions. Photo by Rhoda Sidney.

- Working women.
- Consumers with special needs.
- Minority groups.
- Urban, suburban, and rural consumers.

Working Women

Dramatic growth in the number of working women

The number of women in the work force will continue to escalate. According to Census Bureau projections, this group will account for more than two-thirds of the labor force growth through the 1990s (Figure 3-5). At present, over 60 percent of married women under age 65 are working. By the year 2000, 4 out of 5 women between the ages of 25 and 54 are expected to be in the labor force.

Implications for Retailers. Studies indicate that the interests and needs of working and nonworking women differ. Working women are concerned about outside interests, appearance, and convenience in doing household chores. Consequently, retailers who deal in fashionable items, convenience products, recreation, and the like should devise strategies to attract this segment of the market.

Some consumers are willing to pay more at strip retail centers in order to save time, rather than shop at the lower-priced stores and supermarkets. Although working women have additional purchasing power, they are "time poor."

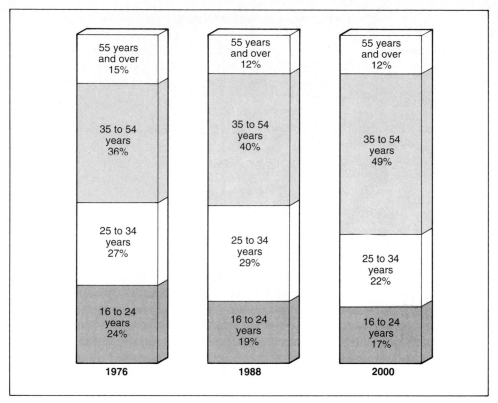

Figure 3-5   The age distribution of the labor force is changing. *Source:* U.S. Department of Labor, Bureau of Labor Statistics, *Occupational Outlook Handbook,* 1990–1991 edition.

Therefore, merchants who help reduce the number of stops required for shopping, offer more conveniences, and provide additional facilities (e.g., banking) will undoubtedly benefit. Creative retailers who are action minded have already targeted this group for special treatment. J. W. Robinson grouped business attire and accessories in its Career Shop in Los Angeles, while Abraham & Straus created The Office for its working consumers in New York. Others with a similar approach are Marshall Field & Company in Chicago, Filene's in Boston, and Sanger-Harris in Dallas. These stores concentrate on the working woman's need for quick shopping, good value, and special services. Women who shop there have courier service for deliveries to home or office within 24 hours, and are able to charge on long-term accounts. This special merchandising captures the working woman's loyalty.

Catalog shopping and in-home shopping services should benefit working women because they save shopping time. In-home computer terminals are expected to become widespread in the 1990s.

The Consumer with Special Needs

The handicapped have special needs

There are approximately 39 million people for whom shopping is not a routine experience. Members of this group, a sizable market segment, suffer physical and sensory disabilities. Included among them are 24 million in the 18–64 age bracket.

Implications for Retailers.   This is a potentially lucrative market for sensitive merchants. Through physical improvements and service accommodations in their stores, some retailers have already taken steps to "welcome" this special group. For example, Sears recently installed an experimental teletype ordering system that allows deaf customers in the Los Angeles area to place catalog orders. In fact, Sears and J. C. Penney have catalogs to meet special-needs customers.

In another instance, Braille menus have been built into counters at selected McDonald's locations.

Minority Groups

Minority groups are increasingly important to retailers

Minorities and immigrants will make up a larger share of the U.S. population in the year 2000 than they do today. By the year 2010, as many as 38 percent of Americans under the age of 18 will belong to minority groups. Substantial increases in the number of blacks, Hispanics, and Asians are anticipated. In fact, the Hispanic population will grow by one-third, while the U.S. population as a whole will grow by less than one-tenth. Higher birth rates in minority groups are expected despite the predicted decline in the total number of births in the year 2000.

Ethnic and religious backgrounds are somewhat influential in consumers' preferences for different stores and products. Although race and religion are difficult to use as a means of predicting consumer behavior, they are factors to observe. A reasonable forecast regarding minority groups is that the market will be more lucrative and more diverse.

Implications for Retailers.   The growing size of the affluent black market segment represents an opportunity for retailers to satisfy this market's demand for upgraded merchandise. Similarly, merchants who are interested in reaching the growing Hispanic group will consider bilingual store signs and specially designed promotion materials. For example, Penney has introduced the J. C. Penney Spanish U.S.A. shopping guide in Miami. In addition, Burdines department stores publish Spanish brochures and promotes special events for Hispanics in Florida.

Urban, Suburban, and Rural Consumers

The location of consumers very often affects how they buy. City dwellers have briefer but more frequent shopping experiences than rural and suburban shoppers. The latter groups generally "stock up" more and tend to buy in a more organized fashion (shopping lists, coupons, etc.).

Knowing the type of dwelling in which consumers live is also helpful to retailers. People who live in apartments do not spend heavily on certain items that homeowners purchase, such as window treatments, fixtures, and so forth. Apartment dwellers buy items that are more fashionable, trendy, and movable, whereas homeowners spend more time shopping and are more interested in guarantees and durability.

Consumer purchases reflect different lifestyles. Van Bucher.

Implications for Retailers.   Every shift of consumers has strong implications regarding where expenditures for new household products, durables, and nondurables will be made. Retailers located in urban areas might capitalize on the more frequent shopper by offering special in-store promotions and setting up displays for various impulse items.

LIFESTYLES

Our lifestyles are changing radically   **Lifestyles** are often affected by demographic background because age, income, and education have a great deal of influence on the way a person chooses to live. By definition, lifestyle is the unique way in which a particular group sets itself apart from others. A comprehensive study of an individual's lifestyle involves an understanding of the following influences: social class, reference groups, and cultural influences.

Social class

Social classes are homogeneous divisions within a society into which families and individuals can be classified for comparative purposes. In some societies, these groups may be so clear-cut that movement between them is not permitted. In others, the dividing lines are not so definite and movement may be easier. Nevertheless, divisions always exist. Consequently, it is important to understand the concept of social class and how it applies to consumer behavior.

Warner's class system

A social class division involves a structure for ranking individuals in the United States according to occupation, source of income, education, family background, dwelling, and other factors. According to Lloyd Warner, the class system is divided into six levels.[4]

1. Upper-upper
2. Lower-upper
3. Upper-middle
4. Lower-middle
5. Upper-lower
6. Lower-lower

The following are some of the characteristics of each class.

Upper-upper: 1 percent of population

This group possesses "old wealth" and is composed of second- and third-generation families. Because of their great affluence, its members are secure in their status and reside in exclusive areas. Their children attend prestigious schools and are graduated from some of the best-known institutions in the world. People in this group are active in charities and the arts. Money is not a factor in their purchasing activities.

Lower-upper: 1½ percent of population

This group is sometimes called *nouveaux riches*, French for "new rich." Its members are high-income earners who are usually educated for professional careers in private schools. Active in community work, they are socially aggressive and value possessions highly. As with the upper-upper class, money is not a factor in their purchasing activities.

[4]W. Lloyd Warner, *Social Class in America* (New York: Harper & Row, 1960).

Upper-middle:
10 percent of
population

This class contains both professional and businesspeople. It relates its social status to money, attempting to "mirror" an upper-class style of living. It is a highly educated group, with a substantial number of members who attend prestige schools. The group values quality possessions—and purchases accordingly.

Lower-middle:
30 to 35 percent of population

This is essentially a white-collar group that reflects middle-class values. Its members are conscientious workers with steady incomes who place great value on higher education for their children. They shop often, with price an important factor in their purchasing activities. Their possessions are related largely to their occupations.

Upper-lower:
40 percent of
population

While this group is generally involved in blue-collar occupations, individual members' incomes are sometimes higher than those of members of the lower-middle class. Members of this group have limited education, seek job security, and are family oriented. They are not socially active outside of their own circle, and their living style is highly routinized. While sta-

Blue-collar workers comprise an important target market for retailers. Owen Franken/Stock Boston.

tus image is unimportant in their purchases, they do show brand loyalty. Money is a strong factor in their purchasing activities.

Lower-lower:
15 percent of
population

This group has low incomes and unsteady employment. With poor education and depressed living conditions, its members are uninformed and often in need of public or private subsidization. They have limited ability to purchase goods other than necessities and use credit whenever possible.

Some retail firms operate effectively with particular social classes by planning merchandise and service offerings for those classes. Table 3-3 indicates shopping preferences and merchandise appeals for each social class.

Reference Groups

Lifestyles are affected by people whose status, achievements, or activities cause others to emulate them. They are also influenced by the manner in which particular groups function. In the former instance, we are dealing with reference groups; in the latter, with cultural influences.

Groups that are influential in shaping attitudes and opinions have an impact on the lifestyle an individual chooses. Known as **reference groups,** they include opinion leaders and the family.

TABLE 3-3   Social Classes: Shopping Preferences and Merchandise Appeal

Social Class	Shopping Preference	Merchandise Appeal
Upper-upper	Prestige stores	Expensive jewelry, antiques, expensive homes, elegant and conservative clothes
Lower-upper	Prestige stores	More ostentatious, less conservative, original designer clothes
Upper-middle	Department stores for furniture and fashion goods (goods others would notice), discounters for goods not easily noticed by others	Spending on mass market designer labels, better furniture and clothing
Lower-middle	Discounters, department stores, small shops	Do-it-yourself products, modest housing and clothing
Upper-lower	Neighborhood stores that extend credit, discount stores	Sports products, outdoor equipment, do-it-yourself products; spend less on clothing, late-model cars
Lower-lower	Stores extending credit, neighborhood stores	Buy primarily to provide necessities

Opinion Leaders

Opinion leaders exist in all groups

Members of a group who exert influence on consumer decision making are called **opinion leaders.** They are generally the avant-garde and are regarded as a source of information and advice. They have a very strong impact on the decision-making process involving purchases of conspicuous goods and services. They are the first to adopt new styles and are instrumental in having those styles accepted more widely. For example, Michael Jackson, the rock star, popularized flashy and colorful garments that caught the fancy of many young music fans. Opinion leaders are found on all social levels and are selected by their followers for several reasons: They are considered important, possess recognized expertise, and are highly visible to the group. These leaders have the ability to promote sales through their consumption patterns.

The Family

Most of our attitudes are probably shaped by family influences. Consequently, the family is considered one of the most influential of all reference groups. Since attitudes toward stores and products are developed within the household, individuals remember the countless articles used in their first homes. These include types of cars, brands of food, toothpaste, and much more.

Young married women often buy the brands that were used in their early households. Similarly, parents sometimes influence the spending patterns of young married couples who may shop the same stores looking for the same services.

Family Life Cycle.   The **family life cycle,** as shown in Table 3-4, is another tool used to examine and understand the consumer. The traditional life cycle describes how a typical family evolves from bachelorhood to couples to children to retirement. To be successful, a store's program must take into account each family member's role. Ultimately, the retailer must fit comfortably into the customer's lifestyle. In other words, the retailer's strategy should communicate that the store's merchandise and services are compatible with the consumer's lifestyle.

Cultural Influences

Culture and lifestyles are inseparable

According to *Webster's* dictionary, culture is "behavior typical of a group or class." Culture and values affect the types of lifestyles individuals choose, as well as their buying patterns. For this reason merchants should be sure that their product offerings and services do not conflict with the cultural values of a targeted group. The social meaning attached to a product within a culture is critical in assessing how the product might be accepted. For example, in some countries higher-status people do not engage in any form of manual labor because it is considered demeaning. Consequently, it is common for members of this group to

TABLE 3-4   Family Life Cycle

Stages	Lifestyle Characteristics	Consumer Decision Maker	Implications for Retailers
Single			
Young	Inexperienced; independent; concerned with starting career; establishing own lifestyle; low income	Individual	Entertainment; cars; travel; clothing
Mature	Independent; more set in lifestyle; few financial burdens; greater discretionary income	Individual	High-quality home furnishings; convenience; eating out often
Couples			
Young Married	Relative independence; two incomes; future oriented	Joint	High level of entertainment; recreation; travel; household furnishings
Cohabitating	Independent	Independent	Entertainment; convenience oriented; low-cost home furnishings
Married with Children			
Full Nest I	Youngest child under six; one income; some financial pressure; future oriented	Joint	Spends primarily on children and items for family use; family vacations
Full Nest II	Youngest child between 6 and 15; some wives work part-time; financial position better	Joint	Will spend for main interests; family, home, and children
Full Nest III	Older married with dependent children; more wives work; pressure for children's education	Joint, with children's input	Interested in home furnishings, automobiles, travel, and recreation; can be limited by educational expenses
Empty Nest I	Mature couple; children are on own; head of household still working; some wives work part-time; good income	Joint	More time and money for travel and luxuries; independent; spend on recreation
Empty Nest II	Retired couple; fixed income; downsized lifestyle; economical	Joint	Travel; recreation; medical-health; little interest in luxuries
Sole Survivor I	Employed; enjoys autonomy; pursues personal interests; helps offspring in many cases	Independent	Involved with job and friends; clothing; health concerns
Sole Survivor II	Retired, limited income; tightened purse-strings; economical lifestyle	Independent	Travel; recreation; appeal to economy and social activity

hire laborers. It follows, then, that the introduction of do-it-yourself products would meet with social resistance.

We are concerned primarily with several key aspects of American culture: religion, economic relations, status, and grouping. Religious beliefs in American culture affect consumer behavior in many ways. For example, religious groups prohibit the use of products ranging from certain foods to birth control devices;

others frown on Sunday business hours; still others ban the consumption of alcoholic beverages.

Economic relations and status have a powerful influence on consumers' buying preferences and habits. They include work achievement, the work ethic, the need for security, and striving for better things. The motivation to achieve sparks the competitive drive to purchase products that identify with success, such as big cars and other expensive items.

Grouping or conforming is an aspect of American society that prompts people to dress like, act like, and follow the trends or fads of their group. Attempts to retard the aging process are another reflection of American culture. Progressive retailers respond to these behavior patterns by supplying products and services that are in demand.

Some of the changing American values that have implications for retailers are the stress on instant gratification as opposed to postponement of pleasure, naturalism in foods versus preservatives and artificial additives, and gender equality instead of male dominance. In addition, the greater emphasis on individualism and the improved status of the aging have influenced lifestyles significantly. Merchants who recognize these changes fare better by integrating new ideas into their sales strategies.

Psychographics

The study of lifestyles and consumer behavior patterns is another way by which retailers learn about their target market. **Psychographics** is a method that measures trends in consumer lifestyles and behavior patterns. The monitoring of consumer values and lifestyles helps narrow the market so that businesses can communicate their messages more directly to the appropriate consumer group. Consequently, lifestyle analysis, or psychographics, is an attempt by researchers to develop consumer profiles based on their ways of living.

The following is an example of psychographic research. In a study to determine how Americans aged 55 and older would want to live in retirement, four psychological factors that influence preference were identified.

1. autonomy-dependence (need to be on their own)
2. introversion-extroversion (degree to which people need to be socially involved)
3. self-indulgence–self-denial (degree to which people seek gratification)
4. resistance to change–openness to change (degree to which people are adaptable).

The study was conducted with 3,600 people aged 55 and older and considered their health status as well as their socioeconomic positions. Some of the highlights are: the six distinct psychographic segments of older adults that were identified and are shown in Figure 3-6.

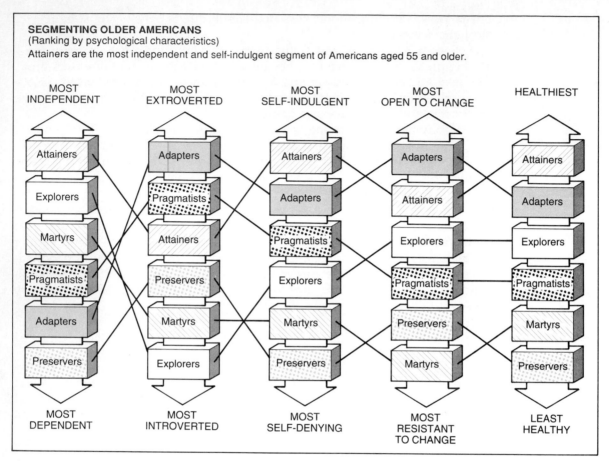

SEGMENTING OLDER AMERICANS
(Ranking by psychological characteristics)
Attainers are the most independent and self-indulgent segment of Americans aged 55 and older.

Figure 3-6   *Source:* J. Gollub and H. Javitz, "Six Ways to Age," *American Demographics* (June 1989), pp. 28–35, 56.

- Attainers are the youngest, most autonomous, self-indulgent, healthy, and wealthy. Some older adults in the study want services, while others prefer to remain independent.
- Pragmatists are the second most likely group to live alone and least likely to have thought about moving.
- Adapters are the most extroverted and are open to change. Personal relationships and material possessions play an important role in their sense of well-being.
- Explorers want to do things their way. They are self-reliant and less likely than any other segment to feel that children have an obligation to help parents.

- Martyrs are resistant to change, most self-denying, and more likely to live with children
- Preservers are the least healthy segment and are resistant to change. They are highly need driven and are concerned with preserving what little they have. They are most likely to look for help and a total health care package.

Implications

Businesses that are concerned with opportunities in retirement housing and so on should develop options that appeal to the divergent lifestyles and values of older Americans.

Retailers in the 1990s will face the challenges of a slowing population and household growth, an aging society, an evolving ethnic composition, and fragmentation of consumer markets. Retailers who choose to meet consumers' demands will have to respond by keeping track of their attitudes, lifestyles, and preferences.

NEW TERMS

apparent self	motivation
biogenic motive	opinion leader
blue-collar worker	patronage motive
buying motive	perception
constant dollars	personal income
consumer behavior	personality
demographics	psychogenic motive
discretionary income	psychographics
disposable income	rational motive
emotional motive	real income
Engel's laws	real self
family life cycle	reference group
ideal self	self-concept theory
learning	self-image
lifestyle	social class
market segmentation	target market
Maslow's hierarchy of needs	white-collar worker

CHAPTER HIGHLIGHTS

1. The process whereby consumers decide whether, what, when, and how to buy the goods they use is known as consumer behavior.

2. The study of consumer behavior involves an understanding of motivation and its effect on purchasing patterns.

3. An analysis of consumers' needs and motives helps retailers understand why consumers buy.

4. Maslow's theory of needs is used to explain how consumers are motivated to satisfy needs in a specific order.

5. Motivation studies and learning theories help retailers decide how to appeal to consumers.

6. The self-concept theory is used by retailers to analyze consumer personalities.

7. Understanding the various steps in the buying process is another way of understanding the consumer.

8. Two major factors that influence consumers' buying decisions are demographics and lifestyles. Demographics is the breakdown of a population into statistical categories based on age, education, sex, occupation, income, household, and family status. Lifestyle is the unique way in which a particular group sets itself apart from others.

9. Through market segmentation retailers can reach special markets, such as the elderly, teenagers, and working women. These market segments provide retailers with important information for store promotions.

10. Social class is the ranking of individuals according to occupation, source of income, education, family background, dwelling, and so forth.

11. Warner's class system is divided into six levels: upper-upper, lower-upper, upper-middle, lower-middle, upper-lower, and lower-lower.

12. The social class structure has many implications for retailers regarding the purchasing behavior of each class.

13. Reference groups, including opinion leaders and the family, affect the attitudes, opinions, and actions of consumers.

14. The family life cycle is another tool used to examine and understand the consumer.

15. Culture and values play an important part in the lifestyles that individuals choose. Alert retailers benefit from the recognition of changing social values.

16. Psychographics is a method that measures trends in consumer lifestyles and behavior patterns.

REVIEW QUESTIONS

1. What are the influences and factors that affect consumer behavior?
2. How would you relate the order of needs in Maslow's hierarchy to consumer purchases?
3. What kinds of products are purchased because of emotional and rational buying motives?
4. What are the implications for retailers when consumers attempt to enhance their egos?
5. List and explain the various steps that a consumer goes through during the buying process.
6. List and explain how any three of the demographic categories outlined in this chapter affect the retailer's strategy.
7. How do members of the upper and middle classes differ in their buying needs?
8. Explain how the traditional life cycle of a family affects the retailer's strategy.
9. How do consumer lifestyles affect buying behavior? What factors should the retailer consider?

DISCUSSION QUESTIONS

1. Using specific examples, show how retailers rely on consumers' conditioned responses to communicate their messages.
2. How are retailers affected by the social class structure?
3. Identify special consumer segments that are not listed in the text and explain why they are important to retailers.
4. What impact can psychographic profiles have in developing retail services and product offerings?

CASE 1

Marble Arch to Manhattan

"Taking Marks & Spencer to the world's largest retail market is the challenge facing its U.S. team, based in New York."*

*M&S World, Autumn 1988 (company publication).

Marks & Spencer, one of Britain's largest apparel and food retailers, had been trading up for some time. Traditionally known as the place to go for solid, no-nonsense goods of undisputed quality at unspectacular prices, Marks & Spencer has embarked on a fast track for expansion into the U.S. market.

In the United Kingdom, although the stores are attractive, with carpet and other trimmings, merchandise is piled on open tables under plain, bright lighting. In many stores, a no-dressing-room tradition is maintained (no questions asked on refunds), and signs around the store put renewed stress on "lower prices/quality maintained."

Marks & Spencer claims that it is neither the cheapest nor the most fashionable retailer. The company's very British, very stolid image is so strong that former Prime Minister Margaret Thatcher once posed at M&S butchers' stalls in order to identify herself as a thrifty homemaker looking for a good product at a sensible price.

In January 1987, against this background of substantial reputation in the United Kingdom, the chairman, Lord Rayner, outlined a policy for international expansion. The U.S. team was to examine and identify the best strategy for a Marks & Spencer entry into the U.S. market.

Since Marks & Spencer is known for both apparel and food, the U.S. team proceeded to investigate thoroughly U.S. apparel and food retailing.

The team traveled widely throughout the United States, meeting many people and spending a great deal of time observing the major malls and supermarkets. The members experienced U.S. culture firsthand, people's attitudes, customer behavior, various stores, and different standards. In essence, the team began to understand the dynamics of the American retail scene.

U.S. demographic trends are similar to those in the United Kingdom—more working women, more singles, greater affluence, longer working hours for management categories, and more time being spent in organized leisure.

On the other hand, the U.S. retail market is very different from that in the United Kingdom. Basically, there are three differences between the two.

First, although in the United States the industry includes outlets such as general merchandise discount stores and food warehouse stores that have sizable pieces of business, there are no retailers as dominant in the United States as Marks & Spencer is in Britain. For example, the top three U.S. general merchandise retailers—Wal-Mart, Sears, and K mart—have among them less clothing market share than does M&S. And there is no food retailer that is truly national—the largest, Kroger, has less than 6 percent of the national market.

The second significant difference is the importance the American customer places on price, or bargains. Quality becomes an important factor only at the upper end of the food or clothing markets.

A third difference is that stores, especially department stores, specialty apparel stores, and better supermarkets, are expected to provide a dramatic presentation of their merchandise. It also was clear that with price as the main competitive factor, and with many stores selling the same brands, store interiors, decor, and image become competitive weapons.

The team then evaluated the areas of opportunity against the Marks & Spencer strengths and weaknesses in an American context. The conclusion was reached that start-up entry in the United States would require too much revision and that acquisition was a better route into the U.S. market.

"The acquisition of Brooks Brothers and Kings Super Markets will give Marks & Spencer much more than established chains of shops—it also brings experience and knowledge of the U.S. retail industry."*

a. Brooks Brothers is considered a very conservative company appealing to an affluent market. How will Marks & Spencer affect the chain's strategy?
b. What class of shoppers do you think the Marks and Spencer team was targeting? Do you think these shoppers would respond to M&S? Why?
c. Of the three differences between the U.K. and U.S. market, which is most significant and why?

*Ibid.

CASE 2

Targeting New Consumers

Family Dollar Stores, Inc., is one of the most profitable discount retailers in the United States. Figures from a recent statement show a 6.9 percent profit on sales of $377 million, one of the highest in the business. The company has built its success thus far in one region of the country—the Southeast. From its headquarters in Charlotte, North Carolina, Family Dollar operates and maintains strict control over 889 stores in 20 states.

The company's profitability is due in large part to a strategy that has worked since the enterprise was founded 28 years ago and that the management of the company has steadfastly followed. The formula calls for small stores, set in rural areas (usually areas with populations under 15,000). Each store carries only 5,000 items in stock. The stores serve low- and lower-middle income groups who are largely blue-collar. Generally the yearly income of Family Dollar customers is about $17,000, almost 31 percent below the median family income in the United States.

All Family Dollar stores are self-service and sell merchandise of adequate quality at a low price, usually under $17. Customers spend slightly over $6 each time they shop at a Family Dollar store. All sales are cash only: Family Dollar stores have no charge accounts and take no credit cards.

But although the Family Dollar formula calls for low-priced merchandise, very little of it is irregular or "seconds." Most goods carry a manufacturer's label and 30 percent of the merchandise is name brand.

Industry analysts attribute much of the company's success to "superb execution and professional management." It is also highly centralized management and execution. The independent owners manage and exercise close control over all aspects of the business, from the design of the stores and ad campaigns to buying decisions, merchandise mix, inventory, and pricing policies.

The layout and look of all stores are similar. All are clean, air-conditioned, well lighted, and small. No store is more than 8,000 square feet. Goods are positioned the same way in each store. Women's apparel, for example, is to the right of the front entrance, because most Family Dollar shoppers are women and most people walk to the right upon entering a store. Sale goods are positioned at the end of aisles, whereas toys are at the rear in order to draw the customer into and through the store.

The creation and direction of advertising and direct mail are also controlled by management at headquarters, which has proved effective and cost-efficient. Family Dollar places ads in 800 small papers each week and makes heavy use of direct-mail promotions, mailing out 8 million flyers 12 times a year. All copy is created and approved in Charlotte.

The chain has only one warehouse and distribution center from which all goods are shipped, so monitoring the flow of goods is efficient. The warehouse, too, is located in Charlotte. Management at headquarters also monitors buying decisions closely and decides prices and price changes as well as determining to a large extent the merchandise mix—how much of each item a store will carry. Very few decisions are made by store managers themselves.

Tight and centralized direction has helped the company keep costs down and made managing the stores relatively simple. Although the company has an excellent sales and profit record, its stores usually come close to sales potential in the first year of operation and then grow slowly. Generally, stores have sales volume of $500,000 to $550,000 consistently, but few reach a volume of $1 million. Same store growth (sales growth in stores open over a year) is not the factor that will keep the chain prospering. To continue its success at the same rate, the company must keep opening new stores and in new locations.

Family Dollar has now expanded beyond its traditional southeastern base and opened stores in other regions from Texas to New Jersey and plans to keep expanding nationwide. For the immediate future, the expansion will be paid for in cash—the company has no debt.

Analysts have found the company's growth impressive and predict that sales and earnings will grow at a substantial rate: retailers point out that expansion entails risks.

As Family Dollar opens stores in areas of the North and West, the company will have to adjust the mix of merchandise to accommodate varying seasonal needs and regional preference. The company will no longer be able to sell the same mix in every store throughout the chain. Inevitably, the number of items carried and warehoused will increase, which can be costly.

New stores create the need for more new managers and carry the risk of choosing some poor ones. Expansion can also mean that some of the present management policies may not prove efficient or easy to implement as the company adds stores rapidly.

Some retailers believe that to maintain the rate of growth and profit, Family Dollar will have to expand its customer base and appeal to more than just blue-collar, low-income customers. And they point out that blue-collar jobs are expected to continue to decline in the next several years.

Several major competitors in the discount field have already opted to change their strategy for growth. Discounters such as Wal-Mart and K mart now seek to attract more middle-income consumers by increasing the kinds of goods they carry and offering more expensive lines of merchandise.

Family Dollar does not plan to change its orientation, however. The company has grown from 12 stores in the late 1960s to almost 900 today without deviating from its strategy for success. It has used that strategy to generate record sales and earnings for over nine straight years. As the company implements its major expansion program, its management plans to maintain the strategy that has proved so lucrative: small stores, located in rural sections, carrying a limited number of items and serving low-income, mainly blue-collar customers.

a. Do you think that Family Dollar will be successful using its formula on a nationwide basis? Explain.

b. Can Family Dollar continue its commitment to low-income, blue-collar customers in rural areas and still achieve substantial growth in sales and earnings? How?

c. What changes in strategy, if any, do you foresee the company management making? Give your reasons.

REFERENCES

"Adult Boom: Aging of the Wunder-generation." *Chain Store Age Executive*, **61** (May 1985), pp. 27–30.

BLOCK, C. E., AND K. J. ROERING. *Essentials of Consumer Behavior: Concepts and Applications* (Hinsdale, IL: Dryden, 1979).

REDDING, A. "You Don't Turn 50 and Change What You Read." *Advertising Age* (May 22, 1989), pp. S-4, S-6.

RICHE, M. F. "Psychographics for the 1990s." *American Demographics* (July 1989), pp. 24–26, 30–31.

ZEITHAML, V. A., AND M. C. GELLY. "Characteristics Affecting the Acceptance of Retailing Technologies: A Comparison of Elderly and Nonelderly Consumers." *Journal of Retailing*, **63** (Spring 1987), pp. 49–68.

Part 2

Retailing Structure

Having read about the development and growth of retailing, we turn our attention to how retail institutions are structured. Chapter 4 identifies retail businesses by type of ownership. After studying the general characteristics of business organizations, we examine specific forms of retail ownership, which range from chains to consumer cooperative associations. We also discuss acquisitions and mergers in retailing.

Chapter 5 continues the discussion of the structure of retail institutions by identifying them according to the type of merchandise they sell. We then study the characteristics of general-merchandise and limited-line stores. The discussion includes a description of new types of general merchandise stores. Next we focus on nonstore selling methods, including in-home retailing, vending machines, mail order/catalog retailing, telephone selling, and electronic retailing.

In Chapter 6 we study store organization by analyzing line and line-and-staff structures. The material includes organizational arrangements for small retailers, department stores, branch stores, and chain stores. It also outlines the differences between store centralization and decentralization.

In dealing with the management of human resources, we cover the recruitment, hiring, and training of new employees. We also examine problems associated with the transfer, promotion, and discharge and performance appraisal of employees. After studying the establishment of wage and compensation scales and fringe benefits, we cover the organization of store communication in both informal and formal modes. Finally, we determine what retailers should know about labor unions and the law.

Chapter 7 is concerned with the very important topic of store location. We look at the major factors in determining location and identify the types of shopping areas available to retailers. Next we analyze the criteria used in site selection and canvass the alternatives of buying or renting a retail outlet. The chapter closes with a listing of trends in store location.

Chapter 8, the last chapter in Part Two, deals with the physical aspects of a store's exterior and interior. We discuss the physical structure, visibility, entrances, and parking facilities of stores, as well as aspects of lighting, modernization, and layout. We also see how air conditioning, in-store transportation, and store services contribute to a store's success. Finally, we explore the store's responsibility for customer safety and conveniences.

Chapter 4

Retail Institutions, by Ownership and Organization

After completing this chapter, you should be able to:

- Identify business and governmental groups that use retail statistics.
- Identify six categories that are used to analyze retail institutions.
- List the important characteristics of sole proprietorships, partnerships, and corporations.
- Identify the types and characteristics of retail store ownership.
- Discuss acquisitions and mergers as they affect retail businesses.

Because retailing is so important to various segments of our economy, it receives much attention in newspapers, periodicals, and government publications. Hardly a day goes by without some reference in the media to retail statistics regarding sales volume, merchandise lines, and employment. For example, it is estimated that retail sales account for about one-third of overall economic activity in the United States and are closely watched as a measure of the health of the economy. The data are studied by various groups for information about retail trends, and they provide facts to be used in intelligent decision making.

Among the groups that use retail statistics regularly are retailers, retail suppliers (manufacturers and wholesalers), government agencies, and lending institutions. Retailers use the information for a variety of purposes, including the updating of current plans and the formulation of new ones. Retail suppliers develop production and distribution schedules on the basis of the latest data. Some governmental units study retail sales for estimates of sales tax receipts, while others are concerned with employment figures. Banks analyze the statistics for clues about the extent of borrowing by retailers and the levels of consumer credit.

RETAIL CATEGORIES

In order to compile useful retail information, it helps to classify retail institutions in understandable categories. This is not easy to do because some retail organizations fall into more than one category. For example, while A&P is a supermarket, it is also a chain operation. Again, while Sears, Roebuck maintains department stores, it also conducts a mail order catalog business.

Basically, retail organizations can be arranged in six categories.

Six categories of retail institutions

- **Ownership** This refers to the way control of an organization is exercised. Such control may range from independent ownership to corporations.
- **Types of merchandise sold** This category consists of stores arranged by the types and variety of merchandise they carry. Included are general and limited-line stores.
- **Extent of nonstore selling** This includes retailers who contact consumers in other ways than through stores.
- **Types of services offered** In this category, stores are arranged by the extent to which services are offered to customers. While some stores make available a full line of services, such as delivery, credit, and sales assistance, others are on a self-service, cash-and-carry basis.
- **Extent of departmentalization** This category involves the degree to which stores are departmentalized. Although most small stores are not arranged

this way, department and large specialty stores show an astonishing variety of departmental organization.

- **Location of outlets** This category identifies stores by their location: central-city shopping districts, suburban malls, neighborhood locations, and so forth.

In this chapter we analyze retail institutions by form of ownership, an arrangement that permits us to structure retail statistics for easy and useful reference.

TYPES OF BUSINESS ORGANIZATION

Three types of business organization

Before discussing specific types of retail store ownership, mention should be made of the three ways in which a business may be organized (Table 4-1). First, it may be started as a **sole proprietorship.** This means that one person owns the business, investing both money and time. The owner makes decisions about the business and assumes personal responsibility for its debts. Most small retail establishments, and some moderate-sized ones, are sole proprietorships.

A business may also start as a **partnership,** a form of organization in which two or more people invest their money and time. On the basis of a partnership contract, the partners agree on how the business is to be operated, the amount of time each partner is to devote to it, and how profits and losses are to be shared. The partners are personally liable for the debts of the partnership. As with sole proprietorships, most retail partnerships are small establishments.

The third way in which a business may be organized is as a **corporation.** The owners who invest in the company are called stockholders, but they do not necessarily share in its management. Instead, major decisions are made by a board of directors, while day-to-day operations are conducted by executives and other employees. A major advantage of owning stock in a corporation is that stockholders have limited personal responsibility for the company's debts, being limited to the amount of their investment. Virtually all large retail organizations

TABLE 4-1 Types of Business Ownership

	Sole Proprietorship	*Partnership*	*Corporation*
Ownership	Single owner	Two or more partners	Stockholders
Investment	Money and time	Money and time	Money
Decisions made by	Owner	Partners	Board of directors and executives
Owner responsibility for debts	Unlimited	Unlimited	Limited to amount of investment

TABLE 4-2   Single (Sole) Proprietorships, Partnerships, and Corporations in the Retailing Industry—Number and Receipts, 1986

Type of Business Organization	Number	Percentage of Total	Business Receipts (billions)	Percentage of Total
Single proprietorship	1,886,000	71%	$160.4	11%
Partnership	151,000	6	44.2	3
Corporation	621,000	23	1,298.4	86

Source: Bureau of the Census, *Statistical Abstract of the United States, 1989* (Washington, D.C.: U.S. Government Printing Office, 1990), Table 859, p. 521.

are corporations, and some small retailers are family-owned corporations with few stockholders.

Table 4-2 contains a breakdown of retailing firms in 1986 by type of business organization. It also lists business receipts for each type. It is interesting to note that although sole proprietorships accounted for 71 percent of all retail firms, their share of total receipts was only 11 percent. On the other hand, corporations, with 23 percent of the total number of retail businesses, had 86 percent of the receipts. Obviously, sole proprietorships dominate the field of retailing in number of enterprises, whereas corporations garner the lion's share of sales volume. The table also indicates that partnerships, with 6 percent of the total number of firms, registered only 3 percent of the receipts.

TYPES OF RETAIL STORE OWNERSHIP

Ownership of retail businesses may take any of the following forms.

1. Chain
2. Ownership group
3. Manufacturer-retailer
4. Independent
5. Leased department
6. Franchise
7. Consumer cooperative association

Chain Ownership

As indicated in Chapter 1, a chain organization consists of multiple retail outlets under common, centralized ownership. Some chains have only a few outlets, while others have hundreds or thousands. The major functions of a chain

Chain ownership covers a variety of institutions. *Courtesy:* Hampton Inn and Grand Union.

(buying, advertising, hiring, record keeping, and planning) are controlled by a central headquarters.

Because a chain store usually sells identical merchandise in all its outlets, it buys in large volume and, thus, can sell at lower prices than smaller retailers. The volume of its purchases gives a chain organization important competitive advantages in establishing selling prices for its merchandise, and enables it to deal with manufacturers and wholesalers from a position of strength.

Because of their economic power and centralized management, chains have a distinct advantage in advertising their products. Specialists design advertising campaigns for the organization and have access to all forms of national and regional media. While a chain can afford to send its message to the consumer through newspapers, periodicals, radio, and television, a retail organization with less economic strength has fewer options.

Chain organizations maintain personnel departments that are responsible for hiring and training employees for their stores. Specialists in personnel management outline employee responsibilities so that store procedures are standardized. Potential employees are sometimes attracted to chains by the availability of fringe benefits and the possibilities for advancement.

Advantages and disadvantages of chains

Owing to their financial strength, chains can utilize sophisticated computers for record keeping and other purposes. The most modern equipment and techniques are used for inventory control, customer records, payroll data, sales forecasting, and credit analysis. The availability of up-to-date information from the computer enables chains to make critical decisions quickly.

Many chains recognize the lessons to be learned from failure to adapt to new conditions. They maintain planning departments, employing specialists to analyze economic events, people's habits, and emerging lifestyles. As a result of their long-range planning, they are better prepared than most retailers to meet

THE VARIETY CHAIN BUILDER

Frank Winfield Woolworth

Not all merchants are successful in their first attempt at retailing. A case in point is that of Frank Winfield Woolworth, the famous variety store innovator, whose first store in Utica, New York, failed in 1879 almost as soon as it opened.

Banking on the idea that the public would respond to a store that sold items at prices no higher than 10 cents, Woolworth immediately started another business in Lancaster, Pennsylvania. As this store flourished, he opened additional outlets, so that by 1900 there were fifty-nine "5-and-10" stores.

In 1909 Woolworth went international with the opening of stores in Liverpool, England. Shortly thereafter he consolidated his chain with stores owned by several of his relatives and friends, forming the F. W. Woolworth Co.

The basic merchandising technique exploited so well by Woolworth was this: People would pay "cash on the barrelhead" for what they perceived as a bargain. Woolworth's genius lay in his ability to acquire goods that consumers wanted—that could be sold at low prices (5 cents and 10 cents!) and would result in profits. With proper management, he reasoned, those profits would mount considerably as sales volume increased.

The new F. W. Woolworth Co. comprised 611 stores, but the total grew to more than 1000 by 1919. Annual sales were over $60 million in 1909; they reached $119 million in 1919. Judged by the standards of those days, Woolworth's business receipts were remarkable.

In addition to the "5-and-10" concept, Woolworth's success was ascribed to a variety of business practices. These included purchasing goods directly from manufacturers, thereby excluding wholesalers; the absolute reduction of operating costs; the purchase and sale of merchandise for cash; and the development of accessible store displays.

future needs. For example, on the basis of extensive research, K mart has developed two apparel chains targeted to different economic groups. One, Designer Depots, is geared to consumers of some means, whereas the other, Garment Rack, caters to the blue-collar trade.

It is ironic, but true, that the organizational structure of chains, which gives them competitive advantages, sometimes results in disadvantages. For example,

Bakers, a chain store, is part of the Edison Brothers Stores, Inc. ownership group. *Courtesy:* Edison Brothers Stores, Inc.

the centralization of control makes it difficult to respond quickly to local changes in customers' desires and needs. Centralization also places severe pressure on top management to respond quickly to problems and inefficiency in dispersed branches. Finally, the very large investment needed to locate, outfit, and stock new branches and maintain existing ones ties up significant sums of money.

The extent of chain ownership in the United States is illustrated by the following partial list of well-known chains that were doing business at the beginning of the 1990s.

DEPARTMENT STORES	SPECIALTY STORES
Carter Hawley Hale	Charming Shoppes
Dayton Hudson	Deb Shops
Dillard	The Gap
J. C. Penney	The Limited
Mercantile	Merry-Go-Round
May	Neiman Marcus Group
Nordstrom	Paul Harris Stores
	Petrie Stores

DISCOUNTERS

Ames
Family Dollar
Jamesway
K mart
Roses Stores
Wal-Mart

OFF-PRICE RETAILERS

Burlington Coat
Dress Barn
Ross Stores
Syms
TJX

MASS MERCHANDISERS

K mart
Sears, Roebuck
Wal-Mart
Woolworth

Ownership Group

The "parent" retail corporation
Some of the best-known department and specialty stores in the country are now owned by parent corporations. While the stores maintain their own names and basic functions, the parent corporations exercise control in the areas of long-range planning, financing, and data sharing. However, unlike chain organiza-

Courtesy: Neiman Marcus.

tions, in which individual stores have little to do with policy formulation, stores (known as divisions) in **ownership groups** conduct business almost as though they were self-owned. In fact, the public is largely ignorant of the existence of the parent corporation. For example, in 1989, Filene's, the Boston-based department store chain, announced that it planned to open six new stores and remodel eight others over the next five years. Few persons, customers or not, were aware that Filene's was a division of the parent owner, the May Department Store Company.

Among the larger ownership groups (several of their divisions are listed) are the following:

R. H. Macy & Company (department stores)
   Bullock's
   I. Magnin
   Macy's

F. W. Woolworth Company
   Afterthoughts (fashion accessories boutiques)
   Champs (sporting goods)
   Five-and-Dime (variety)
   Herald Square (party goods)
   Kid's Mart (children's clothing)
   Kinney Shoe (Foot Locker, Kids Locker, Lady Foot Locker)
   Woolworth Express (variety—drugstores without prescription drugs)

May Department Stores Company
   Filene's (department stores)
   G. Fox & Company (department stores)
   Lord & Taylor (department stores)
   Venture (discount stores)

In these days of acquisitions and mergers (buying, selling, or combining stores), it is difficult to keep track of chains and their parent owners. For example, shortly after the Campeau Corporation acquired Allied Stores in 1986, it sold its Ann Taylor fashion stores (a division of Allied Stores) to a group formed by the Ann Taylor chain management. The Campeau Corporation itself went into bankruptcy in 1989.

RETAIL STRATEGY

Williams-Sonoma to Group Stores

Williams-Sonoma's mission to be the leading home-centered specialty retailer continues to gain strength through the synergistic exploitation of its niche store and catalog concepts.

It finds that the demographics of its customers who shop its stores or who buy through its catalogs is largely the same. The customer for **Williams-Sonoma** kitchen products is generally the same customer who would stop in its **Hold Everything** for household storage needs and its **Pottery Barn** for glass and table ware.

Though the same customers will receive a host of Williams-Sonoma catalogs, the company has never taken advantage of the interest overlap at the point-of-sale. Its three retail concepts have each gone their own way in locating their units. But that is changing. Hoping to take advantage of the natural synergism, the company has started to group its stores, testing the concept in both urban and mall locations. In New York, it put the three side-by-side in a busy down-town Manhattan location; in Portland, Ore., it chose a mall location for a test.

Both have worked out well, according to W-S President Kent Larson, and multi-concept grouping will be one of its key strategies for its future store growth. Besides the merchandise impact that will be achieved by locating these units side by side, there is little question but that it will give the chain a decided leasing edge.*

*Williams-Sonoma to Group Stores, *Inside Retailing* (February 4, 1991), p. 3.

Manufacturer-Retailer

In this type of ownership, which includes only large companies, the manufacturer operates its own retail stores. This eliminates the need for involving wholesalers in the distribution process, and gives the manufacturer-retailer absolute control of the distribution of its products. On the other hand, the high investment costs and operational difficulties discourage many retailers from engaging in manufacturing, and vice versa. The retail outlets in this type of ownership arrangement are usually specialty stores. They include such well-known companies as Kinney Shoes and The Gap.

There are, of course, risks in undertaking a manufacturing-retailing activity. As reported in *Inside Retailing*, Kurt Barnard, executive director of the Federation of Apparel Manufacturers, cautioned manufacturers who consider opening their own retail outlets. He said, "Manufacturers thinking of taking a plunge into retailing will find that running a store is a totally different ballgame from manufacturing. Don't be deluded into thinking that you can long operate a store selling only the line that you make . . . soon you will have to add other lines as well. That means a quick plunge into the full-blown world of retailing."[1] Nevertheless, the continued success of some factory outlet malls, in which manufacturers maintain their own retail stores, indicates the rising popularity of this trend.

Faced with dwindling sales from their department and specialty store customers, more manufacturers are opening their own stores. This trend is illustrated by a new complex of retail outlets in Reading, Pennsylvania. Called the Store-

[1] "What About Manufacturer-Operated 'Outlet' Stores?" *Inside Retailing* (February 6, 1984), p. 1.

house Shops, the center houses more than 50 manufacturer-operated shops. While the manufacturers continue to produce for other retailers, they protect themselves with sales from their own stores.

Independent

An independent store has one outlet

The most prevalent type of retail ownership is the **independently owned store.** Although this type of business may be a sole proprietorship, a partnership, or a corporation, it usually has only one outlet. Unlike a chain store, which is controlled by a parent company, the independent has its own management.

Independents can be found in every community in the country and are located wherever people need the convenience of shopping outlets. You can find them on Main Streets and in movie theaters; in office buildings and at roadsides; on busy city streets and in village squares. However, they are almost never found in very large shopping centers.

Independent retailing is the most common type of ownership. Photo by: Teri Leigh Stratford.

Because most small independents are owner managed, the proprietors devote much energy and time to the business. Though the store may have one or more employees, the owner tries to control all aspects of the operation. This absolute control may work to the owner's advantage because he or she can make decisions and judgments when they are needed. However, with so many responsibilities—purchasing, selling, advertising, and recordkeeping, to name just a few—the owner sometimes finds the burden too heavy to carry alone. Furthermore, limitations in the owner's managerial skills may affect the business adversely. It is no accident, therefore, that new independent retailers have a high failure rate. It is generally accepted that almost one out of every five new independents will fail within the first year. These failures are usually due to insufficient investment funds, lack of business experience, and poor management.

An example of a successful independent retailer is Putumayo, a women's specialty apparel company. It was started in 1975 by its owner, Dan Storper, as a one-person, one-store operation. By 1989, Storper had expanded his operation to seven stores strung from Boston to Washington, D.C. Hard work, a creative combination of designing, manufacturing, and retailing activities, and a vision of sensible growth had changed Putumayo from an independent-type retailer to chain status.

An interesting start in independent retailing is illustrated by the following example:

> Jessica McClintock, a well-known designer of female apparel, felt hemmed in by constraints imposed upon her by her department store clients. In order to control her mix of merchandise and fashion, she decided in 1981 to open her own specialty store. By 1986, she had started two additional stores as a successful independent retailer.

Though independents have the advantages of relatively low start-up costs and direct control over operations, they are at a disadvantage with regard to the prices they pay for merchandise. This is so because they usually buy in small quantities and cannot secure the favorable price terms accorded to chains and other large retailers.

In order to strengthen their bargaining position with manufacturers and wholesalers, some small independents form associations for purchasing their merchandise. In some cases they combine their orders so as to secure volume discounts. With this arrangement, they can compete more favorably with larger retailers while maintaining their independence. In other cases they organize their own wholesale business as a **cooperative chain.** Each cooperating store receives the benefit of discounted prices while maintaining its individuality. Finally, some independents have arrangements with a wholesaler whereby they agree to sell the latter's products and to use the wholesaler's name instead of their own. This **voluntary chain,** exemplified by Associated Food Stores and Independent Grocers Alliance, gives the independents price advantages as well as help in such matters as advertising and financing. Here, too, the stores operate as independent entities.

There are a growing number of people who believe that independently owned retail establishments will face difficult financial problems in the years ahead. If such predictions come true, and there are indications of their coming to pass, many people who plan to enter retailing as independent owners may have to do so in some other way, for example, leased department or franchise.

Leased Department

Leased departments are found in discount, department, and specialty stores

Some discount, department, and specialty stores rent space to other retailers (lessees), who maintain their own departments in the stores. These are called **leased departments.** This arrangement enables the store (lessor) to widen its product or service line without assuming the necessary expertise or investment responsibilities. It also provides the store with additional revenue through rent collection, which sometimes includes a percentage of the lessee's sales. Among the most frequently found leased departments are furs and fur storage, photo studio, shoes, fine jewelry, books, cards, and millinery lines departments.

Many leased departments are operated by chains, which sell standardized products or services in their various leased outlets. Like individually run leased departments, the chains are responsible for all activities in their areas.

To the lessee, the advantages of leasing a department are lower investment costs, access to the store's other traffic, and availability of the store's physical services (parking, etc.). The renting store, of course, counts on the leased department to attract additional customers.

Franchise

Although the term *franchise* may not be known by many people, names like Howard Johnson, Dunkin Donuts, and H&R Block usually bring instant recognition. In fact, each of these companies is involved in a form of ownership known as franchising.

Leased departments can offer services as well as merchandise. *Courtesy:* Piggly Wiggly.

Radio Shack is an example of a popular electronics franchise. *Courtesy:* Radio Shack.

In a **franchise,** a manufacturer, wholesaler, or service company (the **franchisor** or **licensor**) gives a smaller company or an individual (the **franchisee**) the right (i.e., the franchise) to conduct a retail business in a certain way and within a specified period. Though there are a variety of possible franchise arrangements, let's examine a typical situation.

Suppose you want to start a retail fast-food business but don't possess the necessary skills and experience. You may be reluctant to open an independent store for fear of possible failure and loss of your investment. In that case you may try to secure a franchise from a company like Burger King or McDonald's. The advantage to you is that you will be able to rely on a large company for guidance and help.

As the franchisee, you might pay the franchisor a one-time franchise fee for the right to conduct business under the franchisor's name. Depending on the popularity of the franchisor and the cost of equipping the franchise, the fee could run from a few thousand dollars to well into the millions. For example, it costs upwards of $300,000 to start a McDonald's franchise, whereas you might secure one from H&R Block, the income tax franchisor, for a few thousand dollars. A Baskin-Robbins Ice Cream Company franchise might be secured for $75,000 to $95,000, while a Sheraton Inns franchise could cost $5 million to $10 million. Table 4-3 contains the investment fees required for additional selected franchises as of 1991.

Consumer Cooperative Association

A store owned by consumers

In **consumer cooperative associations** consumers own shares in a retail store. Though the owners decide store policy, actual operations are maintained by a managing retailer. The store's products and services are available to all customers, whether owners or not. Each consumer-owner has one vote no matter

TABLE 4-3   Investments Required to Purchase Selected Franchises, 1991

Franchise	Investment
Automotive Products and Services	
AAMCO Transmissions	$48,000
Goodyear Tires	$50,000 and up
Beauty Salons, Services, and Cosmetics	
Hair Replacement Systems	$25,000 and up
Syd Simons Cosmetics	$45,000
Donut Shops	
Dunkin' Donuts	$50,000–60,000
Mister Donut of America	$315,000
Men's and Women's Clothing and Specialty Shops	
Formal Wear Service	$65,000 and up
Just Pants	$108,000–225,000
Printing Services	
Insty Prints	$45,000
Quik Print	$84,500
Retail Stores	
Ben Franklin Stores	$150,000
Computerland	$200,000–500,000
Travel	
Empress Travel	$75,000
Travel Agents International	$44,500

how many shares he or she owns, and membership is open to all. Yearly profits, called patronage dividends, are distributed on the basis of a member's purchases, not the number of shares owned. In addition, members may also earn low interest on their investments in the association.

Though consumer cooperatives have not had a significant impact on total retail sales in this country, they continue to function in the farm supply, grocery, cafeteria, health food, and bookstore fields. The basic cost of doing business affects "co-ops" in the same way that it affects other businesses. As a result, the early expectation of some cooperatives that consumer members would benefit significantly from lower co-op prices did not materialize. With other cooperatives, prices are set at competitive levels to avoid conflict with privately run stores. Co-op members then benefit from the annual distribution of profits.

ACQUISITIONS AND MERGERS

During the last few years, American business leaders have participated in or witnessed the acquisition or merger of a fairly large number of corporations. A significant number of those corporations have been retail companies. An acquisition is the purchase by one company or by individuals of a sufficient number of shares of stock of a second company to control the second company. A merger takes place when two or more companies combine to form a new company. In some instances, the new company retains the name of one or both of the merging firms.

Sometimes a company is bought without the buyer(s) assuming much debt, that is, borrowing money that must be repaid. At other times, the opposite is true. When the latter takes place, it is often called a leveraged buyout (LBO). An LBO involves the acquisition of a company by investors who borrow significant amounts to finance the acquisition. This usually puts the investing company into heavy debt. Often, the investors are stockholders or officers of the company being acquired.

For example, key executives of R. H. Macy & Company joined with outside investors in 1989 in a leveraged buyout of the firm. As a result of the debts incurred by the acquisition, by 1990 the new owners were having difficulty meeting those debts. Another example, this one involving the Campeau Corporation, a Canadian firm, occurred when the company acquired Federated Department Stores and went into immediate debt by selling "junk bonds." Junk bonds, issued by corporations, are bonds that pay higher interest to lenders than most other types of bonds. What makes them junk bonds is that they are not backed up by any tangible assets and are therefore worthless if the company can't pay the interest. Consequently, the only attractive item about the bonds is the high interest rate. The sale of the junk bonds placed a large debt burden on the Campeau Corporation, and it was unable to meet its obligations. The company subsequently went into bankruptcy.

The following list indicates the extent of recent acquisitions and mergers in the retail industry. There were 210 of them in 1988. By no means is it a complete list, nor should we expect the recent pattern of acquisitions and mergers to change in the near future.

- In 1989, K mart Corporation acquired Pace Membership Warehouse, Inc., a warehouse club company consisting of 41 units.
- In 1988, Ames Department Stores acquired 392 Zayre discount stores. Zayre, in turn, merged with its 83 percent owned subsidiary, TJX Companies, owner of T. J. Maxx, a clothing chain; Hit or Miss, a chain of apparel shops; and Chadwick's of Boston, a catalog operator. Ames, itself, went into bankruptcy in 1990.
- P. A. Bergner and Company, a department store chain that already owned Boston Stores, acquired Carson Pirie Scott and Company, a regional independent retailer, in 1989. In 1987, Carson had acquired Donaldson's Department Stores from Allied Stores Corporation.
- In 1989, Dillard Department Stores bought a regional independent, D. H. Holmes.
- In 1989, The Gap, Inc., one of America's largest apparel retailers, negotiated for the acquisition of American Eagle Outfitters, primarily a men's apparel chain. In 1983, The Gap had acquired Banana Republic, a chain that sells

clothing with a safari look. The Limited, another leading retailer, acquired Lerner, Lane Bryant, Abercrombie & Fitch, Henri Bendel, and others.

- In 1988, R. H. Macy and Company acquired I. Magnin and Bullock's Wilshire department stores and, as indicated previously, had itself been bought by a group of investors in a leveraged buyout.

- In 1989, American Stores Company merged its California Alpha Beta supermarket chain with the Lucky Stores Company supermarket chain.

- In the late 1980s, Hooker Corporation, an Australian company, acquired the following department stores: B. Altman, Bonwit Teller, Sakowitz, and The Parisian. Because of heavy debts and poor sales, Hooker went into bankruptcy, closing B. Altman stores and selling its Bonwit Teller operations.

- In 1986, May Department Stores Company obtained Lord & Taylor and Caldor when it purchased Associated Dry Goods. It also owns Filene's, Foley's, Hecht's, Loehmann's, G. Fox, Famous-Barr, and Volume Shoes, a specialty chain with 2,663 units. The May Company subsequently sold Caldor to an investment group in 1989.

- In 1985, the buyout of Seligman & Latz, an operator of leased jewelry departments and beauty salons, was spearheaded by Harold Geneen, former chief executive officer of ITT Corporation.

- After acquiring Coldwell Banker Commercial Group, a company whose clients are commercial and real estate operators and investors, Sears, Roebuck and Company sold the group in 1989 in order to bolster its merchandise activities.

One problem that usually arises when a retailer's leveraged buyout expenses become excessive is the wariness of suppliers in extending credit. In difficult cases, suppliers may cut off shipments, resulting in merchandise shortages in the retailer's stores. This affects sales and puts additional pressure on the retailer's ability to meet debt payments. One consequence of this situation is the competitive edge gained by other retailers. For example, desirable merchandise, once destined for the debt-burdened retailer, may be snapped up by off-price chains, specialty retailers, and even healthy department stores.

The financial impact of acquisitions and mergers has also caused some large retailers to concentrate on price-cutting advertising to generate cash flow. Unfortunately, this comes at the expense of the companies' images and may be harmful in the long run.

Another interesting phenomenon associated with acquisitions and mergers involves consumers who have been "trained" by retail advertising and promotions to pay less than full price for merchandise. Acquisitions and mergers have hastened this process because marketing and merchandising considerations have often taken second place to financial matters.

Even after an acquisition occurs, differences may arise between the buyer and seller. Such was the case when May Department Stores acquired Filene's and

Foley's from the Campeau Corporation. The problem arose from differing interpretations of the accounting procedures for year-end adjustments.

The volatility of retail ownership is demonstrated by speculation that even giant companies like Sears, Roebuck and J. C. Penney have been eyed by investors for acquisition.

NEW TERMS

consumer cooperative association

cooperative chain

corporation

franchise

franchisee

franchisor

independently owned store

leased department

licensor

ownership group

partnership

sole proprietorship

voluntary chain

CHAPTER HIGHLIGHTS

1. Retail statistics are used regularly by retailers, manufacturers, wholesalers, government agencies, and lending institutions.

2. Retail organizations are classified according to ownership, types of merchandise sold, extent of nonstore selling, types of services offered, extent of departmentalization, and location of outlets.

3. A new business may be organized as a sole proprietorship (one owner), a partnership (two or more owners), or a corporation (owners are called stockholders).

4. Though a great majority of retail institutions are sole proprietorships, more than three-fourths of retail sales are made by corporations.

5. Ownership of a retail business may take the form of a chain, ownership group, manufacturer-retailer, independent store, leased department, franchise, or consumer cooperative association.

6. Chain organizations have several advantages over smaller competitors: Buying in large volume enables them to pay lower prices for goods; their economic strength and centralized management allow them to advertise in all kinds of national and regional media; they employ specialists to hire and train employees, they have the means to utilize sophisticated computers, and they

maintain planning departments to prepare for future needs. Chains sometimes suffer disadvantages: the difficulty of responding quickly to customers' needs and to problems in individual stores, and the large investment needed to start new stores and maintain existing ones.

7. Ownership groups own and exercise control over their stores. However, the stores usually operate as though they were self-owned.

8. Manufacturer-retailers make and sell their own products. Though they control distribution of their products, they have high investment costs and must contend with operational difficulties.

9. Independent retailers have the advantage of relatively low start-up costs and direct control over operations. Because they usually purchase in small quantities, they pay higher prices for goods than those paid by chains and other large retailers. To meet this problem, some independents form associations, cooperative chains, or voluntary chains in order to purchase merchandise at lower prices.

10. A leased department is a rented area in a discount, department, or specialty store. The store receives rent and the lessee sells its own products. Many leased departments are operated by chains.

11. A franchise exists when a manufacturer, wholesaler, or service company (the franchisor) gives a smaller company or an individual (the franchisee) the right to conduct a retail business in a certain way within a specified period.

12. A consumer cooperative association consists of consumers who own shares in a retail store. Though the owners decide store policy, a managing retailer runs the store.

13. Many acquisitions and mergers have taken place in the retail industry during the last few years.

REVIEW QUESTIONS

1. Why are most large retailing companies organized as corporations?
2. Corporations account for more than 80 percent of retail sales volume. Why, then, are most retailers organized as sole proprietorships?
3. What advantages do small retailers have over chains in the operation of their business?
4. What are the advantages of a division in an ownership group (such as Bullock's of R. H. Macy & Company) operating as though it were self-owned?
5. What are some advantages of operating a leased department in a department store?
6. What are the advantages of owning a franchise?
7. What is the difference between an acquisition and a merger?

DISCUSSION QUESTIONS

1. What are the benefits of arranging a store into departments? Why aren't most small stores arranged departmentally?
2. Of what advantage is it to a manufacturer-retailer such as the Thom McAn Shoe Company to have absolute control over the distribution of its products?
3. What advice would you give to someone who is thinking seriously about opening an independent retail store?
4. Do you think that consumer cooperative associations will someday have a larger share of total retail sales than they do today? Explain.
5. Why might a retailer agree to a merger with another company?

CASE 1

The Pushcart and Kiosk Movement

A form of ownership that can be characterized as both old and new has emerged on the retail landscape. This seeming contradiction involves "temporary," or short-term, retailers who sell in shopping malls from pushcarts or kiosks. The main advantage to the retailers is low start-up costs, while the mall developers garner additional revenue from these renters. The result, at least to date, has been a mutual-benefit relationship.

So successful have these operations been that more and more mall owners are adopting the idea by either establishing landlord-tenant relationships with individuals or franchising the concept. Annual sales from this form of retailing run into the hundreds of millions.

Most of the products sold from pushcarts or in kiosks are exotic or fun provoking, for example, craft items, specialty foods, stuffed animals. Shoppers are attracted to the merchandise by colorful displays and easy viewing. Prices are usually low to moderate.

To avoid angering their conventional retailer tenants—department and specialty stores—mall owners attempt to limit the types of stock sold by temporary tenants. However, the urge to expand product lines and thus increase profits exerts pressure on the owners. And because pushcarts and kiosks are found in some malls only during busy seasons, for example, Christmas and Easter, owners must also deal with dissatisfaction from consumers (with complaints) who cannot locate the temporary retailers.

a. If you owned a specialty store in a shopping mall, what might be your attitude toward pushcarts and kiosks in the mall?
b. Recognizing the need to avoid antagonizing their regular tenants as well as the desire to maximize profits, what factors should a new mall developer consider when renting space to temporary retailers?

CASE 2

Fraction of the Action

Sambo's Restaurants, the food service chain that began 30 years ago in California, achieved rapid growth and profitability as the concept of fast-food dining became popular.

The first Sambo's restaurant opened in 1957 at a beachfront location in Santa Barbara. Sambo's took its name from the two partners who owned and operated the business: Sam Battistone, who had run a diner in town for 20 years, and Newell Bohnett, a salesman for restaurant equipment. Both the restaurant's location and its menu, featuring a wide variety of pancakes, attracted customers. Although the business went through an initial sluggish period, Sambo's soon became extremely successful and the owners decided to expand.

The choice of location for its second unit was somewhat unusual. Instead of opening a unit close to the original Sambo's, the owners elected to establish the second unit in Sacramento, several hundred miles away. Customarily, the operator of a successful retail operation establishes a second unit and eventually several units nearby to develop a broad, cohesive marketing area.

The decision to open in Sacramento raised problems of long-distance supervision and quality control for Sambo's owners. To ensure success, it was absolutely essential to choose a manager who could be trusted to make sound operational decisions.

To solve the problems, Sambo's owners came up with a plan that offered the managers a share of ownership in the unit in return for investing a certain amount of money. This concept they termed the fraction of the action plan. The plan was designed to appeal to entrepreneurs whose long hours and hard work in making a unit successful would be rewarded by a share of the unit's profits. A prospective manager put up $20,000 for a 20 percent share in a unit. Each unit was set up as a separate corporation with both the unit manager and the original Sambo's owners as participating shareholders. The $20,000 investment was refundable, under certain conditions, if the manager decided to leave the operation.

The fraction of the action plan fell between two common forms of ownership-operation: On the one hand, there were companies such as Denny's that totally owned and financed their stores; on the other hand, there were companies such as McDonald's that offered franchising arrangements to prospective operators. With the shared-interest concept, Sambo's believed that they had designed an excellent strategy for profitable operation and expansion.

For several years, they were right. By the time six years had passed, Sambo's restaurants had opened throughout the West, generating $17 million in sales and $2.5 million net profit. Such successes prompted the ready sale of its stock when the company went public.

After the company went public, the original partners retired and turned management of the company over to others, including Mr. Battistone's son. Under the new management, Sambo's embarked on a major expansion program: Its goal was to become the largest full-service restaurant chain in the country. So intense was this effort that, at one point, Sambo's opened a new unit every $4\frac{1}{2}$ days.

The company's amazing growth and seeming financial health attracted many investors to the stock. In 1972, the company realized $12.8 million on a 400,000 share offering of stock, enabling it to eliminate its long-term debt.

But there was trouble ahead for the Sambo's chain. Rapid expansion carried with it a heavy price. Although the fraction of the action plan had worked for more than a decade by attracting responsible, ambitious individuals, qualified unit managers now became increasingly difficult to find and there was little time to provide necessary training for the personnel. Quality control also suffered.

Despite such difficulties, the company continued its policy of expansion by opening more units, and by diversifying to reach the specialty dinnerhouse customer.

A far more serious problem arose in 1977 concerning the fraction of the action plan. After eight years, the Securities and Exchange Commission found that Sambo's practice of treating a manager's $20,000 investment as revenue was misleading. The SEC maintained that such money should be held in escrow, because it was refundable if the manager resigned. To comply with the SEC finding, the company had to revise its financial statements, which had a profound and negative effect on earnings and on the financial outlook for the company.

Sambo's developed a new compensation plan in response to the SEC, but the plan was unpopular with unit managers. Morale among store managers and their staffs dropped and sales began to sag.

Although the company subsequently tried several strategies to reverse its decline, none was successful. The company continued to founder. Finally, in 1981, in order to avoid full failure, Sambo's declared bankruptcy for the purposes of reorganization.

a. Sambo's shared unit ownership plan was both successful and popular. What were the benefits to the company and to unit managers? What kind of problems do you think could arise with such a plan?

b. In your estimation, what are the most serious risks a company faces with an extremely rapid expansion plan?

c. If you were the owner of a successful retail enterprise and wanted to open new outlets, what plan for growth would you find most suitable: company-owned outlets, franchised outlets, or shared ownership outlets? Explain.

d. What plan do you think a prospective manager would find most attractive? Why?

REFERENCES

"Apparel Designers Take Control of Image," *Chain Store Age Executive* (October 1988), pp. 192–196.

BOND, R. E. *The Source Book of Franchise Opportunities*. Homewood, IL: Dow Jones-Irwin, 1985.

HAWKINS, C., AND S. PHILLIPS, "Campeau Is Up on That High Wire Again." *Business Week*, May 15, 1989, pp. 108–110.

PEPPER, B. P. "Fast Forward." *Business Month* (February 1989), pp. 24–30.

"The Storehouse Shops Project Is on Track." *Chain Store Age Executive* (October 1988), pp. 90–95.

Chapter 5

Retail Institutions, by Merchandise Sold and Nonstore Selling Methods

---

After completing this chapter, you should be able to:

- List the reasons for the classification of merchandise.
- List four major ways of classifying merchandise and explain how they serve to identify stores.
- Identify retail institutions according to the merchandise they carry.
- Explain nonstore selling methods: in-home retailing, vending machines, mail order/catalog retailing, telephone selling, and electronic retailing.

In Chapter 4 you learned how retail institutions are classified by form of ownership. You saw that retail ownership assumes an astonishing variety of forms. The discussion indicated that large retail organizations are usually corporations and small retail institutions are owned and operated as sole proprietorships, partnerships, or corporations.

In this chapter we continue our discussion of retail institutions by identifying them according to the types of merchandise they sell; again the diversity of retail outlets will be surprising. You will also be reintroduced to the "moving" wheel of retailing.

MERCHANDISE CATEGORIES

Scrambled merchandising

One of the most significant phenomena in retailing has been the often successful attempt by merchants to widen their assortments of merchandise. We see evidence of this all around us: Supermarkets, once selling only food products, have branched into nonfood items like housewares; drugstores, traditionally offering prescriptive medicines and drug-related goods, have added an inventory of toys and games; and variety stores, previously restricted to the sale of knick-knacks, have expanded into health food products, such as vitamins. This movement toward increasing the types of goods carried in a store is known as **scrambled merchandising.** We can expect to see a continuation of this trend as merchants seek new ways to maintain or increase their share of sales.

For example, Larry's Market in Aurora, Washington, started an upscale combination supermarket-cafeteria store in 1978. The addition of the restaurant aspect to the basic supermarket business appealed greatly to shoppers who were seeking more than just low-priced food items. Shopping became more of a social outlet as consumers responded positively to the store's scrambled merchandising and food service approach.

As the variety of available goods has grown, retailers have had to put them into manageable groups for the following reasons.

1. To provide a system for recordkeeping, including statistics on inventories, sales, and prices
2. To establish systems for controlling inventories and orders
3. To organize merchandise so customers can find out what they want (or acceptable substitutes)
4. To study customer buying patterns and find ways to increase sales

The categories that retailers have developed to meet their needs are as follows.

Scrambled merchandising in an Albertson store. *Courtesy:* Albertson's Inc.

Merchandise categories

1. **General or Limited-Line Merchandise.**   **General merchandise** consists of a variety of goods (e.g., clothing, home furnishings, appliances) while **limited-line merchandise** refers to goods within a particular line (e.g., ladies' wear).

2. **Staple or Fashion Goods.**   **Staple goods** are products that are constantly in demand and are infrequently influenced by fashion changes (e.g., pencils, shoelaces, ladders). **Fashion goods** consist of items that are popular at a particular time (e.g., miniskirts, men's vests).

3. **Seasonal Goods.**   **Seasonal merchandise** is usually in demand at a certain time of the year; examples are skis, bathing suits, surfboards, and Christmas decorations.

4. **Convenience, Shopping, Specialty, or Impulse Goods.**   **Convenience goods** are items that consumers buy because of immediate and usually pressing needs (e.g., shampoo, flashlights, bread). **Shopping goods** are products that consumers buy after spending time and effort to evaluate them (e.g., appliances, cars, clothing). **Specialty goods** are particular brands for which a consumer shops (e.g., Jordache jeans, Ford Escorts, Estee Lauder perfume). **Impulse goods** consist of items that consumers purchase with little or no planning. For example, while waiting to pay at the checkout counter, a shopper might purchase an additional item because the display of the item reminds him or her of a need. Attractive layouts and displays often stimulate the purchase of impulse goods.

Retailers do, of course, classify merchandise in other ways, but the additional categories usually apply only to specific, internal store functions. For example, managers and buyers may sort merchandise by department, price line, color, size or computerized inventory category. Although all of these classifications are useful, only one system is used in classifying stores: general or limited-line.

GENERAL-MERCHANDISE STORES

These stores carry a wide selection of goods and attempt to satisfy most of their customers' needs. Some stores, of course, stock a greater variety of merchandise than others. Included among general-merchandise stores are department stores and their offshoots (branches and twigs), discount department stores, variety stores, catalog showrooms, convenience stores, flea markets, barn stores, and some new types of general-merchandise stores.

Department Stores

Merchandise carried by department stores

Department stores, as you have seen, consist of a collection of specialty operations under one roof, with one owner. The variety of goods carried by department stores is wider than that carried by any other kind of retail store. Some department stores carry more lines than others, but the Bureau of the Census has specified that in order to qualify as a traditional department store a retail outlet *must* sell merchandise from each of the following lines: (1) furniture, home furnishings, appliances, radio and television sets; (2) general apparel for the family; and (3) household linen and dry goods.

Department stores are run on the principle that the way to increase revenues is through high sales volume. Managers of these stores believe that sales volume depends on meeting as many consumer needs as possible. Even though some retailers believe that computerized in-home shopping may one day challenge the primacy of department stores, these stores are still the giants of retailing. What's more, other types of stores occasionally grow into department stores. This happens when a limited-line store scrambles its merchandise successfully and thereby appeals to a larger number of customers. As the store expands through the addition of more merchandise lines, it casts off its previous image as a variety, dry goods, or apparel store and begins to resemble a small department store. When furniture, large appliances, and other high-priced merchandise are introduced, it qualifies as a full department store.

Certain kinds of merchandise require specific selling methods. Department stores are able to capitalize on the most appropriate selling techniques by varying them from one department to another. For example, many types of goods lend themselves to self-service merchandising, but some goods, such as furniture, fine jewelry, and furs, require a more personalized approach. So, in addition to a wide variety of merchandise and one-stop shopping, department stores offer a variety of services tailored to the goods being sold.

The former chief executive officer of Federated Department Stores, Howard

Goldfeder, feels that department stores have six advantages over smaller stores, even off-price ones. He lists them as

1. **Flexibility**—the ability to respond quickly to changing conditions.
2. **Variety of values**—the ability to offer a mixed package of *value* elements: merchandise assortment, presentation, convenience, and so on.
3. **Variety of merchandise**—the offer of a broad array of merchandise.
4. **Variety of services**—the ability to provide more varied services to customers.
5. **Stability**—the credibility and integrity earned by department stores over the years.
6. **Character**—a combination of all the ways in which department stores serve their customers.[1]

Nevertheless, more and more observers have come to realize that in many instances specialty retailers are showing better earnings than department stores. This trend has been with us for some time and has affected the strategic plans of several department store chains. For example, Macy's, on Herald Square in New York City, has reorganized itself so that it looks and feels like a group of specialty stores under one roof.

An interesting study comparing department stores with off-price stores revealed that

- In response to off-price retailing, department stores have become more promotional and price competitive.
- Store brand programs have been developed by department stores so they can offer exclusive merchandise and receive higher profits than those provided by national brand merchandise.
- Off-price retailers are successful because they sell identical or comparable items at lower prices than department or specialty stores.
- A disadvantage of off-price stores is their location outside shopping malls. This denies the consumer one-stop shopping. However, off-price malls have been developed to reduce this inconvenience.
- Department and specialty stores offer more services than off-price stores: customer satisfaction with products, liberal return policies, broad assortments of fashion merchandise, their own credit cards in addition to major cards.
- The cost of operating off-price stores is rising.
- The cost of maintaining professional management skills in off-price stores is rising.[2]

[1] *Inside Retailing* (January 10, 1983), pp. 3–4.

[2] G. H. Kirby, and R. Dardis, "A Pricing Study of Women's Apparel in Off-Price and Department Stores," *Journal of Retailing*, **62** (Fall 1986), pp. 321–330.

Branch stores follow customers
to the suburbs. *Courtesy:*
Filene's.

For about 100 years department stores were located primarily in cities, where they catered to large concentrations of people. However, the population explosion and the need for new residential areas in the 1940s and 1950s affected the stores' traditional marketing strategies. Like all perceptive executives, many department store managers recognized the need to meet this new challenge, so onto the retailing scene came the kinds of outlets called branches and twigs.

Branches

When towns and cities grow, their central business districts expand and many inner-city residents eventually move to the suburbs. As growth continues, the distance between new communities and downtown shopping centers increases. Travel between the suburbs and the central city becomes complicated and inconvenient. To avoid this inconvenience, consumers begin to buy at stores in or near their neighborhoods. These stores prosper and expand their lines to meet customer demands, thereby taking more and more business away from the downtown stores.

Although downtown stores stay in business and continue to serve consumers from outlying communities as well as those in the city, they are eventually forced to find a way of following consumers to the suburbs. By observing how new communities and shopping areas develop, department store executives are usually able to identify high concentrations of potential suburban customers in specific areas. When this happens, the downtown store usually opens a **branch store** designed to meet the needs of consumers in that particular area.

Branches are scaled-down versions of department stores

Branch stores are usually scaled-down versions of the main store, but the size of any one branch depends on the population it serves and on the branch's competition. Branch stores generally cater to smaller, local populations of consumers whose needs, lifestyles, and purchasing patterns are similar and readily identified. This allows the store to tailor its mix of products by concentrating on merchandise that is in frequent demand and limiting or eliminating merchandise that is not.

Because of its size and product mix limitations, a branch generally sells less

Discount department stores
offer one-stop shopping.
Courtesy: K mart.

than a main store; but since there is usually more than one branch, total branch sales usually exceed main store sales. In fact, two-thirds of all department store sales are branch sales.

Twigs

Twigs are department stores' specialty stores

Twigs are small department store branches that stock only one kind of merchandise or perhaps several similar lines. By all rights, they should be classified as limited-line stores, but because they are part of the department store branch network, they are considered extensions of general-merchandise stores. A Sears auto center is an example of a twig.

Discount Department Stores

Bradlees, K mart, and Caldor are discount department stores

Discount department stores, also known as full-line discounters, like Caldor, Bradlees, and K mart, are very much like traditional department stores in the merchandise they carry. However, the quality and price of their merchandise differ, as do the personal services they offer. Discounters sell nationally known brands below the manufacturer's suggested retail price. Like traditional department stores, discounters offer a wide variety of merchandise and one-stop shopping. Until recently, discounters had a fairly wide selection of merchandise, with a narrow range of manufacturers or brands from which to choose. This was partly due to the fact that some manufacturers would not sell to discount stores. They felt that their product's image would be damaged by association with discount stores, which lacked status because of their locations, the way they sold and displayed merchandise, and their lack of personal services. However, this situation no longer prevails, largely because of federal legislation such as the Sherman Antitrust Act, the Robinson-Patman Act, and the Federal Trade Commission Act. In addition, off-price retailing has grown so that manufacturers cannot ignore it.

Another reason for discounters' narrower selection of brands is rooted in their operating principle. Although discounters believe in providing customers with one-stop shopping, their biggest selling point is the savings they offer. To provide these savings, they buy in large quantities, take advantage of close-outs by manufacturers, concentrate on fast-moving merchandise, and in many instances offer no-frills service.

Because thrift is such a large selling point for discounters, they seek money-saving methods in order to pass on savings to customers. Naturally, this affects the discounter's selling methods and services. At one time discounters offered few, if any, personalized services. In order to save on salaries for salespeople, they used self-service wherever it was practical. To some extent, they still do, but today they all provide some degree of personal services. Examples of these services are gift wrapping and delivery of merchandise to customers. Also, in order to minimize costs discounters once refused to extend credit to customers, but now most discount department stores accept major credit cards like VISA and Mastercard.

Discount department stores are a far cry from the original discount stores described in Chapter 1. Departing from the exclusive sale of appliances and other hard goods, they now carry a wide assortment of general merchandise. In fact, the differences between traditional department stores and discount department stores have become so blurred that it is increasingly difficult to distinguish between the two. This is another instance of how the "wheel of retailing" turns.

An interesting departure from the discount department store's way of doing business was the successful attempt by Caldor to continue its discount practices on selected merchandise only. At the same time, Caldor tried to cast off its discounter image by selling quality brand names of both hard and soft goods. In addition, it upgraded its personal services and provided customers with department store surroundings, that is, attractive interiors, carpeting, good-looking showcases, and the like. Caldor managed to combine high management standards and a shrewd merchandising strategy with its discount operation. Making its stores accessible to small-town populations, it has developed a large number of steady customers.

An even more prominent example of a successful discount department store chain catering to small-town populations is Wal-Mart. Numbering some 1,300 stores in 1988, the company offers discounted merchandise as well as popular services that appeal greatly to consumers in those areas.

Variety Stores

In Chapter 1 you learned that variety stores sell a wide assortment of merchandise and, according to the Bureau of the Census, carry goods in the low-to-popular-price range. Because Woolworth's was probably the most successful of the variety chains, the name "five and dime store" became synonymous with variety-type outlets. As inflation eroded the reality of the name, consumers came to refer to variety stores by their names—Woolworth's, Kress, and so forth.

Some variety stores sell higher-priced merchandise, too

Though variety stores have always carried general merchandise in limited-price lines, their competition with department and specialty stores rarely extended into more expensive merchandise. However, as they tested the possibility of carrying a wider and more expensive range of goods, they found that consumers responded positively. So, in addition to maintaining loyal customers who continued to buy such low-priced items as cosmetics, hardware, and toys, variety stores were able to induce the same customers to purchase higher-priced goods. This favorable change was not without its drawbacks; the sale of higher-priced merchandise required a larger sales force to assist customers. It must be remembered that variety stores have always counted on self-service, with little or no help from cashiers.

In 1975 W. T. Grant, one of the largest variety store chains, failed and went into bankruptcy. At that time it was the largest bankruptcy in retailing history. Because most other variety stores were also chain operations, Grant's failure caused many variety store owners to reconsider their merchandising policies. In order to survive, some have reorganized and have shifted their outlets into discounting. Wal-mart has already replaced K mart as America's number two retailer, a notable example of this trend. Interesting, however, was Woolworth's experience in the early 1980s that ran counter to the trend. Having eliminated its unprofitable Woolco discount division, the chain provided new funds and energy for the development of fashion-oriented specialty stores. It maintains its presence in the variety store field by operating small stores called Express.

In many ways the rise and partial decline of variety stores is a classic example of how consumer buying patterns change and how competitive changes encourage or discourage different kinds of retailing and different kinds of stores.

Catalog Showrooms

An addition to the wide array of retail outlets found in many communities is the **catalog showroom.** The showroom is actually a store in which customers order through catalogs. The assortment of merchandise is extensive, ranging from tennis balls to lawn equipment. In general, these stores sell nonclothing, nonfood items that can be taken home immediately upon purchase.

Catalog showrooms are stores in which customers shop through catalogs

Many catalog showrooms have inventories on the premises of almost all its catalog merchandise. Most of the merchandise that is sold is selected, ordered, paid for, and picked up in one trip. The stores have desks at which customers can examine the catalog. In some areas catalogs are mailed to consumers. To help customers, some stores have a limited number of samples on display.

The use of catalogs as a primary selling device benefits the retailer in several ways.

1. It reduces overhead costs.
2. It reduces shoplifting.
3. The catalogs are partially financed by manufacturers and wholesalers.

Catalogs reduce overhead costs by minimizing the space required to store goods for customer inspection, by reducing sales staffs, and by minimizing security needs. All merchandise, except for the samples, is kept in storage areas or

Best Products Catalog Store displays a wide variety of products in many categories. *Courtesy:* Best Products.

stockrooms, which take up the majority of the store's space. Admittance to the stockrooms is limited to employees, so merchandise is out of the public's sight and reach. This feature alone has meant tremendous savings for the catalog store because it virtually eliminates shoplifting.

Further savings derive from the fact that catalogs are heavily financed by manufacturers and wholesalers, who often supply photographs, illustrations, and copy for them. For additional savings, some catalog showrooms use customer-oriented computerized ordering systems.

Though catalog showrooms received their greatest impetus during the 1970s, they started out in the early 1960s as a form of discount retailing. Their main attraction is their claim to offer low prices on housewares, appliances, jewelry, sporting goods, luggage, hand tools, garden equipment, and other medium- to high-priced merchandise.

Even though there are usually samples of some items in the store, the catalogs are heavily illustrated and contain descriptions, specifications, and other information about the merchandise. This is inherent in the nature of catalog selling because the retailer relies on the catalog instead of a salesperson or the merchandise itself to do the selling.

One of the problems experienced by catalog showroom companies is the difficulty of keeping up with price changes. Since market prices change, these retailers are often stuck with "locked-in" catalog prices. To overcome this disadvantage, firms like Best Products combine their showrooms with discount store features, permitting customers to shop with or without a catalog.

Though catalog showrooms burst onto the retail scene with great expectations of success, their progress slowed during the mid-1970s because of their inability to undersell other discounters consistently. Difficulties in operating the showrooms, caused by inefficient systems for getting goods to customers, also contributed to slowing the growth of these operations. However, toward the end of the decade they managed to lower their overhead below that of other retailers and once again challenged conventional discounters. Among the top 20 catalog showrooms in operation today are Best Products, Service Merchandise, H. J. Wilson, and Consumers Distributing.

Convenience Stores

Convenience goods are low in cost and easy to obtain

In observing consumers' buying patterns, retailers long ago recognized the special status of convenience goods. They also knew that consumers do not like to waste time shopping for these items or even to go out of their way to buy them.

A closer examination of these goods reveals that they share the following characteristics.

- They are inexpensive.
- They are consumed daily or frequently.
- They are purchased frequently.
- They are easy to sell because no measuring, matching, or trying on is required.

As retailers added line after line of these goods, they developed a special mix of merchandise that they called convenience goods, which led, of course, to the name **convenience,** or **bantam store.**

To qualify as a true convenience store, a retail outlet must be a small neighborhood store whose principal business is the sale of a balanced mix of convenience items from the following lines.

- *Food products,* such as beverages, dairy and bakery goods, frozen foods, groceries, limited produce, and delicatessen items
- *Health and beauty aids,* such as aspirin, adhesive bandages, cough drops, soap, shampoo, combs, and shaving supplies
- *Tobacco products* such as cigars, cigarettes, and pipe tobacco
- *Printed materials,* such as newspapers, magazines, paperback books, and greeting cards
- *Small housewares,* such as can openers, fuses, drinking glasses, kitchen gadgets, and small hand tools

7-Eleven franchise chain of convenience stores. *Courtesy:* Southland Corp.

Many stores are called convenience stores even though they do not carry all of the items listed here.

Convenience stores operate on the principle that the way to increase profits is to maintain a high sales volume of staple goods by reducing competition through convenient location and extended store hours. This is why many convenience stores stay open most hours of the day and seven days a week.

However, these are not the only means that convenience stores use to increase profits. They sometimes carry unusual items, such as prepared food, to attract customers. As a matter of fact, the addition of fast foods and prepared products like fried chicken appears to be the trend. For example, the Majik Market convenience store chain operates some 1,300 units, primarily in the Southeast. Nearly all of the stores sell fast foods cooked in microwave ovens: sandwiches, soups, stews, and a breakfast menu of pancakes, eggs, and sausage.

Convenience stores keep their operating costs low by maintaining small inventories and low labor costs. This means that most of the store is devoted to display and very little space is required for storage. Since the displays are largely self-service or counter, the store can be run by one or two people whose basic job is to act as cashier. In some stores, such as delicatessens, counter service provides the bulk of the store's income. As for their percentage of profits on sales, convenience store sales are usually higher than most other stores with similar product assortments.

For the consumer, convenience does have a price. Convenience stores usually charge more than their competitors because customers are willing to pay a little more rather than spend the extra time traveling or waiting at a checkout counter.

Convenience stores are usually either mom-and-pop or franchise operations. The largest single operator of convenience stores is Southland Corporation's

7-Eleven Stores, with some 13,000 outlets in the United States and foreign countries. (At this writing, Southland is in bankruptcy and is operating under court reorganization.)

Flea Markets

Flea markets are derived from fairs

Strictly speaking, flea markets are fairs. Fairs have existed in one form or another since early European times and were sometimes associated with religious festivals. Today vestiges of them remain in the form of church bazaars. Most European fairs were regulated, but from time to time unregulated fairs sprang up in various districts. Goods sold at these fairs were of lesser quality and sometimes secondhand.

In addition to their low-quality goods, unregulated fairs were also known for dishonest merchants, beggars, pickpockets, and unsavory practices. One such fair, in Paris, was dubbed Marché aux Puces, or "market of fleas"; hence the term **flea market.**

Characteristics of flea markets

A flea market is composed of a collection of independent retailers selling different lines of goods, old and new, at bargain prices. Though at one time flea market operators offered merchandise that is not generally found in retail stores (e.g., old furniture, used clothing, and handmade crafts), they have expanded their offerings to include practically all types of merchandise, old and new, and now compete with most retail stores. Because many consumers are willing to trade attractive surroundings, gift wrapping, and credit options for bargains, flea markets have gained in acceptance. Once considered transient and found in such places as parking fields and vacant lots, they are now locating in more permanent sites. Some of the vendors even accept credit cards.

In America, flea markets are enjoying a revival. While many flea market vendors are part-time merchants and on the fringes of retailing, some people have carved out careers in flea marketing, and flea markets are attracting conventional retailers.

The kinds of used merchandise found in flea markets is almost unlimited. Shoppers can locate anything from kitchen gadgets to cars, from clothing to books, and from craftware to stereo equipment. Many flea markets also have food and beverage stands.

Flea markets may be open permanently, for limited periods, or only on weekends. The market itself may be indoors (e.g., in an arena) or outdoors (e.g., in a drive-in theater or a parking lot), or both. Space is rented to independent retailers, who set up stalls, tables, or other open displays.

The popularity of flea markets has risen to the point where many conventional retail stores operate in them. For some, it is a way of attracting customers to their main store. For others, it is an inexpensive way of opening a small outlet for the sale of selected items from their main store.

Many flea market merchants purchase their goods from wholesalers. In fact, there are now wholesalers that specialize in selling merchandise to flea market operators.

Barn Stores

Throughout retailing history certain kinds of merchandise have been considered unsuitable for selling in conventional retail outlets and have often created problems for manufacturers and merchants alike. Table 5-1 describes these goods and indicates why they create problems for conventional stores.

In the past, **factory seconds, distressed and salvage goods, closeouts, overruns,** and **abandoned goods** were customarily destroyed, discarded, sold for scrap, or given to charity. Fearful of tarnishing their image, many manufacturers and retailers preferred to destroy imperfect goods rather than allow them onto the market. Later, cost-conscious manufacturers and retailers tried to find satisfactory ways of selling these goods without damaging the reputation of the business. Some factories maintained small company stores in which they sold seconds to employees and local townspeople. Retailers experimented with basement stores in which merchandise was racked, binned, and priced for clearance. The **barn store,** also called a **bargain store,** specializes in salvaging job lots (end-of-season manufacturer leftover merchandise) and has proven a successful answer to this retailing problem. It provides an outlet for otherwise nonmarketable goods, and enables consumers to purchase goods at very low prices.

TABLE 5-1   Barn Store Merchandise

Type of Merchandise	Description	Problems for Conventional Stores
Factory seconds	Imperfect merchandise with manufacturing flaws	• Detracts from other merchandise • Lowers image of the store
Distressed goods	Items that have been damaged or soiled in shipping or handling	• Detracts from other merchandise • Lowers image of the store
Salvage goods	Shipments of goods that have been damaged in transit or storage	• Detracts from other merchandise • Lowers the image of the store
Closeouts	Discontinued merchandise or inventories of stores that have closed or gone into bankruptcy	• Limited selections • No reorders
Manufacturers' overruns	Quantities of custom-made articles in excess of retailers' orders	• Limited selections • Specialized items • No reorders
Abandoned goods	Unclaimed merchandise at post offices, customs offices, shippers' storehouses, etc., sometimes sold in sealed shipping cartons	• Quantities and types of goods unknown when sold in unopened containers • Limited selections • Specialized goods • Difficult to inventory • No reorders

Barn stores are also known as bargain stores

The inventory carried by barn stores is unpredictable, and there are no reorders. Barn stores buy almost anything they think they can resell. The merchandise ranges from canned goods and apparel to home furnishings and small appliances. The quality of the merchandise is usually low, but there is an occasional high-quality "find." The stores pay so little for their merchandise that they can sell at a price that most consumers consider cheap, and still take a high profit. Since everything is sold as is, there are no exchanges or returns.

Close-Out Store

A similar type of retail outlet, but with a decidedly different merchandise emphasis, is the **close-out store.** Increasing numbers of middle-income families are shopping in these stores because of the values they offer. With an attractive mixture of brand names and lower prices, this fast-growing retail segment shows signs of continuing its popularity. Contrary to what some people think, close-out stores carry first-quality goods for the most part.

New Types of General-Merchandise Stores

Large, self-service stores

The most recent types of general-merchandise stores to emerge on the retail scene are the following.

1. Box stores
    Warehouse stores
    Limited-item stores
2. Combination stores (combostores)
3. Superstores
4. Hypermarkets

All of them are large and carry both food and nonfood products. **Box stores** include both warehouses and limited-item stores. Warehouse stores stock up to 10,000 items, including limited lines of perishables and meat. They are inexpensively constructed, are under 30,000 square feet, and show high unit sales. Merchandise is often displayed in cartons, and the stores are likely to be open 24 hours a day. **Limited-item stores** carry fewer than 1,000 products, with few perishables and a limited number of brands. There is no item pricing on goods, and customers bag their own purchases. **Combination stores,** sometimes called **combostores,** offer more services than box stores and carry full lines of food products, including perishables. In addition, they maintain substantial quantities of health, cosmetic, and drug items. They carry at least 40 percent of their merchandise in nonfood items and are over 45,000 square feet. These stores attempt to create one-stop shopping for customers. Combostores such as Albertson's, Giant Food, and Pathmark record high-average sales transactions. Recently,

Kroger (a grocery company) opened a 64,000-square-foot combostore at Braelin Village Center in Peachtree City, Georgia, containing such areas as a bakery, flower shop, and drugstore.

An extremely interesting version of a combostore is the Meyer Company's emporium in the North Benson Center in the state of Washington. The 173,000-square-foot store contains four divisions: Food Market, Clothing Shop, Variety Store, and Home Improvement Center. Each division is divided into separate specialty areas.

Superstores are similar to combination stores, but their inventory includes a greater proportion of food products than the combination stores. They occupy at least 30,000 square feet of space. Both combination and superstores feature wide displays of general merchandise.

Hypermarkets originated in France and Germany during the 1960s as extremely large self-service retail outlets. Forgoing fancy furnishings and fixtures, they create a warehouse setting, with 10- to 15-foot-high racks and hundreds of wire containers loaded with goods. The merchandise consists of food and non-food items, including furniture. The Hypermart USA in Garland, Texas, owned by Wal-Mart, is a 220,000-square-foot hypermarket that is purported to be the largest-volume retail outlet in the United States. Its gigantic inventory includes both food and nonfood items, with the latter including such merchandise as sporting goods, apparel, toys, housewares, crafts, and health/beauty aids.

At the 78th annual convention of the National Retail Federation in January 1989, top executives of K mart Corporation and Wal-Mart Stores were optimistic about their new hypermarkets. Containing about 220,000 square feet—the size of several football fields—these stores offer an enormous variety of products.

Albertson's Combo stores feature a wide display of merchandise. *Courtesy:* Albertson's.

K mart's version of the hypermarket, called American Fare, was opened in Atlanta in 1989.

One of the chief cautions in opening a hypermarket is the ability of the area's population to support the store with sufficient sales volume. Because of the tremendous size of a hypermarket (as much as 300,000 square feet!), there is constant pressure to generate sales. Despite the initial modest success of hypermarkets established by large companies like K mart and Carrefour (a French company), there is considerable disagreement in the retail industry about the American public's readiness to accept the hypermarket concept.

Mass sales basis   The new general-merchandise stores operate on a mass sales basis. Safeway Stores, Inc., one of the nation's largest supermarket chains, has converted a number of its stores into no-frills discount warehouses known as Food Barns. These outlets contain the following features: *Customers bring bags and bag their own purchases* (there is a small charge for the store's bags!), cigarettes are sold by the carton only, produce comes unpackaged, and customers are charged for check cashing. A&P has converted six conventional stores to warehouse stores in Chicago, calling them Super Plus Stores.

The Pathmark "Super Center" in Woodbridge, New Jersey, is one of some 20 that the chain's owner, Supermarkets General Corporation, has opened. Meijer, Inc., operates a gigantic hypermarket in Grand Rapids, Michigan, with almost 70 cashier stations. Chicago, Detroit, and several other cities contain large stores covering acres of land. Although most of these outlets now carry essentially staple products (goods for which demand is constant), in the future they may branch into higher-priced merchandise such as furniture.

LIMITED-LINE STORES (SPECIALTY STORES)

Limited-line stores adopt a different strategy than general-merchandise stores. They attract customers by specializing in a particular line of merchandise (specialty goods), such as sporting goods or women's apparel, and offer extensive selections within that line.

These stores cater to a specific market and have a distinct image. They make no effort to offer one-stop shopping as general-merchandise stores do. They seek, however, to meet the special needs of customers, who often require personal service. For example, K mart recently opened stores called Sports Giant, selling a wide assortment of athletic equipment and apparel. In addition to the sale of merchandise, the stores provide many services, such as bicycle repairs and stringing of tennis rackets. Another example of specialty store retailing today is Woolworth, which operates more than 20 different specialty formats. Among them are some 1,600 Kinney family shoe stores and over 600 Foot Locker stores.

As if to accentuate the trend toward specialty retailing, the Wayne Towne Center mall in Wayne, New Jersey, increased the number of specialty stores from 33 to 51. This dramatic move in 1989 also featured a replacement of most of the previous tenants by upscale specialty retailers. Anchored by Fortunoff, J. C. Penney, and Neiman-Marcus' Last Call (a store that features clearance merchandise at attractive prices), the Center is another example of the importance that retail executives place on specialty retailing.

In an effort to improve its sagging sales and profit performance, Sears, Roebuck, still America's largest retailer, undertook in 1988 to emulate some of the successful specialty retailers. For example, the company started in-store appliance and home electronics sections called Brand Central in which national as well as store brands are sold. This was a departure from its previous policy of stocking store brands primarily. It also opened freestanding McKids stores selling children's apparel and toys. In addition, the firm acquired the following specialty chains: Western Auto Supply Company, Eye Care Centers of America, and Pinstripes Petites, a women's apparel chain.

Despite the impressive gains made by specialty stores in the decade of the 1980s, a perceptible expansion slowdown was detected at the start of the 1990s. Seeking a new approach, some specialty chains were examining the feasibility of opening new units in "anchorless malls filled with other traffic-drawing specialists rather than anchored by large department stores or general merchandise retailers."[3]

The outstanding characteristics of specialty stores are

1. Personalized service
2. Wide assortment of limited categories of merchandise
3. Product expertise

Personalized Service

Understanding their markets, specialty store buyers often purchase with particular lifestyles in mind and select merchandise to meet specific customer needs and demands. Salespeople often develop one-to-one relationships with shoppers, getting to know steady customers by name.

Wide Assortment of Specific Categories of Merchandise

Specialty stores carry limited lines of merchandise in wide assortments for a specific target market. Because they deal in fewer categories of goods, they stock these items in great depth. In fact, customers travel to these shops because they expect to find better selections. For example, a shopper looking for a particular toy or game has a much better chance of finding it at a Toys-Я-Us store than in the toy department of a general-merchandise store. A golfer looking for a new set of clubs has a wide selection from which to choose at a pro shop or a sporting goods store.

A good example of a limited-line store carrying a rich assortment of inven-

---

[3] David P. Schulz, "Specialty Expansion Slowing," *Stores* (December 1990), pp. 35–38.

Specialty store. *Courtesy:* IKEA, Inc.

tory items is Tower Records, located in New York City's Greenwich Village. It is probably the largest musical record shop in the world, stocking some 500,000 records and tapes. Catering to rock fans, classical music lovers, and others, Tower provides an in-depth inventory for all tastes.

Product Expertise

Shoppers expect more from the sales help and staff in specialty stores than from employees in most general-merchandise stores. They feel that these people know more about the merchandise they sell and instill greater confidence as advisers. For example, in a shop that specializes in photography equipment and supplies, it is not uncommon for the entire staff to be well versed in the operation of the equipment. Even though shoppers expect more product knowledge from specialty store personnel, some general-merchandise stores provide similar expertise.

Specialty stores: independents and chains

The major competition in specialty store retailing pits independents against chain specialty stores. Chain specialty retailers have the advantage of strength through numbers. Since they are large operations, they purchase merchandise, store fixtures, and equipment in large quantities and thereby receive better prices. They also have the advantage of benefiting from wide area advertising that ranges from newspaper ads to television commercials. On a per-store basis, even the advertising is cheaper because to advertise one store is to advertise many in the chain.

Food and Nonfood Limited-Line Stores

Supermarkets are limited-line departmentalized food stores

Although there are many examples of limited-line stores, it is helpful to mention one type that is essentially a food store and another that sells only nonfood items. They are supermarkets and warehouse outlets.

Supermarkets

Although supermarkets are known largely for food products, they are classified as limited-line stores with departmentalized sections of food—dairy and meat products, produce, groceries—and many nonfood products. Even though supermarkets stock more food items than anything else, they have added so many nonfood items that they often appear to be combination food and variety stores. The nonfood merchandise commonly sold by supermarkets includes books, magazines, greeting cards, hardware, housewares, clothing and accessories, plants, and toiletries. Some of these products are provided by **rack jobbers,** wholesalers that the store allows to install and maintain displays. Rack jobbers are paid only for what is sold. The jobbers, not the store, are responsible for selecting assortments, stocking and replenishing displays, and removing outdated merchandise. Books, housewares, and toys are examples of the types of goods that rack jobbers place in stores.

This rack jobber is checking a store display. Joel Gordon.

In one study involving rack jobbers, supermarkets reported better profits per linear foot of shelf space when general merchandise and health and beauty aids were handled by rack jobbers than when merchandise was purchased direct by the stores.[4]

Some retailers have extended their food-nonfood mix to form somewhat different types of retail outlets. Pathmark, for example, operates both supermarkets and discount drugstores. In some locations it combines the two operations and increases the number of nonfood items carried by its supermarkets.

Supermarket sales strategy: self-service, low prices

Supermarkets appeal to customers on the basis of low prices. This appeal is enhanced by a wide variety of merchandise that allows one-stop shopping for *basic* household items. Self-service display is another important supermarket feature from which the consumer and the store benefit: the consumer, through faster selection of goods and lower prices; the store, through a reduced sales force and lower costs.

Supermarkets helped pioneer self-service retailing. Early experiments with self-service displays showed that customers were inclined to buy more if they did not have to ask for items or be advised about what to buy. Other types of retailers started to adopt self-service on the basis of the supermarket's success with product displays and reduced labor costs.

A significant trend, in fact, is the increasing availability of self-service opportunities in both supermarkets and other types of stores. Witness the myriad ways in which this trend is manifested: pumping one's own gas at gas stations, trying on shoes in a department store without the help of a salesperson, airport vending machines dispensing floral products, and banking by automatic teller machines in banks and supermarkets. The desire to cut costs is not the only reason for the expansion of self-service outlets. Some retailers maintain that customers prefer serving themselves to avoid waiting for salespeople.

Supermarkets have also contributed to retailing in another way. They were among the first retailers to study the importance of merchandise location and the customer's movements through a store. Since then other retailers have conducted sophisticated studies in order to increase the profitability of their selling space.

In addition to low prices, supermarkets attract customers by fast checkouts and clean, attractive layouts. Some supermarkets, such as Byerly's in Minneapolis and Food Emporium in New York State, are upscale gourmet outlets, catering to more affluent consumers.

Although some independents have succumbed to supermarket and warehouse-type competition, many specialty food stores, including delicatessens, bakeries, cheese stores, gourmet shops, and health food stores, have not been affected significantly. This is because their products require special handling, customized service, or a wider assortment than supermarkets can provide. Certain of these stores are even able to carry on their business next door to supermarkets. Some, however, have been co-opted into leasing departments *within* supermarkets.

[4]R. C. Curhan, W. J. Salmon, and R. D. Buzzell, "Sales and Profitability of Health and Beauty Aids and General Merchandise in Supermarkets." *Journal of Retailing,* **59** (Summer 1983), pp. 77–99.

Warehouse Outlets

Warehouse outlets specialize in a particular line of nonfood merchandise

Another type of limited-line store is a **warehouse outlet.** It specializes in a particular line of nonfood merchandise, such as furniture, toys, or sporting goods. A typical outlet contains large quantities of merchandise (some still in cartons) ready for immediate sale. Projecting a low-price image, such no-frills operations are usually located in low-rent districts. Even though warehouses are sometimes in out-of-the-way places, consumers are attracted by the prospects of savings and immediate pickup.

Warehouses offer delivery services, but customers can avoid delivery charges and delays by taking the merchandise with them. These retailers usually do business on a cash-and-carry basis, which further lowers costs to the customer. Although minimal services provide savings to customers, some find the lack of service unsatisfactory. Also, because many items are in cartons, they are difficult to inspect, may be damaged, and may have to be returned.

The Levitz Furniture Corporation is a well-known retailer that has been successful with warehouse outlets, possibly because it has showrooms connected to its warehouses. After browsing through attractive displays arranged in home settings (living rooms, bedrooms, etc.), shoppers can take immediate possession of the merchandise they purchase because it is stored on the premises. K mart operates specialty stores called Office Square that sell office supplies, furniture, and business equipment. An interesting aspect of the company's strategy is that these stores appeal to consumers because they resemble warehouse outlets. Still another example of a warehouse outlet is BJ's Wholesale Price Warehouse.

One of Lowe's Home Center Warehouse stores. *Courtesy:* Lowe's Company, Inc.

NONSTORE SELLING METHODS

We have already identified retail institutions by ownership and types of merchandise sold. We saw that in both categories selling takes place in stores or in physical settings that are closely related to stores. However, retailing includes methods of selling that do not require stores; hence the description "nonstore" selling. These methods include in-home retailing, vending machines, mail order/catalog retailing, telephone selling, and electronic retailing.

In-Home Retailing

In-home retailing can be traced to the itinerant peddler. In analyzing this form of retailing, it is interesting to note its major, although perhaps obvious, underlying assumption: that there is a large consumer population that is, by choice or circumstance, at home a good deal of the time. At one time this population consisted mostly of mothers, homemakers, disabled people, and retirees. But affluence, technology, the large-scale entry of women into the labor force, and the development of alternate lifestyles have led to greater mobility for each of these groups and for the population at large. Consequently, with fewer people at home at predictable times, these person-to-person salespeople have had to adjust their selling schedules.

Although products sold in homes have been oriented more toward women, today's changing lifestyles have directed merchandise to both sexes. Typical products are cosmetics, vacuum cleaners, small housewares, encyclopedias, dairy products, newspapers, and clothing.

Canvassing, route selling, consultive selling, and party plans are types of in-home retailing

In-home retailing involves four principal methods of selling: convassing, route selling, consultive selling, and party plans. **Canvassing** is the method most people think of when they hear the term **door-to-door selling.** Canvassing is usually a one-time effort by a salesperson to cover an entire area. The salesperson arrives unannounced at each home and makes a "sales pitch"—a planned speech emphasizing product benefits. Companies selling siding and roofs for houses often use canvassing.

In a variation of this type of selling, the retailer or salesperson screens customers by telephone to qualify them as prospects.

Route selling is a method of in-home retailing that is used by retailers who sell frequently-purchased convenience items such as newspapers, cosmetics, and food products. In the past, route selling was the accepted means of selling certain products. Owing to the availability of other retail outlets, however, route selling is on the decline.

Consultive selling is not just an in-home selling technique. It is a method of selling in which the salesperson consults with the consumer to identify the consumer's problems or needs and determines what products and services will satisfy those needs.

Among in-home retailers, consultive selling is used by decorator consultants who work for home furnishing businesses or department stores. Although these salespeople usually operate out of a store, their operations are still considered a type of in-home retailing. And though they sell in the consumer's home, the interaction is almost always initiated by the consumer and a home visit arranged *at the consumer's request*. Decorator consultants usually consult about and sell upholstery, drapes, floor coverings, and other custom work that requires measurement, estimates, and selection of materials.

Ethical consultive selling benefits consumers by providing convenient, personalized service and complete demonstrations in a relaxed atmosphere that is familiar to the consumer. Psychologists and researchers also point out that in this situation the consumer is in a position of greater power than in many store environments. However, the salesperson still controls the direction of the interaction.

How party plan selling works

Cold-call resistance, greater consumer mobility, and low sales force productivity caused some traditional in-home retailers to update their selling methods. Their response to these difficulties was the **party plan,** a direct-sales method of retailing in which a salesperson enlists the aid of one consumer in selling to others within a community. Party plans usually work something like this. A community resident becomes a sales representative or dealer for a party plan retailer. Friends are then invited to an in-home party for refreshments and a presentation or demonstration of the products.

At the party the dealer delivers a planned talk (lecture-demonstration) about the product or products. After the presentation, the dealer takes orders and approaches interested guests about hosting parties for other friends. In exchange for giving a party, the dealer offers the hostess-to-be a collection of selected items from the line, plus assistance with party preparations.

Mary Kay Cosmetics and BeautiControl sell cosmetics and beauty aids through party plans. Tupperware, a division of Dart Industries, uses party plan retailing to sell household plastic goods. Stanley Home Products distributes household products in this way, too.

Vending Machines

As retailers added impulse and convenience items to their lines, they found that they spent the same amount of time collecting money, making change, and recording transactions for low- as for higher-priced items. In many cases this caused difficulties because of the cost and effort involved. The invention of **vending machines** helped retailers minimize this problem.

The history of vending machines

Early automated vending machines dispensed small quantities of a single item, such as candy, gum, or nuts, that sold for a penny. The machines were placed near cashiers so that customers who needed change could get it. For the cashier, the occasional service of making change involved less time than a full sales transaction, and customers could still be served quickly.

Some retailers found that they already had dispensing machines that could be automated. Nickelodeons were early hand-cranked "movie theater" machines that dispensed entertainment in the form of rapidly changing cards. Operators of nickelodeons charged a general admission fee (5 cents—hence the name *nickelodeon*), and customers were free to wander about and view a different show in each machine. The development of coin-operated machines allowed these retailers to increase sales by charging each time a show was viewed. As the popularity of the machines increased, nickelodeon owners added other amusement devices, such as music boxes and fortune-telling machines. Eventually the wider assortments and 1-cent machine prices gave rise to the name *penny arcade*.

In tourist areas other enterprising retailers took advantage of the developing technology and installed pay telescopes and binoculars. Telephone companies began selling their services through pay telephones. Advances in refrigeration led to the development of machines that dispensed cold soft drinks in bottles.

As the technology expanded, so did the lines of products sold in vending machines. Retailers installed machines in transportation and entertainment centers, stores, and other service establishments, and eventually in factories, business offices, hospitals, and schools. Today there are vending machines that sell goods like handkerchiefs, combs, paperbacks, aspirin, toiletries, newspapers, snacks, and other food products. Other vending machines sell such services as shoeshines, photocopying, and rides for children.

Some stores have installed vending machines in areas that are accessible to shoppers after the store has closed. Retailers in Europe have installed large machines that sell hundreds of items. In Sweden retailers have even experimented with fully automated stores.

Advantages and disadvantages of vending machine retailing

For retailers, the advantages of vending machines are as follows.

1. They eliminate the need for salespeople and cashiers.
2. They are always open for business.
3. They may be located indoors or outdoors.
4. They can be installed where other types of selling would be disruptive or prohibitive.

Vending machines. USDA Photo.

Although vending machine retailing has merit, it also has disadvantages. First of all, vending machines require maintenance. Even when they are well maintained, breakdowns are inevitable. Unless machines are checked regularly, broken ones can sit idle—and unprofitable—for long periods. Second, machines require correct change, and while some machines give change, many do not. Finally, the inability to inspect or exchange goods has caused many customers to resist buying them from a vending machine.

The future of vending machines will depend on developing technologies and new retailing techniques. However, the sales statistics for this form of retailing are impressive. In 1990 vending machine sales amounted to more than $20 billion. Soft drinks and tobacco products accounted for about 60 percent of this total.

Mail Order/Catalog Retailing

As outlined in Chapter 1, **mail order retailing** developed as a means of selling to customers over a wide geographic area without the use of stores or a field sales force. Using this retailing method, mail order merchants were able to minimize the overhead costs arising from store operations and sales salaries. Selling was oriented toward consumers in isolated areas whose needs could not be satisfied by distant stores.

There have been many changes in mail order retailing since its early days, but the following characteristics still qualify it as a special category of retailing.

Characteristics of mail order retailing

1. Customers use published materials or direct-mail offerings to shop or pre-shop for merchandise.
2. Customers place orders with the mail order retailer. Today many mail order houses have toll-free long distance numbers that customers may use to place orders.
3. The retailer arranges for delivery of the goods to the consumer.

Early mail order retailing relied almost exclusively on catalogs. Today mail order retailers inform customers about merchandise and solicit orders in several ways. In addition to catalogs, they utilize magazines, newspapers, direct mail, clubs-of-the-month, and television. Although the use of these media has increased mail order sales, catalogs are still responsible for the majority of those sales.

The three mail order giants

Mail order retailers handle very narrow to very wide assortments of merchandise. General mail order houses are the mail order equivalent of general-merchandise stores. They carry assortments of merchandise as wide as those at some department stores. In fact, two of the three top mail order companies—Sears and J.C. Penney (Spiegel is the third)—also operate department store chains.

Unlike the top two mail order retailers, Spiegel maintains catalog stores and some national surplus outlets. The latter are used to dispose of goods that have been difficult to sell. In the late 1970s, Spiegel adopted a new marketing strategy

Covers of the Horchow and L.L. Bean Catalogs. These firms are well-known specialty mail-order retailers. *Courtesy:* Horchow and L.L. Bean, Inc.

by upgrading its catalogs and by appealing to upscale, more affluent consumers. In an attempt to attract particular consumer segments, the company started a series of specialty catalogs in the late 1980s. Instead of targeting its potential customer base in shotgun fashion, Spiegel pinpointed a group, for example, large-sized women, and developed a fashionable-looking catalog that appealed to that group. The strategy has resulted in a more diversified customer population and increased sales.

A surprising casualty in mail order retailing was Montgomery Ward & Company, which decided to discontinue its catalog sales operations at the end of 1986. Having lost some $250 million in its catalog division from 1980 through 1985, the company announced its intention to focus on store sales. Ironically, Montgomery Ward, the "granddaddy" of mail order retailing, was the first of the giants in its field to cease catalog sales. (In addition, at this writing Sears, Roebuck was considering the cancellation or sale of its catalog operation.)

Although selling through catalogs is a long-standing practice, it has expanded recently because of an increase in the number of working women and the growing popularity of nonstore retailing. After receiving a catalog from a firm, the consumer studies its contents and orders merchandise according to the retailer's instructions for purchasing. Catalogs may contain general, specialty, or seasonal merchandise assortments. For example, Sears publishes a general catalog of more than 1,000 pages as well as numerous specialty catalogs of a few hundred pages.

One of the most successful catalog retailers is Lands' End, a Dodgeville, Wisconsin–based clothing and luggage company that started as a yacht supply catalog store. Relying on its constantly updated mailing list of some 9 million names, the firm maintains a successful sales record and image by providing excellent service, niche merchandise (goods appealing to a special consumer category), and attractive catalogs. In addition to no-nonsense layouts, the catalogs include articles of general interest (such as how madras is made), a letters-to-the-editor section, and a corrections box. On a good business day, the company handles about 30,000 telephone calls. It also has an excellent return policy.

However, in 1989–90 higher product costs began to affect Lands' End adversely. Executives at Lands' End and other catalog companies—New Hampton, Inc., J. Crew, and Talbots—complained about the steep price increases to which they were being subjected. Retail analysts were watching the situation carefully to determine the short- and long-term effects on these catalog giants.

Processing more than 10,000 mail orders a day via its automated, computer-run system, Barnes & Noble, the world's largest bookseller, credits its success largely to its ability to fill orders promptly. With catalogs being mailed every three weeks, the company recognizes the importance of speed and accuracy in complying with customers' needs. This is a good example of a happy marriage between a dynamic mail order retailer and computer technology.

So popular are catalogs that the Catalog Retail Corporation installs catalog display kiosks in a variety of retail locations. Stores such as Bloomingdale's, Gumps, and Bergdorf-Goodman are represented. Though the catalogs must be

J.C. Penney and Spiegel publish general catalogs and reach additional customers through seasonal and specialty catalogs. *Courtesy:* J.C. Penney and Spiegel.

purchased by shoppers, the cost is nominal, example, $5, and the money is usually refunded when the customer purchases via the catalog.

Victoria's Secret, a lingerie specialty retailer, keeps its catalog operation separate from its stores. Thus far, its experience with the arrangement has been successful.

While a retailer's costs and selling prices are lower with **catalog retailing,** the firm must contend with more frequent merchandise returns as well as different notification techniques for announcing price changes.

We can look forward to increased use of a modified catalog retailing system in which merchandise specifications are contained on video discs. The consumer selects items by using a hookup between the discs and the home TV set.

Telephone Selling

In the early 1900s many small retailers accepted telephone orders and delivered merchandise to customers. However, **telephone selling** was not widely used until the 1930s.

Department stores use telephone selling methods

Many department stores that are closed on Sundays keep their switchboards and order departments open to handle responses to ads on special catalog and newspaper offerings. Other stores list special numbers and have orders taken by a service. Still other stores, such as Simpson-Sears in Canada, have made arrangements through which owners of touch-tone phones can call in orders and communicate directly with the store's computer.

When retailers take the initiative in reaching customers by telephone, solicitations must be handled carefully. Otherwise the salesperson may encounter cold-call problems and resistance. To avoid this, some stores have salespeople initiate calls by offering to extend credit to the potential customer in the form of a store card or by calling customers to revive inactive credit accounts. Consumers sometimes resist telephone solicitations because unethical companies and overly aggressive salespeople have abused this method of selling.

Some stores use telephone selling to contact customers who have not made purchases for some time. Others use it to notify long-standing customers about upcoming sales or about the arrival of a new merchandise shipment. There are retailers that use telephones controlled by computers to contact consumers and accept orders.

Electronic Retailing

Technological advances such as two-way cable television, videophones, and personal computers are already affecting retailing. For example, the Electric Mall is a videotex shopping service using written descriptions of merchandise on a video terminal to help consumers make purchasing decisions via electronic mail. Subscribers pay an initial subscription fee and an hourly access rate, depending on the time of day.

However, the costs involved and the limited amount of equipment in consumers' homes render **electronic retailing** an emerging form of merchandising at present. Nevertheless, customers in some areas can already view merchandise and demonstrations on command by calling up tapes or files displayed on television monitors in their homes. For example, the Home Shopping Club, with headquarters in Tampa, Florida, sells through cable television. Touch-sensitive panels on television screens even eliminate the need for consumers to do anything but check the items they want.

Electronic retailing consists of five areas:

1. Home television shopping—expected to be a $5 billion sales area by 1992. Example: Telaction, a J. C. Penney–owned service featuring merchandise by Penny, Marshall Field, Dayton Hudson, Neiman-Marcus, Foot Locker, and Sears.
2. Interactive shopping—the TV viewer communicates with the program being watched.
3. Mail order/direct mail.
4. Home information services.
5. General merchandise.

With store-based electronic retailing, it is possible for a customer to buy difficult-to-find shoe sizes in the store's central warehouse by using what is known as an in-store ByVideo system and receive the goods at home via a delivery service. The video terminal records what was bought, what was browsed for, and in which stores the browsing took place.

One of the more successful electronic home shopping services is that developed as a partnership between Sears, Roebuck and the International Business Machines Corporation (IBM). Called Prodigy, the program boasts such additional retail customers as The Broadway, Sam Goody, Crabtree & Evelyn, and the King Soopers supermarket chain.

Sometimes referred to as telecommunication merchandising, electronic retailing still has its skeptics as well as its proponents. The former feel that the widespread use of electronic in-home ordering is years away, whereas the latter point to changing consumer lifestyles, preferences, and behavior as indicators of a coming revolution in the way people shop. Regardless of their expectations, most retail executives keep abreast of technological developments affecting the industry. Not to do so in so dynamic a field could prove damaging or fatal to even a large company.

Other Forms of Nonstore Selling

- **Street vendors** sell merchandise without the need to maintain a store. Often compared to the peddler, the street vendor can be found in many communities and is particularly active in large cities. Merchandise sold by these retailers ranges from food to clothing.

- **Syndicators** operate in conjunction with credit card companies such as VISA and American Express Company. Included with monthly statements sent to cardholders by the card companies are syndicator advertisements of merchandise. The advertisements contain simple mail order forms. Syndicators pay the credit card companies a percentage of their sales.
- Shows are sponsored by civic and charitable organizations as fund-raising methods. The organizations invite retailers to display and sell their goods at the shows. In return, the retailers pay the organizations a fee for the use of space. In some respects, shows resemble flea markets. However, flea market operations are usually ongoing, whereas shows are single events.

RETAIL STRATEGY

Specialty Store Diversifies Merchandise Offering

Specialty stores, for the most part, have remained committed to a merchandise mix centered on a specific product area, for example, women's apparel, sports items, leather goods. Along comes Fry's Electronics, a computer supplies retailer, that sells food and drinks along with its stock of computer programs and parts.

Why the inclusion of noncomputer products in its inventory? "Simple," say Fry's engineer and computer customers. "The nature of our work requires frequent relaxation periods. So while shopping for our computer needs at the computer outlet, we also buy junk food there to quiet our nerves. It's a great combination."

So which is it—a specialty store or a modified convenience store? Whatever the answer, the strategy works.

NEW TERMS

abandoned goods	general merchandise
bantam store	impulse goods
bargain store	in-home retailing
barn store	limited-item store
box store	limited-line merchandise
branch store	mail order retailing
canvassing	overrun
catalog retailing	party plan
catalog showroom	rack jobber
closeout	route selling

close-out store   salvage goods
combination store   scrambled merchandising
combostore   seasonal merchandise
consultive selling   shopping goods
convenience goods   specialty goods
convenience store   staple goods
discount department store   street vendor
distressed goods   superstore
door-to-door selling   syndicator
electronic retailing   telephone selling
factory seconds   twig
fashion goods   vending machine
flea market   warehouse outlet

CHAPTER HIGHLIGHTS

1. A widening of the number of types of goods carried by a store is known as scrambled merchandising.
2. Merchandise is classified as follows: general or limited line; staple or fashion; seasonal; and convenience, shopping, specialty, or impulse.
3. General-merchandise stores include department stores, discount department stores, variety stores, catalog showrooms, convenience stores, flea markets, barn stores, close-out stores, box stores, combination stores, superstores, and hypermarkets.
4. Many department stores have extended their operations to suburban areas by opening smaller stores called branches and twigs. Branches are scaled-down versions of the main store, while twigs stock only one kind of merchandise or several related lines.
5. Though similar in some respects to department stores, discount department stores differ from the latter in the quality and price of their merchandise as well as in the services they offer customers.
6. Variety stores sell a wide assortment of goods in the low-to-popular price range. Some also carry higher-priced merchandise.
7. Catalog showrooms are stores in which customers shop and order through catalogs. They stock nonclothing, nonfood products.
8. Convenience stores carry merchandise that is consumed daily or frequently, purchased frequently, and easy to sell. The merchandise includes food, health and beauty aids, tobacco products, and small housewares.

9. Flea markets consist of independent retailers who rent space indoors or outdoors in which to sell a great variety of used and new merchandise. Though most flea market merchants operate on a part-time basis, some also own conventional retail outlets.

10. Barn stores, also known as bargain stores, sell factory seconds, distressed and salvage goods, closeouts, manufacturers' overruns, and abandoned goods at low prices. Close-out stores carry quality goods at low prices.

11. Limited-line (specialty) stores specialize in a particular line of merchandise. They compete with general-merchandise stores by offering wide assortments within their product line, rendering personal services to their customers, and maintaining product expertise.

12. Supermarkets use self-service techniques to sell food and nonfood products at low cost. Despite encroachment by supermarkets, independent specialty food stores continue to thrive.

13. Nonstore selling methods include in-home retailing, vending machines, mail order/catalog retailing, telephone selling, and electronic retailing.

14. In-home retailing includes four principal methods of selling: canvassing, route selling, consultive selling, and party plans.

15. A vending machine is an automated piece of equipment that dispenses a wide variety of goods and services. Soft drinks and tobacco products account for most vending machine sales.

16. Mail order catalog retailing is carried on by general mail order firms like Sears, Roebuck and J. C. Penney and by special-line mail order houses like Horchow Mail Order, Inc., and Sunset House. This type of retailing has expanded considerably in recent years.

17. Telephone selling is a feature of both mail order and store retailing.

18. Electronic retailing contains promise for the sale of goods and services through store-home communications. It involves computers and video equipment.

REVIEW QUESTIONS

1. Why is scrambled merchandising considered a powerful retailing concept?
2. What was the main reason for the development of department store branches and twigs?
3. How have variety stores responded to changing consumer buying patterns?
4. What methods do convenience stores use to remain competitive?
5. Why do conventional retailers sometimes expand their operations by renting space in flea markets?

6. How have department and discount store chains begun to meet the challenge of specialty store retailing?
7. What is the major assumption underlying the attractiveness of in-home selling as a retail method?

DISCUSSION QUESTIONS

1. How are today's discount department stores different from the original discount stores of the 1940s and 1950s?
2. How does the use of catalogs as a primary selling device benefit catalog show-room retailers?
3. Do you think there are limitations to self-service retailing? Why?
4. Do you think electronic retailing will be accepted by consumers to a greater extent than it is today? Why?

CASE 1

Retailing by Telecommunications

Telecommunications, combined with other advanced technologies, can transform retailing from stores to nonstore systems. The rapid growth of nonstore retailing is beginning to take a larger share of sales away from the traditional stores.

Reasons for the growth of nonstore selling include

- Exclusive offering through TV of many products, such as hardware specialties, records, and the like.
- Increased use of catalog shopping.
- Increase in mail shopping using credit cards.
- Large volume of telephone and mail order retailing done by traditional stores.
- Use of cable TV to order merchandise.

Advanced technology makes it possible for customers to shop at home for a variety of products. The use of the computer and an in-home video catalog enables consumers to order goods and services. Retailers equipped to do business via telecommunication merchandising systems can deliver merchandise without seeing the customer. This method of operation affords the retailer access to larger trading areas, benefits of reduced operating costs, no traditional store overhead, lower inventory costs (stock can be replenished as needed), and a 24-hour, 7-days-a-week operation.

Retailers that utilize this type of operation include Video Tex, a computerized shopping service with computer and telephone link-up, with customers ordering goods shown on their television screens. Comp-U-Card is another computerized shopping service that operates a video service on cable television. Also, video catalogs and video ordering are currently used on a small scale by traditional retailers such as Sears, J. C. Penney, and Bloomingdale's.

A growing number of consumers are interested in the system for a variety of reasons.

- It is a time-saving convenience.
- Television clearly illustrates the product in action.
- It saves the cost of car use and gasoline.
- Consumers can avoid crowded shopping areas and the carrying of products from stores to home.
- In-home use of several catalogs is an ideal way to comparison shop.

In conclusion, if cable TV systems offer consumers the possibility of ordering at home, having the product delivered, and paying through financial transfer systems, all that is needed to produce a retail revolution is large-scale acceptance of nonstore shopping by consumers.

a. What will be the effect on traditional retailing of the emergence of two-way cable TV retailing systems?

b. What effect will the system have on small, independent stores that sell convenience products?

c. How might the physical structure of communities and cities change if stores are no longer needed?

d. As consumers place more value on their time, which types of stores might be endangered most?

e. Can this system actually replace personal shopping? Consider that many people view shopping as a social activity as well as a necessity. Explain fully.

CASE 2

"Wish Book"

On August 2, 1985, Montgomery Ward & Company held a news conference in Chicago. Bernard F. Brennan, president and chief executive officer, announced that Montgomery Ward, the company that had invented the mail order business, was closing its catalog operation. Montgomery Ward would issue its last catalog in December 1985, thus ending 113 years in mail order retailing.

The first mail order catalog was a one-page flyer printed and distributed in Chicago by an enterprising young salesman named Aaron Montgomery Ward. The year was 1872. Lee's surrender at Appomattox had ended the Civil War only seven years earlier. The first transcontinental railroad link was only three years old. Homesteaders were still carving out their farms and ranches in the West, and cowboys were still driving cattle herds north to Abilene, Kansas, along the Chisholm Trail. Custer's Battle of Little Big Horn was still four years in the future.

When Ward's first catalog appeared, nearly 75 percent of the U.S. population lived in rural areas. It is nearly impossible today to imagine the isolation and drabness of farm life in the late nineteenth century. The telephone wasn't invented until 1876, the radio not until the 1890s. Roads were poor and travel by horse or on foot was slow. In 1890, only four automobiles were on the road in the United States. The electric light bulb was invented in 1879, but many rural areas went without electricity until the Rural Electrification Assistance Act was established in 1935.

Montgomery Ward's mail order catalogs soon became the mainstay of the farm family. Few of America's small towns had much in the way of retailers, often just a general store or a dry goods store with a very limited selection of merchandise. "Monkey Wards" filled the gap. The great "wish book" provided everything the family needed—including entertainment and a window on the outside world. Between its paper covers, one could find everything from long woolen underwear and whalebone corsets to yard goods for a new dress and, just maybe, a pair of kidleather shoes.

Of course, the catalog had more than just clothing—the Ward's customer could send away by mail for a plow or a barrel of nails, for a set of china or the latest in iceboxes, for a cradle or a coffin.

For decades, the catalog business flourished, as did Montgomery Ward's chain of retail stores. A century after that first catalog, Montgomery Ward was the sixth-largest retailer in the United States. The company had 365 retail stores, 150 distribution centers, and over 100,000 employees. The twice-a-year catalog had multiplied into 20 separate books each year, with a circulation of 5 million. Catalog operations were supported by nearly 200 company-owned catalog stores and over 1,200 independent catalog sales agencies.

The Montgomery Ward catalog, reflecting its origins, continued to appeal to the small-town and rural customer, even though urban singles and suburban young marrieds had become the major buyers of goods and services. The catalog was still being published as a multiproduct book, with no differentiation by audience. Most of the newer mail order retailers (and there were many) tended to produce specialized catalogs that carried only selected merchandise categories. Even the venerable Spiegel, Inc., made a highly successful move from an all-purpose catalog to a mail order business specializing in apparel and home furnishings.

In 1974, Mobil Oil Company bought Montgomery Ward & Company for $1.7 billion. The acquisition was part of a diversification strategy common among oil companies at the time. What Mobil bought, according to some analysts, was a dinosaur—a company that was too large, too slow-moving, and out of touch with the times. The catalog operation had fallen to third place, behind longtime competitor Sears, Roebuck & Company and behind J. C. Penney, which hadn't even entered the mail order business until 1962. Mobil invested over $600 million in an attempt to improve Montgomery Ward's performance, but the company continued to have lackluster results. The catalog operations lost heavily for 10 years, with losses of over $260 million in the six years from 1979 through 1984.

By the middle of 1985, despite the fact that catalog sales were rising, Montgomery Ward's management decided that the operation could not be profitable in the foreseeable future. Even though the direct-mail market in the United States was booming and was expected to exceed $32 billion in 1985, revenues and profits of Ward's catalog division were not growing as rapidly as those of other divisions. Montgomery Ward's management decided to discontinue the catalog operation. The action would free up nearly $1 billion in capital, money that was badly needed to finance Montgomery Ward's five-year plan to revamp their retail stores into a nationwide chain of specialty stores.

Today, nearly 7,000 different mail order catalogs are produced by more than 250 companies. Not one of them carries the name of the company that started it all—Montgomery Ward's.

a. What caused the Montgomery Ward catalog operation to fail? Could the downward trend have been reversed? If so, how?

b. What factors have led to the enormous growth of the mail order business in the United States? Do you think the industry will continue to grow? Why or why not?

c. Why do you think specialty catalogs are more popular today than multiproduct catalogs such as Montgomery Ward's?

REFERENCES

"Changing Times in Retailing." *Retailing Today,* (December 1990), p. 3.

GILL, P. "Targeting Direct Mail." *Stores* (July 1990), pp. 42–47.

"Is U.S. Hypermarket-Ready? Carrefour Is Not Sure." *Chain Store Age Executive,* **65** (January 1989), pp. 49–50.

"Specialty Catalogs Boost Sales at Spiegel." *Chain Store Age Executive,* **64** (October 1988), pp. 84–88.

"Specialty Shops—Is the Shift Booming to Landslide?" *Inside Retailing,* A Special Report from Inside Retailing (March 27, 1989), pp. 1–2.

Chapter 6

Organizing and Managing the Store; Human Resource Management

After completing this chapter, you should be able to:

- Differentiate between line and line-and-staff organizations.
- Explain store organizations for small retailers, department stores, branch stores, and chain stores.
- Distinguish between centralization and decentralization of store management.
- List the methods used by retailers to recruit and hire new employees.
- Identify the techniques used to train and retrain new employees.
- Explain the responsibilities of a store's human resource department with regard to the transfer, promotion, discharge, and performance appraisal of employees.
- Identify compensation scales and fringe benefits administered by human resource departments in retailing.
- Identify informal and formal methods of communication.
- Explain the responsibilities of human resource departments in dealing with organized labor.

A retailer's prime objective

It is safe to say that the primary objective of any firm is to be successful. It is difficult to imagine a merchant beginning an operation with any other intent. But what does "successful" mean to a retailer? If retailing involves the selling of goods and services to the ultimate consumer, it follows that successful retailers satisfy the wants and needs of their customers and thereby earn a fair profit.

For retailers to achieve their primary objective, an organizational structure must be developed so that the work necessary to achieve the objectives of the organization can be accomplished. Answers to the following questions must be secured: Who will actually do the work? Who has the overall responsibility? To whom does each worker report?

As a retail store expands, organization is vital

Some organizational structures develop as companies grow. For example, the owner of a small retail shop is generally in charge of all facets of the business. (e.g., buying, selling, and financing). As the store grows, more employees are hired, larger quantities of merchandise are purchased, and greater sums of money are involved. When it becomes too difficult for one person to handle all these functions, division of responsibility and authority becomes necessary. In very small firms no formal organization is needed, since each person's job is easily understood. However, when many people are involved, a more formal organization is required in order to separate the functions and responsibilities.

To develop an effective store organization, the retail decision maker should have an understanding of management principles, organization structures, and a process for operating the firm. Management principles that can assist the retailer in developing a sound company structure are as follows.

Management principles

- **Principle of Authority and Responsibility** The employee who is assigned the responsibility and accountability for a particular job should also have the necessary authority to complete the job.
- **Principle of Unity of Command** A worker should not receive orders from or be required to report to more than one supervisor.
- **Principle of Unity of Direction** Only one plan should be in operation for the achievement of an objective and all involved employees should follow that plan.
- **Principle of Span of Control** The number of workers reporting to the same supervisor should be manageable. The span of workers assigned to any supervisor should be in direct proportion to the complexity of the job. When the number of workers exceeds that which a manager can control effectively, the quality of decision making is affected.
- **Principle of Division of Work** Large tasks should be divided into smaller ones, with people specializing in performing them. Reducing the span of work can improve the quality of performance.

- **Principle of Chain of Command (Hierarchy of Authority)** Authority is linked in a ladder-type form from the highest management position to the lowest employee level. This chain of supervisors and subordinates outlines the reporting relationships within the company.

Having identified several important management principles, we turn our attention to how retail firms develop operational structures for carrying out those principles.

ORGANIZATION CHARTS

Organization charts pinpoint responsibility

Diagrams that clearly indicate lines of authority and responsibility are known as **organization charts.** They pinpoint the people who will do the actual work and those who are responsible for getting the job done. Charts indicate the flow of communications by establishing a hierarchy of authority because organization charts are custom made to meet the specific needs of retail institutions. Therefore, they differ for small stores, department stores, branches, and chains.

Organization charts are developed according to the number of employees, the specific activities to be carried out, and the departments in which those activities are to take place. Depending on the size of the firm, they can be simple in design or greatly detailed.

The types of retail positions most commonly used today are (1) line and (2) staff.

Line Positions

Line organization: direct communication

Line positions are characterized by direct authority and responsibility as shown in the **line organization chart** in Figure 6-1. On an organizational chart each worker's position is shown in relation to his or her immediate superior or super-

Figure 6-1   Line organization.

visor. In terms of the flow of communications and delegated authority, questions regarding responsibilities are eliminated. In Figure 6-1, the salesperson reports to the assistant buyer, who reports to the buyer, and so forth. The advantages of this form of organization are that (1) it is easily understood, (2) communications are direct, and (3) supervision is obvious. The disadvantages are that (1) there can be too much responsibility and authority at the top, (2) coordination can be difficult without crossing lines, and (3) each supervisor needs to be a specialist in several areas of management.

Staff Positions

Specialists perform staff functions

Staff positions are advisory or support, and include all work performed by nonline employees as shown on the **line-and-staff organization chart** in Figure 6-2. The advantages of a line-and-staff organization are that it (1) allows for specialists to consult with and advise line people, and (2) maintains the ease of direct communication (each employee reporting to one supervisor). The disadvantages occur (1) when staff employees try to exert authority over line personnel (in order to have their ideas carried out), (2) when line employees follow staff suggestions that fail, and (3) when there is jealousy or friction between line and staff members. Nevertheless, line-and-staff is the organizational form that is most often used today.

It should be noted that in a staff department there are also lines of authority. For example, in a personnel department the personnel manager supervises other employees within the department (Figure 6-3).

It is important to keep charts up to date. Since the charts contain the names of employees, they must be revised whenever personnel changes take place. In firms with a high rate of employee turnover, this is considered a disadvantage.

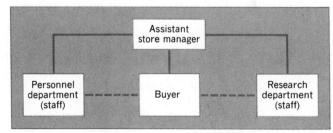

Figure 6-2   Line-and-staff organization.

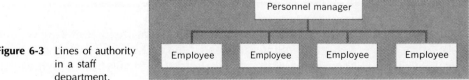

Figure 6-3   Lines of authority in a staff department.

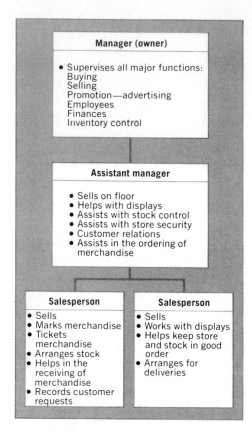

Figure 6-4   Organization of a small store.

ORGANIZATION FOR THE SMALL RETAILER

The structure of small independent retailers is simple, even though they perform the same functions as large retailers. Because a small store has few employees, little specialization, and many tasks to be performed, each employee is responsible for several functions. A typical small-store structure is shown in Figure 6-4.

As a small store expands, there is more opportunity for specialization and departmentalization. When departments are created, salespeople are assigned to particular sections, such as men's wear, women's wear, and so forth.

ORGANIZATION FOR DEPARTMENT STORES— THE MAZUR PLAN

Mazur plan: organization by four functions

Many medium-sized and large department stores are organized according to the various retailing functions. One of the plans widely used by department stores is the **Mazur plan,** which divides all retail store activities into the following four major areas.

1. Merchandising
2. Publicity
3. Store management
4. Control

Merchandising

This is considered the most important function of all and includes responsibility for all the activities involved in buying and selling merchandise. This area is headed by the general merchandise manager, who supervises all the merchandising activities in the main store and other locations. The major activities in this area include buying, selling, planning merchandise promotions, and merchandise inventory management control.

Publicity

This operation is concerned with all nonpersonal selling activities (e.g., sales promotions, advertising, and public relations). The public manager (or advertising manager) heads this area and works with all other areas. The major activities of this operation are planning promotions for the entire store (adviser to the merchandise department, advertising, public relations, and displays (interiors and window).

Store Management

This area is concerned with all activities in the store except buying, selling, promotion, and finance. The store manager oversees personnel, store maintenance, purchasing of supplies and equipment to operate the store, operations, customer services, and store security.

Control

This division is responsible for protecting the firm's financial status. The use of computers and data processing has increased the need for specialists to run this division. The controller, sometimes called the treasurer, heads this operation. Its major activities include accounting and record keeping, credit and collections, budgeting, and inventory control.

Application of the Mazur Plan

Use of the Mazur plan allows for greater specialization and utilization of staff talent. The organization chart in Figure 6-5 indicates how the Mazur plan divides the four areas of responsibility in a department store. Under this arrangement the four area managers provide staff functions for each other. For example, the

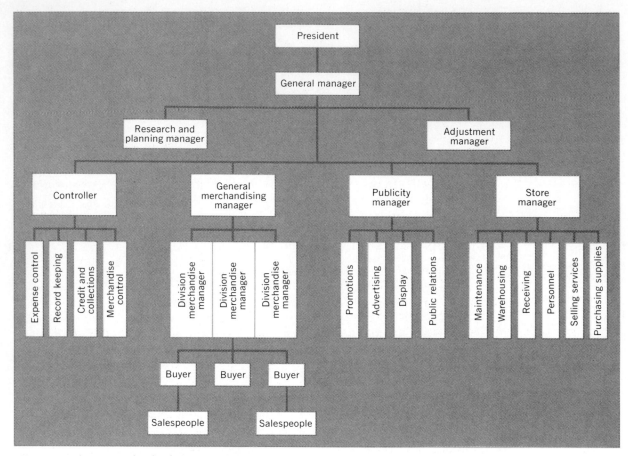

Figure 6-5   The Mazur plan for department stores.

merchandise manager, who is responsible for planning promotional events related to merchandise, such as clearance sales, consults with the publicity manager, the person who is responsible for executing store promotions. The two managers plan merchandise promotions together.

It should be emphasized that although no single plan meets the needs of all retail organizations, the basic Mazur plan, with adjustments, can be adapted to most department and specialty store needs. For example, the complex changes in personnel activities brought about by such considerations as labor laws and unions have led to the treatment of personnel as a separate function. In fact, a five-function organizational plan is the most commonly used structure in department and large specialty stores.

Department stores that use the Mazur plan combine the responsibilities for buying and selling. With the growth of branch stores, however, the tendency has been to separate the buying and selling activities. This is similar to the structure developed by chain store organizations. In fact, a major criticism of the Mazur plan has to do with the responsibility for selling.

Critics of the Mazur plan claim that selling, the most important function in retailing, should be concentrated in one area. Instead, two areas besides the merchandise division are involved in the selling activity. For example, the publicity division becomes involved when a sales promotion is planned. On the other hand, the management division, through its personnel department, is responsible for the training of salespeople.

ORGANIZATION FOR BRANCH STORES

Different forms of the Mazur plan are utilized for branch stores. One approach is to treat these stores as wings of the main store (Figure 6-6). This arrangement is sometimes called the **brood hen and chick** approach; that is, the main store operates the branch by performing functions both for itself and for the branch. The drawback to this arrangement occurs in cases of branches whose customers reveal buying preferences different from those of main store customers.

Another approach (Figure 6-7) is to have the branch operate as a separate

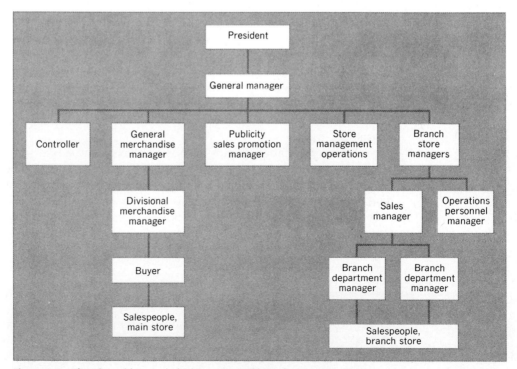

Figure 6-6   The "brood hen and chick" concept of branch store organization.

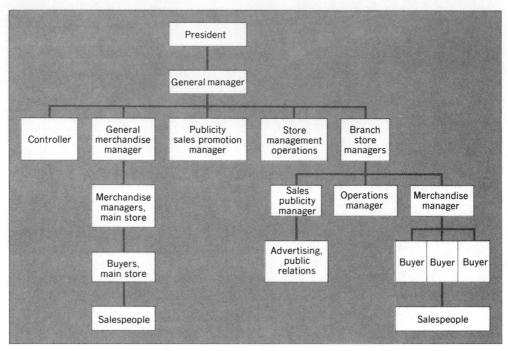

Figure 6-7 The separate-unit concept of branch store organization.

unit with a great deal of autonomy. Under the **separate-unit concept,** customer needs are easily identified because each branch is responsible for its own buying and selling functions. This structure is found where the number of branches increases so that main-store buyers cannot carry out these functions effectively. Under an autonomous arrangement, however, the company risks the loss of a consistent image.

Another variation (Figure 6-8) is known as the **equal store,** in which the buying and selling activities are separated. The buying is done through a central or regional office, with central buyers responsible for the branch stores' merchandise needs. The branches are responsible for the remaining activities of sales and promotion. This form of organization is closer in concept to the chain store structure.

ORGANIZATION FOR CHAIN STORES

Chain stores perform many of the same functions as department stores. However, they differ somewhat in organizational structure because of the products handled, the size of the outlets, the number of units, and geographic spread. Most

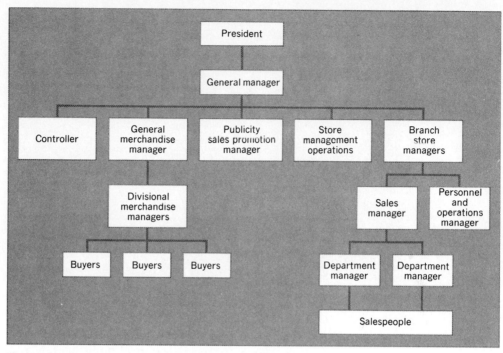

Figure 6-8   The equal-store concept of branch organization.

chain store organizational patterns have the following characteristics (Figure 6-9).

Centralization and control of operating functions administered in chain's home office

1. **Centralization** of the major store functions (buying, personnel, promotion, control, etc.), which are controlled through a regional or home office. **Decentralization** of the selling and sales promotion activities is the main departure from the chain store's commitment to centralization.
2. A larger number of divisions than department stores, including real estate, warehousing, personnel, and transportation.
3. Trained specialists in the home office, who assume a great deal of the individual store manager's burdens.
4. Highly centralized, autocratic lines of authority and responsibility, which coordinate the total operation.
5. Control of individual stores through the filing of up-to-date reports with the home office.
6. Standardized operations regarding merchandise, prices, credit, services, store layouts, and fixtures.

Rickel Home Centers is a chain that operates 51 stores in the states of New

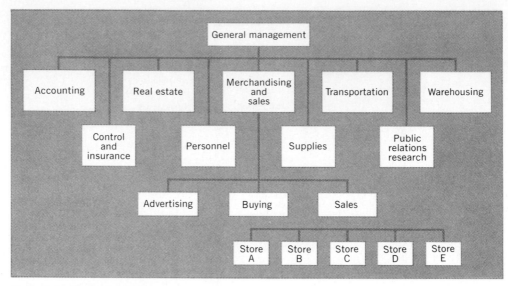

Figure 6-9   Chain organization.

Jersey, New York, Pennsylvania, Delaware, Connecticut, Maryland, and Rhode Island. Rickels is known as a hard goods retailer servicing the "do-it-yourselfer" with a large selection of home improvement products. Figure 6-10 illustrates the organization chart for a store in the Rickel Home Center chain.

RETAIL STRATEGY

Decentralized Structure—Longs' Profitable Operation

Longs, a West Coast self-service drug chain, operates with strong independent store managers and with profit sharing for those managers as well as other employees.

Longs' decentralized structure is the basis for a strong, very profitable operation. Store managers are given great autonomy in running the stores and provide a great deal of service despite the chain's self-service status. Stores are customized to the needs of those they serve. Eighty-five percent of the merchandise is purchased at the store level, either from manufacturers or from local wholesalers and jobbers. The majority of purchasing and advertising decisions is made by the stores, not the general office. The stores show a high level of sales productivity per employee, which is attributed to the chain's autonomous structure. Store managers make decisions and are promoted from within.

Inside Retailing (September 26, 1988), p. 3.

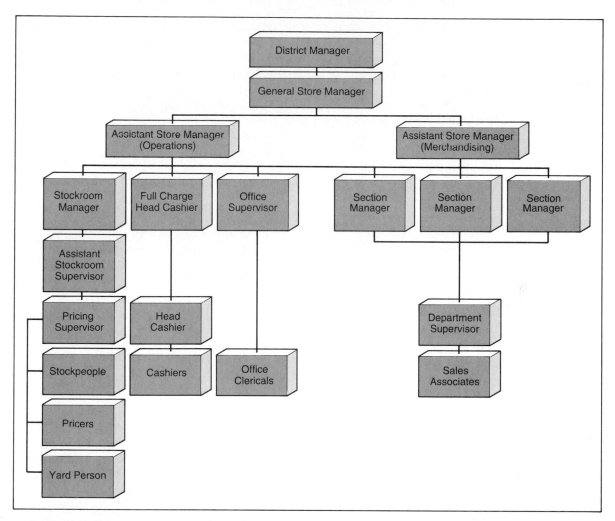

Figure 6-10   Rickel Home Centers store organization chart.

CENTRALIZATION AND DECENTRALIZATION

Centralization and decentralization are the two main types of retail control. Centralization and control of the major retailing operations have made the chain store organization one of the most efficient and economical forms of retailing. The advantages of centralized buying, standardized operations, and control have made it possible for many chains to benefit from major savings, large profits, and expansion. For example, Family Dollar operates more than 1,000 stores from a single headquarters in North Carolina.

Despite many successes, however, some chains have found it necessary to change their methods of delegating authority between individual stores and the central office. In fact, some chains have become more decentralized, giving store managers greater autonomy in making decisions about merchandising and operating policies.

The rationale for decentralizing the buying function is to make the buyer of the goods responsible for the sale of the merchandise, too. Those who favor this position argue that under centralization the buyers are removed from the customers and stores. Consequently, they are not in the best position to recognize local needs and problems.

J. C. Penney is an example of a firm that promotes more management flexibility at the store level. It grants store managers more decision-making responsibility with regard to local merchandising, advertising, and promotion. Penney's also stations buyers away from headquarters in regional markets where there are substantial localized vendors. In these cases, they buy for their own *area* stores. In addition, Penney's sends videotapes to store buyers to choose merchandise from centralized offerings.

In addition, there is evidence of decentralization among other retailers, including Montgomery Ward, Kroger, Sears, and A&P. Montgomery Ward's merchandising structure has been reorganized so that its four major merchandise categories have their own field organization similar to that of a specialty retailer. District managers are responsible for implementing merchandising and sales training at the store level.

Sears has also restructured its retail store merchandising organization. In addition to paring down size and overhead, the merchandise group has been realigned along six vertical business lines. Each one is treated as if it were a separate specialty business headed by a merchandise executive.

Another retailer that has great flexibility at the store level is Nordstrom, Inc., the third-largest specialty retailer in the country. Its organizational structure follows merchandising and management techniques that most retailers gave up long ago. While its competitors became more centralized as they grew. Nordstrom split up responsibility. Consequently, each individual store has its own staff of buyers who also spend three to four hours a day waiting on customers. Furthermore, store managers, not division heads, are responsible for cost control. When Nordstrom expanded to California and the East Coast, it stationed buying staffs in those areas so they would be closer to important vendors.

Regional decentralization Competition among supermarket chains has led to some decentralization of merchandising decisions regarding price and promotion policies, allowing individual units to respond to local competition more effectively.

Despite these trends, some chains with a wide geographic spread continue to move toward centralization because it allows for greater control. This is especially so because of improved computer equipment that transmits information at ever-increasing speeds to the central office.

In another vein, the increase of department store branches has stimulated centralized buying for some large department stores. By considering all their branches as similar units, these retailers find that centralized buying is efficient.

Regional decentralization attempts to achieve a balance between centralization and decentralization. At K mart, for example, the buying is done through central headquarters, but the individual store manager can specify merchandise for his or her store, hire and train employees, and maintain control in conjunction with the home office. Another example is Wal-Mart, which supervises through regional offices, with main control at headquarters. At Sears, the reorganization of its field management divides the chain's 800-odd stores into six sharply focused businesses. As shown in Figure 6-11, the new structure changes the store manager's responsibilities to those of an administrator.

Because chains differ in products sold, size, and geography, it is difficult to construct an ideal form of organization for chain management. Nevertheless, retailers continue to search for a structure to blend the efficiency and economic advantages of centralization with some degree of decentralization. Having exam-

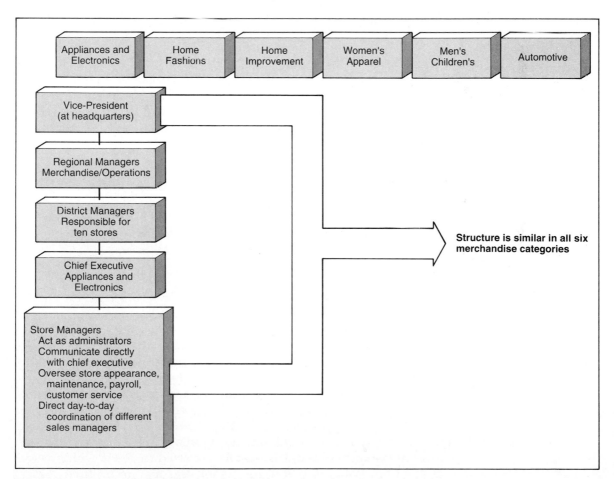

Figure 6-11   Sears' organizational structure for its field management (six sharply focused businesses). Based on various articles.

ined the organization of a store, we turn our attention to the people who work there. To a large extent, the success or failure of a retail firm is dependent on its employees.

This section examines the staffing of a store and the responsibilities of its personnel department. It considers the hiring and training of new employees as well as policies concerning existing staff. It also identifies wage and compensation scales and fringe benefits. Informal and formal methods of communication are discussed, as well as personnel departments in their relation to labor organizations.

THE HUMAN RESOURCE DEPARTMENT

A vital aspect of operating a successful retail store is managing the company's human resources, that is, its employees. As businesses become larger and more complex, the human resource department, also known as the personnel department, has more responsibility for maintaining an adequate labor force. Modern personnel management, then, is concerned with hiring, training, motivating, and understanding the needs of employees in order to develop a productive work force.

In large companies the human resource department is concerned with

Personnel functions

1. Recruiting and hiring new employees.
2. Training and retraining employees.
3. Working with personnel transfers, promotions, discharges, and performance appraisal.
4. Establishing wage and compensation scales.
5. Establishing and managing employee fringe benefits.

Recruiting and Hiring New Employees

The retail employment environment has special characteristics. Among them are a very high employee turnover, the existence of many part-time jobs, and the need for extra hiring at peak periods (e.g., Christmas and Easter).

The types of jobs and the qualifications for them must be determined prior to recruitment. To accomplish these ends, jobs analyses and job descriptions are developed. A **job analysis** is a detailed study of the duties and abilities needed to perform a job efficiently. The information from a job analysis is written up to create a **job description.** A **job specification** sets forth the qualifications required by the job. Using these tools, personnel managers who recruit for new employees can determine exactly the types of people and qualifications needed for specific jobs.

Sources of personnel

Sources from which new employees can be selected are found within as well as outside the firm. Within the firm, new employees may result from present employees' recommendations. Outside sources include advertising in newspapers, trade papers, radio, the store window, employment agencies (public and private), schools, colleges and universities, and walk-in applications (large, prestigious firms attract unsolicited requests for employment).

The most common means of advertising for new employees is to use the classified advertising sections of newspapers. Two types of advertisements are generally used: the **open ad** and the **blind ad.** An open ad supplies all the information about the job, as well as the name, address, and telephone number of the store. A blind ad does not identify the store and provides only a post office box number. There are advantages and disadvantages to both types. An open ad (Figure 6-12) encourages a great many applicants to write and call. This often requires additional personnel to handle the responses and screen applicants for interviews. On the other hand, a blind ad eliminates hours of work because the mail can be reviewed before applicants are told when or where to apply. Though this is somewhat of an advantage, it should be noted that many employed people who are looking for a job change hesitate to answer blind ads for fear of writing to their own employer.

MANAGER

Price Club
THE PRICE COMPANY

Our continuing success & expansion has created management opportunities throughout major East Coast markets.

We are seeking high level managers who have a minimum of 2 years experience successfully managing in a "high volume" ($30 Mil annually) mass merchandise, retail, wholesale, grocery or home improvement environment with total P&L responsibility.

Candidates must possess strong leadership skills & have extensive experience in both merchandising & operations.

Send a confidential resume to:

THE PRICE COMPANY
Attn HR Manager
Suite 150 Countryside Shopping Ctr
37 Pidgeon Hill Drive
Sterling VA 22170
EOE
Price Club is a registered trademark of
THE PRICE COMPANY.

Figure 6-12   An open ad for recruitment of executives.

RETAIL STRATEGY

A Ten-Step Program for Sensible Hiring

Looking for some sound principles to guide your hiring practices during the '90s? Then you'll be interested in these ten points presented by Kathy Fyock, president of Innovative Management Concepts, to the NRF at its recent Human Resource conference.

1. Segment your audience and target your recruiting messages to that audience.
2. Use messages that sell. Think about what that candidate wants. Meet those needs.
3. Make it easy for candidates to explore the opportunities with you. Provide easy access for application and information.
4. Treat job candidates like customers; they are, in fact, shopping for a job with you!
5. Create the right image with candidates—don't send a "desperation" message.
6. Collaborate. Work with others to achieve your goal.
7. Be competitive. Know what your competitors offer and be prepared to define your "unique competence."
8. Don't be afraid to be imaginative and creative. Candidates respond to unique and appealing activities and messages.
9. Don't put all your eggs in one basket; use a variety of recruiting messages and activities to attract the best.
10. Be persistent.

Inside Retailing, (October 22, 1990), p. 2.

The Process of Hiring New Employees

The initial screening is known as the rail interview

In small stores the hiring procedure is informal, with the owner or manager interviewing the potential employee and recording the necessary information. In large firms the procedures are more formal. Prospects may have to go through an initial screening known as the **rail interview.** This is a brief interview before a prospective applicant is asked to fill out an **application form.** This technique is used to eliminate candidates who are clearly unqualified. For example, if a particular job specification includes certain educational requirements and the interviewee does not possess the appropriate background, there is no need to continue the recruitment procedure. When a rail interview is successful, the prospect is asked to fill out an application form similar to the one in Figure 6-13.

Dayton's application for employment adheres to the federal Civil Rights

DAYTON'S ⟫⟫ Application for Employment

EQUAL OPPORTUNITY EMPLOYER

NAME - PLEASE PRINT - LAST, FIRST, MIDDLE	DATE APPLIED

CURRENT ADDRESS - ADDRESS, CITY, STATE, ZIP

PRIOR ADDRESS - ADDRESS, CITY, STATE, ZIP

HOME TELEPHONE NUMBER	SOCIAL SECURITY NUMBER	IF NOT U.S. CITIZEN PROVIDE VISA NUMBER

	NO ☐ YES ☐	IF YES TO ANY OF THE FOUR QUESTIONS, PLEASE EXPLAIN:
HAVE YOU BEEN REFUSED BOND?	NO ☐ YES ☐	
HAVE YOU BEEN CONVICTED OF A FELONY OR MISDEMEANOR?	NO ☐ YES ☐	
HAVE YOUR WAGES EVER BEEN GARNISHED WITHIN THE LAST 7 YEARS?	NO ☐ YES ☐	
HAVE YOU FILED BANKRUPTCY IN THE LAST 7 YEARS?	NO ☐ YES ☐	

NAME OF HIGH SCHOOL	ADDRESS	GRADE COMPLETED	DATE COMPLETED

ADVANCED EDUCATION	ADDRESS	YEAR COMPLETED	DATE

POSITION(S) DESIRED	☐ FULL TIME ☐ PERMANENT
	☐ PART TIME ☐ TEMPORARY

DAYS AND HOURS AVAILABLE	WAGE DESIRED:

995 (5/79)

PREVIOUS EMPLOYMENT RECORD *(List most recent employer first, if none list reference other than relatives.)*

EMPLOYER	DATES	POSITION(S)	WAGE	WHY LEFT
1. CO. NAME	FROM	START	START	
CO. ADDRESS	TO	FINAL	FINAL	
CO. PHONE NUMBER	SUPERVISOR(S)			
2. CO. NAME	FROM	START	START	
CO. ADDRESS	TO	FINAL	FINAL	
CO. PHONE NUMBER	SUPERVISOR(S)			
3. CO. NAME	FROM	START	START	
CO. ADDRESS	TO	FINAL	FINAL	
CO. PHONE NUMBER	SUPERVISOR(S)			

HAVE YOU EVER BEEN EMPLOYED BY DAYTON'S?	FROM TO	WHAT STORE?	WHAT DEPT.?

LIST ALL FRIENDS AND RELATIVES EMPLOYED AT DAYTON'S. (Specify Store Location)

IF CURRENTLY EMPLOYED ☐ Yes ☐ No   MAY BE CONTACT YOUR PRESENT EMPLOYER ☐ Yes ☐ No

HOW WERE YOU REFERRED TO DAYTON'S?

IMPORTANT: READ BEFORE SIGNING!   I understand and agree that: (a) any false statement on this application will be cause for dismissal, (b) I will abide by the policies of Dayton's as a condition of my employment, (c) I will be bonded, (d) reference investigations may be made regarding my credit status, character and work record as it relates to my employment.

SIGNATURE

Figure 6-13 A typical department store application form. Reproduced by permission of Dayton's.

Act of 1964, which makes it illegal and discriminatory to request information about

1. Race, color, creed, or national origin.
2. Age, except to ask if you are under 18 or over 65.
3. Sex.
4. Marital status.
5. Disabilities. Questions may be asked only if the disability is related to the applicant's ability to do the job.
6. Arrest record. An interviewer may ask if you have ever been convicted of a crime, but may not ask if you have ever been arrested.

It is illegal to hire or favor one applicant over another solely on the basis of race or sex. However, the application form does ask for necessary information so that a proper determination can be made as to the prospect's qualifications and background. Educational background, past work experience, and references are required. References are people or past employers who can be contacted regarding the character and ability of the person applying for the job.

Checking references is one of the procedures that is required in the employment process. Background checks are made to gain additional data and to verify information given by the applicant on the application form. Reference checks are made by phone or mail, and many retailers use simple forms that are mailed to the applicant's references. Some firms will not hire employees until their references have responded favorably.

Another method of checking job seekers' honesty was the use of **polygraph instruments,** commonly known as **lie detectors.** By checking a person's pulse, blood pressure, and breathing, and with proper interpretation, these devices

This prospect is being interviewed for a retail job. Photo by Ken Karp.

indicate with some degree of certainty whether the answers to questions are lies or the truth.

Since polygraphs have been banned by law since 1988 from playing a role in the hiring process, employers have been using paper-and-pencil **honesty tests** to screen out undesirable job applicants. One such employer, Super D Drugs, Inc., a Southwestern drugstore chain, has found that a basic test asking straightforward questions has reduced employee theft, absentee rates, substance abuse, lateness, and other forms of counterproductive behavior.

Testing

Testing is another step in the employment process. It includes data on aptitude, skills, personality, and the like. The personnel department must be careful to avoid any type of discrimination so as not to break the law. Although the Civil Rights Act of 1964 permits testing, the tests must be the same for all applicants. Large firms generally administer and evaluate these tests themselves. Smaller firms may use private testing bureaus. Some firms evaluate academic records, courses, and grades, while others use school **internship programs** as a means of "testing" future employees. This is a form of on-the-job evaluation. If a prospect is successful during a prescribed period, he or she is offered the job. Another aspect of testing has been the use of physical examinations. Today many firms test applicants for drug use and acquired immune deficiency syndrome (AIDS). In fact a Reid psychological systems study points up the increased use of drugs as discussed in reemployment interviews. Table 6-1 indicates the extent of drug abuse of the interviewees.

TABLE 6-1   Abstract of Reid Psychological Systems Study

Most Frequent Drug Abuses	Number of Admissions
Uses marijuana before or at work	178
Uses speed before or at work	119
Uses marijuana away from work	71
Uses hallucinogens away from work	54
Uses cocaine before or at work	53

Source: Reported in *Inside Retailing* (January 7, 1991), p. 4.

Interviews

Interviews are another important aspect of the employment process. Further information concerning the applicant's aptitude, verbal ability, and reasons for wanting the job are revealed during an interview session. Additional information concerning different experiences can be advantageous to the applicant. The personal interview also gives the prospect an opportunity to ask questions about the job, the store, and opportunities for promotion.

Training and Retraining

Training

Training for new employees

Another major responsibility of the personnel department is to plan and implement the training of new employees. Small and large firms have some form of instruction in order to supply employees with the skills and knowledge to do an effective job.

Orientation training covers such topics as the history of the firm, procedures and policies, and rules and regulations regarding payroll, promotions, fringe benefits, and so forth. (See Figure 6-14.)

With small firms, **on-the-job training** is very common. The inexperienced employee is assigned to a more experienced person, frequently the owner or manager, until he or she has gained enough experience. (See Figures 6-15 and 6-16.)

INTRODUCTION TO STORE

OBJECTIVES

During the first week you should, with the help of attachments, aim to gain a basic knowledge of the management structure of the store and their respective roles. You should also gain an understanding of the training program and apprasial procedure, and understand your own responsibility for self-development during your training.

JOB KNOWLEDGE	PROBES/QUESTIONS TO CONSIDER
Introduction to all senior members of staff, and their roles.	
Appointment of a suitable sponsor for the trainee.	
Introduction to Customer Service at Marks & Spencer	What type of service do we offer? What are the 5 Steps of a Sale? What can you do to improve our present level of customer service?
Conditions and contract of employment staff regulations.	How does the management team work?
Outline of training program and details of appraisals.	
Fire tour.	
Reporting of accidents.	Where are the accident forms kept?
Working knowledge of the Management Guide.	
Actual square footage of the store, yearly budget, and progressive figures.	
Telephone numbers.	
Orientation of store/stock/customers.	

Figure 6-14 Insert from *Training Guide*, orientation training for new employees at M&S (Marks & Spencer Worldwide). Reprinted with permission from Marks & Spencer, Canada.

STORE MANAGEMENT TRAINING PROGRAM

Area of Training	Approximate Time	
Store Induction	2 days	} Month 1
Receiving/Warehouse	2 weeks	
Office	1 week	}
Head Office Induction Course	3 days	
Sales Assistant Training	3 weeks	}
Textiles	10 weeks	} Month 2–4
Head Office Textile Course	1 week	
Foods	10 weeks	} Month 5–7
Head Office Foods Course	2 days	
General Office	2 weeks	} Month 7
Loss Prevention Workshop	1 day	
Personnel	2 weeks	} Month 8–10
Role of the Manager	10 weeks	
Relief Management	8 weeks	} Month 11–12

**Approximate Length of Program:
10 Months**

Figure 6-15   Example of store management training program at M&S (Marks & Spencer). Reprinted with permission from Marks & Spencer, Canada.

THE ROLE OF THE SPONSOR

1. To provide the trainee with an experienced individual to whom they can turn to for

   ● Advice.
   ● Answers to questions on varied aspects of the business.
   ● Giving vent to frustrations encouragement.

2. To follow up on the trainees, program, ensuring the program is being followed and that the trainee is not being used as "an extra pair of hands."

3. To develop, motivate, and challenge the trainee to reach the very highest standards they are capable of.

4. Through regular contact with the trainee, assist in overcoming the isolation trainees often experience.

5. To do regular store visits with the trainee so that from the earliest stages of their training they become accustomed to handling Head Office visitors with ease.

6. To criticize constructively.

   N.B. The store manager is still responsible for the day-to-day training of the trainee.

Figure 6-16   Example of the trainer's responsibilities at M&S (Marks & Spencer). Reprinted with permission from Marks & Spencer, Canada.

Dayton's is one of the many stores that uses classroom training for newly hired employees.

In larger firms, trainees are assigned after some formal training has taken place. While lectures and seminars are used for large-group instruction, tapes and audiovisual equipment are other commonly employed techniques. When employees are trained prior to assignment, the stores use their own classrooms. This type of instruction is sometimes referred to as **vestibule training.** For example, retail stores train employees in the use of the cash register before they are assigned to the selling floor.

Retraining

Older employees may require additional training for various reasons, such as new technology, transfers, upgrading, and promotions. Employees who need to be retrained are instructed by the personnel department or consultants, or take special courses in schools.

Some firms institute management training or executive training as part of their inservice training or for promotions. This type of training utilizes seminars and job rotation. **Job rotation** moves the employee from one area to another and gives the worker an opportunity to view the total business operation prior to permanent assignment.

Sensitivity training needed to handle people problems

Many stores use outside consultants or educational programs for employees who need skill in handling delicate problems. Sensitivity training is often used in an attempt to improve human relations within a firm by helping the employees develop insight and greater understanding. The employees participate in groups, classes, simulations, or games in which they learn about themselves. Within this group setting, they observe and discuss human behavior. They ask such questions as

Job rotation allows new retail employees to view different aspects of a store's operation.

- What they dislike about a certain manager.
- What causes them to be nonproductive at certain times.
- What happens outside the job that interferes with their concentration on the job. This "insight" training also deals with such topics as feeling stronger about yourself and handling anger.

Employees may be asked to look at the ways in which they are unconsciously or unintentionally counterproductive to the firm. Some personnel consultants consider it useful in a work situation for people to be able to talk about their feelings. However, in order for them to make positive behavioral changes, they must be in an atmosphere that does not pose a threat because of what they say. They must also be motivated to change.

In many cases programs like these help supervisors improve their sensitivity to people with whom they work, thus reducing employee turnover.

Transfer, Promotion, Discharge, and Performance Appraisal

Transfer, promotion, and discharge are other responsibilities of the personnel department. Assigning an experienced worker to another job within the store or to a branch store is known as a **job transfer.** Employees are transferred either because their skills are needed elsewhere or because they are unhappy with co-workers or the job situation.

When an employee is moved to another position that carries greater responsibility and an increase in salary, it is defined as a **promotion.** A promotion generally advances the worker to a job that requires greater skill and ability.

Many corporations are adopting promotion-from-within policies. That is, they attempt to upgrade employees from within the organization and to promote

Your Future With Us
A Career Path Leading To Success.

So how do you fit into this success story? Strawbridge & Clothier has always considered people as our most valuable resource. Therefore, it should come as no surprise that we want to make your career with us as rewarding as possible. Our long-standing policy of promotion from within assures that ambitious individuals will experience success. In fact, over 95% of our management is developed from within.

Our Executive Development Program complements your on-the-job training. It sets you on a career path that will take you to Buyer in just 4 to 5 years.

The goal of this nine month program is three-fold. You will develop management skills, merchandising knowledge and communication abilities. Lectures and workshops in retail math, merchandise reports, merchandise presentation, inventory control, fibers & fabrics, and seminars in supervision and customer services will aid you in your quest for success.

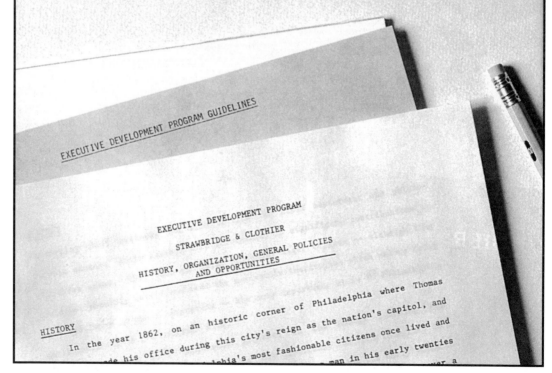

Strawbridge & Clothier considers personnel its most valuable resource and develops over 95 percent of management from within.

from among their own staffs. Sears, Roebuck and Company is known to use this method. This policy minimizes hiring from outside the company and makes internal training more important because employees must be trained to do upper-level jobs when necessary. Firms that promote from within usually have employees with good morale and motivation.

Strawbridge & Clothier, another retailer dedicated to employee development, has a special Career Opportunities Program for its employees. The program was developed to inform employees of regular job openings and to maintain a quick and direct way of applying for promotional opportunities within the firm.

When a job becomes available, the personnel supervisor prepares a Career Opportunities Bulletin that includes a job description and skills requirements. The bulletin is posted (usually at an employee entrance or in an employee lounge) for five working days. During that time, regular and part-time employees who feel qualified may secure a Career Opportunities Application form from the personnel department. If the applicant's performance reviews are good, he or she is eligible for further consideration.

For several years, many employees have utilized the program and have found new and more challenging careers with the firm. The success of the program reflects the company's attitude toward its employees. Francis Straw-bridge, chairman of the board, was quoted as follows: "We at S&C feel that our people are the greatest strength we have."

Discharged and *fired* are synonymous

When employees are **discharged,** they are permanently separated from the company. The word *discharged* is synonymous with the better-known term *fired.* Reasons for being fired range from incompetence and dishonesty to not getting along or "fitting in" with other store personnel.

When an employee is temporarily or permanently terminated owing to an economic slowdown or problems within the firm, it is known as a **layoff.** For example, when the B. Altman department store chain, closed its stores in 1989, it terminated all of its employees permanently.

Performance appraisal measures employee performance and training

In order to carry out the responsibilities of transfers, promotions, and discharges effectively, many personnel managers use performance appraisal to evaluate employees. **Performance appraisal** is a personnel tool that measures employee performance and the effectiveness of training. In most retail firms the methods used to rate employees involve observation and written reports.

Observation

Immediate supervisors, such as department managers, assistant buyers, and buyers, observe the salespeople and stock clerks in their departments. They take note of their appearance, their attitudes toward customers and staff, and how well they comply with store regulations and procedures. To a large degree, well-kept stockrooms and healthy sales are measures of productivity. In small stores the supervisor is generally the owner or assistant manager.

Sometimes salespeople are observed and evaluated by professionals who pose as customers. They rate the salesperson's selling performance, compliance with rules and regulations, personal behavior, attitude, and grooming. This is known as a **shopper's report.**

Written Reports

Reviews and ratings are less complicated for first-level jobs (sales help, part-timers, stock). These reports are usually completed by the employee's immediate supervisor.

More complicated forms are used by most large retailers to rate management trainees. An example of an individual trainee evaluation form used by Dayton's is included in Appendix A at the end of this chapter. This form has three sections to be completed, one each for the buyer, the department manager, and the divisional manager.

The buyer determines the training objectives for the trainee two weeks after the latter has joined the department. Four months later the trainee is reviewed by the buyer, the department manager, and the divisional manager.

Trainees are evaluated by the buyer, the department manager, and the divisional manager

The buyer rates the individual, explains the rating, and makes recommendations as to the type of improvement program needed. The department manager rates the trainee's overall progress as a management trainee, whereas the divisional manager comments about the trainee's potential and possible advancement.

Other forms are used to evaluate the performance of the more advanced trainee. Appendix B is another example of a form used by Dayton's to measure the trainee's ability and leadership characteristics.

Trainees rate branch store training

Trainees, too, have an opportunity to give management their opinions and ratings regarding their training experience. As noted in Appendix C, trainees are requested to complete a written report regarding their training experience at Dayton's.

Employees need assurance that they are doing a good job. Consequently, evaluations can either serve as a morale booster or decrease employee motivation. Skill in handling ratings is very delicate and important. Because of their potential impact on job performance, evaluations and ratings are usually discussed with employees and trainees. In some instances the employee must sign a review.

Ratings and evaluations are used as a basis for raises and bonuses. Many large retailers review employees twice a year, at which times raises may be recommended. Ratings are also used to decide on promotions, discharges, and transfers.

Establishing Wage and Compensation Scales

Developing wage and compensation plans is a function of personnel

Establishing wages for employees is another very important aspect of the personnel function. Compensation plans are developed according to several factors: the nature of the job, prevailing wages within the industry, competition for qualified employees, and availability of capital.

The various forms of compensation include the following.

Guaranteed annual wage
Straight salary
Hourly Wage
Straight salary plus commission
Salary plus bonus
Straight commission
Quota bonus

Guaranteed Annual Wage

Workers are paid every week despite business conditions.

Straight Salary

A fixed amount of wages is paid by the week, by the month, or on some similar basis.

Hourly Wage

Workers are paid according to hours worked. The prevailing minimum wages for the retail industry are generally used as a guideline. Sunday and holiday store hours usually call for higher hourly wages.

Straight Salary Plus Commission

This method is used in many retail stores for different jobs. Cosmetics, shoes, and furniture are generally sold with commission as an added employee incentive. This form of compensation usually motivates the worker to try harder for sales.

Salary Plus Bonus

This form of compensation includes a special addition to salary. It is generally given to executives when business is good or to regular employees at certain times of the year, such as Christmas.

Straight Commission

Straight commission subjects workers to pressure

In this case salespeople are paid a percentage of their total sales. This arrangement is common in the sale of high-ticket items like furniture, furs, and jewelry. The amount of commission varies according to the product and the store. This type of compensation arrangement provides the greatest incentive for salespeople and makes them more service oriented and more attentive to consumers. Although some retail chains have adopted commission compensation programs, for example, Nordstrom, Jordan Marsh, Marshall Field, others have discontinued the programs in some of their departments, for example, The Broadway and The Emporium. Commission arrangements have been maintained for big-ticket items as well as some apparel departments.

However, commission workers are subjected to pressure because earnings are reduced during low-sales periods. As a result, employees may have difficulty budgeting for their living expenses. For this reason, many salespeople are on a **drawing account.** They "draw" or take a set amount each payday regardless of their sales. This "draw" is subtracted from the total commission earned. If the amount is below what the salesperson should receive, that person receives the difference. When salespeople overdraw (take more than they earn), the excess amount is deducted the next month.

Quota Bonus

Salespeople must meet quota set by management

In this system salespeople are paid according to quotas set by management, and each salesperson is expected to meet a certain quota. A predetermined percentage (bonus) is paid on all sales above the established quota. For example, if the sales quota is set at $6,000 and the salesperson has made sales totaling $8,000, he or she will be entitled to a bonus based on $2,000. J. L. Hudson uses a base pay formulated on selling goals, with compensation paid for exceeding a set goal. This system reduces selling costs while providing incentives. The system is more flexible than straight commission because individual selling goals can be adjusted.

Additional Compensation Plans

In order to motivate workers and reduce turnover, many firms have adopted plans known as **profit sharing, stock options,** and **salary supplements.** Whereas some companies offer these incentives only to management, others include all workers who are employed beyond a probationary period.

Profit Sharing. In this plan the employee is given an opportunity to share in the success (profits) of the firm. A certain percentage of the profits is distributed to employees according to their salary levels. Some large retailers, such as Sears, Roebuck and Company, offer profit sharing to their employees. This plan is said to keep labor turnover to a minimum. Indeed, as a result of profit-sharing accumulations over long periods of employment, many of Sears' employees have retired with large sums of money.

Stock Option Plans. Some firms allow employees to buy company stock at inside prices, that is, prices that are lower than the market value of the stock. These investments have generally been lucrative and have served to motivate workers.

Salary Supplements.   In order to increase the sales of a particular type of merchandise, salespeople are sometimes offered additional money or prizes. The terms **spiffs** and **PMs** (premium, prize, or **push money**) are used to identify this practice. The extra commissions are sometimes paid for by manufacturers. Prizes may consist of vacations or high-ticket merchandise.

Establishing and Managing Fringe Benefits

Fringe benefits add to job attractiveness

The human resource department is also responsible for the management of fringe benefits, or employee services. Fringe benefits involve the indirect payments that workers receive, such as health insurance, paid vacations, sick leave, retirement plans, employee discounts, employee services, credit unions, and the like (Figure 6-17). These benefits add to the attraction of the job and help maintain good employee morale.

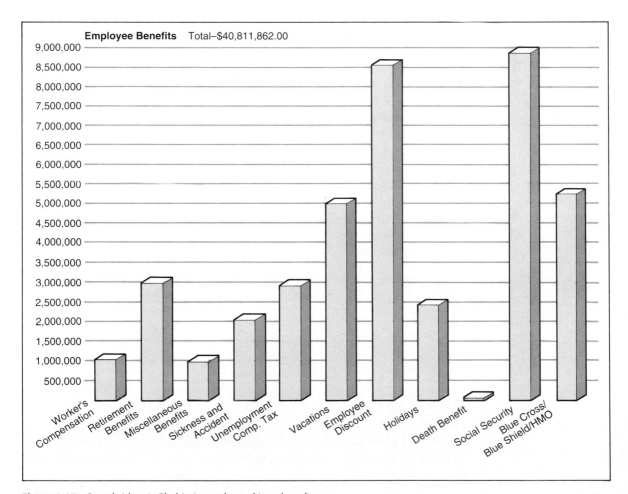

Figure 6-17   Strawbridge & Clothier's employee fringe benefits.

Insurance Plans

Some form of dental, medical, and/or hospital plan is offered to all full-time employees. Some retailers pay the entire cost of these plans, whereas others share the costs with the employee. Some retailers allow medical coverage to be offered to part-time regulars.

Retirement Plans

Retirement benefits (pension plans) are also available as a fringe benefit. Pension plans are benefits that help develop company loyalty, motivate the worker, and reduce personnel turnover. A variety of pension plans are offered by large retailers. Some are paid entirely by the company and others are funded jointly by the firm and its employees. Some are transferable, whereas others terminate when employees leave the firm. A good plan has a tendency to "lock" the employee into staying with the company, thereby reducing labor turnover.

Credit Unions

Credit unions operate as banks and give employees an opportunity to save or borrow money at favorable interest rates.

Discounts For Employees

Employees can buy at the store for less

Many retailers offer their employees reductions from regular store prices. The usual discounts run from 10 percent to 30 percent of the selling price and are supposed to act as incentives for better employee performance. Because discounting for employees is so prevalent, however, it is difficult to judge its long-term effect on employee morale.

Employee Services

Some firms include miscellaneous services to attract desirable workers. Examples are recreational facilities, eating places, attractive lounges, professional counseling, and medical departments.

Additional options some retailers offer are

Flex-time, employees can choose their working hours.

Flex-place, employees can work in the most convenient retail outlet.

Flex-benefits, "Cafeteria Plan," employees can select their own fringe benefit combination from a list of offerings such as enhanced medical coverage or extra vacation time.

PRACTITIONER'S CORNER

What follows is the summary of an interview with James O'Beirne, operations manager of a suburban Abraham & Straus department store. Mr. O'Beirne has been in store management for more than ten years, with prior experience as a buyer.

1. Mr. O'Beirne feels that future growth in retailing lies with large department stores that offer a wide variety of merchandise.

2. There are many career opportunities for young people who like to work in department stores. Although good training is available, candidates must be prepared to work hard. The key to success is to spend sufficient time on the job and to become one of the team. If a worker is involved in merchandise or operations, he or she has excellent advancement opportunities.

3. Career paths in merchandising generally begin with employment as a trainee during busy seasons such as Christmas or as assistant department manager assigned to a department manager. The trainee or assistant manager usually remains in this position for about two years. After satisfactory evaluation based on sales performance, he or she may be promoted to assistant buyer; after a few more years, to Buyer.

4. The career path in operations usually begins with an assignment as operations assistant; then, on to another sales supporting area, perhaps as a manager, for example, receiving manager. It's also possible to start in the Security Division and move on to operations. Although work in both areas

can be rewarding, merchandising offers more opportunities because there are more jobs available in that area.

5. Training in merchandising and operations may take place in a classroom or on the floor working with a department or operations manager. The managers evaluate trainee performance.

6. In most stores, videos and films are part of the training process.

7. During the last ten years, managers have been exposed to many technological advances. For example, information is available almost instantaneously from fax machines, computerized registers, scanning equipment, and excetara. Because reports are transmitted so quickly from the home office, all store managers have the same information at the same time. Conference telephone calls enable several people to "meet" over long distances. In addition, mail can be sent and received via a computer.

8. Most merchandise is vendor marked or is marked at distribution centers. Very little re-marking is done. Discounts and markdowns are computed at cash registers.

9. Employees receive discounts on all merchandise.

10. Retailing is rewarding and not boring; each day brings new experiences.

COMMUNICATION

Communicating with employees is essential for successful retail management.

Effective interaction between employees and management helps employees understand store objectives, policies, and employee opportunities. On the other hand, communication gives management a means for recognizing the wants and needs of its employees and customers.

Communication channels are vertical and horizontal

Commonly used channels of communication are downward vertical, upward vertical, and horizontal. Most organizations depend on the line of command for communications, such as managers sending messages to subordinates (downward vertical). When messages originate with employees and progress to management levels, the channel is known as upward vertical. Horizontal communication is passed along on the same level (managers to managers, salespeople to salespeople, etc.).

Informal and Formal Communication

Communication methods are informal and formal

The methods used to communicate through the channels are either informal or formal. **Informal communication** is the use of vertical and horizontal lines for verbal communication. This system has its limitations because messages may be misunderstood or deliberately distorted.

FILENE'S ECHO

5 FILENE'S FIVE

1. **GREET** the customer
2. **DETERMINE** the customer's needs
3. **SELL** merchandise features and benefits
4. **SUGGEST** multiple/alternative sales
5. **CLOSE** the sale nicely

Filene's helps employees understand store objectives by using written communications.

An unofficial communication network is referred to as a **grapevine.** (See Figure 6-18.) Grapevines interweave throughout the firm and are speedy. Not surprisingly, messages usually travel faster through them than through official channels. Sometimes the grapevine is used deliberately to convey messages that management prefers to keep unofficial.

Unfortunately, some messages are distorted by the time they reach the end of the line. Also, grapevines often spread rumors, some of which are harmful to employee morale.

Formal communication

It is essential for management to kill damaging rumors before they get out of hand. Management must keep the upward and downward channels open so that employee reactions to policy and change are known and understood.

Formal communication involves the use of employee handbooks, suggestion systems, house organs, bulletins, and meetings.

Handbooks are distributed to new employees by most large retailers. They generally contain information about the company's history, wages and hours of work, employee benefits and services, company policies and rules, and the union contract (if there is one).

A suggestion system is a formal way to encourage communication upward through the firm. Using this method, employees have an opportunity to suggest

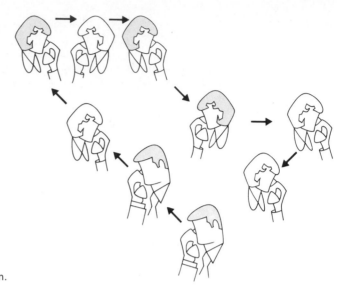

Figure 6-18 The grapevine is an informal means of communication.

ways to improve or change conditions. This type of communication develops loyalty and helps build employee morale. Some firms go further by rewarding employees for useful suggestions. Suggestion systems should give prompt feedback to all employees who submit suggestions.

A house organ may take the form of a newspaper, magazine, or store newsletter. It generally contains news about the store, its operations, and employees and their families. It provides information about employee promotions and retirements, and often includes letters written by employees. The publication serves as a vehicle for good internal relations and keeps employees abreast of store news.

General meetings are effective face-to-face communication

Bulletins are issued when important information needs to be announced quickly. They are a fast way of informing employees of some activity or change.

General meetings are effective for face-to-face communication. In most large retail firms, however, it is difficult to find a time when all employees are available.

LABOR AND THE LAW

Unions—another responsibility of the personnel department

Another responsibility of the personnel department is dealing with organized labor. The growth of unions in the retail industry has been slow. Until recently only a small percentage of salespeople were organized. Union membership was confined essentially to nonselling personnel, such as warehouse workers, truck drivers, and maintenance employees.

To some extent, sales personnel have been reluctant to join unions because they are not anxious to have their wages reduced by union dues, while part-time workers do not view their jobs as careers. Furthermore, salespeople do not view themselves as blue-collar workers; they tend to identify themselves as white-collar workers aspiring to management positions. However, the current trend is toward unions.

At present, most large supermarkets are unionized, most often with the Retail Clerks International Association. Macy's Northeast is a large department store that is unionized.

The efforts of unions in the retailing industry are similar to those in other industries. They strive for better working conditions, more fringe benefits, jobs security, more objective criteria for promotion and salary increases, and the like. Unions and retail firms have worked together to help retailers maintain ample employee coverage to match traffic peaks. For example, supermarkets and other firms have developed fragmented work shifts to keep staff levels matched to busy hours. As a result, a variety of "flextime schedules" (a departure from the traditional approach to scheduling employees' work weeks) has come about. One such example allows employees to start at a different time each day for the same number of given hours a day. In another case, employees are permitted to vary the number of hours worked in a day as long as they total the expected number of hours per week. Furthermore, employees may also elect to work a compressed work week, that is, to work enough hours some days to complete their requirement in less than five days and take a day off.

The personnel department is involved with union negotiations, employee grievances, and the monitoring of rules and union contract guidelines.

NEW TERMS

application form	honesty tests
blind ad	informal communication
brood hen and chick	internship program
cafeteria plan	job analysis
centralization	job description
decentralization	job rotation
discharged	job specification
drawing account	job transfer
equal store	layoff
flex-time	lie detector
flex-place	line-and-staff organization chart
flex-benefits	line organization chart
formal communication	line position
grapevine	Mazur plan

on-the-job training

open ad

organization chart

orientation training

performance appraisal

PM

polygraph instrument

profit sharing

promotion

push money

rail interview

salary supplement

separate-unit concept

shopper's report

spiff

staff position

stock option

vestibule training

CHAPTER HIGHLIGHTS

1. The prime objective of every retailer is to be successful. Successful retailers satisfy the wants and needs of their customers and should have an understanding of management principles.

2. The management principles that can assist the retailer in developing a sound structure are authority and responsibility, unit of command, span of control, division of work, and chain of command.

3. Organizational structures develop as companies grow. In small firms with few employees, no formal structure is needed. When many workers are involved, a more formal organization is required.

4. Line-and-staff positions are shown on organization charts. Line charts show each worker's position with relation to his or her immediate superior. Line-and-staff charts combine the lines of delegated authority with specialists (staff) who act as consultants. Depending on the size of the firm, charts can be simple or complex. The organization chart for small independent retailers is simple. Employers carry out many functions in small firms.

5. Many department stores are organized according to the functions their employees perform. The Mazur plan divides all retail store activities into four major areas: merchandising, publicity, store management, and control. With adjustment and tailoring, the basic Mazur plan can be applied to most department and individual stores.

6. Basically, there are three approaches to branch store organization. They are the "brood hen and chick" approach, the separate unit, and the equal-store concept.

7. In chains, centralization and control of the major functions are performed through a home office. There are more divisions in chain organizations than in department stores. The additional divisions include real estate, warehousing, personnel and transportation. The chain organization is one of the most efficient, economical retailing systems yet devised.

8. Trends indicate an increase in decentralization among some large retail chains, whereas others have become more centralized. Regional decentralization is a combination of both centralization and decentralization.

9. Personnel management is composed of the following activities: recruitment and hiring, training and retraining, transfers, promotion and discharge, performance appraisal, wage and compensation scales, and fringe benefits.

10. Recruitment involves solicitation of job applicants. Sources of new personnel exist both within the firm and outside it (employment agencies, schools, advertisements).

11. The selection process includes job analyses, job descriptions, application blanks, interviews, and testing. After selection, employees often undergo training.

12. Performance appraisal used in transfer, promotion, and discharge includes observation and written reports.

13. Employee fringe benefits include insurance and retirement plans, credit unions, and employee discounts.

14. Compensation plans include a guaranteed annual wage, straight salary, hourly wage, straight salary plus commission, salary plus bonus, straight commission, and quota bonus.

15. In order to reduce labor turnover and motivate workers, many firms adopt profit sharing, stock option plans, and salary supplements.

16. Effective communication helps employees understand store objectives, policies, and employee opportunities.

17. Channels of communication are vertical (upward and downward) and horizontal. The methods used to communicate through channels may be formal or informal. An unofficial communication network is referred to as a grapevine. Sometimes grapevines are used to convey messages that management prefers to keep unofficial. Formal communication involves the use of handbooks, suggestion systems, house organs, bulletins, and meetings.

18. Until recently retail sales personnel were reluctant to join unions. The efforts of retail unions are similar to those in other industries, involving better working conditions, increased fringe benefits, and job security. As a result, the human resource department must sometimes deal with unions.

REVIEW QUESTIONS

1. Why is it important for retail firms to develop organization charts?
2. Explain the four functions associated with the Mazur plan.
3. What are the major differences between centralization and decentralization?
4. What are the main activities of the personnel department?

5. How does the training of new, inexperienced employees differ from the retraining of older, experienced workers?
6. Which methods of compensation are most motivating for the salesperson? Explain.
7. List three examples of a horizontal channel of communication in a department store.

DISCUSSION QUESTIONS

1. How is confusion minimized when a retail firm follows the principle of unity of command? What is the main consequence of a violation of the principle of span of control?
2. Why do retailers need both line-and-staff personnel?
3. How can effective performance evaluation help both employees and management?
4. What is the rationale for retailers offering fringe benefits that are not required by law?
5. How will the growth of unionization affect communication between store managers and employees?
6. How can effective communication help retailers carry out their objectives?

CASE 1

His Job—Her Job

A large variety store chain has found that there are many problems associated with its plan to transfer promising executives to another branch in a different geographic location. To a large extent, this is due to the increased number of women in the work force. The fact is that people who are happy in their own jobs are not interested in their spouse's relocating without some assurance of a good job for themselves as well.

In the case of one particularly talented executive who is willing to transfer, his wife's job status has also become pertinent. Not only is her job important to her, but the couple recognizes that her income is vital to the family's budget.

At first the personnel director tried to deal with the problem by providing lists of employment agencies at the new location, tips on handling job interviews, and the like. The couple did not consider these suggestions adequate and requested a position for the wife within the chain organization at the new location.

Unfortunately, the personnel director cannot offer a job to the wife because of the chain's rule against nepotism, that is, a restriction on husbands, wives, or other family members working for the firm at the same time. However, the couple in this case has asked that the rule be waived so that the transfer can be achieved.

a. If you were the personnel director, what action would you take?
b. What type of program might be developed to help with problems like this one in the future? List and explain some of the details.

CASE 2

Preventing Job Dissatisfaction

WANTED: Well-educated, highly organized self-starter to work long hours in a job with relatively low pay, no clear career path, ambiguous reporting relationships, unclear performance objectives, and little opportunity for personal growth.

Not interested, you say? Yet this is the way some people describe the job of a retail store manager. Why is it that some managers grow dissatisfied with their jobs, perform poorly, and leave their companies, whereas others enjoy their work, stay with their companies, and contribute to the success of the businesses they work for?

The success or failure of a retail chain depends on the skill and productivity of the store manager. The importance of the store manager's role, together with the hidden costs of high employee turnover, have prompted some researchers to look for the key factors that contribute to job satisfaction among retail store managers.

Most of the current research on job satisfaction is based on work done by psychologist Frederick Herzberg.* Herzberg started with the belief that an individual has two distinct sets of needs: the first is a set of lower-level needs to avoid hunger, pain, and similar deprivation; the second is a set of higher-level needs for psychological growth.

In the late 1950s, Herzberg and his associates wanted to see how this concept applied in the workplace. They interviewed 100 accountants and engineers who

*Frederick Herzberg, Bernard Mausner, and Barbara B. Snyderman, *The Motivation to Work*, 2nd ed. (New York: John Wiley & Sons, 1959) and Frederick Herzberg, *Work and the Nature of Man* (Cleveland: World, 1966).

worked in and around Pittsburgh, Pennsylvania. They asked each person to describe situations in their work that made them feel more satisfied and situations or events that made them feel less satisfied.

The survey revealed two distinct groups of job factors. Herzberg called one group of factors *motivators,* because they appeared to motivate the employees to work harder and to try to achieve peak performance. Motivators included job factors such as recognition of one's accomplishments, enjoyment of the work itself, a sense of achievement, and opportunities for growth.

The second group, called *hygiene* or *maintenance factors,* included such factors as pay, working conditions, company policies, and so on. These factors tended to be external to the work itself. They were frequently stated as causes of dissatisfaction, but rarely listed as causing positive job satisfaction.

What conclusions can be drawn from Herzberg's findings? The hygiene factors are important in preventing job dissatisfaction. If salaries and benefits are too low, if working conditions are inadequate, if company policies are cumbersome or unfair, employees will be discontent. But even if all these hygiene factors are adequate, employees still may not be motivated to peak performance. By themselves, the hygiene factors do not create a high level of job satisfaction or job performance. Hygiene factors and motivators must exist together to create a work environment in which employees can satisfy their needs for growth and fulfillment.

Following Herzberg's lead, most of the people who have studied job satisfaction have assumed the existence of two separate types of job satisfaction. *Intrinsic job satisfaction* is related to the nature of the job itself and the opportunities for growth and accomplishment. *Extrinsic job satisfaction* comes from factors that are related to the job, but external to the actual work, such as pay, job security, or working conditions.

In one study that focused specifically on job satisfaction among retail store managers, George H. Lucas, Jr., attempted to identify the relationships among intrinsic job satisfaction, extrinsic job satisfaction, quality of performance, and turnover.* Lucas mailed a questionnaire to 294 store managers employed by a national retail chain. The questionnaire asked about satisfaction with the job itself, as well as with external factors such as pay, benefits, and working conditions. It also asked managers to evaluate their own competency at the job and to provide information about such personal characteristics as age, tenure in the job, educational level, and inclination to leave the organization. Information provided by the store managers was compared with the performance evaluation forms prepared by their supervisors.

One of Lucas's key findings was that the store managers' self-evaluation of their own competency was closely related to their intrinsic job satisfaction. In other

---

*George H. Lucas, Jr., "The Relationships Between Job Attitudes, Personal Characteristics, and Job Outcomes: A Study of Retail Store Managers," *Journal of Retailing,* **61** (Spring 1985), pp. 35–60.

words, a manager who felt he or she was doing key tasks well was likely to be highly satisfied with the job. Lucas concludes that retailers can enhance job satisfaction by providing good initial training programs and ongoing development programs for store managers.

The length of time a store manager had been in the job was strongly related to the supervisor's performance rating. That is, a manager who had been in the job for a relatively long time was most likely to be doing well. Lucas concludes that the way to ensure peak performance from store managers is to concentrate on factors that will reduce turnover. He proposed that retailers tie managers' pay closely to their performance, thus increasing extrinsic job satisfaction. He also advises efforts to increase the managers' intrinsic job satisfaction, by establishing open communications between store managers and their supervisors and by trying to structure the managers' job better and make it more rewarding.

a. What factors have the most impact on your level of satisfaction with a job? Are they hygiene factors or motivators?

b. In the retail chain that Lucas studied, what measures would you propose to increase store managers' intrinsic job satisfaction?

c. Would you expect store managers to have higher job satisfaction in a centralized or decentralized organization. Why?

d. Most businesses still tend to base their management policies on the assumption that extrinsic rewards are the most important factors in employee motivation. Why?

REFERENCES

BANIK, J. A. "Communication—The Marketing Approach to Communicating with Employees." *Personnel Journal*, (October 1985), pp. 62, 67, 68.

BARMASH, I. "How They Plan." *Stores*, **65** (August 1983), pp. 7–15.

CAMENITI, S. "What Ails Retailing." *Fortune* (January 30, 1989), pp. 61–63.

PEPPER, C. B. "Fast Forward." *Business Month* (February 1989), pp. 25–30.

"Rewards for Collectors: Salary vs. Incentives." *Stores* (April 1989), p. 28.

APPENDIX A

Individual Trainee Evaluation

TRAINEE NAME: _____

DEPARTMENT NAME/NUMBER: _____

DATE STARTED IN DEPARTMENT: _____

DATE OBJECTIVES SET: _____
(Within two weeks after joining department)

BUYER: _____ EXT: _____

REVIEW DATE: _____
(Four months after joining department)

QUESTIONS ON SETTING OBJECTIVES OR EVALUATING THE TRAINEE SHOULD BE DIRECTED TO _____, EXTENSION _____.

cc: (Cover sheet and objectives)
    Divisional Merchandise Manager
    Manager, Manpower Planning
cc: (Completed review)
    Manager, Manpower Planning

Section I

	Points Assigned	Points Earned
A. Objective: Communications		
1. Relate counts on basic, non-basic and clearance merchandise to stores monthly.	_____	_____
2. Maintain a product description book, reviewed monthly.	_____	_____

Section II (To be filled in by department manager after four months)

How do you rate the trainee's overall progress as a Management Trainee? *(Score your evaluation according to this scale for each item.)*

Unsatisfactory 0–5	High 8–9
Satisfactory 6–7	Excellent 10

                                                                         Points Earned

A. Planning
Keep in mind the opportunities you have given the trainee to plan. Did he/she draw on the knowledge of the people around in planning? Did he/she come reasonably close to reaching the established objectives, or were they unrealistic?   _____

Explain rating: _____

_____

_____

_____

_____

Section III *(To be filled in by divisional manager after four months)*

A. Comments

_____

_____

_____

_____

_____

_____

_____

_____

B. Potential
What is the next step ahead for this individual and doe he/she have further potential beyond the next step? If so, outline:

_____

_____

_____

An individual trainee evaluation form used by Dayton's. (Reproduced by permission of Dayton's.)

APPENDIX B

Dayton's Management Trainee Evaluation

NAME _____
TRAINEE'S NAME _____
STORE _____   DEPT. _____
EVALUATION PERIOD: FROM ____   TO _____

Part I: Management Traits

Rate the following factors by circling the letter which indicates the most accurate appraisal of the trainee's behavior:

1. **Initiative**
   a. Constantly searches for improved methods; suggests new concepts and procedures.
   b. Resourceful; usually alert to opportunities for improvement.
   c. Makes occasional suggestions for improvement. Usually does the same thing every day.
   d. Not an independent thinker. Rarely initiates innovative ideas.
2. **Planning**
   a. Plans work to avoid difficulties. Establishes excellent priorities.
   b. Sets good priorities. Usually plans well enough to prevent major problems.
   c. Cannot always distinguish important from unimportant. Difficulties sometimes arise through lack of planning.
   d. Firefighter; no predetermined plan or program to accomplish tasks effectively.

Directions
Parts II, III, IV, V, VI

Indicate your judgment of the trainee's performance by checking the appropriate box for each item. Please use this scale:

    4 = Excellent, reflects superior performance.
    3 = Very good, reflects highly competent performance.
    2 = Good, reflects average performance.
    1 = Adequate, reflects minimally acceptable performance.
    0 = Unsatisfactory, reflects substandard performance.

Part II: Selling Skills	4	3	2	1	0
1. Completes sales documents accurately and legibly.					
2. Greets customers promptly and positively.					
3. Seeks understanding of customer wants.					
4. Directs customer interest toward appropriate merchandise.					

Part III: Management Skills					
1. Accepts and carries out responsibility as well as authority.					
2. Demonstrates willingness to delegate authority as well as responsibility.					
3. Follows through on all tasks previously mastered with minimum supervision.					

Part IV: Operational Skills	4	3	2	1	0

1. Learned location of merchandise, by department, through-out store.
2. Exhibits understanding and acceptance of merchandise trend concepts.
3. Demonstrates dedication to profitable operation.

Part V: Personnel Skills

1. Demonstrates ability to train and supervise all personnel in the store.
2. Eager to know aspects of the job of each employee.
3. Demonstrates ability to plan effective work schedules.

Part VI: Personality

1. Demonstrates a pleasant, businesslike attitude toward both customers and co-workers.
2. Exhibits respect and courtesy toward others.
3. Exercises patience in dealing with customers and coworkers.

Dayton's management trainee evaluation form. (Reproduced by permission of Dayton's.)

APPENDIX C

Management Training Program Evaluation

NAME _____

Please complete the attached evaluation of your branch store training in detail. Rate each question according to the following guidelines and explain your answer fully and completely.

1 = UNSATISFACTORY
2 = MARGINAL
3 = AVERAGE
4 = VERY GOOD
5 = SUPERIOR

(To be completed by the trainee).

Evaluate your branch store experience:

1. Consider: quality and quantity of time spent with you; willingness to teach; clarity of instruction; thoroughness of instruction.

2. Consider: follow-up and discussions of your required activities; constructive suggestions and help given to enable you to accomplish all your activities; constructive criticism given.

3. Consider: observed strengths and weaknesses of your Sales Manager; quality and quantity of work produced; organizational skills; competence in human relations; effect of the above factors on you and your performance.

4. Consider: exposure received to various duties and responsibilities; exposure to other managers; Store Manager, Group Manager, other departments.

5. Additional comments.

A form used by trainees to evaluate the store's management training program. (Reproduced by permission of Dayton's.)

Chapter 7

Store Location

After completing this chapter, you should be able to:

- Identify the reasons why store location is important.
- List the factors that determine the location of a store.
- List the six categories of retail locations.
- Identify the factors that retailers consider when choosing a site.
- Discuss the advantages and disadvantages of buying or renting a retail outlet.
- Identify trends in store location.

In the previous two chapters you learned about the ways in which retail stores are organized and staffed. You saw that planning is essential to the development of sound business procedures, and that lines of organization depend on the type of retail outlet under consideration. It was pointed out, however, that no organizational plan is effective without the involvement of trained personnel.

Stores usually locate according to carefully developed plans

In this chapter we turn our attention to the location of retail stores. Have you ever wondered why supermarkets are usually surrounded by a variety of small stores? Or why several department stores frequently occupy space close to one another? There are logical reasons for these patterns, and they emerge from carefully developed plans. In fact, for large stores these plans are so elaborate that computers are often used to analyze information and make decisions. In this chapter we will examine the various aspects of store location.

THE IMPORTANCE OF STORE LOCATION

Some retailers feel that the location of a store is the most crucial factor in determining the store's success. These people reason that despite the importance of prices, services, and store features, the specific location of the store is its main attraction to consumers. Although their contention is debatable, no knowledgeable retailer denies the significance of location. Let's see why this is so.

Return on Investment

Since the opening of a store usually requires a substantial initial investment, the retailer seeks a location that will return that investment within a reasonable time. Even starting a small store can cost many thousands of dollars, while department stores and other large retail organizations entail investments of millions of dollars. Since investment funds are either borrowed or accumulated, or both, it is crucial that a store's location provide the new owner with a good chance of recouping that money.

The Need for Profits

Needless to say, retail businesses, like any other type of business, must show profits. In the case of retailing, however, the extent of those profits depends in large measure on the store's location. From this point of view, for example, opening a store to sell maternity clothes in a fast-growing community with many young couples makes good business sense, while starting a similar enterprise in a stable, older area does not.

Convenience to Consumers

Since consumers require a variety of products, they need convenient access to stores that satisfy those requirements. In addition, the locations of these stores should meet their particular shopping needs. For example, establishments like food, drug, and dry cleaning stores that sell convenience items and services should be within easy reach of the shopper. This is so because people make frequent trips to such stores and expect them to be close to their home or place of business. On the other hand, consumers are willing to travel longer distances for less frequently purchased items (shopping goods), such as clothing, appliances, and furniture. As a result, department, specialty, and discount stores that sell such merchandise are often located farther away. Frequently, too, several department stores are located close to each other in order to attract more customers.

DECISION FACTORS IN STORE LOCATION

Definition of a trading area

Before discussing the factors that determine the location of a store, we must identify the types of areas in which stores are located. The term that is most frequently used to describe a store's customer potential is **trading area.** Basically, a trading area is a geographic section from which a store draws the bulk of its customers. For stores that sell convenience items, the area might encompass a few city streets; in a suburban setting, it might include several distinct residential developments; in a rural district, it could encompass several square miles. On the other hand, the trading area for larger stores is usually much greater. For example, Filene's department store in Boston attracts customers from the entire Boston metropolitan area as well as from outside of the state. The Metrocenter in Phoenix, a well-known shopping center, caters to consumers from the newly developed suburban areas surrounding Phoenix as well as from the sunbelt city itself. It follows, then, that retailers that are planning new stores must select locations with a clear understanding of the extent of their trading area. Once this is understood, the retailer is ready to consider the factors that determine the store's location.

The Population of the Trading Area

Current Population Figures

Obviously, the trading area should contain a sufficient number of potential customers to satisfy the new store's planned sales. Population counts can be secured from municipalities, chambers of commerce, and trade associations. The federal government takes a population census every ten years (the last one was done in 1990), and those figures are valuable for planning purposes. Of course, supplemental local and regional data should be used when a community's census information is no longer reliable.

Filene's trading area includes Boston residents as well as consumers from outlying areas. *Courtesy:* Filene's.

Income Levels and Occupations in the Trading Area

A close look at the people in the trading area

Every effort should be made to determine the income levels and occupational clusters in the trading area. Opening a specialty store selling high-priced jewelry in an essentially working-class district would be unwise. Similar situations can be imagined with regard to low-priced merchandise. Information about income levels and occupations can be secured from census reports and local banks.

Seasonal Changes, Trading Area Business, and Industry

Most retail firms depend on year-round sales to sustain their revenues. Consequently, they must avoid locating in areas that cater mostly to tourists and vacationers. On the other hand, quite a few retailers sustain themselves on revenues that come in during short periods of each year. These firms generally operate in resort areas that attract skiers, boat enthusiasts, sightseers, and the like. These retailers might close their doors during off-peak months, or reduce their stock accordingly.

The importance of business and industry in a trading area

Another important consideration is the business and industrial composition of the trading area. A community that depends on one industry for its sustenance is subject to that industry's problems. So are the retailers who serve that area. A case in point is the Texas oil industry, which experienced terrible reverses in the 1980s. As a result of high unemployment resulting from lowered oil prices, local retailers suffered greatly. That experience has been duplicated elsewhere and has caused new retail businesses to seek more industrially diversified trading areas.

Another example of the adverse impact of industrial reverses on retailers occurred in the early 1980s and 1990s. As a result of severely reduced demand for automobiles, car manufacturers laid off large numbers of workers and even closed plants. This had the "ripple effect" of closing many retail car dealerships and damaging a variety of stores that depended on car workers' patronage.

Age Groups—Sexual Composition of the Trading Area

Singles, young marrieds, senior citizens, etc.

To a large extent, success in a trading area is tied to the number of consumers in particular age groups. Thus, it is important that the new retailer consider such age-related statistics as the numbers of singles, young marrieds, families whose children no longer live at home, senior citizens, and teenagers living in the trading area. The types of merchandise carried and the selling strategies employed are obviously tied to the needs and lifestyles of these groups.

The retailer who intends to sell primarily or exclusively to members of one sex must know the approximate proportion of that population in the trading area. In addition, a breakdown of the data by age within each sex category helps the retailer gauge the potential market. These data can be secured from census reports.

Ethnic, Religious, and Special Consumer Groups

As indicated earlier, our society contains many distinct ethnic and religious groups. Consequently, retailers must know whether consumers in those groups have special needs that reflect their cultures and religious practices. For example,

The elderly are frequent buyers of drugs and prescriptions.
Courtesy: Giant Food Inc.

the dress requirements of the Pennsylvania Amish differ radically from those of California's Chicanos. In the same vein, the food preferences of Chinese Americans are quite unlike those of other ethnic groups in our country.

Special consumer groups

Special consumer groups, such as college youth, gays, and the handicapped, are also found in communities. To a large extent, these groups have particular buying needs that can be turned into profitable sales by sensitive and perceptive retailers.

Apartments versus Homes

Some trading areas consist largely of homes, others of apartments, and still others of a combination of the two. Since the needs of homeowners differ to some extent from those of apartment dwellers, retail location planning should consider the mix of dwellings in the trading area.

Population Dynamics

Growth, decline, and constancy of trading area populations

Having considered the basic population characteristics of a trading area, the retailer must determine whether the population is expected to grow, decline, or remain constant. This is important for two reasons: (1) because it enables the merchant to estimate short-range sales (perhaps one to three years) and (2) because it is a predictor of long-range business possibilities. Obviously, a trading area with a growing population presents a radically different profit potential than a stable or declining one.

Socioeconomic Conditions in the Trading Area

Employment and Unemployment

Employment levels affect retailing

As indicated earlier, the extent of business and industry in a trading area is an important consideration in locating a retail outlet. Associated with this factor is the normal level of employment provided by firms in the area. Needless to say, retailing flourishes best where employment is steady. The new retailer, then, should examine the employment history of the area, using census data, state labor department reports, and chamber of commerce statistics.

The Vitality of the Trading Area

Some communities are active places, while others are not. Some areas boast fine schools, socially conscious trade associations, frequent community events, and even tourist attractions. Other areas show few signs of vitality and poor interrelationships among community groups. It should be obvious that the retailer with a choice of location will opt for the more dynamic community, expecting (correctly) that that community will provide a more favorable setting for retail businesses.

An example of the impact of a changing neighborhood on retailing is the establishment by Merry-Go-Round, a specialty clothing chain, of its flagship store in New York City's Empire State Building. As lower-priced discount stores left the area, they were replaced by more upscale retailers. The move by Merry-Go-Round, an upscaler, signaled the importance it attached to location as a symbol of retail image.

A very interesting development relating to store location occurred in 1989 when three builders—Melvin Simon & Associates, Silverstein Properties, Inc., and Zeckendorf Company—opened a retail center in midtown Manhattan, New York City. Containing an anchor department store, Abraham & Straus, and called A&S Plaza, the project has been described by some as a suburban center in an urban area.

Located close to the very successful Macy's store in Herald Square, and including 125 specialty retailers such as Barnes & Noble and The Limited, the center has targeted a largely middle-class group as its customer base. Its proximity to a large work force and its accessibility by mass transit are factors that induced the retailers to participate.

A negative note, however, has been sounded by some retail analysts about A&S Plaza's chances for success. Citing the closing of the now defunct Gimbel's and Korvette department stores (both had been in the A&S Plaza area), they reason that only a successful merchandise strategy, outstanding service, and tight security can overcome the problems experienced there by other retailers. In other words, location *plus* other considerations determine success.

Laws That Affect Retailers

The retailer seeking a new location should check local and state laws that affect retail enterprises. These laws generally refer to taxes: income, sales, property, occupancy, and so forth; credit regulations, such as maximum interest rates that may be charged on customers' past-due accounts; license requirements; and store business hours. When the trading area encompasses communities in more than one state, these items must be checked carefully for their impact on sales, expenses, and profits.

Traffic Considerations

Stores depend on smooth traffic flow

You have already learned that some types of retail outlets, such as convenience stores, are located close to their potential customers. On the other hand, consumers are willing to travel to other types of retail stores, such as warehouse outlets and combination stores. Nevertheless, whether they are shopping on foot, by car, by bus, or by rail, consumers should be able to reach their destination without great inconvenience. When cars are involved, highways and access roads should service customers without frequent bumper-to-bumper tie-ups.

A retail store should also be located a reasonable distance from its suppliers. This allows the store to restock items quickly for the convenience of customers.

Referring to decision factors in store location, Melvin Simon, a major shopping mall developer, believes that "Traffic isn't the only tangible in a community center's success. Our researchers also identify the number of households in a trade area, the number of persons per household, the average household income, the consumers' goods buying potential, and the average age and educational levels in an area."[1]

Miscellaneous Socioeconomic Considerations

Several other factors affect the location of a retail store. Among them are the following.

Local attractions, adequate parking, banks, police and fire protection, advertising outlets

1. Local attractions like museums and parks often bring people from outside the trading area to the area's retail outlets.
2. Parking space should be adequate. Potential customers are turned off by their inability to park comfortably and quickly.
3. The trading area or its vicinity should contain banks that welcome retail businesses. Since retailers borrow funds from time to time, they need bankers with an appreciation of retailers' needs.
4. A trading area should provide satisfactory police and fire protection. In some cases private guards and even guard dogs must be employed to augment local police forces. In such instances the cost of the additional protection is an added expense for the retailer.
5. Since many retailers advertise on a regular basis, the community and surrounding communities should contain adequate advertising outlets. These media might include local and regional newspapers, radio, television, public vehicles (buses and trains), and local magazines.
6. A store's location can influence its merchandising mix. For example, several of J. C. Penney's Los Angeles stores, located in areas with significant Hispanic populations, carry goods like christening outfits and *guayaberas* ("wedding shirts") to meet their customers' needs. The chain also caters to Hispanic shoppers by offering bilingual service, Spanish-speaking telephone operators, and Spanish-printed credit applications.

Competition

Assessing the competition

Another factor to consider in locating a store is the nature and extent of competing outlets. The following matters should be studied.

1. The number and types of competing stores. If the trading area already contains a sufficient number of such stores, it may be unwise to open a new one.

[1] *Inside Retailing,* September 12, 1988, p. 4.

2. The extent of chain ownership among competitors. This is important to know because of the drawing power and financial strength of chains.

3. The existence of shopping facilities in the trading area that attract large segments of the trading area's population. If the new retail outlet cannot be located in those facilities, it must be prepared to do business with smaller groups of people.

4. The possibility that existing stores may try to destroy the new store's chances of success by underselling and developing irresistible sales promotions. Existing stores are sometimes willing to spend substantial sums to stifle new competition.

Geographic Concentration of Stores

A chain may limit store operations to one section of the country so that they are close to the main office and central distribution center. Consumer preferences are well known, and the chain has a clearly defined reputation.

Market Saturation

A company may locate a number of stores strategically in a metropolitan area, where the consumer has to drive no further than 15 to 20 minutes to reach one. K mart and Radio Shack are good examples of this strategy.

Out-of-the-Way Locations

Retailers sometimes select less than perfect locations purposely, even when there are inferior traffic patterns and no shopping centers nearby. Obviously, these sites offer more attractive rental charges. An example of this thinking is the Lee Wards Craft Company, whose stores draw customers because of the specific type of merchandise they carry (and which very few other stores sell).

Impact Fees

Impact fees are charged to developers

Impact fees are costs imposed on shopping center developers by communities in which the centers are located. All developers feel that the fees should reflect environmental costs arising only from the development of the centers. In some instances, however, they have been used as a way of extracting money from developers for general community use.

Additional Decision Factors in Store Location

Merchants often use one or more of the following items in their evaluation of a trading area:

LOCATION FACTOR	SOURCE OF INFORMATION
Newspaper circulation data	Newspaper advertising departments
Auto license analysis	Motor vehicle departments
Charge account data	Credit bureaus
Shopper surveys	Interviews of shoppers

USING MATHEMATICS TO ANALYZE A TRADING AREA

Instead of relying on relatively expensive data such as shopper interviews to analyze a trading area, a retailer can use mathematical techniques based on already available facts. One popular formula, devised in 1929 by William J. Reilly, is known as Reilly's law of retail gravitation.[2] The formula indicates the relative consumer drawing power of two towns or cities. It is stated as

$$\text{Breaking point (in miles) between town (city) A and B} = \frac{\text{Distance between A and B}}{1 + \sqrt{\dfrac{\text{Population of B}}{\text{Population of A}}}}$$

The breaking point is the furthest point from a town or city from which a retailer located in that town or city can reasonably expect to attract shoppers.

Example. Towns A and B are 30 miles apart. The population of town A is 60,000; that of town B is 15,000.

$$\text{Breaking point (in miles) between town A and B} = \frac{30}{1 + \sqrt{\dfrac{15,000}{60,000}}} = \frac{30}{1 + \sqrt{\dfrac{1}{4}}}$$

$$= \frac{30}{1 + \dfrac{1}{2}} \qquad = \frac{30}{1\dfrac{1}{2}}$$

$$= 20 \text{ miles}$$

Solution. Thus, the limit (breaking point) in the direction of town B from which town A can expect to draw consumers is 20 miles. On the other hand, town B can expect to draw consumers in the direction of town A up to 10 miles from town B.

---

[2]William J. Reilly, *Method for the Study of Retail Relationships*, Research Monograph No. 4, University of Texas Bulletin No. 2944 (Austin: University of Texas Press, 1929).

TYPES OF SHOPPING AREAS

From your reading in previous chapters you have already learned that retail outlets are diverse in their purposes, appeal, and selling strategies. Tied to this diversity is the community area or facility in which they locate. Let's examine the types of shopping locations found in our country.

Six categories of retail locations

Basically, there are six categories of retail locations. They are

1. Central (downtown) shopping districts
2. Secondary shopping areas
3. Neighborhood shopping districts
4. Shopping centers
5. Highway outlets, including freestanding stores
6. Specialty shopping areas

Each of these categories contains retail outlets whose appeal is reflected by their location. Let's take a closer look at these shopping areas.

Central (Downtown) Shopping Districts

Every city and town has at least one **central shopping district,** also called a **downtown shopping district,** that contains a variety of stores. These range from department stores to chain and independent specialty shops. Customers in such areas consist of local residents, workers in area businesses, and shoppers from

Located in Seattle's central shopping district, this was J.C. Penney's first city store. *Courtesy:* J.C. Penney.

outlying communities. As a result of this high concentration of consumers, retail space in a central district is generally valuable and expensive.

The typical cluster of stores selling shopping goods in a downtown area allows the consumer to comparison shop for best values and selections with a minimum of travel and inconvenience. It is no accident that so many of the best-known stores are located so close to each other. Contrary to what many beginning students of retailing believe, the stores actually benefit from each other's attempts to attract customers to their stores.

A number of convenience stores are usually found alongside the shopping goods establishments. Capitalizing on the presence of out-of-area consumers, stores that sell food, drug, and variety items depend on these consumers to augment their revenues. The mix of shopping goods and convenience stores, coupled with the high population density of the downtown area, provides a picture of bustling activity. This, in turn, creates a psychological appeal to consumers to shop "where the action is."

RETAIL STRATEGY
Ungluing the Flagship Store

A flagship store is the main unit of a department store chain. Historically, this store, large in size and usually located in a downtown area, has served as the biggest profit maker in a chain's holdings.

In recent years, however, many branch stores have registered larger profits per square foot of space than their flagship stores. Recognizing the excessive costs of midtown flagships, chains have tackled the problem in different ways. For example,

- Associated Dry Goods closed its Stewarts flagship in Baltimore and went the discount route with its branches.
- Hochschild-Kohn, a division of Supermarkets General, also stopped operations at its Baltimore flagship store and devoted energy to its suburban branch stores.
- Carter Hawley Hale's Los Angeles Broadway flagship was closed and replaced by a smaller store not far from the shuttered flagship.

At least for the present, the strategy adopted by some chains appears to involve the pumping of funds into less costly branches and the cessation of flagship operations. This does not necessarily mean the demise of flagship stores. It does suggest the need for new strategies to revitalize the flagships. Thus, Macy's and Bloomingdale's in New York City and Filene's in Boston have redesigned their images successfully by appearing as in-store specialty shops instead of as one gigantic store.

Although downtown shopping districts have suffered fairly recently from urban blight, we are witnessing a resurgence of such districts. In many areas (e.g., Chicago and New York) large numbers of suburbanites are moving back to the cities, bringing with them the buying power of affluent consumers.

Parking and traffic congestion discourage some shoppers from frequenting downtown shopping areas. This is why some stores provide parking for customers on their premises or at nearby locations. In addition, many shopping districts are revitalized by the rerouting of traffic, the planting of shrubs and trees, and the remodeling of outdated stores.

As part of their urban renewal programs, some communities have constructed new shopping centers in their central districts. Contrary to fears expressed by other merchants in those areas, the new centers have attracted additional shoppers to the downtown areas, thereby aiding the merchants already there. In some places, however, as in Troy, New York, the addition of new centers has done little for their downtown districts.

Another example of an attempt to revive an area was the East India Mall in Old Salem, Massachusetts. It was meant to reignite interest in the inner stores in Salem, near the historic Peabody Museum and waterfront. Unfortunately, however, a proposed connector road from Salem was never built, and the mall remained situated in a basically inaccessible part of town. Today, the mall is empty, aside from a movie theater and a few stores. And, with the demise of the mall, more stores in the center of town have closed.

On the other hand, an example of a successful downtown project is the rehabilitated Union Station in downtown Washington, D.C. Using the refurbished train shed to house the stores, the complex also contains restaurants and movie theaters. Leading retailers such as The Limited, Benetton, Ann Taylor, Chico's, and Putumayo are tenants in the center. With all this, the trains still come and go at Union Station.

Secondary Shopping Areas

Secondary shopping areas are smaller than central districts

In addition to central districts, cities contain other shopping areas that are similar to, but smaller than, the downtown district. Known as **secondary shopping areas,** they also contain a mix of shopping goods establishments and convenience stores. These areas attract local consumers as well as those from nearby communities who are unwilling to travel to the central district.

Compared to central districts, secondary shopping areas provide consumers with a limited selection of merchandise. Nevertheless, the proximity of these areas to consumers' homes, the availability of public transit, and the adequacy of parking attract sufficient numbers of shoppers to make secondary shopping areas desirable retail locations. Rents are usually lower in these areas, too.

Until recently, most developers of large shopping malls shied away from building in or near cities whose populations were under 1 million. That policy has begun to change, and a prime example of that change has taken place in Columbia, South Carolina. With projected increases in population *and* household income, that area has been targeted by the developers as a primary, rather than a secondary, market.

Neighborhood Shopping Districts

Neighborhood shopping districts contain convenience stores

Undoubtedly, the neighborhood in which you live contains stores that provide you and members of your family with the food and nonfood items you require daily. These stores, plus an occasional specialty store, comprise what is known as a **neighborhood shopping district.** In addition to supermarkets, a typical district has a selection of the following types of stores: bakery, hardware store, drugstore, meat market, grocery and produce stores, florist, laundromat, and variety store. Among specialty outlets, the most common types are those that carry ready-to-wear merchandise.

In an effort to rehabilitate run-down areas, some localities have constructed neighborhood malls that contain both convenience and specialty stores. Though they are modest in design, these malls enable consumers to shop in pleasant surroundings and encourage retailers to maintain attractive stores.

Shopping Centers

To understand the development of shopping centers, you should know that before World War II the United States was made up of urban and rural areas, with few suburbs. With the return of veterans and the start of many new families, however, the intense need for housing impelled builders to construct suburban communities. This fact, plus the mobility provided by automobiles, led to the development of suburban shopping centers.

Shopping centers are regional, community, or neighborhood

These centers are of three types: regional, community, and neighborhood. A **regional shopping center (mall)** serves consumers from a number of communities, with the trading area containing 100,000 to 200,000 people. It is built either by a developer who rents the stores to retailers or by a large retailer, such as May Department Stores, that operates a main (anchor) store in the center and rents the remaining stores to other retailers. The center usually has one or more large department store branches plus an assortment of limited-line, convenience, and variety stores. Chains invariably have outlets in these centers. Banks and offices are found there, too. Additional features to attract shoppers are added to many centers. For example, one of the world's largest shopping centers, located in Edmonton, Canada, contains an artificial lake, an ice rink, and thrill rides.

Planners of the Mall of America in Bloomington, Minnesota, with four major department stores, four junior department stores, 600 to 800 specialty shops, restaurants, nightclubs, and theaters, see their primary trading area as 150 miles, with a secondary market of 400 miles. This retail center, probably the largest in the world, is banking on a significant increase in the size of its trading area over traditional measurements. In addition to major department stores such as Nordstrom and Bloomingdale's, the center will feature an indoor amusement park, 18 theaters, more than 100 restaurants and nightclubs, a health club, a miniature golf course, and more. In short, it will be a place for socializing and recreation, as well as shopping.

Another example of special features in a shopping center is the Forest Fair Mall just north of Cincinnati. Containing some 115 tenants, it is anchored by such prestigious stores as Elder-Beerman, Benetton, Parisian, and a Biggs hypermarket. The center's nonstore features include a carousel, a miniature golf course, children's rides, a video arcade, movies, a food court, a child care center, and a stage/performance area for almost 2,000 people.

The activities permitted to retailers in regional shopping centers are usually specified in their leases (rental contracts). Thus, the number and types of competitive outlets are controlled; business hours are regulated; and sharing of advertising and promotion costs is generally required. In return for compliance with these controls, however, the center provides convenient parking, pleasant surroundings, easy access, and in many cases, enclosed malls.

At first, regional shopping centers met with little resistance from cities and towns. Recently, however, the picture has changed considerably. As a result of pressure by municipalities and environmental groups, the federal government has issued a policy called community conservation guidance. In effect, it gives a community the right to object to projects undertaken by another community if it feels that such projects will damage its interests. In the case of planned shopping centers, it requires federal agencies to study and report on community opposition to the centers. If the report agrees with a community's position, the shopping center's developers can be prevented from proceeding with their plans. Though some of the protest against new shopping centers is based on energy and environmental considerations, much of it stems from the commercial conflict between urban retail centers and suburban developers. The U.S. Department of Housing and Urban Development has indicated that many municipalities have filed protests.

Deciding on whether to rent space in a particular mall is a complex matter. Referring to the relationship between a mall developer and a retailer, Frank Pasquerilla, chairman of Crown American, a development and retailing company, says, "A department store has to have its own officers and staff making major decisions—including where a store will be located."[3] Robert S. Taubman, an executive of another development and retailing company, has this to say about store location: "The merchant must feel that the decision is warranted from the sales standpoint and also from a strategic, management, marketing, delivery, and warehousing standpoint."[4] Obviously, store location decisions are made only after the most stringent investigations.

Mixed-use centers   Due to the shrinking space available for the building of productive regional malls, as well as the overbuilding of small shopping centers in some areas, we are

[3] "Developers Climb onto Department Store Ownership Bandwagon," *Chain Store Age Executive,* **64** (May 1988), p. 40.

[4] Ibid.

witnessing the increasing construction of mixed-use centers. Consisting of retail *and* commercial space, merchants in these centers rely heavily on office workers for their sales. These projects are already in operation in such diverse areas as Minneapolis, Chicago, Cambridge (Massachusetts), Jersey City (New Jersey), Washington, D.C., and Plantation (Florida).

An unusual suburban shopping center expansion occurred in 1991 when the St. Louis Galleria mall in Richmond Heights, Missouri, more than doubled its space to 1.18 million square feet. The mall's trading area consists of almost 16,000 households, with an average household annual income of $85,350. In order to attract additional shoppers, the developers signed leases with the Lord & Taylor and Famous-Barr department stores. Along with the existing Dillard's department store, the mall now boasts three well-known anchor stores.

A **community shopping center** is smaller than a regional one, and has as its largest tenant either a scaled-down department store or a specialty store. Its trading area consists of 40,000 to 150,000 people, and it has much in common with secondary shopping areas. Owners of community shopping centers provide adequate parking, planned competition, and easy access. The centers also contain a variety of convenience stores.

A **neighborhood shopping center,** sometimes called a **strip center** or a **string street,** is a relatively small group of stores alongside each other. Its largest tenant is usually a supermarket, a variety store, or a drugstore, and its trading area population runs between 7,000 and 40,000. Convenience stores comprise the remaining tenants, and the "strip" is generally constructed on main neighbor-

This strip center is located on a well-traveled road. Photo by: Marjorie Pickens.

hood roads that carry substantial traffic. Thus, neighborhood shopping centers attract mainly residents who live in the vicinity of the strip.

High-fashion strip-size centers in square shapes are new to the retailing scene. Consisting of a dozen or so small shops, they locate in communities of above-average income and cater to consumers who are willing to pay higher prices to avoid shopping at larger stores. Examples of such centers are those in Woodbury, New York, Los Angeles, California, and Caldwell, New Jersey.

In an attempt to attract consumers, strip centers are being built with unusual architectural designs. Some are constructed in wooded areas; others use beautiful landscaping, atriums, and canopies to create an atmosphere of gracious living. Still others develop their buildings and stores around special themes to strike a note of originality and individuality.

A relatively new term, **power center,** has entered the retail scene. It is a shopping center containing the following characteristics, as identified by the International Council of Shopping Centers:

- Multiple promotional anchors—two or three, but as many as five
- Category leaders selling hard and soft goods
- Size ranging from 225,000 to 400,000 square feet
- Location on or near major highways

Power centers are based not so much on the traditional shopping center principle that development should be based on growth, but rather on job growth, population distribution, and the average number (and ages) of people per household. In addition, shopping center developers rely heavily on retailers' suggestions as to where power centers should be located. Examples of power centers are Ross Plaza in Los Angeles and Yorkshire Plaza in Aurora, Illinois. Power center tenants include such well-known retailers as Marshall's, TJ Maxx, Pier 1, and Dress Barn.

Highway Outlets, Including Freestanding Stores

Anyone who has traveled on major or secondary highways has seen stores of all kinds along the way. You may come across a large furniture outlet with attractive window displays; or you may pass a shoe discount store with imposing posters announcing low prices; you will probably also find a well-known discount department store.

Highway outlets are either strings of stores or freestanding

In recent years **highway outlets** have become more popular with shoppers. This is due to the ease of reaching them, the excellent parking they provide, the low prices they offer, and the extensive advertising done by the stores. Unlike shopping centers, in which stores benefit from each other's ability to attract customers, highway stores rely on their own efforts to bring in customers.

A highway outlet may stand by itself (**freestanding**) or be one of a number of stores. For example, it may be a lone discount center or a chain operation surrounded by fast-food and convenience stores. In some cases the arrangement of stores is planned and in others it results from unplanned and uncoordinated decisions by retailers. Highway outlets generally have higher advertising costs per customer than stores in shopping centers or malls.

An interesting fast-food center concept is emerging on the retail scene. Instead of freestanding restaurants, clusters of food shops are grouped to attract larger numbers of people. Called food courts by some, they contain some of our best-known fast-food franchises. Some food courts are in shopping malls, while others are in urban areas. Cleveland, New York City, and Columbus (Ohio) are in the forefront of this trend, featuring outlets such as Pizza Hut, Kentucky Fried Chicken, and Taco Bell under one roof.

For the most part, department stores are not freestanding stores. Cognizant of the gentrification of many urban areas, however, Sears, Roebuck opened a pilot freestanding store in downtown Chicago in 1987 to tap the dense population in that area. This departure by Sears from its usual position in shopping centers is being watched closely by other retailers. If successful, additional large retailers may follow suit.

Specialty Shopping Areas

Specialty shopping areas contain limited-line stores that sell similar merchandise

Most cities have shopping areas containing a number of stores that sell the same kind of limited-line goods. Known as **specialty shopping areas,** they cater to consumers who are willing to travel in order to have a choice among wide selections of merchandise and prices. The following illustration indicates the attraction these areas hold for shoppers. Suppose a woman wants to buy a particular type of ring. She might go to a central or secondary shopping area or perhaps to a shopping center for her purchase. She will probably find a good selection of rings at those locations. However, a shopping area that specializes in the sale of jewelry would undoubtedly widen the choices available to her. With a

Highway outlets provide comfortable parking for shoppers. *Courtesy:* A&P.

minimum of inconvenience, she could walk from one specialty shop to another and examine hundreds of rings.

In addition to areas that specialize in jewelry, there are specialty shopping areas devoted to home furnishings, trimmings, art galleries, automobiles, boats, and many other types of merchandise. It is conceivable that this type of location will grow in popularity as cities become more attractive places in which to shop.

Interesting specialty shopping centers have developed in the Seattle-Tacoma area in the state of Washington. Containing separate spaces and shops for car washes, mufflers, automotive glass, quick lubes, tires, tune-ups, car stereos, and parts, car owners find all their car needs concentrated in one shopping area.

PRACTITIONER'S CORNER

What follows is the summary of an interview with Neal S. Kaplan, partner in Kabro Associates, a real estate development company that owns Woodbury Common, a shopping center in Woodbury, Long Island, New York.*

1. Woodbury Common, an upscale specialty shopping center containing 40 stores, does not fit into a conventional shopping center classification. In fact, it may be setting a trend in retail center architectural style and concept. Constructed by its present owner, the center has been expanded three times during its 17-year existence.

2. The original site contained 1.7 acres, but after expansions in 1981, 1985, and 1990 now consists of 7 acres.

3. The tenant mix today is different from what it was five to seven years ago. At first the complex contained local service-type stores, but as the community

*Interviewed by the authors.

developed and became more upscale, the owners, recognizing this trend, shifted the focus to what is now a distinctively upscale specialty center having a mix of local, national, and international stores.

4. Changes to tenancies are made only after careful consideration of the existing tenant mix, the needs of the community, and the direction of the center's growth. The center has a continuing list of prospective tenants waiting to open at the center. Even though the center could be rented many times over from this list, the owners still actively seek out specific retailers that would enhance the merchant mix.

5. In order to attract the most desirous tenants, the landlord may, in very specific cases, restructure rent obligations to attract a particular tenant who would enhance merchant mix and therefore benefit the center and its present tenants.

6. The owner is active in promoting and advertising the center. The tenants contribute to a fund which the owner uses for promotional activities (such as banners, seasonal lights, etc.) as well as a comprehensive print advertising program.

7. Because of the European village design and configuration of the shopping center, the owners traded off the ability to construct more square feet of stores in exchange for being able to create the uniquely charming atmosphere. While this configuration does not maximize the property (in terms of intensification of use), it does now allow the owner to receive a higher return per square foot because the market recognizes this unique and beneficial atmosphere.

8. There is no anchor store in the shopping center. The wide range and diversification, as well as the number of quality tenants, becomes the center's "draw" or anchor.

9. The owner is entitled to audit tenants' books to verify gross sales receipts for percentage rent purposes. The landlord's election to audit and the frequency of such audits is dependent on the particular tenant.

CHOOSING A SITE

Factors in selecting a store location

Having examined the decision factors used in locating a retail outlet, and having discussed the various types of shopping areas, we turn our attention to the selection of a specific store location. There are a number of matters that the new retailer should consider if the enterprise is to get off to a good start. They are

1. Closeness to competitors
2. Correct blend of stores
3. Potential sales

4. Traffic and traffic patterns
5. Visibility of the store
6. Parking
7. Zoning laws
8. Miscellaneous items

Closeness to Competitors

Competition can work for or against new retailers

Curious as it may sound, competition may work for or against new retailers. As you have seen, department stores are often grouped in the same shopping area. Since each store brings different consumers into the area, there can be benefits for all. The same situation prevails in specialty store areas.

On the other hand, competition can sometimes be damaging to a new store. For example, an enterprising young man with little retailing experience decided to open a hardware store in a secondary shopping area. Neglecting to check the trading area carefully, he overlooked the fact that it already contained another hardware store, an auto supply store that carried hardware items, and a discount center that also sold hardware. Unfortunately for the young man, his store failed in its first year because the trading area's population was insufficient to support an additional hardware outlet.

Correct Blend of Stores

A new retailer must be careful to locate where the store will be compatible with other stores nearby. That is, neighboring stores should attract consumers who may also be willing to shop in the new store. For example, opening a children's clothing store close to women's-wear stores makes sense. On the other hand, the same store surrounded by bars and grills, office equipment outlets, or auto repair shops makes little sense. The merchant, then, should survey the immediate and surrounding areas carefully in order to make a correct assessment of the planned store's compatibility with other stores.

An example of the importance of a correct blend of stores is the Tyler Mall in Riverside, California. For some time the center had been losing shoppers to more upscale centers in nearby areas. To stem this loss, the mall's owner pumped $90 million into a major renovation in 1989. The centerpiece of this move was the acquisition of Nordstrom, an eminently successful department store chain, as a tenant. The expectation was that the project would be completed in 1991, and that the addition of Nordstrom would justify the location of the mall.

Potential Sales

Techniques for estimating potential sales

You have already learned that a trading area should be studied for population size and composition, income levels, occupations, and so forth. This information helps the new retailer judge the number of potential customers for the planned store. However, more precise figures are needed to estimate the new store's sales. These may be determined from

1. A count of people who pass by the location of the store.
2. A check of how well competitors appear to be doing. This can be accomplished by visiting these outlets and counting the number of customers, employees, departments, and so on.
3. Interviews with manufacturers, jobbers, and wholesalers.
4. Discussions with chamber of commerce members, bank executives, and municipal officials.

Traffic and Traffic Patterns

A new retailer who will depend on travel convenience as a means of attracting customers should examine several traffic factors. In the case of suburban shopping centers and highway outlets, consideration should be given to road conditions and the number of cars passing by or close to the store. If the store is to be located in an urban setting, attention should be paid to the availability of mass transit facilities (buses, trains, etc.) and, where automobiles are involved, the condition of roads and access streets.

The retailer should be more concerned with his or her target population than with the volume of traffic per se. For example, if the store's appeal is to affluent consumers who dislike crowds, it makes little sense to locate the store in an area where crowding is common.

Visibility of the Store

The more visible a store, the higher its potential sales

You have probably visited shopping areas where traffic is heavier on one side of a street than on the other. You may also have noticed that corner stores usually have more window space than other stores. Of course, the more visible a store is to passing pedestrians and cars, the more valuable the location. Since rents are usually higher in such locations, the new retailer must judge whether it is worth paying the additional cost. This decision can best be made by estimating the number of potential customers—and, hence, sales—that may be derived from the favorable location of the store.

Parking

Though suburban shopping centers almost always provide parking for customers, the parking area must be large enough to accommodate shoppers adequately. In the case of urban stores, parking should be available to customers who drive to the shopping area. Consideration must also be given to the cost of parking in municipal and private parking facilities.

Zoning Laws

Communities enact laws governing building projects   The continuing emphasis on environmental problems has caused municipalities to strengthen their **zoning laws,** also known as **zoning codes.** These regulations generally restrict the types of building that are permitted in a community. The new retailer should check zoning laws carefully for their possible impact on both short- and long-term business prospects. At times it is necessary to secure the services of an attorney for careful consideration of the regulations.

Since the advent of suburban shopping malls, most large centers that have been built require shoppers to use their automobiles. That concept appears to be in question today as retail planners try to overcome traffic glut and parking lot inconveniences. The suggestion has been made that, whenever possible, new retail centers should consist of stores, housing, and offices in intelligently designed complexes. Such planning requires cooperation among mall developers and community planners. When such cooperation is lacking, chances of retail success are reduced.

Such has been the case with Forrestal Village in Plainsboro, New Jersey. Despite an attractive layout, including a hotel, day care center, and office space, the complex has shown poor retailing results. This is because zoning regulations in the community forbid new housing in Forrestal Village. As a consequence, retailers there are suffering a dearth of shoppers. This unfortunate situation appears to be due to faulty planning.

Miscellaneous Items

During site selection, additional questions should be asked, such as

- Are there active businesses in the area?
- What are the hours of operation of nearby stores?
- Are nearby stores and buildings in good condition?
- Are environmental factors a problem, for example, noise and smoke?

BUYING OR RENTING A RETAIL OUTLET

One final matter must be considered by the new retailer. This is the question of whether to purchase or rent the store. Let's examine both possibilities.

Purchasing A Retail Outlet

Though ownership of a store (and possibly the site) may be expensive, it has its advantages. These include the following.

1. The ability to make physical changes in the store without interference. (Zoning laws must be checked, however.)
2. The possibility of renting store space to other retailers, thereby increasing income.
3. The possibility that the store (and the property) may increase in value over time.
4. The profit that accrues to the owner if the property is sold at a price that is higher than the purchase price.

On the other hand, the new owner must also contend with the following disadvantages.

1. Maintenance costs.
2. Potential tax increases.
3. The possibility of a decrease in the value of the location.
4. Losses due to fire, flood, or natural disasters.

Renting a Retail Outlet

When renting a store, a retailer signs a *lease* (i.e., a contract) with a landlord. Leases are often renewable for nonshopping-center stores, and the retailer (tenant) is usually required to pay a fixed sum each month for a number of years. In some leases the sum increases after a certain period. In both cases, the rent remains fixed regardless of the amount of business the retailer does.

Shopping center leases are generally tied to the retailer's sales volume. A typical lease guarantees the landlord a certain minimum amount plus a percentage of sales. Thus, if the retailer guarantees $25,000 a year plus 8 percent of sales, the landlord will receive a total of $89,000 for a year when sales amount to $800,000 [$25,000 + (.08 × $800,000)]. In addition to the payment of rent, shopping center leases often require tenants to contribute to the center's advertising and maintenance costs.

A retail tenant is usually expected to bear the finishing costs of the store. These include carpentry and plumbing work, fixtures, shelving, flooring, and the like.

Store rents have skyrocketed recently in some urban areas and popular shopping centers. This phenomenon has hurt many retailers, both large and small, and has changed the retail character of the trading areas. The situation has become so serious in the borough of Manhattan (New York City), for example, that there is talk among knowledgeable people of instituting rent control for commercial properties. Obviously, stores that own their premises are insulated against this overhead item. A good example is Alexander's, a discount promotional department store chain, whose flagship unit is located in a truly affluent section of New York City. Early in 1986, in fact, Alexander's announced that it "will close its doors for redevelopment into a higher yielding nonretail property. The site is an extreme example of land value overtaking the earning capability of the store."[5]

The advantages of leasing a store are as follows.

1. No initial investment for a building and/or land.
2. The opportunity to move elsewhere at the expiration of the lease.
3. The ability to concentrate on merchandising instead of on real estate problems.

The main disadvantage of leasing involves the restrictions imposed on the retailer by the lease. These may involve business hours, store alterations, types of merchandise carried, and limitations on displays.

TRENDS IN STORE LOCATION

Though retailing is a volatile field in which any prediction is fraught with danger, the following trends appear to be emerging.

Retailing is an ever-changing field

1. A revitalization of downtown retail stores. Aided in many cases by federal funds, some decaying cities and towns show signs of renewed vigor. St. Louis and Detroit are two examples of this trend.
2. Challenges to the construction of regional shopping centers by communities, planners, and environmental groups.
3. Subleasing by retailers of part or all of their leased store buildings. This allows the retailers (prime tenants) to cut costs.
4. A move toward strip shopping centers.
5. A preference for enclosed and multilevel malls.
6. A tendency for owners of real estate in urban areas not to renew the leases of large-area tenants like supermarkets. Instead, the vacated space is divided into smaller spaces for specialty stores and convenience stores, thereby earning the landlord higher rents.
7. Larger shopping centers combine retail outlets with recreational and amusement facilities. Families make shopping a "day out," with activities provided for children while the adults shop.
8. The acquisition and redevelopment of existing shopping centers rather than the construction of new ones. This is due to the expense of building and to the overpopulation of centers in many trading areas.
9. A move toward fewer and smaller supermarkets in cities because of spiraling rents and soaring energy costs.

[5] *Inside Retailing* (January 20, 1986), p. 1.

This enclosed multilevel shopping center in Philadelphia attracts consumers with its many stores and recreational conveniences. *Courtesy:* Philadelphia City Planning Commission.

Tivoli, a retail center, formerly a factory building. *Courtesy:* Trizec Properties, Inc.

10. The remodeling of factory buildings as retail locations containing a variety of shops: boutiques, restaurants, galleries, and so forth.

11. With about 30,000 shopping centers in the United States, almost every major trading area contains at least one regional mall.

12. There are areas in which overdevelopment of retail centers has taken place.

13. There is a move to specialty shopping centers, other strip centers, and mixed-use complexes.

14. Mall development in the near future will probably consist mostly of rehabilitation, renovation, and expansion of existing centers.

15. In addition to entertainment outlets, shopping malls are emphasizing special services, seasonal events, merchandise exclusivity, and luxurious amenities to enhance their images. Included are baby strollers, wheelchairs, package checking, sale of lottery tickets, and carryout service.

NEW TERMS

central shopping district
community shopping center
downtown shopping district
freestanding store
highway outlet
impact fee
neighborhood shopping center
neighborhood shopping district
mall

power center
regional shopping center
secondary shopping area
specialty shopping area
string street
strip center
trading area
zoning code
zoning law

CHAPTER HIGHLIGHTS

1. Retailers seek store locations that will provide an adequate return on investment within a reasonable time.

2. While consumers are willing to travel some distance for shopping goods, they expect stores selling more frequently-used goods to be located near their home or place of business.

3. A trading area is a geographic section from which a store draws the bulk of its customers.

4. In describing the population of a trading area, a retailer is interested in current population; incomes and occupations; seasonal changes; the character of the trading area's business and industry; age groups; sex composition; ethnic, religious, and special groups; apartments and homes; and the dynamics of the population.

5. The following socioeconomic conditions of a trading area should be studied for their retail potential: employment and unemployment, vitality of the trading area, laws that affect retailers, traffic considerations, local attractions, parking, the attitude of banks toward retailers, police and fire protection, advertising outlets, and merchandising mix.

6. When analyzing the nature and extent of competing stores in a trading area, a new retailer should consider the number and types of competing outlets, the extent of chain ownership among competitors, the existence of large shopping facilities, and the possibility that existing stores may try to destroy the new store's chances of success by means of underselling and special sales promotions.

7. Other location decision factors include the geographic concentration of stores, market saturation, out-of-the-way locations, and impact fees.

8. Some retailers use Reilly's law of retail gravitation to analyze a trading area.

9. The categories of retail location are as follows: central (downtown) districts, secondary shopping areas, neighborhood shopping districts, shopping centers, highway outlets (including freestanding stores), and specialty shopping areas.

10. In selecting a specific store location, a new retailer should consider the following matters: closeness to competitors, blend of stores, potential sales, traffic and traffic patterns, visibility of the store, parking, and zoning laws.

11. A new retailer must consider whether to buy or rent a store. While a store owner has more freedom in the use of property, he or she must contend with maintenance costs and taxes. Renting a store involves paying either a fixed amount for the duration of the lease or a minimum amount plus a percentage of sales.

12. Trends in store location range from revitalization of downtown shopping districts to the increased popularity of strip shopping centers.

REVIEW QUESTIONS

1. How can a poor location hurt a store that is managed efficiently and that maintains effective merchandising policies?

2. Where can a new retailer secure a population count for a particular trading area?

3. Why should a retailer be interested in the incomes and occupations of a trading area's population?

4. How are seasonal changes related to the retail sales potential of some trading areas?

5. Why is it important to know whether a trading area's population is constant, growing, or declining?
6. What is the strategy behind the inclusion of recreational facilities in shopping malls?
7. What are some of the characteristics of highway outlets that make them attractive to shoppers?
8. If you were opening a women's shoe store, what types of stores would you not want nearby? (List at least five types.)

DISCUSSION QUESTIONS

1. Name several special consumer groups in addition to those mentioned in this chapter. How do retailers benefit from understanding the needs of these special groups?
2. In what ways might an existing shopping center attempt to undercut a new competitor? In your opinion, is this practice ethical? Why?
3. What do you think will happen to downtown shopping districts during the next ten years?
4. If you had the option of buying or renting a freestanding store, which might you prefer? Why? (Assume that you have the funds to start the store.)

CASE 1

Leases: Rights and Obligations

In 1990 a well-known discount department store locked its side entrance doors during business hours to reduce the security problems brought about by a reduction in staff. As a result, smaller stores in the shopping strip lost sales because customers had previously used the side entrance to walk through to get to the smaller stores. Many shoppers apparently were unwilling to walk around the discount store to get to the smaller stores.

Prompted by the complaints of the small retailers, the shopping center's landlord reminded the discounter that its lease required it to pay a rental based on a percentage of sales. The landlord also stressed that by closing its side entrance doors, it had broken its implied obligation to produce the highest possible volume of sales. However, the landlord indicated that the store would not be breaching its lease if it could show that it had not lost sales by closing the side doors.

a. Do you think the discounter had the right to close its side doors? Why?

b. How do you feel about the smaller retailers' complaint?

c. If the discounter's sales did decrease, do you think the landlord would take further action? What do you think would be the outcome?

CASE 2

A Site for Convenience

River Grove is a rapidly growing new community on the outskirts of a large sunbelt city. It is a largely residential neighborhood, made up of moderately expensive single-family homes and town house condominiums.

Most of the River Grove residents who work are employed in white-collar and professional jobs in the city. They commute to work by car, driving either on Route 73, a heavily traveled four-lane highway, or on Dixon Drive, a two-lane road that is the main north-and-south artery through River Grove's residential section.

The management of Thimble Marts, a well-established chain of convenience stores, has decided to open a new store to serve the River Grove trading area. Four sites are available in the areas zoned for commercial use. The sites are shown on the map (shown on the facing page).

Site 1 is on the north side of Route 73, about a mile west of the intersection with Dixon Drive. This location is on one of the direct routes to and from the city. On the other side of the highway, about a quarter mile farther west, is a competing convenience store that has been in business for just over a year. Several fast-food outlets are in operation along the same section of Route 73.

Site 2 is also on the north side of Route 73, about 2 miles east of the intersection with Dixon Drive. The nearby businesses include a liquor store, a dry cleaner, and a movie theater. About a quarter mile farther east is a large supermarket.

Site 3 is about a half mile beyond the supermarket, on the south side of Route 73. The area to the east of this site is still mostly farmland, but it is likely to be subdivided into building lots for housing developments within the next three to five years.

Site 4 is immediately to the south of River Grove, on Dixon Drive. The area has recently been rezoned for commercial use, and a number of small buildings are being converted for occupancy as offices and retail shops.

All four sites have adequate selling space and sufficient storage. All have large, convenient parking areas. They are all zoned for retail use, and they are comparable in price.

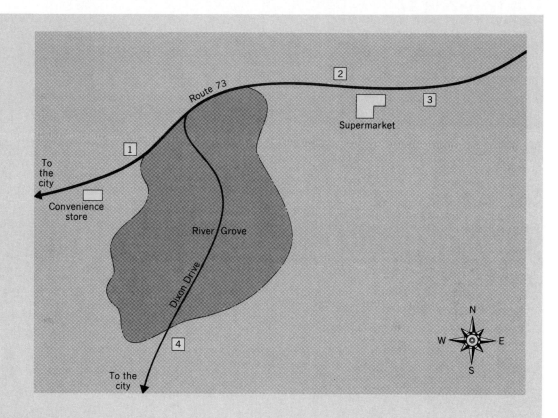

a. What are the advantages and disadvantages of each site?
b. Which location should the management of Thimble Marts select? Why?
c. What other type(s) of retailing businesses might be successful in a new community like River Grove? Where should they be located?

REFERENCES

CRAIG, C. S., A. GHOSH, AND S. MCLAFFERTY. "Models of the Retail Location Process: A Review." *Journal of Retailing*, **60** (Spring 1984), pp. 5–36.

"Location Can Influence Merchandise Mix, Too." *Chain Store Age Executive*, **65** (January 1989), p. 60.

"Mixed-Use Enters a New Generation." *Chain Store Age Executive*, **64** (September 1988), pp. 29–32.

"Power Centers! Now!" *Stores* (March 1989), pp. 61–64.

WRIGLEY, N., ED. *Store Choice, Store Location and Market Analysis*. London: Routledge Kegan Paul, 1988.

Chapter 8

Store Image: Design, Layout, and Store Services

After completing this chapter, you should be able to:

- Identify the important aspects of a store's exterior.
- Identify the important aspects of a store's interior.
- Explain store modernization in terms of the growth of an enterprise.
- Explain store layout in terms of guidelines, space, merchandise placement, and type of store.
- Discuss the following aspects of store interiors: displays, air conditioning, transportation within the store, store services, safety, and conveniences.

You have already learned that the proper location of a retail outlet is essential to its financial success. Having secured a favorable location, the new retailer turns to the store itself. It cannot be emphasized too strongly that, in addition to the site, the nature of the store's image is crucial to its continued acceptance by customers.

Among the aspects of store image to be studied in this chapter are the exterior and interior designs of the store, the importance of modernization, layout and design factors, the impact of displays, the movement of merchandise and customers, and store services.

THE EXTERIOR OF THE STORE

A store's image distinguishes it from its competitors

A store must present a distinct image that distinguishes it from its competition. This image, which is projected through the store's exterior and interior design, layout, displays, and services, gives it an identity that shapes customers' objective and subjective perceptions of the store. These perceptions define the store for the customer and position it relative to other stores with regard to its merchandise, staff, policies, services, and convenience. Called **impression management,** it is a major consideration in planning a store. Most stores must provide a pleasant environment in which to shop. On the other hand, the store must be functional and meet the operating needs of the business in terms of providing adequate facilities for sales, storage, administration, maintenance, customer traffic, security, and the like.

The old Lazarus building reflected the store's image, just as the new one does in a modern vein. *Courtesy:* Lazarus.

Preparing the Store for Occupancy

Once a retailer has chosen a site for a new store, it becomes necessary to prepare the physical plant for occupancy. Depending on the real estate involved, this may require constructing a new building or renovating an old one. In either case, the retailer must consider four major areas in terms of utility and image when planning the store: (1) building size, height, and exterior design; (2) interior layout and design; (3) interior decoration; and (4) displays and arrangement of products and services within departments. Attractive exteriors draw customers into stores; interiors keep customers' attention, and influence them to stay and buy.

Using consultants to design a store

Store design and planning require extraordinary amounts of technical knowledge. Retailers do not have all this expertise. They often retain designers and architects as consultants to develop property in a way that best suits their needs. The retailer must, however, clearly define the needs of the business in terms of store policy, long-range plans, current and projected sales, services, selling techniques, merchandise, support activities, and flexibility. In developing a store plan, retail managers may also consult with suppliers to learn about the most up-to-date equipment and fixtures available. Large and small stores may resort to outside consultants. Large stores are better able to afford the expenses of such consultation and also avail themselves of professional discounts on equipment and supplies that they might not be able to get without the aid of the consultant. Even when larger stores have their own planning staffs, they may occasionally retain independent consultants to provide a fresh point of view. Although smaller retailers sometimes use independent consultants, their budgets often require that they determine their needs as best they can and then work directly with contractors to have store plans implemented. In the long run this may prove more costly than hiring a consultant because, as we have seen, the retailer may lack the requisite knowledge and experience. In some cases, suppliers provide free design services to their retail customers. This is a great help to small stores.

Physical Structure

A store's physical structure can be a selling device

The physical structure of the store is a major component of the store's image and is itself a selling device. Large, tall buildings can either intimidate customers or give them an impression of permanence, solidity, and success. While the height of a building can be disguised by the construction of floors below street level, it is often difficult to disguise the size of a building. Still, architects and retailers have worked together to find creative structural and cosmetic solutions.

Because supermarkets are a significant and distinct segment of retailing, certain aspects of their exterior design warrant comment. First of all, most supermarkets are similar in basic construction. That is, they are rectangular or square one-level stores that are distinguished from one another by architectural variations in their roofs or fronts. Surprisingly, the reasons for this basic design appears to be the public's expectation that supermarkets will be constructed in this manner. Nevertheless, some supermarkets are built as multilevel structures. Second, though they take on some general characteristics of other neighborhood stores, supermarkets are designed to look different from their competitors. Finally, supermarket fronts show a surprising variety of appearances. Some storefronts are almost entirely glass, revealing much of the interior. Others are made completely of brick or some other opaque material, precluding any interior visibility. Still others are composed of glass and opaque materials, providing some interior visibility as well as interior display or storage space.

Visibility

The storefront and any show windows should be visible to both pedestrians and vehicular traffic. Some shopping centers, however, are constructed in such a way that not all of the stores are visible from the highway. In such cases stores often make use of billboards or signs to make their presence known.

These storefronts can easily be seen by passersby. *Courtesy:* Montgomery Ward and A&P.

It is important that the architecture of a store be in keeping with that of the buildings that surround it. It should also to some degree be in keeping with the lifestyles of the residents of the neighborhoods it serves. Unusual architectural devices and design help give a store a distinctive identity in the minds of customers. The costs of constructing such features can be quite high, however.

Show windows and store images

Show windows often emphasize the presence of a store and project its image. Stores that feature low prices often have price tags on the items that they display. On the other hand, stores like Tiffany's, an expensive specialty store, which have an image of exclusivity and prestige, often do not display prices. Tiffany's windows sometimes feature one-of-a-kind items that are integrated subtly in the display. The window design, not the merchandise, is what stands out. By displaying very expensive merchandise in this seemingly offhand way, Tiffany's image projects a concern for aesthetics that goes beyond considerations of price. Tiffany's assumes that the customer can afford the merchandise no matter how expensive it is. It is selling taste and service.

Retailers also use seasonal or holiday themes that feature specific merchandise. Sometimes they devote show windows to displays that have nothing to do with merchandise. During the Christmas season, for example, many stores feature animated window displays that portray traditional or fantasy scenes that represent the holiday season.

Some stores' windows look into the interior of the store so that shoppers can observe the sweep of merchandise, decor, and activities. Other stores—for example, some supermarkets—have their interiors completely shut off from outside view. In these cases the owners have decided that visibility of the store's interior from the outside is unimportant.

Entrances

The number and location of entrances are influenced by such factors as shoplifting, security, customer mobility, and safety. Entrances should be wide to provide easy access to the store. One of the more popular types of entrances is the air curtain, which keeps out dust and dirt. It maintains the internal temperature of the store, yet allows customers to move freely into and out of the store without bothering with doors.

Two interesting entrances that reflect the stores' images are F. A. O. Schwarz's Imaginerium in Canoga Park, California, and Bergdorf Goodman's Fifth Avenue building in New York City. The former is constructed of blocks resembling children's building blocks (F. A. O. Schwarz is a toy retailer), while the latter has an elegant appearance to represent Bergdorf's upscale appeal. Another example is Car's the Star, an auto gift store located in Kansas City's Crowne Center. In an attempt to blend its exterior with its interior fixtures and merchandise, the company built a transparent storefront to resemble the back end of a 1957 Chevrolet. The effect is a dramatic representation of the goods carried by this specialty retailer.

Automatic doors have long been a feature of supermarket entrances. The idea is spreading to other types of retailers. For example, two Michigan-based drugstores chains—Perry Drug and Arbor Drug—have installed the doors, with enthusiastic consumer response. From senior citizens to parents carrying children, the reception has been positive and rewarding.

Parking

Inadequate parking is sometimes unavoidable

Parking facilities and their distance from the store are other important considerations. You read in the last chapter that retailers try to provide customers with convenient parking. However, this is not always possible, especially during major holiday seasons or prior to special occasions like Mother's Day. At such times, even though parking may be inadequate, customers tend to understand the situation and show more patience than at other times.

One of the reasons for the resurgence of downtown shopping is the construction of attractive, safe, and convenient parking areas close to the main stores. Virtually every city has developed such areas as part of its master plan for the revitalization of decaying urban centers.

As though to emphasize the importance of parking to retail success, the Newmark center in Hampton, Virginia, started its overhaul design with a revamped parking lot strategy. In addition to planning for smooth traffic flow, management also considered innovations: more attractive signage, alternative parking on weekends, short-term parking in association with food courts, and canopies. The lesson, of course, is that mall (and, therefore, store) attractiveness begins with the shopper's first impressions, that is, the parking lot.

Construction Costs

Cost-effective construction is related to better planning

The costs of materials and labor have led retailers to seek more efficient and cost-effective construction through better planning. Retailers have also sought to minimize construction costs by using less costly materials and fixtures. In some cases they have used pre-fabricated structures that are manufactured in parts and assembled on site. Chain stores have avoided some cost increases by adopting a uniform design for their units. This saves on architectural fees and allows the chain to negotiate a quantity discount with contractors and suppliers when there are several construction sites and installations in a given area.

Exterior Lighting

The importance of exterior lighting

Store planners must also consider exterior lighting needs. First and foremost, customers must be able to find a store after dark. Electric or illuminated signs and dramatically lit storefronts not only draw and guide customers to a store but also keep the presence of the store in the customer's mind. Even if the store is closed, its lighted sign and facade serve as an advertisement and reminder to passersby. Parking lots, too, require illumination for convenience and safety. Adequate exterior lighting is also a deterrent to would-be thieves.

Entertainment

The latest addition to nonstore features in shopping centers is the entertainment area. Malls like Underground Atlanta in Atlanta, Georgia, Spatz's Metro Centre in Northbrook, Illinois, Hollywood Promenade in Hollywood, California, and the projected megamall in Bloomington, Minnesota, recognize the pulling power of entertainment complexes. We can expect to see a continuation of this trend in the foreseeable future.

Additional Exterior Considerations

Depending on the nature of the store, there are other exterior factors to consider. For example, effective store signs, even nonilluminated ones, attract shoppers who might otherwise ignore those stores. You have only to think of such signs as Toys "Я" Us to realize how powerful a magnet they are. Also, the quality of a building's construction may be of great importance in guaranteeing shopping comfort and in assuring reasonable maintenance costs. Then, some stores on the sunny side of a street may require awnings or tinted glass to enable shoppers to view window displays comfortably.

THE INTERIOR OF THE STORE

Interiors must be appealing and make a favorable impression on customers. Spacious aisles, appropriate lighting, and imaginative, well-thought-out displays are far more inviting than narrow, crowded aisles, stark fluorescent lighting, and a hodge-podge of unrelated displays provided by manufacturers. Decorative floor, wall, and ceiling treatments also make shopping more pleasant and merchandise more attractive, as do well-planned placements of elevators, escalators, and other store fixtures and equipment.

Lighting

Store lighting serves many purposes

Lighting has both practical and dramatic applications. It is used to call attention to the store; to illuminate the store's interior so customers can examine merchandise and see price tags; to create atmosphere; to draw attention to specific areas, displays, or merchandise; and to illuminate nonselling areas. Color, position, and type of lamp and fixture all work together to produce the desired effect. Lighting design is a specialty. Lighting a store can be as intricate as lighting a play in a theater. It is no wonder that many department stores hire professional consultants to assist with or create the store's lighting design. The need for these consultants was heightened by the energy crisis of the 1970s, which caused stores to try to cut energy costs wherever possible.

Lighting Levels

Stores have the same lighting needs as always: however, the high cost of energy has caused retailers to reevaluate their lighting designs. So far, the most noticeable effect has been that retailers have reduced the general level of lighting in their stores. This has allowed store owners to lower the levels of spotlights used to accent merchandise or special areas. Generally speaking, lighting designers feel that it is preferable to have many low-wattage spotlights than just a few high-wattage ones.

Reductions in the intensity of background lighting have been achieved in many ways. One of the simplest ways of reducing the general level of lighting is to

Lowe's, catering to the homeowner, illustrates how the exterior and interior of a store focus the consumer's attention on the store's image. *Courtesy:* Lowe's.

use fewer lamps in fluorescent fixtures. Many stores have cut energy costs by using only half the lamps that their lighting fixtures were designed to hold. When Abraham & Straus eliminated lights over the aisles between departments, the results were effective in terms of both reducing costs and creating more subtle contrasts between departments. Stores also find that lower lighting levels produce a more intimate look and that customers are drawn into the more brightly lit areas. Manufacturers also respond to high energy costs by producing energy-saving lamps in both their fluorescent and their incandescent lines.

Types of Lighting

Incandescent, fluorescent, and metallic-vapor lights

Incandescent lights like those found in the average home are generally used for accent lights because they provide a full spectrum of color. It is easier to determine the true color of merchandise under incandescent lights than under fluorescent or metallic-vapor lights. Fluorescent and metallic-vapor lights, although less expensive to operate, emit a blue light that gives colors an unnatural blue cast: therefore, they are generally used for background lighting. Some stores, which traditionally used only incandescent lighting, experimented successfully with improved fluorescent lights for general lighting purposes. Some of the improved fluorescents have coatings that compensate for the blue light and therefore simulate daylight, thereby providing a warmer, broader-spectrum light than the cold, blue fluorescents. In their furniture departments many stores have substituted portable table and floor lamps for most of their overhead lighting, particularly in model rooms. This has the added benefit of displaying additional merchandise in a "lifestyle" setting.

Newer stores and shopping centers have been designed to make better use of daylight in such areas as entrances and courtyards. However, there are limits on the use stores can make of daylight. Two of the main reasons that stores cannot use more natural light are that (1) it is inconstant because of changes in weather and (2) prolonged exposure to sunlight bleaches, discolors, and otherwise damages goods and fixtures. Besides, fewer windows in a store mean fewer distractions and give a store greater ability to direct customers' attention toward merchandise.

Using skylights in dramatic fashion, Big Y Foods, an East Longwood, Massachusetts, supermarket, welcomes shoppers into its expanded quarters with attractive lighting and colorful banners.

In an effort to improve its illumination system, Filene's department store engaged the services of Lumentech, a lighting design consulting firm. By changing fixtures, lamps, and color combinations, the retailer succeeded in transforming the store into a brighter, more attractive place—without sacrificing energy efficiency.

One successful attempt to cut lighting costs involves the use of reflector material. The mirrorlike units increase reflectivity and allow store planners to focus light more effectively. In addition, the use of fewer lights reduces heat and, consequently, air-conditioning costs.

Modernization

Store growth is the ultimate purpose of modernization

Remodeling or renovating a store will not solve problems arising from poor management decisions, untrained personnel, or poor store location. It can, however, maintain or improve a store's image, increase efficiency and productivity, make shopping more pleasant, and improve employee morale. In time, all buildings, fixtures, and equipment deteriorate or become obsolete. Outdated, run-down exteriors and interiors detract from a store's image.

Actually, the term *modernization* as it applies to retailing implies growth. Perceptive owners recognize that modernization is done for two reasons: (1) To maintain and increase the store's appeal to customers through new appointments and fixtures. For example, J. Brannam, an off-price division of Woolworth, has changed its no-frills image by upscaling its decor. By doing so, it appeals to consumers who want both department store ambience and apparel discounts. J. C. Penney uses dropped ceilings and elaborate floor patterns to separate its departments. (2) To reduce expenses through the installation of labor-saving devices and more efficient merchandising techniques. For example, Montgomery Ward's Kid Stores use brightly designed fixtures to develop exciting and lively atmospheres. Particularly outstanding items are bright yellow wire grids on walls that also serve as merchandise frames.

Experience has shown that retailers who are the first to institute intelligent modernization programs reap the benefits of their efforts to a greater extent than their imitators. For example, a change from conventional exteriors to more exciting façades has weaned consumers away from their customary shopping centers to the modernized ones. Even when competitors followed suit, many of their former customers continued to patronize the new centers. Retailers like Marshall Field have benefited greatly from modernization. Forward-looking retailers like Strawbridge & Clothier give high priority to remodeling.

Modernization programs, of course, require money, and substantial sums are usually involved. Most large retailers have little difficulty securing the necessary financing and expertise. Smaller stores, however, are often unable to modernize for lack of funds, or can do so only in limited ways. In some instances they secure advice from suppliers, manufacturers, and trade associations. In connection with the cost of modernization, it is interesting to note that in a survey conducted by *Chain Store Age Executive* magazine, chains reported that remodeling resulted in an average earnings increase of 17 percent per square foot.[1]

A good example of store modernization tied to image is provided by J. C. Penney. As it took on higher-fashion merchandise, additional brand name goods, and an efficient in-house communications system in the late 1980s, it also remodeled its stores in a $1 billion rebuilding program. The retailer installed parquet walkways, attractive carpeting, and quarry tile. Shopping carts were replaced by distinctive wood cabinets, and specialty areas were developed through the use of

---

[1] "Remodeling Pays Off in Higher Profits," *Chain Store Age Executive*, **61** (April 1985), pp. 27–29.

Forward-looking retailers like Strawbridge & Clothier give high priority to remodeling. *Courtesy:* Strawbridge & Clothier.

glass partitions. The net effect was the increased patronage of more upscale shoppers.

Layout

Store layout: making the most productive use of space

In terms of store design, layout refers to the planned arrangement of selling and administrative areas, fixtures, equipment, and merchandise. When store planners decide on the layout of a store, they must consider the size and shape of the building and how many floors it has, the kinds of merchandise sold and the fixtures and equipment involved in handling it, the need for service areas, the shopping patterns of customers, and the competition. The chief goal in planning a layout is to make the most productive use of space by apportioning it according to the profitability of the various departments and then determining the optimum arrangement of merchandise, fixtures, and equipment within individual and common areas.

Layout Guidelines

In planning a store's layout, the major guidelines are:

1. To provide aisles that are wide enough to avoid crowding customers, allow customers to move quickly from one department to another, and allow for the movement of equipment to deliver merchandise to the selling floors.

2. To provide unobstructed views of the selling floors. This encourages customers to visit other departments and allows closer surveillance of customers by the security force.

3. To group related merchandise together in order to encourage purchases of related items.

4. To reduce resistance to shopping by creating a familiar arrangement of departments. This involves studying and paralleling the layouts of competitors.

5. To provide a means of moving customers quickly through or past departments in which they may feel uncomfortable. For example, women are generally more willing than men to shop for personal garments for members of the opposite sex. This is due partly to the traditional roles of men and women, in which women were often expected to make these purchases for their husbands and sons. Although some men now make similar purchases for their wives, many still feel uncomfortable in a lingerie department.

6. To combine merchandise according to ensembles and lifestyles. However, this may cause problems by duplicating merchandise sold in other departments (making it difficult to determine who is responsible for buying and managing the merchandise) and requiring salespeople who have experience and expertise in selling several kinds of merchandise.

Layout Patterns

Layouts determine in-store traffic patterns and shopping atmospheres. Therefore, the design of the selling floor is of prime importance.

The most common layout arrangements are the grid pattern, free-flow pattern, and boutique pattern. The **grid pattern** is designed to route traffic in a straight, rectangular fashion. The design of the grid creates a series of aisles similar to those found in most supermarkets, variety stores, and discount houses. The grid utilizes space efficiently, simplifies shopping, creates the proper environment for self-service, and reduces problems with inventory and security. This pattern, however, creates a rigid atmosphere, inhibits browsing, and is not suitable for most shopping or specialty goods.

On the other hand, a **free-flow pattern** creates a more relaxed atmosphere. Merchandise is arranged so that the shopper has more room to move and browse. Impulse and unplanned purchases are encouraged in this casual environment, and customers tend to stay longer. The disadvantages of the free-flow pattern are that space is not utilized fully, there are more problems with inventory and security, and fixtures are generally more expensive. This pattern is desirable for department and specialty stores.

The **boutique pattern** creates a small specialty shop within an area of the selling floor. This arrangement utilizes the free-flow pattern in a "little shop" setting such as a "Bed and Bath Corner." The boutique pattern makes it easy for the consumer with a particular interest to see complete offerings in one area.

Carefully-planned store layouts and well-planned lighting result in good traffic flow and dramatic effects. *Courtesy:* A & S.

K mart uses this pattern as part of its upscale transformation. The company has refixtured its stores so that merchandise is housed in a series of mini shops (e.g., Home Center, Kitchen Korner, and Gloria Vanderbilt for Bed, Bath, and Kitchen).

A key trend in new store prototypes is the use of flooring to channel store traffic as well as to create an image.[2] We will undoubtedly witness a continuation of this trend as cost-conscious retailers seek to improve store ambience.

Best Buy, a Minneapolis-based electronics retailer, has no one design format for its 40-plus stores. Instead, each store is planned by a company committee to fit the socioeconomic patterns of the community. Specific design features are related to desired effect, for example, low-price atmosphere, quality ambience.

An exciting innovation in store design is Montgomery Ward's Tucson, Arizona, building. Using clever architectural techniques, the exterior gives the impression of a one-stop mall. The interior, however, is structured into a group of

[2]"Flooring Functions as a Funnel and a Fashion Feature," *Chain Store Age Executive,* **61** (February 1985), p. 30.

specialty areas with appropriate names: The Kids Store, The Apparel Store, Music Express, Auto Express, Home Ideas, and so on. Thus, the shopper can enjoy the "feeling" of one-stop shopping in a carefully designed layout of merchandise areas to facilitate that goal.

Lamston, a variety chain with almost 30 stores in New Jersey and New York, showed how a redesigned store could increase sales. Allocating space in its four prototype stores to Plymouth Stores, a women's ready-to-wear chain, Lamston registered a 30 percent sales increase in its variety store section. With common ownership of both chains, the parent, Plymouth/Lamston Stores, demonstrated the economic potential of a creative store redesign.

Allotting Space

The amount of space that is allotted to a particular department is determined by the retailer's judgment of how much space is required to display a proper assortment of the merchandise. The location of departments and of merchandise within departments is decided primarily on the basis of their contribution to profits, which is usually figured on the basis of profits per square foot of floor space. The departments and merchandise that have the highest profit margins are given the best locations in the store. The process of determining these locations is called **mapping.**

The most valuable space is near entrances on the main floor

Research on customers' traffic and shopping patterns has shown that the most valuable space in a store is near the entrances on the main floor. Merchandise in these locations receives the most exposure because customers see it upon entering and leaving the store. Perfumes, cosmetics, handbags, shirts, neckties, and umbrellas are among the items that retailers most frequently place on the main floor. The least valuable space is on the topmost floor at the greatest distance from the elevators and escalators. Restaurants, furniture departments, and floor covering departments are customarily located on upper floors. These two locations—main and upper floors—represent the extremes of space value within a store.

An interesting example of the relationship between layout and merchandise strategy is the move by Sears, Roebuck in the late 1980s to restructure its stores for increased sales. Spurred by the trend toward specialty areas within department stores and by its own entrance into discount operations, Sears began an analysis of how its stores should be restructured. The emphasis on layout, design, and traffic patterns is testament to the crucial part that such factors play in a store's success. (At this writing, Sear's restructuring has shown fair-to-poor results. In 1991, the company took the drastic step of dismissing a significant number of employees and freezing the 1991 salaries of some 20,000 others at 1990 levels.)

Another example is Higbee's, a Cleveland department store. By a series of changes involving lights, color, entrances, materials, and space allocation, the company transformed its old look into a modern, exciting one. Judging from the jump in sales volume, shoppers responded enthusiastically to the change.

The most outstanding feature of Woolworth Express stores, spinoffs of Woolworth variety stores, is the tremendous merchandise assortment. With close to 10,000 different items for shoppers to select, each store is designed to allow maximum customer exposure to the goods. Wall and floor space are packed with merchandise, but intelligent layouts and colorful decor make shopping pleasant and easy.

Merchandise Placement

Convenience goods are located differently than shopping goods

Convenience, impulse, and other inexpensive items that sell quickly are located in high-traffic areas next to entrances, elevators, and escalators. Shopping goods, which are more expensive items and are purchased infrequently, are placed on the upper floors. In order to draw attention to merchandise on upper levels, retailers sometimes split departments. That is, they set up areas on the main floor that contain representative samples of merchandise from departments on upper floors. For example, men's apparel as well as women's may occupy one or more floors and offer a complete assortment of clothing ranging from socks and underwear to topcoats and from blue jeans to formal wear. On the one hand, this provides a convenience to shoppers who have very general ideas about the merchandise that will fill their needs. It allows them to survey the full range of available goods, define their needs and preferences, and select items that are coordinated with and complement their wardrobes.

However, many customers undoubtedly purchase socks and underwear on a routine basis and do not want to make their way through several departments in order to make such small purchases. Therefore, stores may feature trimmed-down versions of their full departments on the main floor. In the case of men's clothing, these main floor departments usually stock socks, underwear, shirts, ties, toiletries, and accessories like belts, cuff links, tie pins, cologne, and lotions. There may even be a limited section of ready-to-wear slacks. The idea is to provide convenience shopping and a sample of goods to be found in the full department.

Other considerations in planning a store's layout are the location of departments in relation to inventories stored off the selling floor, and the location of departments in relation to one another.

Supermarket and Specialty Stores

Supermarket layouts are also planned on the basis of selling, storage, and administrative requirements. Though not generally considered as such, supermarkets are highly departmentalized. There are distinct areas for groceries, produce, meat, and so forth. In deciding the amount of space needed for each department, planners consider such matters as display equipment (e.g., freezers), the store's concentration on special merchandise categories, space for rack jobbers, and departmental profit expectations. The latter means simply that more space will be allotted to the departments that give the store its largest profits. The size of storage and administrative areas is kept to a minimum consistent with the smooth flow of merchandise, employees, and customers.

Merchandise placement in specialty stores has changed

At one time specialty stores tended to minimize the amount of merchandise on the selling floors. This policy was consistent with their emphasis on service and consultive selling. Today, however, the reverse is true, with only the most exclusive stores clinging to the earlier practice. The fact is that the soaring costs of space compel most specialty stores to maximize the size of their selling areas and to display as much merchandise as possible.

Small-Store Considerations

When deciding on layout, proprietors of small stores should plan for aisles that allow customers easy movement and afford them an opportunity to view and handle merchandise in comfort. Space for goods that will be on sale, or for slow-moving merchandise, should be located in areas of highest customer concentration. The guidelines used for departmentalizing large stores also apply to smaller ones.

Securing Help With Layouts

Retailers can obtain information about layouts from trade magazines like *Chain Store Age* and *Stores;* trade associations like the National Retail Federation, the Institute for Store Planners, and the National Retail Hardware Association; and the U.S. Department of Commerce.

Displays

Displays have much to do with the volume of a store's sales. In fact, some retailers estimate that more than one-fourth of their sales are generated through displays. To prepare a display properly, one must understand the effects of combining merchandise with color, lights, and tasteful props.

The knowledgeable use of glass, metal, plastic, cloth, and wood results in displays that interest customers. The idea is to create a mood that induces the shopper to buy. This is true for displays in supermarkets as well as for those in department stores and styled specialty shops.

A good display often suggests merchandise that may not even be an intrinsic part of the display. For example, a scene showing a backyard on a summer day emphasizing lawn furniture may contain a few nicely designed dishes and silverware as well. If the display is done artfully, these related items will cause some shoppers to look for the merchandise. Depending on the size of the store and its

Attractive fixtures contribute to the effectiveness of displays.
Courtesy: Neiman Marcus.

staff and policies, decisions about interior displays may be made by a display department, an experienced salesperson, or a team of designers, merchandise managers, and salespeople.

A more thorough treatment of displays is contained in Chapter 14.

Air Conditioning

Stores today are designed with central air conditioning, and enclosed shopping malls have total climate control. Air conditioning provides a clean, comfortable environment in which to shop and work. Customers expect to find adequate climate control in stores, and most retail outlets, particularly large department stores, must provide it to maintain a competitive position. Some small independent stores have not installed air conditioning because of space or financial limitations.

Transportation Within the Store

Elevators and escalators

Stairs are generally adequate for two- or three-level stores, but elevators or escalators are needed in taller structures. Escalators eliminate the waiting required by elevators, and reduce congestion. Also, escalators take up less space than a bank of elevators and give customers a bird's-eye view of one floor as they ascend to the next. Large stores still provide elevators to move customers quickly between departments that are several floors apart. Elevators are also provided as an accommodation for the aged and the handicapped.

RETAIL STRATEGY
A Customer-Oriented Home Center*

Hechinger (Washington, D.C.), like most home improvement centers, got its start in life as a lumberyard with building accessories. In more recent years, as the do-it-yourself market expanded, it revised its outlets to aim at the householder. One of our staffers visited a Hechinger unit in Richmond, VA, and reported thusly:

> This Hechinger unit, located in a relatively new strip center in Richmond, VA, looks on the outside as it does on the inside: bright, new, clean, and totally customer-oriented. This home center is as different as it could possibly be from the typical "yard" I visited just a half hour before. Whereas the "competitor" was a semi-warehouse and cleanliness was not a necessary option, this Hechinger store was immaculate. It was well lit, music was coming over the PA system, the aisles were wide. Goods displayed on the shelves were stocked right out to the front, each with its label turned so that the consumer got a direct look at what was being merchandised. The gondolas the stock was kept in went to about 8-feet high but that was not a problem as the same goods that were 8-feet high were also at eye level. Whereas the competitive store kept one selection of each product, this store had numerous selections of each product. The store also had many how-to-do-it displays set up within an aisle on a particular product group. Example: decorative interior shutters. Smack in the middle of the decorative shutters' selection was a good six feet devoted to how to install these shutters, with step-by-step directions and showing the shutters in various stages of assembly. This was not unique to shutters either-
> . . . many other product categories that required installation had similar displays . . .

*"Hechinger Formats Its Home Improvement Store in Consumer Mode," *Inside Retailing* (November 28, 1983), p. 3.

Customer traffic flow is manipulated in many stores by placing such items as impulse merchandise and food products within sight of escalators. In some cases up and down escalators are widely separated so that shoppers must move through large sections of the store to get from one to the other. While this arrangement exposes customers to more merchandise, some people find it inconvenient.

A major consideration in the design of in-store transportation is the desire to pull or push customer traffic to areas with the highest profit potential. Little wonder, then, that architects and engineers pay great attention to a retailer's instructions in the development of a store's physical plans.

STORE SERVICES

In planning a store, consideration must be given to the types of services offered to customers. With some stores, the development of an image and the promotion of sales depend greatly on the extent and quality of such services. With others, such

Customer services are often tied to store image

as no-frills operations, customers expect and receive little in the way of services, looking for low prices instead.

To the extent that customer services require store space—either exterior or interior—planners must include proper facilities for them. Listed here are examples of the kinds of services found in retail establishments. By no stretch of the imagination is this list complete; in fact, in their quest for additional customers, innovative retailers seem constantly to invent new services.

Adding to the importance that some retailers attach to customer service, in 1988 K mart appointed a director of customer service. That office was charged with establishing new standards for customer service and stressing the inclusion of service as part of the sales concept.

Proper customer service has been defined by many people. One of the best explanations is that offered by Dr. Leonard Berry of Texas A&M University. He says,[3]

Service excellence is a never-ending journey; the only option is to plug away towards better quality every day of every week of every month of every year. Quick quality of service fixes do not exist. Magic formula for permanent quality do not exist. Service quality is an attitude, a mind-set, a commitment. It is also competence. Retail executives cannot build a service-minded culture by investing in service when earnings are good and placing service on the back burner when earnings are poor. You cannot build a service-minded culture by turning the service issue on and off like a water faucet. Service excellence requires a full-court press—all of the time.

Nordstrom is a good example of a retailer's commitment to service.

Phone and Mail Orders

In Chapter 5 you learned that some retail outlets, especially department stores (mail order houses do all their business by mail), depend on phone and mail orders for a modest percentage of their sales. To conduct these operations, adequate space and modern facilities must be provided.

Personal Shoppers

A **personal shopper** is a store employee who, upon request, selects (pre-shops) merchandise for a customer prior to the customer's store visit. Relying on the personal shopper's expertise enables the customer to save shopping time (Figure 8-1). Macy's, Barneys, and Lord & Taylor are examples of chains that provide this service. Some retailers include corporations as well as individuals.

[3] *Inside Retailing* (August 15, 1988), p. 4.

Figure 8-1   The Silver Key Club is a unique personal shopping service tailored to the needs of today's fast-paced lifestyle. It is specifically for the woman or man on a tight schedule and with an ongoing need for maximum service and efficiency. *Courtesy:* Neiman Marcus.

Gift Wrapping

Customers expect this service in department and certain specialty stores. Consequently, an area that is convenient to shoppers must be set aside for it. In some stores customers are charged a modest fee for gift wrapping. This is also true for services such as delivery and returns of merchandise.

Gift Certificates

This service enables customers to purchase gifts without having to shop for specific merchandise. The shopper receives a certificate in exchange for cash or a credit charge. The holder may redeem the certificate in the store's merchandise. Proper space for the sale of gift certificates must be planned.

Delivery

Delivery service is not restricted to large stores. Historically, even the smallest retail outlets have delivered merchandise to customers. Today, however, the existence or extent of delivery service depends on the nature of the business. As a general rule, the more personalized the operation, the greater the commitment to delivery.

To provide delivery service, adequate packing and vehicular space must be planned. Though generally out of sight to shoppers, these areas are integral parts of a store's physical arrangement.

Instead of providing delivery service themselves, some department stores lease this service to outside companies. This relieves the stores of the burdens of delivery personnel and equipment. "Leasing out" is also maintained by some stores for installation and repair work requested by customers.

Eating Facilities

In-store food service keeps customers in shopping areas longer

Many specialty stores, department stores, and shopping centers feature restaurants, snack bars, or luncheonettes. Their main purpose is to keep shoppers in the stores longer, thereby increasing the possibility of sales. Until recently, in-store eating places were money losers but were maintained for the convenience of customers. Having learned some basics about food services, however, many stores are realizing profits from their eating facilities. On the other hand, some stores lease their food services.

Since eating quarters require substantial investments in space, equipment, furniture, and appointments, retailers make careful judgments before committing themselves to food services.

Alterations

Stores that sell ready-to-wear men's and/or women's clothing frequently provide alteration services for customers, with or without an added cost. Obviously, space is required to do alterations properly. This includes working space for tailors and fitters, equipment, and storage. This space is normally located near the selling areas.

Layaway Plan

A **layaway plan** is used for customers who want to buy specific merchandise but are unable or unwilling to make payment at the time of sale. Instead, the store holds the merchandise until it is fully paid for. A down payment is usually required and, in some cases, installment payments are due until the final payment is made. At that time, the customer receives the merchandise.

Other Store Services

In addition to those already discussed, store services include prepackaging of certain types of merchandise, information booths, classes—for example, sewing—merchandise returns, baby-sitting, refunds and exchanges, extended store

Consumers use store-provided scanners to tally purchases and save time.
Courtesy: Bull HN Information Systems Inc.

hours, bridal registry, fashion shows and consultations, gift mailing, beauty salons, fur storage, check cashing, and credit. This last service will be discussed fully in Chapter 18.

In a bridal registry, a bride and groom specify their choice of wedding-related gifts at a store that maintains a registry. Friends and relatives can then check with the store to determine which gifts have already been purchased. The system enables the newlyweds to receive the gifts they want and guides gift givers in their choice of gifts. In some cases, special salespeople are available to help customers who speak a language other than English.

In connection with registries, AT&T Information Systems sells a computerized Gift Registry System. It provides centralized information for bridal, baby, cosmetic, and wardrobe registries. The system also tracks sales results and identifies slow-moving items.

In addition to *stores* that provide delivery and other services, some mall developers offer limited services. For example, Harry Newman, Jr., a California developer, provides carry-out and gift-wrapping services to shoppers. For an additional personal touch, he has mall personnel wear badges reading, "Can I Help You?"

In a surprising departure from generally accepted beliefs, a 1988 survey of shoppers conducted by Impact Resources, Inc., revealed that store service ranked well below other considerations. The results showed the following:

ITEM	RANK
Broad merchandise selection	1
Quality of goods	Tied for 2 and 3
Price	
Location	4
Service	5

With the great emphasis on service today, it may be that consumers are becoming accustomed to better treatment in stores and are concentrating more on merchandise factors. Whatever the reason, it is doubtful that merchants will reduce their attention to store services in the near future.

Customer Safety and Conveniences

Fire procedures and controls are essential

A word should be said about providing for the safety of customers. With so many shoppers passing through most stores, it is absolutely essential that management provide for fire emergencies. This involves installing fire extinguishers, developing and posting procedures to be followed in the event of a fire, and, at least in the case of large stores, installing automatic sprinkler systems. In addition, the many tragedies in which people in public places have been unable to reach exits during a fire have made us more conscious of the need for adequate and identifiable exits. All communities have building codes with specific fire safety regulations, and most retailers have conformed to them.

Store owners and managers must also insist on aisles that are free from debris, exit signs that are properly lit, and safe parking areas. They should be certain that electrical and plumbing fixtures are in proper working condition, and that electric wires and outlets are checked periodically. Elevators and escalators are subject to municipal inspection and must be repaired quickly.

Needless to say, many stores provide at least minimal toilet facilities for customers. Larger ones offer other conveniences, such as attractive lounges, dressing rooms (individual or communal), selling area seating, lockers, drinking fountains, pay telephones, coatrooms, play areas, first aid treatment, and doormen. Some firms supply customers with coffee or other refreshments, and others pipe tasteful music into their selling departments.

A good example of a retailer's attention to service is the new Abraham & Straus department store in New York City's A&S Plaza. In an attempt to establish a service image, the store employs many more salespeople than do most other similar stores. Red telephones are located strategically for customers to secure information, and doormen stand at all entrances. The store even has a concierge desk whose personnel make the shopper's stay more pleasant and productive by providing help.

Another example of the importance of customer comfort is the use of air destratifiers in stores. Based on the fact that hot air rises while cool air falls, this equipment modifies air flow to achieve a comfortable balance for shoppers. Well-known retailers that have installed the system include J. C. Penney, Dayton Hudson, Target, and Sears, Roebuck.

Lucky Stores, a chain of almost 500 supermarkets, opened new stores in 1988 with a major emphasis on customer convenience and service. Called Advantage, these stores feature special in-store traffic patterns to help shoppers in a hurry, lighting that highlights particular product categories, easy-to-read informational banners that are colorful and attractive, and plastic degradable grocery bags.

NEW TERMS

boutique pattern   lay away plan
free-flow pattern   mapping
grid pattern   personal shopper
impression management

CHAPTER HIGHLIGHTS

1. Large stores use consultants to prepare a store for occupancy. Small stores generally lack this capability; they work directly with contractors.
2. A store's physical structure is an important part of its image.
3. A store's architecture should blend with that of surrounding stores and neighborhoods.
4. The number and location of store entrances are related to concerns of shoplifting, security, and safety.
5. Though adequate at most times, parking space may be insufficient during busy holiday seasons or special-occasion shopping days like Mother's Day.
6. Exterior lighting and signs add to a store's image.
7. Store lighting has both practical and dramatic applications. Exterior lighting is important for reasons of safety, convenience, and appearance. Management is conscious of energy consumption, making every effort to maintain a good appearance at a lower cost. Incandescent, fluorescent, and metallic-vapor lights are used for particular effects.
8. The ultimate purpose of store modernization, which involves remodeling or renovating, is the growth of an enterprise. Stores are modernized to increase their appeal and reduce expenses.

9. Store layout involves identifying guidelines, establishing layout patterns, allotting space, and arranging merchandise and departments. Today, contrary to past practice, most specialty stores maximize the size of their selling areas and display as much merchandise as possible.

10. Displays of merchandise contribute significantly to a store's sales. Good displays motivate shoppers to buy.

11. Store services include phone and mail orders, personal shoppers, gift wrapping, gift certificates, delivery, eating facilities, alterations, layaway plans, prepackaging, information booths, classes, merchandise returns, baby-sitting, refunds and exchanges, extended store hours, bridal registry, fashion shows and consultations, gift mailing, beauty salons, fur storage, check cashing, and credit.

12. Customer safety calls for fire protection, aisles that are free from debris, well-lit exit signs, and safe parking. Customer conveniences include rest rooms, lounges and dressing rooms, selling area seating, lockers, drinking fountains, pay telephones, coatrooms, play areas, first aid treatment, doormen, refreshments, and music.

REVIEW QUESTIONS

1. What is meant by impression management? Of what significance is it to retailers?
2. In order to use a consultant properly, what needs must a retailer identify when planning a new store?
3. How have chain stores minimized the rising costs of store construction?
4. How is interior store lighting related to a store's image?
5. What are the two basic reasons for store modernization, and what is its ultimate purpose?
6. What are some of the objectives to consider in the development of an in-store display?

DISCUSSION QUESTIONS

1. Can a store's image be judged from its show window displays? Explain.
2. If you were opening a store to sell men's clothing and accessories, what merchandise items would you place near the entrance? Explain.
3. Of the customer services listed in this chapter, which might be suitable to a large independent food store? Which ones would be unsuitable?

4. How might piped-in music add to a store's image? Can you think of any objections to such music? Explain.

Is Supermarket Upscaling Worth the Cost?

One type of supermarket in the city of Atlanta covers an area of 20,000 square feet. In addition to groceries, produce, and other food products, it sells a variety of nonfood items, including hardware, kitchen gadgets, and health and cosmetic merchandise. Its windows are usually covered with advertisements, without any planned attempt to create an attractive exterior.

The stores are divided into merchandise areas, with each section identified by the type of products stocked. Advertised specials are located either near the checkout counters or in the appropriate merchandise areas. Lighting is uniform throughout the store and consists mostly of fluorescent fixtures. Customer traffic is aided by wide aisles.

Though some of the stores feature gourmet food sections, they depart little from traditional supermarket offerings and displays. Emphasis is placed on a suffused consumer mix, with little attention paid to specific ethnic or social needs. However, the stores do offer such personal services as check cashing and assistance with packages.

With this situation in mind, Len Rolson, a former supermarket manager, has been thinking about opening two supermarkets in the same city—using a radically different concept. Banking on the expectation that many consumers will respond positively to innovative supermarket designs, offerings, and practices, he is considering the following.

- 12,000-square-foot stores, resulting in lower rents.
- Ethnic food sections catering to the needs and desires of the majority of ethnic groups in the trading areas.
- Elaborate gourmet areas with international displays and special lighting effects.
- A reduced emphasis on nonfood items and a corresponding broadening of food selections, with each food area entered through decorated archways.
- Tastefully lit signs announcing the day's specials in each section of the store.
- An information desk at the entrance to the store that is staffed full time and stocked with advertising materials.

While Rolson recognizes that many of his costs will be higher than those of other supermarkets, he feels that shoppers will pay more for selected items because of his stores' uniqueness. He hopes that visits to his stores will be "shopping experiences."

a. What is your opinion of Rolson's planned innovations?
b. Do you think shoppers will pay higher prices for some items, as Rolson hopes? Why?

CASE 2

Marshall Field—Upstairs and Downstairs

December 19 at New York's LaGuardia Airport—a Manhattan publishing company executive boards a flight to Chicago. She's going to Marshall Field to meet her sister, who is flying up from Indiana. They'll have lunch at the Walnut Room of the State Street store, then ride the escalator downstairs to spend the afternoon Christmas shopping. They've done it every year since they were children—it's a tradition.

Tradition abounds at Marshall Field, one of the oldest and best known of all U.S. department stores. In the late 1970s and early 1980s, though, it began to look as though sagging profits and diminishing market share were going to become a part of the Marshall Field tradition as well.

In 1982, Marshall Field, with stores concentrated in the Chicago area and in Texas, was acquired by the Batus Retail Group. Profits were down to 5 percent that year, and Marshall Field was steadily losing market share. The new management, headed by Chairman Philip Miller, decided it was time for a change of direction—it was time for Marshall Field to regain its position as the Midwest's premier retailer. Plans were drawn for a major shift in emphasis. Marshall Field budget lines were dropped and the chain launched a campaign to regain strength in the upper end of its market.

The company soon embarked on a $100 million modernization program. Planned capital expenditures included a thorough renovation of the main store on Chicago's State Street, as well as remodeling of six Chicago-area branch stores. Remodeling at the branch stores gained substantially more selling space for men's and women's apparel and accessories, by reducing the size of storage and loading areas. In stores with high shrinkage, more effective security measures were instituted. Utility costs were reduced by installing a computerized energy-management system.

Inside many of the chain's stores, selling space was redesigned to install a number of in-store boutiques, with a heavy emphasis on boutiques stocked with upscale designer accessories. Shoppers in several of Marshall Field's Chicago and Texas stores can now buy a sweater in the Liz Claiborne shop, choose a belt or a scarf from a Gucci or Chanel boutique, add a handbag from a Bottega Veneta or Fendi boutique, and top it off with a necklace or earrings from the Angela Cummings fine jewelry boutique.

Construction of the boutiques ran to nearly $450,000 apiece. Yet by mid-1985 most were contributing much higher sales per square foot than had been planned. Sales in the Louis Vuitton boutiques, for example, were targeted at $250 per square foot; in the first half of 1985, sales averaged nearly $1,000 per square foot.

In several Marshall Field stores, the designer-apparel customer can now find fashions by well-known European and American designers in the new Field Afar shops. Together with collections by designers such as Karl Lagerfeld, Giorgio Armani, Anne Klein, and Perry Ellis, Field Afar also offers an expanded line of private label merchandise. Marshall Field's contemporary division also plans a substantial increase in sales of private-label women's apparel.

In many branches, the young-teen shopper, a customer Marshall Field has been losing to other retailers, can now choose her purchases in a thoroughly remodeled juniors department. Merchandise displays include stylized mannequins arranged on elevated platforms, amid video monitors and stereo music. Boutique shopping is available for juniors, too, with the installation of ultramodern Esprit shops in a number of Marshall Field stores.

A major part of the renovation at the State Street store involved the basement level. Downtown Chicago is built on a maze of underground streets. In recent years, the city has developed much of its underground area into a system of pedestrian walkways called Pedway. Heavily traveled during the morning and evening rush hours and at lunchtime, part of the Pedway runs adjacent to Marshall Field's basement level. Long neglected and underutilized, the enormous basement space had for years been given over to budget-priced and clearance departments. Renovation plans called for a large section of the basement to be redeveloped into a series of retail shops catering to the commuter traffic. Connected to the upper levels of the store only by elevators, the new departments were to include high-end, fast-food retailers and a sizable newsstand and sundries shop, all opening directly onto the Pedway.

The unifying goal behind all the changes at Marshall Field was to increase profits by expanding its upper-end businesses.

a. What risks do you see for a long-established, well-known store like Marshall Field when it embarks on a major renovation? What are the risks of *not* modernizing?

b. Does the extensive use of in-store designer boutiques compete with Marshall Field's attempts to increase its private-label business?

c. As Marshall Field develops its basement level into shops that serve the Pedway commuter trade, how can it ensure that its "upstairs" and "downstairs" images are compatible? Or, does it matter?

REFERENCES

BELLIZZI, J. A., A. E. CROWLEY, AND R. W. HASTY. "The Effects of Color in Store Design." *Journal of Retailing*, **59** (Spring 1983), pp. 21–45.

"Entertainment Anchors: New Mall Headliners." *Chain Store Age Executive*, **65** (August 1989), pp. 54–65.

"Lighting Costs Cut: It's All Done with Mirrors." *Chain Store Age Executive*, **65** (July 1989), pp. 58–60.

"Nordstrom Defines Services." *Retailing Today*, (January 1990), p. 3.

"Woolworth Express: On a Fast Growth Track." *Chain Store Age Executive*, **64** (January 1988), pp. 146–148.

Part 3

Merchandising

Part Three is concerned with merchandise policies and procedures: how the buying of goods is organized and planned, how products are priced, and how merchandise is handled and protected.

Chapter 9 analyzes the buying function by detailing the manner in which it is organized and implemented. We study the services rendered by resident buying offices and examine the major merchandise sources available to retail buyers. We also see how retailers manage their buying operations through the utilization of retailing cooperatives and store-owned merchandise resources.

In its treatment of merchandise planning, Chapter 10 deals with the determination of *what* and *how much* a store should buy. On the basis of a compilation of consumer and trade information, we see how buyers are able to make informed decisions on the types of goods to buy. We then deal with desired levels of purchasing by studying open-to-buy techniques and assortment plans. The chapter ends with a discussion of vendor relations, including terms of purchase, sales and profit experience, and negotiations.

The pricing of merchandise follows its purchase, and Chapter 11 outlines the ways in which retailers determine prices. We analyze the customer, competition, costs, and laws as elements in pricing decisions. Then we look at the variety of price policies used by retailers. Next we study the arithmetic of pricing by calculating markups, and we complete the chapter with an examination of markdowns.

Part Three ends with a discussion of how stores handle and protect merchandise. In Chapter 12 we follow the path taken by merchandise as it is received, checked, marked, stored, and distributed. We also indicate how retailers are coping with the crucial problem of employee and shopper theft.

Chapter 9

The Buying Function: Organization for Buying

After completing this chapter, you should be able to:

- List the personal qualifications of buyers.
- Identify the buying elements that are basic to all types of stores.
- Identify the approaches used in organizing the buying activities of different retail organizations.
- Compare the chain store buyer's responsibilities and authority under centralized buying, decentralized buying, and centralized distribution.
- List the services performed for retailers by resident buying offices.
- Identify the reasons for selecting a resident buying office.
- List the major merchandise sources available to retail store buyers.

In the last chapter you read about the importance of merchandise placement and space allocation for the variety of goods that a store carries. In Chapters 9 and 10 we turn our attention to methods of buying merchandise.

"Goods well bought are half sold"

It is commonly stated in retail circles that "goods well bought are half sold." The best window displays, location, and sales help are of little use if goods are not available when a customer wants them. Although a store may be well financed, it may suffer losses or even business failure for lack of good buying sense—knowledge of when and what to buy and at what price.

The buyer is responsible for this aspect of retailing, that is, for stocking the store with the proper merchandise assortment at a price that customers are willing to pay and at a time when the goods are needed. If merchants were able to achieve this, they would reach the ideal state of merchandising, in which all goods are on hand when needed and are sold without any need for price reductions. This is no small task, and a good buyer must be intelligent, well trained, and able to make appropriate decisions.

PERSONAL QUALIFICATIONS OF BUYERS

Managerial and Planning Skills

A good buyer is a good manager and planner. Timing of merchandise purchases is all-important: Goods must be available to the consumer when they are needed.

Buyers must plan for delivery of merchandise at the proper time. For example, purchases of dresses are commonly made 10 to 12 weeks in advance, while basic lines like underwear, lamps, and housewares require three to five months; Christmas orders might be placed in August. Purchases made overseas may take even longer to allow for shipping.

Skill in Analyzing the Market

A good buyer is a good market analyst. Buyers must be able to look ahead and sense what customers will want and the prices they will be willing to pay. In order to interpret consumer demand, they must be skilled in gathering information from such sources as consumer surveys, past sales records, trade publications, manufacturers, other merchants, and store personnel.

Buying is complicated because the basic question is seldom what consumers want today but, rather, what they will want tomorrow. In fact, some merchants feel that buyers need a sixth sense. In spite of all the sophisticated tools for forecasting demand, buyers still need the ability to make good decisions.

More and more buyers are being freed from operational tasks. Instead, they are concentrating on working closely with vendors long before they make actual purchases. This approach enables them to influence vendor lines and to gauge

A buyer's activities include managerial as well as merchandising activities.
Courtesy: Henry Doneger Associates, Inc.

consumer needs and preferences more accurately. As told to Mark Stevens by Ralph Lauren, "A Bloomingdale's buyer acts as the store's eyes and ears. She is in the market every day, sensing new developments and learning early on where her resources are headed."[1]

When a buyer's flexibility and decision-making authority are restricted, the result is often a poor profit picture for the retailer. Such was the case in 1989 when Consolidated Stores, a leading retailer of closeout goods, reduced its buyers' freedom and autonomy. Acknowledging its error, the company changed its policy by recognizing that the art of buying should not be stifled by bureaucratic rules. Not surprisingly, the change in policy resulted in an upsurge of sales and profits.

Understanding of Finance

A good buyer must be interested in the financial status of suppliers and the quality of the merchandise they carry. The vendor's financial position, work force, and production capabilities generally affect the delivery and quality of merchandise. Consequently, the buyer must investigate these aspects prior to selecting merchandise.

Understanding of the Consumer

Qualifications of a good buyer

A good buyer should be a consumer advocate in the sense that he or she conveys consumer wants and needs to vendors. The buyer should be sensitive to potential consumer satisfaction with new products, materials, and product

---

[1]Mark Stevens, *Like No Other Store in the World* (New York: Harper & Row, 1979).

changes. Buyers also serve as advisers to manufacturers—they supply them with market information and investigate product quality and value.

With the growing sophistication of computers, buyers are basing decisions more on consumer preferences than on vendor-available lines. This market-tuned approach is reaping large dividends for many retailers. As noted in the magazine *Advertising Age*,[2]

> *The consumer is still the boss, and getting consumers to seek out a brand remains the best guarantee that a product will find a place on the shelf. Consumer choice is everyone's bottom line.*

Buyers should also understand a consumer's primary motivations. It is generally agreed that the most important factors affecting consumer selection of a store are price, breadth of merchandise, and merchandise quality.

Skill in Public Relations

Good buyers represent their stores. As such, they have a responsibility to vendors, store personnel, the retail industry, and the community for which they buy. They therefore should project a positive image and abide by all aspects of the law.

Skill in Communicating

In addition to the qualities just noted, buyers must have the ability to motivate sales personnel. Whether written or verbal, information to promote sales is necessary, and buyers must take the lead in providing the facts. For example, many buyers conduct merchandise and fashion clinics for their sales personnel.

Skill in Negotiating

Buying is not simply a matter of accepting or rejecting a seller's price and conditions. Buyers must have acute negotiating skills because there are many other matters that must be agreed upon by both parties. These include delivery, return privileges, the availability of merchandise on reorder, price guarantees on reorders, discounts, and promotional aids.

THE ELEMENTS OF BUYING

Sound buying procedures contain certain elements that are basic in all types of retail establishments, large or small. Buying involves the following steps.

1. Determining the demand for a particular product.
2. Evaluating merchandise in stock.

[2]"Store Label Threat Returns," *Advertising Age* (May 22, 1989), p. 16.

DATE RECEIVED IN OFFICE			OVERSTOCK LIST AND TRANSFER SHEET			Vendor Date Store # Mgr. For office use only		
Comm. #	Description	Reg. retail	Current retail	Overstock qty.	Transfer to	Qty.	Date/comments	

Figure 9-1   Keeping track of merchandise. This form indicates overstocked and transferred merchandise.

3. Planning for the type, brand, and quantity of merchandise needed.
4. Selecting the sources of merchandise (suppliers, resources).
5. Negotiating for the purchase of goods and placing the orders.
6. Receiving and inspecting the merchandise, placing the goods in stock, and pricing.
7. Checking the selling pace or movement of the merchandise. Systems for keeping track of merchandise are discussed later in this chapter (see Figure 9-1).
8. Reordering merchandise that remains in demand (see Figure 9-2).

			VENDOR _____ Pg. ___ Of ___										
			DATE _____ MANAGER _____										
Speedy Order List			STORE NAME _____ STORE NO. ____										
STYLE NUMBER	QTY.	UNIT RETAIL	STYLE NUMBER	QTY.	UNIT RETAIL	STYLE NUMBER	QTY.	UNIT RETAIL	STYLE NUMBER	QTY.	UNIT RETAIL		

Figure 9-2   An order form used by a small or medium-sized store.

Several approaches are used in organizing the buying function

All of the foregoing steps should lead to effective buying, which in turn should make for ready sales. A major goal of the buyer, then, is to purchase a steady flow of profitable merchandise for resale. But first it is necessary to develop a system that gets the job done.

Even though the buying activities are the same for all retailing institutions, several approaches are used in organizing the buying function because stores vary in size and type.

ORGANIZATION FOR BUYING

Small Retailers

In small stores, buying is not treated separately from other functions. In fact, as stated in Chapter 6, the owner or manager of a small retail shop is generally in charge of all facets of the business, including buying.

Because the sales volume of a small store is lower than that of large retailers and there are fewer employees, the buying task is not as clearly defined as it would be in a more formal structure. In fact, because the buyer-owner makes the decisions, there is greater flexibility with much lower operational costs. Often the smaller retailer becomes affiliated with independent buying offices. As indicated later in this chapter, these resident buying offices advise retailers on the best sources of merchandise and work with them on merchandise selection.

Many small store buyers rely on help from manufacturers' sales representatives, who come to the store with samples of new items and up-to-date merchandise information. In stores that carry fast-moving products like food and drugs, it is not uncommon for sales representatives to make daily or weekly visits. In the apparel industry, visits are scheduled much less frequently. During the major market seasons (see Figures 9-3 and 9-4), manufacturers show their products to buyers at showrooms in the market and at trade shows.

Large Retailers

Buyers may specialize in one product category

Larger retailers treat the buying function as a separate activity. Experienced people are assigned to a specific department to carry out the task of buying. The size of the department depends on the store and its merchandise needs. Some stores have buyers who specialize in only one product category, for example, coats, lingerie, or shoes. This arrangement requires a larger staff, with correspondingly higher costs. The advantage of specialized buying is the in-depth knowledge that buyers develop. Although actual buying is left to individual store buyers, some large chains employ specialists who gather market information for their subsidiaries.

Stores with Branches

Buyers in department stores with branches are responsible for buying for the branches as well as the main store. Their offices are generally in the main store. The number of lines for which each buyer is responsible depends on the size of the department and the sales volume of each line. Some stores have several buyers in one merchandise area, each buying a separate line. For example, in the children's department, infants' wear might be handled by one buyer while children's wear is purchased by another buyer.

Buying for branches can present complications when the branch store's customers have different needs from those of the main store's customers. In these cases, some branches have their own buyers. In other cases, **associate buyers** work with the main store buyer. While the main store buyer carries the responsibility for running a profitable department in the main store as well as in the branches, the associate buyer's major responsibility consists of ordering merchandise for branch store customers.

Dallas Market Center Company
1991 Market Calendar

Women's and Children's Apparel Market
January 24-29*
April 4-9*
June 6-11*
August 15-20*
October 24-29*

Men's & Boys' Apparel Market
January 19-22
April 6-9
July 20-23
September 21-24

Dallas Western Market
January 19-22
April 7-9
September 22-24

Dallas Apparel Mart/Menswear Mart
Market Mondays
February 25
May 13
July 22
September 23
November 18

* Tuesday by appointment only.

Figure 9-3   A calendar of market dates for the Dallas Regional Market Center. Reprinted by permission of Dallas Market Center.

1991 Dallas Market Center Calendar

Call DMC Travel Services: 1-800-634-2630

JANUARY

S	M	T	W	T	F	S
		1	2	3	4	5
6	7	8	9	10	11	12
13	14	15	16	17	18	19
20	21	22	23	24	25	26
27	28	29	30	31		

January 9
Day of Education

January 10-17
DALLAS SUPERMARKET
International Lighting Market *January 10-15*
Dallas Spring Gift Market *January 10-17*
Bath, Bed and Linen Show *January 10-17*
National Decorative Accessories Market *January 10-17*
Temporary Gift and Home Furnishings Exhibits *January 11-15*
Winter Home Furnishings Market *January 12-17*

January 19-22
Men's, Boys and Western Apparel Market

January 24-29
Women's and Children's Summer Apparel and Accessories Market *(January 29 - Appointments Suggested)*

January 26-28
JAM - Jewelry and Accessories Market *(Apparel Mart)*

January 28- February 1
Dallas Fabric Show

FEBRUARY

S	M	T	W	T	F	S
					1	2
3	4	5	6	7	8	9
10	11	12	13	14	15	16
17	18	19	20	21	22	23
24	25	26	27	28		

February 4
First Monday *(Home Furnishings/Gift)*

February 23-26
Southwestern Shoe Travelers Fall Show *(February 26 - Appointments Suggested)*

February 25
Market Monday *(Apparel/Menswear Mart)*

MARCH

S	M	T	W	T	F	S
					1	2
3	4	5	6	7	8	9
10	11	12	13	14	15	16
17	18	19	20	21	22	23
24	25	26	27	28	29	30
31						

March 10-13
Dallas Toy Show

March 10-13
Dallas Holiday Early Buy Market

APRIL

S	M	T	W	T	F	S
	1	2	3	4	5	6
7	8	9	10	11	12	13
14	15	16	17	18	19	20
21	22	23	24	25	26	27
28	29	30				

April 1
First Monday *(Home Furnishings/Gift)*

April 4-9
MEGA MARKET *(April 9 - Appointments Suggested)*
International Women's Apparel and Special Sizes Show *April 4-9*
Active Sportswear Show *April 4-9*
Group III Collections *April 4-9*
Studio? Directives *April 4-9*
Childrenswear Super Show *April 4-9*
Accessories Showcase *April 4-9*
Bridal Fashion Fair *April 4-9*
Men's Designer Gallery *April 6-9*
Men's and Boys' National Apparel Market *April 6-9*
Western Market Roundup *April 6-9*
National Imprinted Sportswear Expo *April 5-7*
Visual Merchandising Idea Symposium *April 4-9*

MAY

S	M	T	W	T	F	S
			1	2	3	4
5	6	7	8	9	10	11
12	13	14	15	16	17	18
19	20	21	22	23	24	25
26	27	28	29	30	31	

May 6
Spring First Monday

May 13
Market Monday *(Apparel/Menswear Mart)*

JUNE

S	M	T	W	T	F	S
						1
2	3	4	5	6	7	8
9	10	11	12	13	14	15
16	17	18	19	20	21	22
23	24	25	26	27	28	29
30						

June 3
First Monday *(Home Furnishings/Gift)*

June 6-11
Women's and Children's Christmas/Holiday Apparel Market *(June 11 - Appointments Suggested)*

June 9-10
Fashion Footwear Preview

June 28
Gift Day of Education

June 29 - July 5
Dallas Christmas Gift Market *(Temporary exhibits close at noon July 3)*

June 29 - July 5
Bath, Bed and Linen Show

JULY

S	M	T	W	T	F	S
	1	2	3	4	5	6
7	8	9	10	11	12	13
14	15	16	17	18	19	20
21	22	23	24	25	26	27
28	29	30	31			

July 12
Dallas Home Furnishings Day of Education

July 13-17
Dallas International Lighting Market

July 13-18
Dallas National Decorative Accessories Market
Dallas Summer Home Furnishings Market

July 20-23
Men's and Boys' Apparel Market

July 22
Market Monday *(Apparel/Menswear Mart)*

July 29 - August 1
Dallas Fabric Show

AUGUST

S	M	T	W	T	F	S
				1	2	3
4	5	6	7	8	9	10
11	12	13	14	15	16	17
18	19	20	21	22	23	24
25	26	27	28	29	30	31

August 5
First Monday *(Home Furnishings/Gift)*

August 15-20
Women's and Children's Holiday/Resort Apparel Market *(August 20 - Appointments Suggested)*

August 24-27
Southwestern Shoe Travelers Spring Show *(August 27 - Appointments Suggested)*

SEPTEMBER

S	M	T	W	T	F	S
1	2	3	4	5	6	7
8	9	10	11	12	13	14
15	16	17	18	19	20	21
22	23	24	25	26	27	28
29	30					

September 21-24
Dallas Fall Gift Market *(Temporary exhibits close at 3 p.m. September 24)*

September 21-24
Men's, Boys and Western Apparel Market

September 23
Market Monday *(Apparel/Menswear Mart)*

September 24-26*
Dallas Toy Show

* Date subject to change

OCTOBER

S	M	T	W	T	F	S
		1	2	3	4	5
6	7	8	9	10	11	12
13	14	15	16	17	18	19
20	21	22	23	24	25	26
27	28	29	30	31		

October 7
First Monday *(Home Furnishings/Gift)*

October 24-29
Women's and Children's Spring Apparel Market *(October 29 - Appointments Suggested)*
Childrenswear Super Show *October 24-29*
Bridal Fashion Fair *October 24-29*

November 4
Fall First Monday

November 18
Market Monday *(Apparel/Menswear Mart)*

NOVEMBER

S	M	T	W	T	F	S
					1	2
3	4	5	6	7	8	9
10	11	12	13	14	15	16
17	18	19	20	21	22	23
24	25	26	27	28	29	30

DECEMBER

S	M	T	W	T	F	S
1	2	3	4	5	6	7
8	9	10	11	12	13	14
15	16	17	18	19	20	21
22	23	24	25	26	27	28
29	30	31				

December 2
First Monday *(Home Furnishings/Gift)*

December 8-9
Fashion Footwear Preview

LEGEND

MEGA MARKET
- Women's and Children's Apparel
- Men's/Boys'/Western Apparel
- Market Monday
- Jewelry and Accessories
- Shoes
- Active Sportswear
- Bridal
- Children's Apparel

SUPER MARKET
- Home Furnishings/Lighting/Decorative Accessories/Floor Covering
- Gift/Bed, Bath and Linen
- Fabric
- Toy
- First Monday

Dates subject to change.

An Extra Large Invitation For An Extra Large Event.

You're invited to the biggest fashion event of the year — the 2nd annual MEGA MARKET.

Last year's MEGA MARKET was a huge success. This year will be even bigger. With more lines, more fashion shows, more parties, more fun. More of everything. Call **1-800-MEGA-630** for market information and advance registration materials.

It's all here April 4-9, 1991.

Plus, Extra Large Savings On Airfare And Hotel Rates.

Call **1-800-MEGA-630** today, and book now to receive your biggest travel discounts. You'll be getting the most for your travel dollar because DMC Travel Services always offers the guaranteed lowest airfare and hotel rates.

DMC TRAVEL SERVICES
Time is money.
We save both.
1-800-MEGA-630

THE DALLAS APPAREL MART/MENSWEAR MART/MARKET HALL.

2300 Stemmons Freeway
Suite 5G51
Box 586442
Dallas, Texas 75258

Accessories Showcase
April 4-9

Active Sportswear Show
April 6-8

Bridal Fashion Fair
April 4-9

Childrenswear Super Show
April 4-9

Group III Collections
April 4-9

International Women's Apparel and Special Sizes Show
April 4-9

Studio Directives
April 4-9

Visual Merchandising Idea Symposium
April 4-9

National Imprinted Sportswear Expo
April 5-7

Men's Designer Gallery
April 6-9

Men's and Boys' National Apparel Market
April 6-9

Dallas Western Market
April 7-9

Bulk Rate
U.S. Postage
PAID
Permit No. 7
Dallas, Texas

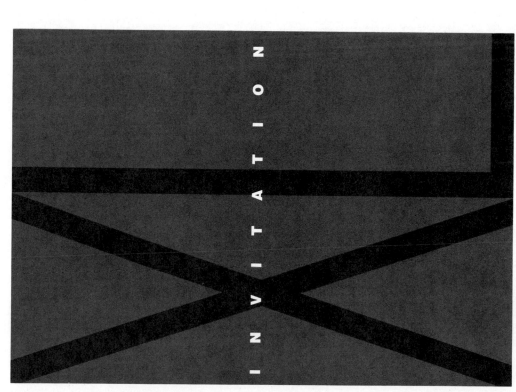

Figure 9-4 An example of how buyers are invited to a market. Reprinted by permission of Dallas Market Center.

When branch store involvement becomes too great a burden for a main store buyer, the buyer's responsibilities may be changed. For example, it is not uncommon to see store buyers actually selling during peak hours. This is done because contact with customers gives the buyer firsthand information regarding their needs and wants. However, because of their branch store responsibilities, many buyers are relieved of selling functions and rely on reports from associate buyers and their assistants. Assistant buyers help buyers and associate buyers perform their duties.

Specifically, associate and assistant buyers aid main store buyers with reorders and follow-up orders. At times they accompany buyers on visits to suppliers. A good buyer uses the input from assistants who maintain consumer contact through floor selling.

Some very large retailers maintain offices for their buyers away from the stores. This is similar to the central buying arrangement used by chain stores (Chapter 6), in which buying and selling activities are separated. In these cases the branches are responsible for all merchandise activities other than buying.

Chain Stores

Chain store buyers generally are trained specialists

In most chain organizations control of the buying function is exercised by trained specialists through a regional or home office. The practice of employing buying specialists for each kind of merchandise is demonstrated by chain stores like J. C. Penney and Sears, which may have a buyer who purchases only, say, carpets. This buyer is responsible for researching the market for carpets, comparing the quality and prices of competing goods, and buying the product at the best price.

Chain store buyers' responsibilities and authority differ from one chain to another because the buying structures may be different. The method used depends on the kinds of merchandise and the amount of autonomy delegated to store managers.

Once a decision regarding direction or policy is made by top management, a buyer's role is to implement that decision with intelligence and dispatch. For example, when Sears, Roebuck committed itself in the 1980s to the development of a fashion image, a separate inventory management system was established for fashion apparel. Sears' buyers then had to adapt to a revised category of goods.

Centralized Buying

Some chains use a **centralized buying** system in which the buyers make all the decisions regarding selection, quantities, and distribution to stores. This system is most commonly used for fashion goods because it allows for speedy action. The central buyer has full authority to order and plan each store's inventory.

This system of centralized buying has made it possible for chains to amass great savings and profits. In fact, in 1912 F. W. Woolworth wrote: "The success of our organization may be attributed to great buying power and the ability to take advantage of all cash discounts combined with economy of distribution." This could equally well describe the policy of most chains today.

Decentralized Buying

Some chains equip each of its divisions with its own buying staff (**decentralized buying**). This is done to establish buyers closer to their customer base. Nordstrom has demonstrated the effectiveness of this plan as it continues its expansion to new territories and its emphasis on good customer relations.

Centralized Distribution

Other chains use a **centralized distribution plan** (central warehousing). Under this plan buyers make all the purchasing decisions. However, the individual store managers have control over the depth of their stock because they order what they need from a distribution center. This method is most often used in food and drug chains because it works best with items that are in steady demand. Since the store managers are provided with checklists from which to order, they are responsible for maintaining sufficient stock of items that are in demand.

Price List Agreements

In still other arrangements the central buyer develops merchandise catalogs or lists that are distributed to the different store managers for selection. Under these **listing plans,** also known as **price list agreements,** the central buyer shops for the merchandise and arranges price agreements with vendors. The store managers may order directly from these sources, and they have greater say regarding the merchandise stocked in their units. The catalogs and lists are prepared often so that a continuous flow of new merchandise is available to the stores. Variety chains generally use price list agreements for staple and semistaple merchandise.

Specification Buying

Specification buying gives the retailer unique merchandise

Concentration of buying power in one place contributes to lower costs because of volume discounts, and allows for savings and quality control through **specification buying.** In this method buyers develop product specifications for their purchases rather than selecting from what is available in the market.

Specification buying allows the merchant to design unusual goods that are not in direct competition with branded merchandise. Manufacturers are willing to produce such products when the orders are large enough. The obvious advantage to the retailer is a product that is exclusive. Generally, only large retailers can take advantage of specification buying because small retailers cannot order in sufficient quantities to make it worthwhile for a manufacturer to produce the desired item.

J. C. Penney is notable for its use of this practice. Since Penney does not manufacture the merchandise it sells, it must buy from others. Eighty-five percent of Penney's domestic merchandise is purchased by specification buying, which involves negotiations by buyers for the development of J. C. Penney items of predetermined quality and design. The specifications are issued in writing and usually are highly detailed. The Penney specifications for a dress shirt, for example, may run to eight typewritten pages.

Private Labels

Private labels (store brands), like specification buying, require a fairly high degree of purchasing power. Large stores or groups that buy together use private labels to give the stores some individuality and freedom from direct price competition. In order to satisfy the demands of upscale retailers, some national brand vendors manufacture designer labels for the former while continuing to produce traditional labels for mass merchants.

Private labels are often used effectively to differentiate products from similar name-brand merchandise. In fact, one of the reasons for Nordstrom's success is its offering of distinctive private-label goods that remind customers and alert others to the retail source of these products.

J. C. Penney and Sears, Roebuck are examples of chains that have switched from selling private labels exclusively to offering both private labels and national brands.

One reason for the retail industry's interest in private labels was summarized as follows by Wendy Warren, a retail buying expert:[3]

> *Branded merchandise is being sold by off-price retailers. And, in a mall, the same brand could be sold in 80 of the 100 stores. All the stores look alike. A store may have a one-day sale event and all the others are affected by an item and are forced to meet that price. Private label gives the store opportunities to have a distinctive image.*

Private labels are available to small retailers through cooperatives, for example, Tru-Value Hardware, and buying offices.

[3]Muriel J. Adams, ''Private Label: Now Trump.'' *Stores* (June 1988), pp. 12–24.

Despite the trend by major retailers to go the private-label route, national brands outsold house brands in the late 1980s. This was particularly true in the sale of designer jeans and fleecewear.

Buying and New Technology

Computers are the key to efficiency and lower costs

Because chain organizations are much larger than independent stores, they have the means to operate more efficiently at lower costs and to save their customers money. Today buyers for chains with hundreds of units can keep track of merchandise through the use of computers. Applying new technology to buying makes it easier, as buyers say, to "have the right merchandise in the right place at the right time in the right colors, sizes, and styles and at the right price." Computerized cash registers, for example, compile information on the movement of merchandise and other data needed by management.

A **semiautomatic stock control system** replenishes stocks of nonseasonal merchandise quickly and almost automatically. J. C. Penney, for example, uses punched tickets that are mailed from the store to the nearest Penney data center. The information is transmitted overnight to the data center in New York, where the system processes the information and then issues orders to the many thousands of Penney vendors.

A **buyer's commitment system** is connected directly to the company's corporate information data base. This system provides the buyer with the facts required to respond immediately to the merchandise needs of the stores.

A **retail merchandise management system** tracks the performance of merchandise, reordering hot items ("checkouts") and identifying the cold ones ("dogs"), which are then reduced in price. The information generated for point-of-sale transactions enables store buyers to make timely decisions about reorders, price reductions, item promotions, and cost control.

Retailers often use a **stockkeeping unit (SKU)** as the basis for a merchandise management system. An SKU represents one item of inventory that has distinct characteristics. For example, if a store has 18 identical ceramic jars in stock (same shape, glaze, size, etc.), it recognizes them as 1 SKU. If at the same time the store also has 15 units of the same type of jar in stock (but with a different glaze), it has 2 SKUs. In other words, the store is carrying 33 jars, but 2 SKUs. By using SKUs, computers can be programmed to keep track of quantities and types of merchandise, thus aiding the buyer in making inventory decisions.

A pilot project initiated by J. C. Penney in the late 1980s demonstrated the effectiveness of an inventory control system called Quick Response. (Quick Response is explained in Chapter 17.) Based on point-of-sale data by SKU, the results included improved customer service, reduced markdowns, lower alteration expenses, and increased first-price sales.

Independents buy cooperatively to get lower prices

New technology has also resulted in an increase in central buying for others, such as voluntary groups of independents. These small retailers pool their orders and buy cooperatively, thereby obtaining lower prices. This practice enables them to compete more effectively with the large chains.

RETAIL STRATEGY

The Woolworth Corp.: Strategies for the 90s

1982 was a critical year for the Woolworth Corp. It turned its back on its general merchandise past for the uncertainty of a specialty store future.

Harold Sells, Chairman and CEO, in a recent interview with *Inside Retailing* alluded to the trauma surrounding the decision when he said, "We were in greater trouble than Federated today. We never went into Chapter 11, but we were in a very difficult position in 1982. We decided to close the 772 Woolco store chain and put 35,000 people out of work overnight."

In 1983, the company adopted a strategic plan that has guided it since and will continue to provide the framework for Woolworth actions into the 90s.

Has it worked? Today Woolworth is a $9 billion corporation with 40 companies operating more than 8,000 stores in 15 countries on 4 continents. Over the past 7 years its net income has increased at a compound annual growth rate of 22%.

In view of the challenges facing the retail market place of the 90s—saturation, segmentation and globalization—*Inside Retailing* sought out Mr. Sells to learn how his company is going to deal with them.

Inside Retailing: Is the current gloomy business outlook in any way altering the implementation of your strategic growth plan?

Harold Sells: No. It hasn't. If every time you have a blip in the economy you speed up or cut back on your store opening rate, you will never hit anything right. We are working now on 91 and 92. By the time we get to 91 or 92 had we cut, we might find ourselves in the teeth of a strong movement upward. So you are never right if you try to adjust. We just set a 5-year plan. This is the way we want to grow, and we'll pretty much stick to it as we try to plow through.

We don't expect 1990 to be a real boom year in retailing, yet we also don't expect a recession either. In fact, we just stepped up our store expansion program for this year. We originally planned to open 735 stores and we've stepped this up to 825.

IR: You operate about 40 companies, but your growth is concentrated in just a few of these.

HS: Seventy percent of our expansion will be concentrated in 5 or 6 chains. Foot Locker has been our big growth vehicle of the 80s, and by the end of the year we will have about 1,500 of these and we will continue to open them. Worldwide we plan about 200 with 165 of these in the United States.

IR: Is there any fear of saturation?

HS: Yes, at some point, but that is still quite a way down the road. There is probably room for another 800 to 1,000 in the U.S. We feel that every mall can take a Foot Locker and a lot of downtown areas as well. The growth will probably continue at 100 stores a year for the next 7 or 8 years. Lady Foot Locker is newer than Foot Locker. We will have about 500 or 600 of those by the end of the year. So we can open another 1,000 of these.

IR: Are they complimentary or competitive to one another?

HS: We don't feel that they cannibalize one another. The overlap is so slight you can hardly see it in the sales rate. The Foot Locker is primarily a male oriented store; it's a locker room atmosphere and I don't think that women are really comfortable going in there. So when we opened Lady Foot Locker they loved that, and I think we pulled those customers away from department stores or other places where they had been buying these products before. So they really don't hurt the Foot Lockers. In fact, in some of the bigger centers we have opened a third one called Kids Foot Locker.

IR: Foot Lockers have been your prime area for growth. What are some of the other areas?

HS: We are not putting all of our eggs in the Locker baskets. We feel that the greatest growth vehicle we will have in the 90s will be Champ Sports. Now this carries a lot of apparel and a lot of equipment. Exercise equipment, tennis racquets, golf clubs and things of that nature. We have about 210 of those today, and we'll open 75 in the next year. We will probably be opening 100 more a year right through the 90s. We think this is something we can move across the country into every regional mall and some day have 1,000 or 1,200 of them.

IR: Now that you are so heavily into the specialty store area, what is happening to Woolworth US, your general merchandise division?

HS: I want to point out that though we have far fewer stores, our sales are at an all time high and our profits have almost doubled in the past 8 years. What we did was pull out of a lot of weak small stores and concentrated on the better stores. We remodelled them, we refurbished them and they have responded well, but not one that is going to grow rapidly in its present format.

We are going to grow that business with a small store called Woolworth Express. They are 5 to 6,000 sq. ft., a fourth or fifth of the size of the conventional store. We think there is a future for this division. It's a convenience outlet with such core departments as health & beauty aids, candy, greeting cards, paper supplies, notions—all of the old variety store staples.

IR: In areas such as the Foot Lockers are you doing any central buying?

HS: Each of our divisions operates autonomously. We have computerized a lot of staff functions, but operations we leave to the people who run the stores. They understand better than we what their needs are. What might be right for one, might not be right for the other.*

*"The Woolworth Corp.: Strategies for the 90s," *Inside Retailing*, **15:** 24 (August 13, 1990).

RESIDENT BUYING OFFICES

Buying can be performed internally or by outside consultants

Retailers must decide whether buying is to be performed by staff, consultants, or a buying organization. When merchants utilize store personnel to perform the buying task, they bear the cost of staff buyers. To save these operating costs, small merchants often do the purchasing themselves, while others use outside sources to assist them.

Trips to the market are time consuming and costly. In order to have up-to-the-minute merchandise information and complete market coverage, both large and small retailers utilize the services of **resident buying offices.** These are service organizations that help retailers buy merchandise. Small stores that are located far from manufacturers' showrooms find it vital to engage the services of resident buying offices in order to have complete market coverage, good prices, and help in promoting sales.

Resident buying offices are situated in the major market centers. The largest concentration of buying offices is in New York City; however, substantial offices exist in Dallas, Los Angeles, Chicago, St. Louis, and Miami.

Resident buying offices employ personnel to scan the market for new merchandise and supplier resources. They also provide **trending services** (information bulletins on current fashion trends) and act as buying agents for stores. Some offices render aid in private labeling and import merchandising. Furthermore, they offer merchants the use of office space and services when they travel to the markets. (See Figures 9-5 and 9-6.)

Resident buying offices can be independent, store-owned (private), cooperative (associated), or corporate (syndicated).

Independent Office

Stores pay a fee to an independent office

An **independent resident buying office** serves both large and small noncompeting retailers. The office charges fees that are generally based on the types of services performed and the volume of merchandise purchased. Fee arrangements differ and are spelled out in one- to two-year contracts.

One of the largest independent resident buying offices is Henry Doneger Associates, a firm that represents more than 600 retailers. As the number of major retailers with which manufacturers do business decreases, companies like Doneger become increasingly important to the market. The number of buying offices in the field has been shrinking recently, with firms like Henry Doneger involved in acquisitions and mergers.

Store-Owned Private Office

A private office is limited to its own firm

A **store-owned** or **private resident buying office** is owned by the firm it serves. For example, the Montgomery Ward resident office buys exclusively for stores in that organization. In fact, Ward's maintains resident buying offices in several of the major market centers, including New York, Los Angeles, Dallas, and Chicago.

Store-owned offices are very costly operations and are generally limited to the giant chains, department stores, and large specialty stores. However, some of the large retailers do not maintain their own offices. They reason that the exchange of market information in a store-owned office is too limited because it is confined to their own noncompeting stores. Because of this, many very large firms use other types of resident offices.

An interesting example of a private buying office is the one maintained in

CATHERINE HALL INTERNATIONAL LTD.

STYLE #: 03-6005A   SEASON: Holiday '91
DEPT: Better Misses   LABEL: To Be Advd
COST: 30⁸⁰   DELIVERY: 10/1 -10/15/91
TERMS: Net 7 days   COUNTRY: Imports
DESCRIPTION: Cotton/Lurex Cardigan

SIZES: S - L   PREPACK QUANTITY: 16

COLORS	SIZES		
	S	m	L
WHITE/SILVER	2	4	2
CREAM/GOLD	2	4	2

1126

STYLE #: 03-6005 B   SEASON: Holiday '91
DEPT: Better Misses   LABEL: To Be Advd
COST: 30⁸⁰   DELIVERY: 10/1 -10/15/91
TERMS: Net 7 days   COUNTRY: Imports
DESCRIPTION: Cotton/Lurex Cardigan

SIZES: S - L   PREPACK QUANTITY: 8

COLORS	SIZES		
	S	m	L
WHITE/SILVER	1	2	1
CREAM/GOLD	1	2	1

1126

Figure 9-5 A bulletin from a resident buying office notifying clients about important import information and order form. Reprinted by permission of Henry Doneger Associates, Inc.

DONEGER MENSWEAR

TOM TAILOR

TOM TAILOR creates excitement for Spring by offering newness in novelty wovens. Great prints on chambrays, rayon blends, and the newest cotton/linen blends. With casual shirts being the strength of the contemporary market, we strongly recommend picking up on some of these new items, incentively priced at 8% off the line cost for Doneger Mens.

534

539

1722

#630-2775

Figure 9-6 (a) Sample bulletins that a resident buying office sends to its clients about new merchandise and fashion trends. Reprinted by permission of Henry Doneger Associates, Inc.

UPDATED SPORTSWEAR

DON'T STOP CLASSICS

Colorblock and novelty suede are the things to look for for Fall ... and you need to look no further than DON'T STOP. A must stop for Fall.

L3003

L2000

#125-0322

Figure 9-6 (b) Sample bulletins that a resident buying office sends to its clients about new merchandise and fashion trends. Reprinted by permission of Henry Doneger Associates, Inc.

Figure 9-6 (c) Services performed for retailers by this resident buying office.

Hong Kong by R. H. Macy & Company, the department store chain. Using manufacturers in the Far East, the company agreed in 1989 to make its private-label merchandise available to Kintetsu department stores of Japan. This arrangement affords Macy a lucrative outlet and enhances the Macy name.

Chains sometimes find it advisable to abandon their own buying offices and use other services. Such was the case in 1988–89 when Allied Stores Corporation closed its six overseas buying offices and switched to the foreign offices of Associated Merchandising Corporation.

Cooperative (Associated) Office

When a group of stores owns and manages a buying office cooperatively, it is known as a **cooperative** or **associated resident buying office.** The stores share the operating expenses according to the size of each store and the services it requires. Although this type is more expensive than an independent office, it more than compensates by offering its members a high degree of information exchange and mutual assistance. Even though they exchange a great deal of confidential information, the member stores do not feel threatened because they do not compete in the same areas.

One of the better-known cooperative offices is the Associated Merchandising Corporation. Its member stores include various divisions of Federated Department Stores, Parisian, and Dayton Hudson department stores.

Corporate (Syndicated) Office

A corporate office is a division of a parent company

A **corporate resident buying office** is owned and operated by a parent company for its own stores. The office is a division of a large corporation that owns a number of retail chains. Though the chains may not be alike, the corporate buying office meets the needs of each by maintaining a well-staffed group of specialists.

Because a corporate office buys and distributes merchandise for all its stores, it has a great deal of buying power. Examples of this type of office are the Allied Stores Marketing Corporation and Macy's Corporate Buying Office.

SELECTING A BUYING OFFICE

In selecting a buying office to represent them, many small retailers are limited to an independent office or a cooperative arrangement because they are too small to absorb the costs of separate offices.

Selecting an office that meets the store's service needs

It is important to select an office that provides all the services a merchant requires. The following are a few of the services that a resident office may provide to its members.

1. Market and resource information.
2. Appropriate mix of store members to allow for meaningful data exchange.
3. Proper merchandise specialists (buyers).
4. Access to imported merchandise.
5. A good private-label program—development of private brands (mostly in accessories and apparel).
6. A good communication system so that information is accurate, timely, and meaningful (see Figure 9-7).

In addition, a resident office usually does the following.

1. Places orders for store buyers (see Figure 9-8).
2. Sends bulletins on fashion trends and current prices (see Figure 9-6).
3. Arranges for vendor showings.
4. Makes arrangements for and accompanies store buyers on visits to vendors.

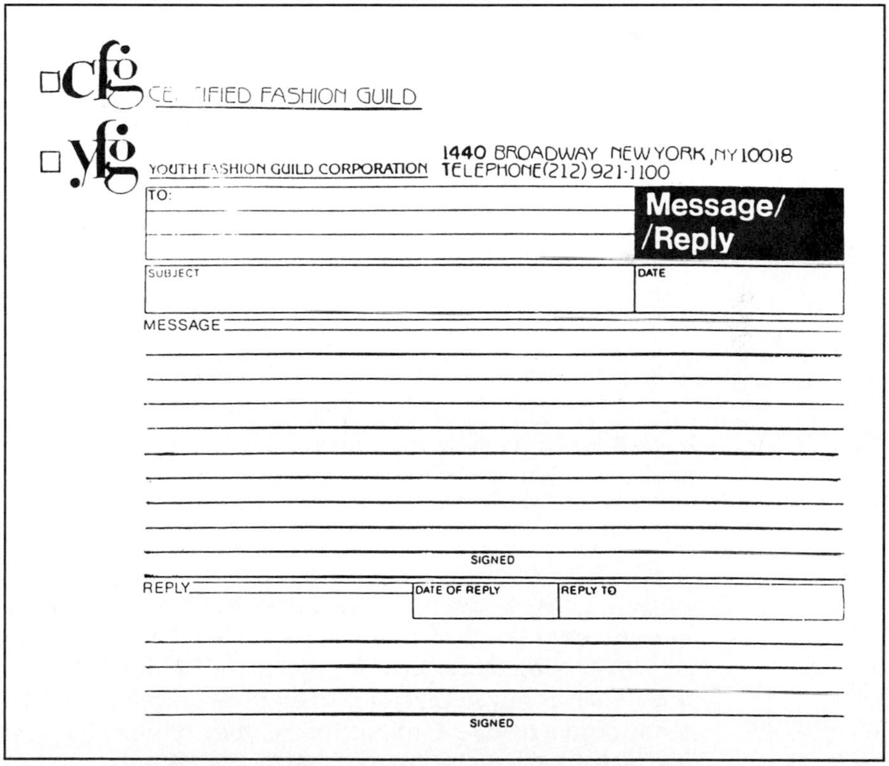
cfg CERTIFIED FASHION GUILD

yfg YOUTH FASHION GUILD CORPORATION 1440 BROADWAY NEW YORK, NY 10018 TELEPHONE (212) 921-1100

Message/ /Reply

TO:

SUBJECT

DATE

MESSAGE

SIGNED

REPLY

DATE OF REPLY

REPLY TO

SIGNED

Figure 9-7 A form used by a resident buying office to communicate with its clients. Reprinted by permission of Certified Fashion Guild.

CERTIFIED FASHION GUILD

CONFIRMATION OF ORDER NOTICE

YOUR ORIGINAL ORDER HAS BEEN PLACED FOR YOU AS FOLLOWS:

STORE .... CITY .... DATE .... 19 ....

ATT'N: .... RE: ....

MANUFACTURER	ORDER # OR DATE OF ORDER	DELIVERY DATE	REMARKS (CHANGES - IF ANY)

BUYER: ....

Figure 9-8 This form is sent to stores to confirm orders placed by the resident buying office with the manufacturer for the retailer. Reprinted by permission of Certified Fashion Guild.

5. Arranges for fashion shows for new merchandise.
6. Keeps track of deliveries and cancellations (see Figure 9-9).
7. Organizes and assists with promotions and advertising.
8. Is available for advice.

Merchants view their need for a buying office in various ways, and make their selections accordingly. When interviewed regarding the role of a buying office, store executives made comments like these: "We need fashion strength as well as promotional buying from our resident office"; "The office is a good bird dog"; "Cross-pollenization of information is another reason for joining a buying office"; "Private labels and import programs are important for many stores in budget areas."

Special areas important to the merchant

A buying office provides merchandise to fill the need for goods in special areas such as private labels for small stores, promotional items, and imports. Since many stores require a unique image, they rely on the services of a resident office for such merchandise to establish that identity.

CANCELLATION NOTICE

TO [MFR.]_____

_____

_____ Date_____19__

Gentlemen:
Kindly cancel the following orders.   Your cooperation in this
instance is very much appreciated.

STORE NAME_____

_____

Order #   Style #   Placed   Due Date

HENRY DONEGER ASSOCIATES, INC.
463 Seventh Avenue, New York, N.Y. 10018

CANCELLATION NOTICE

Certified Buying Service, Inc.

119 WEST 40th STREET
NEW YORK, N. Y. 10018

MFR._____   Date,_____19____

Address_____

Please cancel the order for:

_____

_____

Order Date_____Order No._____Dept. No._____

Style No.:_____

Acknowledged by:

MFR._____   CERTIFIED BUYING SERVICE, Inc.

Per_____   Buyer_____

Figure 9-9 Cancellation forms used by resident buying offices. These forms are
sent by the buyer to the vendor and store as notification of a stopped
shipment. A copy is retained for the buyer's files.

MAJOR MERCHANDISE SOURCES FOR RETAIL BUYERS

Buyer links merchandise resource, store, and customer

You have seen that the buyer is a key figure in the success of a retail store. Every time a customer purchases a suit, he or she is exercising "demand." To meet that demand, the retail buyer must, in turn, have purchased the suit from some resource. In anticipating consumer demand, therefore, the buyer links the merchandise resource, the store, and the customer.

The sources of merchandise include wholesalers, manufacturers, retailing cooperatives, resident buying offices, store-owned suppliers, and foreign sources.

Wholesalers

Traditionally, wholesalers have been a major source of supply for retailing. They are middlemen who buy from manufacturers in large quantities and sell to retailers in substantially smaller quantities. The wholesaler carries a stock of merchandise, sometimes makes deliveries, extends credit, and provides sales help to retailers. To a large degree, wholesalers act as buying agents for their retailer customers in the same manner that retailers act as "purchasing agents" for store customers.

Full-Service Wholesalers

Wholesalers are middlemen

Full-service wholesalers are particularly valuable to small retailers because of the services they perform. For example, they research the market in order to stock merchandise for resale to the retailer. In addition, they provide storage, prompt delivery, credit, valuable market information, and help with displays and advertising. These services are particularly valuable to small and medium-sized retailers, who use this source of supply most frequently. A large retailer, such as Sears or A&P, often takes over many of the functions of a wholesaler. However, even large retailers utilize wholesalers when it is more economical for them to do so.

Limited-Function Wholesalers

Though **limited-function wholesalers** do not provide many services, they render a warehouse service and stock fast-moving items that are available to retailers in small quantities. Because they eliminate sales help, credit, and delivery service, they are able to offer lower prices to retailers, an important factor for small merchants.

Rack jobbers maintain stock, replace slow items with fast-moving goods

Rack jobbers, as discussed in Chapter 5, stock and maintain assortments of goods on special display racks. They select the goods, arrange the displays, price the merchandise, and provide materials for selling assistance. In addition, they guarantee a specified profit to the retailer. Thus, the retailer is relieved of all risks other than providing selling space. Rack jobbers generally check merchandise on a weekly basis and charge the retailer only for the goods sold.

The Regional Market in Dallas conducts fashion shows that enable buyers to preview manufacturers' lines.

Although rack jobbers work with a variety of retail outlets, they are credited with the growth of scrambled merchandising in supermarkets, a departure from the traditional food merchandising policy. Rack jobbers introduced nonfood items like hardware, toiletries, cosmetics, books, and toys. L'eggs is a well-known product handled by rack jobbers.

Manufacturers

Many retailers buy their goods directly from manufacturers. When this happens, the services that are usually performed by wholesalers are assumed by the manufacturers or the stores themselves.

Direct buying is common among large chains like Montgomery Ward because they can purchase merchandise at lower prices. In addition to obtaining a volume discount, large retailers can purchase goods made to their own specifications, and they may have their own labels (private labels) attached to merchandise.

In the fashion field, direct buying enables the retailer to get merchandise into the store faster than would be the case if a wholesaler (middleman) were involved. Since customers' tastes in fashion goods change rapidly, time is an important consideration. It is too risky for both the retailer and the manufacturer to chance storing large inventories of fashion goods that may become outmoded.

In the case of physically perishable items, not only is it important to buy directly from the producer, it is necessary to purchase more often.

Other benefits of direct buying include lower prices, market information, help in training salespeople, and assistance with advertising and displays.

PRACTITIONER'S CORNER

What follows is the summary of an interview with Judith Ann Eigen, designer and co-owner of Judith Ann Creations, a company that specializes in the manufacture of high-fashion beaded garments and exciting novelty leathers.

1. With regard to the merging of resident buying offices, Ms. Eigen misses some of the input those offices used to provide to her company and her customers (retailers). Resident buyers are in touch with small retailers all over the country, and their close contact is invaluable.

2. The soft goods business does not operate well in a strict corporate structure. As a designer, your independence of expression may be restricted by the loss of available funds; that is, stores don't have sufficient latitude for an expansion of expression. Consequently, she is anxious when she learns about impending acquisitions or mergers.

3. Judith Ann Creations considers opening its own stores constantly. The company is a family business, and at present there is no real middle management. As yet, the firm lacks the personnel to commit to a role as a retailer. However, it might consider expansion through the purchase of a small specialty chain that has a strong staff.

4. The company's distribution system involves in-house salespeople and territorial representatives. Salespeople are sent to all shows to help the territorial representatives. The firm caters to small stores, with some 20 percent of its market in the major department stores. Stores are supported heavily with trunk shows and promotions. The company also mails printed notices, and in territories where people travel, it helps with advertising.

5. The company reaches small specialty stores by communicating with them and offering them services. They are helped with special orders, and salespeople follow up each order personally. In addition, the stores' catalogs are subsidized, and aid is offered with local advertising.

6. Before a new line is developed fully, the firm communicates with retailers as to their needs.

7. Ms. Eigen sees tremendous growth opportunities in the senior market.

8. The company is now diversifying with licensing deals in loungewear and children's dresses.

9. Judith Ann Creations employs more than 10,000 families in the New Delhi and Calcutta areas of India, and much of what they hand produce is for the large-size market.

Retailing Cooperatives and Resident Buying Offices

Voluntary groups are an important source for small retailers

As noted previously, independent retailers have formed groups to secure greater strength in buying. For example, voluntary chains have been organized by wholesalers, which assume the burden of supply to enable small retailers to compete with the chains. The retailers buy all needed goods from the wholesaler and benefit from lower prices through volume purchases. The Independent Grocers' Alliance and Western Auto Stores are examples of voluntary chains. A recent trend toward cooperative buying exists in the hardware line, with such participating companies as Tru-Value Hardware and American Hardware Co.

We also noted earlier that resident buying offices are also vital to retailers' access to major merchandise markets. Because they exist to link the two, resident buyers are important for both retailers and the manufacturer.

Store-Owned Merchandise Resources

In Chapter 4 you learned that some manufacturers, for example, Benetton, have their own retail outlets. The reverse is true, too. In both instances, the arrangement is known as **dual distribution.**

Store-owned resources require high investment

Several chains, franchised retailers, and mail order houses own their own factories and produce the merchandise that their stores request. This arrangement is found mainly in the apparel and household drug industry. It makes it easier to

Retailers have the opportunity to examine a manufacturer's line of merchandise at the showroom of the manufacturer's representative. *Courtesy: Telisman Sales, Dallas Mart.*

coordinate customer demands with production. However, depending solely on one's own facility involves more risk and higher investment, and restricts assortments.

Evidence of the risk involved in retailers owning their own resources is

---

A WOMEN'S APPAREL SUCCESS STORY

Liz Claiborne

Rising to the top of the women's apparel trade doesn't happen overnight, to say the least. Take Liz Claiborne (Elizabeth Claiborne Ortenberg), for instance. Before attaining prominence in the designer and retail trades as founder of Liz Claiborne, Inc., she held a variety of related jobs: model, design assistant, and dress designer. Before striking out on her own, she worked for Junior Rite Company, Rhea Manufacturing Company, and Youth Guild, the junior dress division of Jonathan Logan.

With personal savings and loans from others, in 1976 Ms. Claiborne became head designer and president of Liz Claiborne, Inc., a manufacturer of women's apparel. Achieving success from the start, the company's sales increased rapidly and became a billion-dollar firm by 1986. Ms. Claiborne's ability to anticipate the fashion desires of women in different walks of life was a key reason for her achievement. So was her willingness to seek consumer and professional advice.

In 1988, the company opened its own retail stores on Long Island, New York, called First Issue. Ms. Claiborne's interest in retailing stemmed not only from a desire for pecuniary gain, but also from a desire to demonstrate how Liz Claiborne apparel should be presented.

With few honors left to achieve, Ms. Claiborne felt secure enough to withdraw from active management of the company in 1989, retaining her role as a member of the board of directors.

Source: Current Biography Yearbook, 1989. Maritz, Charles, ed. H.W. Wilson Company, NY, 1989.

---

supplied by A&P, which had to close its large food processing plant near Elmira, New York. This occurred because the chain's large output of its own private labels overloaded its store shelves, preventing it from carrying sufficient assortments of other brands. Some companies that do their own manufacturing also purchase a portion of their goods from others. For example, Sears, Roebuck and Company has arrangements with manufacturers to produce a portion of the merchandise it sells. On the other hand, Thom McAn Shoe Company produces all its own shoes.

In some cases, manufacturers become competitors of their retail customers. Examples include such hard goods vendors as Black & Decker and Corning, and soft goods producers as Hanes, Lee Jeans, and Van Heusen.

Foreign Sources

Stores use foreign merchandise for several reasons: The items are more expensive, more difficult to comparison shop, may be less expensive to purchase and are not available from American sources. On the other hand, delivery is slower, it is difficult to inspect goods before shipping, contacting foreign sources is complicated, travel is expensive, and shopping and import duties are costly. In addition, currency changes are difficult to anticipate, so that goods can cost more than originally expected.

Some American buying offices have representatives in foreign markets. If a store requires foreign goods, it is advisable to use such a buying office because it assists with all purchases, and reduces the risk of merchandise not meeting specifications.

Foreign goods

Foreign buying offices located abroad are known as **commissionaires.** Like American resident houses, they provide various services, and charge a fee or a percentage of purchases.

Importers are located in this country, but they research merchandise and buy in foreign markets. They are like other wholesalers that buy in large quantities and sell to retailers in smaller quantities.

In the next chapter we will see how buyers actually select resources from among manufacturers, middlemen, and other intermediaries.

NEW TERMS

associate buyer	limited-function wholesaler
associated resident buying office	listing plan
buyer's commitment system	price list agreement
centralized buying	private label
centralized distribution plan	private resident buying office
commissionaire	resident buying office
cooperative resident buying office	retail merchandise management system
corporate resident buying office	semiautomatic stock control system
decentralized buying	specification buying
dual distribution	stockkeeping unit (SKU)
full-service wholesaler	store brand
importer	store-owned resident buying office
independent resident buying office	trending service

CHAPTER HIGHLIGHTS

1. The personal qualifications of buyers include the following skills: managerial and planning skills, ability to analyze the market, understanding finance, understanding the consumer, skill in public relations, communications skills, and negotiating skills.

2. The buying procedure contains eight basic elements for both large and small retailers. Because stores vary in size and type, several approaches are used in organizing the buying function.

3. In contrast to larger retailers, small stores do not treat buying as a separate function.

4. Some stores have buyers who specialize in only one product category.

5. In department stores with branches, main store buyers have the added responsibility of stocking the branches. When these responsibilities become excessive, they are relieved of selling functions and rely on assistants and associate buyers for customer feedback.

6. Chain stores hire specialists to buy for their units. They perform the buying function in a regional or home office away from the stores.

7. Centralized buying gives the buyer the responsibility for ordering merchandise and controlling inventory in all stores. Centralized buying has made it possible for chains to obtain great savings and profits. In decentralized buying, each of a chain's divisions is equipped with its own buying staff.

8. A central distribution plan is basically a warehousing setup. This plan gives store managers an opportunity to select merchandise for their units.

9. Under price list agreements store managers have greater input regarding the merchandise stocked in their stores.

10. Specification buying and private labeling help the retailer cut down on product competition, but they require a large amount of purchasing power.

11. New technology has made it easier to "have the right merchandise at the right place at the right time."

12. Buying offices provide a host of services to their members, including market information, access to import merchandise, private labels, and trending services. In addition, they usually perform such activities as placing orders and arranging for store buyers' visits.

13. Resident buying offices are situated in the major market centers. They can be independent, store owned, cooperative, or corporate.

14. Sources of merchandise for the retail buyer are wholesalers, manufacturers, retailing cooperatives, resident buying offices, and company-owned suppliers.

15. Foreign buying sources include American buying offices in foreign countries, commissionaires, and importers.

REVIEW QUESTIONS

1. Buying functions are the same for large and small retailing organizations. Explain how a buyer's job in a small independent store differs from that in a department store.
2. How has the increasing number of branch stores complicated the department store buyer's job?
3. How does centralized buying differ from decentralized buying?
4. What are the main reasons for small stores using outside buying consultants and resident buying offices?
5. What criteria should be used by a retailer in selecting a resident buying office?
6. The major merchandise resources for retail buyers are either direct or indirect. Explain.
7. What are the advantages of using wholesalers as a source of merchandise?

DISCUSSION QUESTIONS

1. What are the advantages of buying plans that afford the store manager greater autonomy?
2. Why do many retailers maintain their own market representatives in a resident buying office in addition to their store-based buying operations?
3. How can small retailers compete with the buying power of large chains? Be specific.

CASE 1

Dual Distribution

The Hartmarx Corporation, a manufacturer of men's clothing including Austin Reed, Hickey Freeman, and Hart Schaffner & Marx, also owns retail stores that sell both its own brands and others. In order to reduce losses, the company began to sell off more than 16 percent of its stores (all marginal ones) in 1990. Despite the selloff, Hartmarx was still committed to the concept of dual distribution. In fact, the company believed that the trend in the industry would continue.

Marketing analysts acknowledge that dual distribution helps manufacturers by providing outlets for their products that are not otherwise available. This lack of distribution channels is due primarily to the volatility of the retail industry. In Hartmarx's case, a little less than 20 percent of its products are sold through its own stores.

Other reasons advanced for dual distribution include better cash flow, reliable consumer feedback, and more efficient production cycles. A manufacturer's own stores can also be used to test new products and to serve as models for retailers that sell the manufacturer's products.

Despite the entrance of more producers into the dual-distribution field, their customers' (retailers') needs continue to be a major concern. Without constant attention to these needs, manufacturers can lose favor in the marketplace. When this happens, the manufacturer's own outlets suffer as well.

a. Do you think the trend toward dual distribution will continue in the 1990s? Why?
b. If a dual distribution trend does continue, can you foresee a rise in retailer resentment? Explain.
c. If you were a retailer contemplating business with a dual distribution manufacturer, what might be some of your concerns?

CASE 2

Kickbacks

The buying function is essential to the successful operation of any retail business. Good buyers are specialists who know and understand all aspects of their markets. A buyer also has the responsibility of representing his or her employer to manufacturers and wholesalers and of conducting business in a reputable and ethical manner. Although most buyers do so, there are and have long been instances in retailing when buyers have participated in the illegal (unethical) practice of taking kickbacks.

A kickback can be defined as the return of part of a sum of money received, generally prompted by threat of force, coercion, or secret agreement. In retailing, this means that the seller (a manufacturer or wholesaler) pays back to a buyer a sum of money in exchange for getting the buyer's order.

One recent case involved a buyer for Stop and Shop Cos., a Boston-based chain of stores that sell health products and cosmetics. According to court records, a health and beauty products supplier in New York paid back to the Stop and Shop buyer the equivalent of 1.5 percent of all goods ordered over a period of eight years. During this time, the buyer placed orders for products worth $17 million and received kickbacks of $256,000. To cover the cost of the kickbacks, the supplier increased the amount billed to Stop and Shop.

The buyer held an important position in the company's management, with the responsibility for checking to make sure that other workers were not taking kickbacks. But because the buyer reported directly to the vice-chairman of the company, it was difficult to check on the buyer's own actions.

The buyer pleaded guilty to fraud and was ordered to repay the $256,000 with interest and to pay a fine of $3,000. The court also imposed a two-year suspended sentence and placed the buyer on probation for three years.

The practice of offering gifts to buyers in retailing is not new. Apparel manufacturers and wholesalers, for example, have long sought to influence buyers' decisions through gifts, expensive meals, and so on. But, according to retailing experts, the practice of taking kickbacks has increased sharply in recent years.

Heightened competition for orders and the expanded involvement of foreign manufacturers in U.S. retail trade are often cited as major reasons, as is the growth of imports. For example, over 30 percent of the clothing sold in the United States today is imported, compared with 12 percent in 1973.

With estimates of the amount of money involved in kickbacks varying from $100 million a year to over $500 million, the problem has become a major concern in the retailing industry.

It is not always easy to discover and document a kickback scheme. Often, as in the case mentioned, the person taking kickbacks is a head buyer and a company officer with the responsibility for seeing that kickbacks do not occur. Frequently, more than one person in a company is involved.

Kickback schemes can be initiated by either buyer or vendor. They may be simple in structure or complex. For example, a kickback payment can simply be made directly to a buyer, or in a more complex arrangement, one or more "dummy" corporations can be set up for the purpose of receiving the kickback payments.

Even when a company discovers that a buyer is taking kickbacks, often the case is not prosecuted. Instead the company merely fires the person, thereby avoiding embarrassment.

Kickbacks are costly both to the retailing industry and to the consumer. Because vendors often raise the amount billed to the buyer's company to cover the kickback cost, the company is paying more than it should for merchandise. Eventually these higher costs mean higher prices to the consumer and/or lower profits for the company. In some cases, the company can even suffer an outright loss. Nor is the cost to the buyer's company limited to the amount of kickback. A company that decides to take a kickback case to court also incurs investigation expenses, legal fees, and perhaps most costly of all, damage to the company's reputation.

a. Do you think that kickbacks are a common or accepted part of the retailing industry?
b. What measures, if any, do you think a company could take to protect itself from such practices?
c. What would you do if you suspected a buyer at your company of taking kickbacks?
d. What would you do if you were offered a kickback?

REFERENCES

ADAMS, MURIEL J. "Private Label Programs: Major Changes." *Stores* (June 1989), pp. 10–19.

BIVINS, JACQUELYN. "Buying Office Status Report." *Stores* (May 1989), pp. 54–61.

GALLAGHER, DENISE. "Tabletop Shops." *Stores* (February 1989), pp. 39–40.

ROBINS, GARY. "New Planning Systems," *Stores* (July 1989), pp. 61–64.

"Store Label Threat Returns." *Advertising Age* (May 22, 1989), p. 16.

Chapter 10

Merchandise Planning

After completing this chapter, you should be able to:

- List the ways in which buyers determine what merchandise to buy, how much to buy, from whom to buy, and when to buy.
- Identify sources of information for interpreting consumer demand.
- Compute open-to-buy and define stock turnover and assortment plans.
- Identify the factors that determine the value of a vendor resource.
- Identify common discount and dating terms.
- List the major aspects of vendor-retailer negotiations.

What, when, how much to buy
As stated in Chapter 9, the elements of buying are similar for small and large stores. In this chapter we will deal with the planning aspect of buying merchandise.

A major consideration that confronts buyers is the ability to stock their stores with merchandise that can be sold profitably. In order to do this, it is necessary to plan for the "right merchandise to be at the right place, at the right time, in the right quantities, and at the right price."[1] In other words, the buyer is faced with the decision of *what* to buy, *how* much to buy, from *whom* to buy, and *when* to buy.

WHAT TO BUY—CONSUMER DEMAND

Since a store's image depends a great deal on the type and price of merchandise it sells, the desired image determines the goods that must be purchased. Uppermost in the buyer's mind, therefore, must be the needs and desires of the customers that the store wishes to attract. For example, Henri Bendel, an exclusive shop in New York City, caters to upscale customers who demand ambiance, service, and unique merchandise.

The merchandise that this store sells is expensive, trendy, and sophisticated. Bendel does not extend the welcome mat to oversized people in its ready-to-wear areas. The Lane Bryant chain, on the other hand, caters to "the big woman." Both stores have decided on a target customer and buy accordingly.

Misunderstanding consumer demand can be disastrous for retailers. For example, when Ames department stores acquired the Zayre discount chain in 1988, it changed the Zayre name to Ames and altered Zayre's product mix. This created confusion among Zayre's essentially ethnic customers and resulted in drastically reduced sales volume. Added to other problems, the Zayre debacle caused Ames to declare bankruptcy in 1990.

A good example of a retailer that is tuned to consumer demand is Merry-Go-Round, a company that sells trendy fashions to people in the 14- to 35-year-old bracket. Applying technology to fashion, this avant-garde retailer knows daily which items sell and which don't. Using these data, the firm makes quick decisions about its inventory.

Predicting *what* the consumer will want is not easy. Because buyers must avoid stocking inappropriate goods, they seek information to use in interpreting consumer demand. Sources of reliable information include the consumer, the trade, and store records.

[1] Committee on Definitions. *Marketing: A Glossary of Marketing Terms* (Chicago: American Marketing Association, 1960).

Retailers often survey consumers to determine their merchandise needs and preferences.

Consumer Information

Anticipating consumer demand is not easy

It is important for merchants and buyers to "listen" to their customers. After all, it is the consumer who decides what and where to buy. The retailer is able to study the consumer by keeping track of buying habits. For example, merchants can assess customers' "taste" requirements by tracking fast-selling items (Figure 10-1). They can also observe the most popular shopping hours and how purchases are paid for. They sometimes resort to the use of direct mail inserts and questionnaires.

Through the use of telephones and in-store interviews, merchants use surveys to determine merchandise preferences. They also mail printed questionnaires, which are sent to charge customers to obtain feedback on store brands, merchandise performance, and the like. Some retailers conduct consumer panels for direct contact regarding customers' purchase plans as well as their likes and dislikes. Other research techniques utilized by retailers are discussed in depth in Chapter 19.

Whatever the technique used, a retailer must understand consumer preferences. Sears Roebuck, a giant retailer, has struggled with this problem for years. At this writing, its changed strategy of offering lower prices instead of conducting sales and expanding its name brand appliance inventory has still not changed its fortunes. This is about as good an example as one needs of the trickiness of consumer preference.

BEST-SELLERS
Include the top five selling items in each department for the November/December period.

Dept. #	Style #	Vendor Name	Description of Item	Class	Price	Units Sold	Comments

Figure 10-1 A department store form used to determine best-selling merchandise.

Trade Information

Suppliers

Manufacturers, wholesalers, and other intermediaries do their own research in analyzing the market. Since vendors must also study consumer demand, they can provide the retailer with information that might be helpful in making buying decisions (Figure 10-2).

Competition

Information can come from suppliers, competitors, or others

It is important to observe how the competition analyzes consumer demand. Retailers can comparison shop at other stores and study the stock they carry. They can also investigate displays and analyze competitive promotions and advertising.

Noncompeting Stores

Retailers in different markets often exchange predictions regarding merchandise, trends, and special promotions. For example, a Chicago merchant who sells giftware might share information about successful items with another giftware retailer in Michigan.

Publications, Trade Shows, and Market Weeks

There are many publications that contain excellent information for buyers. They include *Women's Wear Daily, California Apparel News, Chain Store Age, Daily News Record, Stores* magazine, and *Home Furnishings Daily*. These trade papers report on new products, business statistics, demand trends, and important items for the specialty retailer.

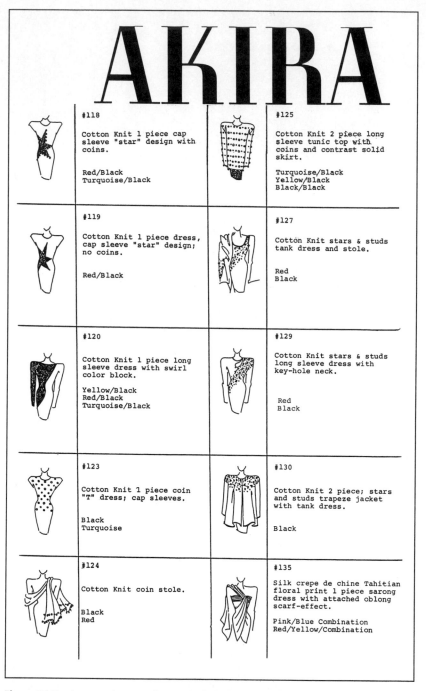

AKIRA

#118	#125
Cotton Knit 1 piece cap sleeve "star" design with coins. Red/Black Turquoise/Black	Cotton Knit 2 piece long sleeve tunic top with coins and contrast solid skirt. Turquoise/Black Yellow/Black Black/Black
#119	#127
Cotton Knit 1 piece dress, cap sleeve "star" design; no coins. Red/Black	Cotton Knit stars & studs tank dress and stole. Red Black
#120	#129
Cotton Knit 1 piece long sleeve dress with swirl color block. Yellow/Black Red/Black Turquoise/Black	Cotton Knit stars & studs long sleeve dress with key-hole neck. Red Black
#123	#130
Cotton Knit 1 piece coin "T" dress; cap sleeves. Black Turquoise	Cotton Knit 2 piece; stars and studs trapeze jacket with tank dress. Black
#124	#135
Cotton Knit coin stole. Black Red	Silk crepe de chine Tahitian floral print 1 piece sarong dress with attached oblong scarf-effect. Pink/Blue Combination Red/Yellow/Combination

Figure 10-2   A page of a manufacturer's showroom catalog for the placement of seasonal orders by buyers. *Courtesy:* Akira.

Manufacturers often present their new merchandise at trade shows (Figure 10-3), which are generally organized by trade associations. Vendors usually have representatives at these shows to explain their products, provide current product information and market trends, and take orders. For example, the Gift Show has suppliers who deal in items that are usually sold in specialty or department stores. As a result, buyers have a firsthand opportunity to see new products that vendors feel will be in demand during the coming season.

In some lines, such as toys, a large part of the purchasing is often done at the annual trade show, where some of the major retailers place toy orders a year in advance. Other well-known shows are the National Boutique Show, the International Fur Show, and the Jewelers' International Showcase.

Several months prior to the start of a new season, retailers are able to view new merchandise during "Market Weeks." The major regional markets (Atlanta, Chicago, New York City, Dallas, Los Angeles) sponsor new showings of merchandise for a specific line of goods.

The Resident Buying Office

Another valuable source of information that helps store buyers make intelligent merchandise decisions is the resident buying office. Since resident buyers are in the market every day, they see new products almost immediately and maintain reliable lists of suppliers. Also, retailers belonging to a resident buying office often check with other retailers in that same office on what merchandise is selling and what is not selling.

Store Records and Personnel

Information about the consumer

Some retailers maintain a "want slip" system for consumer requests about out-of-stock or unstocked goods. These records are possible indications of consumer demand. Records produced by computers via POS registers provide buyers with up-to-the-moment information (spreadsheets) about customer merchandise selection and fast- and slow-moving lines (Figure 10-4). Sales personnel can also provide valuable feedback because they are in direct contact with customers and can observe their buying habits. Information regarding prices, desired styles, and merchandise lines are passed along to the buyer (Figure 10-5).

A store's position regarding fashion leadership is another factor in considering the potential demand for certain product lines. The buyer needs a clear picture of how the store's clientele fits into the fashion adoption process. As discussed in Chapter 2, the buyer must determine whether the store's customers are the avant-garde, who buy in the early stages of style development, or the latecomers, who wait for the style to become established.

Top management must be certain that buyers use their expertise when selecting goods. Unfortunately, buying decisions are sometimes made on the basis of financial considerations rather than on wise merchandise choices. This

It's All Here
April 4-9, 1991

DALLAS MEGA MARKET

- *Accessories Showcase*
- *Active Sportswear Show*
- *Bridal Fashion Fair*
- *Childrenswear Super Show*
- *Group III Collections*
- *International Women's Apparel And Special Sizes Show*

- *Studio? Directives*
- *Visual Merchandising Idea Symposium*
- *National Imprinted Sportswear Expo*

- *Men's Designer Gallery*
- *Men's And Boy's*
- *National Apparel Market*
- *Dallas Western Market*

THE DALLAS APPAREL MART/
MENSWEAR MART/MARKET HALL

SATURDAY, APRIL 6

DISCOVERY! FASHION SHOW - 7:30 am cash breakfast buffet, 8 am show. Great Hall. Featuring Sunny Sport.

CHILDRENSWEAR SUPER SHOW - 7:30 am breakfast buffet co-sponsored by *Earnshaw's Review*; 8 am fashion show. Fashion Theatre, 3rd floor. Guest designer Amy Bahrt for Ruth Scharf is featured.

ACCESSORIES SEMINAR - 8 am, 6th floor, front lobby. Join T.J. Reid for "Hot New Trends in Accessories - Spring/Summer '91."

MENSWEAR WELCOME BREAKFAST - Saturday and Sunday, 8 - 10 am, Menswear Mart lobby, compliments of Van Heusen.

WELCOME ENTERTAINMENT - 8 - 10 am. Apparel Mart lobby. Sponsored by Mel and Evelyn Cannon in showroom 2B374.

MEGA MARKET ORIENTATION - 9 - 9:30 am, 1st floor, West Atrium, Independence Room. A must for menswear buyers new to Dallas. Continental breakfast compliments of Du Pont.

BRIDAL SEMINAR - 10 - 10:30 am, Suite 2C30. "Getting Intimate With The Bride," co-sponsored by The Southwest Intimate Apparel Association and *Elegant Bride Magazine*.

BLOOD DRIVE/DESERT STORM - 10 am - 4 pm, front entrance of Dallas Apparel Mart. Show your patriotism by giving blood. All donations help support our troops in the Middle East. Hosted by Parkland Hospital.

IMPRINTED SPORTSWEAR SEMINAR - 10:30 - noon, 2nd floor, Market Hall. "10 Deadly Sins of Management."

ACCESSORIES FASHION SHOW - Noon, 6th floor, front lobby. Featuring guest designer Patricia Von Musulin.

SWIMWEAR 1992 FASHION SHOW - Noon - 1 pm, 2nd floor, front lobby. See the newest swimwear lines ready for June delivery. Sponsored by the Southwest Swimwear Association.

INFORMAL MODELING - Noon - 2 pm, Terrace Cafe and Great Hall Cafeteria. Featuring fall lines from the George Elphand & Associates showroom.

BRIDAL SEMINAR - 2 - 2:30 pm. Suite 2C30. Marilyn Nason, contributing editor for *VOWS Magazine*, discusses key bridal business tools. Co-sponsored by *Elegant Bride Magazine*.

CAJUN COCKTAILS - 5:30 - 6:30 pm, Menswear Mart, 3rd floor. Informal munchies and drinks with the menswear 3rd floor exhibitors.

GROUP III COLLECTIONS FASHION SHOW - 5:30 pm cocktails, 6:15 pm show. Fashion Theatre, 3rd floor. Featuring Dallas' own Todd Oldham as guest designer. Tickets are $9 in advance, $10 Saturday, and include cocktails. Co-sponsored by Stavros with pre-show informal modeling and a drawing for a free fur and leather coat.

MATERNITY FASHION SHOW - 6 pm cocktail reception, 7 pm fashion show, 5th floor, Lookout V. Sponsored by the Dallas Maternity Representatives.

BRIDAL AND FORMALITIES PARTY - 6:30 pm buses depart from the front of the Menswear Mart, 7 - 10:30 pm party at the Circle R Ranch. Tickets are $25, including transportation. Join the bridal industry in a toast to Fall '91 with barbecue, two-steppin' and Texas-size fun. Co-sponsored by *Elegant Bride Magazine*.

JUSTIN BOOTS CONCERT EVENT - 6:30 - 8:30 pm, 1st floor lobby, Menswear Mart. Bar hosted by Australian Outback.

HOTEL

THE DALLAS APPAREL MART/
MENSWEAR MART/MARKET HALL

2300 Stemmons Freeway
Suite 5651
AM Box 580142
Dallas, Texas 75258

Figure 10-3 An announcement to the retail apparel trade about market week in Dallas. Reproduced by permission of Dallas Market Center.

N·O·V·E·M·B·E·R

MONDAY	TUESDAY	WEDNESDAY	THURSDAY	FRIDAY
			1	**2**
5	ACCESSORIES SHOW *9:00 A.M.* IMPORT COAT SHOW-FALL '91 *10:00 A.M.* JUNIOR SPORTSWEAR SHOW *1:00 P.M.* MISSY SPORTSWEAR SHOW *2:00 P.M.* SPRING '91 CATALOGUE MEETING *3:00 P.M.* DESIGNER & COUTURE DRESS SHOW *5:30 P.M.* Election Day **6**	**7** LINGERIE SHOW *9:00 A.M.*	**8**	**9**
12	ACCESSORIES SHOW *9:00 A.M.* IMPORT COAT SHOW-FALL '91 *10:00 A.M.* JUNIOR SPORTSWEAR SHOW *1:00 P.M.* MISSY SPORTSWEAR SHOW *2:00 P.M.* SPRING '91 CATALOGUE MEETING *3:00 P.M.* DESIGNER & COUTURE DRESS SHOW *5:30 P.M.* **13**	**14** LINGERIE SHOW *9:00 A.M.*	**15**	**16**
19	**20** IMPORT COAT SHOW FALL '91 *10:00 A.M.*	**21**	**22** OFFICE CLOSED Thanksgiving Day	**23** OFFICE CLOSED
26	**27** IMPORT COAT SHOW FALL '91 *10:00 A.M.*	**28**	**29**	**30**

CERTIFIED FASHION GUILD
1440 BROADWAY, NEW YORK, N.Y. 10018
TELEPHONE (212) 921-1100

A calendar of events to help retailers plan. *Courtesy:* Certified Fashion Guild.

Y 1 DEPT 20 CLSS SEQUENCE REPORT THRU 12-06

STYLE DESCRIPTION			ALL STORES COMBINED						
VEND. / STYLE / STYLE NAME CLASS CODES LAST ACTION & DATE	COST INT. MU%	CURR. RETAIL 1ST RETAIL	LIFE HISTORY	RECENT SALES & STOCK HISTORY 4 WEEKS AGO	3 WEEKS AGO	2 WEEKS AGO	1 WEEK AGO		ALL STORES
117 924 CREW HEATHER			SLS 260		23	65	32	CURR SLS	65
62 00	.01	16.99	RCPTS 378	302	279	215	183	ON HAND	118
RECPT 11-22	100.0 %	20.00	RETURNS 17	LAST RCPT 2 WKS AGO				PRV 1WKS	32
				FIRST RCPT 14 WKS AGO				LIFE	260
117 925 V HEATHER			SLS 339	9	40	54	48	CURR SLS	74
62 00	.01	16.99	RCPTS	-.1	-.2	-.2	-.3	ON HAND	-.3
TRANF 11-26	100.0 %	20.00	RETURNS 21	LAST RCPT ** WKS AGO		ORD	1	PRV 1WKS	48
				FIRST RCPT ** WKS AGO				LIFE	339
117 860 PROMO LAMBSWOOL			SLS 3.5	123	153	215	240	CURR SLS	584
62 00	.01	20.00	RCPTS 5.1	2.8	2.6	2.4	2.2	ON HAND	1.6
RECPT 12-03 *CUM MD $ 7205.00	100.0 %	22.50	RETURNS 197	LAST RCPT. WKS AGO				PRV 1WKS	240
MD#1 11-08 2882 PCS.				FIRST RCPT. 10 WKS AGO				LIFE	3.5
851 13102			SLS					CURR SLS	
62 00	.01	20.00	RCPTS 78			78	78	ON HAND	78
RECPT 11-19	100.0 %		RETURNS	LAST RCPT. 2 WKS AGO				PRV 1WKS	
				FIRST RCPT. 2 WKS AGO				LIFE	
851 102 BLEND V NECK			SLS 4.8	170	253	430	340	CURR SLS	2.4
62 00	2.17	21.00	RCPTS 9.2	2.2	2.8	3.7	5.2	ON HAND	4.4
RECPT 12-06	90.0 %		RETURNS 220	LAST RCPT. WKS AGO				PRV 1WKS	340
				FIRST RCPT 21 WKS AGO				LIFE	4.8

Figure 10-4 Computer-generated data sheet showing the movement of merchandise lines.

SALES RESULTS

Dept. # & Name	Week Ending		Week Ending		Week Ending		Week Ending		Week Ending		Week Ending		
	TY 11/22	LY 11/24	TY 11/29	LY 12/1	TY 12/6	LY 12/8	TY 12/13	LY 12/15	TY 12/20	LY 12/22	TY 12/27	LY 12/29	

Figure 10-5 A comparative sales results form.

occurs when computer projections are considered more important than consumer preferences, and is particularly true in the fashion business.

ASSORTMENT—HOW MUCH TO BUY

After determining what to buy, the buyer must choose the assortment and quantity of stock to carry. Merchants must buy in large enough quantities to avoid running out of stock and thereby lose sales. On the other hand, they should not overbuy and wind up with too much inventory. In order to buy in proper amounts, buyers should make carefully developed plans and check current details. This is done several months before the selling season. One way the buyer begins to accomplish this task is through a six-month seasonal merchandise plan (Figure 10-6). Plans used by retailers before buying include **open-to-buy (OTB),** which sets the dollar amount of merchandise that a buyer can order for a particular period, and assortment plans, which ensure a proper variety of stock for a particular period.

Open-to-Buy

Open-to-buy helps buyers plan purchases

Open-to-buy is the difference between planned purchases and stock already ordered (commitments) and on hand. The OTB, therefore, is the amount of money a buyer has left for ordering merchandise at any time during a certain period.

Six-Month Merchandising Plan

Fall 1987		**Aug.**	**Sep.**	**Oct.**	**Nov.**	**Dec.**	**Jan.**	**Total**
Sales	Last year							
	Plan (this year)							
	Revision							
	Actual							
Inventory (beginning of month)	Last year							(Inventory
	Plan (this year)							Jan. 31)
	Revision							
	Actual							
Reductions (markdowns + shortages + discounts)	Last year							
	Plan (this year)							
	Revision							
	Actual							
Purchases	Last year							
	Plan (this year)							
	Revision							
	Actual							

Figure 10-6   This is a typical form used by retailers for developing their merchandise plans in advance of the period to which they refer. Plans should always be completed before actual buying for the season begins.

OTB is computed by the following formula.

Merchandise Needed	−	Merchandise Available	=	OTB
Planned sales for period + Planned end-of-month inventory + Planned reductions		Planned opening inventory + Commitments (stock on order)		Amount left to spend on merchandise for period

Suppose a furniture merchant plans to sell $120,000 worth of goods during the month of October. The planned inventory is $80,000 for October 1 and $70,000 for October 31. Planned reductions (discounts, shortages, markdowns) for the month are $9,000. Stock on order is $25,000. (All amounts are at retail prices.)

Merchandise needed
Planned sales $120,000
Planned end-of-month inventory   70,000
Planned reductions   9,000
                                                                                    $199,000

Merchandise available
Planned opening inventory $80,000
Stock on order   25,000
                                                                                    $105,000

Open-to-buy = $199,000 − 105,000 = $94,000

The buyer's open-to-buy for the remainder of the period is $94,000.

The OTB concept is important for several reasons. First of all, it gives the buyer some flexibility in replacing goods that are sold. Second, it avoids an improper balance between inventory and sales. Thus, it is easier for the buyer to maintain planned inventories without overbuying or underbuying. Third, it indicates how the retailer can adjust purchases at any time during the buying period. Fourth, it gives the buyer an opportunity to purchase additional "hot items" (fast-moving products) or order something new. Finally, and most important, it is a control against acquiring more inventory than needed.

There are times when buyers need to know the open-to-buy figure before the end of the planned period. For example, a buyer may have good reason to expect that sales will be better than anticipated or that business conditions may warrant quick steps to reduce the stock on hand. In either event, by simply adjusting the example to include the sales actually recorded and the actual reductions, the open-to-buy can be computed for any date (October 13 in our illustration).

Merchandise needed, October 13–31		
Planned sales, October 1–31	$120,000	
Actual sales, October 1–12	−70,000	
Balance of planned sales		$50,000
Planned EOM inventory		70,000
Planned reductions, October 1–31	9,000	
Actual reductions, October 1–12	−2,000	
Balance of planned reductions		7,000
Total merchandise needed		$127,000
Merchandise available, October 13–31		
Planned opening inventory	$80,000	
Merchandise received, October 1–12	+14,000	
Total merchandise handled, October 1–12	$94,000	
Actual sales, October 1–12	−70,000	
Merchandise on hand, October 12	$24,000	
Merchandise on order, October 13	+21,000	
Total merchandise available		$45,000
Open-to-buy, October 13		$82,000

RETAIL STRATEGY
C.E.O. Antonini Defines K mart's New Creed on Merchandise Development

"I believe the great retailers of the 1990's will exhibit a new partnership arrangement with vendor resources. Retailers are at the forefront of contact with the consumer. They know what the consumer wants and what he or she is asking for. They should be far more involved in the whole product development, packaging, resourcing process. In the future, the great retailers will take on much more of the *product development research* and planning process and let the manufacturers concentrate on other important elements of successful product development such as up-to-date facilities and up-to-date procurement of raw materials. The great retailers will also be using their tremendous information base to take advantage of economies of scale *across* divisions and product categories in addition to those economies of scale within product categories. The key phrase will become product procurement, an entirely different concept than the traditional vendor/retailer, buyer/seller relationship. Product procurement is a joint effort by the retailer and the manufacturer to serve the customer better. Product procurement is the natural evolution of the marketing process as it takes hold within the retailing organization. Marketing, with its focus on the customer, requires that the retailer take the lead in the development of the product assortment and merchandise diversity within his own categories. The retailer that does not take the lead in product procurement cannot make each category of merchandise truly stand for something specific in the minds of the consumer."*

* C.E.O. Antonini Defines K mart's New Creed on Merchandise Development," *Inside Retailing* (March 27, 1989), p. 4.

Stock Turnover

An important measure for comparing the volume of sales for a given period to the volume of unsold inventory accumulated in that same period is called **stock turnover.** It is a mathematical indication of how quickly merchandise is replaced in a store. It enables retailers to plan their purchases more accurately, and reduces the possibility of over- and understocking their inventory. A high stock turnover means that merchandise is selling faster than when there is a low turnover. The computation of stock turnover is discussed in Chapter 17.

With their gigantic size and costly initial investment, hypermarkets are particularly sensitive to profitable stock turnovers. Inasmuch as 30 to 40 percent of their products consist of food and related items (which usually show low profit margins), high turnover is essential.

Assortment Plans

Assortment plans help the buyer achieve merchandise balance. A stock of merchandise is properly assorted when it is composed of lines of goods that are suited to the demands of customers. One drugstore, for example, may have a proper assortment when it carries prescription and nonprescription items, cosmetics, and toiletries, but another drugstore might have a proper assortment when it carries prescription and nonprescription items, cosmetics, giftware, small games, and stationery. In other words, the merchandise lines carried bear a direct relationship to consumer demand.

Many specialty stores have expanded their assortments by enlarging the number of their product lines. For example, The Limited has introduced lingerie and fragrances, and Ann Taylor has added stockings, handbags, and costume jewelry. Combined with a personalized sales approach, this expansion attracts more and more consumers to the specialty store sector.

Retailers must decide whether their inventory composition should have breadth or depth. **Breadth,** or **width,** refers to the number of product classifications that a merchant stocks. **Depth** refers to the number of styles or brands within a product classification. There are three types of relationships between breadth and depth (Figure 10-7).

1. **Narrow and deep.** Only a few selections are offered, but they are stocked in depth (e.g., two styles of jeans, but in all sizes and colors).
2. **Broad and shallow.** The merchant carries a little of many styles in a product class (e.g., a large variety of designer jeans, with limited size selection).
3. **Combination.** A combination of (1) and (2) (e.g., four styles of jeans, in several colors and sizes).

Macy's is a good example of a department store that follows a narrow and deep strategy. Among others, its sportswear section is a good illustration of this policy.

In an effort to dominate a particular category of merchandise, some stores

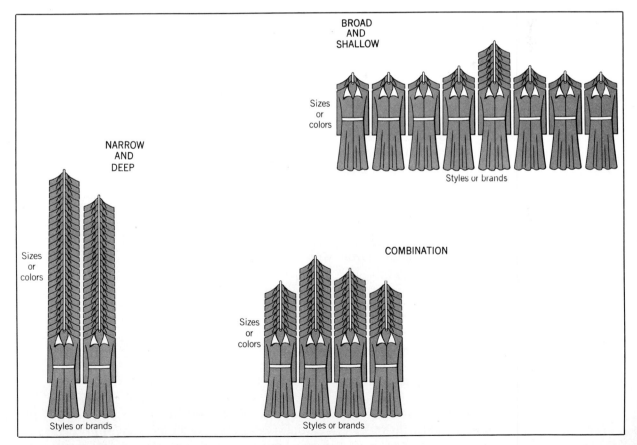

Figure 10-7   Types of breadth and depth assortment plans.

present overwhelming assortments. This technique is used by such chains as Kitchen Etc., Today's Man, and S&K Famous Brands.

K mart's hypermarket division, American Fare, is relatively narrow in assortments but very deep in the categories it sells. This arrangement has the advantage of focusing its marketing image for consumers.

Specialty stores that carry only one type of goods, for example, leg wear, must obviously have great depth to satisfy their customers. Stores such as Sock Shop International, Sock Express, and Sox Appeal maintain deep inventories of popular items that sell well—pantyhose, short socks, knee-high socks, and so on.

FROM WHOM TO BUY

In Chapter 9 we discussed the major merchandise sources for retail buyers. We will now see how buyers actually select among those resources.

Merchants always look for goods that can be sold in their own stores. Although improvements in production, distribution, and communications aid retailers in their search for merchandise, their buying depends on their ability to find good sources of supply (Figure 10-8). As indicated previously, they do this through visits to showrooms, vendors, and trade shows.

Vendor Relations

In selecting resources, buyers must find vendors who can supply merchandise reliably and consistently. To determine the value of a resource, the retailer should consider the following factors.

Quality of merchandise
Vendor's reputation
Location of vendor
Advertising and promotion of sales
Vendor's brand policy
Reorder availability
Terms of purchase
Sales and profit experience
Retailer-vendor cooperation

Quality of Merchandise

The quality of goods must meet the needs of the store's clientele

The vendor's merchandise must be suitable for the retailer's clientele. The market to which the retailer caters may prefer low-, medium-, or high-priced lines. The preference may be avant-garde (advanced) or conservative styles. It may also be either staples or specialty goods that cannot be substituted for or found

| Y | | 1 DEPT 5 | | | VENDOR NAME LIST | | REPORT THRU 2-06 | | | D125 |

		STYLE DESCRIPTION				ALL STORES COMBINED						
	VEND.	STYLE	STYLE NAME			LIFE HISTORY	RECENT SALES & STOCK HISTORY				ALL STORES	
CLASS CODES				COST	CURR. RETAIL		4 WEEKS AGO	3 WEEKS AGO	2 WEEKS AGO	1 WEEK AGO		
LAST ACTION & DATE				INT. MU%	1ST RETAIL							
	11		KOU FENG			SLS						
	11		DORA KNITTERS			RCPTS						
	11		MANFARE			RETURNS	LAST RCPT.	WKS AGO				
	11		AFASIA				FIRST RCPT	WKS AGO				
	14		ORIENTAL KNIT			SLS						
	15		FOLIE			RCPTS						
	22		NYSE			RETURNS	LAST RCPT	WKS AGO				
	25		BERNETTE				FIRST RCPT	WKS AGO				
	28		PURITAN			SLS						
	29		LAHM			RCPTS						
	51		MILFORD/DIMENSION			RETURNS	LAST RCPT	WKS AGO				
	72		HUK A POO				FIRST RCPT	WKS AGO				
	73		MEDIA INC			SLS						
	85		ROBERT BRUCE			RCPTS						
	85		CATALINA			RETURNS	LAST RCPT	WKS AGO				
							FIRST RCPT	WKS AGO				

(Left margin label: STYLE)

Figure 10-8   An example of a vendor name list stored by a computer that helps buyers determine good sources of supply.

Retailers check merchandise to evaluate the performance and reliability of their vendors.

elsewhere. Whatever the preferences of customers, the retailer must consider them when selecting vendors. Those who do not carry the quality of goods required are not good sources of supply. No matter how attractive their prices or how desirable they are to deal with, the buyer cannot consider them as suppliers.

The importance of merchandise quality is a major concern in the new businesses mushrooming in Eastern Europe. For example, rejecting the poor quality of local goods in a certain area of Poland, Michel Badre, a French retailer, opened Warsaw's first 24-hour convenience store in 1990 and stocked it almost totally with imported merchandise. Although he could have purchased many items from local vendors, his concern for first-rate products caused him to look elsewhere. The results were excellent, and Mr. Badre looked forward to franchising his business in other parts of Poland.

Vendor's Reputation

A vendor's reputation is indicated by the guarantee that it places behind its merchandise. Ethics are also an important standard by which to choose. Perhaps the size of the vendor's business or how long it has been in business are good indications of its reliability.

An unethical vendor is not likely to remain in business long. Sometimes buyers secure information about suppliers through merchantile agencies that issue confidential reports. Inquiries from noncompeting retailers are another way of learning about vendors.

Large retailers investigate vendors in an attempt to judge their ability to deliver quality goods. In addition, they check on their reputations for honesty. Unfortunately, errors regarding quantities, prices, and the like are not always innocent. Also, since a weak supplier may go out of business and thereby interrupt the supply of merchandise, retailers are interested in the financial strength of their vendors.

Some financially weak vendors are good sources but lack capital. In some cases large retailers that are interested in these vendors' merchandise advance funds against future orders.

Location of Vendor

Transportation costs may be a deterrent

Obtaining merchandise from distant vendors generally entails higher transportation costs than does obtaining merchandise locally. Higher costs, of course, can be a deterrent to handling such merchandise. On the other hand, if transportation costs are not a significant factor, and especially if the supplier is dependable, it may be advisable to use such a vendor.

When goods are sold, the buyer and seller must agree on which of them will pay the cost of transportation. There are two terms used to indicate responsibility: **FOB shipping point** and **FOB destination.** FOB stands for "free on board."

If the terms are FOB shipping point, the seller delivers the merchandise to the starting point of shipment. From that point on, the buyer pays transportation costs, has title (ownership) to the goods, and suffers any loss if the merchandise is damaged during shipment. When the terms are FOB destination, the seller pays the costs of transportation to the buyer's location, retains title to the goods while they are in transit, and suffers any loss if the merchandise is damaged during shipment.

It goes without saying that vendors that are reliable are preferred over those that renege on delivery promises. Buyers therefore should keep records regarding delivery performance so that vendors can be evaluated fairly.

Advertising and Promotion of Sales

Some vendors are well aware of how important it is for the retailer to move goods into the hands of the consumer. Such vendors help the retailer sell the goods by providing assistance with displays, advertising, and sales promotion. This type of help is very important to small retailers.

A good example of a major retailer that receives important help from its vendors is Marks & Spencer, the British department store chain. Without a manufacturing facility of its own, the company works closely with its suppliers in developing successful assortment plans. Because of this relationship, Marks & Spencer's buying personnel are called selectors, not buyers.

A novel in-store advertisement supported by vendors is Home Depot's use of salespeople's polo shirts. Inscribed with the Home Depot logo in front and specific product advertising on the back, these store-provided shirts are furnished free-of-charge to retailers by vendors who approve of the technique.

Vendor's Brand Policy

Some retailers need vendors for both branded and unbranded goods

A vendor's brand policy is another standard for selection. Some retailers prefer to handle only nationally advertised goods. Others prefer to develop and promote their own brands. For example, Henri Bendel employs some 35 designers who develop a constant flow of unique merchandise. The very large retailers find it worthwhile to develop and promote their own brands and, at the same time, handle some nationally advertised merchandise. In these instances vendors of both branded and unbranded merchandise must be selected.

Reorder Availability

Some vendors reserve additional merchandise at the time of the initial order so a buyer can be assured of fast delivery for a follow-up order. On the other hand, vendors dealing with financially pressed retailers are usually wary about shipping merchandise without some assurance of payment. For example, during the 1989–90 collapse of the Campeau Corporation, many vendors refused to ship goods to Federated Stores (Bloomingdale's, Abraham & Straus, Jordan Marsh, and others) until they were guaranteed payment by the bankruptcy court.

Terms of Purchase

An important standard by which vendors should be selected are the credit terms they offer. Although there is a good deal of standardization of terms, individual vendors often differ. Credit terms also vary with market conditions. Specific terms are treated later in this chapter.

According to a 1988 Supreme Court decision, vendors have the right to refuse to sell to retailers if the refusal is *not* based on price maintenance. For example, if the sale of a product requires a special store service, such as an alteration room, and the retailer doesn't supply such a service, the vendor may refuse to sell to that merchant.

Terms of purchase are also affected by another consideration. Due to the increased tempo of price sales and "everyday-low-price" approaches, stock turnover has taken on greater importance in retailers' plans. As a result, buyers now stress reorder time as part of terms almost as much as they do price.

Sales and Profit Experience

Careful records should be kept on vendor performance

Retailers should keep careful records of vendor performance. Comparisons can be made over time on the basis of customer returns, extent of markdowns, competition, markups, and the total sales picture. Obviously, the larger the sales volume, the more valuable the vendor.

Retailer-Vendor Cooperation

The sometimes bitter relations between vendors and retailers, caused by such factors as misunderstanding and unfulfilled promises, has given rise to suggestions for improved dealings. The following statement indicates a possible change in this relationship.[2]

> *Partnership between retailer and vendor is in the wind, and no one is a greater advocate of this relationship than Jack Shewmaker, former vice chairman of Wal-Mart and one of the leading architects of that firm's partnership program.*
>
> *Speaking before the recent IMRA meeting, he called for the end of the adversarial and confrontational relationship between vendor and retailer. He said, "Much too often the adversarial position led to mistrust, misguided plans and strategies and supersecretive attitudes. We fostered our own 'cold war.' "*
>
> *Here then are Shewmaker's thoughts on how to end that war and foster the partnership relationship.*
>
> **Suggestions for the retailer:**
> *Identify from 20 to 50 of your suppliers. Accumulate and collect all the data you can on these suppliers, then decide upon a partnership approach and*

---

[2] "Partnerships: A Necessity for the 90s and Beyond," *Inside Retailing* (July 1990), p. 1.

Retailing has come a long way since the old-style department store came on the business scene. Today, we visit attractive shopping malls, seafront store centers, and upgraded inner city emporiums. We also shop at home using video equipment and computers. Yes, retailing is an exciting world, and the photographs that follow reveal how new and refreshing that world is.

Service Businesses like the Hampton Inn chain are a

Unobtrusive security devices blend into a store's decor. *Courtesy*: Sensormatic Electronics Corp.

This shop looks like a store unto itself. It isn't; it's part of the Neiman Marcus flagship store...a "shop within a shop." *Courtesy*: Neiman Marcus.

As shown by the helpful employee and grateful shopper, customer service is uppermost in the strategy of successful retailers. *Courtesy*: Wal-Mart.

Colorful displays attract shoppers and stimulate purchasing. *Courtesy*: Neiman Marcus.

Saks Fifth Avenue

The ambiance of the North Star Mall in San Antonio, Texas is enhanced by stores such as Saks Fifth Avenue. *Courtesy*: Saks Fifth Avenue.

The increase of in-home shopping causes retailers to reassess their marketing strategies. The use of videos permits merchants to develop new techniques for tapping a "goldmine" of at-home consumers. *Courtesy*: AT & T.

Governor's Square in Tallahassee, Florida provides more than just stores. It makes shopping a social as well as a buying experience. *Courtesy*: Rouse Company.

Resident buying offices help retailers and store buyers make intelligent merchandise decisions. They employ specialists to scan the market for new merchandise and supplier resources. *Courtesy:* Henry Doneger Associates.

This unique layout of a store provides access and visual impact at every level. *Courtesy:* A & S

This 7-Eleven Store in the United Kingdom is an example of the increasing presence of American retailers in foreign countries. *Courtesy*: 7-Eleven Stores, Southland Corporation.

This shopping crowd at Faneuil Hall, Boston illustrates the changing lifestyles of American consumers. *Courtesy*: Rouse Company.

The Banana Republic—an unusual name for a retail store. But the name and the store's design communicate a clear message; we carry out-of-Africa, safari-type merchandise. *Courtesy*: Banana Republic

Youth Fashion Guild

Resident buying offices prepare catalogs for their clients. *Courtesy*: Certified Youth Fashion Guild.

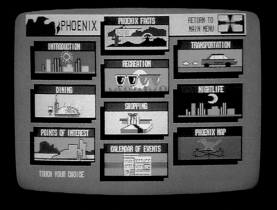

One touch makes information come alive with the IBM InfoWindow System. Virtually any information that the retailer needs to present to the seller can be obtained effectively with this interactive technology. *Courtesy*: International Business Machines.

A & P's SAV-A-CENTERS feature superstore size, variety, and a pleasant one-stop shopping environment. These spacious superstores communicate value to consumers who demand low prices along with an extensive assortment of private-label and national brand products.
Courtesy: A & P.

Strawbridge & Clothier's commitment to customer service and quality merchandise at any price is symbolized by their Seal of Confidence. *Courtesy*: Strawbridge & Clothier.

Shoppers enjoy seeing well-designed interiors and exteriors. *Courtesy*: The Limited, Inc.

Regional Marts are important sources of information and contacts for retailers, buyers, and vendors who meet during market week. *Courtesy*: Dallas Apparel Mart.

spread this word throughout your organization by continuous buyer-group meetings. Then expand buyer meetings into meeting with all the support-functions personnel.

In the process of doing this, recognize that we, through delegation, over-delegation and adversarial encouragement have created 'power zones' wherein individual buyers or departments have been given authority which preclude partnership relations. Convert them to modern management techniques.

Above all don't forget that in today's age of information technology, many support functions are really in the mainstream of the buying and selling of merchandise. Transportation, distribution, data processing, accounting and store operations are integral to the buying function in today's high-tech environment.

With this being the case, many of us must redefine the buyer's role . . . because it must change.

Now, while you are in the process of collecting data on your suppliers, identify all known problems which apply to each. Then contact senior personnel of the suppliers along with their salesmen and their sales team. Request an audience, assign your own support team, then schedule meetings between the two groups.

At these meeting discuss known problems, but be sure to devote equal time to discussing mutual opportunities and long range planning objectives. Take an actionable point of view where individuals on both teams are assigned responsibility with deadlines and goals. At the senior management level maintain responsibility for follow-up.

Suggestions for the supplier:

First, identify your key retail accounts. Then develop an internal plan for addressing those accounts in a very straightforward way. In this process, you will need to redefine your salesmen's role giving them new responsibilities and a new understanding of your business plan. Assign key team members from the various support functions including R&D, transportation, accounts receivable, data processing, manufacturing and marketing.

Aggressively set out, to seek an audience with the retail counterparts. Many a time I have heard my vendor friends say,—'If I go over the buyer's head, my chances of trying to sell the organization will be zero.' Getting rid of this notion is a key step in building the first leg of trust. Sure, tell the buyers what you want to do, tell them you intend to talk with senior management, but you would like to do it with them and involve them in the process. Your goal: to enhance the partnership by seeking out and visiting with several levels of the retailer's management.

Above all, be prepared to address and solve problems with your new partners. Offer new ideas, conceptualize and strategize about long range-planning issues.

Negotiations

Some vendors have set terms that are the same for all retailers. These terms vary from one resource to another and change as business conditions change. In a seller's market, the terms are not so liberal for the retailer. In a buyer's market, however, retailers can sometimes insist on their own terms.

Terms of purchase also vary according to the trade. In the food trade, for example, the terms of purchase are not as liberal as in the apparel trade. As a rule, the faster the merchandise is sold, the shorter the terms and the smaller the discount. Discounts alone, however, should not lure a buyer into a purchase that is not suitable for the store's clientele.

Because of depressed profits during the last decade, many retailers have become more demanding in their relationships with vendors. Attempting to minimize risk, the former have increased their requests for advertising aid, promotional support, and reduced-price contributions on poor-selling merchandise.

Discounts and Dating

Cash Discounts

The most common terms of purchase are **cash discounts.** The discounts are listed in percentages of total purchase price and are offered in return for prompt payment. A cash discount has three elements: a percentage figure, a discount period consisting of a certain number of days, and a net period.

The date of the invoice usually determines when the discount and net periods expire. If the retailer does not take advantage of the cash discount by paying early, the full amount must be paid within the net period computed from the date of the invoice.

Suppose the terms of an invoice are 2/10, net/30 and the invoice date is May 1. The retailer may deduct 2 percent of the bill if it is paid within 10 days (May 11), but must pay the full price if it is paid after May 11. In any case, the bill must be paid no later than May 31 (30 days from the invoice date). Since discounts mean additional capital for retailers, they make every effort to pay bills early.

Anticipation is an extra discount that retailers ask for if they pay their bills before the expiration of the cash discount period. The rationale for this additional discount is that the vendor has the use of the retailer's money and any interest it might earn. As interest rates have risen, retailers are demanding higher anticipation discounts. It is not uncommon for stores to request rates as high as 1 percent monthly or 12 percent a year. When anticipation is granted by the vendor, it is deducted from the invoice price.

Dating

Dating refers to the period allowed by vendors to buyers for the payment of bills. It includes both the discount period and the net period. These periods vary and may include any of the following.

ROG (Receipt of Goods).   The cash discount period begins with the receipt of the merchandise rather than the actual date of the invoice. If goods are bought under terms of 2/10, net 60 ROG, the 2 percent discount may be taken if the bill is paid within 10 days after the receipt of the goods. This is generally used when the invoice date and the date of arrival of merchandise are not the same because of long distances between retailer and vendor.

DOI (Date of Invoice).   This is called ordinary or regular dating: payment starts with the invoice date.

EOM (End of Month).   The discount period starts at the end of the month in which the invoice is dated. For example, if an invoice date is April 8 and the terms are 2/10 EOM. net/60. the retailer can deduct a 2 percent discount if the bill is paid by May 10.

Extra Dating.   Sometimes a retailer requests additional time in which to take advantage of a cash discount. When the discount period is extended, it is known as **extra dating** and is denoted by a capital *X* or the term *extra*. For example, "2/10 − 30X" or "2/10 − 30 extra" on an invoice extends the regular discount period from 10 to 40 days (10 + 30) from the date of the invoice.

Postdating.   Similar to extra dating, **postdating** is a common practice in the apparel industry. It extends the cash discount period for an additional month when the invoice is dated on or after the twenty-fifth of the month and end-of-month terms are given. For example, if an invoice is dated September 26 with terms of 6/10 EOM, the retailer has until October 10 in which to take the discount. With postdating, the retailer has until November 10 to qualify for the discount.

Advance Dating.   When ordering goods during a slow period, the merchant may sometimes arrange to pay for the merchandise after it has been sold. The merchant arranges to have the credit date based on a date later than the invoice date. Toys and Christmas items are often ordered in this way. Because retailers are motivated to purchase early, manufacturers benefit by not having to store the merchandise. Thus, an invoice for a shipment of toys could be dated July 1, effective November 10. If a cash discount of 2/10 were in order, the 2 percent discount could be deducted through November 20.

Advance dating is a help to retailers with seasonal products

Trade Discounts

Trade Discounts are given by vendors according to the type of customer. That is, they are given according to the quantities purchased and the functions performed by the purchaser. In most cases wholesalers receive larger discounts than retailers. This is due either to the volume of purchases made by wholesalers (**quantity discount**) or to the many marketing functions they assume, functions that ordinarily are handled by the manufacturers. In the latter case the manufacturers pass along their reduced costs in the form of trade discounts. Since large chains and department stores buy much larger quantities than some wholesalers, they are able to secure trade discounts, too. Another type of trade discount is a **seasonal discount** given to retailers willing to order, receive, and pay for goods during the "off season."

Other Aspects of Negotiations

Sometimes there are other concessions that make a buyer select a particular vendor. The following are among those that are considered most often.

Other factors in selecting a vendor

Market Exclusivity. For some goods, limits on the type or number of competitors may be required if a store is to make a reasonable profit. For example, a ladies' handbag line that is discounted within a particular trading area might not be a wise purchase for a traditional department store in that area. Exclusivity may also involve confining a style to a particular store even though the vendor's line is sold by competing stores.

Lower Costs. Lower costs are always of interest to buyers, especially for merchandise categories in which competition is severe.

Advertising. Vendors may offer financial assistance to support retail advertisements. (Retail advertising and cooperative arrangements are discussed in Chapter 15.)

Guaranteed Sales. Under a system of **guaranteed sales,** before an order is received from a retailer, the vendor agrees to take back merchandise that the retailer cannot sell within a specified time. For example, a dress manufacturer could make such an agreement to move end-of-season stock. The buyer benefits from the arrangement because no OTB dollars have to be committed if the dresses do not sell.

Consignment Buying. In **consignment buying,** the vendor permits the retailer to pay only for goods that are sold. In this arrangement the seller retains ownership of the goods and more or less dictates the terms of sale. It is used with high-priced specialty goods that a store might want to "try."

Service. Some vendors offer additional services that attract purchasers. For example, vendors take stock counts (in the store) of merchandise that they supply, offer sales assistance in the store, and help train salespeople.

Another valuable vendor service is **premarking,** also known as **source marking.** Premarked merchandise arrives in the store completely marked (i.e., ticketed) by the vendor according to the merchant's specifications (price, style, size, etc.). The advantages to the retailer are reduced store marking costs, more accurate ticketing, and the ability to get the merchandise onto the selling floor earlier. (Premarking is covered in greater detail in Chapter 12).

Backup Stock.   **Backup stock** is merchandise that a vendor will reserve without the store's having any obligation to purchase it. This arrangement allows the merchant to buy in smaller quantities and still "have" stock.

Special Features.   Some manufacturers are willing to add a distinctive merchandise feature to a regular item for some stores. This can give added value by creating a degree of exclusivity.

Suggestions for Retail Negotiators

Obviously, negotiations require skill on the part of retailers. The following suggestions can be of great help to merchants in their dealings with vendors:[3]

- *"Throughout the negotiating process,* try to learn what the vendor needs and correlate those needs to your needs.
- *"Maintain constructive relationships* during negotiations. Avoid defend/attack spirals. Paraphrase what you've heard to show you're taking the vendor's proposal seriously. Build on areas of agreement rather than pointing out where you disagree. Read the cues you see and hear.
- *"Move forward* when you've gotten agreement rather than tack on weaker points the vendor might attack.
- *"Asking questions* lets you clarify *and shape* the other party's proposals. If you feel the proposal is inappropriate, you probably need more information on the reasoning behind it.
- *"Questions also allow you* to avoid disclosing information prematurely; handle the situation when you don't know what to do; and avoid being pressured.
- *"Use preparatory statements* to change pace and direction with minimum disruption. Examples: I wonder if we can backtrack a moment? Let's make sure that we're on track with each other. How would you feel about this:
- *"While you should give the other party* as little information as possible during negotiations, there are times when revealing your *feelings* will encourage more openness and trust from the other party.
- *"When it looks like you and the vendor* can't work out a solution to a problem, look "outside the box" for possible answers. Examine your assumptions. You may believe, wrongly, that the vendor is locked into certain shipping times. The vendor may mistakenly think your open-to-buy doesn't allow for a larger order."

[3] "Today's Scheme of 'Produce-or-Perish,' " *Inside Retailing* (October 23, 1989), p. 3.

ETHICS

Legal and ethical constraints on negotiations

Buyers have the obligation to negotiate the best possible terms of sale for the goods they purchase. The negotiations, however, are subject to certain legal and ethical constraints. A handy tool for buyers is *The Buyer's Manual*.[4] which lists unethical buyer-seller practices. The following list contains common abuses, some of which can be attributed to retailers, some to manufacturers, and some to both.

- Attempts to evade contractual obligations
- Excessive demands for service
- Unjust price concessions
- Abnormal credit extensions
- Discrimination based on the superior bargaining power of large groups
- Lack of sound business methods
- Unjust cancellations

Many difficulties arise in buying and negotiating for merchandise. Ethical practices are necessary for a store's public relations. For example, when the buyers of three well-known retail firms arranged with vendors to raise, fix, and maintain the retail prices charged for women's clothing, their carefully developed public images were tarnished.

NEW TERMS

advance dating	FOB destination
anticipation	FOB shipping point
assortment plan	guaranteed sales
backup stock	narrow and deep plan
breadth	open-to-buy (OTB)
broad and shallow plan	postdating
cash discount	premarking
combination plan	quantity discount
consignment buying	receipt of goods (ROG)
date of invoice (DOI)	seasonal discount
dating	source marking
depth	stock turnover
end of month (EOM)	trade discount
extra dating	width

[4] David E. Moeser, *The Buyer's Manual* (New York: National Retail Merchants Association, 1965).

CHAPTER HIGHLIGHTS

1. Buyers must stock the store with merchandise that can be sold profitably. They are faced with the decisions of what to buy, how much to buy, from whom to buy, and when to buy.

2. A store's image and the clientele it attracts depend to a large extent on the type of merchandise it sells.

3. Purchasing the right merchandise involves interpretation of consumer demand. Retailers seek information from their consumers, the trade, and company records.

4. A "want slip" system is a definite indication of consumer merchandise requests at a given time. These systems are helpful to buyers.

5. It is important for the buyer to understand the store's fashion position and how its clientele fits into the fashion adoption process.

6. The open-to-buy sets the dollar amount of merchandise that a buyer can order for a particular period. It provides the buyer with flexibility and results in a proper balance between inventory and sales.

7. Assortment plans help the buyer achieve merchandise balance.

8. The success of retailers depends on their ability to find good sources of merchandise. Several factors should be considered in selecting a vendor: quality of merchandise, vendor's reputation, location of vendor, advertising and promotion of sales, vendor's brand policy, reorder availability, terms of purchase, sales and profit experience, and retailer-vendor cooperation.

9. Negotiations involve terms of purchase, exclusive arrangements, and special vendor considerations and services.

10. Terms of purchase vary from one trade to another and involve a variety of credit terms.

11. Buyers have the obligation to negotiate the best possible terms of sale within certain legal and ethical constraints.

REVIEW QUESTIONS

1. What are the major decisions that a buyer has to make with regard to stocking a store?

2. How can a retailer assess consumer demand? How are consumers helpful in the interpretation of consumer demand?

3. What might be the consequences of a retailer's financial needs conflicting with his choice of merchandise?

4. Why is open-to-buy a valuable tool for the buyer? For the store?
5. How do assortment plans relate to consumer demand?
6. What are the factors to be considered in selecting a vendor?
7. What kinds of records should be kept by a store once a vendor has been used as a source of supply?

DISCUSSION QUESTIONS

1. How does merchandise play an important role in creating a store's image?
2. When selecting a vendor, is the quality of merchandise sold by the vendor more important than the vendor's reputation? Why?
3. How might the financial strength of a retailer's vendor affect the retailer?
4. How might a charge of unethical buying practices affect a store's image?

CASE 1

Key Vendors

Recently two executives made a presentation to the president of a large retail firm regarding a new way to plan purchases. Basically, it was an integrated system for programming merchandise with the retailer's key vendors. The plan consisted of the following.

- The merchant's chief executives and the top-level personnel of several key vendors would jointly develop a merchandise plan.
- The plan would take into consideration several factors.

Merchandise, including basic stock, fashion assortments, and profit structures.
Sales training by vendor specialists.
An advertising and promotional program to include displays, feature promotions, and printed advertising.
A detailed organization chart designating the responsibilities and directions for carrying out the plan.

When the plan was presented, the following arguments for adoption were made.

- The store would become a "known" quantity and would benefit as a preferred customer.
- The key vendors would concentrate on providing the store with better service, premarked merchandise, and better shipping arrangements.
- Vendors would work directly with the store's inventory and reordering schedules.
- The relationship between the store and key sources would be closer, with fewer problems and simpler procedures for solving misunderstandings.
- Because decision making would involve only top-level executives, it would be easier to make necessary changes.

After listening to the presentation, the president indicated that he would consider the proposal and make a decision within a week.

a. If you were the president of the retail firm, would you adopt this plan? State your reasons for acceptance or refusal.
b. What types of stores might benefit from a programmed merchandising system? What types of stores might be handicapped by this arrangement?

CASE 2

K mart Changes Course

In the 1970s and early 1980s, K mart emerged as one of the nation's largest discount retailers. For over 19 years, the K mart chain had based its planning on four strategies: Sell very low-priced merchandise, underprice all competitors, rapidly open stores in new locations to establish markets faster than competitors, and realize profits by running a "no-frills" operation to hold costs down.

Its huge volume of sales combined with low operating costs and few services offered customers contributed to record sales revenues for many years. By 1979, K mart was second only to Sears in nonfood retailing sales.

But in 1980 the company's fortunes began to turn downward. Although sales volume continued to increase, the company saw its net income decline. It is estimated that one key indicator of productivity—net income generated per square foot of selling space—fell from approximately $3.80 in 1979 to $1.90 in 1981, even though the company continued to open new stores. Company projections for future productivity were similarly pessimistic.

K mart's commitment to very-low-priced merchandise meant that, despite increasing sales volume, the dollar value per sale was low. Changed economic conditions, mainly inflation, meant rising costs of operation that outpaced K mart's dollar intake per customer. K mart's position at the low-price end of the extremely competitive discount market meant the chain could not raise its prices to match inflation.

Changes had also taken place in consumers and in their demands that made K mart's strategy less viable.

There were a growing number of two-income families who could afford to spend a little more for the goods they purchased. On a larger scale, there was a broad segment of consumers who were more interested in getting quality and value in their purchases than in paying the lowest possible price. In the minds of many consumers, a K mart store was the place to save money, but not the place to find the values they wanted.

The company's own research revealed that, although more than half of all shoppers in the United States walked into K mart stores, they purchased only a few basic items. K mart simply did not get the customer's money for other items.

For customers seeking better quality at a slightly higher price, K mart stores could not meet the need, because they did not carry such merchandise. For example, a customer who was prepared to pay about $6 for a better bath towel had to go elsewhere, because K mart's top price was around $4 for a towel of lesser quality.

Smaller chains such as Caldor had already proved more flexible in responding to changing consumer demands by upgrading merchandise and store appearance.

Realizing that the economy and consumer demands and expectations had changed by the end of the 1970s, K mart's management determined that its merchandising and marketing strategy also needed to change. And they decided to accomplish this in several ways.

It slowed down the rate of expansion, opening stores at a slower pace. It decided to seek a more affluent customer, in addition to its traditional price-conscious consumers. In order to do so, K mart upgraded merchandise to provide better quality and expanded the price range of goods. The chain added national brands to the merchandise carried. The company also expanded the variety of merchandise sold in its stores. For example, women's apparel was expanded to include dresses and suits as well as slacks and tops.

The chain installed specialty shops and groupings, including designer collections such as Gloria Vanderbilt, to attract the more well-to-do customer.

K mart also decided to refurbish existing stores to reflect its changing image by installing new fixtures, changing merchandise presentation, utilizing modular displays, and giving specialty (fashion) treatment for related merchandise.

To improve its profit picture, the company sold a number of divisions that were not producing well. For example, it spun off its Designer Depot and Jupiter variety store operations. The firm enhanced its private-label image through attractive lines of women's clothing and arranged to carry an exclusive line of Jaclyn Smith apparel.

It improved its customer services by such innovations as an automated layaway plan, and it refined its purchasing procedures.

Despite the changes, by 1991 K mart had slipped to number three behind Sears and Wal-Mart among the top American retailers. The company continued its role as a strong discounter, and management was not hesitant about making bold moves for improvement.

a. K mart developed its business as a low-price discounter over many years. Do you think K mart can successfully change its mix of merchandise to attract the higher-income customer permanently?

b. Do you see a trend among "no-frills" discount retailers to upgrade merchandise in order to attract more affluent buyers? What kind of competitors will they face? Who will their competitors be?

c. Can you foresee any dangers for a discounter that upgrades in order to offer better merchandise and more customer amenities?

REFERENCES

BIVINS, J. "Buying Office Status Report." *Stores* (May 1989), pp. 54–56, 60–61.

"Category Killers Take Different Forms." *Inside Retailing* (April 9, 1990), p. 3.

KRIENKE, M. "Home Fashions Business." *Stores* (April 1989), pp. 41–44.

MICHALS, D. "Living with the Tough Stores." *Women's Wear Daily* (February 14, 1989), pp. 6–7.

"Retailers and Vendors Playing a New Game with New Rules." *Inside Retailing* (June 18, 1990), p. 1.

Chapter 11

Pricing

After completing this chapter, you should be able to:

- Discuss the three elements in pricing decisions: the consumer, the competition, and the laws.
- Identify common price policies followed by retailers.
- Explain and compute markups.
- List the reasons for markdowns and calculate markdown percentages.

In Chapter 9 we discussed the factors that retailers consider when buying merchandise. Buying methods and the buyer's role were explored, and sources of merchandise were examined. Chapter 10 dealt with the planning aspect of merchandise: its objectives, stock strategy, and buying levels.

Retail pricing is a complex process

Having decided on a general approach to the purchase of goods, the retailer must consider the prices at which to sell the merchandise. Contrary to what many people think, retail pricing is a complex process involving a variety of factors. In addition, pricing is a key element in the eventual success or failure of an enterprise. That being so, it is essential to study this critical aspect of retailing.

THE IMPORTANCE OF CORRECT PRICING POLICIES

The pricing policies established by a retail enterprise must appeal to its customers. This holds true for high-priced fashion shops as well as for low-priced convenience stores. The essential point is that the store's overall price levels must match the image it projects. Without this blend of price and image, customers become confused and frequently turn elsewhere for their needs.

A retail price includes the cost of the goods, overhead, and profit

Correct pricing policies are essential to the profitability of a business. This is so because the price of an item must cover the cost of the product, the **overhead** (e.g., rent, salaries, advertising, telephone, delivery) of the business, and the profit the retailer wants to make. For example, if a retailer buys an item for $6, estimates overhead at $4, and desires a profit of $2, the item must be sold for $12 (Figure 11-1). Though many other factors enter into the determination of price, the

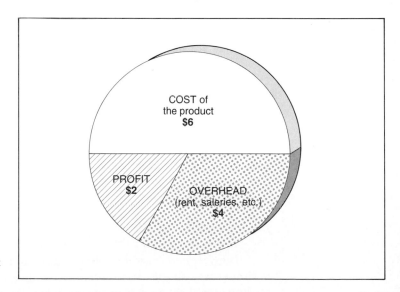

Figure 11-1 Price components of a product that sells for $12.

355

retailer's ultimate consideration must be the maintenance of a satisfactory profit level.

It goes without saying that the lower the overhead, the lower the price at which a retailer can sell a product. This translates into a possible advantage over competitors. For this reason, astute retailers keep a constant watch on expenses, going so far as to reward employees for cost-saving suggestions.

MEASURING A STORE'S SUCCESS

One measurement of a store's success is the sales generated per square foot of selling space. For example, if a store's sales for a year total $20,000,000 and its selling area contains 100,000 square feet, its sales per square foot are $200. Whether or not this is a satisfactory figure depends on the size, type, and location of the store. A large urban department store probably experiences sales per square foot in excess of $200. In fact, some stores register more than $300.

Another measure of a store's performance related to *sales* per square foot is *profit* per square foot. Many retailers feel that the latter measure is more significant as an indication of a store's performance. This is because the measure indicates the true level of a store's success, that is, the "bottom line." Comparisons of both measures are made frequently with those of competing stores and with a store's own history, and retail industry analysts pay close attention to the findings. The National Retail Federation publishes per square foot figures of member stores in its *Merchandising Operating Results,* published yearly.

ELEMENTS IN PRICING DECISIONS

The Consumer

As indicated previously, the consumer is one of the retailer's main concerns in the development of a price structure. An analysis of this concern takes into consideration the following aspects of the consumer's status.

1. Income levels
2. Consumer motivation
3. Psychological aspects
4. Store image concepts
5. Value concepts

Income Levels

With a good understanding of the public's buying capabilities, it is possible to draw some simple, yet valuable, conclusions about price levels. For example, a trading area that consists primarily of low-income people could not be expected to support a variety of high-priced stores. On the other hand, stores that carry products with prices keyed to the area's ability to pay might do quite well.

Retailers must watch for changes in consumers' income levels

Retailers must be alert to changes in consumers' income levels because even subtle shifts in neighborhood populations can have a serious effect on sales. For example, the closing of an auto factory can change the character of a community and, with it, the public's purchasing potential. Therefore, price policies need to be reviewed periodically in the light of possible changes in the population of a trading area.

Consumer Motivation

Despite the importance of income levels in the determination of consumer spending, other factors often influence shoppers when they buy. These include personal services offered by retailers, the availability of discounts, and the assortment of merchandise carried by stores. In addition, a consumer's purchases may be affected by his or her age, education, ethnic group, personality, and occupation. Though prices cannot take all of these influences into account, retailers should consider those that appear to have the greatest impact on their sales.

Psychological Aspects

Odd pricing is still used, but its effectiveness is declining

Have you ever wondered why stores sometimes sell merchandise at such odd prices as 59¢, $8.95, and $16.99? After all, amounts of 60¢, $9.00, and $17.00 are much simpler for both retailers and consumers to use. The most commonly accepted reason appears to be the customer's feeling that **odd prices** (prices just below even amounts) result in real savings. Though this psychological approach to pricing may have been effective in the past, it has lost some of its appeal in today's market. Many consumers have become too sophisticated to be taken in by such price arrangements, and pay little attention to them. However, because of tradition or custom, a significant though declining number of retailers still cling to the practice.

A humorous sidelight to the use of odd pricing occurred late in 1982 during competition between Macy's New York and Zabar's, a gourmet food specialty shop. At a time when Beluga caviar from the Caspian Sea was in plentiful supply, Macy's lowered its price for a 14-ounce package to $149. Zabar's countered with a reduced price of $139.95. Macy's then went to $135, and Zabar's responded with $129.95. Could Zabar's have reasoned that its odd pricing gave it an additional advantage over Macy's?

Store Image Concepts

Store image can be molded by price

Not all consumers buy on the basis of price. For some shoppers, a store's image is the main reason that they shop there. This is particularly true for prestigious stores like Neiman-Marcus and Marshall Field. Such factors as display, decor, atmosphere, and store reputation appeal more to these consumers than low

Pricing to meet the competition. Notice the odd pricing. *Courtesy:* Giant Food Inc. and Safeway Stores.

prices. The stores maintain their reputations—and their customers—by cultivating a clearly defined affluent image.

Of course, store image can be molded by price, too. For example, consumers generally think of discount operations in terms of money-saving merchandise. Whether shoppers actually pay lower prices at such stores depends on the specific products purchased, the competition, the store itself, and similar factors. What draws them to these stores is the images the stores project through years of advertising, word of mouth, and personal contact with other shoppers.

Supermarkets sometimes use posters to provide shoppers with price information. This supermarket poster provides the shopper with price and product information.

Value Concepts

People have general ideas about how much they expect to pay for most items. For example, they know that designer products cost more because of the status of a well-known name, that fruits and vegetables fall into specific price categories, and that well-made furniture costs hundreds or thousands of dollars. With these understandings in mind, shoppers expect to pay prices at or close to their perceptions. When consumers' value judgments are jarred by unexpected prices, not only are sales lost, but particular customers may be lost for good.

The danger of jarring customers' price expectations

A relevant comment about value is provided by the following excerpt from *Inside Retailing:*[1]

> *Every retail sage, from Stanley Marcus to Sam Shoestring, will report that today's (and future) customers are super-sensitive to value. But what is value? You can pay $250 for a custom-made shirt at New York's Sulka. You can pay $6.99 for a shirt at most discount stores. Which is the better value? The answer, of course, is that it depends on the customer . . . on the specific*

[1] "What Is Value?" *Inside Retailing* (May 16, 1983), p. 1.

blend of ego and pocketbook. *That's why the specialty store has outrun the department store. It is easier for the specialist to target his customer base and buy and sell what represents value to that segment of the market. The tragic error is that so many "merchants" equate value with price. Not so. When major stores promote $20 shirts in a one-week sale at 20% off, it should be a cleanup, right? Wrong. When the store invites customers to paw through tables of shirts to find the right collar size and sleeve length in the right pattern, we suspect a large portion of potential buyers turn away and say it isn't worth $4 to contend with the hassle.*

Raising prices to convey the impression that merchandise is upscale fools few consumers. Recognition of this attitude is the fact that retail giants like Sears, Roebuck and The Limited acknowledge shoppers' demands for value by pressuring vendors for upgraded manufacturing techniques, attractive packaging, and package inserts carrying personal touches.

Competition

Having considered the factors that influence consumer buying habits, the retailer must analyze the competition. This involves asking such questions as "Am I competitive?" "Should I offer some additional service to my customers?" "Should I sell some products close to cost to attract additional customers?" and "Can I change prices without affecting the level of my sales?"

All retailers use pricing techniques to remain competitive

Obviously, large retailers have more options for meeting competition than small ones. Nevertheless, an astute small retailer can use a number of pricing techniques to remain competitive. To deal with competing stores, both large and small retailers usually consider the following.

1. Competitors' prices and services
2. Pricing to meet the competition
3. Private brands

Competitors' Prices and Services

Without knowing their competitors' prices, most retailers would be hard pressed to establish realistic prices. For example, it would be wise for a new women's-wear store specializing in **misses merchandise lines** (clothing for mature women) to check prices in competing department and specialty stores. Ignorance of those prices could have disastrous consequences for the new retailer.

In addition to being aware of competitors' prices, some types of stores must also know the nature of the customer services offered by competitors. Gift wrapping, free delivery, alterations—these are often the factors that help shoppers decide which stores to patronize. The addition of even one new service can sometimes attract new customers or retain old ones.

Comparison shoppers check competitors' prices and services

In order to maintain current information about rival stores, larger retailers employ **comparison shoppers.** Their job is to check the merchandise sold by competitors for price, assortment, and the like. They also note the services offered by competitors. At times they purchase selected items in competing stores for purposes of analysis and planning by their own buyers. Since smaller retailers cannot afford the luxury of comparison shoppers, they carry out this function themselves or send out employees to do so.

Pricing to Meet the Competition

A retailer's control over prices depends on the nature of the business

The nature of a retail establishment has much to do with its degree of freedom in setting prices. With some types of businesses, such as gas stations and newspaper/magazine stores, there is little leeway to depart from prevailing prices. This is so because there are so many stores in each category, all of which compete directly with each other and sell the same kinds of products. Even a one-cent reduction in the price of gas, for example, can cause drivers to switch from one gas station to another. Unless a station offers unusual services or is located away from competition, it must maintain competitive prices in order to survive.

On the other hand, other types of retailers can sometimes exercise considerable control over prices. For example, specialty stores often carry a wide assortment of merchandise that customers find appealing. Department stores may offer services that are not available elsewhere. Convenience stores are located close to where people live or work. Whatever the reason, such stores attract shoppers who are more interested in assortment, services, or convenience than in price. Consequently, these stores can maintain higher prices and still be competitive.

RETAIL STRATEGY

If You Can't Beat 'Em, Join 'Em

Not so many years ago prominent department store executives were predicting the early demise of discount stores. So certain were they of the disappearance of the discount store industry that they trumpeted their pronouncements at meetings and seminars.

Needless to say, their rosy predictions never materialized. In fact, discount operations became powerful competitors to traditional department stores. So much so, that full-line discounters now account for more than $70 billion in annual sales.

Faced with a general price challenge and unwilling to forego its preeminent position with upscale consumers, many large department store chains established or purchased discount divisions of their own. Their strategy was simple: to have their cake and eat it, too. This novel approach to servicing price-different target populations is illustrated today by the following examples:

DEPARTMENT STORE CHAINS	**DISCOUNT DIVISIONS**
Dayton Hudson	Target, Mervyn's
May	Venture

Having succeeded in attracting and retaining customers, these retailers have additional options open to them. For example, they can stock brands that other retailers cannot afford to carry. They can also be more selective about pricing individual items; that is, they can lower prices in direct competition with other stores, or raise them when they see little danger in doing so.

Consumers do not automatically react favorably to price discounts. Although retailers agree that shoppers respond positively to steep price discounts, they recognize that moderate discounts (e.g., 10 percent) may be unavailing. Despite all the experience with off-price retailing, discounting strategy, and no-frills operations, many consumers are still attracted by pleasant surroundings, store services, and wide assortments.

Nevertheless, because the selling price differential between discounters and department stores on many items is in the 25 percent range, the discounters exercise a powerful price advantage. Successful department stores respond to this price pressure by providing special services and amenities to their customers. In many instances this strategy neutralizes the price differences. On the other hand, too many department stores still rely on their past performances, images, and loyal customer patronage. They have reduced services to cut down on costs, but have maintained or increased prices, leaving some customers disillusioned.

Price wars are harmful to most retailers

From time to time retailers that sell similar types of merchandise engage in ruthless competition, slashing prices on specific items in an attempt to steal customers from each other. In the past these **price wars** involved such products as clothing, gas, food, and liquor. Until the retailers themselves, or their suppliers, put a stop to the "war," consumers have a field day, whereas the retailers usually suffer financial losses. These price struggles illustrate the often harmful consequences of fierce competition.

When a retailer experiences a cash flow problem (insufficient cash on hand to pay current debts), one of the ways he copes is by cutting prices to stimulate sales. Such was the case with the Campeau Corporation in 1989. The company, owner of such well-known chains as Bloomingdale's, Stern's, A&S, Bon Marché, and Jordan Marsh, found itself pressed for cash to meet mounting debts. Selective price promotions, coupled with an outside loan, enabled Campeau to pay some of its obligations.

Private Brands

Private brands give some retailers a competitive edge

One of the ways in which retailers sometimes gain a competitive edge is through the sale of private brands (private labels). As you recall, these are products that carry the retailer's or middleman's label instead of a manufacturer's national brand. Since national brands usually cost more than private brands because of the extensive advertising and other marketing expenses borne by manufacturers, retailers can sell private-label goods for less. As a result, the savings can be passed along to consumers in the form of lower prices, with the retailer still making the desired profit.

In order to give customers a choice, many retailers stock both private and national brands of particular products. For example, Waldbaum, Inc., a supermarket chain, sells cans of chunk pineapple under its own label as well as under the label "Dole," a national brand distributed by Castle & Cooke Foods of San Francisco. Since the Waldbaum pineapple is sold for less than the Dole pineapple, shoppers have the opportunity to either save money or purchase a better-known product with a national name. It should be noted that the ingredients and size of the products are similar.

Some stores that cater to affluent shoppers sell some of their own brands at higher prices than manufacturer-labeled goods. This occurs when the retailer's reputation is more important to customers than the manufacturer's name. For example, a man's suit sold at Saks Fifth Avenue and carrying that famous store's label is more attractive to many of Saks' customers than even well-known manufacturers' brands. Thus, the Saks name enhances its prospects for success against competitors.

Because of their reputations and advertising power, some chains have devel-

This Grand Union store carries both private and national brands. *Courtesy:* Grand Union.

oped their private-brand merchandise into products with national recognition. A&P's Ann Page line and Sears, Roebuck's Kenmore selection are examples of this achievement. In these cases the chains have great flexibility in developing their product assortments and prices.

Laws and the Setting of Prices

Small retailers require legal protection against price discrimination

In some instances any consideration of customers, competition, and costs is superseded by laws—local, state, and federal—that affect retail prices. At one time competitive practices were so blatant and discriminatory that state and federal legislation was necessary to restrict them. By and large, this was essential for the protection of small retailers, which were hurt by the greater purchasing power of larger firms.

For example, the Sherman Antitrust Act of 1890 was passed to prevent **horizontal price fixing** in any type of business. Acting within a general prohibition of restraint of trade, this federal law makes it illegal for retailers, wholesalers, or manufacturers to fix prices. Thus, a group of retailers act illegally if they conspire to set specific prices. The obvious purpose of such an agreement would be to stifle competition, a situation that in the past hurt small retailers most.

A number of states have passed unfair trade practices laws, sometimes called **minimum price laws,** which require retailers to charge a minimum price for goods based on the cost of the merchandise plus a percentage for overhead. These acts, too, protect small retailers that might otherwise be undercut by larger stores.

The Robinson-Patman Act imposes restrictions on both manufacturers and retailers in the setting and receiving of prices that discriminate against other retailers. For example, manufacturer A and retailers B and C are guilty under this federal act if they agree on the price of an item that is not offered to other retailers in the same trading area at the same price. However, the act allows manufacturers to establish price differentials based on cost differences in selling to retailers if they can prove that specific price agreements do not hinder competition. Like the Sherman Antitrust Act and minimum price laws, the Robinson-Patman Act protects small retailers from adverse effects of price favoritism.

An interesting situation involving pricing practices is taking place in England, where book publishers set the prices to be charged in retail bookstores. This regulation, dating to the year 1900, has been under attack by booksellers and authors. They charge that the policy reduces sales and that it is nothing more than price protectionism for the publishers. In 1989, at least one large bookselling chain (Pentos, P.L.C.) indicated its intention to break with the practice, known as the Net Book Agreement. It remains to be seen how this action will be met by the government and the publishers.

Item pricing

Item pricing requires stores to put prices on each piece of merchandise. While this procedure allows shoppers to compare products or detect overcharges, it adds to a store's costs by requiring clerks to stamp or attach prices to goods. Some states require item pricing; others do not.

PRICE POLICIES

Price policies are designed to fit a retailer's needs

By now you have probably guessed that a store may establish a number of different price policies to fit its needs. For example, it might set only high or low prices for all its products. Or it might vary its price levels, charging high prices for some classes of merchandise and lower ones for others. The determination of prices involves considerations of customers, competition, and other factors. Although many price policies are found in the retailing industry today, we will examine only the more common ones.

1. One price versus variable prices
2. Multiple pricing
3. Unit pricing
4. Price lining
5. Manufacturers' prepriced labels
6. Matching competitors' prices
7. Leader pricing and loss leaders
8. Single pricing
9. Automatic price reduction policy
10. Everyday low prices

One Price versus Variable Prices

One-price policy: all customers pay the same price

A one-price policy means that all customers pay the same price for the same product.

Customers benefit from a one-price policy by the assurance that all shoppers in the store pay the same price. Thus, they have no fear that they will be "cheated." This sense of security develops consumer confidence and ultimately benefits the retailer as well. Since the turn of the century, a one-price policy has been the rule among most retailers in this country.

To retailers, the advantages of such a policy are as follows.

1. It reduces the time needed for selling merchandise. Since no bargaining is involved, fewer salespeople are required to conduct transactions.
2. It permits self-service retail operations. Customers select their goods with full knowledge of the nonnegotiable prices.
3. Since it speeds sales transactions, mass merchandising operations are possible. For example, supermarkets and discount stores are able to sell large quantities of goods quickly.
4. It facilitates catalog and vending-machine retailing. Imagine trying to operate a catalog showroom with indefinite prices listed in the catalog!

A variable-price
policy encourages
bargaining

A **variable-price policy,** also called **flexible pricing,** enables customers to bargain over prices. Contrary to the attitude of most consumers, who prefer a set price, some shoppers enjoy the challenge of haggling with retailers. Because sales transactions involving bargaining require time and attention, retailers must pay for additional salespeople. Consequently, variable pricing is generally restricted to high-ticket merchandise, such as furniture, cars, and appliances. This type of retailing also involves fewer customers and less frequent purchasing by shoppers.

A variable-price policy gives retailers flexibility in dealing with customers. For example, they can take trade-ins from shoppers or offer services in order to secure the desired price. However, self-service retailing is out of the question, and retailers also run the risk of reduced customer confidence.

Multiple Pricing

Multiple pricing
acts as a
"psychological
pull" on shoppers

Stores that follow a **multiple-price policy** offer two or more of the same item at a unit price that is lower than if only one item is bought. For example, four boxes of Jell-O gelatin dessert might be sold for $1.54, making the unit price 38.5 cents, whereas a single box might sell for 39 cents. Thus, the customer must choose between a larger quantity at a lower price and a smaller quantity at a higher price. Although the retailer's profit per unit is reduced with the larger quantity, the result is usually an increase in overall profits on sales.

The psychological pull of multiple pricing works with many shoppers and is a regular policy at supermarkets and variety stores. Consumers expect to find such "bargains," and retailers continue to offer them.

Unit Pricing

Over the years supermarket shoppers have complained about the difficulty of comparing prices of a product that is packaged in different quantities. For example, they are unable to judge whether a 16-ounce can of Del Monte peas and carrots selling for 65 cents is a better buy than an 8½-ounce can selling for 47 cents. The only way they can decide which can costs less per ounce is by dividing the cost of each can by the number of ounces in it. Needless to say, many consumers either cannot or will not perform the necessary arithmetic.

Unit pricing helps
consumers make
shopping
decisions

As a result of the consumer movement, many supermarkets have adopted **unit pricing** to aid customers in making shopping decisions. In effect, the stores do the computations for their customers. Without the computer, this would be a considerable printing and clerical chore.

Under unit pricing, a can containing 5 ounces might show a regular total price of 50 cents and a unit price of 10 cents an ounce; a box containing 15 ounces might show a total regular price of 75 cents and a unit price of 5 cents an ounce. Labels containing unit prices are often attached to the shelf on which the merchandise is displayed (Figure 11-2).

Figure 11-2 Supermarket unit pricing labels.

Price Lining

A progressive retailer makes shopping as easy and understandable as possible for customers. One way to accomplish this objective is to establish a **price lining** policy. The retailer sells several lines of a given product, each with a different price, and carries an adequate assortment of goods at each price. For example, sweaters may be sold for $17, $25, and $35. Customers then have a choice between low and high prices for the item, as well as a price in the middle range. Contrast this policy with one that offers sweaters at $17, $20, $23, $26, $30, and $35. With this expanded price range, a customer would probably be confused about the differences in quality among products with such closely related prices.

Price lines are planned on the basis of past sales, competitive prices, and suppliers' suggested prices. Though a particular price line may contain as many as six different prices, most lines contain three prices.

Advantages of price lining

The advantages of price lining are as follows.

1. Reduced confusion among customers about merchandise selection.
2. A wider assortment of goods within each price range.
3. A possible reduction in the total inventory carried by a retailer.
4. Easier buying for the retailer.
5. Easier for salespeople to remember prices; fewer customer questions about merchandise quality.
6. The opportunity to trade up a customer to a higher-priced item. **Trading up** takes place when a salesperson persuades the customer to buy a more expensive item or a larger quantity, than originally intended. Although trading up increases sales, it must be used with care to avoid pressuring customers.

The year 1989 witnessed vigorous price competition between Sears, Roebuck and K mart. After Sears announced its "everyday low price" policy, thereby challenging K mart and other discounters, the two retail giants engaged in active trading up policies. They did this by increasing the number of brands they carried in an effort to attract more affluent consumers.

Disadvantages of price lining

The disadvantages of price lining are as follows.

1. The necessity of changing price ranges during inflationary periods. Without such action, profitability is endangered.
2. The difficulty of maintaining a price line in the face of lower prices offered by competing stores.
3. A restriction in the variety of goods available to a store's buyer, since purchasing must be done within certain price ranges.
4. The danger of selecting a price range that does not appeal to shoppers.

Pricing lining is common in furniture, apparel, and department stores where shopping goods are prevalent. It is not popular in supermarkets and other stores that sell staple merchandise.

Manufacturers' Prepriced Labels

Many types of merchandise have the price printed on the outside of the product (e.g., magazines). Retailers may, and often do, sell the goods for less than the manufacturer's suggested price. Shoppers often feel that this policy allows them to compare merchandise on the basis of both price and quality.

Matching Competitors' Prices

"We will not be undersold"

You have probably seen store advertisements announcing. "We will not be undersold!" or "We'll meet any competitive price!" This policy acts as an inducement to a store's customers to buy at the store even when a competitor's prices are lower. Assuming that the store continues to provide the customer with the services to which he or she has become accustomed, matching the competition reinforces the customer's loyalty to the store. However, the store is sometimes obligated to employ comparison shoppers to verify competitors' prices.

When Sears, Roebuck adopted its everyday low price policy in 1989, its chairman, Bernard Brennan, guaranteed that his company would refund to the customer any difference between its price and the advertised sales price of a competitor. While this policy was not new to retailing, it was a first for Sears.

Leader Pricing and Loss Leaders

Leader pricing attracts shoppers

The highly competitive nature of retailing, as you have seen, impels retailers to devise ways of attracting shoppers. In one of the methods used, called **leader pricing,** the retailer sells one or more products at lower-than-usual prices, with reduced profits. The idea is to induce customers to shop for the "leader" merchandise in the hope that they will purchase other, regularly priced goods as well. In the final analysis, the objective is to increase customer traffic, sales volume, *and* profits.

Leader items are found in many types of stores and consist of merchandise that shoppers generally need and are purchased frequently. The goods are neither high priced, attracting a limited number of consumers, nor so low priced that customers can't perceive a bargain. In order to avoid customer resentment, retailers must carry sufficient leader merchandise to satisfy demand. To do otherwise is to invite charges of trickery. In fact, some states require retailers to give "rain checks" to customers when they run out of advertised leader merchandise.

In the past some retailers sold items at or below cost. Called **loss leaders,** sales of this type hurt small retailers badly. Today loss leader selling is found infrequently, is disdained by reputable retailers as unfair competition, and is prohibited in some states by minimum price laws. In some cases, loss leader policies have damaged manufacturers and distributors. In the milk industry, for example, some distributors have been driven out of business.

Single Pricing

A single price for all items in the store

With a **single-price policy,** all the merchandise is sold at one price, as, for example, in a tie shop that prices all of its ties at $3. Relying on favorable consumer response to the appeal of a single price, the store can select goods only within a limited range. Many consumers enjoy the ease and novelty of single-price shopping.

Small variety and clothing stores have had success with single pricing, but the restriction on merchandise selection often precludes expansion. In an effort to widen their product assortments, single-price stores pay various prices for their merchandise. The average cost, however, must allow the stores to make a reasonable profit from the single retail price.

A basic appeal of one-price stores is the reduced pressure on shoppers having to make purchasing decisions. Instead of the uncertainty associated with price choices, they feel more comfortable in their selection of one-price merchandise. This simplicity of choice is the basic reason for the increased popularity of one-price shops. The largest of these chains include One Price Clothing Company, Bargain Town/Simply 6, Only $1, and Everything's a $1.00.

Automatic Price Reduction Policy

Some stores follow a procedure of reducing prices on an automatic basis. Known as an **automatic price reduction policy,** its purpose is to attract shoppers as part of a regular promotional appeal. For example, a retailer might adopt the following practice:

TIME	PRICING PROCEDURE
Merchandise placed on floor for sale	Original selling prices
Two weeks later	Prices reduced 20 percent on unsold merchandise
One week later	Prices reduced an additional 20 percent on unsold merchandise

Best known for their automatic price reduction policies are Filene's Automatic Bargain Basement in Boston and SYMS, the apparel chain.

Everyday Low Prices

An everyday low price policy indicates that most, if not all, of a retailer's merchandise is being discounted. This policy has paid big dividends for chains like Wal-Mart and Toys "Я" Us. Instead of waiting for sales—which both of these retailers run rarely—shoppers expect that on any given day the prices these chains maintain *are* sales prices, that is, that it would be unusual to find lower prices at their competitors' stores.

The move by Sears, Roebuck in 1989 to cut prices by up to 50 percent on some 50,000 items affected big discount retailers like K mart, Wal-Mart, Circuit City Stores, and Ames more than it did large department stores. This was because Sears targeted the same lower economic groups that comprised the bulk of discounters' customers. Sears' new low-price policy is a decision that was taken to reverse flat sales and earnings.

MARKUPS

Having considered the elements that go into price decisions as well as several specific pricing policies, we turn our attention to the computation of retail prices. We will examine the basic arithmetic concepts that all retailers should know as well as some arithmetic terms used in the retail trade.

Calculating Markups

Markups

Suppose the Reddy Wear Store purchases dresses costing $18 each and sells them for $30 each. The difference between the two unit prices, $12, is called the **markup.** In other words, markup is the difference between the original selling price (retail) and the cost. It may be stated as follows.

$$\text{Markup} = \text{Retail} - \text{Cost}$$
$$\$12 = \$30 - \$18$$

The relationships may also be shown as follows.

$$\text{Cost} + \text{Markup} = \text{Retail}$$
$$\$18 + \$12 = \$30$$

Markups Expressed in Dollars and as Percentages

In the Reddy Wear illustration the markups were stated in dollars and cents. Though some retailers feel comfortable with this way of expressing markups, most stores—especially large ones—prefer to use percentages. This permits more direct comparison of markups with those of previous periods, even though prices may have changed. It also enables a store to compare its markups with those of competitors.

Though some retailers compute markups as percentages based on cost prices, most merchants use selling prices as the base. A major reason for doing this is the common practice of reporting such expenses as advertising and salaries as percentages based on selling prices. In this way a store's markups can more easily be compared with its expenses. Other reasons include the relative ease of securing company data on a retail, rather than a cost, basis; the fact that profits are shown more conservatively (see Table 11-1 for comparative markup percentages); the availability of retail industry data on a retail basis; and the practice of some vendors who use retail prices as a base on which to compute discounts.

TABLE 11-1   Equivalent Markup Percentages Based on Cost and Retail Prices

Markup Percentage Based on Retail	Markup Percentage Based on Cost
4.0%	4.2%
6.0	6.4
8.0	8.7
10.0	11.1
10.7	12.0
12.5	14.3
13.0	15.0
18.0	22.0
23.1	30.0
30.0	42.9
40.0	66.7
50.0	100.0
60.0	150.0 (see example)

Computing a markup percentage

Let's see how a markup percentage based on selling price (retail) is computed. Assume the following.

$$\text{Cost} + \text{Markup} = \text{Retail}$$
$$\$12 + \$4 = \$16$$

Solution: Divide the markup by the retail price.

$$\frac{\text{Markup}}{\text{Retail}} = \frac{\$4}{\$16} = \frac{1}{4} = 25\% \text{ markup percentage}$$

As indicated previously, the 25 percent markup can be used for comparative purposes.

Using the same illustration, the markup percentage based on cost is

$$\frac{\text{Markup}}{\text{Cost}} = \frac{\$4}{\$12} = \frac{1}{3} = 33^{1}/_{3}\%$$

Notice that the markup based on retail results in a lower percentage than that based on cost. This is so because the retail price (*denominator*) is higher than the cost (*denominator*), and the fraction is therefore smaller.

Equivalent markup percentages   Table 11-1 contains some equivalent markup percentages based on cost and retail prices. For example, a 10 percent markup based on retail is equivalent to an 11.1 percent markup based on cost. Here is an illustration.

$$\begin{array}{ccccc} \text{Cost} & + & \text{Markup} & = & \text{Retail} \\ \$90 & + & \$10 & = & \$100 \end{array}$$

Markup based on retail:

$$\frac{\$10}{\$100} = \frac{1}{10} = 10\%$$

Markup based on cost:

$$\frac{\$10}{\$90} = \frac{1}{9} = 11.1\%$$

Additional markup equivalents can, of course, be computed in similar fashion.

As you can see, markups based on cost can be greater than 100 percent. For example,

$$\begin{array}{ccccc} \text{Cost} & + & \text{Markup} & = & \text{Retail} \\ \$80 & + & \$120 & = & \$200 \end{array}$$

Therefore,

$$\frac{\text{Markup}}{\text{Retail}} = \frac{\$120}{\$200} = \frac{3}{5} = 60\%$$

and

$$\frac{\text{Markup}}{\text{Cost}} = \frac{\$120}{\$80} = \frac{3}{2} = 150\%$$

Markups based on retail can approach but never equal 100 percent.

Composition of the Markup

Markup consists of overhead and profit

Since markup is the difference between retail and cost, it consists of two items: the store's overhead and the desired profit. For example, a $10 markup might include $6 to cover expenses (rent, salaries, etc.) and a $4 profit. Therefore,

$$\text{Cost} + \text{Markup (overhead + profit)} = \text{Retail}$$
$$\$10 \qquad (\$6 + \$4)$$

Markups by Category

A markup can be set for each category of merchandise

Sometimes a retailer uses a separate markup for each merchandise category. The individual markups reflect such considerations as the ease with which the merchandise can be sold and the nature of the products themselves. Higher-priced goods, for example, might carry higher markups than more frequently sold convenience items. Regardless of how the individual markups are constructed, the dollar total of the markups is designed to equal the total planned markup for the store.

Let's examine a specific example. Suppose a toy store sets a 20 percent markup on its inexpensive toys and a 40 percent markup on the more costly ones. It plans total sales of $60,000, with an overall store markup of $33\frac{1}{3}$ percent. Assume the following additional information.

Planned sales of inexpensive toys	$20,000
Planned sales of more costly toys	$40,000
Total sales	$60,000

Therefore,

	Markup Percent		Planned Sales		Dollar Markup
Inexpensive toys:	20%	×	$20,000	=	$ 4,000
More costly toys:	40%	×	$40,000	=	$16,000
				Total	$20,000
Overall store markup:	33⅓%	×	$60,000	=	$20,000

Table 11-2 contains representative markups for various merchandise categories.

TABLE 11-2   Markups by Selected Merchandise Categories

Merchandise Category	Markup Percent
Bath shop	47
Dairy	18
Frozen foods	22
Gift shop	52
Health and beauty aids	27
Luggage	49
Shower curtains	43
Tables	40
Women's suits	52

Initial Markup

In the Reddy Wear example we used previously, the markup computed before any merchandise had been sold is called the **initial** or **original markup.** Let's review the example:

If

$$\text{Retail (selling price)} = \$30$$

and

$$\text{Cost of merchandise} = \$18$$

then

$$\text{Initial markup} = \$12 \text{ or } 40\%$$

$$\frac{\text{Markup}}{\text{Retail}} = \frac{\$12}{\$30} = \frac{2}{5} = 40\% \text{ initial markup}$$

Maintained Markup

Of course, there are many instances when the actual selling price is different from the original price. This may happen because of business conditions, selling strategy, competition, or internal errors. In addition, the markup may be affected by factors like shoplifting and employee discounts. As a result, the new markup, called the **maintained markup,** will differ from the initial markup. If the original price remains unchanged, however, the two markups will be equal. To summarize,

1. The initial markup is based on the original price.
2. The maintained markup is based on the actual selling price.

Example.   Suppose Reddy Wear sells the originally priced $30 dress for $24. What is the maintained markup?

Solution:

$$\text{Cost} + \text{Markup} = \text{Retail (selling price)}$$
$$\$18 + \$6 = \$24$$

$$\frac{\text{Markup}}{\text{Retail}} = \frac{\$6}{\$24} = \frac{1}{4} = 25\% \text{ maintained markup}$$

Determining the Cost of Merchandise

Transportation charges and cash discounts alter the cost of merchandise

In the preceding example the cost of the dress ($18) included only the invoice cost of the merchandise. Sometimes, however, this cost is increased or decreased by other factors. Suppose, for example, that the store had to pay an additional $2 for transportation, for a total cost of $20. Also assume that Reddy Wear took advantage of the supplier's offer to reduce the invoice cost by 3 percent by taking a cash discount. As a result, the actual cost to the store was $19.46.

Invoice cost	$18.00
Less: 3% cash discount	0.54 (0.03 × $18)
	$17.46
Plus: transportation	2.00
Actual cost	$19.46

Other factors that affect the final cost of an item are trade and quantity discounts (subtracted from cost) and installation and alteration expenses (added to cost).

The size of a markup depends on a number of factors. Among them are the type of merchandise sold (e.g., food items carry lower markups than furniture), the degree of competition, the extent of store promotions and sales, the influence of manufacturers, and seasonal concerns.

Example.   A retailer purchases a dozen tennis rackets at $40 each. He pays total transportation of $28 and takes a 2 percent cash discount off the cost of the rackets (not off the transportation cost). Subsequently, he sells all ten rackets for $60 each. What was the retailer's maintained markup percent?

Solution:

Invoice cost of ten rackets	$400 (10 × $40)
Less: 2% cash discount	8 (0.02 × $400)
	$392
Plus: Transportation	28
Actual cost of ten rackets	$420
Selling price of ten rackets	$600 (10 × $60)
Less: actual cost of ten rackets	420
Maintained markup	$180

$$\frac{\text{Markup}}{\text{Retail}} = \frac{\$180}{\$600} = \frac{3}{10} = 30\% \text{ maintained markup}$$

Keystone Markup

When the retail price of a product is determined by doubling its cost, the resulting 100 percent markup on cost (50 percent on retail) is known as a **keystone markup.** Although used by some retailers, keystoning can backfire when important pricing variables are not considered (e.g., competition).

MARKDOWNS

Reasons for Markdowns

A reduction in selling price is known as a **markdown.** Markdowns may occur for any of the following reasons.

1. Judgments by store buyers
2. Misjudgments in setting prices
3. Faulty selling techniques
4. Unpredictable factors
5. Use as a promotional tool

Judgments by Store Buyers

Despite the most careful planning, a buyer may purchase too much of a particular item, resulting in leftover inventory. In order to stimulate sales, the merchandise is sold at a marked-down price. Sometimes an item has lukewarm appeal to customers, perhaps owing to design, color, or changes in consumer taste. In this case a price reduction may overcome purchase resistance.

Misjudgments in Setting Prices

When the price of an article is set too high, a markdown is inevitable in order to move the merchandise. It should be understood, however, that pricing is based on judgments made by management. As such, prices that prove to be unrealistic must be changed to stimulate sales.

One markdown policy that has been subject to criticism by some retailers involves "an additional—% off our already reduced price." For example, suppose a retailer sets an initial markup of 60 percent on an item, resulting in an original selling price of $40. After offering a markdown of 20 percent, the item now sells for $32 ($40 less $8). Subsequently, the retailer decides on an additional markdown of 30 percent, resulting in a new selling price of $22.40 ($32 less $9.60). While some shoppers may respond positively to the additional markdown, critics contend that the 60 percent initial markup was "phony." They maintain that the original selling price of $40 was set at that level only to make the markdowns look attractive. By such actions, they feel, retailers hurt their credibility.

Faulty Selling Techniques

In Chapter 8 you learned that poor displays and layouts affect sales volume adversely. When this happens, markdowns are necessary to spur sales. Merchandise may also move slowly because of improper actions by salespeople. For example, an employee who sells a particular line of VCRs aggressively, but ignores a less popular line, may cause an early markdown on the latter line. In the case of the first line of VCRs, pressure selling may cause customer dissatisfaction and merchandise returns. When this results in merchandise that is returned soiled or damaged, markdowns become necessary.

Unpredictable Factors

Poor economic conditions, sudden changes in weather, slow-moving merchandise, and the appearance of new, competing merchandise all affect sales. Appropriate markdowns must then be taken to move merchandise and maintain a competitive edge.

At times, consumers bargain-hunt to the extent that some retailers are forced to discount prices to remain competitive. This price resistance by shoppers often causes tensions between retailers and their suppliers. In some instances, retailers seek new or additional vendors, while the latter may drop some merchants and seek others as replacements.

Use as a Promotional Tool

Markdowns are often used to stimulate sales. Recognizing that many consumers respond positively to price reductions, retailers frequently use markdowns to promote their products. Some stores mark down certain items during major sales events such as Presidents' Day and Mother's Day. Overall, markdowns should fit into a retailer's short- and long-term strategic plans; they should not be applied helter-skelter.

When Markdowns Are Taken

Markdowns are a strategic part of selling

Contrary to popular impressions, retailers view markdowns as a strategic part of selling. Some stores apply markdowns early in order to generate more cash for further purchases of stock.

In some prestige stores markdowns are not noted on price tickets. Instead, the merchandise is shifted to an area devoted to a lower price line. Other prestige stores delay taking markdowns in order to discourage bargain hunting. The timing of markdowns often depends on the type of merchandise involved. For example, fashion goods that are unlikely to be salable next year call for markdowns at times that will ensure sales. On the other hand, staple goods like stationery are often marked down when they become shopworn. Regardless of the product, retailers must be alert to establish markdowns at the most favorable times because unsold merchandise represents an investment that is not producing earnings.

How Large a Markdown?

The size of a markdown is important

Markdowns must be sufficiently large for customers to respond favorably. For example, a chair that is marked down from $54.99 to $47.99 will probably sell, whereas a reduction to $53.99 might not. Through experience retailers learn how large a markdown is required to attract customers.

Retailers use markdowns as a strategic part of selling in order to generate more cash.

NEW TERMS

automatic price reduction policy
comparison shopper
flexible pricing
horizontal price fixing
initial markup
item pricing
keystone markup
leader pricing
loss leader
maintained markup
markdown
markup

minimum price law
misses merchandise line
multiple-price policy
odd price
original markup
overhead
price lining
price war
single-price policy
trading up
unit pricing
variable-price policy

CHAPTER HIGHLIGHTS

1. The price of an item must cover the cost of the product, the overhead, and the profit.
2. The success of a store is often measured by the sales generated per square foot of selling space.
3. An analysis of the consumer as an element in pricing decisions includes consideration of income, motivation, psychological aspects, store image, and value concepts.
4. Odd pricing (59¢, $16.99) is used as a psychological pricing technique by a significant but declining number of retailers.
5. Some shoppers buy on the basis of price. Others are influenced by a store's image.
6. People have general ideas about the prices they expect to pay. Purchase resistance develops when their expectations prove wrong.
7. In order to deal effectively with competing stores, retailers consider competitors' prices and services, pricing to meet the competition, and private brands.
8. The nature of a retail business has much to do with its freedom in setting prices.
9. Private brands carry a retailer's or middleman's label instead of a manufacturer's national brand. The use of private brands often gives retailers a competitive edge.
10. There are local, state, and federal laws regulating retail price practices. The

Sherman Antitrust Act prevents horizontal price fixing, that is, conspiracies to arrange prices for the purpose of stifling competition. State unfair trade practices laws (minimum price laws) require retailers to charge a minimum price for goods based on the cost of the merchandise plus a percentage for overhead. The Robinson-Patman Act prohibits manufacturers and retailers from engaging in discriminatory price practices.

11. Among the price policies in use today are the following.
    a. *One price versus variable prices.* Under a one-price policy all customers pay the same price. A variable-price policy allows customers to bargain.
    b. *Multiple pricing.* Under this policy a customer can buy two or more of an item at a unit price that is less than the unit price if only one item is bought.
    c. *Unit pricing.* Merchandise is labeled with the unit price as well as the total price.
    d. *Price lining.* Several lines of a given product are carried, each with a different price.
    e. *Manufacturers' prepriced labels.* These selling prices, printed on the outside of containers and boxes, are sometimes lowered by retailers, allowing consumers to compare merchandise on the basis of price and quality.
    f. *Matching competitors' prices.* A retailer guarantees to match or beat the competitors' prices.
    g. *Leader pricing and loss leaders.* Leader pricing involves the sale of merchandise below the usual selling price in order to attract customers. A loss leader is an item that is sold below cost. In some states loss leaders are prohibited by minimum price laws.
    h. *Single pricing.* All goods in a store are sold for the same price.
    i. *Automatic price reduction policy.* The reduction of prices on an automatic basis.
    j. Everyday low prices. Most, if not all, of a retailer's merchandise is discounted.

12. Markup is the difference between the retail price and the cost of goods. Initial markup (original markup) is the first markup, whereas maintained markup is the markup based on actual sales.

13. Markups may be expressed as dollars or percentages. Retailers usually base markups on retail prices. A markup consists of overhead and profit, and may be computed for each category of merchandise and/or for an entire store.

14. The cost of merchandise is increased by transportation charges, installation expenses, and alteration expenses. It is decreased by cash, trade, and quantity discounts.

15. A reduction in a retail price is called a markdown. Markdowns are due to judgments by store buyers, misjudgments in setting prices, faulty selling techniques, unpredictable factors, and use as a promotional tool. The timing of markdowns is dictated by the nature of the store and its selling strategy. Part of this strategy involves the size of the markdown.

REVIEW QUESTIONS

1. How does comparison shopping help a store remain competitive?
2. Considering similar merchandise, are there stores that sometimes sell private brands for more than manufacturers' national brands? Explain.
3. What is the significance of "sales generated per square foot of selling space"?
4. Why is price lining feasible in stores that sell shopping goods?
5. If an invoice price is $42, transportation charges $2, and the cash discount 2 percent, what is the cost of the merchandise if the retailer pays the bill within the cash discount period?
6. If an article costs $9 and is marked up $3, what is the markup percentage based on retail? On cost?
7. Why do retailers consider markdowns a strategic part of selling?
8. If a skirt selling for $40 is marked down $10, how would a retailer express the markdown as a percentage?

DISCUSSION QUESTIONS

1. Why is it important for retailers to review their price policies regularly?
2. Why must a retailer consider shoppers' value concepts in the setting of prices?
3. Under what circumstances might a store charge higher prices than its competitors and still attract customers?
4. If competition is the lifeblood of free enterprise, why are there laws that regulate competition? How do you feel about them?

CASE 1

Pricing to Meet Competition

The Dali Fashion Center is a ladies'-wear shop located in a strip shopping center in a suburban community. It carries low- to middle-priced merchandise and maintains three price lines. The store has been at the same location for 26 years and caters to women of all ages. Its customers are basically middle-income consumers who have demonstrated consistent loyalty to the store over the years.

A popular feature of Dali's is an alcove containing specially discounted merchandise. Started 15 years ago by the owner in an attempt to sell slow-moving merchandise, the innovation became an instant hit with Dali's steady customers. Interestingly enough, the discount alcove had little effect on the sale of other goods.

From the outset, prices were set at even dollar or half-dollar amounts. For example, a particular style of sweater might be price-lined at $28, $32, and $35, or at $16.50, $19.50, and $23.50. The owner's negative attitude toward odd pricing is based on the feeling that most consumers are not influenced by this "psychological" approach to pricing.

Because Dali's is located some distance from another strip center and even farther from the nearest regional shopping center, it has had little serious competition. The store has, however, lost some business to shops in those centers because of its decision to remain closed on Sundays, Sunday opening being permitted under a two-year-old law.

Several months ago Dali's owner learned about the construction of a competitive freestanding store within its trading area. The newcomer is to occupy three times the space of Dali's store and has advertised itself as a "quality discount fashion shop." As near as Dali's can determine, the new store will stock merchandise in direct competition with its own. In addition, the new shop will be open on Sundays.

a. How might Dali's alter its price policies to counter the competition?
b. Should Dali's change its Sunday closing policy? Why?

CASE 2

Quantity Surcharges—Fair or Unfair?

Suppose your recipe for tuna casserole calls for 13 ounces of tuna fish. Instead of buying two 6½-ounce cans of tuna fish for 79¢ each, you buy one 13-ounce can for $1.89. Like most shoppers, you assume that the larger size costs less per ounce. But does it? At 79¢, the 6½-ounce can costs a little over 12¢ per ounce. The 13-ounce can, at $1.89, costs 14½¢ per ounce—2½¢ per ounce more.

Surprised? You shouldn't be. More often than not, a large can of tuna fish costs more per ounce than the 6½- or 7-ounce can of the same brand. This is just one example of a pricing practice called a *quantity surcharge*. When the larger size of a particular brand of merchandise has a higher unit price than the smaller size of the same brand, the consumer is paying a surcharge for buying the larger quantity.

Many shoppers are unaware of quantity surcharges, and nearly everyone is surprised to learn how common the practice is, especially in food stores. In some supermarkets, you might find as many as one out of three major brands priced with quantity surcharges.

Some consumer activists would claim that quantity surcharges are used intentionally to exploit the naive food shopper, who more than likely believes that larger sizes are less expensive per unit measure.

Sometimes, a quantity surcharge is the result of a simple mistake in pricing. For example, the stock clerk might simply put the wrong price stickers on the "giant economy" boxes of laundry detergent or mix up the price tags for the "regular size" and "family size" jars of peanut butter.

Other quantity surcharges exist because of special promotions. If, for example, a retailer has a sale on one-liter bottles of soft drinks, the customer who buys a two-liter bottle at its regular price will probably pay more per ounce.

Stanley M. Widrick is assistant professor of marketing at Rochester Institute of Technology in Rochester, New York. Professor Widrick has been studying quantity surcharges for several years. In one study, he made a random selection of grocery stores in Monroe County, New York. Then he chose several product categories that are used in the majority of U.S. households and analyzed their prices in each supermarket. Out of nearly 2,200 brands studied, more than 18 percent were priced with quantity surcharges.* More detailed analysis of the prices revealed the following patterns:

1. Some product categories were far more likely than others to have quantity surcharges. Tuna fish, for example, was priced at a surcharge more than 75 percent of the time. Quantity surcharges were also common in canned beans, laundry detergents, peanut butter, jams and jellies, frozen orange juice, and instant tea. The occurrence of quantity surcharges in certain other product categories was significantly lower.

2. Some supermarkets had a much higher incidence of quantity surcharges than others. The highest was a supermarket in which 28.2 percent of the brands checked had quantity surcharges; the lowest was a supermarket in which only 3 percent of the brands had surcharges.

3. Some manufacturers are much more likely than others to have their brands priced at a surcharge. For example, nearly 90 percent of the brands owned by Starkist Food and by SSC International had quantity surcharges; not one of the brands owned by General Foods or by Purex Corporation had surcharges.

4. If a large number of package sizes were available, the brand was more likely to have one or more sizes priced at a surcharge.

5. Very few products were packaged in sizes that are even multiples of one another. Those that were packaged in even multiples, such as 8-ounce, 16-

*Stanley M. Widrick, "Quantity Surcharge; A Pricing Practice among Grocery Store Items—Validation and Extension," *Journal of Retailing,* **55** (Summer 1979), pp. 47–58.

ounce, and 32-ounce packages, had a relatively low incidence of quantity surcharges. It is more difficult to compare unit prices for brands with odd-sized packages—for example, 5¼-ounce and 12½-ounce packages. These brands were also more than three times as likely to be priced with quantity surcharges.

6. Only a little over 10 percent of the quantity surcharges found in the survey were the result of manufacturers' promotions or retailers' specials.

Widrick concluded that most quantity surcharges could not be explained by pricing errors or promotional specials, suggesting the likelihood that quantity surcharges result from a conscious pricing policy.

a. Do you agree with Widrick's conclusion? How does the evidence from his study support your statement? Can you think of any other reason(s) that might explain quantity surcharges?

b. Who is most likely responsible for intentional quantity surcharges—the manufacturer, the wholesaler, or the retailer?

c. The Fair Packaging and Labeling Act requires packages and labels to "facilitate value comparisons." Do quantity surcharges violate the spirit of the act? Is a quantity surcharge unethical, or is it an acceptable form of competition?

d. How should a supermarket manager respond if a customer complains about a quantity surcharge?

REFERENCES

BIVINS, J., "One-Price Clothing Stores." *Stores* (October 1989), pp. 39–41.

KIRBY, G. H., AND DARDIS, R. "A Pricing Study of Women's Apparel in Off-Price and Department Stores." *Journal of Retailing* (Fall 1986), pp. 321–330.

U.S. Department of Commerce, Small Business Administration, "Boost Profits by Cutting Markdowns," *Bulletin 78* (Washington, D.C.): U.S. DOC.

WIDRICK, S. M. "Quantity Surcharge: A Pricing Practice Among Grocery Store Items—Validation and Extension." *Journal of Retailing*, 55 (Summer 1979), pp. 47–58.

"You Have to Watch Your Prices." *Retailing Today*, **25:** 8, (August 1990), pp. 1–2.

Chapter 12

Handling and Protecting Merchandise

After completing this chapter, you should be able to:

- Identify and describe receiving area facilities and records found in stores.
- Describe checking and marking procedures used in stores.
- Identify procedures used by retailers for the storage and distribution of merchandise.
- List security measures taken by retailers to control the theft of merchandise by employees and outsiders.

Having established merchandise pricing policies, a retailer must consider the physical handling of the goods. Without a smooth flow of inventory from the receiving area to the selling areas, a store can lose customer goodwill and actual sales. In addition, merchandise must be checked for quantity and quality, marked with prices, and stored carefully for ready movement to appropriate departments. Finally, attention must be paid to the security of goods in receiving and storage areas and on the selling floor. This chapter explores each of these concerns.

HANDLING THE MERCHANDISE

Receiving merchandise from suppliers

As shoppers, our exposure to store merchandise is usually limited to what we see on shelves, in displays, and so forth. The retailer, however, must perform a number of functions before goods reach the selling areas. Of these, the first involves procedures for receiving merchandise from suppliers. This is true for both large and small stores, with the former requiring rather elaborate arrangements. Small retailers, on the other hand, establish simple routines for the receipt of merchandise. In this chapter we will deal mainly with the physical handling of goods in large retail organizations.

Figure 12-1 outlines the usual steps in the handling of merchandise. Each

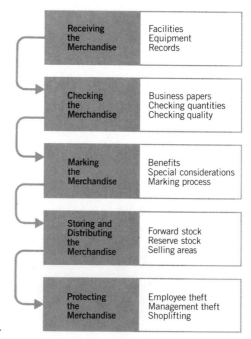

Figure 12-1 Steps in the handling of merchandise.

step will be discussed as it relates to eventually getting the goods into selling areas for display and sale.

RECEIVING THE MERCHANDISE

Receiving Facilities

The need for a receiving area   Since the receipt of goods is an important activity in all retail organizations, it is essential that proper facilities exist for accepting deliveries. When you consider the tremendous volume and variety of merchandise reaching a large store each day, you can appreciate the need for adequate receiving areas.

Loading Platforms

Sometimes called a **loading dock** or a **receiving dock,** a **loading platform** accommodates trucks or other vehicles for the unloading of merchandise. The area must be large enough to service the oversized trucks in use today. In most cases the platform is located either in the back or on the side of the store.

Delivery of merchandise to small stores usually takes place on a sidewalk or at the rear. Since the quantity of goods is limited, no special unloading facility is required. Instead, goods are carried directly into the store by the most convenient or accessible entrance.

The size and composition of a receiving area depend on the type and volume of the merchandise carried. Sybil Shelton/Monkmeyer.

Warehouses

Large stores that sell major appliances and furniture generally maintain warehouses for storage of these goods until delivery to the customer. In instances in which a store also carries other types of goods, the receiving function may take place at the warehouse for the large-ticket items and at the store for the remaining merchandise. In busy urban areas warehouses are sometimes used to carry out the main receiving functions.

RETAIL STRATEGY
Strategic Warehouse Location

Bentleyville is a tiny dot on the map of Pennsylvania . . . 30 miles south of Pittsburgh. Its special importance is that it marks Family Dollar's first location north of the Mason-Dixon line. It's fairly typical of F.D.'s 626 discount-variety units: it occupies 6,700 square feet, split down the middle with soft goods on one side and hard lines on the other. Up until now, the steady spread of its origin in Charlotte, NC, has been in the Sunbelt States . . . a triangle bounded by Florida, Louisiana, and West Virginia. Its strategy of small stores in small markets enables it to plan expansion in closely contiguous markets. That, in turn, provides a very efficient distribution flow from its warehouse in Charlotte. And *that*, in turn, enables stores of 6,000 to 8,000 square feet to carry in-depth assortments on low price points, mostly under $15. The formula has been profitable, providing a base for steady physical expansion.*

*"Family Dollar Opens Beachhead into the North," *Inside Retailing* (November 14, 1983), p. 4.

Although many warehouses are one-story structures, large retailers are constructing multistory buildings today to reduce real estate and operating costs. With 24-foot forklifts and computerized conveyors available, storage heights can be enlarged, and merchandise can be reached more quickly and efficiently.

An interesting warehouse innovation involves retailers that interface (tie in) their store/warehouse computers with vendor computers, thereby reducing reorder cycle time. This arrangement also cuts the retailer's inventory investment. For example, suppose a department store has immediate need of ten popular-selling dishwashers. Through its tie-in with the vendor's computer, the merchandise is ordered automatically and is shipped quickly to either its store or warehouse for further routing. An increasingly popular vendor-retailer tie-in is called Quick Response and will be discussed in detail in Chapter 17.

In the design of their merchandise distribution centers, some retailers place a very high priority on employee safety and comfort. A chief proponent of this approach is Rich's department stores, a New England discount chain. Its center is colorful, attractive, well lighted, and quiet.

To upgrade its warehouse system efficiency, the Burlington Coat Factory, an off-price specialty retailer with more than 130 stores in 37 states, uses checkout counter scanners that can read bar codes on moving merchandise from up to 5 feet from the goods. With a computer involved, this dual capacity enables the company's warehouse personnel to track merchandise more efficiently than had been done manually.

Receiving Areas in the Store

When goods are brought into the store, they should be placed in an area that is large enough to accommodate checking and marking functions and close enough to stockroom and selling areas for quick transfer. Precious time that can be translated into lost sales is wasted when the facilities are far apart. An exception exists in stores that utilize electrical and mechanical equipment for speedy movement of merchandise.

Receiving areas are not conducive to selling

Store planners recognize that selling space is extremely valuable. Consequently, receiving sections are located in areas that are not conducive to selling. Upper floors, with adequate freight elevator service, are usually used in stores that contain several levels, while one-story structures utilize back-room space. Though selling space is crucial to the profitability of a business, the receiving area must be large enough to allow for the smooth handling and flow of goods. Any other arrangement results in delays before merchandise reaches the selling areas, in possible loss or damage of goods, and in inefficient use of employee time.

Adequate planning considers seasonal and special-occasion receiving requirements. For example, receiving and stockroom areas that are just large enough for normal business activities may be inadequate during intense selling periods like Christmas and Mother's Day. Unless the store can rearrange space to accommodate heavy shipments during these periods, it must plan the size of its receiving areas accordingly.

Receiving Area Equipment

Using elevators, conveyors, and chutes for merchandise

There are a number of ways in which merchandise may be transported from a loading platform to a receiving room within the store. Mechanical equipment is widely used to minimize the need for human labor and to maximize operating efficiency. The type of equipment employed depends on the physical characteristics of the store. For example, a multistory building might be serviced by elevators or by conveyors that connect with receiving rooms. A one-story edifice might utilize a horizontal beltlike conveyor that carries goods directly to checking areas. When a basement serves as a receiving room, merchandise is slid down chutes to checking stations. Of course, there are other types of equipment, for example, electric trucks.

Tables, conveyor mechanisms, and bins are used to prepare goods for selling

Within the store, equipment and furniture must be available to prepare the merchandise for delivery to selling areas. A basic arrangement utilizes **stationary tables** for receiving goods after they have been unpacked. In some instances, merchandise is separated by department, with tables assigned to particular departments. In other cases, tables are designated for each type of merchandise.

Checking and marking are done on the tables, after which the goods are taken either to a stockroom for future use or directly to a selling area.

A variation of this arrangement involves the use of **portable (movable) tables.** In this design, merchandise is put on tables that can be wheeled to other areas. This allows the checking of goods to be done in one area and the marking in another without the merchandise itself having to be moved. The division of functions ensures better control over the merchandise, since quantity checking is completed before goods are marked. After the merchandise has been checked, it is wheeled, still on the same tables, to separate marking areas.

A more elaborate system used in many large stores involves **conveyor mechanisms** that carry goods from receiving areas to stockrooms or selling spaces. On the way to their destination, the goods are checked and marked. Clothing is generally moved by overhead conveyor rollers, while most other merchandise is transported on belt systems. Goods on roller equipment or belts may be removed at specified points for inspection. However, care must be taken to prevent anxious buyers and selling personnel from removing merchandise before it has been fully processed.

One further checking–marking arrangement is worth mentioning. Some stores use **bins** as receptacles for incoming merchandise. After merchandise has been unpacked and checked in one section of the receiving area, it is placed in bins for movement to the marking area. Since checking is done at a separate location, unauthorized personnel can be kept away more easily.

Receiving Department Records

The constant burden of handling incoming merchandise requires that stores maintain accurate receiving records. Large stores, of course, have more elaborate records than small ones, but no store can ignore the need for sensible records without suffering losses.

Goods are checked against a **delivery receipt** supplied by the **carrier** (transporter), the **invoice** (bill) itself, or the **bill of lading** (a receipt from the transporter giving title to the goods being shipped). (See Figure 12-2.) If packages are missing or damaged, the details are written on the document so that the store can justify the adjustments.

Standard receiving practice involves recording incoming goods in some kind of **receiving book** or on a form (Figure 12-3). The information recorded usually

Function	Record
Checking accuracy of shipment	• Delivery receipt • Invoice • Bill of lading
Recording incoming goods	• Receiving book

Figure 12-2   Receiving department functions and records.

Week Ending _____				Store No. _____ Location _____	
		Received from			No. of
Date Received	Interstore Transfer Control No.	Store No.	Store Name	Received Via (Freight Co., UPS, etc.)	Cartons Received

Figure 12-3 A receiving record.

includes quantity of packages, date and time of receipt, weight of packages (if appropriate), type of transportation, name of carrier, shipping costs, damaged containers, and name of vendor or intercompany store. (Figure 12-3 is a receiving record for interstore transfers.) In addition, the supplier's invoice number and the invoice amount are recorded when they are available, which they usually are since invoices generally arrive before merchandise is received.

Receiving records and computers

For companies that use computers to process information, receiving records are tied into the overall recordkeeping system. Since purchasing data are stored in the computer, information supplied by receiving clerks is compared electronically with the stored data for immediate verification.

Small stores usually confine their receiving records to the maintenance of delivery receipt files. Since the owner either handles or supervises deliveries, all that is required is a simple system for tying merchandise received to timely payment of bills.

CHECKING THE MERCHANDISE

The next step in the handling of merchandise involves procedures for determining the specific goods received. The basic reason for checking merchandise is to be certain that payment is made only for goods that have actually been delivered. Shortages and damage in deliveries might go undetected without a sound system for checking incoming shipments. (See Figure 12-3.)

Business Papers Used in Purchasing Goods

Purchase orders and invoices

Before discussing the procedures for checking merchandise, we need to examine two common business documents that are used in purchasing. One is called a **purchase order** (P.O.); the other is the invoice.

As shown in Figure 12-4, a purchase order is prepared by the purchaser (the retailer), in this case the Ted Lane Co., and is made out to the supplier, Vicki Spar, Inc. In addition to information concerning dates, shipping instructions, and terms, the document indicates what the store wants to buy and how much it has agreed to pay. A copy of the purchase order is often sent to the receiving department. Upon receiving the original of the purchase order, the supplier prepares and sends an invoice to the store and ships the goods. Figure 12-5 shows that the invoice contains information similar to the purchase order. If the supplier does not fill the entire order, however, the invoice omits the missing items. Notice that the customer's order number on the invoice, 1453, matches the number on the purchase order. This cross-referencing is useful to the store when checking incoming merchandise.

When a purchase order is prepared, many buyers insert a cancellation date on which the order is automatically cancelled if the merchandise has not arrived. Receiving departments have to be told about such cancellation dates so that they will not take in merchandise that the store may no longer want or need. This is of particular importance for seasonal goods such as clothing.

Procedures for Checking Goods

Checking Quantities

Though there are a variety of methods for checking quantities, most stores employ one or a combination of the following procedures.

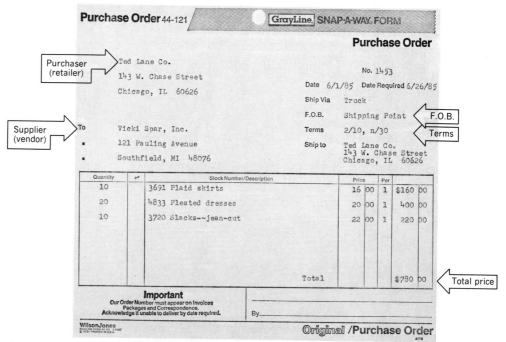

Figure 12-4   A purchase order. (Product of Wilson Jones Company.)

1. Direct checking
2. Indirect checking (blind checking)
3. Semi-indirect checking (semiblind checking)
4. Spot checking
5. Bulk checking
6. Universal vendor marking checking

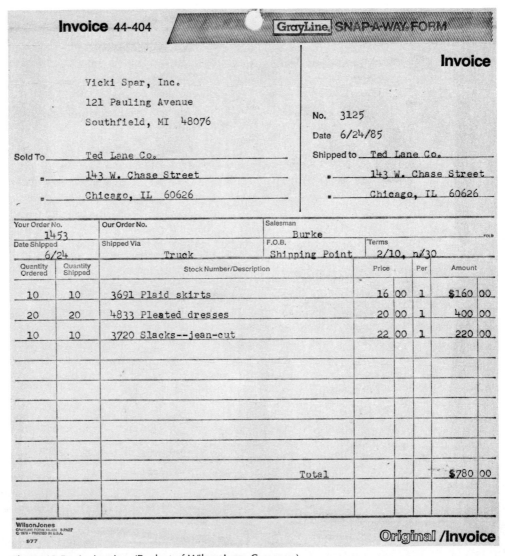

Figure 12-5 An invoice. (Product of Wilson Jones Company.)

Direct checking is quick and relatively inexpensive

Direct Checking.   In **direct checking,** as goods are unpacked, the items are checked against the invoice for accuracy. This allows the checker to indicate any shortages or damages on the invoice. If the checker is a reliable employee, the store is assured that payment will be made only for merchandise received. On the other hand, a careless checker may not count the shipment accurately, simply assuming that the items received are exactly the ones listed on the invoice. It is obvious, therefore, that direct checking is effective only when it is done by careful employees. This type of checking is quick and relatively inexpensive.

In cases in which an invoice has not arrived, the store must make a decision: either to count and list the merchandise and send it on for marking or to leave the shipment unopened until the invoice is received. In the first instance, merchandise reaches the stockroom or selling areas quickly, but rechecking the goods is difficult or impossible. In the second instance, shortages may occur in selling areas owing to delayed processing, but accurate checking can be done. Despite the risks in checking without the benefit of an invoice, many stores adopt the first policy in the desire to get merchandise to selling areas as quickly as possible. Because retailers are anxious to have invoices for checking purposes, however, suppliers sometimes enclose them with the shipments.

Indirect Checking.   When a store does not want a checker to rely on invoices, **indirect** or **blind checking** may be used. As goods are unpacked, the checker lists them on special forms. Not having an invoice to work from, the checker is compelled to conduct a more thorough check. When the count has been completed, the forms are compared with the invoices. While indirect checking usually results in a more accurate count of goods, the time required to list the contents of packages makes it more expensive than direct checking.

What if invoice quantities are omitted?

Semi-indirect Checking.   Suppose you were a checker using an invoice with the quantities deliberately omitted by the store. Wouldn't you have to count the packages received, knowing that your figures would be compared with the missing invoice quantities? On the other hand, wouldn't you save considerable time by not having to write the names of the items received, as in indirect checking? Using this procedure, called **semi-indirect checking** or **semiblind checking,** gives the store better information about merchandise received while reducing the time spent by the checker.

Spot Checking.   Unwilling to spend much time or effort on checking and assuming that most shipments are correct, some retailers **spot-check** large deliveries. That is, the checker counts the number of cartons and the contents of particular ones. If they coincide with the invoice or purchase order quantities, the merchandise is sent on for marking. If not, the remaining items are checked and shortages are noted. This method is far less accurate than other procedures.

Bulk Checking.   In **bulk checking,** when goods are packed in specific bulk quantities by number or weight (e.g., 100-dozen packages or 50-pound containers), they sometimes are not opened. Instead, the supplier's quantities, as listed on the cartons or other containers, are compared with the invoice figures.

Universal Vendor Marking Checking.   This method of checking is discussed in the following section, "Marking the Merchandise."

Follow-up of Shortages or Damaged Goods

Notification of damaged goods and shortages upon arrival

A shortage of merchandise or damage of various kinds may be caused by either the supplier or the carrier. Whichever one appears to be responsible for the problem, the store must protect itself. In all cases, the supplier or carrier must be notified immediately. Sometimes damaged goods are returned and replaced with new merchandise; at other times, financial adjustments are made with the supplier or carrier. In some instances shortages are made up by subsequent deliveries. However, if a new delivery will arrive too late, the store deducts the amount of the missing goods from the invoice total.

Checking Quality

Though checkers can make superficial judgments about the quality of incoming merchandise, they are unqualified to make reliable decisions. Checking the quality of goods, therefore, is left to those who specialize in merchandising: buyers, store managers, and the like. To make certain that the merchandise conforms to specifications, many large retailers compare incoming items with samples that are secured at the time of purchase. Whether a store is large or small, displaying or selling inferior merchandise damages its reputation.

MARKING THE MERCHANDISE

Customers entering a store, whether it is a clothing shop, a supermarket, or some other type of store, expect to find prices identified clearly. The exception may be a high-fashion store whose image calls for discreet discussion of prices. Since most stores therefore require precise indication of prices, they develop systems for achieving that objective. **Marking** is the recording of a retail price on an item of merchandise.

The Benefits of Marking

Marking goods helps customers, salespeople, and the store

Since stores commit significant amounts of time and money to the marking of goods, they expect their efforts to produce positive benefits. For example,

1. Customers appreciate quick identification of prices.
2. Because salespeople need not check prices with other personnel, they can devote their time to making sales.

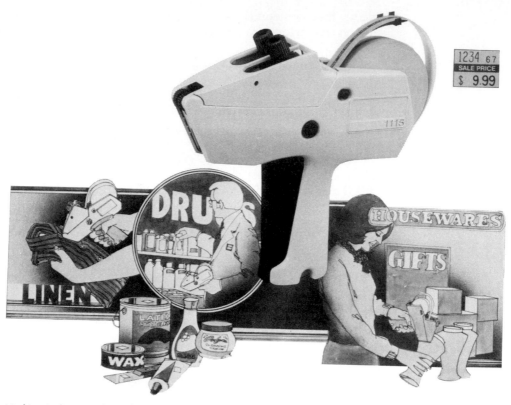

Marking is the recording of a retail price on an item of merchandise before it reaches the selling floor. *Courtesy:* Monarch Marking Systems, Inc.

3. Customers generally feel secure in the knowledge that they pay the same prices as others.

4. Listing on the price tag the date on which the merchandise was placed on the selling floor helps the store decide on markdowns and clearances.

5. Marking enables retailers to maintain self-service features. As a matter of fact, supermarkets and other stores with self-service features could not function without proper marking of prices. Instead of marking merchandise, some supermarkets mark shelves instead and use scanners at registers to record prices from bar codes on the merchandise.

6. With additional accounting information placed on price tags, such as size, style, and department name, stores can compute total costs, sales, and profits more easily. This can be done for each department or merchandise category. This is especially helpful with seasonal merchandise.

Special Marking Considerations

There are several special concerns related to marking that should be noted before we discuss marking procedures.

Expediting Marking with Preretailing

Preretailing speeds up the marking process

In order to speed up the marking process, some retailers follow a procedure called **preretailing.** It requires the buyer to list retail prices on purchase orders. Subsequently, copies of purchase orders are sent to receiving locations and are used for marking purposes as soon as merchandise has been checked. Though preretailing works well with goods whose prices remain stable, it is not suitable for merchandise with fluctuating prices.

Saving Time by Premarking

In some instances, as you read in Chapter 11, suppliers or manufacturers mark prices on merchandise in actual figures. Called premarking or source marking, this involves stamping prices on packages or attaching price tags to the merchandise itself. For example, items like magazines often have prices preprinted on them. Though premarking saves retailers time, the expenses involved are passed along to the stores as part of the cost of the goods.

Computerized Marking

In Chapter 2 we discussed the use of computerized operations at checkout stations through the stamping of universal product code symbols on packages. Since UPC marking is generally done by manufacturers, retailers are relieved of the need for marking merchandise with detailed cost and related information. Of course, stores must still indicate retail prices on packages, shelves, or bins.

Food stores using UPC marking benefit from the reliability of computerized price tallies. Instead of relying on checkout clerks to list prices, human error is eliminated—or at least minimized greatly—through the use of computerized equipment. The resulting accuracy of sales slips assures the retailer of correct data and reduces customer annoyance.

Another system for marking and controlling inventory is known as **universal vendor marking (UVM).** Similar in purpose to UPC, UVM involves the premarking of merchandise by manufacturers and includes manufacturer identification, size, color, and style. Unlike the markings of UPC that can be read only by machines, UVM uses numbers and letters that can be read by both people and equipment.

The classification system used in UVM is called **optical character recognition—font A (OCR-A).** Font A refers to the type of print used with OCR. UVM is used in department and specialty stores, whereas UPC is found more often in the food industry.

Retailers that use UVM add a department code, price, and additional information to their price tickets by imprinting a label and attaching it to the vendor's ticket. As indicated earlier in this chapter, **UVM** is also valuable for checking purposes.

Although UVM OCR-A has been used since 1975, there has been significant movement recently to replace it or to supplement it with UPC bar code marking.

For example, in 1988 Sears, Roebuck and Company purchased hand-held scanners for its more than 800 stores. The change is based on the belief that UPC, once used primarily by supermarkets, reduces sales counter time and improves accuracy.

A major consideration in department store use of UPC centers on the responsibility for marking goods with bar codes. While department stores are understandably reluctant to do so, most vendors agree to do the marking. Although many observers believe that UPC will ultimately replace UVM, vendors are careful to accommodate retailers who prefer UVM or want to use both UVM and UPC. What does appear certain is that vendors will be responsible for marking goods with either system.

The Marking Process

The marking process involves techniques for indicating a price of a product. It may involve tags, tickets, labels, stamping, and so on. Because retailers use a variety of marking procedures, we need to examine the more common ones.

Price Tags and Price Tickets

The information on tags and tickets can be printed, stamped, or punched by equipment or by hand (Figure 12-6). Tags are usually attached to goods with string, while tickets may be stapled, held fast by buttons, or looped around items like bracelets.

The use of cost codes

Some stores put cost codes, which indicate the cost of an item, on tags or tickets. This is valuable in instances in which bargaining over price is store policy and the retailer wants the cost known to salespeople but not to customers. Knowing the cost enables the salesperson to determine the range of possible retail prices of an item.

Using a ten-letter code, any cost can be listed on a tag or label. For example, using the following scheme, a $16.50 cost would be coded as PTIE.

$$\begin{array}{cccccc} P & R & O & F & I & T & \quad L & A & N & E \\ 1 & 2 & 3 & 4 & 5 & 6 & \quad 7 & 8 & 9 & 0 \end{array}$$

Gummed Labels

After information has been listed on labels, the labels are attached to products by means of a gummed substance. This type of marking is commonly used on hard surfaces like boxes, glass, and plastic.

Stamping

Instead of using gummed labels, many stores apply prices with rubber stamps. This saves time and is a popular method with convenience stores and supermarkets. Other hand-operated marking devices include the band stamp,

(a)

Your Logo

DEPT.   CENTS

C05 $12.00

DP CL VEN   STYLE CTL CODE

0569644062263439

00 1300   **13**

COL   SIZE

U053778095

DEPT.   SKU NO.

JUNIOR

22⁰⁰ **$12**⁰⁰

(b)

(c)

FURNITURE
CLEARANCE
CENTER

**SALE
PRICE**

ALL SALES FINAL – CASH & CARRY

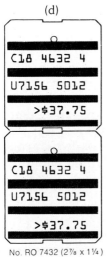

(d)

C18 4632 4

U7156 5012

>$37.75

C18 4632 4

U7156 5012

>$37.75

No. RO 7432 (2⅞ x 1¼)
SKU, Department and
Price with duplicate stub
for batch reading

(d)

I   O   I

C32130012

P39149336 14½

M30210 $125.00

No. RO 4845 (1⅞ x 1¾)
Full SKU, Department and
Price (plus non-OCR size)

(e)

C614 78421

U54364 538

>$44.50

No. RP 3530 (1⅜ x 1³⁄₁₆)
SKU, Department and
Price

C192 42207

U618 49214

>$29.95

No. RP 3837 (1½ x 1⁷⁄₁₆)
SKU, Department and
Price

Figure 12-6 Types of price tags, tickets, and labels. (a) and (b) Kimball tickets, (c) ordinary tag, (d) tags containing SKUS, and (e) Kimball labels containing SKUs. *Courtesy:* Kimball Systems, Division of Litton Industries.

which contains rotating number columns, and the label gun, which affixes price labels to merchandise. Marking machines may be hand operated or electrically powered.

Marking by Hand

Many small stores continue to mark by hand, using grease pencils and multicolored pens. While it is relatively slow, this method serves the modest needs of cost-conscious retailers.

Nonmarking

In an effort to save time and money, some retailers do not mark merchandise. Instead, prices are listed on shelves, posters, bins, showcases, and so forth. For example, stores that sell record albums generally categorize the albums by type (e.g., rock, jazz, classical). Using a letter or color code, the customer checks prices on posters located at strategic points in the store. An added benefit of **nonmarking** is the ease of changing prices on posters as contrasted with doing so on the merchandise itself.

Remarking Merchandise

Remarking is used to show markdowns or markups

To avoid preparing new price tags or tickets when markdowns occur, some stores simply cross out the old price and write in or stamp the new price. This is called **remarking,** and is sometimes done when merchandise is returned by customers, when it is damaged, or when it remains unsold after a certain period. To maintain control over remarked merchandise, buyers in large stores authorize price changes via special forms.

Store policy dictates whether markdowns are shown on the original tag or a new tag is prepared. The policy depends on the store's perception of customers' feelings: Do customers think they are getting a bargain, or do they conclude that the merchandise was overpriced originally? Obviously, the nature of a store's clientele determines which course the store will follow.

STORING AND DISTRIBUTING THE MERCHANDISE

Efficient storage provides for forward and reserve stock

In many retail stores an important nonselling area is the area where merchandise is stored. The nature of the store's physical handling of goods determines the size and location of the storage area. Consequently, careful planning must be done to ensure an efficient flow of merchandise from the time it is received, to the time it is placed in storage, and finally to the selling area. Even a minor mistake in routing

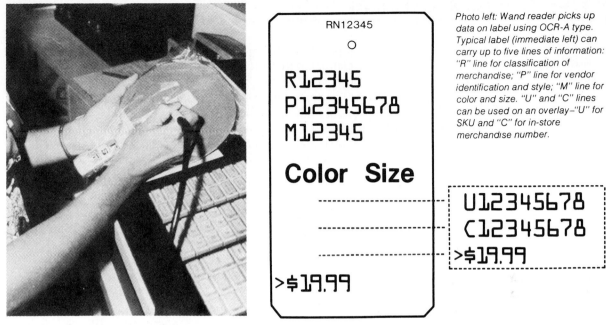

Retailers use wand readers and OCR-A type on price labels for universal vending marking. *Courtesy:* Kimball Systems, Division of Litton Industries.

goods can be costly in terms of employee time, space needs, and energy consumption. Sometimes merchandise is stored in drawers or bins, or on racks in or close to a selling area. This is called **forward stock.** At other times it goes to a central stockroom within the store or to the individual stockroom adjoining each department. This is known as **reserve stock.** However, some large stores do not maintain reserve stock. Instead, all merchandise on hand is displayed. When goods are needed, they are requisitioned from a strategically located distribution center.

When a business consists of more than one store, the goods may be sent from one store, in which receiving, checking, and marking are done, to one or more of the other stores.

Though small stores have limited storage space, they too must make merchandise readily available to customers. Owners, managers, and salespeople in these stores follow established routines for maintaining stockrooms and forwarding goods to selling areas.

One consequence of the 1988 move by Sears, Roebuck and Company into discount retailing was the need to overhaul its merchandise distribution system. This came about because receiving and shipping areas had to be redesigned to accommodate a greater number of brands. Without a physical restructuring, the company could not hope to compete with mass merchandisers like K mart and Wal-Mart.

PROTECTING THE MERCHANDISE

Shoplifting is costly to consumers

At the first national Shoplifting Prevention Conference, held in Atlanta, Georgia, in August 1980, it was estimated that shoplifting was costing retailers (and, hence, consumers) $16 billion a year! Stated another way, Americans were paying 5 percent of every dollar they spent in stores on shoplifting. By 1984, the Nicolette Consulting Group Ltd. of Chicago had estimated annual losses at $24 billion! Other retail industry estimates set shoplifting losses at $22 billion annually.[1] In 1989, average shrinkage as a percentage of sales was about 1.9 percent. It was highest for drug chains and lowest for supermarkets.

This is not to say that shoplifting is the only type of crime committed in stores. Far from it! Others include burglary, robbery, pilferage by employees, arson, and vandalism. How does a store defend itself against these criminal acts? The following are some features of store security that tend to minimize the damage caused by retail crime.

1. Clerk and cashier stations are positioned to bring most or all of the selling areas under surveillance.
2. As far as possible, in some stores exits are accessible only after the customer has passed through a checkout counter. This is particularly true in self-service stores.
3. Closed-circuit television systems and carefully placed cameras discourage potential shoplifters. Though some shoppers complain about the threatening nature of the equipment, on the whole this technique is accepted by most consumers. A new system on the market conceals the equipment in ceiling inserts that look like fixtures.
4. Electric alarm systems are used at entrances and around windows. When an illegal entry occurs, an alarm sounds in specific locations.
5. Mirrors are placed at strategic locations to reveal customer activities that would otherwise be hidden.
6. Warning signs are located in certain areas to caution against shoplifting. The effectiveness of this technique is still being debated in the retail industry.
7. Safes are used to store particularly valuable merchandise, such as jewelry and furs.
8. Although they present no serious problem to professional burglars, locks and barred windows are used with some success.
9. The persistence of burglary has caused many retailers in crime-ridden areas to fasten their storefronts with accordion steel gates upon closing. Though it is unsightly, a well-constructed metal "fence" acts as a fairly good deterrent to burglars.
10. Camouflaged blinds are installed in certain selling areas, allowing store personnel to view customer activity without being seen themselves.

[1] "Confessions of an Ex-Shoplifter," *Chain Store Age Executive*, 61 (February 1985), pp. 15–18.

11. Some stores use electronic systems that transmit high- or low-frequency radio beams that pick up signals from tags attached to merchandise. If someone leaves the store with an item to which a tag is still attached, the system alerts security forces in the store.

12. In-store private detectives and security guards are additional deterrents.

13. There are tags that explode a green dye when taken off merchandise in a nonprescribed way.

14. Special mannequins can contain hidden cameras placed inside them.

15. Some apparel stores use a technology called Tell Tag. If a shopper attempts to remove a tag from a garment, an alarm sounds. The technique is particularly effective in preventing dressing room theft.

The preceding list obviously could be expanded, particularly since new techniques are being perfected constantly. Nevertheless, the list should give you some idea of the efforts retailers have made to reduce store crime.

It must be understood that inventory shortages (**shrinkage**) have a variety of causes, not all of which involve crimes. For example, a broken jar in a supermarket reduces inventory, as does an honest mistake by a salesperson in packing goods for a customer. In addition, vendor theft and errors are reasons for shrinkage.

According to a survey of department stores, mass merchants, and specialty stores, conducted in 1988 by the National Retail Group of Arthur Young & Company, a leading accounting firm, the three departments with the highest shortage rates were women's apparel, records/tapes, and radios/TVs/stereos. The departments showing the lowest rates were fine jewelry, men's apparel, and shoes.

Thefts by Employees

Though difficult to confirm, many retailers believe that the amount of merchandise stolen by store personnel is greater than the amount stolen by outsiders. Whether this is due to the ease with which merchandise can be stolen by employees, to job dissatisfaction, to the low pay received by some workers, or to some other reason, the fact remains that internal theft is a serious problem.

The following internal warning signals should alert retailers to possible theft problems in their stores:

- Preparation of invoices by only one person
- Poor management supervision
- Noncompetitive purchasing
- Preference by a vendor to deal with the same buyer constantly
- Buyer's refusal to change a vendor even when the vendor's competitor offers lower prices
- Persistent vendor shortages

Thefts by employees generally occur in the following store areas:

The Receiving Area

Opportunities for theft in receiving areas

As you saw earlier in this chapter, the receiving area is a hub of activity where store personnel mingle with truck drivers, delivery people, and others. With virtually all merchandise moving through the receiving, checking, and marking functions, it is here that potential thieves have their best opportunity to steal goods. Working by themselves or in collusion with other employees or outsiders, the thieves develop a variety of techniques.

Controlling Receiving-Area Theft. Security personnel may be assigned to receiving areas, allowing only authorized people into or out of specific sections. Cartons, trash containers, and bags are inspected for hidden goods. Some stores require employees to leave by certain exits. Owners and managers of small stores try to maintain control of back and side doors, using signs, warnings, and door mechanisms to prevent unauthorized people from using them. In some instances employees attempt to steal merchandise by hiding it in empty cartons for later removal. To combat this possibility, some retailers require all empty cartons to be disposed of through compactors that destroy their contents.

The Front Area(s)

Retailers have always known that checkout areas are places where dishonest employees plan thefts. Operating by themselves or in collusion with "customers," they develop ingenious ways to pilfer merchandise. For example, they put more goods into bags or boxes than the collaborating "customer" pays for; or, where there is no security guard, they deliberately overlook a "customer" leaving the store with unpaid merchandise.

Accounting control systems minimize theft

Controlling Front-Area Theft. Large stores have accounting control systems for tying receipts (cash, checks, and credit cards) to merchandise purchased. For example, accounting department personnel might check total receipts against price tags or tickets removed from sold merchandise. Many stores post security guards at exits to make sure that packages containing goods purchased at the store have sales receipts attached to them. Some stores use cameras to survey activities in checkout areas.

With increased attention being paid to internal theft, some supermarkets and discount stores have installed split-screen monitors at checkout counters that check merchandise prices against the cash register tape. Used for items not suitable for scanning equipment, the system identifies the merchandise, establishes its price, and determines whether the cashier has rung up the correct price.

Thefts by Management Personnel

Though not so common as thefts by other employees, there are instances of managerial personnel stealing goods. Since managers supervise and control store operations, their merchandise crimes are more difficult to uncover and often involve large dollar amounts.

Controlling Theft by Management Personnel.   The most effective way to control thefts by managers is to encourage and develop store loyalty. This is usually accomplished through opportunities for promotion, satisfactory pay levels, incentive programs, and recognition of effort.

General Approaches to Reducing Employee Theft

Basic employee honesty is a store's best protection against employee theft

While the techniques mentioned previously for controlling the theft of merchandise by employees have some effect, store owners and managers recognize that basic employee honesty is by far the store's best protection. Consequently, strong efforts are usually made to hire people of integrity. As discussed in Chapter 6, employment procedures generally include the completion of application forms and the screening of applicants.

Screening is a continuous process

The screening of employees is a continuous process, necessitated by the possibility that current workers may be susceptible and even involved in merchandise crimes. Only a naive person would assume that financial and home problems, career frustration, and difficulties with supervisors or other workers might not cause some employees to steal. Therefore, managers must be sensitive to changes in employee behavior and their living standards, using discreet screening techniques to detect possible malfeasance. If there is any suspicion of an employee's honesty—even if his or her record has been satisfactory—the situation should be investigated immediately.

At least one retail executive believes that neither sophisticated equipment nor a large security department is necessary to control merchandise shrinkage. Shelley Connors, regional loss prevention manager for Best Products, a catalog showroom retailer, maintains that "Security-conscious employees are the most effective deterrent against inventory shortage. If motivated properly, they can help reduce shortage and improve a company's bottom line."

Ross Stores, an off-price apparel retailer, offers incentives to employees who try to stop shoplifting and internal theft. Bonus points, redeemable in merchandise, are awarded to those who help reduce shrinkage.

A program called Watchline encourages employees to register complaints and suggestions anonymously over a 24-hour, toll-free telephone line. Surprisingly, security improves as employees report internal theft and other crimes committed by fellow employees.

Theft by Shoppers

Shoplifters run the gamut of society

People who enter stores with the intention of stealing merchandise may act alone or in collusion with others. Surprisingly, they include representatives of all levels of society: well-to-do and poor, young and old, educated and uneducated, and so forth. With so varied a potential security population, retailers must devise systems for minimizing (elimination is probably impossible) the amount of merchandise theft.

The use of electronic beams alerts security forces to possible thefts of merchandise. A leading manufacturer of electronic merchandise security systems, the

Sensormatic Electronic Corporation, produces sophisticated equipment and supplies for most types of retailers. Other major manufacturers include Knogo North America and Checkpoint of Thorofare.

Reusable tags sensitive to electronic beams can prevent shoplifting

A commonly found design is the Sensormatic system. It employs reusable tags that contain semiconductor materials. A tag is attached to every merchandise item that requires protection, and when a sale is made, the tag is removed by an employee. Scanning pedestals or overhead units are located at the store's exits; these broadcast an electronic signal that can detect tags entering the scanning field. If shoplifting is attempted, the tag activates an alarm when it is near an exit. The alarm, which may be either audible or visual, is located near the exit or monitored in a remote security room.

Sensormatic's analysis of the shoplifting menace and its involvement in **electronic article surveillance (EAS)** display the increasing concern of retailers and security equipment manufacturers in the protection of merchandise.

Retailers using EAS

Sophisticated EAS systems are being used by many retailers, for example department stores like Lord & Taylor, Jordan Marsh, Rich's, and Sears, Roebuck; specialty stores like Lerner Shops, Elizabeth Arden, Dallas Carriage Shops, and Peaches Records & Tapes; and discounters and hypermarkets like Ames, Ayr-Way Stores, Fed-Mart, and Woolworth.

Until the late 1980s, EAS devices were designed only for soft goods. A breakthrough occurred when products were developed to protect hard goods as well. EAS firms like Sensormatic Electronics, Knogo North America, and Checkpoint of Thorofare pioneered the effort.

Hypermarkets in Europe now use electromagnetic paper strips on packaged goods to forestall theft. An alarm is sounded if merchandise goes past a checkout counter without its passing over a demagnetizing plate. The system is being used in this country by an increasing number of retailers, including Eckerd Drugs.

Another illustration of an electronic system for the control of theft is that used by Martin's Aquarium, one of the world's largest pet retailers. Having suffered greatly from shoplifting, Martin's now uses package stickers that trigger an alarm system when merchandise is taken past a counter. With the new system, Martin's has apprehended a much larger number of shoplifters than it had previously.

Stores in areas containing a significant number of homeless people, transient hotels, and criminals can be a risky venture. However, executives at New York City's new A&S department store in A&S Plaza are confident that they can control theft there much as they have done in their other stores. Relying heavily on EAS devices provided by Knogo North America, the store also uses detectives, guards, and a special system to monitor POS transactions. Nevertheless, the chain feels that its best security deterrent is its well-trained sales force.

A novel attempt at reducing shoplifting involves the rehabilitation of convicted shoplifters. For example, Shoplifters Anonymous, a company that deals with shoplifting problems, secures permission from court systems to run theft rehabilitation courses. Ex-shoplifter "students" pay for the course, which covers

Reusable tags are sensitive to electronic beams located at store exits to alert the store's security personnel. *Courtesy:* Sensormatic.

such areas as the costs of shoplifting to society and the effects of theft on businesses and prices. In addition, shoplifters' personal problems are discussed.

Shoplifting and Drugs

It is estimated that shrinkage is normally above 2 percent of sales. Due to the increased use of narcotics by the public, sales employees, and management personnel, retailers are exhibiting a greater awareness of the connection between drugs and merchandise theft. Increasingly, merchants are adopting packages of techniques to reduce theft. Included are the use of more detectives, a greater willingness to prosecute for shoplifting, more use of EAS tags, the employment of closed-circuit television (cc TV), and the initiation of employee awareness/reward programs.

Shoplifting and Civil Recovery

One of the new laws used by retailers in dealing with shoplifters is known generally as **civil recovery.** It allows merchants to collect a sum of money from someone caught shoplifting without the need of criminal prosecution. Almost 40 states have such laws, and retailers using them attest to their effectiveness. The appendix at the end of this chapter contains the history and a more detailed discussion of the intent of civil recovery laws.

Security Guard Training

The importance of security guard training was illustrated in 1989 when Bloomingdale's was compelled to pay $2.3 million in damages to a shopper who had been accused incorrectly of stealing a $99.50 jacket. Security officers had beaten and slapped the shopper when he refused to sign a confession of guilt.

POS and Store Security

One of the most recent contributions to store security is the spin-off benefits of POS (point-of-sale) terminals. With appropriate programming, the equipment can do the following.

- Enable salespeople to alert store security personnel to a problem by entering a code into POS terminals.
- Permit store personnel to detect shoplifting trouble spots quickly by matching POS sales and inventory data against actual merchandise counts.
- Alert the security department automatically for a cash pickup when a cash register contains more than a certain amount of money.

NEW TERMS

bill of lading
bin
blind checking
bulk checking
carrier
civil recovery
conveyor mechanism
delivery receipt
direct checking
electronic article surveillance (EAS)
forward stock
indirect checking
invoice
loading dock
loading platform
marking
movable table

nonmarking
Optical Character Recognition—
   Font A (OCR-A)
portable table
preretailing
purchase order
receiving book
receiving dock
remarking
reserve stock
semiblind checking
semi-indirect checking
shrinkage
spot checking
stationary table
universal vendor marking (UVM)

CHAPTER HIGHLIGHTS

1. Large stores that sell major appliances and furniture maintain warehouses for the storage of these goods until delivery to the customer.
2. Since selling space is valuable, receiving sections are located in areas that are not conducive to selling; receiving equipment within a store may consist of elevators, conveyors, and chutes.
3. The preparation of merchandise for delivery to selling areas is facilitated by the use of stationary tables, portable tables, conveyor mechanisms, and bins.
4. Information about incoming goods is entered in a receiving book and includes quantities, date and time of receipt, weight, type of transportation, name of carrier, shipping costs, damaged containers, and vendor's name.
5. A purchase order prepared by a retailer specifies the goods ordered. Upon receipt of the purchase order, the supplier sends the retailer an invoice and ships the goods.

6. In the receiving process, quantities may be checked by a variety of procedures: direct checking, indirect checking or blind checking, semi-indirect checking or semiblind checking, spot checking, bulk checking, and UVM checking.

7. Preretailing is a procedure that requires a buyer to list retail prices on purchase orders.

8. The marking process may involve the use of price tags, price tickets, gummed labels, stamping, or hand marking. Computerized marking is done by manufacturers through use of the universal product code and universal vendor marking.

9. Remarking prices on goods may be used when goods are returned by customers, when they are damaged, or when they remain unsold after a certain period.

10. Forward stock is stored in or close to selling areas. Reserve stock goes to a central stockroom or to an individual stockroom adjoining each department.

11. Thefts of merchandise by store personnel occur in both receiving and front areas. Stores must institute procedures to control theft. Because the basic honesty of store employees is probably the store's best protection against employee theft, large and moderate-sized stores screen employees continuously.

12. Many well-known department and specialty stores, discounters, and hypermarkets use electronic article surveillance to control shoplifting.

13. Civil recovery laws enable retailers to collect money from convicted shoplifters without the need of criminal prosecution.

REVIEW QUESTIONS

1. Why is it important for retailers to interface their store and warehouse computers with their vendors' computers?

2. What is the purpose of comparing information supplied by receiving clerks with purchasing data that is stored in the computer?

3. What is one of the items found on both a purchase order and an invoice that is used for cross-referencing? Of what importance is this feature?

4. How does direct checking of merchandise differ from indirect checking? What is the major advantage of each?

5. What is a common method used by large retailers to check the quality of incoming goods?

6. How do computerized marking and premarking help the retailer?

7. Why is it dangerous for retailers to permit noncompetitive purchasing by their buyers?

DISCUSSION QUESTIONS

1. Why is it important to restrict access to checking and marking areas by buyers and selling personnel? What should be done in the case of buyers who ignore the restriction policy?
2. Why is spot checking sometimes used for large deliveries? Do you think it is a reliable checking method? Why?
3. Can the screening of employees as a continuous process cause friction? Explain.
4. How does electronic article surveillance reduce the opportunities for shoplifting? Is it practical for all retailers? Explain.

CASE 1

Shrinkage

The J. T. Mandy Company, a discount department store with annual sales of over $40 million, is plagued by merchandise theft. Its inventory shortage rate was 1.9 percent of sales in 1980, but had risen to 2.5 percent by 1985. Despite the installation of such equipment as hidden closed-circuit television cameras and receivers, theft remains a serious problem.

Mandy's executives know that the firm's largest volume of thefts occurs in its leather goods department, followed closely by the costume jewelry and sporting goods departments. Consequently, it recently stationed uniformed security personnel in those areas to maintain constant observation of shoppers.

The head of Mandy's security department has suggested that the store develop an employee incentive program in an effort to reduce theft. He recommends that employees who notify security personnel about dishonest employees and on-the-spot shoplifting be awarded cash sums for their help; the reward could be either a flat amount or one based on the value of the goods involved. He also feels that cooperating employees should be considered for promotion.

Another of his suggestions is that many part-time workers be dismissed and replaced with full-time personnel. He reasons that full-timers are more reliable, honest, and loyal than part-timers. While recognizing the payroll savings that accrue from staffing the store with substantial numbers of part-time people, he contends that these savings would be more than offset by reduced inventory shortages.

Though top management is anxious to control the theft problem, it does not want to create other problems by adopting new procedures. Since its members are concerned about employee morale and customer comfort, management intends to proceed carefully and prudently.

a. What arguments would you advance for and against the employee incentive program?
b. What is your opinion about the suggestion regarding part- and full-time personnel?
c. Should new security procedures be applied storewide, or should they be tested in the leather goods, costume jewelry, and sporting goods departments?

CASE 2

Confessions of an Ex-shoplifter*
by Holly Klokis

As a professional shoplifter for 20 years, William "Dick" Deal managed to pull down a tax-free $100,000 a year, one-quarter of the retail value of the merchandise he stole. Together with his booster team, Mike and Tootsie, Deal estimates they stole $1.2 million at retail, every year.

The 47-year-old Kansas City native began his dubious occupation in the mid-1960's to support a heroin habit. He acted as a "stall," distracting the attention of salesmen while his two partners helped themselves to merchandise.

Deal was a natural. At 6 ft., 280 lb., with a beard and shaved head, he attracted attention easily. Generally, his gift of gab was enough to keep a salesman occupied. When that didn't work, he'd resort to acting crazy: "I'd walk in and start picking up $200 blouses and throwing them on the floor. I knew everyone in the store would come over to see." Meanwhile, Mike and Tootsie did their thing.

Today, Deal operates on the other side of the law. He is, ironically, a locksmith. He is also employed by the Nicollette Consulting Group Ltd. of Chicago to give seminars on how stores can avoid shoplifting. Like Deal's former occupation, his drug habit is a thing of the past.

But when you get him going, Deal still talks about shoplifting in the present tense. Obviously an expert in his field, Deal tells of being undaunted by the myriad security devices on the market—cameras, electronic surveillance tags, and the like—which can be misused or improperly manned by store personnel.

In fact, he says, there was one thing—and one thing only—that ever prevented

*Courtesy of *Chain Store Age Executive*, February 1985.

him, or any other professional shoplifter for that matter, from stealing: a knowledge-able, persistent, good salesman.

"I don't care about locks. Locks only keep honest people honest," he says in a surprisingly soft-spoken Midwestern drawl. A large part of the problem, he notes, is that retailers commonly buy the cheapest locks to protect their most expensive merchandise.

"I don't care about [two way] mirrors. If I go into a store and there are only two salesmen on the floor, are you going to convince me that you're paying someone $8 an hour to stand behind the wall and peek through a hole at me? I know there's no one there."

The list continues. "I don't care about electronic devices because I can beat or remove any of 'em." (Often, says Deal, the emergency tag-removal devices, which are supplied by electronic surveillance manufacturers, are left lying around the store, accessible to any thief.)

"I don't care about a policeman standing at the front door. That's an open invitation to come in and steal. . . . The one thing he wants to do is come to this store for four hours, drink a cup of coffee, read the paper and try to get a date with the gal at the cash register and rap because his old lady really don't understand him.

"Cameras? That's crazy," he remarks with a laugh. They're not manned properly either. "I know that half of them are blanks and aren't taking a picture of anything. And those that are, who's watching the monitor? It's generally a 16- or 17-year-old high school girl who also has to do her homework, answer the telephone, receive packages, let people in and out the back door, and fend off the advances of the cop who's trying to get a date with her."

"No," he says, "there's only one reason that I would not go into a store to steal: they got a salesman in there who drives you nuts. The fool wants to try to sell you something; you can't get rid of him. He wants to help you; he wants to show you things; he wants to make money because he's on commission."

Despite the potential availability of such an effective deterrent, Deal managed to maintain his career for two decades. Not only didn't he ever get caught, he boasts of never being with anyone who ever got caught.

He attributes his success to two things: poor store planning and misinforma-tion about shoplifting.

"The way stores are built today it almost seems that they were designed by a thief," he states flatly. "When a store is built or designed, the architect never takes into consideration the security. . . . Everything is off in little rooms or boutiques. If you can't see what's going on in your store then you're gonna lose your merchan-dise."

To make matters worse, he continues, "The merchandisers and display peo-ple come in—and they don't know a damn thing about security. They'll have built a display that's absolutely beautiful. Unfortunately, the people have stolen it all."

Another of Deal's pet peeves is window displays. "A window is made to be a window," he says emphatically. "But they [the visual presentation staff] fill it full of things. I don't worry about people in the store ever telling on me [when I'm shoplifting]. They generally won't because they don't want to be involved. But people outside parking their cars or walking in the mall, if they see you through that window, they'll tell on you in a New York second. They'll run to the telephone and describe you down to the color of your socks.''

Deal's on a roll now and no detail of merchandise presentation gets away unscathed: ''They can't even leave a post or a pillar alone. They'll drill holes in it; screw rods in it and hang things from it. That isn't a 2-ft. square post anymore. It's an 8-ft. wall. And every time you build something that blocks the view of the store, I can get behind it—and you'll lose.''

Aside from store planning, says Deal, retailers could avoid shoplifting by professionals if their salesmen knew what to look for. ''I can't impress on you enough the bad information that has been fed to salesmen, retail people, managers, security people. And unfortunately it's generally by the police department.''

Law enforcement agencies compile their statistics from people who have been caught, he points out. A real professional rarely gets caught—and they're the ones responsible for the majority of theft that goes on, according to Deal.

While he admits he has no statistics to back him up, he speaks from experience. ''We would steal more in one day, money-wise, than 40, 50, or 100 amateurs would in two years. To steal $6,000 or $8,000 worth of merchandise a day is child's play.'' With a dollar volume like that, Deal has no trouble accepting the industry estimate of $22 billion ($40 billion in 1989) lost to shoplifters annually. By way of comparison, that's nearly as much as Sears, Roebuck, the nation's largest retailer, grosses on sales.

''Go into any town of any size and ask the police department if they have a film on shoplifting. They will bring you down a film that will show you black people stealing with a booster box. A booster box is a wrapped box with a spring loaded trap door that no one has stolen with since 1938,'' he says with a touch of frustration.

The three biggest myths about shoplifting, according to Deal, are that ''black people do all the stealing, that they're poor, poorly dressed and illiterate and that we use gimmicks like booster boxes and booster bloomers and saxophone hooks to hang things on. And all those are lies.''

Quite the contrary, he says, ''Professional shoplifters are not stupid people. They're some of the most inventive, industrious, intelligent people you will meet. Unfortunately, they steal. They do it seven days a week and they're very good at it.''

Unlike the image the word ''shoplifter'' conjures up, they are, says Deal, ''the best dressed people in your store. They're white; they're between the ages of 25 and 50—and there's a reason for that. Ninety percent of all professional shoplifters are drug addicts. And it takes you till about the age of 25 to become a dyed-in-the-wool, knock-down, screamin' dope fiend. You don't see 'em over 50 because they're dead.''

Shoplifters tend to be well-dressed, he explains, because ''when you steal clothes for a living, you wear the best. You don't steal clothes from K mart. A $35 K mart leisure suit and an $800 Oxford cashmere sportcoat are the same size package when you roll it up and steal it. So, simple economics will tell you where I steal clothes—the best places in town."

Salesmen need to know facts like these in order to prevent shoplifting. "You have to have someone tell your salesmen how it's done, who does it and why they do it. It's not the black people wearing Red Ball Jet tennis shoes—it's the best dressed white couple in the store, with a little touch of gray at the temples. Who takes all their money out to spend it? White people between 25 and 50 years old. Now, that's one hell of a disguise we use."

During the course of one of his presentations, Deal also explains the technique he used over the years. It never varied: The female half of the booster team always carried the merchandise. She secreted it in a tailor-made elastic girdle worn under a loose fitting dress or top, preferably maternity clothing. Deal stalled the salesman while the team worked together loading up the girdle with merchandise—always facing one another for a full field of vision.

To a knowledgeable salesman, says Deal, the stall tactic noted earlier would have been a dead giveaway. "Nine out of 10 times when something bizarre happens in a store, there's a reason for it," he claims. "I tell people that whenever they see something weird, crazy or bizarre, they have to say to themselves, 'Hold it, what the hell is really going on here?'"

Another tactic shoplifters use, says Deal, is intimidation; "It's the biggest tool we have." When approached by a salesman offering assistance, a shoplifter will commonly respond belligerently, he reports, because in most cases the salesman will leave. With a saleswoman, Deal says, "you just go up and whisper something obscene in her ear. You know the young saleslady will turn around, blush and get the hell away from you."

By the same token, says Deal, "men are just as easily intimidated by women shoplifters—maybe not with violence or the threat of violence," he admits, but with sex. A woman can "just whisper in his ear or expose a breast," to send a salesman running the other way.

In addition to clothes, there was little Deal didn't steal. And when he wasn't stealing, he operated as a fence—a person who buys stolen goods for resale. Together with a partner Deal owned a 2,000-sq.-ft. retail store, "a very nice store," that bought and sold only stolen merchandise.

"We had everything from tools to the finest men's and women's fashions," he recalls. "We bought $60,000 to $80,000 worth of merchandise a week from shoplifters."

The ease with which stolen goods can be fenced to another retailer makes every merchandise category, as well as every store, a target. There are only two kinds of merchandise Deal wouldn't touch: anything with a serial number and guns. "Those are two things that'll get you arrested faster than anything." The only exceptions to the rule are expensive furs; the pelts are branded with a serial number on the inside. In that case, Deal sold them out of the trunk of his car behind his store.

Curiously enough, some shoplifters have specialties. When illustrating that most shoplifters are drug addicts, Deal relates the following anecdote:

"I only knew of two people who were shoplifters who were not drug addicts. One of the men is retired now. He lives in a $250,000 home and goes to the Bahamas five months out of the year. All he ever stole—and I laugh even thinking about it—was paint brushes and fishing lures. Everyone thinks you wouldn't want to steal a paint brush, but look at the price of a good one. And they put them in places in the store that are out of the way because 'nobody's gonna steal a paint brush.'"

"But they have a tremendous market because every painter's got to have them, so why wouldn't they buy them for a third of the price instead of full price? And this man never went into a place that he didn't also steal a handful of fishing lures. They're easy, they're handy, they're hanging there."

Deal concludes by offering retailers a word of advice about shoplifters. "One thing you must do with everybody that comes into your store: look him in the eye and say 'hi.' You don't say, 'Can I help you?' and you must look them in the eye.

"Several things will happen when you do this," he continues. "He'll either wink, smile, frown, say 'hi,' tell you why he came in the store, or he'll leave. But he can't ignore you. When I went into a store and someone looked me in the eye and said, 'hi,' the first thing I thought of was, 'Where does this fool know me from? Did they knock us off the last time we were in this store, but just didn't catch us?'"

At that point, Deal says, he left the store. "We never stopped to think. I knew I could go next door and they'd leave me alone. I don't have the time to let a salesman follow me around the store for 15 minutes. Time is money to me, just like it is to you."

a. William Deal, the ex-shoplifter, maintains that store security devices are minor deterrents to professional shoplifters. Do you agree? Why?

b. Mr. Deal also feels that trained store personnel are a store's best antidote to shoplifting. Do you agree? Why?

c. What are your reactions to Mr. Deal's comments about shoplifting myths such as poorly dressed people, gimmicks, and so on?

REFERENCES

ABEND, J. "Narcotics Cited as Key Threat." *Stores* (June 1989), pp. 56–59.

"Employee Involvement Is Key to Store Security." *Chain Store Age Executive*, **65** (April 1989), p. 80.

FRENCH, W. A., M. R. CRASK, AND F. H. MADER. "Retailers' Assessment of the Shoplifting Problem," *Journal of Retailing*, **60** (Winter 1984), pp. 108–115.

"Loss Prevention Can Be Profitable."

Chain Store Age Executive, **64** (December 1988), pp. 72–73.

"Shortages, the Game of Blind Man's Bluff." *Inside Retailing*, March 16, 1987, p. 4.

APPENDIX

History and Intent of Civil Recovery Laws

History

Civil recovery is not a new concept. It is as old as common law. What is new are the civil demand laws being passed across the nation. These statutes are written to make it easier administratively for merchants to collect for damages incurred as a result of increasing losses due to theft.

The first civil recovery statute was enacted in Nevada in 1973. Prior to this, the legal damages available to the retailer for shoplifting offenses, if any, were small, attorney's fees were generally not recoverable, and such fees would typically outweigh any recovery of damages, placing the financial burden of pursuit of the shoplifter and security costs in general on the retailer and ultimately, through increased prices, on the nonshoplifting customer.

Civil recovery statutes, in general, by establishing automatic, preset ranges of penalties directed at the shoplifter, tend to shift this financial burden from the consumer to those who commit acts of shoplifting and theft. Basically, civil recovery statutes were enacted in order to compensate the retailer *and* provide for deterrence.

Intent of the Laws

1. To help offset the tremendous costs of theft and security by passing on the burden to the offenders and not by raising prices to consumers.
2. To serve as a deterrent—especially to repeat offenders.
3. In some states it can be viewed as a possible alternative to criminal action, although both can be used simultaneously (Ohio being the exception in that a retailer is permitted to pursue either the criminal *or* civil remedy, but not both).
4. To provide a source of revenue to retailers for funding of loss control training, programs, and equipment.

Part 4

Promotion: Communicating with the Customer

Preparing goods for sale is of little value unless customers know they are available. Part Four covers the ways in which retailers communicate with consumers. Chapter 13 is devoted to retail selling, and we note the differences between order taking and creative selling. We then explore the principles of effective retail selling, with an explanation of the selling process. Finally we examine the major aspects of sales training programs.

Chapter 14 continues our coverage of the retailer-customer communication process with an examination of visual merchandising techniques. First we see how window displays convey information to shoppers. Then we study interior displays in two categories: merchandise and point-of-purchase. The chapter ends with a discussion of responsibility for displays and a list of guidelines for interior arrangement and display.

In Chapter 15 we see how advertising acts as a communication medium for retailers. After examining the different kinds of advertising that merchants use, we study the development of an advertising plan. Our discussion includes a plan's objectives, the media available for communicating with customers, the formulation of an advertising budget, and evaluation of the plan.

Chapter 16 takes us through the communication areas of sales promotion and public relations. We identify the types of promotions that retailers use, such as trading stamps and contests, and learn how responsibility for their implementation is shared. We also study public relations and publicity activities, ranging from community services and fashion shows to the use of free space and time in various media.

Chapter 13

Retail Selling

After completing this chapter, you should be able to:

- Identify and define the types of selling found in retailing.
- Explain the step theory (AIDA) of retail selling.
- Explain suggestion selling, substitute selling, and turnover.
- Explain the rationale for out-of-store selling.
- Identify the skills included in an effective sales training program.

Interaction of salesperson and customer	Of all the retailing activities designed to generate sales and serve customers, the most important may be the selling that takes place when a customer and a salesperson interact. **Personal selling** differs from other means of communicating with consumers in its face-to-face nature. It can best be explained as the methods used in helping customers solve their buying problems.
It is difficult to develop a good sales force	Although many stores have turned to self-service in an effort to cut selling costs, it is difficult to buy such items as cars, sewing machines, or fine jewelry without the help of a salesperson. Merchants often suffer lost sales because the quality of their sales effort is poor. Despite attractive decor, merchandise, and prices, a poor sales team can lose sales and affect store image. Although retailers are aware of this, the development of a good sales force is no easy task.

TYPES OF RETAIL SELLING

Order Taking

Routine selling

Order taking, or clerking, takes place when the clerk in a store does little more than fill a request, make change, or wrap items. Order takers generally work in a highly structured environment, such as McDonald's, Consumers Distributors, and Pizza Hut, or in stores with a strong mix of self-services. This form of selling may require a combination of skills, including the ability to operate quickly and to handle several customers at the same time. Order takers may also function as checkout clerks and cashiers.

Creative Selling

Creative selling requires more product knowledge than order taking. It also calls for the ability to persuade and an appreciation of customers' needs. For example, Nordstrom is known for its extraordinary personalized service. Each Nordstrom store directory carries this message: "Our sales staff is genuinely interested in seeing that all your needs are met. They are professionals who will help you with everything from gift suggestions to complete wardrobe planning. They even accompany you from department to department until you find exactly what you're looking for." At Nuovo Contemporary Menswear, Inc., a New York retailer, salespeople assist shoppers in several unusual ways. They coordinate wardrobes with an understanding of the customer's skin tones and hair coloring. They help put together new looks, working with items their clients may have bought the previous year. This technique is important because every season brings change in shapes, textures, color tones, and so on. Employees who do creative selling are sometimes called sales consultants, or sales associates. They

Personal selling is as important today as it was in the 1925 Sears store. *Courtesy:* Sears, Roebuck.

generate sales by reaching out for new business. For example, many salespeople in apparel and better department stores develop their own customer mail and telephone lists and alert customers of special discounts, sales, and so on. Salespeople who develop their own loyal customer lists are very much in demand and can generally negotiate much better salary and commission arrangements.

Employees affect store image

A salesperson's personality traits and communication skills are very important because the impression a salesperson conveys often influences a customer's buying decisions. In fact, a store's image is directly associated with the type of employees it has. Retailers who are anxious to build a favorable image, therefore, are advised to consider the personality of any employee who comes into contact with customers.

Personal qualities such as appearance, speech, tact, friendliness, resourcefulness, and initiative are additional traits that help build good customer-salesperson relationships. Studies indicate that the quality of store employees is the most frequently mentioned reason for patronizing a particular store.

Even in shops that rely predominantly on self-service, employees are an important consideration. This is so because they may be called upon to answer questions about the quality of particular products, the location of certain items, and so forth. Consequently, they, too, affect the general atmosphere of the store.

Figure 13-1   Dimensions of retail selling. Van Bucher.

Their friendliness and helpfulness become part of the store's "personality" (Figure 13-1).

To underscore the importance of proper selling qualities, Bernard Marcus of Home Depot, a chain of warehouse-style home centers, maintains that "most important, we are different because all of our sales personnel are trained to offer professional advice on how to select building materials and tools for any do-it-yourselfer, and this is the critical factor."[1]

[1] "Bernie Marcus of Home Depot Tells All," *Inside Retailing* (October 3, 1983), p.3.

EFFECTIVE RETAIL SELLING: THE STEP THEORY

Effective selling matches merchandise with customer needs

In order to sell effectively, salespeople must learn all they can about the merchandise, find out what their customers require, and use appropriate selling techniques to satisfy them. Salespeople are obliged to help customers make the best buying decisions with regard to their needs and economic resources. Personal selling in retailing, then, is essentially the process of matching the store's merchandise and services with the customer's needs. Although there are a number of theories regarding effective selling, the most commonly used one is the **step theory.** In this theory, also known as formula selling, the customer follows a pattern of easily identifiable steps that leads to a decision to buy or not to buy. When a salesperson understands the theory, he or she is better able to lead the customer to the successful close of a sale. The process, commonly known as AIDA, involves attention, interest, desire, and action.

Attention The customer's attention must be gained before a sale can be made. This can be accomplished by an advertisement, a display, or the salesperson's approach.

Interest Interest is basically prolonged attention. It is aroused when the salesperson recognizes the customer's wants and presents the correct merchandise to meet those buying needs.

Desire Desire to possess the goods can be stimulated by demonstrating the product. For example, a customer who is looking at a tennis racket or golf club should be encouraged to grasp the handle and execute a swing. Customers who are interested in clothing should be persuaded to try on a suit or dress. In other words the psychological effect of touching or trying an item increases the desire to own the product.

Action Action takes place when the customer is convinced the product is acceptable. During this phase the customer orders or takes the goods.

The salesperson's role in this process involves

1. Approaching the customer.
2. Determining customer needs.
3. Presenting the merchandise.
4. Answering questions and meeting objections.
5. Closing the sale.
6. Suggesting additional merchandise.

Approaching the Customer

When approaching the customer, the salesperson should try to gain the person's attention, create interest, and then proceed with the sale.

A *simple greeting* like "Good afternoon, Mrs. Jones," or "Good morning" is informal, friendly, and welcoming. *Service approaches* like "How may I be of assistance?" and "How may I help you?" may not be effective with a browsing customer, but they are particularly useful when a customer needs someone to explain how a product works, or when the customer appears to have made a selection. *Merchandise approaches* are comments by a salesperson about articles that a customer has stopped to examine. For example, an effective opening might be, "These shirts are featured in *Sports Illustrated*."

Carter Hawley Hale and Neiman-Marcus train their sales associates to approach the customer immediately rather than waiting to be asked for help. In its trainer's package, Marks & Spencer includes a list of 15 ways to approach customers. (See Appendix A)

Determining Customer Needs

The salesperson must ask good questions and be a good listener in order to understand what the customer is searching for. For example, "How will you use the product?" "When do you need it?" and "What size do you need?" are acceptable questions. By asking appropriate questions, the salesperson gains a better idea of what goods to present or demonstrate. In the trainers' package mentioned above, Marks & Spencer also includes guidelines for good listening. (See Appendix B)

Presenting the Merchandise

Even though much merchandise is tagged or labeled, there are many items that require a salesperson's demonstration or explanation. Examples are typewriters, cameras, stereos, and appliances. Technical equipment should be operated so that the buyer is convinced that it is easy to use (e.g., test-driving a car). Special features or selling points should be emphasized.

Answering Questions and Meeting Objections

Questions and objections by the customer are strong signs of interest. A salesperson with good product knowledge can often turn objections into reasons to buy. For example, when a customer says, "This quilt seems too light to be warm," the salesperson might say, "Because it is made of 100 percent down, it has warmth without much weight. It is very comfortable to use."

Some objections to a product are really excuses not to buy. By means of careful questioning, the salesperson can separate quality or price objections from

The salesperson attempts to match a customer's needs with the retailer's merchandise and services.

excuses. Thus, by asking, "What exactly don't you like about the product?" or "What would you care to spend for a product of this kind?," the salesperson can gain a better understanding of the customer; in other words, salespeople should learn to treat objections as unanswered questions.

Closing the Sale

As the objections are answered, the salesperson should attempt to close the sale. Up to this point the entire process has involved getting the customer to make a buying decision. Some decisions are made quickly, as in the case of a customer who knows exactly what he or she wants. At other times, however, a more creative close is required. This is especially so when the salesperson must assist a customer who has difficulty making decisions or does not have the confidence to express a decision. There are several closing techniques that may be used in such cases.

**Closing
techniques**

1. Asking pointed questions such as "Will this be cash or charge?" "Shall we send it gift wrapped?" or "When would you like this delivered?"
2. Watching and listening for signals from the customer. For example, questions like "Can this be returned?" or "How long will it take to be delivered?" are signals. Facial expressions may also indicate that a buying decision is close.
3. Offering inducements or special services (when appropriate). These are typical comments: "The sale price is available today only"; "Free alterations are available today"; "We will not charge you for delivery." Customers are tempted to say yes under these conditions, and generally are pleased with the salesperson's suggestions.
4. Recognizing that the customer might need the approval of another member of the family when dealing with expensive items. In this case the salesperson should try to arrange another meeting. A resourceful salesperson tries to guarantee the customer's return by taking the customer's telephone number and other information. It is important to remember that even if a sale is not made, the customer is a potential future buyer. In other words, spending a little more time with the customer promotes goodwill.

Suggesting Additional Merchandise

Suggestion selling is another way in which a retail salesperson can add to sales and profits. After a sale has been made, a customer is usually receptive to further discussion, and it may be wise to suggest additional items that relate to the original purchase. For example, the salesperson might suggest a beach hat to complement a bathing suit, a tie for a shirt, a belt for a dress, and so forth. In addition, suggesting a special store promotion that may or may not be related to the item already purchased is sometimes effective. However, good suggestion selling keeps the customer's interest in mind and does not simply "add on" to the sale.

Special Retail Situations

In cases in which a customer asks for a special brand that the store does not carry, the salesperson may offer an alternative item to satisfy the customer's needs. This is known as **substitute selling.** Without this additional effort, the sale is usually lost. On the other hand, it was indicated in Chapter 11 that trading up persuades the customer to buy a more expensive item or a larger quantity than originally intended.

Another important selling practice is the use of a **TO,** or **turnover.** This involves turning over a customer to someone else when it appears that a sale will not be closed. Depending on the store, the turnover person is generally someone in authority or someone with particular expertise. This may be the manager, the assistant manager, a buyer, or a senior salesperson.

A TO is used only when the salesperson realizes that he or she will not be successful in making the sale. The main reasons for the TO are

1. To save the sale.
2. To serve customers by doing what is necessary to solve their buying problems.
3. To change salespeople when a personality clash has occurred.

When a TO is used, the salesperson introduces the designated individual to the customer by name. The introduction might go as follows: "Madam, this is Mr. Worth, our department buyer. I know he will be able to find what you want." In this case the salesperson has given the customer the impression that the TO person will be able to do more than he or she did. There must be a valid reason for effecting a TO if the customer is to accept the new "salesperson" with confidence. Two commonly accepted reasons are the following.

1. A person with greater authority has greater leeway than the salesperson.
2. The new person has a special ability or expertise that may be used to solve the customer's immediate problem.

A TO is also called for when, at a particular point in the sale, the customer is too confused or discouraged to buy. The move is made to prevent the customer from giving up. The introduction of a new person can make a customer think, "Ah, this person knows more about my problem and will be able to help."

Personal Selling Outside the Store

Product specialist

Interior designers and decorators are employed by many department stores to sell outside the store. These salespeople visit the customer's home equipped with samples and illustrations of fabrics, wallpaper, carpets, and other home furnishings. They attempt to help the customer solve decorating problems by selecting appropriate merchandise. Retailers that sell air conditioning, kitchen and bathroom fixtures, and remodeling often send salespeople to the customer's home to help design the layout of the room.

Out-of-store, house-to-house sales forces are gaining in popularity with customers because of the convenient services they offer, as well as the help they render in making buying decisions. For customers who lack shopping time, an out-of-store seller often provides the service at times that differ from regular store hours.

Better opportunity to demonstrate the product

In situations in which the customer requires more product information, the out-of-store seller gets a chance to demonstrate the product where it will be used—in the home. For example, customers who are interested in slipcovering their livingroom furniture have an opportunity of seeing fabric samples on their furniture in the correct setting. These customers need not worry about the appropriateness of their selections.

To be successful, the out-of-store seller must develop strong sales skills in addition to becoming a product specialist. In a brief visit, the salesperson must gain acceptance, win the confidence of the customer, develop an interest in the product, create a desire to buy, and close the sale. Even if the sale is not closed, enough interest and motivation may be developed to produce future sales.

TRAINING THE RETAIL SALESPERSON

In recent years the quality of retail selling has been criticized, suggesting that there is a need for change. For example, in stores where customers expect service, they are sometimes disappointed because of insufficient numbers of salespeople. And if one is lucky enough to secure a salesperson, he or she may lack merchandise information. Furthermore, in outlets where customers need directions or simple answers, the sales help is often misinformed, lacking proper information and less than sufficiently attentive.

The trend toward self-service and the marketing strategy of preselling merchandise through advertising, displays, and such has diminished the role of retail selling. This is especially true in self-service stores such as supermarkets and discount merchandisers. In department stores and specialty shops, where a wide range of services is offered, personal selling still plays an important role.

Because personal selling influences a customer's buying decisions and perceptions, adequate sales training is a must. Training can increase employee productivity, lead to better morale, reduce job turnover, and motivate employees to foster good customer relations.

A good training program stresses

1. Sales techniques and customer service.
2. Product information.
3. Standards and evaluation.

Sales Techniques and Customer Service

A program aimed at improving salespeople's skills should deal with the following.

1. Train salespeople to recognize and handle different types of customers and special problems.
2. Train salespeople to sell from the viewpoint of customers by understanding their buying motives.

3. Instruct sales personnel as to the steps needed for effective selling.
4. Instruct salespeople in providing customer service.

Handling Different Types of Customers

Salespeople encounter many types of customers. The manner in which the salesperson pays attention to them can mean the difference between closing or losing a sale. Customers may be of either sex, and any age, race, or nationality. The more common types are the following.

The argumentative customer who disagrees with many statements and tends to disbelieve what he or she is told. The salesperson should avoid trying to win an argument, since the sale may ultimately be lost. Instead, the salesperson needs to overcome objections with facts and strong emphasis on merchandise benefits.

The procrastinator lacks confidence in his or her own judgment, but will listen to the salesperson. This customer likes to postpone buying decisions with statements like "I'll wait till next week." The salesperson must help this customer decide by reinforcing his or her judgments. The astute salesperson narrows the selection by putting away the merchandise to which the customer appears indifferent. In other words, the salesperson must help this person decide.

The looker may be a customer who is "shopping around," making comparisons, or on the way to another department. When greeted by the salesperson, this customer frequently replies, "I'm just looking." The salesperson might answer, "That's all right, we're glad to have you. I'll be over there if you need assistance." By offering help and making the customer feel welcome, the salesperson lays a foundation for future sales.

The silent customer talks little, but pays attention. The salesperson must ask direct questions that require more than a yes-or-no answer.

The decided customer knows what he or she wants and is confident about making decisions. Though not generally interested in other opinions, this customer respects quality, service, and so forth.

The angry customer, recognizable by his or her "chip on the shoulder" attitude, is easily provoked. The salesperson should stick to facts and avoid arguments.

Training sessions that illustrate various types of customers and how to handle them can be very helpful to inexperienced salespeople. Some stores use role playing to dramatize selling situations with difficult customers. Role playing consists of acting out the customer-salesperson relationship. One person plays the part of the customer and the other that of the salesperson. This method enables salespeople to see various sales situations from the customer's point of view. The skill of "sizing up" a customer (learning to recognize his or her needs) can be cultivated through role playing.

Handling Special Problems in Retail Selling

There are certain situations that all salespeople encounter, such as the need to handle two or more customers at once, the parent with a child, and the group shopper. Each of these situations requires special handling.

Handling More than One Customer at a Time.   Most customers want attention and service, and sometimes salespeople find that they must handle several customers at once. This is not an easy task, even for the most experienced salesperson. Nevertheless, some salespeople are adept at doing this without antagonizing customers, and are able to increase sales thereby.

When waiting on one customer, it is wise to acknowledge the others by some greeting or comment, such as "I'll be with you as soon as I can." While one customer is looking at merchandise, the salesperson might excuse himself or herself and attempt to serve another customer. People are usually considerate when they see that a salesperson is trying to help them. Nevertheless, dealing with two or more customers requires tact and patience.

Parent and Child.   Many customers shop with their children. This situation can be difficult if the salesperson is not aware of the potential problems. In order to go through the selling process quickly and efficiently, the salesperson needs the customer's undivided attention. If the shopper is distracted by efforts to keep the child out of mischief, the situation becomes difficult and the customer may say, "I'll come back later *alone*." The salesperson's best technique is to befriend the child. This generally flatters and pleases the parent, who will probably attempt to keep the child quiet. By paying attention to the child, the salesperson enlists the cooperation of both parties.

The Group Shopper.   When friends or family accompany the customer, they do so to provide advice about the purchase. This situation presents a real problem to the salesperson unless diplomacy and tact are used. The salesperson must avoid the slightest disparagement of the views of any member of the group.

The salesperson should determine which member of the group has the greatest influence on the customer. With the aid of that person, the sale may be closed quickly. The strategy is to include the person in the sales talk. For example, as a product is presented to the customer, the salesperson should direct one or two comments to the other member as well. By doing this, the salesperson indicates that his or her opinion is valued, and an ally is gained. Most selling is needed when two or more people are involved, but care must be taken to direct enough remarks to the friend to win his or her support while not seeming to exert pressure.

The Customer's Viewpoint

Effective salespeople develop the ability to sell from the consumer's point of view by putting themselves in the customer's shoes. They can better understand the shopper's needs because they become the buyers rather than the sellers. When this happens, the salesperson develops awareness of the customer's motives for buying.

All merchandise satisfies some consumer need

Customers buy because they are motivated by certain emotional or rational motives, such as pride, beauty, convenience, or romance (Chapter 3). For example, when a person desires recognition as a leader, the pride motive may stimulate the purchase of a large boat or car. On the other hand, if time is a factor, the convenience motive may prompt the purchase of a microwave oven.

When salespeople become familiar with the individual drives that cause people to buy, they are in a better position to match the qualities and benefits of a product with the consumer's motive for buying. For example, Wal-Mart trains its sales associates to make eye contact with their customers and develop a more personal relationship. It provides them with an understanding of their patrons' tastes, natures, and prejudices and can generally feed information to buyers about what is likely to sell. Eye contact also establishes trust between buyer and seller. It is difficult to believe someone who can't or won't look you in the eye.

Training for Effective Selling

Instructional methods used in training

There are various techniques for training salespeople. Among them are role playing, video tapes and cassettes, sales meetings, and seminars.

Role Playing.   As indicated earlier, this involves acting out a scene between a customer and a salesperson in order to experience situations commonly encountered and be better prepared to handle them.

Videotapes and Cassettes.   Many large firms have taped instructions for their employees. This form of teaching is becoming popular because employees can watch and listen at their convenience. Some tapes demonstrate the sales presentation from start to finish. Sometimes they indicate right and wrong ways to approach a customer, meet objections, and close a sale. Instructional tapes can be developed by the store or purchased from professional organizations. Some tapes are developed by manufacturers to aid in the selling of their products. These are very specific regarding the selling qualities and benefits of the merchandise.

Sales Meetings and Seminars.   These methods are generally helpful because they afford managers an opportunity to discuss the features of new products, changes in store policies, new merchandise strategies, or other matters related to the store's merchandise and services. Sessions conducted regularly prompt the interchange of ideas because salespeople enjoy sharing their "tales of sales."

Store training involves customer-salesperson simulation. *Courtesy:* Dayton's.

Training for Customer Service

In addition to selling, the salesperson is often faced with nonselling activities that involve customer contact. These include following up on orders, wrapping packages, handling returns, answering complaints, and arranging for alterations and installations.

Following Up on Orders.   Following up customer orders may be part of the job when one is selling major items like appliances and furniture. Checking to see that customers are satisfied develops goodwill and customer loyalty. Salespeople may also call a list of regular customers when the store runs sales or when new merchandise is expected.

Wrapping Packages.   Some salespeople are responsible for wrapping packages for their customers. When they do so with speed and care, they have an opportunity to add to the customer's satisfaction. Customers generally like this arrangement because one individual is able to complete the entire transaction.

In some stores the salesperson is responsible for goods that are to be mailed, or for carrying merchandise to a delivery vehicle. Even though a sale has been made, the follow-through to avoid errors is important for the development of customer goodwill.

Handling Returns and Answering Complaints.   Handling returns properly can change a discontented customer into a happy patron. For example, in many stores merchandise is returned directly to the selling departments. If the salespeople show concern and are helpful in resolving return problems, customers are generally satisfied. Since refunds and credit policies are keys to the level of store service, most stores are willing to accept merchandise returns in order to maintain customer goodwill.

Complaints are a tangible way in which customers inform the store of their dissatisfaction. Though there are many reasons for complaints, in this chapter we are concerned with those that arise from poor salesmanship, incorrectly filled orders, damaged merchandise owing to negligent packing, and unwanted purchases made through excessive sales pressure.

Figure 13-2 shows the front and back of a reminder card issued to all Marks & Spencer salespeople.

Learning about the Store

It is important for salespeople to be cordial and helpful even when they are called upon to answer questions that are not related to their area. In order to have salespeople build customer goodwill, training should also include information about the store and its policies. In this way salespeople are able to provide the customer with correct information concerning the locations of departments, services, and special events.

THE CUSTOMER
ALWAYS
COMES FIRST

CUSTOMER SERVICE SELLING STANDARDS

1. Acknowledge each customer and smile.
2. Find out what the customer needs.
3. Show appropriate merchandise or share your product knowledge
4. Use Suggestion Selling:
   - Better Value Promotions
   - How many would you like?
   - May I show you something to go with that item?
5. Express appreciation to customer, say "Thank you." Use their name; invite them back. Smile..
   Make that lasting impression.

Figure 13-2 A reminder card for salespeople. *Source:* Marks & Spencer.

Product Information

Salespeople should have a thorough knowledge of the merchandise they are selling because

- It develops selling confidence.
- It makes for a better sales demonstration.
- It helps match the selling qualities of the product with the customer's needs.
- It provides a basis for overcoming objections successfully.
- It makes for a smoother transaction.

If salespeople are to have the necessary product information, they should become familiar with sources of product information. Most merchants, managers, and buyers have access to trade materials that provide information about the products they handle. Manufacturers and wholesalers provide them with product information (literature, periodic sales meetings, etc.), which serves as resource material for salespeople.

Available Sources of Product Information

Buyers

Buyers are very concerned about how merchandise sells in their departments. Resourceful buyers hold instructional programs or seminars about their merchandise, identifying particular selling features and explaining what the merchandise can do for the customer. For example, when selling an expensive hand cream one should stress its importance to soft, smooth skin or its function as protection against cold weather. In other words, a salesperson should sell product benefits.

Vendors

Salespeople must be confident about the merchandise they sell in order to instill confidence in their customers. Consequently, when products are technical or require special demonstrations, vendors prepare information for their merchandise and sometimes conduct sales lectures at the store.

Labels

Merchandise tags and labels offer information regarding fiber content, instructions for care, quantities, and so forth. The purpose of an informative label is to enable the consumer to buy wisely and to minimize the likelihood of returns and customer dissatisfaction. The salesperson can use labels to point out specific benefits to customers. The following list contains information found on labels and is mandated by federal law.

- Manufacturer (name and address—how to contact)
- Performance (color, permanence, strength, resistance to water and perspiration, light, etc.)
- Content (kind of fiber, metal, leather, plastic, etc.)
- Construction (how the product is made, size, weight, finish, hand or machine made, etc.)
- Care and uses (most suitable uses, instructions for washing, cleaning, storage, etc.)

Catalog Descriptions

Many mail order companies send catalogs filled with product information and descriptions. These can be helpful to the salesperson because they are easy to understand and explain product quality in specific terms.

Government Standards

Another excellent resource for salespeople consists of government publications that contain standards and regulations for many products. They are available through agencies like the Department of Commerce and the Office of Consumer Affairs.

Private Agencies and Testing Laboratories

There are agencies that operate testing laboratories for the guidance and protection of consumers. In these cases, labels or seals are used to show that the articles have met certain standards. *Consumer Reports, Good Housekeeping,* and *Parents* magazine are examples of publications that perform tests on products and make the public aware of the results. Large retailers like J. C. Penney operate their own testing facilities to check the quality of the products they sell.

RETAIL STRATEGY
Combining Service with Selling

Reverting to the concept of one-on-one selling, Carson-Pirie-Scott has established a specialty shop in two of its suburban Chicago stores. Called Corporate Level, the shops cater to the career woman by providing her with one-stop shopping for personal items, as well as a host of personal services.

Wardrobe consultants (well-trained salespeople) assist patrons with individual garments, outfits, complete wardrobes, and accessories. Working by appointment, Corporate Level customers pay $50 a year for such services as 24-hour alterations, a complimentary treatment in the Hair Studio, wardrobe consultations at home, and reminders of such dates as anniversaries and birthdays.

Salespeople are paid on a commission basis and are motivated to sell full wardrobes. With their in-depth training and product knowledge, it is expected that the sales staff, the stores, and the customers will benefit.

Publications and Professional Organizations

Trade papers like *Women's Wear Daily, Daily News Record,* and *Chain Store Age* are just a few of the publications that keep salespeople up to date. Trade organizations like the National Retail Federation also publish a great deal of material of value to management and salespeople.

Standards and Evaluation of Sales Performance

All training programs should include guidelines or standards so that employees know what is expected of them and how they are evaluated. Sales records provide specific information that can be used to measure the effectiveness of the individual salesperson. Although some people are more productive than others, the dollar volume and number of transactions handled by an employee are important measures of sales performance.

It is important to compare salespeople in similar departments with similar responsibilities because salespeople are often involved in related activities such as stock work, maintaining merchandise and work areas, arranging displays, handling returns, and awaiting customer arrivals. Studies indicate that sales personnel may spend only 50 percent of their time actually selling. Consequently, another consideration should be the value of the salesperson's performance in nonselling activities. In fact, stores like May Company have been experimenting with a revision of their salespersons' responsibilities. In an attempt to increase sales productivity, they have removed some of the salespersons' non-selling tasks to allow them to concentrate on serving customers. Regardless of the standards set for evaluating sales performance, it is essential that they are understood by the salesperson so that they are easy to measure and calculate.

A RETAIL TREND SETTER

Charles Tiffany

Of all the well-known glassware, jewelry, and silver retail firms in this country, Tiffany & Co. is probably the most famous. Catering to the wealthy as well as the middle class, the store, located on Fifth Avenue in New York City, is a major attraction for tourists as well as shoppers.

Started in 1837 by Charles Tiffany and John P. Young, the store originally sold stationery and variety goods. Like so many other retail ventures, this one would have failed but for the determination and energy of its two young owners.

In addition to an uncanny knack for selecting salable merchandise, Tiffany dared to try out new ideas. For example, he marked every piece of merchandise with its selling price—a radical departure from the prevailing practice. He also disproved the contention that women of the time lacked taste by successfully selling a line of Parisian jewelry. This feat convinced Tiffany to discontinue the sale of costume jewelry and carry only genuine goods.

Tiffany's recognition of the importance of publicity involved him with such celebrities as Jenny Lind, the famous Swedish singer, P. T. Barnum, the American showman; and Cyrus W. Field, the American financier who built the first transatlantic telegraph cable. These publicity stunts promoted Tiffany's name worldwide and added enormously to its success.

One of Charles Tiffany's unsuccessful ventures was his attempt to manufacture watches in a factory in Geneva, Switzerland. Because Swiss craftsmen would or could not adapt to assembly-line production methods, the factory closed. Nevertheless, Tiffany continued to purchase Swiss watches from others and to sell them with great success.

Tiffany's is known for many other exciting possessions and designs, among them the Tiffany diamond (a 128.51-caret gem), the magnificent Mackay silver service, and the famous Tiffany stained glass lamps. Today Tiffany's is a far cry from the knick-knack store opened in 1837, and Charles Tiffany's genius as a merchant endures in its preeminent position in American retailing.

NEW TERMS

creative selling	substitute selling
order taking	suggestion selling
personal selling	turnover (TO)
step theory (AIDA)	

CHAPTER HIGHLIGHTS

1. Personal selling can best be explained as the methods used to help customers with their buying problems. The face-to-face nature of the activity distinguishes it from other forms of communication with the consumer.

2. The two basic categories of selling are order taking and creative selling. In general, order taking has little to do with helping customers make buying decisions, whereas creative selling involves the use of selling techniques to help solve customers' problems.

3. The quality of a store's employees affects the extent to which customers patronize the store. Personality factors and appearance influence salesperson-customer relations. Effective salespeople match a customer's needs with the store's merchandise and services.

4. The step theory (AIDA) involves attaining the attention, interest, desire, and action of the customer.

5. Although different selling techniques are used in retailing, they all involve approaching and greeting the customer, determining needs, showing merchandise, answering questions and meeting objections, closing the sale, and suggesting additional purchases.

6. Special retail situations may call for substitute selling, trading up, or TO (turning over a customer to another salesperson).

7. Because some situations require more product information, many department stores employ interior designers and decorators to sell outside the store. They visit customers' homes and demonstrate products where they are most likely to be used.

8. Because the quality of retail selling has been criticized, greater attention to training is suggested. Training can increase employee productivity, lead to better morale, reduce employee turnover, and motivate employees to foster good customer relations.

9. The manner in which a salesperson deals with different types of customers can mean the difference between closing or losing a sale. Retail selling entails handling special problems, such as dealing with more than one customer at a time, the parent and child, and the group shopper.

10. Retail training methods include role playing, videotapes and cassettes, sales meetings, and seminars.

11. Training for customer service involves following up on orders, wrapping packages, handling returns and answering complaints, and arranging for alterations and installations.

12. Sources of product information for salespeople include buyers, vendors, labels, catalog descriptions, government standards, private agencies and testing laboratories, and publications and professional organizations.

13. Training programs should include guidelines or standards so that employees know what is expected of them.

REVIEW QUESTIONS

1. Explain how face-to-face communication affects a store's image. How can the salesperson's personality influence the customer?
2. Part of a salesperson's job is to approach customers promptly in a friendly manner. Cité an example of each of the common types of approaches. When should they be used for maximum effectiveness?
3. How can a salesperson anticipate when to close a sale?
4. What are some of the dangers of trading up?
5. How can salespeople become product specialists? What information is available to them?
6. In what ways does an effective training program increase employee productivity?
7. When should the salesperson consider using the practice of TO?

DISCUSSION QUESTIONS

1. Why do merchants have difficulty in attracting high-caliber applicants for retail sales positions?
2. How does suggestion selling help the customer?
3. Which factors do you consider most important in the evaluation of a salesperson's performance? Explain.

CASE 1

How Do You Account for Customer Loyalty?

When the William F. Gable department store, a 96-year-old institution in Altoona, Pennsylvania, was scheduled to go out of business, the city's residents rallied in an attempt to keep the store open.

The store, located in the heart of the downtown shopping district, was closed as part of the bankruptcy proceedings ordered by a federal judge. After the store applied for a going-out-of-business license, many of Altoona's 60,000 residents made it clear that they would fight the decision to close the store.

The executives at the store, as well as city officials, received hundreds of calls from customers complaining about the closing. A number of customers visited the store to pay off their charge account balances early. Multitudes of shoppers, as many as 15,000 a day, poured into the store for the final sale, not only to buy but to complain about the closing.

These actions by Gable's customers created such a stir that the bankruptcy proceedings were reconsidered.

a. How do you explain the actions of Gable's customers?
b. What types of selling services do you think Gable's offered? Can you see this happening where you live? Why?

CASE 2

Pressure and Productivity

Commission selling as an element in the development of good salespeople is a topic of some controversy in the retailing industry. Some retailers maintain that the industry must move toward a system of incentives and rewards inherent in commission selling as a necessary step toward solving one of retailing's most critical problems—how to improve productivity.

Others believe that a commission on sales program costs too much and leads to high pressure, hard-sell tactics on the part of the sales force that alienate customers.

In the industry as a whole, commission selling has been declining since the 1960s as more and more retailers adopt the self-service concept and reduce the number of their salespeople, commissioned as well as salaried.

In the same time period, consumer complaints about customer service have risen sharply. These include complaints about stores that maintain sales staffs, such as department stores, and self-service outlets, as well. Often customers complain about sales personnel not knowing their merchandise, not answering customer questions, and not seeming to care about the customer—a situation that has been characterized as "The Clerk versus the Enemy." Low employee morale and lack of motivation are commonly given as prime causes for these problems.

Yet there are retailers, primarily better department stores and specialty stores, where morale and motivation of the sales force are high and, moreover, so is productivity.

This is particularly remarkable in a segment of the industry that is facing slow expansion and the loss of customers to off-price retailers. Retailers such as Neiman Marcus, J. L. Hudson, and the Parisian chain of specialty stores all utilize commission selling with great success. Each, however, incorporates this kind of incentive system in their overall plans for developing and maintaining a highly skilled sales force in a slightly different way.

Neiman Marcus is on a straight commission plan in all departments and is known for its highly professional sales staff. Neiman Marcus executives acknowledge that commission selling and extra support staff do cost more, and they say that such costs must be expected. However, they also claim such costs are offset by lower advertising outlays and lower personnel turnover (16 percent average). Lower turnover has meant lower costs for training personnel, has provided continuity in the sales force, and has enhanced the store's reputation for a highly professional and knowledgeable staff.

J. L. Hudson uses a commission system in a team selling format together with a rating system that includes sales totals and customer service measures. The company evolved its present system because it found that a straight commission system did not work for them, but led to high-pressure selling. Using the new system, Hudson has found that selling costs have fallen, while providing incentives for the sales force. The company provides a base pay that is formulated on sales goals with compensation paid for exceeding goals. Hudson believes that one of the benefits for the company and the sales force is the flexibility provided in its system, because individual sales goals can be adjusted easily.

At Parisian stores, a chain of specialty stores, commission selling is part of a benefit and career progression package that has been described by an employee training specialist as one of the most successful in retailing. The Parisian plan evolved from two major elements. One was a study of turnover problems that revealed the following: The sales force had no clear idea of what was expected of it; rigid, set sales goals resulted in survival rates of personnel as low as 5 percent; and there was no emphasis in training on developing human relations skills, only cash register skills. The second key element is management's belief that if everyone is paid at a flat rate or receives an across-the-board raise, there are no significant rewards for people who do well. Thus, runs the company's argument, high achievers go elsewhere and retailing is left with low-achieving, unmotivated personnel.

Parisian's system centers on clearly defined goals that offer measurable rewards and a clear career path to the sales staff. In addition to commissions, salespeople earn titles, status, and corporate recognition. Close monitoring of progress occurs at all levels of the organization, and reinforcement of achievement is provided frequently. According to one executive, the sales force is considered by the chain to be the most important element in the organization.

The Parisian chain, like Neiman Marcus and J. L. Hudson, also contends that its selling costs have fallen. The costs have declined from 6.2 to 5.9 percent of sales even though the rate of compensation is now higher. The key difference, according to the company, is that productivity is higher—a lot higher.

Executives at all three companies do agree that instituting an incentive system is a large undertaking, requiring time, a comprehensive training program, and perhaps most critical of all, the long-term commitment of management.

Some executives doubt that many retailers will try such systems, because, as one Neiman Marcus vice-president explained, "It takes a total commitment for years. . . . They have to be prepared for the long pull."

a. Do you agree with Parisian stores executives that sales personnel are the most important people in a retailing organization? Why?

b. If the rate of growth for better retailers continues to be sluggish, do you believe that incentive systems can provide sustained high productivity levels?

c. Do you think that increasing productivity is the most critical problem facing retailers today? Are there strategies other than incentive systems that you think could alleviate the problem? Explain.

d. Many better retailers are part of larger publicly held corporations whose stockholders are interested in profits. Can the costs in time and money be justified in such a situation? How?

REFERENCES

BRUNER, G. C. "Problem Recognition Styles and Search Patterns: An Empirical Investigation." *Journal of Retailing*, **62** (Fall 1986), pp. 281–297.

DUBINSKY, A. J., AND S. J. SKINNER. "Impact of Job Characteristics on Retail Salespeople's Reactions to Their Jobs." *Journal of Retailing*, **60** (Summer 1984), pp. 35–62.

HANCOX, C. "Back to Service." *Daily News Record*, (December 11, 1989), pp. 52–53.

LEVY, M., AND A. J. BOBINISKY. "Identifying and Addressing Retail Salespeople's Ethical Problems: A Method and Application." *Journal of Retailing*, **59** (Spring 1983). pp. 46–56.

SCHILLER, Z. "Stalking the New Consumer." *Business Week* (August 28, 1989), pp. 54–62.

APPENDIX A

Fifteen Ways to Approach Customers*

1. Hello, you are looking at our new Spring collection.
2. Hi, you seem to be looking for something special.
3. Hi, we have not seen you for a long time, welcome.
4. Hello, you have come at the right time, we have just received. . . .
5. Hello, I noticed that you are wearing. . . .
6. Where did you get such a tan?
7. I will be with you in a moment.
8. Hello, is it still as nice out?
9. Hello, I saw you looking at our window display. (Ask customer what made her stop.)
10. Do you work in this mall? I see you regularly.
11. Hello, are you familiar with this label?
12. Hi, how is the weather out? Is it still as cold?
13. What a nice outfit you are wearing!
14. Hello, did you know that. . . . ?
15. Can I help you find your size?

APPENDIX B

Ten Guidelines for Good Listening*

1. **Stop talking.**
   You cannot listen if you are talking.
2. **Put the talker at ease.**
   Help him feel he is free to talk.
3. **Show him that you want to listen.**
   Look and act interested. Do not read your mail or perform other paperwork chores while he talks. Listen to understand rather than oppose.
4. **Remove distractions.**
   Don't doodle, tap, or shuffle papers.
5. **Empathize with the talker.**
   Try to put yourself in his place so that you can see his point of view.

*Marks & Spencer Management Training Guide, *Trainer's Package* (August 1989).

6. **Be patient.**
   Allow plenty of time. Do not interrupt him. Don't walk away.

7. **Hold your temper.**
   An angry person gets the wrong meaning from words.

8. **Go easy on argument and criticism which will put him on the defensive.**
   He may clam up or get angry. Don't argue; even if you win, you lose.

9. **Ask questions.**
   This encourages him and shows you are listening. It helps to develop points further.

10. **Stop talking.***
    This is the first and last, because all other guidelines depend on it. You cannot do a good listening job while you are talking.

---

*This is advisable when a customer interrupts you, agrees with you, acknowledges a thought from you, or is pleased by what you are selling.

Chapter 14

Display—Visual Merchandising

After completing this chapter, you should be able to:

- Identify and describe the two main types of displays: window and interior.
- Define and illustrate the differences between promotional and institutional displays.
- List guidelines for the following window display considerations: amount of merchandise, frequency of change, and planning.
- Discuss the differences between merchandise and point-of-purchase (P-O-P) displays.
- Identify those in retailing who are responsible for displays.
- List the guidelines for interior arrangement and display.

Display is still one of the most important communication devices available to retail management, and is one type of promotion that no store can do without. From the earliest days of retailing, merchants displayed their wares at fairs, in the marketplace, and even along highways so that passersby would stop, look, and buy. Merchants, of course, still display their wares, and while more sophisticated display techniques are used today, the objective is still stop, look, and buy.

A nonpersonal form of selling

Displays are a nonpersonal and unusual approach to the selling process. Through the use of windows, signs, and fixtures, the merchant tries to attract attention, create interest and desire, and prompt the shopper to inquire and buy.

As a promotional device, display involves two major categories: window display and interior display. In this chapter we present an overview and some basic principles of display.

WINDOW DISPLAYS

Window displays create the prospective customer's first impression of the store. Since this is so, shops make certain that their displays reflect their merchandise policies and store image. Effective window displays indicate the quality of merchandise handled, price lines, and whether the store is up to date. They add to the prestige of the store by including unusual creations and generate business in the same way that advertising does. For example, department stores in large cities often design windows that become tourist attractions during holiday seasons, especially the Christmas season.

Windows are "street theater"

Henri Bendel, one of New York City's trendier stores, is famous for its inventive windows. For example, exclusive designs were presented as though the store were a stage. Bendel's window displays were hailed as "street theater." One spring, during the Paris showings of fall styles, pictures of the parading models were flashed in disco style on a screen in a window. At another time Bendel promoted lingerie by means of a boudoir murder scene and generated a great deal of publicity.

Barneys, another retailer known for showmanlike displays, created quite a stir when its window featured one woman being sawed in half and another as a target of a knife thrower.

Windows are traffic builders

As a selling device, window displays attempt to draw people into a store and can become a round-the-clock sales force. In fact, many retailers consider window display space more valuable than advertising because they are nearer to the point of purchase. In addition, the actual merchandise can be displayed more dramatically through the use of mannequins, lighting, animation, and color. When used properly, window displays help tie in other advertising and promotional efforts. For some small stores, show windows are the chief means of creating traffic.

Some merchants consider modern glass fronts, through which passersby look directly into a store's interior, more valuable than street windows. In these cases the whole store interior becomes part of the "window display." The interaction of customers, merchandise, and salespeople produces a lively setting with lots of movement by day and, if lighted properly, an attention-getting scene at night.

Other positive features of glass fronts are the following.

1. They give the store more selling space.
2. They are easier and less expensive to maintain because they eliminate frequent display changes.

New approaches to construction in shopping centers have almost eliminated street windows. In these cases the store windows are built to face the inside of a mall or passageway. The store's exterior faces the parking lot and looks more like a warehouse than a store. Despite the waning interest in glass fronts, window shopping is still a popular activity in large cities where streets are known for their

This glass front allows passersby and shoppers to view the store's interior.
Courtesy: The Limited, Inc.

collections of unusual stores. These include Fifth Avenue in New York, Michigan Avenue in Chicago, Rodeo Drive in Beverly Hills, and Melrose Avenue in Los Angeles.

Window displays, like advertising, help draw people into the store. The window display should harmonize with the store's merchandising policies so that the store's image is clear in the consumer's mind. The window's selling message should reach passersby on sight. For example, many discounters display a sample of most of their items, with the implied message: "We have what you want at low prices." Supermarkets cover their windows with posters announcing specials— "Come in for bargains." Exclusive stores have windows that contain few items, the message being "This is expensive and unique." Some off-price retailers display fewer items than traditional discounters.

What Should Be Displayed

The merchandise displayed depends on the purpose of the display

If the purpose of a show window is to get people to stop and look, the window must attract attention to the displayed merchandise. Although an unlimited variety of arrangements is possible, they fall into two main categories: promotional and institutional. **Promotional displays** attempt to sell merchandise directly and dramatically by displaying

1. Products carried by the store, such as store or national brands.
2. Merchandise that requires great effort to be sold within a reasonable time.
3. New lines of merchandise.
4. Fast-selling lines.
5. Special items related to holidays, seasons, and the like.

Windows that sell the store

Institutional displays attempt to "sell" the store by building goodwill. Merchants often permit charities, schools, famous figures, or the arts to become the central themes of their windows. Customers react favorably to retail outlets that show community interest through their involvement in such activities as charity collections. When Lord & Taylor, for example, renovated its Manhattan flagship store, it removed all goods from the display windows and replaced them with large signs reading, "New York, We Love You."

How Much Should Be Displayed

Image quality versus quantity

A major display objective is to be consistent with the store's merchandising policy. For example, too much merchandise in the window creates an impression of low quality; too little creates an air of distinctiveness and high prices. If a store intends to emphasize bargains and appeal to a price-conscious customer, a considerable amount of merchandise may be shown in the window. This creates the impression that the store has almost everything the shopper may want at low prices. As noted previously, discounters display a little of almost all their merchandise, indicating that the goods are available and cheap. On the other hand, if the store's merchandise policy is to appeal to shoppers who are interested in quality, the quantity of merchandise displayed in windows will not be great. Prestige stores have smaller windows and display relatively few items, indicating that they carry expensive merchandise. For a department store with thousands of items and many departments, window treatments generally highlight merchandise in a fashionable way.

Displaying the merchandise at the right time

Displays should contain timely, coordinated merchandise that has been advertised in newspapers. Today's displays show related items and take advantage of seasonal events, utilizing thematic presentations such as "Easter Parade," "Back-to-School," and "Mother's Day." In addition, these displays "teach" customers how to put together the "look" of the season. Unusual effects are created through imaginative use of appropriate merchandise, fixtures, and mannequins. Creative use of props is often seen in the famous boxlike windows (shadow boxes) at Tiffany's. Such was the case when the Tiffany visual merchandiser made use of a toy truck dumping real sand in which a large diamond was displayed. Good taste in executing and designing displays adds to the total store image.

This Saks Fifth Avenue institutional display depicts the charm of a bygone Christmas. *Courtesy:* Saks Fifth Avenue.

Changing Window Displays

It is important for retailers to consider the frequency with which window displays should be changed. Windows can present a negative image if they are changed infrequently or appear outdated. Windows that become stale suggest an inefficient, stagnant business. The director of visual planning at Henri Bendel works with two assistants and seven free lancers every Wednesday night to decorate the windows: one assistant for the mannequins' hair, and the other for makeup.

Responsibility for window changes

Because window dressing is an art, most large stores assign regular staff members to this important aspect of retailing. Sometimes consultants are engaged to provide plans and materials for special occasions. Large stores plan their changes well in advance so that appropriate merchandise can be selected from the various departments. Usually each department is represented in window promotion at one time or another.

In some chain organizations display specialists are based at the central office. They plan and set up window displays, which are photographed for the various stores. The individual outlets reproduce the displays according to detailed instructions.

Small stores often engage the services of freelance display specialists, who come to the store either on a scheduled basis or when called.

J. C. Penney's instructions for a promotional window are clearly spelled out so that the display can be easily duplicated (see the accompanying photograph). As you can see, the theme, "Fur You," is developed with a snowstorm window effect, using snowy netting and snow floor covering as props.

Good fakes and the genuine article keep out the cold in the poshest possible way, and have a special gift appeal at Christmas. Jackets and full length coats are available in a variety of styles, from sporty to glamourous. Many have this year's wrap belt treatments.

window

Create the snow storm window with supplementals #628 (snowy netting) and #634 (snow floor covering). Add mannequin cards and sign theme with white slant back letters.

For interior mannequin presentation, show one jacket style along with one full coat style. Highlight display with the poinsettia supplemental.
lot numbers: 3907, 3906

J.C. Penney's instructions make it easy to duplicate promotional windows throughout the chain. *Courtesy:* J.C. Penney.

Guidelines for changing windows

There are guidelines which retailers can use to determine how often they should change their windows.

1. **The location and size of the store.** When the same people pass the store frequently, it is wise to change the windows often so that passersby see a variety of merchandise and paying attention to the window becomes a habit.
2. **The pedestrian traffic.** Stores located in large cities are generally exposed to a variety of pedestrians. In these instances a display has a longer "life." Many large stores located in cities change their windows as often as twice a week. Others change them once a week. The value of window displays to the retailer is realized by frequent changes. Small stores should change their displays more often than stores in regional shopping centers because they probably experience the same pedestrian traffic repeatedly.
3. **The types of goods sold.** Fashion merchandise is considered "perishable," and displays of such goods should be changed often. Because fashion-conscious customers are interested in new and different items, styles that are displayed too long become "stale" and lose their appeal. Furniture and hardware displays, on the other hand, are changed less frequently.

Planning Window Displays

Planning allows the retailer to coordinate window displays with other promotional activities. For example, if it is determined that merchandise featured in advertising should also be displayed in the window, advance planning is vital. Visual planning at Henri Bendel is prepared 13 weeks ahead of its actual execution. The director of visual planning meets four times a year with the store president and the store manager. The main considerations for such planning are as follows.

1. Set a policy regarding the relationship between newspaper advertising and the merchandise to be displayed.
2. Set a policy regarding price tags and printed messages in the window.
3. Set a policy with regard to the use of manufacturer displays. While vendor-supplied materials can be helpful to small merchants, they should be selected to tie in with store image.
4. Set a frequency of window changes policy so that displays that should remain longer will have the proper time allotted to them.
5. Schedule window displays in larger stores to give the various departments proper representation.

Planning should consider departments' needs

6. Set a policy with regard to informing salespeople about displayed merchandise. Too often salespeople are not aware of what is "advertised" in the store's windows.

In addition to the considerations just noted, Figure 14-1 lists the guidelines for window displays suggested by the U.S. Small Business Administration.

I. MERCHANDISE SELECTED

1. Is the merchandise timely?
2. Is it representative of the stock assortment?
3. Are the articles harmonious—in type, color, texture, and use?
4. Are the price lines of the merchandise suited to the interests of passersby?
5. Is the quantity on display suitable (that is, neither overcrowded nor sparse)?

II. SETTING

1. Are glass, floor, props, and merchandise clean?
2. Is the lighting adequate (so that reflection from the street is avoided)?
3. Are spotlights used to highlight certain parts of the display?
4. Is every piece of merchandise carefully draped, pinned, or arranged?
5. Is the background suitable, enhancing the merchandise?
6. Are the props well suited to the merchandise?
7. Are window cards used, and are they neat and well placed?
8. Is the entire composition balanced?
9. Does the composition suggest rhythm and movement?

III. SELLING POWER

1. Does the window present a readily recognized central theme?
2. Does the window exhibit have power to stop passersby through the dramatic use of light, color, size, motion, composition, and/or item selection?
3. Does the window arouse a desire to buy (as measured by shoppers entering the store)?

Figure 14-1 Guidelines for a window display. *Source:* U.S. Small Business Administration, *Small Store Planning for Growth,* 2nd ed., Small Business Management Series, no. 33. (Washington, D.C., U.S. Government Printing Office, 1977), p. 77.

INTERIOR DISPLAYS

When customers enter a store, they expect the displays and departments to reflect the store's image. In addition to the decor and furnishings, the general tone or atmosphere of the store is set by the merchandise arrangements, displays, and fixtures. While **interior displays** can take a variety of forms, depending on the merchandise carried and the store's image, the entire interior should be considered from the point of view of promoting sales.

**Self-service
increases
the importance of
interior displays**

Though the value of window displays has been questioned by some retailers, interior displays have become more important with the growth of self-service. In stores where self-service is the key factor in sales, it is the interior display that has to "sell" the merchandise. Good displays are very effective in

Mannequins—a basic fixture in retail merchandising—become uncannily realistic with a few finishing touches. *Courtesy:* Neiman Marcus.

Merchandise settings often reflect the latest trends in interior design. Custom furniture can be found in the men's department at the A & S Manhattan market place. *Courtesy:* A & S.

Capturing the customer's imagination is a hallmark of successful retailing.
Courtesy: Neiman Marcus.

Self-service displays help promote sales. *Courtesy:* Wal-Mart.

creating product awareness and stimulating unplanned purchases (impulse buying). In these cases interior displays rely on the use of descriptive signs and informative labels to encourage customers to try a product. The arrangement of merchandise requires the display of related product lines in settings that interest the customer. For maximum success, supermarkets, variety stores, drugstores, and hardware stores generally coordinate their displays with their advertising.

Interior displays can be classified in two main categories: **merchandise displays** and vendor or store **point-of-purchase (POP) displays.**

Merchandise Displays

Merchandise displays are of several types.

- **Open displays** are shown on tables, carts, and baskets. These displays are designed to make the merchandise accessible to the customer by allowing handling of the products. Sometimes the merchandise is heaped in a pile without any real order (**dump display**). The psychological effect is that the items are available at bargain prices.
- **Closed displays** contain more valuable items like jewelry, cameras, silver, and antiques. The products are behind glass and may be handled only by a salesperson.
- **End-aisle displays** are placed in vacant areas at the ends of aisles in supermarkets, variety stores, and the like and generally carry advertised specials.

The total compatibility of product packaging and environment is evident in the Food Preparation Shop of Sears remerchandised store. *Courtesy:* Sears, Roebuck.

- **Related-merchandise displays,** found in such stores as supermarkets and drugstores, contain arrangements with matching products (e.g., cheese and crackers, pasta and sauces).

- **Area displays** are set up for special lifestyle merchandising or long-term displays such as model rooms in a furniture department or sports equipment (with related clothing) on a seasonal basis. The latter may include ski equipment and clothes for winter, tennis accessories and clothes for spring and summer, and so forth.

- **Special-event displays** are used by department stores and mass merchandisers for thematic storewide promotions. For example, a department store promotion of items imported from China might feature Chinese wares throughout the store, from clothing to gift items, while a supermarket might carry "health foods" in every department.

- **Checkout counter displays** are the last opportunity to communicate with shoppers. These up-front displays always feature "impulse items" close to the cashier and usually contain things like magazines, candy, and cigarettes.

- **Assortment displays** show a complete line of merchandise in depth, including colors, sizes, styles, and prices. The advantages of assortment displays are that they enable customers to help themselves and to make selections quickly.

- **Theme displays** are designed around an idea, such as "Back to School" and "Hunting Season on." The theme should stimulate the interest of consumers.

Theme display. *Courtesy:* Marks & Spencer.

- **Ensemble displays** are those in which the item to be promoted is combined with related merchandise for a complete effect. For example, swimsuits shown in an ensemble display can be combined with robes, slippers, beach hats, and the like.

Good planning is the key for effective store displays. *Courtesy:* J.C. Penney.

RETAIL STRATEGY

Retailers and manufacturers recognize that in-store vendor shops (boutiques) increase sales. With vendors like Liz Claiborne, Esprit, and Ralph Lauren, retailers are just as eager to display the manufacturer-specific shops as they are their own names. When introduced years ago, these shops were treated as extensions of their visual merchandising programs and were generally located in designer and better-price areas. The idea was to add exclusive specialty store environments. Today, the concept is also used with moderate-priced or better goods because visually-attractive selling environments encourage buying. Shops are considered a prime vehicle for creating dynamic visual impact and are part of both merchants' and vendors' marketing plans. Liz Claiborne, a pioneer in in-store vendor shops, offers a breadth of products, while Leslie Fay, a comparative newcomer, introduced the shop concept in moderate-priced departments. In men's wear, Levi's Docker shops have created a strong enough demand to justify its space allocation. According to Levi executives, goods sell better than when placed on regular fixtures.

In creating these shops, there must be special fixturing to differentiate the areas from other parts of the department. Brand identification must be highly visible, and strong displays must help customers visualize their use of the products. This concept has also been adopted by Gitano, a manufacturer that offers mass merchandisers varied products for women.

Point-of-Purchase Displays

POP displays are sponsored by vendors

In-store displays are planned to stimulate customers to buy or to inquire about a product. They encourage unplanned purchases and are largely decorative. Many of these displays are supplied by manufacturers and are a key element of sales promotion.

Point-of-purchase displays are structures or devices that are used in, on, or adjacent to any point of sale. They are usually planned by manufacturers to increase sales of their products at the store. The following are examples of the most commonly used POP displays.

- **On-the-shelf displays** utilize shelf space as the basis for displaying merchandise. Included in this group are "shelf talkers," dividers, and extenders. Shelf talkers provide an on-the-spot communication utilizing signs like SPECIAL, LOW PRICE, or TODAY ONLY. Dividers are constructed so that when they are placed on a shelf the products are displayed at a favorable angle. Extenders are secured at the ends of shelves to create more space.
- **Mobiles** are displays hung from beams on the ceiling. As the name implies, they move and attract attention.
- **Cut-case displays** are packing boxes that are really self-contained displays. By means of cutting and folding, these cases are easily converted into display

units. Retailers appreciate them because they can be displayed immediately, do not require shelf space, and provide a colorful display of the product.

- **Catchall displays** are large containers, such as barrels, baskets, and carts, that hold large quantities of one kind of merchandise. The careless manner in which the merchandise is "dumped" into the container implies that it is a bargain. These units are generally displayed in food, drug, and discount houses.

- **Display stands** are a more permanent kind of self-service display that carry such items as paperback books. They come in various heights and are often made so that they can be rotated by the customer. Retailers like these displays because they are attractive, store a great deal of merchandise, and occupy little space. Furthermore, they often help the retailer convert unused space into a profitable merchandising area.

- **Counter displays** are used in areas where it is easy to sell related merchandise. The more elaborate ones are used in department stores and specialty shops to "suggest" additional items, for example, on counters where costume jewelry is sold. In other areas a counter display may be a simple poster at a checkout counter where impulse items are sold.

POP displays are tied to store image

POP materials are used a good deal with other sales aids, such as coupons, to generate excitement about a product. Because such materials have been so successful, merchants should find out what POP material is available from their suppliers. Manufacturers are more than eager to supply these displays because they mean more sales. Nevertheless, it is important for the merchant to evaluate the use of these displays in terms of store image. Other considerations are the amount of selling space they occupy relative to sales and the cost in terms of lighting needs.

Kiosks

Kiosks are freestanding booths that display and make specialized product lines available for sale. One such example is the Portable Store, a $10 million chain, with a unique market niche. It merchandises small carry-out impulse items like telephones, personal radios, and pocket computers in the $50–200 range. Its stores, spotted in malls, are kiosks averaging 450 square feet.

Kiosks as self-service displays

Interactive kiosks display products and related information on a video screen. Consumers can actually place orders and, with the use of a credit card, complete transactions and have goods mailed to them. This kind of display will be important for retailers planning to enter the European market in 1992. Interactive kiosks, which have already been used by such chains as Sears, Phar-Mor, Pace, and Woolworth Express, may help American marketers overcome language problems and provide shoppers with product-selection guidance. According to some marketers, these kiosks are wonderful self-service displays and can provide in-store merchandising information for the European community.

Kiosks are versatile and can be stationed in most malls, stores, airports, etcetera. In the early 1990s, kiosks are expected to generate several hundred million dollars in sales in the United States, with more than 20,000 of them in operation.

Responsibility for Display

In small stores, the responsibility for displays generally lies with the owner or an assistant. In department stores, the responsibility may rest with the display manager, who, in turn, is supervised by the sales promotion director. In some cases stores have resident window display directors as well as interior display directors. Display personnel, also known as visual merchandisers, dressers, or trimmers, have workshops in the store in which they plan and construct instore displays. They generally have a stock of fixtures and mannequins as well as appropriate background props. In addition, there are many kinds of shelving,

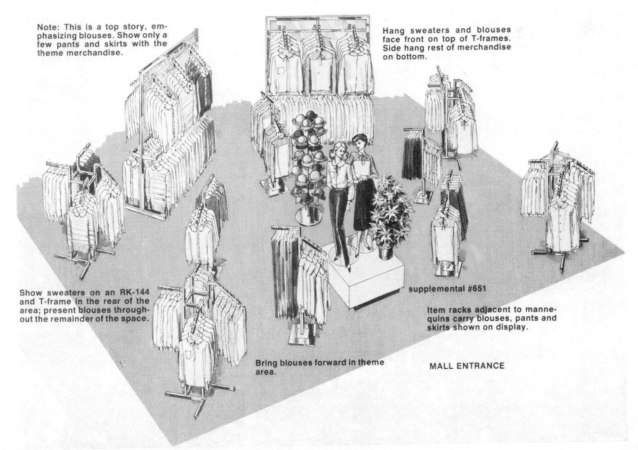

Figure 14-2 Instructions for a store entrance in a mall, illustrating display racks, mannequins, and merchandise. Reproduced by permission of J.C. Penney.

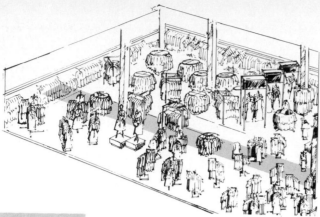

interior aisles

Interior aisles play an important role in outerwear, as in all other fashion departments:
- department store image
- easy for the customer to shop
- make a clear passage for rolling racks, as well as customers

Interior aisles are particularly important for **deep departments,** **breaking up** the **wide** expanse of **carpet** and **allowing more merchandise exposure.**

OUTERWEAR	DRESSES	LARGE SIZES	MISSES SPORTSWEAR

MAIN AISLE

the aisle story

create departments in the children's area
- Using aisles in the children's area provides maximum customer exposure for all age groups.
- Utilize fashion racks (4-way, item, tri-circle) in the forward section of each area, creating "windows-on-the-aisles."
- Highlight each department with a coordinated mannequin display.

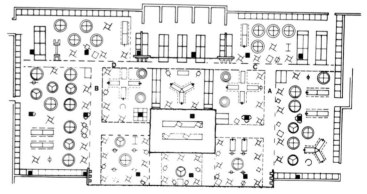

Figure 14-3 Instructions for arranging interior aisles; creating departments by using aisles, racks, and mannequins; and using fixtures and racks to group outerwear. Reproduced by permission of J.C. Penney.

aisle leading to boys' pre-school area

aisle leading to girls' pre-school area

brackets, and display holders that can be used. A creative display artist looks for unique items like an old ship's wheel, a Chinese screen, or a fisherman's net.

Many of the large retail chains distribute detailed display information to their individual branches or stores. Displays are planned, photographed, and diagrammed for the individual stores. This reduces the cost of large display staffs and saves time in the execution of displays. Complete instructions and layouts are sent to the general merchandise manager, the buyer, and the presentation supervisor. Figures 14-2, 14-3, and 14-4 show diagrams, instructions, and fixtures for effective displays.

Some chain stores have crews of window trimmers who travel from one location to another. In these cases the central office usually coordinates all the materials in advance so as to provide directions to the various outlets. Some large chains hire outside consultants and agencies.

Very often supermarket chains give store managers detailed plans showing exactly where each product belongs on the shelf. The most profitable and fastest-moving items are placed at eye level to make them easy for shoppers to reach. Studies indicate that more products are picked up from eye-level shelves than from any other type of shelf. It is not by chance for example that the most popular brands of soap and expensive cheeses are usually displayed at eye level.

Figure 14-5 contains guidelines for interior arrangement and display.

fixtures

R-967A

RK-137

DC-241

DC-274

metro stores/issued march '80   outerwear   page 7

avoid

• merchandising both half and petite sizes on one rack, as it can be misleading and very difficult for the customer to shop.

Figure 14-4   How to display merchandise and what arrangements to avoid. The correct fixtures to use are indicated clearly. Reproduced by permission of J.C. Penney.

I. LAYOUT

1. Are your fixtures low enough and signs so placed that the customer can get a bird's-eye view of the store and tell in what direction to go for wanted goods?
2. Do your aisle and counter arrangements tend to stimulate a circular traffic flow through the store?
3. Do your fixtures (and their arrangement), signs, lettering, and colors all create a coordinated and unified effect?
4. Before any supplier's fixtures are accepted, do you make sure they conform in color and design to what you already have?
5. Do you limit the use of hanging signs to special sale events?
6. Are your counters and aisle tables *not* overcrowded with merchandise?
7. Are your ledges and cashier/wrapping stations kept free of boxes, unneeded wrapping materials, personal effects, and odds and ends?
8. Do you keep trash bins out of sight?

II. MERCHANDISE EMPHASIS

1. Do your signs referring to specific goods tell the customer something significant about them, rather than simply naming the products and their prices?
2. For your advertised goods, do you have prominent signs, including tear sheets at the entrances, to inform and guide customers to their exact location in the store?
3. Do you prominently display both advertised and nonadvertised specials at the ends of counters as well as at the point of sale?
4. Are both your national and private brands highlighted in your arrangement and window display?
5. Wherever feasible, do you give the more colorful merchandise in your stock preference in display?
6. In the case of apparel and home furnishings, do the items that reflect your store's fashion sense or fashion leadership get special display attention at all times?
7. In locating merchandise in your store, do you always consider the productivity of space—vertical as well as horizontal?
8. Is your self-service merchandise arranged so as to attract the customer and assist in selection by the means indicated below?

Figure 14-5 Guidelines for interior arrangement and display. *Source:* U.S. Small Business Administration, *Small Store Planning for Growth,* 2nd ed., Small Business Management Series, no. 33. (Washington, D.C., U.S. Government Printing Office, 1977), pp. 101–102.

a. Is each category grouped under a separate sign?

b. Is the merchandise in each category arranged according to its most significant characteristic—whether color, style, size, or price?

c. In apparel categories, is the merchandise arranged by price lines or zones to assist the customer to make a selection quickly?

d. Is horizontal space usually devoted to different items and styles within a category (vertical space being used for different sizes—smallest at the top, largest at the bottom)?

e. Are impulse items interspaced with demand items and *not* placed across the aisle from them, where many customers will not see them?

9. Do you plan your windows and displays in advance?

10. Do you meet with your sales force after windows are trimmed to discuss the items displayed?

11. Do you use seasonal, monthly, and weekly plans for interior and window displays, determining the fixtures to be used and merchandise to be displayed?

12. Do your displays reflect the image of your store?

13. Do you budget the dollars you will set aside for fixtures and props to be used in your displays, as well as the expense of setting them up and maintaining them?

14. Do you keep your fixtures and windows clean and dust free?

15. Do you replace burned-out light bulbs immediately?

16. Do you take safety precautions in setting up your fixtures?

17. Do garments fit properly on mannequins and fixtures?

Figure 14-5   Continued

NEW TERMS

area display	display stand
assortment display	dump display
catchall display	end-aisle display
checkout counter display	ensemble display
closed display	institutional display
counter display	interactive kiosk
cut-case display	interior display
display	kiosk

merchandise display   promotional display
mobile   related-merchandise display
on-the-shelf display   special-event display
open display   theme display
point-of-purchase (POP) display window display

CHAPTER HIGHLIGHTS

1. Display is a nonpersonal approach to the selling process. Through the use of windows, signs, and fixtures, the retailer attempts to attract attention, create interest, stimulate desire, and prompt the shopper to buy.

2. As a promotional device, display involves two major categories: window display and interior display.

3. Window displays are a reflection of the store, including its merchandise policies and image. As a selling device, window displays draw people into a store and are considered by some retailers to be more valuable than advertising.

4. In recent years many retailers have switched from street windows to modern glass fronts. These retailers feel that it is valuable for potential customers to see movement inside the store.

5. Window displays are generally planned to promote specific merchandise (promotional) or the store itself (institutional).

6. Because window dressing is an art, most large stores have regular staff assigned to plan and execute their displays.

7. Displays should be attractive, imaginative, and timely and should be changed frequently. They should be coordinated with other promotional activities.

8. Interior displays are of two types: merchandise and point-of-purchase.

9. Manufacturers frequently supply retailers with display materials. Retailers must select those that tie in with the merchandise and services offered by the store.

10. Some vendor displays, such as shelf talkers, dividers, and extenders, help retailers get the most mileage out of their shelf space. In addition, display stands enable retailers to convert unused floor space into profitable merchandising areas.

11. Kiosks and interactive kiosks are versatile structures and can be situated most anywhere. According to some marketers, they are wonderful self-service displays and provide valuable in-store merchandising information.

12. The responsibility for display varies with different types of retailers. Some stores have resident display staffs and in-house workshops, while others use consultants. Some chains have floating crews that travel from one unit to another, while others plan and design displays in the central office. Under these conditions detailed layouts and photographs are distributed to the individual stores for execution.

REVIEW QUESTIONS

1. In what types of stores do we still see merchants displaying their wares as they did in the early days of retailing?
2. Explain the statement, "Window displays play a role similar to advertising." Why do some retailers consider window displays more valuable than advertising?
3. How can retailers use displays to communicate the types of merchandise and services they offer?
4. What are the basic considerations for creating an effective display?
5. How do POP displays help the retailer?
6. Explain how centralized planning for displays is carried out in a chain's local units.
7. In what types of stores do you think kiosks will be most successful? Explain.

DISCUSSION QUESTIONS

1. How does window display affect store image? In terms of display, how do retailers communicate whether theirs are low- or high-priced stores?
2. In light of the increase in self-service shopping, what type of display would be effective for a new line of cosmetics targeted to the 18–25 age range?
3. Why have stores changed their merchandise presentations and layouts to allow customers to help themselves?
4. What factors should the retailer consider before using vendor displays?

CASE 1

All that Meets the Eye

Supermarkets are experimenting with the positioning of products to maximize purchases by shoppers of both sexes. The most profitable and fastest-moving products are placed at eye level to make them easy for shoppers to reach. Studies indicate that more items are picked from eye-level shelves than from any others. Because of this, supermarkets and food stores generally display popular brands of detergents, expensive gourmet foods, and imported cheeses at eye level.

Supermarket professionals have some difficulty deciding what should be considered eye-level shelving. The eye-level shelf has traditionally been slightly under 5 feet from the floor, which is the right height for the average female shopper (5 feet 4 inches). However, supermarket studies indicate that more men are shopping than ever before. In one recent study, men did the family food shopping in almost 30 percent of the households. This is not surprising, considering that more than half of the adult women in the United States work all or part of each day.

Since the average male shopper is about 5 feet 10 inches tall, to accommodate males an eye-level shelf would need to be higher than the former standard. The shift in shopping practices has caused planners of supermarket chains to reconsider display positions for many products. One supermarket professional said, "This problem is driving us mad. We have changed the position of Best crackers five times this month, and we still can't figure out where to put them."

Even though the majority of shoppers are women, men almost make up for the difference by making a greater number of impulse purchases. Generally speaking, when a woman goes to a supermarket for a few items, she usually ends up buying eight or ten. On the other hand, a man usually walks out of the store with twice as many impulse purchases. This may be so because men use shopping lists less than half as often as women.

It is easy to see why supermarket planners are anxious to display popular foods on the shelves that will catch the eye of "impulsive male shoppers." At the same time, however, they do not want to place those products out of reach of female shoppers.

a. What suggestions do you have for eye-level displays in supermarkets?
b. Should displays be geared to men and women separately? What types of displays do you recommend?

CASE 2

POP

Retailers constantly seek ways to boost sales of the goods in their stores. Similarly, the manufacturers and wholesalers who supply retailers also seek to increase the volume of orders.

Over the last several years, there has been a marked increase in the kinds of point of purchase display devices designed, it is claimed, to increase sales in the retail setting. These include floor displays (end-cap or aisle-end display), dump bins, shelf talkers, over aisle display, and promotional display on shopping carts.

These various forms of POP displays are supplied by the vendors. For large retailers, like a supermarket chain, the devices are often supplied free of charge and sometimes the goods displayed are offered at a discount. But small retailers must pay for the displays installed in their stores, and the amount of money can be considerable, depending on how elaborate the display is.

Large retailers can also devote considerable time and effort developing for themselves the kinds of POP display that aid their sales and test the prototypes before installing such displays throughout all their stores. At K mart, for example, the modular displays incorporating cubes and end caps now in place permit the display of more goods per square foot and have helped raise sales per square foot of selling space. Small retailers, however, usually cannot spare the time or funds to determine the effectiveness of promotional displays. They generally rely on articles in journals and trade papers, on other retailers, or on the vendors themselves for such information. And vendors often make grandiose claims for their POP displays' effectiveness in increasing sales. Although claims can tend to be exaggerated, POP displays are considered to have the advantages of providing a narrow focus for a product, to offer precise targeting of people who want the product and have the money to buy it, to facilitate impulse purchases, and to appeal to busy consumers who have little time to shop.

Although data are not readily available or very extensive, the studies that are available tend to support the contention that POP displays are effective.

For example, a study was conducted for a pharmaceutical manufacturer on the effectiveness of floor displays in increasing sales of an antibiotic ointment.* The store sampling represented chain grocery stores and both chain and independent pharmacies.

The study was divided into three phases, each lasting two weeks. For one two-week period, the floor displays were placed in the first aid section of half the participating stores and in the baby section of the remaining half of the stores. Then the displays were shifted to a high-volume location in all of the stores for two weeks. During the first or last phase of the study, no floor displays were used. The ointment was stocked in its usual shelf or gondola space.

The study found that the use of the floor displays boosted average sales in the grocery stores and in the drugstores approximately 388 percent and 107 percent, respectively. The high volume locations performed best in all three types of stores: There was no appreciable difference in units sold from a display in the first aid section or in the baby section. Stores that showed an increase of 100 percent or better on display sales over shelf sales were high volume units and thus high traffic

*Jean Paul Gagnon and Jane T. Osterhaus, "Research Note: Effectiveness of Floor Displays on the Sales of Retail Products," *Journal of Retailing*, **61** (Spring 1985), pp. 104–115.

units to begin with. These stores also placed the displays near the cash register at the front of the store. The study concluded that

> Floor displays significantly affect the number of units of a product sold; store managers know their store's high volume locations, and these locations increase a display's effectiveness; [and] the floor displays did not generate sales at the expense of shelf sales.

Such information and validation are useful to both manufacturer and retailer. Not only are the costs of the displays themselves rising at a rapid rate (and therefore the amount of money that a small retailer must pay for a display), but the volume of POP material available to retail store managers is overwhelming. As the number of consumer products continues to grow and competition for shelf and display space continues to intensify, retailers need to be as well informed as possible in order to select the best display options for their operations and to negotiate advantageously with vendors.

a. What questions do you think a retail store manager should ask before deciding to install a POP display?

b. Using the study cited as a guideline, where is the most desirable location for a floor display of nonprescription headache pills in a small grocery store? Would the same location be best for a floor display of another item, such as pantyhose? If you, as a small retailer, wanted to display both the headache pills and the pantyhose, where would you position the display of each item? What factors would influence your decision?

c. What social or economic changes in the customer base do you think contribute to the effectiveness of a POP display?

REFERENCES

ADLER, F. M. "No Shock." *Stores*, **65** (December 1983), pp. 40–47.

FUDA, G. E., AND E. L. NELSON. *The Display Specialist*. (New York: McGraw-Hill, 1976).

GAGNON, J. P., AND J. T. OSTERHAUS. "Effectiveness of Floor Displays on the Sales of Retail Producers." *Journal of Retailing*, **61** (Spring 1985), pp. 104–116.

ROSENWEIN, R. "Whir, Click, Thanks: Merchandisers Turn to Electronic Salesmen in 24-Hour Kiosks." *The Wall Street Journal* (June 23, 1986), p. 23.

"Third Quake in Store Competition: Power Retailing." *Inside Retailing*, Special Report from *Inside Retailing* (June 25, 1984).

Chapter 15

Advertising

After completing this chapter, you should be able to:

- Define advertising and identify the types of advertising used by retailers.
- Discuss the importance of the advertising plan and the setting of objectives.
- Discuss the importance of the advertising budget and how it is used.
- List and explain the advantages and disadvantages to the retailer of the following media: newspapers, magazines, direct mail, telephone directories and Yellow Pages, flyers, radio, television, outdoor, and transit.
- Explain how retailers evaluate the impact and value of their advertising efforts.

Throughout history retailers have advertised in order to increase sales and store traffic. After the Civil War, merchants concentrated on the use of advertising to bring in the local trade. By the 1880s and 1890s, both local and national media were experiencing tremendous growth because of retail advertising.

Marshall Field's approach was expressed by the slogans, "Give the lady what she wants" and "The customer is always right." The Wanamaker company advertised that it consistently followed "the golden rule of business," and John Wanamaker became identified with business virtues.

A large part of Macy's success is credited to aggressive pricing policies that became well known because of advertising. The store's first single-price ad appeared in 1851.

Huntington Hartford and George Gilman, the founders of A&P, advertised their imported tea at "**cargo prices.**"[1] They had these ads printed in circulars and then through newspapers and the mail. They, too, offered money-back guarantees and became known for low prices. Advertised "cargo prices" became synonymous with discounting or lower prices.

ADVERTISING DEFINED

In today's market merchants are still trying to attract as many consumers as possible through **advertising.** The American Marketing Association defines advertising as "any paid form of nonpersonal presentation and promotion of ideas, goods, or services by an identified sponsor." The key terms in the definition are

- **Paid form** The retailer pays for the message so that it will be read in newspapers, magazines, etcetera; viewed on television, movie screens, etcetera; or listened to on the radio and other broadcast devices. The advertiser-retailer controls the placement and content of the message.

- **Nonpersonal** There is no face-to-face communication as in a salesperson-customer transaction. The selling message is communicated through newspapers, radio, television, and other media.

- **Identified sponsor** The name and location of the business or person paying for the advertisement are included.

---

[1] The genesis of the A&P chain was the buying of clipper ship cargoes of tea and reselling them at low or cargo prices.

TYPES OF RETAIL ADVERTISING

The primary function of advertising is to bring customers to a store

Retailers use different kinds of advertising to attract attention to their store, services, and merchandise. These include institutional, promotional, combination, and cooperative advertising.

Institutional Advertising

Some ads sell the store

Institutional advertising attempts to convey an idea about the store. Basically, it is designed to "sell" the entire concept of the store and its image rather than a particular type of merchandise. In fact, some marketers refer to it as image advertising.

When retailers advertise "institutionally" they aim for long-range sales results as opposed to direct sales action. These advertisements concentrate on building the reputation of the store, focusing on unique qualities and services. They help create customer confidence in the store. While some advertisements attempt to build an image of fashion leadership, others stress unique services. In either case, marketing the total store is as important as advertising certain items. For example, during the campaign to restore the Statue of Liberty and Ellis Island, Strawbridge & Clothier advertised an appeal for help in a full-page ad. A patriotic gesture like this creates goodwill toward the store.

A subtle approach to the use of institutional advertising is illustrated by the Southland Corporation. This retailer, owner of the 7-Eleven convenience store chain, features a new theme, "7-Eleven—The Sign of the Times," on spot TV commercials, radio, outdoor advertising, and point-of-purchase materials. This campaign is a change for the 7-Eleven stores. Instead of emphasizing the store or a product, ads focus on the consumer by establishing "an emotional bond" between the two. Spots feature how 7-Eleven fits into people's lifestyles as a convenient, everyday shopping provider rather than as an emergency stop.

Promotional Advertising

Day-to-day advertising

Promotional advertising is routine advertising that attempts to sell specific items or services and is designed to bring customers to a store for immediate action. Retailers depend on this type of advertisement for their day-to-day traffic and sales. Therefore, the bulk of retail advertising is promotional in nature. This category includes advertisements for specific items, special sales, special events, and new items and services.

Sears has embarked on an extensive advertising program to change its image from a full-priced merchant to a merchant with lower prices. The theme of "Everyday Low Prices" is featured in the United States through newspapers, television, and radio. Sears is the nation's number one retail advertiser, with an annual advertising budget in excess of a billion dollars.

Three cheers for the Red, White and Blue

With great pride, we salute our troops, and those of other Allied Forces in the Middle East, for their courage, tenacity and determination in the pursuit of freedom.

We are inspired by the willingness and sacrifice of our service men and women, who have put their lives on the line to defend the rights of humankind.

We are thankful that this mission for liberty in the Persian Gulf was relatively swift, and that our spouses, fathers, mothers, sons, daughters and dear friends will soon be home.

We are saddened at the loss or injury of those who fought for freedom and offer our condolences and prayers to their loved ones.

We fly our flags high and anxiously await the day when we will welcome our soldiers with open arms and untie our yellow ribbons.

We hope and pray for a long and lasting peace in the Middle East, and throughout the world. For it is only through commitment, communication and understanding that we can make this a better world for all people.

Strawbridge & Clothier institutional ad saluting the success of our troops in the Persian Gulf. This ad strengthens the store's image with customers in Philadelphia and the surrounding communities. *Courtesy:* Strawbridge & Clothier.

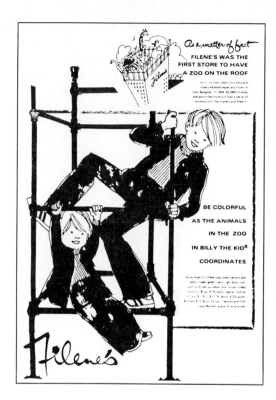

This combination ad is selling apparel by using a human interest story. *Courtesy:* Filene's.

Combination Advertising

Institutional and promotional advertising combined

As the name implies, **combination advertising** combines the functions of promotional and institutional advertising. It advertises a specific item or service for immediate results and builds a favorable image of the store as well. For example, while advertising air conditioners and fans, in the same ad a store may include a list of hints about saving energy and staying cool.

Filene's developed a series of combination ads that were most effective. For a set of apparel ads it used a format highlighting important fashion stories. At the top of the advertisement was a human interest story about why Filene's is considered progressive and innovative. As an illustration, one ad indicated that Filene's was "the first store to have a zoo on the roof." (At the top was a picture of the Filene zoo, and a part of the ad showed children's fashions.) Another read, "In 1913 Filene's opened Boston's first commercial wireless station." These ads demonstrate how combination advertising can sell specific merchandise and the store simultaneously. Combined promotional and institutional advertising has become very popular and appears to be on the rise.

Cooperative Advertising

Shared costs of advertising

When retailers share the costs of advertising with manufacturers, suppliers, or other merchants, it is known as **cooperative advertising.** Such ads can be arranged either vertically or horizontally. Under a vertical cooperative advertising agreement, manufacturers or suppliers pay part of the costs for featuring specified items or brands. Retailers are reimbursed after the ads have been printed or aired. Invoices or documents from the media, such as **tear sheets** (advertising cutouts), are required to substantiate the publication of the advertisements. In some cases the manufacturer supplies a variety of aids to the retailer, such as completed artwork and advertising copy containing open space for the retailer's name.

Horizontal arrangements increase traffic and product demand

In a horizontal cooperative advertising agreement, several retailers sponsor and pay for the costs of advertising to increase traffic to an area or increase the demand for a product. Groups of merchants in shopping centers often sponsor ads jointly in order to draw people to the center. To stimulate demand for certain items, merchants carrying the same product lines in noncompeting areas frequently sponsor ads jointly in order to spread product awareness.

Of the estimated $11 billion a year manufacturers budget for co-op advertising, approximately 60 percent is actually spent. Retailers are making greater demands and manufacturers are beginning to shape cooperative advertising into a tool that helps them meet those demands and still get their message across to consumers. Manufacturers are trying to channel money where it will stimulate sales for their brands. Consequently, they are offering incentives to retailers in targeted regional areas. For example, Sears, in its Brand Central format, has used cooperative advertising dollars for brand name appliances and electronic gear alongside its private-label goods.

Robinson-Patman Act treats small buyers in the same way as large buyers

Manufacturers encourage large retailers to participate in joint advertising more than they do small merchants, partly because it is more costly to administer cooperative advertising programs when many small merchants are involved. However, the Robinson-Patman Act requires sellers to give the same allowance for promotion to all buyers on a ''proportionately equal basis.'' Therefore, if a seller gives a large department store chain a 5 percent advertising allowance, all other buyers (large and small) are entitled to the same arrangement. However, many small retailers are unaware of this money or do not know how to apply for it.

It is predicted that cooperative advertising in local media will increase for several reasons. First, the cost of advertising can probably be reduced for small retailers. Second, many newspapers and radio stations have added staff members to coordinate cooperative advertising funds. In this way small retailers will have help in finding and using money for advertising.

Retailers must look at the total picture before they join a cooperative-advertising venture. For example, the availability of co-op advertising may play a role in merchandise and vendor selection. This may or may not be in the retailer's interest. Listed here are some of the important advantages and disadvantages of such ventures.

ADVANTAGES OF COOPERATIVE ADVERTISING

- Cooperative advertising reduces costs.
- Small retailers are provided with professional ads.
- Small stores are helped to build a prestige image.

Natural Russian Golden Sable

Alixandre

This promotional ad is an example of cooperative advertising. *Courtesy:* Alixandre Furs, Inc.

- Bargaining power with media is increased due to greater quantity.
- The store message reaches a greater number of prospects.
- A positive relationship between suppliers and merchants is promoted.

DISADVANTAGES OF COOPERATIVE ADVERTISING

Cooperative advertising is not feasible for all retailers

- There is less control and flexibility.
- Ads prepared for national coverage may not fit local situations.
- Ads may not fit a store's image.
- Reimbursement is not immediate; the retailer must submit media invoices to suppliers.
- The program may require additional investment in merchandise.

RETAIL STRATEGY
Drive Toward Image Marketing

Major department store chains such as Bloomingdale's, J. C. Penney, and Neiman-Marcus appear to be opening their doors to new marketing strategies that will shape their images during the 1990s. They are building their images with such tactics as new ad strategies, remodeled stores, and a more select grouping of merchandise.

The 1990s will feature a stronger drive toward image-building advertising rather than price promotion ads. Image advertising (institutional advertising) will stress the store, customer service, and a pleasant shopping experience.

THE ADVERTISING PLAN

Retailers that conduct advertising programs must consider what they want to accomplish, how much money they have to work with, and how to reach the widest possible market. In other words, merchants must determine the overall objectives, the budget, and the types of media to use. These make up the **advertising plan.**

Objectives

Develop a profile of the store and its customers

The desired objectives are the results that merchants want to achieve through an advertising program. These include increasing sales and profits, maintaining loyal customers, and attracting additional customers with appropriate offerings. In order to do so, merchants need answers to such questions as

- What is the store's main business?
- What kind of image does the store project?

- What kind of image do we want to project?
- What quality of merchandise does the store carry?
- How does the store compare with its competition?
- What customer services does the store offer?
- Who are the store's steady customers?
- What are the customer's tastes and income levels?
- Why do its customers buy from this store?
- Who are the store's potential customers?
- What are potential customers' tastes and income levels?
- What might attract potential customers to the store?

The answers to these questions help in constructing profiles of the merchant and the customers so that the store's message can be directed to loyal customers, those who already buy from the store, as well as the potential market.

In addition, an examination of customers' taste and income levels will give the merchant insight into *what* to advertise. The most appropriate offerings will vary according to the type of store, economic conditions, the season, and the local competition. Nevertheless, a good rule would be to feature a product that is wanted, timely, stocked in depth, and typical of the store.

In large stores decisions about an advertising plan and the setting of objectives are made jointly by upper-level executives, merchandising personnel such as buyers and merchandise managers, and advertising executives. These decisions include the planned cost of the advertising and the amounts needed to help sales grow.

Establishing a Budget

Advertising is a controllable expense

Advertising budgets are tools for controlling and allocating advertising dollars. The budget establishes guidelines for assessing the amount of advertising as well as its timing.

Several methods are used in establishing advertising budgets, each with its own benefits and problems. These include the **percentage-of-sales method,** the **objective-and-task method,** and the **unit-of-sales method.**

The Percentage-of-Sales Method

The easiest and most commonly used way to prepare a budget is to base it on a percentage of a sales figure such as past sales, anticipated sales, or a combination of the two.

- **Past sales**   The sales figures of the last year or an average for several years are used as the basis for calculating the budget.
- **Anticipated sales**   Estimated future sales volume is used as the basis for

calculating the budget. There is a risk of optimistically assuming that the business and business conditions will be good, however.

- **Past sales and estimated future sales**   This is considered the middle ground between a too optimistic and a too conservative approach. Consequently, this method is a little more realistic during periods of changing economic conditions because it allows for a study of trends and business in general.

By simply multiplying past or future sales figures by a percentage one can calculate the advertising budget for the next fiscal or calendar year. However, the merchant must first decide what percentage will be allocated to advertising.

Percentages vary according to the following factors.

- The condition of the business
- The size of the store
- The extent of the trading area
- The local competition
- The age of the store
- The nature of the merchandise carried
- Merchandising practices
- Media costs
- Store objectives
- Past practices and advertising results

Calculations in the Percentage-of-Sales Method

Department	1985 Sales	Percentage of Sales	Advertising Budget
A	$100,000	6%	$ 6,000
B	800,000	5	40,000
C	900,000	8	72,000
		Total advertising budget	$118,000

Guidance is available from several sources   Trade journals, the Census, and Internal Revenue Service reports offer comparative percentage statistics on an industry-wide basis. The merchant can choose a percentage-of-sales figure on the basis of what other businesses in the same line are doing. Stores should not, however, base their advertising budgets only on the activities of competitors.

The percentage-of-sales method is generally sound for stable merchants and established businesses, but it has limitations for new merchants. The need to attract attention to a new business requires advertising expenditures in excess of what its immediate sales volume would justify. New merchants therefore are generally advised to use the objective-and-task method.

The Objective-and-Task Method

It is difficult to set down specific objectives

The most accurate of all methods of preparing advertising budgets is the objective-and-task method, but it is also the most difficult. Basically, it relates the advertising budget to sales objectives for the coming year. To establish the budget by this method, the merchant must look at the total marketing program and consider store image, location, size, and so forth. For example, certain product offerings, such as women's luxury apparel, require a more aggressive advertising strategy, resulting in a larger budget.

The task method sets down what the merchant must accomplish and what must be done to meet objectives. Although it is difficult to judge the level of advertising needed to achieve specific tasks, expenditures are directly related to the specific task. For example, if the objective is to sell a new product and service to professional women, the merchant must determine what media will best reach this market and estimate how much it will cost to do the job. The tasks and costs are then calculated to achieve this objective.

An Objective-and-Task Method Breakdown

Objective	Task	Cost
Create awareness of the target market— professional women	Use Sunday supplements in local newspapers; full pages; 3 times	$6,000
Gain awareness of professional women	Use professional journals; ½ page; 4 times	3,000
Gain awareness of professional women	Use radio commercials; 5 times; prime time	200
		$9,200

The process is repeated for each of the objectives. When the total has been determined, the projected budget is finished. Since merchants may find that they cannot afford to advertise exactly the way they would like to, it is important to rank priorities and to change them if necessary. The major weakness of this method is the difficulty of setting specific tasks and objectives and then determining the expenditure needed to reach the objectives.

The Unit-of-Sales Method

The unit-of-sales method is not for all retailers

This budget is based on the unit (number) of sales rather than on dollar amounts, with a fixed sum set aside for each unit the merchant expects to sell. For example, if it takes 5 cents' worth of advertising to sell a turkey and the supermarket plans to sell 15,000 turkeys, the store must plan to spend 15,000 × $.05, or $750, on advertising for that product. Past experience is the key to unit-of-sales planning because it is important to know how much advertising it takes to sell a particular unit. This method is most useful for retailers of specialty goods like appliances, china, and cars. It is difficult to use when the merchant deals in many different kinds of products, and it is not dependable in sporadic, irregular markets or for style merchandise.

Allocating the Budget

Once the advertising budget is prepared, the merchant must decide how to allocate the money. This is accomplished by determining the type of advertising (institutional, promotional, cooperative), the merchandise lines to be promoted (departments), the timing of the advertising (calendar periods), and media selection.

Departments

Allocating dollars by percentage of sales, the merchandise lines or departments with the largest sales volumes receive the largest share of the budget. Allocating the budget in this way allows for the promotion of goods that require advertising to stimulate sales.

Timing

The budget must be divided into specific periods. Retailers plan their advertising on a seasonal basis, dividing each season into months, weeks, and days. The percentage-of-sales method is useful in determining the amount of money to allocate according to time periods.

It is convenient for retailers to base their advertising on planned monthly sales. For example, if April contributes 7 percent of the year's sales, they plan to spend 7 percent of the advertising budget during that month. If February accounts for 5 percent of sales, then 5 percent is allocated to that month. Of course, the budget usually requires flexibility. For example, though Christmas might contribute as much as 30 percent of annual sales volume, it would probably be unwise to spend that much of the total budget in that period.

Flexibility is important

Flexibility can be built into budgets when the planning also includes a six-month block. This allows for spending Christmas advertising dollars in October and November in preparation for Christmas. As you might imagine, there is no set pattern, and the budget should allow for changes to meet immediate needs.

Media Selection

The amount of advertising placed in each medium (television, radio, newspapers, direct mail, etc.) should be based on past experience, competition, and advice from specialists.

Where to advertise

Media are the "vehicles" by which the advertiser's selling message is carried to the consumer. If a retailer intends to make an impact with advertising, it is vital for the store's message to reach the correct target market. Media selection is the

Types of Advertising Media

	Medium	Benefits	Limitations
PRINT MEDIA	**Newspaper**	Universal circulation (reaches everybody at relatively low cost) Most people generally see a daily newspaper Products can be illustrated Frequent publication Flexible—booked with minimum advance notice Ads can be in various sizes Routinely used as a shopping guide Offer services to retailers for ad preparation (either free or for low fees) Can offer coupons, savings certificates	Waste circulation when target audience does not match paper's circulation Appearance of ad may be unattractive due to poor reproduction of illustrations or poor color Short life for ad
	Magazines	Repeated exposure (long life because people save magazines) Ads can be produced in high-quality color reproduction Retailer's image enhanced because of expense factor	Sometimes difficult to reach target market with circulation Higher production costs Generally long lead time
	Direct mail	Controlled circulation (reaches select market—goes directly to prospect) Flexibility in terms of timing, message, artwork, color Can be low cost (mailing lists can be maintained and kept current) Personalized	Junk mail image—sometimes never opened (waste factor) High cost for large mailings Difficult and expensive to compile good lists
	Telephone directories	Widespread customer usage and long life, usually one year	Limited to people searching for the product or service Long lead time—cannot change ad easily
	Flyers	Inexpensive Easy to prepare, can be produced immediately	Heavy waste—high nonreadership Expensive to distribute

key to having the right audience read, see, or hear the store's communications. There are three major categories of media that retailers use: print, broadcast, and outdoor/transit. (The merits and limitations of the major retail advertising media are summarized in Table 15-1.)

Print Media

Print media include newspapers, magazines, direct mail, telephone directories, and flyers.

TABLE 15-1 Benefits and Limitations of Major Retail Advertising

	Medium	Benefits	Limitations
BROADCAST MEDIA	Radio	Can stimulate excitement (sound more persuasive than print) Blanket coverage (everyone has a radio at home, at work, in the car) Short lead time allows for last-minute changes Personalized by use of voice Supplements advertising campaigns Can be selective (programs have different appeal to various groups) Relatively inexpensive Good for stores appealing to teens, commuters, etc.	Excess market coverage Nonvisual No tangible attributes (nothing to hold onto); handicap if price or location of advertiser needed Difficult to know who heard message Poor message may annoy listeners Short life for message Needs to be played often for impact
	Television	Product can be demonstrated more effectively because of sound, motion, color Wide market coverage	Production costs are high Expensive for small or middle-sized retailer Message short lived (no tangible attributes) Excess market coverage May not reach target market Complicated to produce
OUT OF HOME	Outdoor advertising	Long life Costs low per person reached Good backup medium Geographically selective Dramatic because of size	Copy limitations Expensive Difficult for good selling message
	Transit	Low cost per person reached Good repeat value Well read Good for commuters	Not suitable to direct selling Evaluation difficult Limited audience
NEW TECHNOLOGIES	Video wall	Entertaining Flexible in terms of timing and programming Products can be demonstrated effectively because of motion and color Geared to mall shoppers Available to small merchants and national advertisers	Limited audience Difficult to evaluate Could be expensive
	In-Store Electronic Devices*	Customized messages Entertaining	Limited audience Must be changed often Difficult to evaluate Message must be brief

*Talking posters, radio, video shopping cart, video display network.

Flexibility and wide circulation

Newspapers. Newspapers are the backbone of retail advertising. Day in and day out the newspaper is the merchant's best medium because it offers flexibility and a short lead time and lends itself to very wide circulation. A major limitation can be the cost of waste circulation. The kinds of newspapers found in large metropolitan areas are as follows.

- **Daily**
  Morning editions.   These are excellent for merchants who are looking for an immediate reaction to the ad. The paper is out early enough to allow readers to act on advertisements the same day.
  Evening editions.   These papers have smaller circulations than morning editions, but the papers are kept longer and read more thoroughly. They are used a good deal by department stores.
- **Weekly.**   These are generally published in rural communities and are considered hometown papers. They have a longer life than other papers, and readers are very receptive to retail advertising.

Printed primarily for the advertising

- **Weekly shoppers.**   These are published primarily for advertising and offer little in the way of news items. They are generally distributed free of charge. Simplified printing methods have made it possible for this type of publication to grow and prosper. Most are tabloids that are either mailed to "occupant" or distributed by hand. In metropolitan areas they are stacked near mailboxes, in lobbies, or on counters in local stores. It is estimated that they are received by more than 75 percent of people over 18 years of age.
- **Sunday newspapers.**   These are usually divided into special-interest sections, which attract ads that are suited to those sections. For example, apparel and ready-to-wear ads could be placed in the family, magazine, or home section. These sections are also excellent for "big-ticket" items for which the whole family takes part in the decision-making process.

Inserts are popular

- **Inserts.**   These are not part of the newspaper run but are distributed by the local newspaper. They are known as supplements, special sections, free-standing inserts, stuffers, free-falls, and tabloids. This category has grown to over $400 million in advertising billings (over 12 billion pieces) and is expected to increase. At one time inserts were found only in Sunday papers, but now many dailies allow them to "ride along" inside the paper on "best buys" day editions. "Best buy" days or "best food" days are usually Wednesdays, when most supermarkets and national advertisers run their ads. Next to the news, inserts have the highest readership, which explains their great popularity with department stores, chains, discounters, and local retailers. Because they are preprinted, they are of much better quality than ads reproduced in newspaper runs.

Local merchants place ads in regional editions of national magazines

Magazines.   In the past, magazine advertising was limited to retail giants like Sears and Penney. The well-known consumer magazines were too expensive for local merchants to use because they had to pay for waste circulation. In recent years, however, many national magazines have introduced regional and even local

Newspaper fashion insert. *Courtesy:* Strawbridge & Clothier.

editions in an attempt to capture a greater share of the local retailer's advertising dollar. This practice is known as a **split run,** a method whereby the publisher divides the national circulation into smaller sections. In this case merchants pay only for the geographic areas that feature their ads. For example, *Time* magazine offers 123 regional editions. Some other magazines that offer regional flexibility are *Better Homes & Gardens, TV Guide, Family Circle, Seventeen, Newsweek,* and *Ladies Home Journal.*

Magazines offer the retailer an opportunity to reach specific audiences (Table 15-2) and feature long ad life and fine-quality color. The limitations include added costs for retailers because ads must be ready for printing and many magazines do not offer free or low-cost production services. In addition, the lead time for publication is generally long (two to three months), a fact that limits the effectiveness of this medium for retailers.

Magazines offer retailers well-defined audiences because they are separated into categories based on readers' interests, sex, age, and ethnic background.

The most direct medium

Direct Mail.   **Direct mail** is the medium that retailers use to send catalogs and brochures to customers. In fact, as a result of increased activity by major department stores and specialty store chains, direct-mail sales through the use of catalogs are increasing much faster than other types of retail sales. Some leading retailers in this regard are Neiman Marcus, Ann Taylor, and Ames. Also in this category are the **stuffers** that accompany billing statements. The main benefits are the advertiser's control over the mailing, the audience it goes to, and the ability to tailor it to a specific promotion or event. In addition, it is highly flexible in that it can be produced in any size or color. The disadvantages include its high cost compared with other media, its negative "junk mail" image, its high throwaway rate, and the risk of outdated mailing lists. Nevertheless, direct mail is widely used by retailers.

Telephone Directories and Yellow Pages.   The Yellow Pages are a great help to merchants because they list types of businesses. Potential customers who are searching for a product or service find these directories most useful. A well-planned advertisement can lead to a great deal of business and has a life as long as one year. Its limitation is that once published the ad cannot be changed for that issue. However, its cost is relatively low.

The Yellow Pages are invaluable for businesses in specific product or service categories, (e.g., restaurants, limousine services), but are much less effective for department stores and similar institutions.

Regular telephone directories are listed alphabetically, and information in them is easy to find. Every telephone user is entitled to one free listing.

Flyers.   Flyers are another means by which retailers reach their target audience. They are single-page ads delivered door-to-door or placed on cars in parking lots and are particularly useful for the small neighborhood retailer. They can be produced very quickly and inexpensively.

TABLE 15-2 Magazines Offer Retailers an Opportunity to Reach Specific Audiences

Automotive, Mechanics, Science	**Fashion**
Car & Driver	*Elle*
Hot Rod	*Glamour*
Motor Trend	*Harper's Bazaar*
Road & Track	*Mademoiselle*
Popular Mechanics	*Mirabella*
Popular Science	*Vogue*
Sports, Travel	**Homes**
Golf	*American Home*
Sport	*Better Homes & Gardens*
Travel & Leisure	*Food & Wines*
Business, Finance, News	*Gourmet*
Barron's	*House Beautiful*
Business Week	*Town & Country*
Entrepreneur	**Sophisticated Editorial**
Forbes	*Harper's Atlantic*
Fortune	*Psychology Today*
Inc.	*New Yorker*
Income	**General Editorial**
Newsweek	*People*
New York	*Reader's Digest*
Time	*TV Guide*
U.S. News & World Report	**Ethnic**
Movies	*Ebony*
Modern Romance	*Essence*
Modern Screen	*Black Sports*
True Story	*Temas*
Youth	*Pimienta*
American Girl	*Revista Rotaria*
Boy's Life	*Reader's Digest* (Spanish edition)
Co-ed	**Women's**
Seventeen	*Cosmopolitan*
Teen Beat	*Family Circle*
Men's	*Good Housekeeping*
Argosy	*Parents'*
Esquire	*Woman's Day*
Penthouse	*Ladies Home Journal*
Playboy	*Working Woman*
True	*Ms.*
	Savvy

Broadcast Media

This category includes radio and TV advertising. Radio is characterized by immediacy in scheduling, lower rates compared with other media, and popularity with retailers. The main benefits are its short lead time, wide reach (home, car, almost anywhere), and ability to reach specific audiences. For example, certain groups tend to listen to particular shows, music, and news.

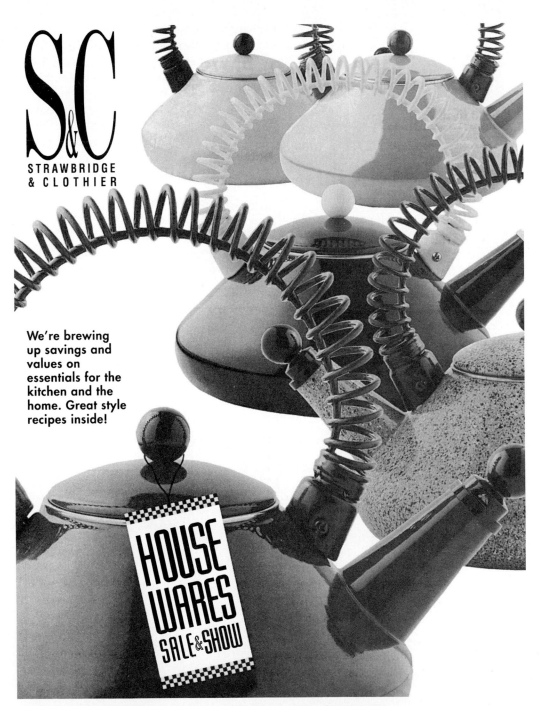

Homestore catalog cover. Strawbridge & Clothier's use of direct mail. Homestore catalog mailed to stimulate housewares sales. *Courtesy:* Strawbridge & Clothier.

Television is also utilized by many retailers, and since the stations sell local ad times, more retailers are taking advantage of this medium. It has great impact because it allows for dramatic demonstrations. Its main strengths are the ability to combine motion, sound, color, music, and drama, and the ability to reach specific target groups. Its main limitations are high costs and limited time slots. At present, only large retailers like K mart, Wards, and Sears use national TV to any degree. The use of local TV is growing not only with these large merchants but also with service institutions and local retailers. In fact, Sears has participated in a tripart venture with CBS and IBM. Local TV owners were provided with a keyboard by which they could order merchandise offerings flashed on their TV screen.

Outdoor Advertising

This category includes outdoor billboards and signs. They are generally located along highways and in strategic metro areas leading to the store. They are designed to appeal to general audiences and are of a fairly permanent nature. Some billboards remain unchanged for many years. In fact, they often become well-known landmarks. They are limited in the amount of copy they can hold, and are not flexible. Prime locations are difficult to obtain and are expensive. In addition, environmentalists sometimes object to this type of advertising.

Local retailers are the second largest users of outdoor advertising. Billboard messages can be selectively placed near points of sale to reach consumers in

Strawbridge & Clothier's commitment to customer service and quality merchandise at every price is symbolized by this outdoor advertisement. *Courtesy:* Strawbridge & Clothier.

seconds. Outdoor advertising relies on simplicity, and, according to a media director at Backer Spielvogel Bates, billboards are the equivalent of seven-second commercials popular in Europe.

High tech has entered the outdoor billboard medium. Backlit panels provide daylong illumination; fiber optics and timed displays create the illusion of colored lights; and inflatable extensions provide three-dimensional effects. There are currently some 500,000 outdoor-ad structures across the country, down from 1.2 million in the 1960s. Income from outdoor advertising accounts for 2 percent of total media spending in the United States. Restrictive zoning laws, sign-free interstate systems, and anti-billboard organizations have adversely affected its usage.

Special video wall in the Northern Mall in North Olmstead, Ohio. The video wall is entertaining as well as an effective selling tool.

Transit

This medium is viewed in and around bus and train stations and also comprises the cards and posters seen in trains, buses, taxis, and platforms. It exploits the commuter's boredom to gain readership. Car cards need a lead time of two to three months and have a limited audience.

New Technologies

Video Wall

Video advertising is now being used on special video walls in shopping centers. These walls are entertaining as well as effective selling tools. One such example is the Northern Mall in North Olmstead, Ohio. A special 20-minute program known as the "Shopping Showcase" features 2- to 3-minute merchant advertisements geared to the mall shopper. The mall wall displays original as well as national advertising videos. The programs are updated to keep pace with in-mall activities and seasonal promotions. Merchants can buy space on the video wall at rates starting at $550 per spot, including production costs. In New York City, Admotion, another mall wall advertising company, expects to have 50 shopping centers featuring its video wall. Admotion walls hold 16 to 27 video monitors that display original videos geared to mall shoppers in addition to those containing national advertising.

According to the Point of Purchase Advertising Institute, point-of-purchase advertising is expected to reach more than 14 billion consumers in 1990. A significant portion of growth will be due to new electronic technologies such as talking posters, POP radio, video shopping carts, and video display networks.

- **Talking poster.** A Japanese product combining body sensors and voice boxes that creates animated displays and "speaks up" when someone approaches.

- **POP radio.** Resembling commercial radio, POP Radio Corporation provides in-store programming for a private network that reaches approximately 65 grocery chains across the country and contains a mix of radio chatter, music, and advertising.

- **Video shopping cart.** A shopping cart with a small video screen that displays advertising for different products. For example, a coffee ad might pop up as the shopper enters the coffee aisle.

- **Video display network.** A computerized, in-store advertising display network using stadium-type scoreboard technology on a small scale to carry customized advertising messages store by store or aisle by aisle.

Evaluation of Media

Selecting the most effective medium is vital to getting the most from a store's advertising dollar. The retailer must determine whether to use a single medium or a media mix. Many merchants have found that a media mix works best for them. For example, some department stores no longer depend solely on newspaper coverage because the increased importance of branch stores has forced them to reevaluate their trading areas. In one case a sales promotion director in a leading department store chain found that in order to reach all its branches it would have to advertise in five newspapers. As a result, the store relies instead on radio and direct mail. Nonetheless, many stores in similar situations claim that newspaper advertising remains their number one vehicle.

Although media use differs according to users' needs, the process for choosing a specific channel is similar. The first step should be a careful review of the benefits and limitations of newspapers, magazines, television, radio, direct mail, and other media. (The various media advertise to attract advertisers; see Figures 15-1 and 15-2.) The next step would consist of examining the effectiveness of the media by checking costs, reach, and frequency.

Costs

CPM (cost per thousand). CPM is the most commonly used formula for assessing a medium's impact. CPM refers to the cost of reaching 1,000 people in a desired audience (viewers, listeners, or readers) and has also been adopted by print buyers. The cost is measured by dividing the cost of an advertisement by the number of people reached. The formula is

$$\text{CPM} = \frac{\text{Total cost}}{\text{Circulation or audience in thousands}}$$

Reach, Frequency, and Continuity

Reach refers to the number of people in a target audience, in other words, the range of people who will view, listen to, or read the advertising message. Frequency refers to the number of times the target audience will view, listen to, or read the advertised message. Continuity refers to the length of time an advertising message runs in a given media schedule.

Evaluation of Advertising

Measuring the effectiveness of the total advertising program involves various research methods that will be discussed in Chapter 19. However, it should be noted that it is important to check the results of specific advertising expenditures.

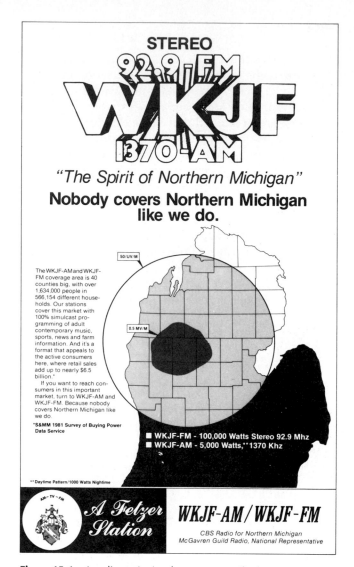

Figure 15-1 A radio station's ad to attract retail advertisers.

Every advertisement should be followed up to determine whether it has fulfilled its objective. In many cases this can be done during the period of the ad. For example, many stores rely on the departmental results on the day of or a few days immediately following the appearance of the ad. They compare their current figures with those for the previous year, when presumably the same ad was not run. Other retailers measure the effectiveness by the mail and phone orders generated, and still others consider the traffic in the store.

Figure 15-2 Magazines often advertise to attract retail advertisers.

NEW TERMS

advertising	institutional advertising
advertising budget	objective-and-task method
advertising plan	percentage-of-sales method
"cargo prices"	promotional advertising
combination advertising	split run
cooperative advertising	stuffers
CPM	tear sheet
direct mail	unit-of-sales method

CHAPTER HIGHLIGHTS

1. After the Civil War, merchants employed advertising to bring in the local trade. Early retailing giants like Marshall Field, John Wanamaker, R. H. Macy, and Huntington Hartford all advertised heavily.

2. The main function of retail advertising is to attract customers to the store. Advertising is a nonpersonal, paid-for sales message using mass media such as newspapers, television, radio, and magazines.

3. Retailers use different kinds of advertising to attract customers, including institutional, promotional, combination, and cooperative advertising. While these methods are directed to the same groups of customers and potential markets, each conveys its message in a different way. Institutional advertising attempts to "sell" the store; promotional advertising is routine advertising designed to sell specific items; combination advertising combines these elements in the same ad.

4. When retailers share the cost of advertising with manufacturers, suppliers, or other retailers, it is known as cooperative advertising. It is predicted that this form of advertising will grow because it offers many benefits to retailers.

5. An advertising plan must reflect the store's objectives, budget, and type of medium to be used.

6. In determining advertising objectives, it is wise to develop a profile of the store and its customers so that the store's message will be directed to the correct market.

7. Advertising costs are a controllable expense. The advertising budget is the means of determining and controlling this expense and dividing it wisely among departments, merchandise lines, and services.

8. Various methods are used in establishing an advertising budget. These include the percentage-of-sales method, the objective-and-task method, and the unit-of-sales method. The percentage-of-sales method is the easiest and most commonly used way to prepare a budget, while the objective-and-task method is the most difficult and the most accurate. The unit-of-sales approach to a budget is more limited than either of the others.

9. Allocating a budget consists of breaking down the total budget by type of advertising, merchandise lines, departments, time, and media.

10. *Media* are the channels by which the advertiser's selling message is carried to the consumer. There are three major categories of media: print, broadcast, and outdoor/transit. Newspapers are the backbone of retail advertising because they offer retailers great flexibility, wide circulation, relatively low cost, and a short lead time.

11. Magazine advertising in the past was seldom used, except for large retailers.

There is greater flexibility today, however, because many national magazines offer regional and local editions.

12. Direct mail is the medium that retailers use to send catalogs and brochures to customers. The advertiser controls the mailing so that it reaches the desired market.

13. Broadcast media include radio and TV advertising. Radio is characterized by immediacy in scheduling, lower rates, and popularity with retailers.

14. Consumers make buying decisions while they're shopping. Consequently, marketers are advertising via supermarket loudspeakers, shopping carts, in-store monitors, and video shopping carts.

15. Video advertising is being used on special video walls in shopping centers. These walls are effective selling tools.

16. The evaluation of media includes a consideration of costs, reach, frequency, and continuity. Advertising is evaluated by specific research methods.

REVIEW QUESTIONS

1. What is the primary function of local advertising?
2. How does promotional advertising differ from institutional advertising?
3. What effect does the Robinson-Patman Act have on cooperative advertising? How does this affect small retailers?
4. What is meant by "advertising is a controllable expense"?
5. What are the major categories of retail advertising media?
6. Why has newspaper advertising been the backbone of retail advertising?
7. Why is point-of-purchase advertising expected to increase?

DISCUSSION QUESTIONS

1. Why does a significant part of the money set aside for cooperative advertising often remain unused?
2. Why is it wise to develop a profile of the store and its customers in determining advertising objectives?
3. How would you determine the overall effectiveness of your advertising effort?

CASE 1

Inserts Taking Over?

As more people have started to use cents-off coupons, co-op couponing has become a popular area of sales promotion. One entry into this field is a weekday "best foods day" free-fall coupon insert that is a monthly feature in newspapers. Wednesday is usually selected as "best foods day" because most supermarkets and national advertisers run their ads on that day.

A firm called Ad-Serts promised advertisers a circulation of more than 29 million home-delivered once-a-month Wednesday inserts in 150 newspapers in 138 markets. Competition in the newspaper insert business consists primarily of insert advertising in Sunday papers. The owner of Ad-Serts claimed that 29 million best foods day Ad-Serts equaled 35 million Sunday inserts.

a. How do you think the Ad-Sert might affect local food stores?
b. Do you agree that inserts are more effective than ordinary newspaper promotional ads? Why?

CASE 2

"Bloomies" Sells Media

Until 1985, a fashion retail store carrying paid advertising in its own catalogs, just like the ads found in *Vogue* or *Newsweek,* could not be found in the United States. But in August of that year, Bloomingdale's by Mail, Ltd., mailed to 1.7 million consumers its fall catalog containing several pages of ads for products that Bloomingdale's does not sell. These included ads for items such as liquor and cigarettes.

In addition, Bloomingdale's by Mail, Ltd., had determined that 12 of its other 30 catalogs would carry advertising, with such ads taking up 2 to 12 pages per catalog. The company had also found that response from advertisers was very positive.

Although this approach was novel enough to attract attention in trade journals, it was not unique in retailing and, in certain respects, not such a radical departure from accepted retailing practice.

For example, both the large English department store, Harrods, and the

French-based Hermes accept paid advertising in their catalogs and have done so for some time.

In this country, Neiman Marcus has sent its customers a publication called *Imprint* three times a year since 1981. Called a "magalog" by people in the trade, *Imprint* contains both editorial material featuring trends and forecasts in fashion and paid advertising.

It is accepted practice in the United States for manufacturers to pay for space in department store catalogs to feature their products. After agreeing to pay, representatives from the manufacturer and the store decide which of the manufacturer's goods will be selected to appear. These catalogs closely resemble cooperative advertising in newspapers, with the manufacturer paying a large part of the cost.

However, Bloomingdale's was the first U.S. retailer to solicit advertising for a straight catalog format. The reasons offered by Bloomingdale's for accepting ads in its catalogs were (1) the bigger the catalog received by the customer, the longer it is kept and the more closely it is read; (2) ads for cars, liquor, cigarettes, fashionable resorts, and similar items enhance interest in the catalogs; and (3) carefully chosen advertisers help round out the impression created by the catalogs of a desirable lifestyle.

Bloomingdale's reputation as a fashionable and sophisticated department store is worldwide, and its ability to sell merchandise by mail in areas where no branches of the store exist led to the creation of Bloomingdale's by Mail, Ltd., a separate subsidiary, in 1982 to concentrate on building catalog sales. So popular are the Bloomingdale's catalogs that one, the Christmas catalog, is even sold for about $3 at newsstands in some isolated areas.

These factors made Bloomingdale's catalogs attractive to potential advertisers who were prepared to pay about $30,000 per page for an exclusive one-time ad in a catalog in order to reach the customers on Bloomingdale's mailing lists.

Bloomingdale's catalog sales are expected to be $200 million in 1990 and to outstrip the sales in every one of its stores except the main one in New York City. Compared with these figures, the amount generated from catalog advertising is slight, only a few million dollars, but Bloomingdale's executives believe the enhancement value from the ads is a much more important factor.

Whether other retailers in large numbers follow Bloomingdale's into catalog advertising is not certain, although a few have such ventures under study. What is also not clear is whether ads for such items as cigarettes and liquor will have an adverse effect on Bloomingdale's customers or whether customers will simply accept the catalog ads in the same way they do magazine ads or, perhaps, not even notice.

a. Do you believe that putting ads in a catalog enhances its appeal to the customer?

b. Are there reasons a retailer might reject the notion of catalog advertising? If so, for what reasons?

c. With so much attention focused on the negative effects of smoking and drinking, do you think catalog ads for liquor and cigarettes could be detrimental to catalog sales? Explain.

d. Does the inclusion of advertising in a Bloomingdale's catalog for products the store does not sell imply a "stamp of approval" by Bloomingdale's?

REFERENCES

CULICOVER, R., "Targeting the Hometown Crowd." *Sales and Marketing Management* (April 1989), pp. 70–77.

FAHEY, A. "Department Stores Spruce Up Images." *Advertising Age* (May 21, 1990), p. 42.

"The Great Outdoors—Billboard's Big Picture." *New York,* (September 4, 1989), pp. 20–22.

SCHILLER, Z., "Stalking the New Consumer," *Business Week* (August 28, 1989), pp. 54–62.

"Seizing the Initiative in Co-op." *Sales and Marketing Management* (April 1989), pp. 78–87.

"Video Advertising—Goes to the Wall." *Chain Store Age,* (November 1989), pp. 104–106.

Chapter 16

Sales Promotion, Public Relations, and Publicity

After completing this chapter, you should be able to:

- Define sales promotion and indicate its primary objectives.
- Identify sales promotion activities conducted by retailers.
- Describe the advantages and disadvantages of sales promotion activities.
- Identify retail personnel who are responsible for sales promotion.
- Identify the ways in which retailers develop goodwill through public relations.

Advertising, display, personal selling, and sales promotion are the means by which a retailer conveys to the customer messages about the store, its merchandise, and its services. Basically, it is how the retailer communicates to the customer in order to sell more merchandise and create goodwill. As noted earlier, advertising and display help attract customers to the store, while personal selling attempts to get them to buy. Sales promotion, on the other hand, supplements the store's advertising, display, and personal-selling activities by attracting additional customers.

SALES PROMOTION

As indicated in Chapter 1, sales promotion includes all the activities through which a merchant attempts to generate immediate sales, attract customers to the store, build customer loyalty, and promote goodwill. These activities include trading stamps, contests, games, premium offers, samples, coupons, price promotions, and special events such as demonstrations and shows.

Reasons for Using Sales Promotions

Retailers use promotions for the following reasons.

Objectives of sales promotion

- To attract new customers
- To introduce a new service or product
- To offset seasonal declines
- To offset competitive promotions

Attracting New Customers

The aim of some promotions is to gain new customers. Because shoppers are creatures of habit, the offerings should be substantial enough to wean potential customers from their usual retail outlets. Samples, free gifts, and special prize inducements are some of the promotions used to encourage customers to patronize a new store.

Introducing a New Service or Product

Some promotions are used to encourage customers to try a product or service for the first time. Wardrobe consultants, 24-hour alterations, service, and express delivery are examples of special services that enhance a store's image, attract new customers, and motivate regular customers to participate.

Offsetting Seasonal Declines

The aim of these promotions is to encourage shoppers to buy off-season merchandise (e.g., to buy Christmas cards and decorations in January) or to stock up on a product before they need it. Successful promotions of this nature brighten the sales picture during slow times. In fact, if the promotional incentives are attractive enough, they encourage the purchaser to buy just to take advantage of the offer.

Offsetting Competitive Promotions

Sometimes merchants must develop promotions to avoid losing business to other retailers who are using sales incentives. They also strive to maintain their image.

Types of Sales Promotions

Care must be taken in selecting a promotion

Merchants must decide what they expect their promotions to accomplish before selecting a particular incentive. The costs must also be evaluated against expectations. It should be noted that good promotions cannot overcome poor product performance or replace sound merchandising strategies. Consequently, merchants should plan and research their offerings carefully.

Trading Stamps, Contests, and Games

The purpose of these incentives is to develop customer loyalty and repeat business. The lure of stamps and the opportunity to win prizes make shopping more exciting for some customers and bring them back to the store again and again.

Historically, the principal users of stamps, contests, and games have been supermarkets, service stations, and small retailers. The customers have the feeling of getting something for nothing, and are given an opportunity to acquire products that they would not normally buy.

Trading Stamps. **Trading stamps** are given to shoppers as a bonus for purchasing goods. The number of stamps a shopper receives is related directly to the size of the purchase. The stamps or coupons are accumulated and can be traded in for merchandise at redemption centers or through a mail order center.

Stamps traded for a variety of merchandise

Redemption centers display products and prizes that are available for designated amounts of stamps. The stamps are "traded" for merchandise that runs the gamut of household products, appliances, and sporting goods. The centers are owned and operated by the companies that issue the stamps. The three national trading companies are S&H Green Stamps, Quality Stamp, and Gold Bond.

Stamps are costly to retailers

Retailers must carefully consider the pros and cons of stamps before offering this form of promotion. Because stamp companies charge retailers a percentage of

A distribution of colorful pictures, cards, and gifts helped bring traffic to the early A&P stores. *Courtesy:* A&P.

sales, stamp promotions in some cases can be more costly than advertising. Also, because many sophisticated consumers are aware that stamps are not free, they often choose to shop at stores that offer lower prices. Furthermore, once a retailer begins a stamp promotion, it is dangerous to stop it abruptly because of customer objections. Trading stamps saturated the market in the 1950s and 1960s. Because so many merchants offered them, they lost their competitive advantage and practically disappeared in the 1970s. Less than 10 percent of U.S. supermarkets now offer trading stamps.

Contests and games must adhere to legal regulations

Contests and Games.   These promotions give the customer an opportunity to compete for prizes. Some are based on skills, such as completing a puzzle, while others resemble a sweepstakes in which prizes or money are awarded on the basis of lucky numbers and the like. Purchases are not necessary, and all the shopper need do is fill out a card or entry blank in the store. Sweepstakes create a great deal of interest and can be an inexpensive form of promotion. It is important for retailers that are interested in contests and games to seek legal advice because such promotions must adhere to legal regulations, and these vary from one state to another. Retailers and manufacturers spend more than $200 million annually on contests and sweepstakes.

Premium Offers and Samples

Premiums are articles of merchandise that are offered to the shopper as incentives to buy. They are either given away free after the customer has bought or tried a product or service, or sold at cost. In either case, premiums leave the consumer with a direct, tangible benefit.

A **direct premium** is the basic type of premium. It is an item that is offered *free* with a purchase and is received by the customer at the time of purchase. This "something extra" philosophy is really the key to all premium techniques. In supermarkets premiums are often physically tied to the product by a special package or container, or banded together. This type of direct premium is generally packaged at the factory and is known as a "factory pack." Its advantages are as follows.

- It is visible at the point of sale.
- It attracts attention on the store shelf.
- It frequently moves more products without destroying a price pattern.

A self-liquidator pays for itself

A **self-liquidator premium,** on the other hand, is *sold* (usually at cost) to the shopper after he or she bought some item or tried a new service. The principle of the self-liquidator is simple: The retailer buys the merchandise at the best possible price, adds handling costs, and arrives at a total that becomes (approximately) the offering price to the shopper. The idea is to make the item very attractive to the customer by offering it at a price that is much lower than the normal retail value of the merchandise.

Traffic builders over longer periods

Some premiums are designed to build traffic over a longer period. One such type is the **purchase privilege offer.** This type of promotion is offered on a limited basis (6 to 10 weeks is common). For example, with a specified minimum purchase—say, $5 or $10 worth of groceries—the customer is entitled to buy the premium at a self-liquidating price. The sale of encyclopedias on a volume-a-week basis is a common program of this type. Kitchen tools, glassware, dinnerware, and flatware are also used in this type of promotion.

Premiums may also be offered as a one-time promotion. Banks use this concept in offering gifts to new depositors. **Referral premiums** are gifts that are awarded to customers who send in the names of potential customers. They are popular with direct sellers such as party plan operators, insurance salespeople, and various service companies.

Whether a premium is used as a direct tie-in with a purchase, a new customer referral, or a traffic builder, the success of the promotion depends on the premium selected. Retailers therefore must decide on the markets they want to reach in order to provide the right incentives.

Valentine's Day ad for him and her includes a contest and bonus gift wrap. Courtesy: Strawbridge & Clothier.

Sampling can create customer awareness

When a retailer offers a **sample** as a premium, it is usually provided by the manufacturer as an inducement to shoppers to try a product. Usually, trial or sample sizes of a product are handed out in the store. Cosmetics companies do a great deal of "sample" promotion. The theory behind sampling is that shoppers need to be convinced by trying a product before buying it. However, the kinds of products that can be sampled are limited.

Bakeries, specialty food stores, supermarkets, and cheese shops often offer free samples in order to get customers to buy or try new items. Sampling is not difficult to arrange and can be relatively inexpensive. It is most suitable for products whose benefits cannot easily be communicated through advertising.

Coupons

This form of promotion allows a specific reduction in the price of an item. **Coupons** for national brands are offered by manufacturers (through newspapers and magazines) and are redeemable at stores that carry the brand. Manufacturers pay for the cost of redemption plus the retailer's handling cost. Even though they are one of the oldest forms of incentive merchandising, with beginnings well before the start of this century, coupon incentive programs have become a separate industry. Newsletters about coupons are distributed, they are discussed on TV and radio shows, and groups have been formed to trade them. The word *couponing* is a recognized term for this industry. According to Summary Scan, a division of the Advertising Checking Bureau, 263 billion coupons were distributed in 1989 through newspapers, magazines, freestanding inserts, and direct mail.

Advantages and disadvantages of coupons

Coupons build brand loyalty for manufacturers and retailers, reduce the costs of products to consumers, and encourage consumers to try new products. Some of the disadvantages are that they can be misused and redeemed fraudulently, with the additional costs passed on to the consumer. Also, retailers are sometimes pressured by customers to redeem coupons even when the product in question is not purchased. This may occur where no proof of purchase is required. Although the paperwork and record keeping involved can also be bothersome to retailers, coupons with UPC and scanning have alleviated this problem somewhat. Furthermore, retailers have little control over this form of sales promotion, because it is initiated by the manufacturer.

Some supermarkets maintain computers that dispense coupons to shoppers based on the shoppers' selection of items from a video screen.

In addition to manufacturers' coupons, some retailers offer coupons that are redeemable only at their stores. This is usually part of a price promotion strategy (see Figure 16-1). In highly competitive markets retailers may offer double or triple coupon values.

Other Types

Retailers are constantly developing innovative sales promotions (e.g., Ladies' Day discounts, Senior Citizen Opportunity Days, Morning to Midnight Sales Day, Free Flyer Point Systems in which consumers earn airline flying points based on accumulated store purchases).

The proceeds from Strawbridge & Clothier's Charity Day benefited nearly 100 local charities while giving shoppers money-saving discount coupons in a day filled with savings, contests and excitement. *Courtesy:* Strawbridge & Clothier.

Figure 16-1   Coupons are popular consumer incentives. *Courtesy:* A&P.

Price Promotions

**Sales affect
store image**

Storewide sales or special sales are common retailer promotions. The purpose is to generate immediate sales, attract customers to the store, and increase profits through higher sales volume. Stores differ in their approaches to sales because of their varied merchandising policies and store images (see Figure 16-2). Although some merchants never hold sales because of their impact on store image, other stores are known for their once-a-year clearance sales. Supermarkets generally have sales at least once a week, whereas other stores sell at "reduced" prices all year long. Still other retailers conduct recognized sales events on special occasions—back to school, Washington's Birthday, January clearance, and so forth.

OPENING WEEK
Be a part of our fabulous King of Prussia Opening Week Celebration, March 3 to 6! It's an exciting world of difference and you're gonna love it!

YOU'RE GONNA LOVE IT! SWEEPSTAKES!

16 GRAND PRIZES PLUS 94 ADDITIONAL PRIZES WORTH OVER $150,000

1 WRAP YOURSELF IN THE MOST ELEGANT COAT OF ALL... A MINK!
Enter to win a luxurious mink coat in the Intimate Apparel Department on the Lower Level. This $5000 value can be yours courtesy of Warner's.

2 A 6-DAY/7-NIGHT TRIP FOR 2 TO THE LOVELY ISLAND OF MARTINIQUE
A cold-weather escape courtesy of Lancome. Includes airfare via American Airlines to the Meridian Hotel. Cosmetic Dept. Upper Level
 AmericanAirlines

3 A VACATION FOR TWO TO SAN DIEGO... COURTESY OF JANTZEN
Includes round-trip airfare and hotel stay. You could also win a 13-foot paddle-ski, the rage of Australia! Men's Swimwear, Lower Level.

4 SPEND 3 UNFORGETTABLE NIGHTS IN SUNNY FREEPORT BAHAMAS
Courtesy of Jantzen. Includes airfare, hotel stay for 2. Also win a $1000 Jantzen shopping spree. Misses' Swimwear, Upper Level.

5 CRUISE THE CARIBBEAN ABOARD THE SOVEREIGN OF THE SEAS
Spend 8 days and 7 nights cruising around Haiti, Puerto Rico and St. Thomas. Courtesy of Trifari. Enter in Jewelry, Upper Level!

6 GAMBLE THE NIGHTS AWAY IN MONTE CARLO ... A TRIP FOR TWO
A vacation made possible by Riviera Sunglasses. Includes airfare via Air France, hotel stay. Enter in Accessories, Upper Level.

7 SEE BEAUTIFUL PALM SPRINGS, CALIFORNIA BY AIR ... BY HOT AIR THAT IS!
A 3-day/2-night holiday for two including a hot air champagne balloon ride. Courtesy of Newport Blue. Men's Activewear, Lower Level.
NEWPORT B·L·U·E

8 SWATCH PRESENTS EXCITING PRIZES, VALUED AT OVER $1000
Prizes include GT Trail Bike, Mullen Powell Peralta Skateboard and Maxi Swatch wall watches. Enter at the Swatch Counter, Upper Level.

9 SPEND A ROYAL WEEK IN HISTORIC LONDON, ENGLAND ... TRIP FOR 2
Enter in the Travel Dimensions Travel Agency on the 3rd Floor. Includes airfare and 6-night hotel stay at the Ritz Hotel.

10 VISIT AN ISLAND WHERE SUMMER NEVER ENDS... A HAWAIIAN TRIP FOR 2
Enter in our Travel Dimensions Travel Agency on the 3rd Floor. Includes airfare and 7-night hotel stay at Waikiki Beach.

11 SONY OFFERS 21 CHANCES TO WIN SONY TELEVISIONS
Enter to win a Sony color 20" Trinitron control monitor receiver valued at $399 each. Enter in the Electronics Dept., 3rd Floor.
 SONY.

12 SPEND A NEW ENGLAND WEEKEND FOR TWO IN HISTORIC BOSTON
Courtesy of Boston Traders. Includes round-trip airfare and 2-night hotel accommodations. Enter in Men's Better Sportswear, Lower Level.

13 HOME GIFTS: ENTER TO WIN LUXURIOUS BED AND BATH PACKAGE
Stearns & Foster mattress, Liberty of London bed ensemble, Fieldcrest gifts, Swan Lake pillows, Woolrest cover. Domestics, 3rd Floor.

Figure 16-2   A new store opening sweepstakes. *Courtesy:* Strawbridge & Clothier.

14 **ENTER TO WIN A SPECIAL DREAM DINNER FOR 2 IN PARIS, FRANCE**
Round-trip airfare on the Concorde. 2 nights at the Hotel de Crillon, all airport transportation. 2 breakfasts, 1 lunch and one dinner.

15 **CRUISE THE SHORE ABOARD A WIND SURFER COURTESY OCEAN PACIFIC**
Enter to win a wind surfer. OP also is giving away 2 exciting surfboards. Enter in the Young Men's Department, Lower Level.

16 **3-NIGHT TRIP TO DISNEY WORLD FOR 2 ADULTS AND 2 KIDS**
Courtesy Travel Dimensions. Includes hotel, Rent-a-car, airfare, admission to Disney World and Epcot Center. Children's Dept, Lower Level.

OPENING WEEK CONTESTS

Pick up your entry ballots for our contest during our exciting King of Prussia Opening Week Celebration, March 3 to 6 . . . No purchase necessary!

THE NAMES YOU LOVE BEST HELP MAKE OUR

17 **"YOU'RE GONNA LOVE IT SWEEPSTAKES" A SUCCESS:**

94 PRIZES WORTH OVER $150,000

Christian Dior
Val Mode
Gilligan & O'Malley
Cinema Etoile
Barad
Miss Elaine
Swirl
Wear-It-Out
Say Lu
Tiffany
Trendsetters
Triumph
Union Bay
Jordache
Palmetto
Ocean Pacific
Sassafras
Gunne Sax
Pant-her
Nell Flowers
Stephen Douglas
Koret
Catalina Bay Club
Comosport
Sync
Norton McNaughton
SK & Co.
Counterparts
Knit DeVille
Beverly Hills Polo Club
Melrose
Personal II
D. Klein & Son
Jantzen II
Villager Women's
Pendleton Women's
Coach
Smith Corona
Lee
London Star
Pegasus
Orare
Solomen Schecter
Downey's
Dotti
Gerson & Gerson

Stiffel
Remington
Westwood
Robert Abby
Cameo
Croscill
Decorama
Graber
Fieldcrest
Regal
Springs
Martex
Speedo
Bill Blass
Anne Cole
Robby Len
Herman Geist
Tahari
Izod
J.G. Hook
Putumayo
Skyr
Ellen Tracy
Counterparts
Liz Claiborne
Chaus Petite
Misty Harbor
London Fog
Tiger Fox
Club Pret
Fleet Street
Gallery
Utex
Mulberry Street
Canon
Summit
Braunstein
Delsey
Sag Harbor
Marchesa
York
Technics
Rafaella
Babytogs

Stevens
Crown Crafts
Fallani & Cohn
Quaker Lace
Sunweave
Vera
Reefer Galler
Chatham
Personal Petites
Nina
Easy Street
Unisa
Stearns & Foster
Sealy
Simmons
Oster
Toastmaster
Farberware
Home Spa
Lladro
David Winter
Henckels
Reed & Barton
Waterford
Oneida
Polder
Revere
Calphalon
Catskill Craftsman
Lenox
Noritake
Wedgwood
Royal Doulton
Burnes of Boston
Gund
Brother
A. Benedetto
Andin
Baltimore
Dreams
K & F
Wings
Jones New York
Fisher
Tapemeasure
Trimfit

I.C. Isaacs Petites
9West
Russ
Catalina
Personal
Young Stuff
I.C. Isaacs
Laura & Jayne
Esprit Sport
Generra
Bongo
Necessary Objects
Rolfs
Arrow
YSL
Rooster
Manhattan
Schoenfield
B.D. Baggies
David Peyser
Members Only
Pacific Trail
Cricketeer
Fenleigh
Porfilo
Austin Reed
Chaps
Perry Ellis
Polo University
Portfolio
Asher
Mannor
Jay Mar
Riviera
Pierre Cardin
Evan-Picone Woman
Totes
Atlantic
Zena
Gemsmith
Samsonite
Peters & Ashley
Shariff
U.S. Luggage
Alexandria
Gucci

Elizabeth
J.H. Collectibles
Seiko
Sony
ABS
Carter's
Hartman
Intro
Schwab
Perugina
Gottex
Calabash
Burlington
Sirena
Evan-Picone Sport
Dooney & Bourke
Panasonic
A. Klein/New Aspects
Citizen
American Tourister
Calvin Klein
Soupcon/Weewear
Godiva
Mainstream
Good Lad
Gold Toe
Rose Marie Reid
Knitwaves
Susan Gail
Sharp
Lloyd Williams
Pulsar
Zenith
C.P. Shades
Buster Brown
RCA
Roxanne
Billy The Kid
Host
La Blanca
Baylis
John Henry

How to enter:
To enter to win any of the prizes , fill in the entry blank coupons in our multi-page flyer and deposit them in the ballot boxes located in the department sponsoring the Grand Prize. Ballot box #17 will be located on the Upper Level of our King of Prussia store.

Multiple entries will be disqualified. Strawbridge & Clothier employees, vendors, sponsors, their subsidiaries, divisions, affiliated companies, successors or their immediate families are not eligible to win. Prizes are not returnable, exchangeable, transferable or redeemable for cash. Any prize not claimed within 30 days will result in an alternate winner. Winner is responsible for taxes on all prizes and trips are subject to availability.

Winner is responsible for his/her own actions and agrees to hold harmless Strawbridge & Clothier, their subsidiaries, divisions, related companies, officers, directors, employees, agents, successors, assigns and licensees from any liability. Entry constitutes permission for Strawbridge & Clothier to use winner's name and data in connection with this contest.

You must be at least 18 years of age to enter.

Figure 16-2   (Continued)

Storewide sales are a major type of promotion that includes displays, advertising, and long-range planning. As stated previously, the price reductions must be significant if the promotion is to be effective.

The most common arguments against the use of special price promotions are the following.

- Some customers who expect a sale postpone purchasing until sale time.
- An excess of price promotions results in a loss of effectiveness.
- Complaints from customers increase when promotions end.
- Special sales sometimes increase expenses with no corresponding increase in profits.

An example of a special price promotion involved Filene's Basement, which mailed lottery coupons to its customer list. The coupon offered bonus prizes of 10 to 40 percent price reductions on top of the normal discounts.

Special Events

Sometimes special activities attract trade to the store because the offerings are excitement, showmanship, or information, rather than lower prices. These events add to the atmosphere and image of the store in addition to stimulating sales (Figure 16-3). Bloomingdale's is well known for special events.

Some products lend themselves to demonstrations

Demonstrations.   Demonstrations can be very effective in promoting such products as cosmetics, cooking utensils, and electronic devices. Because a good demonstration requires someone who is trained in the use of the product, many manufacturers supply professional demonstrators to help promote their products. For example, in order to promote a new pan for making crepes, one manufacturer hired several chefs to demonstrate and instruct customers in the proper use of the product. Demonstrations were held in the housewares departments of a select group of stores, and customers were invited to stop by for the demonstration and a "crepe treat." The chefs prepared various crepes with such ease that some customers ascribed "magical qualities" to the pan. The free food samples attracted large crowds, boosted sales, and enhanced the store atmosphere.

Demonstrations add excitement to a store's image

In-store demonstrations are used by Carson-Pirie-Scott in Chicago to generate excitement about luggage. Luggage and packing seminars are held two to three times a year to increase sales as well as enhance the luggage department's image. Most of the major manufacturers get involved by sending their representatives to help. They teach customers luggage-packing techniques and emphasize major features of the merchandise. The store uses signs in the store to attract walk-

---

Figure 16-3   Example of exciting store promotion. Bigg Saturday combines a sale with special events for the whole family. *Courtesy:* Strawbridge & Clothier.

BIGG
Saturday

TOPS, 12.90
- Campshirts and polos by **Objectives**
- Florals, stripes, beach motifs
- Cotton/polyester basics, brights, pastels
- Classic warm-weather styling for misses

YOUR CHOICE, 19.90
- Ilio shorts and campshirts
- Plus Hasting & Smith tees
- All of soft, pure cotton for misses
- In pretty prints, stripes, solids

THE BASICS OF SUMMER
AT LOW VALUE PRICES

CARDIGANS, 21.90
- By **Objectives** for misses
- Red, fuchsia, turquoise, navy, more
- Soft polyester/cotton knit
- V-neck, patch pocket styling

SHORTS, 24.90
- From Hasting & Smith
- Essentials, too!
- In polyester/cotton and ramie/cotton
- Plus twills and sheetings
- Pick solids, prints, stripes or florals
- All for misses

(584-588-590) Selection varies by store. Sorry, no mail or phone orders accepted. Delivery $5

Strawbridge & Clothier

through traffic. Bloomingdale's in New York also uses demonstrations to help build traffic and sales of luggage.

Video cassettes and tapes are effective in generating customer interest and are used in demonstrations to attract customers. In these cases the demonstrations are taped and can be played at any time. More and more manufacturers are using this method because trained demonstrators are expensive and can be in only one place at a time. Because many stores make video players available, manufacturers supply the tapes or the entire package.

Henri Bendel arranged an unusual window demonstration for its beauty salon. The hair stylists highlighted the salon's services by making over mannequins. The demonstration was successful in luring large street audiences all day.

Shows.   Fashion shows are used widely by most department stores and some specialty shops to display the latest fashions. The main objectives are to sell merchandise and to communicate the store's fashion stance. In many instances, designers sponsor such shows at the stores for customers who are interested in their clothes.

Fashion shows require a great deal of advance preparation, organization, and planning. Usually, the store's fashion director is responsible for selecting the merchandise and the overall theme, preparing the commentary, and working with the models.

Breakfast and lunch hour fashion shows in a store's restaurant are popular and attract a great deal of attention. For one thing, the audience is captive and the models can get very close to the tables. Customers are often able to touch the fabrics and ask questions.

Fashion shows are particularly popular in the sale of furs. In fact, some stores are noted for their fur shows. Neiman Marcus offers refreshments and tries to

Some products lend themselves to demonstrations.
Ken Karp.

This customer is learning how to tie a scarf Western style through the use of the store's video cassette. Ken Karp.

make the show more of a social event than a sale. According to the store's fur buyer, this technique attracts many male customers.

A recent innovation in nonpersonal selling involves Diebold Company, a manufacturer of ATM equipment. The company also markets an interactive video system for retailers. The store designs its own videos which display feature merchandise items. The customer responds to questions displayed on the screen for information about the merchandise. In effect, the video is a catalog that allows the customer to communicate with the store. The concept of the fashion video catalog thus educates consumers about merchandise and builds sales. The use of fashion videos is the best technique for "reading" a customer other than personally seeing her. Designers such as Norma Kamali and Donna Karan use videos as a way of stimulating sales.

Fashion videos are gaining greater exposure by being played in restaurants, hospitals, health spas, beauty salons, airports, cocktail lounges, etcetera. They are used with interactive home shopping systems, such as J. C. Penney's Telaction system. Operated through cable network, the consumer punches in a number on a push-button telephone to bring the program up on a TV screen. Then she selects merchandise from any of the 40 Penney stores linked to the system.

A **trunk show** is another powerful promotion technique used by fashion stores. When a manufacturer (vendor) does a trunk show, the company representative presents the line (goods are stored in the rep's car or van) to store personnel and/or customers in the store. This intimate touch benefits all three parties. An example of a successful retailer that uses trunk shows is Martha, Inc., which stages as many as 70 shows a year. In fact, this upscale women's clothing retailer conducts about 45 percent of its business through trunk shows.

Fashion shows build store traffic and
promote a store's fashion image.
Courtesy: Dallas Mart.

Designers sometimes participate in trunk shows, and often make personal appearances. Shows increase sales, stimulate interest, and enable manufacturers and designers to see the buying public's reactions firsthand.

Theme Promotions.   The important aspect of a theme promotion is the selection of an idea that will stimulate the interest of consumers and attract them to the store. A theme need not be elaborate, but it should develop an idea in a dramatic way. The following examples illustrate a range of thematic promotions.

Themes can involve many store areas

Britian's prestigious department store, Harrods, held a week-long salute to Italy, ''Buongiorno Italia.'' One of the largest storewide promotions ever undertaken by the store, it brought together Italian foods, fashions, furniture, and craftspeople. The Italian theme developed because Harrods found in Italy a wonderful source of exciting, high-quality merchandise. In keeping with the theme, the central exhibition hall was transformed into an Italian villa and courtyard. Over 60 different window displays set the background for fashion, home furnishings, and food displays. In addition, top Italian craftspeople demonstrated decorative wood and cameo carving, illustrated sixteenth-century ceramic reproductions, constructed mosaic pictures with semiprecious stones, and lectured on the art of hand printing on paper. Youngsters were entertained in the toy department by giant Scilian puppets.

During the opening week customers sipped complimentary glasses of Italian wine and Harrods' restaurant offered speciality dishes from well-known trattoria. Two of Italy's best-known restaurant owners discussed the essentials of Tuscan food and wines with interested customers.

A special aspect of the promotion was the great number of Italian artists and craftspeople who demonstrated their skills throughout the store. Harrods also received considerable assistance from the Italian Ministry for Foreign Trade, the Italian Institute for Foreign Trade, and the Italian State Tourist Office, which cosponsored the promotion.

Bloomingdale's has conducted successful theme promotions using foreign country fashions, e.g., China, Spain, India, as well as one involving famous Hollywood figures.

A well-known star or comic figure can be the inspiration for a theme. Here are some examples.

- Stores around the country have cashed in on promotions featuring Popeye, Olive Oyl, and Superman.
- The movie *Teenage Mutant Ninja Turtles* was such a great promotional success that it spawned a successfully licensed toy line.
- When Bloomingdale's rolled out the red carpet for 1,200 guests at the "Vive la France" charity gala, it attracted many socially prominent people and received positive publicity.

A storewide theme promotion about Great Britain, highlighting King's Road, a well-known shopping area in London. *Courtesy:* Neiman Marcus.

- Inspired by Prince Charles's first appearance in New York, many merchants held promotions featuring products made in England. A later visit by the prince and Princess Diana to a Washington, D.C., J. C. Penney store drew record crowds.

Bridal themes can be his and hers

Bridal themes are another popular type of promotion, with many stores putting together programs of equal interest to brides and grooms. For example, tie-in presentations include travel planning information, a his-and-hers trousseau fashion show, and the like. Merchandising the honeymoon has such potential that hotels and travel agencies often supply free champagne, travel cases, and similar items.

RETAIL STRATEGY
New Strategy for Top Community Relations

Shopping centers provide classrooms for adult education programs. In an attempt to educate a work force populated by recent immigrants with English language difficulties, some malls in Kentucky provide classroom space for adult education programs. In concert with the Kentucky Department of Education, shopping centers operated by David Hooker & Associates provide the space, while the Kentucky Department of Education provides the teachers and textbooks. Adult students appear to feel most comfortable in malls. According to some marketing consultants, providing education programs will become the top community relations effort of shopping center managers in the 1990s.

Public Service

Community events build goodwill

Themes that concentrate on public service events attempt mainly to build goodwill. Dayton's, located in Minneapolis, is well-known for its innovative ideas and community involvement. It sponsors many exciting programs and public service events, which are presented in a 12,000-square-foot auditorium. Benefit shows, fashion shows, art exhibits, concerts, and lectures are held there. More than 200,000 visitors attend the store's annual Christmas event and its spring flower show, both of which have become traditions in the Midwest.

Peter Kuntz Co., a do-it-yourself home center, in Dayton, Ohio, sponsors a radio call-in show, "Meet the Pro." Listeners are invited to call with questions about do-it-yourself projects. The answers are broadcast to the Dayton market.

Another illustration of public service is stores that cater to professional women through information seminars (e.g., "Putting Together a Business Wardrobe"). The sessions are held in the store and at other locations, including colleges and graduate schools. At the seminars, which last about 1½ hours, models and slides augment oral presentations and allow for questions and answers. Informative sessions like these are viewed as a true public service, especially by women who are entering the business world for the first time.

Group Promotions

Group promotions help small retailers

Shopping center associations sponsor events that involve all or most of their merchant members. For example, many regional shopping centers or malls conduct auto shows, art shows, auctions, and flower shows. Music, entertainment, banners, and a great deal of advance advertising and publicity accompany these promotions. Merchants generally share the expenses in proportion to the size of their stores. Because of the scope of the event, many people are usually drawn to the center, and while the merchant is not assured of increased sales, increased traffic is generated.

Entertainment facilities are part of the marketing promotions used to create a distinct image for shopping centers. In many communities, a specific entertainment event affords the public a chance to see stars, bands, etcetera. A well-planned event draws people and becomes a community focus. An increasing number of shopping center developers are building in entertainment as a permanent function of the center. Retailers benefit because traffic is the name of the game in retailing. One shopping center that has incorporated entertainment is Franklin Mills, a unique destination mall in North Philadelphia. The Huge Western Development project, a discount, off-price, outlet mall has a resident group of strolling mimes, a full-time clown, a fife-and-drum corps, and a color parade of giant crayons. In addition to the special entertainment events, Franklin Mills has a family recreation center run by the Christensen Co., an operator of theme parks. The center includes a roller rink, bowling alley, softball and baseball batting cages, three 18-hole miniature golf courses, laser tag video games, fast food, and continuous live shows with jugglers, singers, and magic acts, etc. The stores include five anchors: Sears Outlet, J. C. Penney Catalog Outlet Store, Boscov's Department Stores, Reading China and Glass store, Carrefour hypermarket, and several other major chains like Modell's T. J. Maxx, and Filene's Basement. The mall also includes several traditional retailers operating outlet stores, such as Gantos Boutique and Wallach's Outlet. Since the mall opened in May 1989, Franklin Mills has become a tourist attraction—so much so that a full-time "tour director" is employed to book tours for bargain-seeking shoppers.

Cooperative promotions may also take the form of tie-ins with other companies, manufacturers, or institutions. For example, several of the daytime soap operas tie in with local merchants. The TV shows offer exposure of the store's name in exchange for clothing or props used on the show. Such exposure adds a measure of prestige to the shop. Similarly, a travel agency may display luggage and travel accessories for a local merchant. In exchange, the merchant may display brochures regarding the agency. There are unlimited ways in which creative merchants can sponsor or cosponsor events. However, the retailer must always consider the objectives of the promotion, its cost, and the nature of the store. Following are some guidelines for staging promotions of this type.

1. Stay on your own "turf"—aim your promotions at your own market.
2. Make your events frequent enough to develop the impression that something *interesting* is *always* happening at your store.

3. Planning for special events must be very thorough—allow for possible foul-ups.
4. When it is practical, work with vendors or other merchants for their support.
5. Advise newspapers and other media contacts well in advance; follow up several times so that some media coverage is possible.
6. Stick to your sales promotion aim.

Responsibility for Promotion

Who should be responsible for the promotion function? In small firms, the owner or manager generally makes the decisions as to what, how, where, and when to promote. In large retail organizations, the work is generally divided among specialists such as sales promotion directors, artists, illustrators, copywriters, production managers, and display artists. Figure 16-4 is an example of an organizational structure used for carrying out the sales promotion function in a large store. Of course, smaller firms have fewer people on staff to do the work. In these cases one individual may be responsible for several activities.

Sales promotion planning is essential to timely decisions about the types of promotions needed to meet the competition, reach the store's sales goals, and create the right atmosphere for increased customers. Major store promotions are generally planned six months in advance so that all the necessary elements of the promotion are brought together at the right time. For example, the merchandise

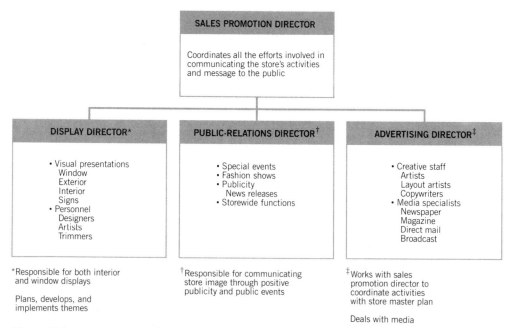

Figure 16-4   An organizational chart for use in planning advertising, display, and public relations activities.

needed for the promotion must be ordered months ahead, the materials needed for display must be prepared, the printing and publicity arrangements must be completed, and the hiring of necessary personnel must take place. Because of these details, large stores also hold periodic reviews as the promotion date approaches. Major theme promotions have been known to start years in advance to achieve the right merchandise mix.

Stores use various tools to keep on top of their promotion activities. A **promotion calendar** is used to pinpoint special events, local and national events, holiday promotions, advertising, and the like. This calendar expands the special days noted on a normal calendar by indicating the dates of retail sales promotions (Figures 16-5 and 16-6).

Planning for promotion costs requires the development of a promotion budget. Each activity involves manpower, media expenses, supplies, printing, and so forth. Preparation for a budget includes the following considerations: the type and size of the store, its location and clientele, the type of merchandise carried, the local competition and business conditions, and the cost of local media.

PUBLIC RELATIONS AND PUBLICITY

Publicity is free coverage by the media

Many special events, such as educational seminars, shows, and charitable functions, are unusual enough to receive special attention from the media. **Publicity** is free space and time provided by newspapers, magazines, radio, and TV for newsworthy events. For example, the famous annual Macy's Thanksgiving Day parade is covered extensively by the media. Stories abound about the celebrities involved, the beautiful floats, the giant balloons, and the parade watchers. This free media coverage is distinguished from advertising because of its nonpaid feature. It should be noted, however, that whereas retailers do not pay for publicity, they cannot always control the time, coverage, or content of the communication.

Retailers interested in good public relations have a more specific role to play regarding issues that are important to the public, such as the environment. Since packaging is a major source of environmental pollution, some retailers have responded by using bagging material that is degradable or recyclable. K mart and Wal-Mart have taken strong, visible positions on this issue. Jewel Food Stores, in concert with the Burlington Northern Railroad and a corrugated box recycler, has launched a "Recycling Express" train that transports tons of used corrugated material for reprocessing. Woolworth Corporation has created a new post of corporate director of environmental management to review corporate environmental activities and plans to respond to environmental issues. After McDonald's and eight of the nation's largest plastics producers set up a national program to recycle plastic hamburger containers and other packages, McDonald's yielded to public pressure by discontinuing its use of plastic. Furthermore, retailers are rushing to introduce environmentally friendly store brands, and manufacturers are following with "green products" such as phosphate-free laundry detergents,

FIGURE 16-5 Promotion Calendar

Date		Events L.Y.	Date		Events T.Y.
S	29	HOLLY DAYS Sale Insert	S	27	HOLLY DAYS Home Insert, NBW/CDH Insert
M	30	HOLLY DAYS	M	28	HOLLY DAYS
T	1		T	29	
W	2		W	30	
T	3		T	1	
F	4	BIGG SATURDAY TABLOID	F	2	BIGG SATURDAY PRE-PRINT
S	5	BIGG SATURDAY	S	3	BIGG SATURDAY
S	6	SALE INSERT	S	4	SALE INSERT
M	7		M	5	
T	8	ONE DAY SALE	T	6	ONE DAY SALE
W	9		W	7	
T	10		T	8	
F	11		F	9	GIFT INSERT
S	12		S	10	
S	13	SALE INSERT	S	11	
M	14		M	12	
T	15		T	13	
W	16		W	14	
T	17		T	15	
F	18	COUNTDOWN SALE BEGINS	F	16	COUNTDOWN SALE BEGINS
S	19		S	17	
S	20		S	18	
M	21		M	19	
T	22		T	20	
W	23		W	21	
T	24	COUNTDOWN SALE ENDS	T	22	
F	25	CHRISTMAS DAY	F	23	
S	26		S	24	COUNTDOWN SALE ENDS
S	27	CLOVER DAY	S	25	CHRISTMAS DAY
M	28	CLOVER DAY	M	26	
T	29	White Sale Catalog Mails CLOVER DAY	T	27	White Sale Cat. Mails
W	30	CLOVER DAY EXTENDED (SNOW)	W	28	
T	31		T	29	CLOVER DAY
F	1	NEW YEAR'S DAY	F	30	CLOVER DAY
S	2		S	31	CLOVER DAY

Note: The Petite Catalog scheduled to mail on November 11 will now mail on *November 14.*

biodegradable diapers, bathroom tissue made from recycled paper, and coffee filters that don't release chlorine. It appears that Americans are ready to change the way they live and buy. Preserving the environment, in fact, improving it, has become the marketing movement of the 1990s.

Publicity also takes the form of reporting a store's newsworthy activities of special seminars, shows, visits by celebrities, and personnel visits to schools and

major special events........week of   September 3, 1984

MONDAY	TUESDAY	WEDNESDAY	THURSDAY	FRIDAY	SATURDAY
Sept. 3	Sept. 4	Sept. 5	Sept. 6	Sept. 7	Sept. 8
Lees Carpet Expo and Sale Last day in Phila. Aud. Store hours Food Hall Demo Booth closed for Labor Day	Food Hall Demo 12:00 - 3:00 p.m. Tips for canning and preserving	Food Hall Demo 12:00 - 3:00 p.m. Watermelon rind	"Executive Decisions" Informal modeling and cocktails to introduce new Bridge Dept. 3rd floor in front of Fur Dept. 6:00 - 9:00 p.m. Food Hall Demo 12:00 - 3:00 p.m. Plum Tart French Apple Pear w/custard Tarts (variety) Irene Rothchild	Food Hall Demo 12:00 - 3:00 p.m. Candied fruit peel	Seventeen Beautyworks/Good Grooming classes Phila. Auditorium Springfield Training room 10:15 - 1:30 p.m. Food Hall Demo 12:00 - 3:00 p.m. Pies Rachel McNellis

major special events........week of   September 10, 1984

Sept. 10	Sept. 11	Sept. 12	Sept. 13	Sept. 14	Sept. 15
Food Hall Demo 12:00 - 3:00 p.m Beef Jerky Bridal Registry Promotion ends All Stores	Food Hall Demo 12:00 - 3:00 p.m. Pickled Celery and other Vegetables	Seventeen Beauty-works/Good Grooming classes 5:15 - 8:30 p.m. Jenkintown training room Men's Suit Seminar Philadelphia Auditorium Food Hall Demo 12:00 - 3:00 p.m. Dilly Beans	Seventeen Beauty-works/Good Grooming classes 5:15 - 8:30 p.m. Concord Training room Food Hall Demo 12:00 - 3:00 p.m. Mint Jelly	Seventeen Beauty-works/Good Grooming 5:15 - 8:30 p.m. Plymouth Meeting Auditorium Burlington training room Food Hall Demo 12:00 - 3:00 p.m. Lemon Curd	Seventeen Beauty-works/Good Grooming classes 10:15 - 1:30 p.m. Philadelphia Auditorium Springfield Training room Food Hall Demo 12:00 - 3:00 p.m. Northern preserved Cabbage Mei Ling Moy

Figure 16-6   Another example of a promotion calendar. *Courtesy:* Strawbridge & Clothier.

other institutions. For example, many personnel directors visit colleges and high schools to discuss career opportunities in retailing. These activities usually receive recognition from school and local papers, as well as from local radio stations. In addition, retailers support the activities of the Distributive Education Clubs of America, a national organization composed of students of retailing and marketing.

Publicity is one of the tools of a total **public relations** program, a continuing management function whose goal is to encourage positive public attitudes. Favorable public relations are another means of promoting a store, its services, and its image. A public relations program is designed to influence the opinions and attitudes of the store's various publics. These include customer publics, community publics (e.g., Boy Scouts and Little League), employee publics, and suppliers.

Public relations programs are not confined to domestic events only. For example, in 1990 an international team of Chinese, Soviets, and Americans climbed Mount Everest as a symbol of cooperative human achievement. The team was outfitted by L. L. Bean, Inc., the well-known catalog outdoor retailer. The televised event, beamed to the three nations, gave the company an aura of environmental and global peace leadership.

Favorable public relations help promote a store's image. Strawbridge & Clothier spearheaded the restoration of the nation's oldest commercial street. *Courtesy:* Strawbridge & Clothier.

Some stores offer discounts to special groups, usually civic, religious, or charitable organizations. By means of these price accommodations the stores develop community goodwill and often secure new patronage from members of the organizations to which the discounts are granted.

A good public relations program includes a store's internal public, meaning the people employed by the store. Happy employees serve the store's customers pleasantly and with dedication. Company publications containing news about store personnel are other important public relations tools.

When handled correctly, customer services such as credit, alterations, and returns are another avenue toward favorable public relations.

Press releases are prepared for the media

Press releases (Figure 16-7) are formal statements prepared by a firm and submitted to the media for publication. The message may be about a product, a special event, a store opening, or some change in store management. If it is newsworthy, the media will print the message at no cost to the store.

The major activities involved in carrying out the public relations function are

Macy's annual Thanksgiving Day parade generates excitement and extensive media coverage. *Courtesy:* Macy's.

THE ATTACHED WAS RELEASED AT 4:30 P.M., THURSDAY, MARCH 14, 1991

The Great Atlantic & Pacific Tea Company, Inc.
Corporate Affairs Department
Two Paragon Drive. Montvale. New Jersey 07645

Michael J. Rourke, Vice President
Communications and Corporate Affairs
(201) 930-4236

FOR IMMEDIATE RELEASE

MONTVALE, N.J. -- MARCH 14, 1991 -- The Great Atlantic & Pacific Tea Company, Inc. today reported record sales and earnings results (unaudited) for fiscal 1990.

For the year ended February 23, 1991, the company said net income rose 3% to $150,954,000 or $3.95 per share compared to $146,698,000 or $3.84 last year, while sales were $11,390,943,000 up 2.2% compared to $11,147,997,000 in fiscal 1989.

In the 12-week fourth quarter ended February 23, 1991, net income was $31,581,000 or $.83 per share compared to $34,509,000 or $.90 cents per share in the same period last year. Sales for the quarter were $2,772,991,000 compared to $2,567,724,000 during the same period a year ago. The results of the 69 Miracle Food Mart stores acquired in November 1990 were included in the 1990 fourth quarter, but not in 1989.

James Wood, chairman, president and chief executive officer, said that sluggish sales caused by a difficult economic climate in several key markets required increased spending on sales programs and advertising to stimulate sales volume during the fourth quarter. "The added spending had an adverse impact on fourth quarter earnings, but we improved our sales trends," he said. "We also partially offset the added promotional expense through the continued expansion of our centralized purchasing program, as well as synergistic savings in purchasing, distribution and administration costs, including one-time purchasing benefits achieved during the integration of Miracle Food Mart into our Canadian operations."

Mr. Wood added that the pressure on sales was expected to continue during the first half of 1991, especially in Ontario, Canada and the northeastern U.S. where A&P has large store concentrations and the economic downturn was having the greatest impact on consumer spending.

#

Figure 16-7 An example of a press release. *Courtesy:* A&P.

This Lazarus public relations advertisement was designed to generate excitement for its new store opening. *Courtesy:* Lazarus.

preparation of press releases, planning of community events, and development of good channels of communication with the media and the community. The mechanics of securing and reporting the appropriate information involves communication skills like writing ability.

NEW TERMS

coupon	purchase privilege offer
direct premium	referral premium
premium	sample (offered as a premium)
press release	self-liquidator premium
promotion calendar	trading stamps
public relations	trunk show
publicity	

CHAPTER HIGHLIGHTS

1. Retailers communicate to customers through advertising, display, personal selling, and sales promotion.
2. Sales promotion attracts additional customers through specific activities such as trading stamps, contests, games, premium offers, samples, coupons, price promotions, and special events. Retailers also use promotions to introduce new services and products and to offset slow periods and competition.
3. Trading stamps, contests, and games help develop customer loyalty and repeat business. The principal users of these types of promotion are supermarkets, service stations, and small retailers. Retailers must consider the use of stamps carefully before they adopt such promotions because they are expensive and difficult to terminate because of negative customer reactions.
4. Contests and games are exciting for customers and can be successful for retailers. However, they must adhere to legal regulations.
5. Premiums are items that are offered as incentives to shoppers. They include direct premiums, self-liquidators, purchase privilege offers, referral gifts, and samples.

6. Coupon incentive programs offer specific reductions in the prices of certain items. They build brand loyalty and reduce the costs of products. Some of the disadvantages are their occasional misuse and fraudulent redemption.

7. Price promotions by way of storewide sales increase customer traffic and generate higher sales volume. Some stores conduct sales on a regular basis, while others never hold sales because they believe sales would hurt their image.

8. Special events utilize excitement, showmanship, or information rather than price inducements. They include demonstrations and shows, theme promotions, and public service events.

9. In large firms, specialists perform the sales promotion function. In small ones, the owner or manager is responsible for decisions about what, how, and when to promote.

10. Major store promotions and promotion budgets are generally planned months in advance. Preparing a promotion budget depends on the size of the store, its location, its clientele, the type of merchandise carried, the local competition, local business conditions, and the cost of local media. A promotion calendar is used for planning special events over time.

11. Publicity is nonpaid-for space and time that is given by newspapers, magazines, radio, and television for newsworthy events like seminars, shows, and visits by celebrities.

12. The public relations program is a continuing management function whose purpose is to create a positive public attitude toward the retailer.

13. Retailers interested in promoting good public relations have a more specific role to play regarding the environment today.

REVIEW QUESTIONS

1. What are the main reasons for a retailer's use of sales promotions?
2. Explain how trading stamps and contests can build customer loyalty. What are some of the drawbacks of trading stamps?
3. What are the reasons for the popularity of coupons?
4. How are premiums used most effectively?
5. What types of special events are suitable for each of the following: department stores, supermarkets, small retailers, shopping centers?
6. Why are major store promotions planned far in advance? Why is the promotion budget so important?
7. How does publicity differ from advertising? In what ways can a store create favorable publicity?

DISCUSSION QUESTIONS

1. How might price promotions affect store image?
2. Why are coupon promotions becoming controversial?
3. Why is it important for a store to communicate with its various publics?

CASE 1

Coupon Controversy

The Department of Agriculture has estimated that 80 percent of American food shoppers use coupons in an attempt to cut their food bills. The average family redeems about 70 coupons annually, at an approximate average value of 18 cents each. Shoppers clip and use coupons from daily newspapers, magazines, and mail brochures and from the products themselves.

Esther Peterson, formerly special assistant to the president for consumer affairs, has commented that coupon promotions should be ended, provided that consumers receive the savings. She feels that coupons are used largely for what some nutritionists describe as "gimmick foods." Nevertheless, she believes that at least some portion of the promotion money spent by food companies has filtered down to the consumer.

The Community Nutrition Institute of Washington also has mixed feelings about coupons. Although it is opposed to coupons, it has not taken any formal position because of the possibility of savings for low-income families. Lower-income people have been increasing their use of coupons, but the highest rate of coupon redemption is still found among middle- and upper-income families.

According to Josephine Swanson, a consumer education instructor and food shopping consultant for Cornell University's Cooperative Extension in Ithaca, New York, coupons can "trap" shoppers, costing them more money in the long run. This is so because shoppers benefit from using coupons only if they use them to buy products that they normally purchase. However, the "trap" occurs when consumers are enticed by coupons into buying something that they wouldn't ordinarily purchase. This is especially so in the case of the double and triple couponing offered by several supermarket chains. This type of promotion actually doubles or triples the value of each coupon redeemed, thereby increasing the incentive to spend money on items that are not considered to be "durable household items." Such spending is a source of concern regarding the use of coupons by lower-income people.

Supermarket professionals support both arguments. Some feel that coupons improve consumer awareness and encourage shoppers to switch brands, thereby broadening the consumer's choices. Other defenders maintain that coupon promotions have not raised prices, but that higher prices are due to increased charges by wholesalers. On the other hand, some stores contend that it might be wise for manufacturers to eliminate coupons because the costs to supermarkets and other retailers are very high, with the savings to consumers insignificant.

Still another area of concern is coupon fraud. It is estimated that almost 20 percent of redeemed coupons are redeemed fraudulently by trade and store personnel. Consequently, the money value of these coupons is not paid to consumers. According to a Procter & Gamble executive, the costs of fraud eventually are reflected in consumer prices. To help curb this problem, the U.S. Postal Service and the Federal Bureau of Investigation probe possible cases of coupon fraud.

a. What do you think will be the outcome of the coupon controversy?
b. Do you agree that ending the use of coupons will save the consumer money? Explain.
c. Since basic foods like fruit, vegetables, milk, and meat are rarely couponed, do you feel that couponed items can be eliminated without affecting the average family's food budget? Explain.
d. Do you believe the costs of fraudulently redeemed coupons are reflected in consumer prices? Why?

CASE 2

Giant Retailers Target a Special Market

"*Grandes ahorras para toda la familia,*" states the announcer as the television screen depicts a smiling Hispanic father and two children dressed in fashionable sportswear and outerwear. The commercial is for J. C. Penney and is part of Penney's campaign to attract Hispanic customers to its stores.

J. C. Penney is one of a number of retailers in various parts of the country who have engaged in efforts to gain minority consumers, with a major effort geared toward Hispanics. These retailers include Sears, Ames, K mart, Burdine's, Walgreen, and supermarket chains such as Safeway, A&P, Kroger, and Ralphs.

Retailers who have targeted the Hispanic market have used a variety of advertising, promotion, and marketing techniques. These include ads in Spanish language dailies, sponsorship of programming and commercials on Hispanic radio and television stations, as well as active participation in community programs.

One of the most successful has been J. C. Penney, which has expanded its radio and television advertising campaigns, has a J. C. Penney USA guide available in Spanish, and has become strongly involved in Hispanic community affairs. Penney's is a participant in the U.S. Hispanic Chamber of Commerce and has sponsored such community programs as "Miami Is for Me" that is intended for the Hispanic populace of South Florida.

In addition, Penney's stores in major Hispanic markets such as Miami have installed bilingual directories and signs and have introduced specific merchandise like *quinceaners* gowns or debutante gowns to enhance the stores' appeal to Hispanic customers.

Burdine's is another retailer interested in the Hispanic consumer. Its department stores in Florida promote special events to attract these consumers, publish brochures in Spanish, and advertise in the major Spanish language media.

In Spanish-speaking areas, some stores have also made heavy use of Spanish language media and designed their promotions specifically for the market.

K mart is yet another retailer that is reaching out to Hispanic shoppers with increased advertising and sponsorship of a weekly variety show on the Spanish Radio Network, which reaches markets where 80 percent of the Spanish-speaking population in the country live.

The reasons for the efforts to reach Hispanic consumers can be found in marketing data that have revealed some extraordinary demographics. The current rate of growth for Hispanics is 6.5 times that of the general population, because of high birth rates and unrestricted immigration. Based on these rates, Hispanics will be the dominant minority in the United States in 1993 with 40 million people. Hispanics are already the dominant minority in a number of U.S. cities, such as Los Angeles, New York, San Francisco, Miami, and Denver. The Spanish-speaking minority currently numbers above 22 million, giving the United States the fifth-largest Hispanic population in the world.

Research also reveals that about 90 percent of Hispanics in the United States speak Spanish and 43 percent speak only Spanish or just enough English to be understood. In addition, surveys have shown that 63 percent of Hispanics believe that Spanish is the only language to use in order to communicate effectively with other Hispanics.

Media studies have found that a vast majority of Hispanics (70 percent) read, watch, or listen to Spanish language media and 63 percent indicate that such media are important to them.

What analysis of such research has concluded is that Hispanics represent a potential consumer market of $50 billion or more, and that, as consumers, they are more interested in name brands and quality products than most other Americans.

Clearly, such studies and the experience of some retailers have shown that Hispanic consumers form a major and expanding customer base for the retailing industry. Despite such statistics, many retailing analysts believe that the Hispanic consumer market has been largely untapped or even neglected by U.S. retailers in general, even as other domestic markets have reached or approach virtual saturation.

a. Why do you think some retailers have not made more serious efforts to reach the Hispanic consumer?

b. To reach the Hispanic customer, what strategies would you as a retailer follow in the areas of personnel, merchandising, customer service, and advertising and promotion? Explain how you might go about implementing these strategies.

c. How might an emphasis on the Hispanic market affect a retailer's traditional customer base?

REFERENCES

BEARDEN, W. O., D. R. LICHTENSTEIN, AND J. E. TEEL. "Comparison Price, Coupon, and Brand Effects on Consumer Reactions to Retail Newspaper Advertisements." *Journal of Retailing,* **60** (Summer 1984), pp. 11–34.

GREEN, P. E., V. MAHAJAN, S. M. GOLDBERG, AND P. K. KEDIA. "A Decision-Support System for Developing Retail Promotional Strategy." *Journal of Retailing,* **59** (Fall 1983), pp. 116–143.

KUNTZ, M. "Taking a Chance on Sweepstakes." *Newsday* (June 21, 1987), p. 76.

PETERSON, E. "New Tools to Create an Image." *Stores* (September 1989), pp. 42–44.

SCOTT, H. "Coupons Go In-Store." *Advertising Age* (May 21, 1990), p. 45.

Part 5

Controls

No retail business can remain successful for long without a system for managing money, records, inventory, and credit. So complex have commercial activities become that even small retailers are conscious of the need for controls. Chapter 17 introduces us to the meaning of accounting and the reasons for its importance. We study basic accounting procedures and delve into the meaning of financial reports. In connection with the reports, we learn about the usefulness of certain balance sheet and income statement measurements. We also discuss the significance and development of budgets.

Next we deal with inventory control, studying the causes of and remedies for inadequate and excessive inventories. We discuss Quick Response and its value to retailers. We then examine the factors that shape a store's inventory control system and show how perpetual and periodic inventory methods are used in dollar and unit control systems. We also learn how to estimate an inventory by the retail method. In order to determine a firm's profitability, we see how ending inventories are computed on a cost basis using the FIFO and LIFO methods.

In Chapter 18 we look at the role that credit plays in retail operations. After studying the different types of credit plans available to consumers, we look at the customer as a credit risk and list criteria for granting credit. Then we analyze the billing and collection techniques used by retailers. Finally, we examine the major federal laws regulating the extension of credit.

Chapter 17

Accounting and Inventory Control Systems

After completing this chapter, you should be able to:

- Explain the sections and terms of a balance sheet and an income statement.
- Compute ratios to measure the success of operations.
- Compute increases and decreases in operating expenses and explain how retailers evaluate expenses.
- Explain expense, cash, advertising, and merchandise budgets and indicate their relationship to accounting data.
- List resources for the development of sales forecasts.
- Identify the causes of inadequate and excessive inventories and suggest remedies for them.
- List the factors that shape a store's inventory control system.
- Describe the use of perpetual and periodic inventory methods in dollar control and unit control systems.
- Estimate ending inventory using the retail method, and list the method's advantages and disadvantages.
- Compute ending inventory by the (first-in, first-out) (FIFO) and (last-in, first-out) (LIFO) methods and explain their effect on income statements during inflationary and deflationary periods.
- Describe Quick Response and indicate its value to retailers.

In previous chapters, the emphasis has been on the following characteristics of retailing: image, location, price, value, and service. Few retailers blend all five in their operations. Instead, the more successful merchants build their sales strategies on a clearly defined combination of them. Some of the outstanding performers over the last few years show why this is so: The Price Company (image, price), The Home Depot and Wal-Mart Stores (image, price, service), and Nordstrom (image, value, service). Through effective promotions and advertising, retailers develop an image, maintain contact with consumers, and seek to enlarge their customer base.

The next matter of concern for a store is the system by which it controls the financial and inventory aspects of the business. Without carefully designed procedures for ensuring accuracy and completeness in the maintenance of records, management could not make the myriad decisions required of it each day. Nor would it have the necessary information for a correct analysis of operations. In this chapter we examine some important features of financial and inventory records.

THE MEANING OF ACCOUNTING

Accounting for control, analysis, and decision making
Accounting is the compilation of financial data for purposes of control, analysis, and decision making. This definition applies to all types of businesses, including retailing. Though retailers need not know accounting techniques to understand financial reports, they should be familiar with some basic terms and concepts found in those reports. Without this knowledge, they are handicapped in efforts to interpret the results of business activities.

Why Accounting Records Are Important to Retailers

Many individuals within a retail business make operational decisions. For example, a buyer needs to know the volume of current sales in order to plan markdowns or additional purchases. A store manager requires information about departmental sales in order to capitalize on strong sales areas and correct the difficulties in weak ones. He or she also needs to know the profit levels in each department. An advertising manager needs sales data to judge the effectiveness of the store's advertising efforts. In short, few planning and control decisions can be made without adequate accounting systems.

UNDERSTANDING FINANCIAL REPORTS

Information contained in financial reports, also known as financial statements, is analyzed to determine a firm's status and progress. The analysis involves many financial aspects of a company's operation, including sales trends, inventory costs, overhead changes, and profitability.

The two most commonly used financial reports are the **balance sheet,** or statement of financial position, and the **income statement.**

The Balance Sheet

The balance sheet: assets, liabilities, owner's equity

This report contains information about the assets (the things a business owns) and **liabilities** (debts) of a business as of a particular date. Subtracting the liabilities from the assets results in the **owner's equity,** or **net worth.** For example, a retailer whose assets and liabilities are $40,000 and $30,000, respectively, has an owner's equity of $10,000.

The amounts may be expressed as follows.

Assets	$40,000
Less: Liabilities	30,000
Owner's equity	$10,000

Stated another way, assets equal liabilities plus owner's equity. Corporations often call their net worth **stockholders' equity.**

For comparative purposes, many retailers list the previous year's figures as well as current ones. This allows them to detect changes from one period to the next. Table 17-1 shows the balance sheet of a retail corporation. The sections of the statement are analyzed in the following paragraphs.

Current Assets

These assets consist of cash and assets that are expected to be either converted into cash or expended within a year. Accounts receivable, for example, represent money owed by customers and usually are collected within a year. Merchandise inventory, or stock, is assumed to be sold within a year. Supplies, including store and office supplies, are generally used within a year of purchase.

Plant and Equipment Assets (Fixed Assets)

These are long-lived assets such as showcases and delivery equipment that are periodically reduced in value (depreciated) because of wear and tear, obsolescence, or inadequacy. Depreciation is a deductible expense for tax purposes and reduces the amount of taxes a business pays. Consequently, retailers should consider the tax effects when planning their purchases of plant and equipment assets.

Current Liabilities

This category consists of debts that will probably be repaid within one year of their assumption. For example, *accounts payable*, which consist of debts owed to *creditors* (those to whom the retailer owes money) for purchases, are customarily

TABLE 17-1 The Balance Sheet of a Retail Corporation

Four-Star Stores Corporation *Balance Sheet* *December 31*	*1990*	*1989*
ASSETS		
Current Assets		
Cash	$150,000	$120,000
Accounts receivable	280,000	250,000
Merchandise inventory	200,000	220,000
Supplies	40,000	18,000
Total current assets	$670,000	$608,000
Plant and Equipment Assets		
Delivery equipment (after depreciation)	$58,000	$62,000
Furniture and fixtures (after depreciation)	85,000	82,000
Office equipment (after depreciation)	22,000	26,000
Total plant and equipment assets	$165,000	$170,000
Total assets	$835,000	$778,000
LIABILITIES		
Current Liabilities		
Accounts payable	$282,000	$236,000
Notes payable	50,000	20,000
Salaries payable	3,000	5,000
Total current liabilities	$335,000	$261,000
Long-Term Liabilities		
Notes payable (due 1994)	40,000	40,000
Total liabilities	$375,000	$301,000
Stockholders' Equity		
Capital stock	$300,000	$300,000
Retained earnings	160,000	177,000
Total stockholders' equity	$460,000	$477,000
Total liabilities and stockholders' equity	$835,000	$778,000

paid in less than one year (e.g., 30 days or 60 days). Notes payable that are included in current liabilities are short-term loans (e.g., 60 or 90 days), which are scheduled for repayment in less than a year. *Salaries payable* are monies that are due to employees at the balance sheet date.

Long-Term Liabilities

These are debts that run for more than a year. For example, the *notes payable* due in 1994 may have arisen from the purchase of furniture and fixtures on a long-term basis, with the retailer not liable for the payment until 1994. Of course, interest will be paid along with the amount of the note.

Stockholders' Equity

This section of the balance sheet contains the net worth of the business. Capital stock refers to the investment by stockholders (owners) in the corporation, while retained earnings are profits made by the company that have not yet been distributed to the stockholders. Distributed profits of a corporation are called **dividends.**

Useful Balance Sheet Measurements

Retailers frequently use balance sheets to determine the relationships among their assets, liabilities, and owner's equity. Through the application of simple mathematical procedures, they can judge the status of a particular aspect of the business. As you will see, they often compare their results with retail industry averages. (For convenience, all financial statement measurements discussed in this chapter are summarized later.)

Current Ratio

Current and quick ratios

By matching current assets (CA) against current liabilities (CL), the retailer learns how well the business is positioned to pay its current debts. Here's how it's done.

$$\frac{\text{Current assets}}{\text{Current liabilities}} = \textbf{Current ratio}$$

Using the 1990 amounts in Table 17-1, we find

$$\frac{\text{CA (\$670,000)}}{\text{CL (\$335,000)}} = \text{CR (2:1)}$$

The ratio is usually expressed as 2 to 1, meaning that there are $2 of current assets available to pay every $1 of current liabilities.

A current ratio (CR) of 2 to 1 or a bit higher is usually considered satisfactory. When the CR is significantly lower, the retailer may have difficulty paying current debts. This may be due to insufficient cash on hand or because sales of merchandise and anticipated collections of accounts receivables are insufficient to meet those debts comfortably. When the CR is too high, the retailer may have excessive cash or merchandise on hand, that is, assets that are not earning money for the business.

Quick Ratio

Though the current ratio is often of value, it is sometimes a deceptive indication of a retailer's ability to pay current debts. This happens, for example, when the merchandise inventory is a very large part of the current assets. Since it is not easy to turn a large inventory into cash quickly, a business with such an inventory may not have sufficient funds for the payment of current liabilities. A more realistic test in this instance would be the **quick ratio,** sometimes called the acid test. Here's how this measure is computed.

$$\frac{\text{Cash} + \text{Receivables}}{\text{Current liabilities}} = \text{Quick ratio}$$

Returning to the 1990 amounts in Table 17-1, we get

$$\frac{\$150,000 + \$280,000}{\$335,000} = 1.3{:}1$$

In other words, the quick ratio is 1.3 to 1, which means that there is $1.30 of current assets (not including inventory and supplies) available to pay each $1.00 of current liabilities. Since banks and other lending institutions usually require a quick ratio of approximately 1 to 1, the Four-Star Stores Corporation may be in a favorable position for securing loans.

Though the current and quick ratios serve useful analytical purposes, they are generally considered along with other important factors. For example, retailers often compare ratios against ratios for previous accounting periods or those of competitive stores. In other words, an informed retailer rarely relies on only one factor in making decisions.

Debt-to-Equity Ratio

The **debt-to-equity ratio** shows the relationship between a company's liabilities and net worth. The *higher* the ratio, the more difficult it is for a company to meet its debts. Using the 1990 amounts in Table 17-1, we see that

$$\frac{\text{Total liabilities}}{\text{Total stockholders' equity}} = \text{Debt-to-equity ratio}$$

$$\frac{\$375,000}{\$460,000} = .82 \text{ to } 1$$

A ratio below 1 is considered excellent, so the .82 ratio in our illustration is a favorable one. However, we are witnessing distressingly higher ratios in the retail industry as we enter the last decade of this century. For example, while a cross section of large retailers showed an average ratio of 1.8 to 1 in 1970, it had grown to 3.32 to 1 in 1989. This statistic is one of the reasons for the increased pace of acquisitions and mergers in retailing. By contrast, Dillards, a department store chain, was able to purchase D. H. Holmes in 1988 because of Dillards' low ratio.

The Income Statement

The income statement: sales, cost of goods sold, operating expenses

An income statement, also known as a profit and loss statement or an operating statement, indicates whether a company has made a profit or sustained a loss over a specific period. It includes information about sales, merchandise costs, and operating expenses. It is particularly valuable when compared to a report for a prior, similar period. For example, it might be helpful to compare operating figures for two successive Christmas seasons in making plans for the next one.

Table 17-2 contains the three sections of an income statement. The first, "Revenue from Sales," shows that after returns and allowances by customers are deducted, net sales increased from $910,000 in 1989 to $970,000 in 1990. The second section, "Cost of Goods Sold," reveals an increase from $400,000 in 1989 to $500,000 in 1990. The amounts in the second section are computed by

1. Adding the merchandise inventory on hand at the beginning of the year to the purchases for the year. The result is the *cost of goods available for sale*.
2. Subtracting the merchandise on hand at the end of the year from the cost of goods available for sale. The result is the *cost of goods sold*.

TABLE 17-2 The Income Statement of a Retail Corporation

Four-Star Stores Corporation Income Statement January 1–December 31	1990		1989	
Revenue from sales				
Sales	$990,000		$920,000	
Less: returns and allowances	20,000		10,000	
Net sales		$970,000		$910,000
Cost of Goods Sold				
Merchandise inventory, Jan. 1	$220,000		$190,000	
Add: purchases	480,000		430,000	
Cost of goods available for sale	$700,000		$620,000	
Less: merchandise inventory, Dec. 31	200,000		220,000	
Cost of goods sold		500,000		400,000
Gross margin (gross profit)		$470,000		$510,000
Operating Expenses				
Salaries	$150,000		$145,000	
Rent	90,000		90,000	
Advertising	75,000		100,000	
Utilities	55,000		50,000	
Insurance	24,000		35,000	
Supplies and postage	30,000		24,000	
Depreciation	16,000		40,000	
Total expenses		440,000		484,000
Net income		$30,000		$26,000

This section also shows that the **gross margin** (profit before deducting operating expenses) decreased from $510,000 to $470,000. The third section, "Operating Expenses," lists a decrease in expenses (overhead) from $484,000 in 1989 to $440,000 in 1990. Finally, the statement shows that the net income (net profit) increased from $26,000 to $30,000. Net income is the difference between gross margin and operating expenses.

Useful Income Statement Measurements

Retailers use a combination of income statement and balance sheet amounts to construct additional ratios and business indicators. As with balance sheet ratios, these measurements enable merchants to assess the effectiveness of business operations and to make important decisions. (The balance sheet and income statement measurements covered in this chapter are summarized in Table 17-3.)

TABLE 17-3   Financial Statement Measurements

Name of Measurement	Financial Statement from Which Information Is Taken	Formula	Purpose
Current ratio	Balance sheet	Current assets ÷ current liabilities	Enables retailer to determine how well the business is able to pay current debts
Quick ratio	Balance sheet	(Cash + receivables) ÷ current liabilities	Used instead of the current ratio when merchandise inventory is a very large part of current assets
Debt-to-equity ratio	Balance sheet	Total liabilities ÷ stockholders' equity	Indicates the level of debt in relation to ownership
Stock turnover	Balance sheet and income statement	Net sales ÷ average inventory at retail	Indicates the number of times an average inventory is sold during the year
Average turnover days	Balance sheet and income statement	Number of days in accounting period ÷ turnover rate	Indicates the number of days it takes to sell the entire inventory once
Average collection period	Balance sheet and income statement	Year-end receivables ÷ average sales per day	Tells retailer the approximate time it has taken to collect the store's debts
Gross margin on sales	Income statement	Gross margin ÷ net sales	Indicates the percent of gross margin on every sales dollar
Sales per square foot of selling space	Income statement	Net sales ÷ square feet of selling space	Indicates how effectively sales are generated
Net income on sales	Income statement	Net income ÷ net sales	Indicates the percent of net income on every sales dollar
Return on investment (ROI)	Balance sheet and income statement	Net income ÷ stockholders' equity (owner's equity)	Indicates the percent earned on investment in the business

Stock Turnover

This measure indicates the number of times an average inventory is sold during the year. It is important to have this information because unsold goods occupy valuable shelf space and also represent a costly monetary investment. To compute stock turnover, use the following formula.

$$\frac{\text{Net sales}}{\text{Average inventory at retail}} = \text{Stock turnover}$$

The net sales are taken from the first section of the income statement. For the purposes of the following illustration, the average inventory at *retail* is an average of the inventory at *retail* prices at the beginning and end of the year. Assuming the following inventories at *retail* price for the Four-Star Stores Corporation in 1989,

January 1	$280,000
December 31	300,000

the average inventory was $290,000.

$$\frac{(\$280,000 + \$300,000)}{2} = \$290,000$$

Computing the 1989 stock turnover, we get

$$\frac{\$910,000}{\$290,000} = 3.1$$

Assuming the following inventories at *retail* price for 1990,

January 1	$300,000
December 31	290,000

the average inventory was $295,000 and the stock turnover was 3.3, computed as follows.

$$\frac{\$970,000}{\$295,000} = 3.3$$

Now, what do turnovers of 3.1 and 3.3 mean? These figures indicate that the average amount of merchandise on hand was turned over (sold) 3.1 times in 1989 and 3.3 times in 1990.[1] These numbers are significant *only* when they are related to

[1] Another way of expressing the figures is this: In 1989, the merchandise was sold in 3.1 times more volume than its corresponding unsold inventory was accumulated; in 1990, the figure was 3.3 times.

the type of retail business involved. For example, stores, such as jewelry shops, that carry high-priced merchandise generally show low turnover rates, while gasoline stations and many food stores have high rates. Merchants compare their turnover rate to rates for previous periods to detect the relative frequency of sales activity. A significant change in a rate may call for an analysis of sales and inventory operations. Some retailers also compare their turnovers to rates reported by other merchants in similar businesses.

Low turnovers may be due to any or a combination of the following additional factors:

- Poor buying decisions or unreasonable pricing policies
- Faulty in-store practices such as inefficient stockkeeping, unproductive salespeople, and wasteful checking/marking procedures
- Acceptance of late-delivery goods, with consequent damaging markdowns
- Ineffective advertising, displays, or promotions

Although high turnovers are usually desirable, they sometimes bring on unfavorable results. For example, retailers whose customers depend on wide, indepth assortments of merchandise must guard against stock shortages in their quest for high turnovers. Without adequate stock to maintain patronage, their customers may seek other retail outlets. The lesson, then, is to balance the advantages of high turnover rates with an intelligent balance of goods.

In the preceding illustration the average inventory was the average of the inventories at the beginning and end of the year. Since inventories are usually low at these times, however, this average may not be representative of the amount of stock that a retailer usually maintains. To reduce the chances of distortion, most retailers include several monthly inventories in their computations. Some, in fact, use the inventory on hand at the beginning of each month (12 months) in addition to the inventory at the end of the year (1 month), thereby obtaining 13 separate inventory amounts for averaging.

It should be noted that many accountants use cost, rather than sales, figures in computing stock turnover.

Average Turnover Days

Having computed the stock turnover, some retailers go one step further and convert the turnover rate into **average turnover days.** This is accomplished by dividing the number of days in the accounting period by the turnover rate. For 1990 the Four-Star Store Corporation shows

$$\frac{365 \text{ days}}{3.3 \text{ turnover rate}} = \begin{array}{l} 111 \text{ average number of days for each} \\ \text{stock turnover (days in inventory)} \end{array}$$

In other words, it took approximately 111 days to sell the entire inventory once. Of course, the shorter the turnover time, the less chance there is for merchandise to become obsolete, soiled, or damaged. Retailers match turnover days against those for previous periods as an additional check on the movement of stock.

Average Collection Period

This measure tells the retailer the approximate time it has taken to collect the store's debts. It is computed as follows.

$$\frac{\text{Year-end receivables}}{\text{Average sales per day}} = \textbf{Average collection period}$$

The average sales per day are derived by dividing the net sales (found on the income statement) by the number of days in the year. For Four-Star Stores at the end of 1990 we get

$$\frac{\$970,000}{365 \text{ days}} = \$2,658 \text{ average sales per day}$$

Next we substitute both the $2,658 and the year-end accounts receivables, $280,000 taken from the 1990 balance sheet, to find the average collection period.

$$\frac{\$280,000}{\$2,658} = 105 \text{ days}$$

In other words, it took an average of 105 days for the company to collect from a customer. The length of a collection period depends on the time a retailer allows customers to pay bills and the extent to which it enforces collections. The more delinquent customers are, of course, the longer the average collection period. To remain operational, therefore, retailers must attempt to extend credit only to reliable consumers and must institute workable collection procedures. (Credit and collections are discussed further in Chapter 18.)

Gross Margin on Sales

This measure indicates the *percentage* of gross margin on every sales dollar.

$$\frac{\text{Gross margin}}{\text{Net sales}} = \text{Gross margin on sales}$$

Both amounts in the formula are taken from the income statement. From Table 17-2 we find the following

1990	1989
$\dfrac{\$470,000}{\$970,000} = 48.5\%$	$\dfrac{\$510,000}{\$910,000} = 56.0\%$

Typical gross margin rates in the retail industry range from 20 percent to as much as 60 percent. As you can see from the figures, Four-Star Stores Corporation's gross margin rate fell from 56 percent in 1989 to 48.5 percent in 1990. Management would have investigated the reasons for the decline, checking sales and purchases amounts as well as inventory levels.

A typical gross margin for discount stores is 23 percent, for warehouse clubs, 13 percent, and for hypermarkets, about 18 percent.

Sales Per Square Foot of Selling Space

More and more, retailers are measuring success in terms of their sales volume as it relates to the amount of store space devoted to selling. Called **sales per square foot of selling space,** this measurement is calculated as follows:

$$\frac{\text{Net sales}}{\text{Square feet of selling space}} = \text{Sales per square foot of selling space}$$

Let's assume that the Four-Star Stores Corporation's selling areas contain 5,000 square feet. Using the 1990 net sales figure in Table 17-2, we see that

$$\frac{\$970,000}{5,000 \text{ square feet}} = \$194 \text{ sales per square foot of selling space}$$

The significance of $194 in this illustration depends on such factors as past performance and retail industry averages.

For a more complete understanding of sales per square foot, one must know some of the characteristics of the retailer under study. For example, drugstores located in skyscraper buildings tap into a tremendous source of potential customers without the need of parking space. Consequently, almost all of their space is devoted to selling, and their sales per square foot are high—even above $1,000 in the case of Duane Reade drugstores located in New York City.

Sometimes, chains project higher sales per square foot when opening a new store. For example, when Hooker Corporation developed its Cincinnati Forest Fair Mall in 1989, it expected its stores in the mall to produce about $150 sales per square foot. This goal was in excess of what Hooker stores elsewhere had been doing.

One caution in the use of sales per square foot of selling space is the composition of those sales. For example, if the sales consist largely of low gross margin merchandise, the net profit (the bottom line) will also be low—or nonexistent. Consequently, an intelligent reading of this measurement must be combined with a concomitant analysis of profits. In fact, most retailers consider profit per square foot of selling space a very critical measurement of success.

Net Income on Sales

This measure indicates the *percentage* of net income (net profit) on every sales dollar.

$$\frac{\text{Net income}}{\text{Net sales}} = \text{Net income on sales}$$

Both amounts in the formula are taken from the income statement. From Table 17-2 we find the following

1990	1989

$$\frac{\$30,000}{\$970,000} = 3.1\% \qquad \frac{\$26,000}{\$910,000} = 2.9\%$$

Of course, the higher the percentage of net income to sales, the more profitable the business. Typical net income rates for retailers are

Fast-food chains	4.0 percent
Specialty stores	3.5 percent
Department stores	3.5 percent
Supermarkets	1.5 percent

There is a good deal of evidence that specialty store divisions of large chains produce higher rates of profit than do the department store divisions. This is the major reason for the start-up and/or acquisition of specialty operations by department store chains.

Return on Investment

How does a retailer or an investor in a retail company determine whether the monetary investment is a sound one? A method that is often used to answer the question is to compute a measure called **return on investment, (ROI).** Here's how it's done.

$$\frac{\text{Net income}}{\text{Stockholders' equity (owner's equity)}} = \text{Return on investment}$$

The net income is taken from the income statement, while the stockholders' equity comes from the balance sheet. The stockholders' equity used is the average of the equities at the beginning and end of the year. Using Four-Star Stores' 1990 figures, the average equity is

$$\frac{\$477,000 + \$460,000}{2} = \$468,500$$

The return on investment for 1990, then, is

$$\frac{\$30,000}{\$468,500} = .064, \text{ or } 6.4\% \text{ ROI}$$

This means that Four-Star Stores earned 6.4 percent on its investment in 1990. Should an investor be content with this return? The answer depends on a number of factors, such as the possibility of the investor's earning a higher return from some other venture or investment, the financial outlook for Four-Star Stores, competitors' ROI, the state of the economy, and so forth.

Figure 17-1 shows how a retail firm might chart its ROI for a number of years. Other significant ratios are

- Gross margin return on inventory investment.
- Gross margin per full-time equivalent (FTE) employee.

RETAIL STRATEGY

Although gross margin is a key measurement in retailing, it is sometimes subject to price strategy. This was the case with K mart Corporation in 1989 when the company lowered its prices as part of a long-term strategy to improve market share. K mart's approach sacrificed some gross margin (temporarily, the company hoped) in order to benefit future earnings.

Measuring Operating Expenses

It is obvious that the lower a retailer's expenses, the higher its possible net income. In order to control operating expenses, the merchant needs to determine the extent to which individual expenses increase or decrease over time. An

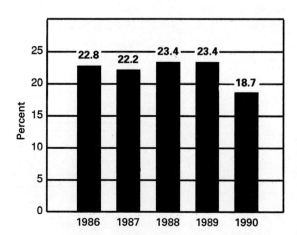

Figure 17-1 Shareholders' return on average equity.

TABLE 17-4 Using Dollars and Percents for Comparisons

| Company | Advertising Expenses | | Increase | |
	1989	1990	Dollars	Percent
A	$200,000	$210,000	$10,000	5
B	50,000	60,000	10,000	20

analysis of this information often makes it possible to reduce particular overhead items.

It is much easier to judge the significance of increases and decreases by using percents rather than dollars. To understand why this is so, look at Table 17-4. Company A's advertising expenses increased by $10,000, or 5 percent, from 1989 to 1990. Company B's advertising expenses also increased by $10,000, but its *percent* increase was 20 percent, four times as much! Though the dollar increases were identical, the percent increases showed the true relative changes. This is why retailers frequently use percentages to compare progress in one period with progress in another, or to compare their statistics with those of competitors.

Table 17-5 shows how a retailer might analyze expenses in terms of its own operations. Utilities expenses increased by $1,000, or 50 percent, from 1988 to 1989. It increased by an even larger amount, $1,200, from 1989 to 1990, yet the *percentage* increase was only 40 percent. The insurance expenses decreased by $1,200, or 25 percent, from 1988 to 1989. It decreased by a lesser amount, $1,080, from 1989 to 1990, yet the *percentage* decrease was 30 percent. In both cases the percentages were a more realistic indicator of change than the dollars.

We turn our attention once more to the Four-Star Stores income statement. Table 17-6 contains the dollar and percentage changes from 1989 to 1990 for net sales and for selected expense categories. On the basis of the changes, management might ask the following questions.

Management questions about expenses

To what extent was the 3.4 percent increase in salaries responsible for the 6.6 percent increase in net sales? Would hiring additional salespeople result in an even better sales performance?

Why was there an increase in net sales despite a 25 percent decrease in advertising expenses? Are advertising expense dollars being used most effectively?

TABLE 17-5 An Illustration of Increases (Decreases) in Expenses

| Expense | 1988 Actual Expense | Actual Expense | 1989 Increase (Decrease) from 1988 | | Actual Expense | 1990 Increase (Decrease) from 1989 | |
			Dollars	Percentage		Dollars	Percentage
Utilities	$2,000	$3,000	$1,000	50%	$4,200	$1,200	40%
Insurance	4,800	3,600	(1,200)	(25)	2,520	(1,080)	(30)

TABLE 17-6   Four-Star Stores Corporation—Analysis of Income Statement Changes, 1989 to 1990

			Increase (Decrease)	
Income Statement Item	*1989*	*1990*	*Dollars*	*Percentage Change*
Net sales	$910,000	$970,000	$60,000	6.6%
Salaries expense	145,000	150,000	5,000	3.4
Advertising expense	100,000	75,000	(25,000)	(25)
Supplies and postage expense	24,000	30,000	6,000	25

Was the 25 percent increase in supplies and postage due largely to inflation and higher mailing costs? Might these expenses be reduced with better management controls?

Evaluating Operating Expenses

Many retailers evaluate each operating expense as it relates to net sales. The assumptions underlying this method are as follows.

1. Sales can be produced only through the outlay of operating expenses.
2. Funds for operating expenses should be used where they are most likely to increase sales.
3. A reduction in expenses does not necessarily result in a decrease in sales.
4. Unnecessary expenditures do not increase sales and should be eliminated.

Table 17-7 shows the relationship of each of Four-Star Stores' operating expenses to net sales for the years 1989 and 1990. On the basis of the statistics, the owners or managers might ask questions like the following.

TABLE 17-7   Four-Star Stores Corporation—Relationship of Operating Expenses to Net Sales, 1989 and 1990[1]

	1990		*1989*	
Operating Expense	*Dollars*	*Percentage of Net Sales*	*Dollars*	*Percentage of Net Sales*
Salaries	$150,000	15.5%	$145,000	15.9%
Rent	90,000	9.3	90,000	9.9
Advertising	75,000	7.7	100,000	11.0
Utilities	55,000	5.7	50,000	5.5
Insurance	24,000	2.5	35,000	3.8
Supplies and postage	30,000	3.1	24,000	2.6
Depreciation	16,000	1.6	40,000	4.4

[1] Net sales: 1989, $910,000; 1990, $970,000.

Salaries	What were the reasons for the decrease from 15.9 percent to 15.5 percent despite a $5,000 increase in actual salaries?
	What accounted for the $5,000 increase in salaries? Employee raises or benefits? Additional personnel?
Rent	How much longer does the store's lease have to run? How would a substantial increase in rent affect the relationship between rent expense and projected sales?
Advertising	Why did net sales increase despite a reduction of $25,000 in advertising expenses?
	Might advertising expenditures be reduced further without hurting sales?
Utilities	Is the increase from 5.5 percent to 5.7 percent reasonable in the light of escalating costs of energy?
	Are there alternate forms of store lighting that should be explored?
Insurance	Does the decrease from 3.8 percent to 2.5 percent have implications for the adequacy of the store's insurance coverage?
	When can the company expect an increase in insurance rates? To what extent?
Supplies and postage	What accounted for the increase from 2.6 percent to 3.1 percent?
	Prices of supplies and/or increased postal rates?
	Can outgoing mail be reduced without damaging sales?
Depreciation	Is the decrease from 4.4 percent to 1.6 percent an indication of aging physical assets?
	Are additional equipment, furniture, and fixtures needed?

BUDGETS

Budgets and accounting data

A budget is a plan that estimates future sales, expenses, or some other financial aspect of a company. The use of budgets to plan, evaluate, and control retail operations is common to well-run stores. Whether it is a simple budget prepared by the owner of a small store or a departmentalized budget designed for a large retailer, accounting information is essential for its preparation. Now we'll identify specific budgets and indicate their relationship to accounting data.

Expense Budget

We have already indicated the importance of controlling operating expenses. In order to do this, many retailers prepare **expense budgets,** which consist of estimated expense outlays over a specific period—six months, one month, one week, and so on. These estimates are based on past experience and future plans. Actual expenses are then compared with the estimates to determine how well specific areas or departments are staying within the estimates.

Budgets must be flexible to accommodate sudden changes in operations. For example, a newspaper strike may affect sales so severely that a store may require additional funds for alternative advertising outlets.

A budget pinpoints responsibility for the expenditure of funds. Consequently, specific store personnel can be held accountable for expense overruns or rewarded for reducing expenses. Ideally, those who are responsible for incurring expenses should be involved in the development of the budget estimates.

Accounting records allow for the listing of specific expenses. In this way the retailer has day-to-day information on expenditures and uses the expense budget to make decisions.

Cash Budget

As you have seen, one of the most crucial financial considerations facing retailers is the need to have sufficient current assets to pay bills as they come due. Of all the current assets, the most essential one is cash. This is so because only cash can satisfy the payment demands of creditors and employees. It should be noted, however, that an excess of cash is wasteful, since idle money does not earn anything for a business. The excess might be used more productively for the purchase of additional stock or for investment.

In order to plan cash activities prudently, retailers develop a **cash budget.** This budget is an estimate of cash receipts and payments for a given period. Receipts are determined from forecasts of cash sales, accounts receivable collections, and miscellaneous income. Payments are based on anticipated expenditures for merchandise, expenses, miscellaneous items, and income taxes. As with expense budgets, actual intakes and outlays of cash are periodically matched against cash budget estimates to evaluate the company's cash position and take whatever action is necessary. Retailers often refer to their cash status as their cash flow position. A sample cash budget is shown in Table 17-8.

The importance of cash flow was demonstrated vividly in 1989 when the Campeau Corporation announced that its two retail divisions—Federated Department Stores and Allied Stores—could not pay their debts without a substantial infusion of cash.

TABLE 17-8 A Cash Budget

Lorel's Toy Room— Cash Budget for Quarter Ended June 30, 1990	April	May	June
Cash balance, 1st day of month	$22,000	$24,000	$25,000
Cash receipts			
Cash sales	12,000	11,000	14,000
Accounts receivable collections	15,000	17,000	18,000
Rent from leased departments	1,000	1,000	1,000
	$50,000	$53,000	$58,000
Cash payments			
Purchase of merchandise	$38,000	$34,000	$31,000
Operating expenses	11,000	10,000	8,000
Installment on notes payable		2,000	2,000
Income taxes	5,000	5,000	5,000
	$54,000	$51,000	$46,000
Cash balance, last day of month	($ 4,000)	$ 2,000	$12,000

Advertising Budget

In Chapter 15 you saw that advertising is an extremely important function in a retail organization. In order to use advertising dollars effectively, many retailers develop advertising budgets. Estimates are usually based on the following factors: an evaluation of consumer demand, a selection of appropriate advertising media, a clear understanding of the retailer's objectives, and an appreciation of past practices and results. Up-to-date accounting information is essential if one is to determine how well the budget is serving as a useful guide to expenditures.

Despite the availability of useful advertising budget techniques, too many retailers base their estimates on a single consideration, such as competitors' practices, a tie-in to estimated sales volume, or an arbitrary determination of available funds. Retailers who fail to identify specific goals in the construction of advertising budgets frequently waste precious funds. For example, a store whose image is unclear might do well to commit some advertising dollars to strengthening its image rather than spending it all on conventional campaigns aimed at increasing sales.

Merchandise Budget

A **merchandise budget** contains estimates of the factors that affect merchandise activities. It guides the retailer in the development of buying and selling plans. In this sense it is also a mechanism for the control and evaluation of employees who are involved in merchandise functions.

The budget considers the following items: projected sales, inventory levels, open-to-buy, and gross margin. It provides for

1. An analysis of changes in the trading area
2. An examination of short- and long-range selling facilities
3. A consideration of additional merchandise categories
4. An identification of competitive practices

It plans for inventory shifts on the basis of opening stock levels, planned purchases, markdowns, discounts, and shortages.

A carefully developed merchandise budget provides a framework for sound business practices. It should be specific yet flexible, and must be attentive to past practices yet open to new ideas. Detailed performance statistics maintained in usable accounting form are essential to its success.

SALES FORECASTING

Sales forecasting: a key element in budgeting

Our discussion of merchandise budgets indicated that one of the key items in such a budget is a projection of sales. This is true because a material over- or under-estimation of sales has a serious effect on merchandising decisions. Consequently, it is essential that the retailer project future sales with a good degree of accuracy. As stated in Chapter 2, this predictive feature is often referred to as sales forecasting.

A small merchant develops forecasts on the basis of

1. Experience.
2. Knowledge of the field.
3. Contacts with suppliers.
4. Opinions of salespeople.
5. Input from professionals (e.g., accountants).

Minicomputers are being used by small retailers with increasing frequency in the development of sales forecasts.

Large retail companies

1. Gather information from their own executives and buyers.
2. Secure data from consulting firms.
3. Study journals of retail opinion, such as *Women's Wear Daily.*
4. Use computers to identify trends and problems.

All retailers rely on consumer attitudes and behavior to chart future actions.

OPERATING AN ACCOUNTING SYSTEM

Large retailers utilize computers for most of their accounting functions. This enables them to secure daily reports on a variety of activities: sales, accounts receivables, inventory, and so forth. Input to computers is accomplished through the use of magnetic tapes, magnetic disks, or cash register tie-lines. In many

THE A&P EMPIRE

George Huntington Hartford

Born in Augusta, Maine, in 1833, George Huntington Hartford worked in a dry goods store in Boston to learn the basics of business. From there he went west to seek his fortune in the meat and hide center of St. Louis. However, the politics and hardships of frontier life convinced him that his merchant mind was better suited to the commerce of the East.

Hartford was hired by Benjamin F. Gilman, a successful businessman, to work in his leather firm and his newly developed tea-importing business. Within a short time the two men had expanded the tea enterprise into a retail and mail order tea business, undercutting competitors by means of a shrewd sales strategy. Thus was born the Great American Tea Company.

In 1869 Gilman and Hartford started a new company called Great Atlantic & Pacific Tea Company. Soon everyone was referring to it simply as A&P. By 1876 there were more than 20 stores extending as far west as St. Paul, Minnesota, and shortly thereafter there was a total of 52 outlets.

In 1878 Hartford secured control and management of A&P and could boast a sales volume of over $1 million. He introduced premium coupons, horse-drawn A&P wagons, and city directory advertising. Meanwhile the number of outlets had increased to over 200. By this time, Hartford's sons were actively involved in the business.

After several terms as mayor of Orange, New Jersey, Hartford became active in turning A&P from a partnership into a corporation. In addition, the company changed its operations from credit-based stores to cash-and-carry stores, with startling decreases in costs and prices. By 1914 there were hundreds of A&P stores across the country.

George Huntington Hartford died in 1917, by which time he owned more than 4,000 stores. By then A&P had become a household name, with the physical similarities of all A&P outlets embedded in the public mind. The concept of mass merchandising in the grocery field had come of age through A&P, paving the way for the emergence of the supermarket.

instances source documents such as sales slips, checks, and credit slips are written by hand and then transferred to an input medium for computer processing. In addition to maintaining their own staffs for handling accounting functions, large retailers retain independent accounting firms to audit their records, prepare tax reports, and advise management.

Small retailers rely on independent accountants to design their accounting systems. Records are maintained by hand, by electromechanical equipment such as billing machines, by microcomputers, or by outside computer service companies. Depending on the size of the store, daily records are kept by the owner or by bookkeepers and clerks. The accounting firm makes periodic visits to summarize and analyze the data. It is also responsible for the preparation of tax reports, and usually provides advice to the retailer.

INVENTORY CONTROL

You have seen that merchandise inventory is an essential element of both the balance sheet and the income statement. The inventory value on the balance sheet tells the retailer the available stock on the last day of the accounting period, while the beginning and ending inventory values on the income statement are used to determine the cost of goods sold and gross margin for the period. Since inventory is so large a part of a store's assets and because it figures so prominently in the determination of profit or loss, it is important that retailers understand its effect on various phases of store operation.

It has already been pointed out that, ideally, a store should contain sufficient merchandise at all times to satisfy customers. Reaching the ideal is not a simple matter, however. It calls for planning, alertness, and, in the case of larger stores, sophisticated recordkeeping.

The importance of inventory control is associated with the distribution of merchandise. The trend toward warehouse-based distribution has been evident for some time. Its basic advantage over in-store stockroom distribution is the reduction of reserve stock requirements. In addition, it results in wider assortment possibilities, more selling space, fewer stockouts, and less shrinkage.

The Adequacy of Inventory Levels

Regardless of the type of inventory, care must be taken to assure adequate stock on hand. This involves constant awareness of the following factors.

1. The quantity of goods in selling areas, stockrooms, and warehouses
2. The frequency of sales of each inventory item
3. The type and quantity of stock on order

With this information, the retailer can make timely decisions on whether to increase the supply of quick-selling products or mark down slow-selling items for speedier sale. For example, a T-shirt with specific appeal to young boys that had been expected to sell only moderately, suddenly "takes off." With proper controls, the store can detect the trend and prepare to replenish the stock in time to tap the shirt's popularity.

Inadequate inventory may result from

1. Improper anticipation of sales.
2. Late deliveries by suppliers.
3. Insufficient funds for purchases.
4. Unexpected customer demand.

Strategies for avoiding inadequate inventory

Though it is not always possible to avoid these problems, the retailer can plan a course of action to avoid at least the first three factors listed. For example, information obtained from manufacturers, distributors, or trade publications is an aid in predicting sales volume. Awareness of a supplier's past delivery record or well-placed pressure on the supplier may minimize late deliveries. Finally, alternate sources of funds (e.g., short- and long-term notes at banks) may bring in the money required for purchases.

The consequences of an inadequate inventory are, of course, reduced sales and disappointed shoppers. While lost revenue may be recaptured through additional promotions and advertising, it is not always possible to entice unhappy customers back to the store.

While insufficient inventory should be avoided, so should excessive quantities of stock. Too much merchandise on hand arises from

IS YOUR INVENTORY MAXI WHEN THE MARKET'S MINI?

The ability to respond quickly to rapidly changing market conditions can mean the difference between getting rich and getting stuck.

But in order to make quick business decisions, you need up-to-the-minute information instantly. And you need it in a form that you, the decision-maker, can use.

Precisely why Sperry Univac created System 80 ESCORT.

ESCORT is software that lets you use the computer to get immediate answers to your questions. Without learning computer language. And without a programmer.

What's more, with ESCORT you can design your own applications. Even add new information to the computer's data base. All by yourself.

And you can do all this even if you've never seen a computer before.

Providing, of course, that the computer you use with ESCORT is the Sperry Univac System 80. Which happens to be the ideal computer for medium-to-large companies anyway.

So if you're not getting all the information you need to make quick business decisions, decide right now to call your Sperry Univac marketing office for a free demonstration.

Or write to Department 100, P.O. Box 500, Blue Bell, PA 19424, for our product brochure.

And we'll show you how Sperry Univac System 80 ESCORT can minimize your problems. While maximizing your profits.

SPERRY✦UNIVAC
The computer people who listen.

This ad emphasizes the importance of computers in making decisions about inventory. *Courtesy:* Unisys Corporation.

1. Poor sales performance.
2. Overordering.
3. Ordering incorrect items.

As in the case of inadequate levels, the keys to preventing inventory overages are obtaining reliable information from suppliers and pinpointing consumer demand.

Excessive stock, as you have seen, ties up funds and space needlessly. Particularly during periods of high interest rates, when it is expensive to borrow money to buy merchandise, retailers must make every effort to maintain sensible stock levels. Otherwise, they may watch their profits dwindle as unnecessary merchandise remains unsold.

INVENTORY CONTROL SYSTEMS

Since it is important to keep inventory at satisfactory levels, a store requires a workable plan to carry out this goal. Whatever system is adopted must provide usable information for decision making and not be too costly to maintain. The system used by any given retailer depends on the following factors.

The Size of the Inventory

Factors that shape inventory control systems

Some owners of small stores attempt to assess the size of inventories by means of observation of merchandise on shelves and in stockrooms, sometimes called "eyeballing." Unfortunately, this approach is fraught with the danger of over- or underestimating inventory levels and indicates lack of managerial know-how. A more objective approach requires written records. Inventories in large stores, of course, require considerably more attention than those in smaller ones because of the sheer quantity and variety of items for sale. Figure 17-2 shows a tie-in between a price ticket and an inventory sheet.

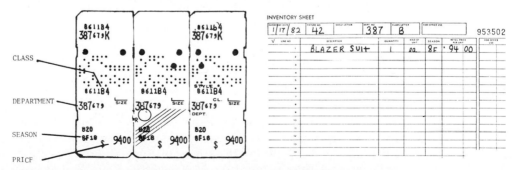

Figure 17-2   Recording information from a price ticket (Kimball ticket) to an inventory sheet. *Courtesy:* Kimball Systems, Division of Litton Industries.

The Assortments Within the Inventory

Stores that have relatively few categories of merchandise can keep tabs on inventory levels fairly easily. However, those with great product diversification are faced with more serious information problems.

The Information Needed by Top and Middle Management

Top management is concerned primarily with overall store performance: sales, cost of purchases, gross margin, net income, and so forth. Middle management, on the other hand, needs more detailed inventory statistics: sizes, styles, colors, and the like. Both levels of management require data about departments and sections within departments.

Two widely used systems for gathering information about inventory are **dollar control** and **unit control.** The former indicates the dollar value of merchandise, while the latter treats merchandise in terms of quantity. Let's look at each system in detail.

Dollar Control

In this system retail dollar values are used for all calculations. Therefore, when one is computing an inventory at any particular time, the inventory is stated at its retail value. As you will see later in this chapter, however, the retail value can easily be converted into the cost price of the inventory.

Dollar control reveals the performance of broad segments of a store; that is, it shows the sales, purchases, markdowns, and ending inventories for the entire store or for some segment of the store, such as a department or a merchandise category. Dollar control does not, however, deal with inventory quantities. There are two methods for maintaining dollar control of inventories. One is called perpetual inventory and the other periodic inventory.

Perpetual Inventory in Dollar Control

The word *perpetual* signifies the continual occurrence of an event. A **perpetual inventory** is defined as a method for knowing the value of an inventory at any given time. This requires an understanding of the flow of merchandise in a business as well as an appreciation of the necessary records.

Basically, inventory in a retail store moves as follows: First it is received and stored or put out for sale; next it is sold; finally, whatever remains unsold is listed as ending inventory. Now examine Table 17-9. You are looking at a perpetual inventory record for a particular style of jeans. It indicates that there was a jeans inventory of $3,000 at the beginning of July. The sales of $700 on July 2 left a balance of $2,300. On July 3 the $1,000 worth of merchandise received raised the balance to $3,300. The sales for July 5 and 6 ($600 and $800) reduced the inventory on hand to $2,700 and $1,900, respectively.

TABLE 17-9   An Inventory Control Card for a Perpetual Inventory System—Dollar Control

Inventory Control Jeans—Style No. 104L Date	Received	Sales	Inventory on Hand
July 1			$3,000
2		$700	2,300
3	$1,000		3,300
5		600	2,700
6		800	1,900

Perpetual inventory with dollar and unit control

As you can see, the inventory on hand is known each time merchandise is received or sold—provided that the inventory control card is kept up to date or a computer is used. The inventory record is valuable for making daily decisions about how merchandise is moving, which items require restocking, which items should be marked down, and so forth. However, the data on the card are only an *estimate* of the inventory on hand each day, since shortages (pilferage, etc.) or customer returns may have reduced or increased the stock.

Notice, too, that each different inventory item requires a separate control card. Depending on the size of the store and its financial capacity, the information may be recorded by computers, by mechanical equipment, or by hand.

Since shortages are inevitable in retail businesses, it is necessary to take a periodic physical count of the merchandise to check the accuracy of the inventory control cards. Any discrepancies between the *estimated* amounts on the cards and the *actual* amounts from the physical count are corrected on the cards. An inventory count is a time-consuming and expensive procedure, but inventory levels can be checked daily by computers. However, most retailers take a physical inventory once or twice a year.

Because record keeping can be costly, the perpetual inventory method is better suited to high-ticket items like cars and appliances than to low-priced products like food and notions. This is apparent when one considers the smaller number of types of inventory carried by a car dealer as contrasted with a variety store. Nevertheless, a perpetual inventory record can be maintained by any retailer whose cash register or credit system is tied to a computer. In fact, increasing numbers of stores are installing cash registers with special sensing devices and "tear-off" price tags to record sales and, thus, inventory changes. Low-priced retailers without computers find the perpetual inventory method too costly to maintain.

Periodic Inventory in Dollar Control

Unlike the perpetual inventory method, the **periodic inventory** method involves finding the value of merchandise at a particular time *only* by taking a physical count of the stock. It is used by retailers who do not require constant knowledge of inventory levels or find the cost of maintaining perpetual inventory records prohibitive.

Some retailers take physical counts several times a year. However, the cost of such counts restricts most merchants to one or two counts a year, usually during January–February and July–August. In effect, then, the difference between a store that uses a perpetual inventory record with one or two physical counts a year and a store that uses a periodic method with the same counts is that the former has a continuous stream of information for decision making. The latter, instead, must rely largely on observation of inventory on shelves and in stockrooms for merchandise information, or on some type of written record.

Taking inventory means making a physical count of merchandise. The specific time when inventory is taken, however, depends on a store's needs. Some large stores take counts based on specific inventory categories (e.g., sportswear). Others stagger their counts, with each department being inventoried during a different month.

To ensure a realistic count, a specific inventory-taking date is set. All transactions that affect the inventory balance on that date are taken into account: receipts of goods, sales, returns, and so on. While some stores check inventory while business is in progress, most retailers do so when their stores are closed (i.e., holidays or after hours). The actual counting is done by employees or by an outside contractor whose staff is trained to take inventories. Records are maintained by hand on specially designed columnar sheets or with the aid of electronic devices that detect sensed markings (codes) on shelves or packages.

Unit Control

As indicated previously, unit control involves quantities rather than dollars. Depending on the store's needs, it provides the retailer with a number of vital facts.

1. The number of items on hand, arranged by size, color, style, or other merchandise classification
2. Products that are selling at fast or slow rates
3. An indication of how well each vendor's merchandise is moving
4. Detection of stock shortages
5. The points at which stock should be reordered, and the quantities needed

As with dollar control, unit control can be maintained through the use of perpetual or periodic inventory methods. Let's examine each of these possibilities.

Perpetual Inventory in Unit Control

Table 17-10 shows an inventory control card for a particular model and color of gas range. On August 1 there were 6 ranges in stock. On August 2 three additional ranges were received, resulting in a new inventory on hand of 9 units.

TABLE 17-10   An Inventory Control Card for Perpetual Inventory System—Unit Control

Gas Range	Inventory Control Model No. L254 Reorder Point: 4		Color: Red
Date	**Units Received**	**Units Sold**	**Units on Hand**
August 1			6
2	3		9
5		2	7
8		3	4[1]
10		1	3

[1] Reorder point.

The sales on August 5, 8, and 10 reduced the on-hand inventories to 7, 4, and 3, respectively. The heading of the form indicates a reorder point of 4 units. This tells the retailer that when the inventory on hand drops to 4, additional ranges should be ordered to avoid running out of merchandise. Notice that the reorder point was reached on August 8. Obviously, the retailer requires a procedure for employees to follow in order to obtain the needed merchandise in the correct style, color, and quantity. Computers meet this need admirably.

As you can see, in the perpetual-inventory method the arithmetic procedures are similar for both dollar and unit control. In fact, the most effective use of the method combines both controls; this approach is used by many retailers. Shortages can easily be checked with unit control by matching inventory control card figures with actual counts.

Taking inventory electronically involves bar code scanning and reduces clerical time. *Courtesy:* MSI Data Corporation.

Computerized registers record sales electronically and help maintain perpetual inventory. *Courtesy: Walgreens.*

Periodic Inventory in Unit Control

Here, as in dollar control, inventory on hand—or ending inventory, as it is usually called—is determined by physical count. Inventory not on hand is presumed to be sold or lost as a result of shrinkage.

When an ending inventory figure has been determined, financial statements are prepared. As discussed earlier in this chapter, from these reports the merchant obtains key results such as gross margin and net income.

Planogramming

Planogramming: a management tool

A relatively new approach to the control of inventory is a process called planogramming. Utilizing a computer, **planogramming** enables a merchant to maintain shelf inventory for maximum efficiency. It takes into account space and employee productivity, profitability, expense reduction, and improved communications. Developed by Michael Tanner, a retail marketing adviser, we can expect to see the increased use of planogramming as a key management tool, especially for discount store operations.

ESTIMATING AN INVENTORY

Though formal financial statements are generally prepared once a year, many retailers require balance sheets and especially income statements more frequently. In such cases accountants usually submit monthly or interim statements (as opposed to formal statements). With data on the cost of goods sold, gross margin, operating expenses, and net income (or loss), merchants can make decisions based on timely information.

A problem arises with regard to the development of the income statement when the periodic inventory method is used. You will recall that an ending inventory is required in order to compute the cost of goods sold as well as the gross margin. Furthermore, for income statement purposes the ending inventory must be the *cost*, not the retail, figure. A review of a section of an income statement may be helpful before we proceed (see Table 17-11).

Since retailers generally maintain inventory records at retail prices, some way is needed to estimate the ending inventory at retail and then convert the figure to its cost equivalent. A very popular method, especially among large and medium-sized stores, is the retail method.

The Retail Method for Estimating Inventory

The **retail method** for estimating an inventory at cost is used by many retailers and is accepted by the federal government for tax purposes. In order to use it, the retailer must have available both the cost and the retail prices of beginning inventories and purchases. You will see shortly why this is so.

TABLE 17-11   An Abbreviated Income Statement

Income Statement		
Net sales		$50,000
Cost of goods sold		
Beginning inventory (at cost)	$18,000	
Add: purchases (at cost)	22,000	
Cost of goods available for sale (at cost)	40,000	
Less: Ending inventory (at cost)	25,000	
Cost of goods sold		15,000
Gross margin		$35,000

Suppose Carol Rich, the owner of Carol's Handmade Pottery, wants to estimate her inventory at cost price on February 28 in order to prepare an income statement for the month. Her records reveal the following.

Inventory, February 1, at cost	$10,000
Inventory, February 1, at retail	20,000
Purchases for February, at cost	15,000
Purchases for February, at retail	30,000

Steps in estimating ending inventory by the retail method

Rich takes the following steps to estimate her ending inventory.

1. She determines the goods available for sale at both cost and retail prices.

	Cost	Retail
Inventory, February 1	$10,000	$20,000
Add: February purchases	15,000	30,000
Goods available for sale during February	$25,000	$50,000

2. She computes the relationship between the goods available for sale at cost and at retail. This is called the *cost ratio.*
   Goods available for sale:

$$\text{At cost } \frac{\$25,000}{\text{At retail } \$50,000} = \frac{1}{2} = 50\% \text{ cost ratio}$$

In other words, for the month of February, the total *cost* of the merchandise available for sale was 50 percent of its *retail* price.

3. From her accounting records she determines the sales for February to be $39,000, markdowns $700, and stock shrinkage $300. The total reduction in inventory of $40,000 is subtracted from the goods available for sale at retail

($50,000, from step 1) to find the February 28 inventory (ending inventory) at retail.

February sales	$39,000	
February markdowns	700	
February shrinkage	300	
Total reduction in inventory	$40,000	
Goods available for sale (retail)		$50,000
Less: Total reduction in inventory		40,000
February 28 inventory (retail)		$10,000

4. Finally, she multiplies the February 28 inventory at retail by the cost ratio found in step 2 to find the February 28 inventory at cost price.

$$\frac{\text{February 28 inventory at retail}}{\$10,000} \times \frac{\text{Cost ratio}}{.50} = \frac{\text{February 28 inventory at cost}}{\$5,000}$$

The $5,000 figure is the ending inventory that is used on both the balance sheet and the income statement prepared at the end of February.

Advantages of the Retail Method

The most important advantages of the retail method are as follows.

1. Interim financial statements can be prepared without having to take a physical inventory. This is a tremendous time-saver for managers who need frequent information about the cost of goods sold, gross margin, and net income or loss.

2. When a physical inventory must be taken, the retail method minimizes the chance of clerical errors. This is so because merchandise is already marked with retail prices, while taking inventory on a cost basis requires coding the merchandise, as discussed in Chapter 12, so that customers are not aware of the cost. Subsequent decoding by store personnel at inventory-taking time can result in a high rate of clerical errors.

3. Since merchandise is marked with retail prices, inventory can be taken more frequently than when coded cost prices are used. Consequently, a comparison of actual counts with estimates shown by the retail method gives management a better understanding of stock shortages as well as fast- and slow-moving merchandise.

4. In the event of damage to merchandise due to fire or some other cause, the estimated inventory computed by the retail method at the time of the loss can be used to submit insurance claims. Since merchandise comprises such a large part of a store's assets, insurance coverage is essential, as are the accompanying records to substantiate losses.

Disadvantages of the Retail Method

The most significant disadvantages of the retail method are the following.

1. The clerical cost of maintaining records at retail prices is considerable. This arises from the need to record price changes due to markups, markdowns, merchandise returns, and so forth. A store must judge the numerous benefits of the retail method against recordkeeping expenses.
2. The cost ratio in the retail method is an *average* based on the total goods available in a store for a given period. It does not account for different markups and frequencies of sales within specific departments. Consequently, the computed ending inventory may distort the actual inventory situation in particular departments. To overcome this problem, some stores apply the retail method for estimating inventory on a departmental basis.
3. Since the retail method depends on accurate sales forecasts, any significant change in retail prices distorts the estimated ending inventory.

ACCOUNTING FOR INVENTORY ON A COST BASIS

You have already seen that when inventory records are maintained at cost prices, taking a physical inventory is an expensive and error-prone process. Nevertheless, some retailers use the cost method because of its lower recordkeeping costs.

Some retailers who operate on the cost basis under a periodic inventory system do not mark merchandise with cost figures, not even in coded form. Consequently, they are unable to specify ending inventory items by their original cost. For example, a music store that stocks all 40-inch guitar cases in one bin without regard to purchase date or cost cannot distinguish among the cases when taking inventory. Yet it must establish an ending inventory value in order to prepare financial statements.

FIFO and LIFO assumptions

The solution to the music store's problem depends on the theoretical assumption it makes with regard to the sale of the guitars. Most stores make either of the following *assumptions*.

1. **First in, first out (FIFO)** Merchandise purchased first is sold completely before any subsequently purchased items are sold.
2. **Last in, first out (LIFO)** The merchandise purchased last is sold completely before any earlier-purchased items are sold.

The second assumption may sound strange, but remember that it is an assumption for computational purposes *only*. Its theoretical explanation is beyond the scope of this book, but it can be found in any elementary accounting textbook. You must also recognize that since all the guitar cases are alike, it makes no difference which ones are *actually* sold.

Now let's see how the music store determines its ending inventory under FIFO and LIFO.

Suppose the store's inventory records of 40-inch guitar cases for a business year ending December 31 show the following.

Date	Quantity	Cost per Case	Total Cost
January 1—on hand	20	$15	$300
April 6—purchase	30	16	480
July 14—purchase	30	16	480
November 2—purchase	40	17	680

On December 31 the store took physical inventory and counted *44 guitar cases on hand*. The question is, On December 31 which 44 cases are in the inventory? Which cost price(s) should be used to compute the ending inventory?

FIFO

Using the FIFO approach, the assumption is that the guitar cases on hand on January 1 were the first ones sold (first in, first out), that the next ones sold were from the April 6 purchase, and so on. Therefore, to determine which cases are on hand on December 31, we start with the ones from the last purchase of the year, that is, the purchase of November 2. This is how the computations are made.

Date	Quantity on Hand	Cost per Case	Total Cost
From November 2 purchase	40	$17	$680
From July 14 purchase	4	16	64
	44		$744

Using FIFO, then, the cost value of the ending inventory of 44 guitar cases is $744. Now we'll use the LIFO assumption.

LIFO

Using the LIFO approach, the assumption is that the guitar cases from the last purchase (November 2) were the first ones sold (last in, first out), that the next ones sold were from the July 14 purchase, and so forth. Therefore, to determine which cases are on hand on December 31 we start with the ones on hand January 1. This is how the computations are made.

Date	Quantity on Hand	Cost per Case	Total Cost
From January 1 on hand	20	$15	$300
From April 6 purchase	24	16	384
	44		$684

Using LIFO, then, the cost value of the ending inventory of 44 guitar cases is $684.

Comparison of FIFO and LIFO

FIFO and LIFO during inflation and deflation

In order to understand how FIFO and LIFO affect profits and losses, refer back to the inventory cost per case at the beginning of the example on page 569. Notice that the cost of the guitar cases rose from $15 each to $16, and then to $17. In other words, since prices increased, there was *inflation* in the economy.

Now we need to compute gross margin (Table 17-12) using both FIFO and LIFO ending inventory figures. When FIFO was used, the ending inventory was $744 and the gross margin was $1,804. The comparable amounts for LIFO were $684 and $1,744. In other words, using LIFO during an inflationary period results in a lower gross margin. That also means a lower net income and, consequently, a lower income tax for the retailer. Of course, the reverse will be true when prices are falling, that is, during a period of *deflation*.

Retailers may select either FIFO or LIFO to compute inventory on a cost basis. However, once they have made a selection they are required by the Internal Revenue Service to use that method consistently. (Exceptions are considered on a case-by-case basis.) Obviously, if inflation continues, the retailer using LIFO will have a tax advantage. Should deflation take place, however, the retailer would pay higher taxes.

QUICK RESPONSE

Quick Response, also known as **electronic data integration (EDI),** is an inventory delivery system in which retailers, manufacturers, and mills work together as partners. The overriding goals are to produce goods quicker, reduce inventory

TABLE 17-12   Effects of FIFO and LIFO on Gross Margin

	Ending Inventory at FIFO		Ending Inventory at LIFO	
Net sales		$3,000		$3,000
Cost of goods sold				
Beginning inventory (at cost)	$ 300		$ 300	
Add: Purchases (at cost)	1,640		1,640	
Cost of goods available for sale (at cost)	1,940		1,940	
Less: Ending inventory (at cost)	744		684	
Cost of goods sold		1,196		1,256
Gross margin		$1,804		$1,744

delivery times, develop more accurate forecasting, reduce out-of-stock problems in stores, increase stock turnovers, and improve profitability. The system requires pinpoint cooperation among the three groups based on specific assumptions of responsibilities and the coordination of computer functions. It appears to work best with staple goods.

The Quick Response partnership started with such retailers as Bullock's, Strawbridge & Clothier, Dayton Hudson Corporation, and Wal-Mart; with such manufacturers as Burlington Industries, Maidenform, and Russell Corporation; and with such mills as Guilford Mills, Mt. Vernon Mills, and Dundee Mills. They were also joined by accounting firms like Arthur Young and by data processing firms like IBM and NCR.

Another way of describing Quick Response is the following: "Quick Response is the establishment of new business policies, new procedures, and new relationships to speed the flow of merchandise and information between retailers and their suppliers in an effort to respond quickly to changing consumer demands."[2] In order for Quick Response to work, merchandise must be ordered, manufactured, shipped, distributed, sold, replenished, marked down, and paid for faster.

As an example of a large retailer's involvement with EDI, K mart's commitment has five phases:

1. POS
2. An automated receiving system
3. Ongoing inventory maintenance
4. Centralized replenishment of inventory
5. Centralized payment to vendors

One significant result of Quick Response has been the increasing replacement of imports by domestic products. The reduction of inventory turnaround time has reduced the disparity in prices between the two. Consequently, more retailers are rethinking their dependence on foreign merchandise.

In order to coordinate and streamline vendor-store merchandise activities, large retail chains like Sears, Roebuck and K mart work with manufacturers in an organization called Voluntary Interindustry Communications Standards (VICS). The group tackles areas like bar code scanning and replenishment cycling. It attempts to eliminate duplication and waste.

Brendle's, a 40-plus store upscale specialty retailer offering fine jewelry, gifts, and name-brand hard goods at low prices, indicated in 1989 that it was planning "a minimum/maximum, just-in-time, seasonally-adjusted inventory system which should lower inventories while maintaining a better in-stock position."[3] This statement, of course, is another way of describing a Quick Response approach to inventory.

---

[2]"Quick Response Adds Speed at Mercantile," *Chain Store Age Executive,* **65** (November 1989), p. 36.

[3]Brendle's First Quarter Report, for the Three Months Ended April 29, 1989.

FACTORS CONTRIBUTING TO EFFECTIVE RETAILING

A summary of characteristics that mark successful retailing indicates the following:

1. Consumer driven
2. Concentration on value
3. Effective management
4. Utilization of the latest technology
5. Commitment to or variation of Quick Response

NEW TERMS

average collection period	liabilities
average turnover days	merchandise budget
balance sheet	net worth
cash budget	owner's equity
current ratio	periodic inventory
debt-to-equity ratio	perpetual inventory
dividend	planogramming
dollar control	quick ratio
electronic data integration (EDI)	Quick Response
expense budget	retail method
first in, first out (FIFO)	return on investment (ROI)
gross margin	sales per square foot of selling space
income statement	stockholders' equity
last in, first out (LIFO)	unit control

CHAPTER HIGHLIGHTS

1. Accounting is the compilation of financial data for purposes of control, analysis, and decision making.
2. The most commonly used financial reports are the balance sheet and the income statement.

3. A balance sheet contains a list of assets and liabilities, as well as owner's equity. Assets are categorized as current or long-lived (plant and equipment), depending on how long they are expected to be available, whereas liabilities are listed as current or long term, depending on when they are scheduled for repayment.

4. Several measurements based on balance sheet figures are useful to retailers. Among them are the current ratio (matching current assets against current liabilities), the quick ratio (matching cash and receivables against current liabilities), and the debt-to-equity ratio (matching liabilities and net worth).

5. An income statement contains three sections: revenue from sales, cost of goods sold, and operating expenses. The final amount on the statement indicates net income (profit) or net loss.

6. A combination of balance sheet and income statement amounts provides retailers with the following measurements: stock turnover, average turnover days, average collection period, gross margin on sales, sales per square foot of selling space, net income on sales, and return on investment.

7. Retailers often analyze expenses in terms of their increases or decreases from one period to another. Percentages are a more realistic indication of such changes than dollars.

8. Operating expenses may be evaluated as a percentage of net sales. This procedure allows retailers to judge the effect of overhead expenditures on sales volume.

9. Budgets are important for planning purposes and are also used to judge current operations. The following budgets are among those used by retailers: expense, cash, advertising, and merchandise.

10. Sales forecasting involves projecting sales. Both small and large retailers rely on internal and external resources to help them develop forecasts.

11. Large retailers use computers for most of their accounting functions, whereas small ones rely on hand methods, electromechanical equipment, microcomputers, or outside computer service companies.

12. Inadequate inventory results from improper anticipation of sales, late deliveries by suppliers, insufficient funds for purchases, and unexpected customer demand. Excessive quantities of stock arise from poor sales performance, overordering, and incorrect orders.

13. The type of inventory control system used by a retailer depends on the size of its inventory, the assortments within the inventory, and the information needed by top and middle management.

14. Dollar control of inventory reveals the performance of broad segments of a store. Control may be maintained by either of two inventory methods: perpetual or periodic.

15. The perpetual inventory method tells the retailer how much stock should be on hand at any given time. Stock records are checked periodically by means of a physical count of merchandise. The periodic inventory method involves a physical count of merchandise without recourse to perpetual records.

16. Unit control of inventory involves the determination of inventory quantities rather than dollars. Control may be maintained by either the perpetual or the periodic method.

17. The retail method for estimating ending inventory is used in the development of interim financial statements.

18. Retailers who account for inventory on a cost basis but do not list cost prices on the inventory items usually use FIFO or LIFO to compute ending inventory. LIFO results in a lower ending inventory, a lower net income, and a lower income tax for the retailer during inflation.

19. Quick Response, also called electronic data integration, is an inventory delivery system in which retailers, manufacturers, and mills work together to reduce inventory delivery times, improve forecasting, reduce out-of-stock problems, increase stock turnovers, and improve profitability.

REVIEW QUESTIONS

1. If a retailer's balance sheet shows current assets of $180,000 and current liabilities of $80,000, what is the current ratio? Is the ratio a favorable one?

2. If a retailer's income statement shows net sales of $230,000, cost of goods sold of $140,000, and operating expenses of $40,000, is the result a net income or net loss? In what amount?

3. Indicate whether each of the following retail operations should normally antici-pate a high or a low stock turnover. State reasons for your answers.
   A Marshall Field furniture department
   A Burger King franchise
   A Sears, Roebuck stereo department

4. A store's net sales for the year total $1,095,000 and its year-end accounts receivable amount to $45,000. What is its average collection period? Of what significance is this measurement?

5. A retailer's store contains 50,000 square feet of selling space. Sales during the year were $10,000,000. What were the retailer's sales per square foot of selling space?

6. Why is the perpetual inventory method better suited to a business that sells high-ticket items than to one that carries low-priced products?

7. Why is the retail method of estimating ending inventory valuable to a merchant in filing inventory insurance claims?

8. How do FIFO and LIFO affect a store's ending inventory, gross margin, and net income during a period of inflation? During a period of deflation?

DISCUSSION QUESTIONS

1. The following information is taken from the first quarter operations of Lindy's Specialty Store for 1989 and 1990. On the basis of the data, answer the following questions.
   a. What may have accounted for the percentage decrease of delivery expenses in 1990 from the 1989 figure?
   b. What questions should be asked about the dollar change in advertising expenses?

Lindy's Specialty Store—First Quarter, 1989 and 1990

	1990		1989	
Operating Expense	Dollars	Percent of Net Sales	Dollars	Percent of Net Sales
Delivery	$ 3,000	5%	$ 4,000	8%
Advertising	12,000	20	10,000	20

Net Sales: 1989, $50,000; 1990, $60,000.

2. Why should a store be as concerned about excessive quantities of stock as it is about inadequate inventory? Is one to be avoided more than the other? Why?
3. What effect has the computer had on the use of the perpetual and periodic inventory methods?
4. Is Quick Response more important to a retailer than to a manufacturer? Why?

CASE 1

A Case for Records

Three partners operate the Orleans Department Store. They have been in business for five years, registering a higher net income in each year. Though he is satisfied with the increasing profits, one of the partners feels that the store has been operating very much in the dark with regard to expense and cash items. He believes that the company should at least prepare expense and cash budgets as well as expense analyses. He argues that the store might do even better with a detailed understanding of its financial operations.

The other partners contend that a knowledge of merchandising is sufficient for business success. They point to the company's profit picture as proof of their position. Their feeling is that increased sales, generated through more advertising, will enable the store to continue its progress. They also claim that the financial aspects of the business should be left to the accountants and that retailers should concentrate on merchandising.

Because he is outnumbered, the first partner recognizes the need to support his position with hard facts. He also understands that the accounting records and financial statements for the past five years may not substantiate his position. Yet he is determined to make his case as strong as possible.

a. If you were the first partner, what information would you ask the accountant to prepare? Would you require data for all five years? Why?

b. Do you agree with the two other partners that increased sales would guarantee continued profits? Why?

c. With whose position do you agree? Why?

CASE 2

FIFO Versus LIFO

The Bristol chain of department stores, a corporation, has been in operation for 36 years. Although its flagship store is located in the center of a large city, the bulk of its units consist of suburban branches. All of the stores carry wide assortments of both hard and soft goods, but the chain's emphasis the last few years has been in the direction of upscale soft goods.

Bristol's management has been satisfied with the firm's fiscal performance as reflected in the previous year's financial statements. Ratios developed from those statements show the following:

Current ratio	2.1 to 1
Chainwide stock turnover	5.8
Gross margin on sales	22%
Net income on sales	8.3%
Return on investment	15.6%

Based on the nature of Bristol's business, management feels that the ratios are reasonable. The chief fiscal officer, in fact, contends that the ratios compare very favorably with those of the competition.

One aspect of the financial statements, however, is of particular concern to several senior executives. This concern involves the basis for inventory valuation used by the company. During its entire history, Bristol has used the FIFO method to cost its inventory. The senior executives who have expressed concern maintain that the company should switch to LIFO.

Despite increasing criticism by such well-known management consultants as Peter F. Drucker, many retail businesses in addition to Bristol continue to follow the FIFO method. The criticism arises from the fact that the use of FIFO results in higher taxes during an inflationary period. Drucker contends that significant tax savings are lost when LIFO is not used.

A further argument for LIFO is made by J. C. Penney Company and Federated Department Stores, which suggest that because it matches the latest inventory costs against revenues, LIFO is more representative of the effects of inflation. An outstanding example of a major retailer that switched from FIFO to LIFO is Lowe's Companies, Inc., a specialty retailer of building materials and related products for the home construction and home remodeling markets.

Although not disputing the criticism, Bristol's chief fiscal officer contends that FIFO results in higher net incomes and that stockholders are impressed by that fact when they study the firm's income statements.

Another reason for the persistent use of FIFO is the fear expressed by retailers who are thinking of selling their stores. They reason that the higher net incomes caused by FIFO are more attractive to potential buyers.

Some retail managers are comfortable with FIFO because it follows the way merchandise is received and sold; that is, the first products to arrive are the first ones sold. LIFO, of course, works in reverse and unsettles some managers who view it as an illogical system.

a. If you were in top management at Bristol, would you consider switching to LIFO (assuming that the IRS grants permission)? Why?

b. How might you use Bristol's recent fiscal performance to support the argument for the continued use of FIFO?

c. Should Bristol's management explore Peter F. Drucker's position further? What questions should it raise?

REFERENCES

"Breaking Profit Source into Smaller Nuggets." *Inside Retailing* (February 29, 1988), pp. 2–3.

"Fast Payback from Quick Response, Study Finds," *Chain Store Age Executive*, **65** (May 1989), pp. 245–246.

"Hooker's Super Mall in Cincinnati to Open." *Women's Wear Daily* (February 23, 1989), p. 2.

"Quick Response Adds Speed at Mercantile." *Chain Store Age Executive*, **65** (November 1989), p. 36.

ROBINS, G. "NEW TECHNOLOGIES FOR 1991." *STORES*, (JANUARY 1991), PP. 120–129.

Chapter 18

Credit

After completing this chapter, you should be able to:

- List the advantages of credit to retailers and customers.
- Identify credit plans commonly offered by retailers to customers.
- List the criteria that retailers use for granting credit.
- Identify techniques for gathering credit information.
- Explain billing and collection procedures used by retailers.
- Identify major federal credit laws and explain the reasons for each.

In Chapter 17 you saw the following items listed in the "current assets" section of a retail balance sheet.

Cash   Merchandise inventory
Accounts receivable   Supplies

The definition of accounts receivable indicated that it represents money owed by customers. In other words, these debts arise from sales made to customers on the basis of credit, not cash. In this chapter we discuss why credit is important to retailers, the types of credit offered by merchants, store credit systems, why stores must be careful about extending credit, and laws that deal with credit.

EXTENDING CREDIT

To be successful, the process of doing business by credit must appeal to both the retailer and the customer. Let's examine the advantages to both.

The Retailer's Point of View

Why retailers extend credit
Retailers know that offering credit increases a store's sales. This arises from a number of factors.

1. The opportunity for shoppers to buy even when they don't have ready cash.
2. The greater attraction by credit customers to impulse buying and attractive promotions.
3. The ease with which credit customers can make telephone and mail purchases.

In addition, the availability of credit creates goodwill for the store. Customers often respond to credit service by continuing their patronage (loyalty) at the store. Another factor is that the ability to buy on credit enables customers to make purchases at any time. As a result, the retailer avoids the tendency of sales to be concentrated around paydays, when customers have more cash to spend. Instead, sales are spread out more evenly.

Studies have shown that shoppers who buy on credit are less concerned about prices than those who purchase with cash. Consequently, retailers are able to sell to such customers with less difficulty and in greater volume. Finally, though some merchants would prefer to sell on a cash basis only, they extend credit because their competitors do so. Significant sales can be lost by adhering to a no-credit policy in a trading area where credit arrangements are popular.

The Customer's Point of View

Why customers like to buy on credit

Many credit customers believe that they receive better service than cash customers do. They point to the relative ease of returning merchandise as well as the special announcements of sales that are mailed to them. Another important factor is that credit customers need not carry substantial amounts of cash when shopping. This relieves them of the risk of loss due to theft and enables them to shop for high-priced items more easily.

"Buy now, pay later" is a slogan that is dear to the hearts of credit customers. The ability to satisfy immediate needs without immediate payment is a great convenience to them. Furthermore, credit transactions provide customers with a record of their purchases. The combination of sales receipts, credit memorandums, personal checks, and the store's statements of account comprises an organized system for personal budgeting and income tax preparation.

CREDIT PLANS OFFERED BY RETAILERS

Open Charge Accounts

In an **open charge account,** the store permits the customer to make purchases without a down payment. Instead, the customer is given a specific period—usually 30 days after receiving the bill—within which to make payment.

For many years the J.C. Penney Company stood for "cash only." Today the company has more than 25 million charge customers. Reproduced by permission of the J.C. Penney Company. Material exclusively owned and part of the J.C. Penney Co. Archives Collection.

Though no interest is charged if invoices are paid on time, most stores charge a penalty on unpaid balances after the stipulated period.

Since stores really finance open charge accounts on their own (i.e., they don't generally charge interest within the payment period), this form of credit is expensive for retailers. Stores that still maintain open charge accounts do so either because their customers are accustomed to this service or because the maintenance of this type of credit gives them a competitive advantage.

Revolving Charge Accounts

Revolving charge account plans are common

In **revolving charge** accounts, too, the store establishes a credit limit for the customer. The latter then has a specific period within which to make full payment without an interest (finance) charge. Though 30 days is the most common period, some stores permit longer periods, such as 60 or 90 days. Still others use 25-day periods.

At the end of the period the customer has the following choices.

1. To pay all current charges in full without a finance charge.
2. To pay a minimum amount. For example, Macy's requires a minimum payment of $15. The remainder is due in the following period and carries a finance charge.
3. To pay part of the amount due without a finance charge, with the remainder of the bill due in the next period, but subject to a finance charge.

Except for a few states, finance charges are normally 1.65 percent per period. This is equivalent to an annual rate of 19.8 percent.

A typical store statement contains the following summary columns.

Previous Balance	Charges	Payments and Credits	Finance Charge	New Balance	Minimum Payment Due
.00	40.60	.00	.00	40.60	15.00

The major advantages of revolving credit plans to retailers are the money they earn through finance charges and the increased sales generated by the popularity of the plan with customers. Customers like this type of credit because it offers them sufficient repayment options for personal budget planning. Revolving credit is now more wide-spread than open credit, and its use is increasing.

Installment Credit

Installment credit is generally extended in the sale of high-ticket items like appliances, cars, and furniture. It involves a written contract in which the customer usually agrees to

1. Make a down payment
2. Make periodic payments (including principal and interest) until the total invoice price has been paid.
3. Return the merchandise if payments are not made as agreed in the contract.

Some installment sales contracts give the buyer title to the merchandise while others, known as **conditional sales contracts,** permit the retailer to maintain title until the final payment has been made. Because the computation of finance charges in installment contracts is complicated, retailers are required to state the actual annual interest rate.

Since the financing of high-ticket items is expensive, retailers generally arrange for banks or other lending agencies to lend money to the customer. In effect, the lending institution owns the installment contract while the retailer does the necessary paperwork. The association with the lender allows the retailer to make money on the sale itself and on a portion of the finance charges.

Credit Cards

Credit cards are sometimes called plastic money

It's hard to believe that relatively few people used **credit cards** prior to 1960. However, the decade of the 1960s witnessed an enormous increase in the use of such cards, and continues to this day to the point where many people now refer to them as "plastic money." There are several types of credit cards in use, each with a different sponsor.

The magnitude of credit card use is demonstrated by the fact that some 3 billion credit card transactions were made in 1989, worth a total of close to $220 billion. Average transaction amounts of credit card sales increased by 11 percent in 1990 over 1989, while average cash transaction amounts during the same period increased by 8 percent.

Desirable credit cards have three attributes: little or no annual fee, a 25- or 30-day grace period for paying bills, and a relatively low interest rate.

Bank Credit Cards

The *best*-known **bank credit cards** are VISA and MasterCard. A retailer who wants to affiliate with either or both arranges to do so through a local bank (Some retailers now issue their own VISA or MasterCard cards.). In return for paying the bank a percentage of the customer's purchase price (usually 3 to 6 percent, depending on the arrangement), the bank collects from the customer and assumes responsibility for delinquent accounts. Before joining a bank card plan, however, a retailer must assess its costs and benefits. For example, a merchant whose markup is 15 percent must judge what bank card rate he or she can afford to pay and still stay in business. (The rate is negotiated between the bank and the retailer and depends on the nature of the business and the trading area.)

Though banks have always levied finance charges on unpaid credit card balances, until 1981 they did not require annual membership fees for use of the cards. However, during that year many banks changed their policy and instituted an annual fee of $15. Today the fee is more likely to be $20. In addition, finance charges were raised significantly, with some banks charging as much as 19 percent. Nevertheless, the public continues to use bank cards in increasing numbers. The system is particularly advantageous to retailers who service tourists, visitors, and businesspeople.

Some credit card holders use their cards to secure discounts at restaurants. For example, the Transmedia Network issues such cards for use at designated eating places. In addition to securing discounts on meals—as much as 25 percent in some cases—the discounted bill appears on the diner's VISA or MasterCard monthly statement.

Travel/Entertainment Cards

American Express, Carte Blanche, and Diner's Club

Since 1950 another type of card has been available to people who desire to charge their travel and entertainment expenses. Of particular use to business people and tourists, these **travel/entertainment cards** include Carte Blanche and Diner's Club cards. For an annual fee ($40 is typical), a member can charge purchases at motels, airlines, restaurants, and the like up to a predetermined limit. At the end of a billing period unpaid balances become subject to finance charges.

Businesses that accept travel and entertainment cards pay the sponsoring card company a percentage of sales. As with bank credit cards, the responsibility for billing customers and assuming delinquent account risks rests with the card company.

Though such cards were, and to a large extent still are, used largely for the purchase of services, increasing numbers of retailers have begun to accept some of them for sales of merchandise. As the cost of bank cards approaches that of travel and entertainment cards, we may see both types of cards in general use by retailers.

The American Express card is a type of travel/entertainment card. *Courtesy:* American Express.

Bank Debit Cards

A new type of third-party card is known as a **bank debit card.** Although technically not a credit instrument, a consumer uses this type of card much as he or she uses a credit card or a check. The difference between the two cards lies in the manner in which customer charges are recorded. With a debit card, the charges are deducted immediately from the customer's bank account balance. In other words, the sales transaction is recorded as an electronic funds transfer.

Debit cards are also being used in vending machine retailing. Instead of coins, cards are used to secure merchandise. The limited use of such cards is found in such places as prisons, corporate buildings, and even at the U.S. Mint in Denver. It remains to be seen whether these isolated instances will be extended further.

There is a feeling among some retail analysts that debit card progress has been impeded by banks that want to protect their credit card business. Since bank credit card rates are much higher than debit card rates, the reasoning goes, banks are reluctant to promote the latter cards. To demonstrate the seriousness of the situation, 12 states—including California, New York, and Texas—filed suit in federal court in 1989, charging MasterCard and VISA with violating antitrust laws by preventing the introduction of debit cards.

Store Credit Cards

Most department stores and large specialty shops issue their own credit cards (**store credit cards**) for use in their establishments. Many shoppers always carry cards issued by their favorite stores in their wallets or purses for convenience in making cashless purchases. Customers pay only a finance charge on balances that are unpaid after a specified period. Store cards contribute to customer loyalty and serve as reminders of past patronage. Some stores accept only their own cards for special and telephone orders.

Payment Option Plan

In an effort to induce its customers to use the stores' own credit cards (proprietary cards), the Dayton Hudson Department Store chain started a Payment Option Plan in 1988. In effect, the plan rewards customers who pay their bills early by reducing the finance charge rates on their outstanding balances. For example, an 18 percent rate could be reduced to 16 percent, 14 percent, or 12 percent, depending on the amount of payment.

Another suggestion for increasing the popularity of proprietary cards is the development of a national card. This would enable a retailer with several divisions to issue one card for use in all its divisions. For example, a Federated Department Stores national card could be used at all Abraham & Straus and Burdine's stores. As of this writing, however, few chains have adopted a national card.

Company Cards

Many companies issue credit cards for use in purchasing their products or services. Businesses that issue **company cards** include oil companies (Gulf, Mobil, etc.), hotels, and even telephone companies. Since customer billing is handled by

Selection from promotional
advertisements sent to active
Gulf Credit Card accounts as
part of the company's shop-
by-mail, direct marketing
program. *Courtesy:* Gulf
Consumer Service Co.

a central office, the individual retail outlet is spared major clerical costs. Though
customers do not pay an annual fee for these cards, they are charged on unpaid
balances after a specified time. Company cards are responsible for heavy sales
volume, with more than 100 million of them in circulation.

Mall (Shopping Center) Cards

We are now witnessing shopping centers that issue credit cards accepted by
retailers within the malls. The first mall to offer its own credit card program was
South Coast Plaza in Costa Mesa, California, in 1984. The program is coordinated
with the Bank of America.

Credit Card Competition

The competition among credit card companies has intensified to the point
where promotions are being used increasingly to improve market share. Examples of this trend are MasterCard's discount program called Master Values, American Express's Weekend Privileges program offering restaurant, airline, resort, and
store deals on weekends, and Sears, Roebuck's Sears-Charge Bonus Club that
returns part of a customer's purchases in the form of certificates.

Checking Credit Card Data

Leased telephone lines are an alternative to telephone dialing when stores
check customers' credit card transactions. Because leased lines maintain continuous communication between the retailer and its credit authorization company,
information is secured more quickly than when dialing is required. Chains such as
Home Depot, a home center company, contracts with Control Data, a communications and processing firm, for its leased line data.

Credit Card Fraud

Some retailers believe that fraudulent credit card applications are the retail industry's biggest credit card fraud problem.

As an example of the extent of credit card fraud, MasterCard International member banks lost about $99 million in 1987. Also, the U.S. Secret Service arrested some 1,800 people that year for illegal credit card activities.

To reduce fraud, credit card companies constantly seek new ways to thwart the illegal use of cards. One promising system involves the scanning of a person's veins (yes, veins!) at the time he or she uses a credit card. If the scanned image matches the pattern stored on the card, the transaction is completed. If not, the merchant does not accept the card.

One of the most effective ways retailers can protect themselves against credit card fraud is to request another identification from the credit card user. However, most retailers do not make such requests because of the fear of inconveniencing their customers. Yet this method, if used consistently, reduces the fraudulent use of credit cards enormously.

Credit Cards in the Fast-Food Business

Although the use of credit cards in the fast-food business is virtually non-existent, the situation may change as companies like Arby's, McDonald's, Wendy's, Burger King, and Domino Pizza experiment with the concept. If certain obstacles can be overcome—such as time-consuming card processing—we may yet see the widespread use of credit cards in fast-food restaurants.

STORE CREDIT SYSTEMS

Before examining the specifics of store credit systems, it should be emphasized that retailers have great leeway in determining who will be granted store-sponsored credit. Retailers are not as concerned about people who use bank or travel/entertainment cards, since outside organizations are responsible for collections and delinquencies. Our concern here, then, is with procedures for the establishment and implementation of a store's own credit plans.

Criteria for Granting Credit

Though retailers strive constantly to increase sales, they try to do so at minimum risk to themselves. Selling for cash, of course, involves no risk. The success of credit selling, on the other hand, depends largely on the degree to which credit customers pay their bills. It is crucial, then, for retailers to extend credit only to those who are likely to meet their obligations.

Millions of consumers use
bank and store credit cards.
Photo by: Kathy Bendo.

**Questions about
extending credit**

How does a merchant determine who should or should not receive credit? What safeguards can be used to minimize the possibility of poor credit risks being approved? What strategic and procedural differences exist between small and large retailers in their design and handling of credit policies?

Credit and the Small Retailer

Many small stores sell on a cash-only basis and follow a strict no-credit policy. Others adopt a variety of credit practices to meet the needs of their customers or to sustain sales. For example, a neighborhood merchant may allow credit because it is a long-standing practice in the trading area. A convenience store owner who knows customers by name may extend credit as a way of strengthening their loyalty to the store.

Whatever the reason, small stores that allow credit must develop and maintain adequate accounts receivable records. They must also establish policies for the collection of debts as well as procedures for the disposition of delinquent accounts.

Credit and the Large Retailer

Large stores develop elaborate credit systems. Without a carefully designed program for dealing with credit, stores risk serious losses. Accurate credit records must be maintained, and effective collection methods should be applied. In addition, sensible criteria must be developed for deciding who is a worthy credit risk. Let's examine several criteria.

**An individual's
history of debt
payments is
crucial**

The Applicant's Personal Qualities.   Stores are not very different from individuals when they are judging personal characteristics. They look for such qualities as reputation, honesty, and industry. They are concerned with the person's job history, recognizing that someone who moves from job to job or has periods of unemployment is a greater credit risk than one whose employment is steady and confined to a few employers. They are also impressed with an applicant's community status, showing greater favor to homeowners and civic-minded individuals than to uninvolved, temporary residents. Most important of all, however, is the individual's history of debt payments. It has been demonstrated countless times that those who pay their financial obligations on time are much more likely to continue to do so than those who have an erratic payment record.

The Applicant's Ability to Pay.   This criterion refers to an individual's earning capacity. Stores are much more likely to extend credit to people with secure, well-paying positions and other sources of steady income than to people with low wages or unsteady jobs. Callous as this policy may sound, stores will point out that they are in business to make money and must therefore screen applicants carefully.

One of the unfortunate consequences of this policy is the inability of some young people—single or married—to secure credit. Without a history of credit experience or a favorable employment record, many retailers are reluctant to accept them as credit risks. It should be noted, however, that a decision in a specific case depends on the strictness of the store's policy and current attitudes about the extension of credit.

The Applicant's Wealth.   In addition to earning capacity, retailers are interested in the applicant's accumulated assets. For example, they place emphasis on size of savings accounts; extent of investments in stocks, bonds, and other securities; and possession of real property such as a house. In some instances specific assets may be pledged by the applicant as security for a credit purchase.

In addition to knowing an individual's assets, retailers also need to know the applicant's liabilities. You will remember that assets − liabilities = owner's equity, or net worth. Therefore, the amount on which retailers rely as a measurement of capacity to pay is the owner's equity.

Assessing Criteria for the Granting of Credit

Screening criteria vary among retailers

It should not be thought that all retailers follow the same strategy and procedures in screening customers for credit approval. On the contrary, each store sets its own priorities for selecting credit risks. For example, store A may be more concerned with an individual's personal characteristics, while store B may stress the person's job history. With experience, store executives who are responsible for administering credit programs recognize which criteria best suit their needs and make decisions accordingly.

Techniques for Gathering Credit Information

The usual methods for obtaining information from applicants for credit are to have them submit application forms and/or respond personally to questions by store interviewers. The required data include the applicant's (or family's) employment history, salary, bank account details, assets, liabilities, references, and so forth. Written questions are designed for brief responses, while interview inquiries are handled tactfully and tastefully. Under no circumstances is an interviewer permitted to be abusive or inconsiderate, since the store recognizes that a turned-down applicant can still use cash or bank credit cards to make purchases.

Application blanks should be easy to complete, unoffensive, and attractive. As a means of judging their adequacy, some retailers test the forms by having store personnel complete them. Credit managers frequently fill out the blanks, too.

Having secured personal information from the customer, the store needs to verify certain facts. Since doing so on its own is a costly process, it enlists the help of organizations known as **credit bureaus.** In effect, a credit bureau gathers personal information about shoppers from stores, employees, banks, and so forth, and develops summary reports for use by stores that request them. However, the bureau does not make recommendations about applicants; rather, it leaves decisions to the individual stores.

Cooperative and entrepreneurial credit bureaus

Credit bureaus are of two types: cooperative and entrepreneurial. The first type is formed by a group of stores through a retail association or a chamber of commerce. Its costs are defrayed by membership fees charged to the retailers. The second category consists of private business to whose services interested stores subscribe.

Techniques for Securing New Accounts

Retailers have devised a variety of techniques to persuade shoppers to apply for credit. Some use a welcome wagon, personally visiting newcomers to the community. Others encourage shoppers to fill out credit application forms by offering them free gifts. Still others use attractive in-store displays as a means of coaxing customers to visit the credit department. Whatever the method, good taste and friendliness must accompany the approach.

In an effort to boost sales, many retailers such as Sears, Roebuck have expanded the variety of credit cards they accept. Sears, for example, now accepts VISA, MasterCard, and American Express cards in addition to its own cards—Sears and Discover. Whether this change in policy will be effective remains to be seen.

RETAIL STRATEGY
Forecasting Consumer Buying Preferences Through Credit Records

With the aid of computers, retailers compile large quantities of information from credit transactions. The data enable them to determine such items as the volume of purchases made by charge customers, the frequency of purchases, the types of merchandise purchased, and so on. In short, the stores develop a history of customer patronage.

With this "profile" of customer shopping habits and preferences, store buyers can make more realistic merchandising decisions. Because future customer purchases can be forecast more accurately, the credit data actually serve as a tool for the development of merchandise strategy and the creation of store promotions.

Billing Procedures

Every retail credit system involves periodic notification of customers regarding the status of their accounts. Both small and large stores must develop careful procedures so that both they and their customers are clear about amounts due, payments made, and finance charges. Three billing methods are in general use by retailers.

Descriptive Billing

Descriptive billing makes use of a computer printout of each customer's account for a monthly period. It lists information about the customer's purchases, including the following.

Dates
Departments in which purchases were made
Descriptions of transactions
Prices charged
Payments
Credits

In addition, the statement contains summary financial information about finance charges and the balance due.

Cycle Billing

Instead of billing all customers at the same time, stores that use **cycle billing** stagger their customer statements. That is, they mail statements in batches at different times of the month, with each batch arranged as an alphabetic group (e.g., A-C, D-F, etc.). Stores that lack data processing equipment may still use cycle billing, omitting detailed information about customer purchases, while those with computer capabilities combine descriptive with cycle billing (Figure 18-1).

Country Club Billing

To save time and clerical work, some retailers use **country club billing.** They mail sales slips to customers at the end of a billing period, including a simple statement listing the end-of-period balance owed by the customer. Copies of the

Additional Payment Information

Payments, accompanied by payment stub, received at the P. O. Box listed on the stub for payments by 2:00 p.m. on any Monday through Friday that is not a holiday, will be posted as of the day of receipt. Although payments made elsewhere may not be posted on the day received, they will be posted promptly within 5 days thereafter.

17-3000

Information Applicable to Both Purchases and Advances

A minus sign (−) preceding any amount indicates a credit (including a Payment) or a credit balance. If the total New Balance is a credit balance, it will be applied to future amounts you owe us or refunded to you upon request. Send these refund requests to the address for receiving inquiries about your account appearing on the face of this statement.

You must make the required total Minimum Payment to avoid delinquency.

The Minimum Payment will be applied in the following order: any **FINANCE CHARGE**, Late Charges, Insurance Premium Charges, principal of Advances incurred before the Conversion Date, principal of Purchases incurred before the Conversion Date, principal of Advances incurred on or after the Conversion Date, principal of Purchases incurred on or after the Conversion Date.

If you wish, you may make additional payments. You may instruct us as to how to apply these additional payments. In the absence of your instructions, 50% of any additional payment will be applied in the reduction of the principal of Advances incurred before the Conversion Date, if any, and 50% in reduction of the principal of Purchases incurred before the Conversion Date, if any. If any portion of the additional payment remains unapplied to balances incurred before the Conversion Date, it will be applied to the principal of Advances incurred on or after the Conversion Date, if any, and next to the principal of Purchases incurred on or after the Conversion Date.

Any **FINANCE CHARGE** At Periodic Rate is computed for the periodic statement only through the Bill Date, but it continues to accrue daily until payment is posted. Any **FINANCE CHARGE** which accrues after the Bill Date will appear on your next statement.

YOU MAY AT ANY TIME PAY YOUR TOTAL INDEBTEDNESS. Under the average daily balance method we use the earlier payments are received during a billing cycle the lower the **FINANCE CHARGE** for that billing cycle will be.

Information About Each Finance Charge At Periodic Rate On Purchases And The Balance Upon Which Each Is Computed

Each Purchases Finance Charge Balance is an average daily balance. To compute each one, we add up all the applicable daily principal balances in the Billing Cycle and divide the sum by the Number Of Days In Billing Cycle. We get the daily principal balance for Purchases incurred before the Conversion Date as follows; each day we begin with the applicable opening principal balance for the Billing Cycle and add all New Purchases And Other Debits incurred before the Conversion Date and posted to principal since the start of the Billing Cycle (including any posted that day) and subtract all Payments And Other Credits applied to Purchases incurred before the Conversion Date and posted to principal since the start of the Billing Cycle (including any posted that day). We get the daily principal balance for Purchases incurred on or after the Conversion Date as follows: each day we begin with the applicable opening principal balance for the Billing Cycle and add all New Purchases And Other Debits incurred on or after the Conversion Date and posted to principal since the start of the Billing Cycle (including any posted that day) and subtract all Payments And Other Credits applied to Purchases incurred on or after the Conversion Date and posted to principal since the start of the Billing Cycle (including any posted that day). However, there is no "purchases finance charge balance" for purchases incurred either before or on or after the Conversion Date in any billing cycle in which you have no previous balance for any purchases or all your payments and other credits applied to purchases for that billing cycle at least equal your previous balance for all purchases for that billing cycle.

A **FINANCE CHARGE** At Periodic Rate is computed for Purchases incurred both before and on or after the Conversion Date by (i) multiplying each portion of the applicable Purchases Finance Charge Balance by the Number Of Days In Billing Cycle, (ii) applying to the resulting products the applicable Daily Periodic Rates, and (iii) adding these products together.

Information About Each Finance Charge At Periodic Rate On Advances And The Balance Upon Which Each Is Computed

Each Advances Finance Charge Balance is an average daily balance. To compute each one, we add up all the applicable daily principal balances in the Billing Cycle and divide the sum by the Number Of Days In Billing Cycle. We get the daily principal balance for Advances incurred before the Conversion Date as follows: each day we begin with the applicable opening principal balance for the Billing Cycle and add all New Advances And Other Debits incurred before the Conversion Date and posted to principal since the start of the Billing Cycle (including any posted that day) and subtract all Payments And Other Credits applied to Advances incurred before the Conversion Date and posted to principal since the start of the Billing Cycle (including any posted that day). We get the daily principal balance for Advances incurred on or after the Conversion Date as follows: each day we begin with the applicable opening principal balance for the Billing Cycle and add all New Advances And Other Debits incurred on or after the Conversion Date and posted to principal since the start of the Billing Cycle (including any posted that day) and subtract all Payments And Other Credits applied to Advances incurred on or after the Conversion Date and posted to principal since the start of the Billing Cycle (including any posted that day), and adding a per item charge of $.25 for each Advance made on the account which will increase the **ANNUAL PERCENTAGE RATE** for any monthly billing cycle in which an Advance is included.

A **FINANCE CHARGE** At Periodic Rate is computed for Advances incurred both before and on or after the Conversion Date by multiplying each Advances Finance Charge Balance by the Number Of Days In Billing Cycle, and applying to the resulting products the applicable Daily Periodic Rates.

Figure 18-1 Finance terms under cycle billing.

sales slips remain with the store and substitute for more formal bookkeeping records.

There are still retailers who send detailed statements to customers at the end of a month. Though it is restricted to small stores, this method affords customers the opportunity to examine a month's activities on a transaction-by-transaction basis. The clerical work involved, however, is considerable.

Collecting from Credit Customers

If a store's screening process is effective, most credit customers will pay their bills on time. Contrary to what some cynics think, most people do not become delinquent payers intentionally. Instead, it happens either because of circumstances beyond their control or because of forgetfulness on their part. Consequently, the retailer's role is to institute an organized collection system that encourages customers to make payments on time.

Handling delinquent accounts

No matter which credit plan is offered, collection procedures should include a series of specific steps. Suppose a customer's account is past due. The store might send a form letter simply reminding the individual about the unpaid bill. If no reply is received within a reasonable time, a second letter is sent, one with a slightly more compelling tone. Neither of these letters should be threatening. On the contrary, they should stress the store's appreciation of the customer's patronage and its desire to be of help. In the event that the second letter does not produce results, the store may either call the customer or, in special cases, send a telegram. When an account is truly delinquent, stores resort to one or a combination of the following actions: Send a personal collector to the customer's home; engage a collection agency; or sue. In the case of small amounts, however, a store may write off the account as a bed debt, that is, take the delinquent amount as a

Part of a store's programmable credit system. *Courtesy:* Unisys Corporation.

loss. Delinquency in installment credit, as you have read, may result in repossession of merchandise.

Collection policies vary among retailers. Some are stricter than others, with the approach depending on the store's image, the affluence of its customers, and its collection experience. In general, stores try to collect from customers on time because delinquent accounts tie up funds and increase overhead. While high finance charges minimize such costs, seriously delinquent amounts are a drain on a store's assets.

CREDIT LEGISLATION

In previous chapters we discussed the effects of consumerism on certain retail practices. We saw how consumer advocates have succeeded in minimizing or eliminating the dubious behavior of unscrupulous retailers. We also took note of the salutary effect of state and federal legislation on retailer-consumer relations.

A significant aspect of the consumer movement has been the passage of legislation to regulate credit. All states have passed laws whose purpose is to protect consumers in their credit dealings with retailers, but the legislation varies too greatly from one state to another to permit discussion here. However, several federal credit laws are particularly important to both merchants and consumers.

The Truth-in-Lending Act

The Truth-in-Lending Act has two goals:

1. To inform consumers about the credit terms of sales transactions.
2. To specify the manner in which finance charges are determined.

Prior to passage of this law, customers were often confused by the language of their credit contracts as well as the details listed on monthly statements. Truth-in-Lending is an attempt to clarify matters for consumers by requiring retailers to state pertinent credit facts. For example, the law requires the retailer to state finance charge rates in annual percentages even when they are already stated in daily ones. Thus, a daily finance charge of .05391 percent must also be listed as a 19.68 percent annual charge. The logic behind this requirement is that it is easier to understand and compare finance charges as annual rates than as monthly ones.

Figure 18-2 contains information provided to consumers as directed by the Truth-in-Lending Act.

The Fair Credit Reporting Act

In our discussion about investigations of credit applicants, the retailer's need for thorough and reliable information was stressed. No mention was made of the consumer's rights and prerogatives. The Fair Credit Reporting Act, however,

EAB European American Bank

Important Information in Case of Errors or Inquiries About Your Bill

Thank you for banking with us. If you have a question about your bill, or think we made an error, you're protected by the Federal Truth in Lending Act.

The Federal Truth in Lending Act requires prompt correction of billing mistakes.

1. If you want to preserve your rights under the Act, here's what to do if you think your bill is wrong or if you need more information about an item on your bill:
   a. Do not write on the bill. On a separate sheet of paper write the following: (you may telephone your inquiry but **doing so will not preserve your rights under this law).**
      i. Your name and account number (if any).
      ii A description of the error and an explanation (to the extent you can explain) of why you believe it is an error.
         If you only need more information, explain the item you are not sure about and, if you wish, ask for evidence of the charge such as a copy of the charge slip. Do not send in your copy of a sales slip or other document unless you have a duplicate copy for your records.
      iii. The dollar amount of the suspected error.
      iv. Any other information (such as your address) which you think will help the bank to identify you or the reason for your complaint or inquiry.
   b. Send your billing error notice to:
      Mail it as soon as you can, but in any case, early enough to reach the bank within 60 days after the bill was mailed to you. If you have authorized the bank to automatically pay from your checking or savings account any credit card bills from the bank, you can stop or reverse payment on any amount you think is wrong by mailing your notice so the bank receives it within 16 days after the bill was sent to you. However, you do not have to meet this 16-day deadline to get the bank to investigate your billing error claim.

2. The bank must acknowledge all letters pointing out possible errors within 30 days of receipt, unless the bank is able to correct your bill during that 30 days. Within 90 days after receiving your letter, the bank must either correct the error or explain why the bank believes the bill was correct. Once the bank has explained the bill, the bank has no further obligation to you even though you still believe that there is an error, except as provided in paragraph 5 below.

3. After the bank has been notified, neither the bank nor an attorney nor a collection agency may send you collection letters or take other collection action with respect to the amount in dispute; but periodic statements may be sent to you, and the disputed amount can be applied against your credit limit. You cannot be threatened with damage to your credit rating or sued for the amount in question, nor can the disputed amount be reported to a credit bureau or to other creditors as delinquent until the creditor has answered your inquiry. **However, you remain obligated to pay the parts of your bill not in dispute.**

4. If it is determined that the bank has made a mistake on your bill, you will not have to pay any finance charges on any disputed amount. If it turns out that the bank has not made an error, you may have to pay finance charges on the amount in dispute, and you will have to make up any missed minimum or required payments on the disputed amount. Unless you have agreed that your bill was correct, the bank must send you a written notification of what you owe; and if it is determined that the bank did make a mistake in billing the disputed amount, you must be given the time to pay which you normally are given to pay undisputed amounts before any more finance charges or late payment charges on the disputed amount can be charged to you.

5. If the bank's explanation does not satisfy you and you notify the bank **in writing** within **10** days after you receive its explanation that you still refuse to pay the disputed amount, the bank may report you to credit bureaus and other creditors and may pursue regular collection procedures. But the bank must also report that you think you do not owe the money, and the bank must let you know to whom such reports were made. Once the matter has been settled between you and the bank, the bank must notify those to whom the bank reported you as delinquent of the subsequent resolution.

6. If the bank does not follow these rules, the bank is not allowed to collect the first $50 of the disputed amount and finance charges, even if the bill turns out to be correct.

7. If you have a problem with property or services purchased with a credit card, you may have the right not to pay the remaining amount due on them, if you first try in good faith to return them or give the merchant a chance to correct the problem. There are two limitations on this rights:
   a. You must have bought them in your home state or if not within your home state within 100 miles of your current mailing address; and
   b. The purchase price must have been more than $50.
      However, these limitations do not apply if the merchant is owned or operated by the bank, or if the bank mailed you the advertisement for the property or services.

230/0609 June 80

Figure 18-2 Consumers' rights under the Truth-in-Lending Act.

allows credit applicants to review information in their files for the purpose of determining its accuracy. It also prohibits use of the information for any reason other than credit or employment. The law makes credit bureau files available to applicants if they are denied credit. Except for bankruptcy data, information that is damaging to a consumer may not be maintained by a retailer or a credit bureau for more than seven years.

At a 1989 meeting of the U.S. Congress Consumer Affairs Subcommittee, the National Retail Federation testified to the effectiveness of the Fair Credit Reporting Act. The organization felt that the act did not require substantial revision.

The Equal Credit Opportunity Act

Consumerism and the women's movement resulted in the passage of the Equal Credit Opportunity Act. This law prohibits retailers from denying credit on the basis of sex, marital status, religion, race, or national origin. Among other things, it protects widowed and divorced women against discrimination for lack of a credit history, if, during the time that they were married, their family credit was listed under the husband's name.

The Fair Credit and Charge Card Disclosure Act

Passed by Congress in 1988, this act requires issuers of credit cards to disclose basic price information when an application is made for a credit card.

The Fair Debt Collection Practices Act

Prohibits harassment by debt collectors and requires that amounts owed be verified.

The Fair Credit Billing Act

This law provides protection for consumers in cases of inaccurate billing by retailers. It gives customers 60 days in which to report billing mistakes. The retailer then has 30 days in which to acknowledge receipt of the customer's letter and 60 more days in which to resolve the problem. If the problem is not solved after 90 days, the retailer may take legal action.

The Holder in Due Course Act

One of the ways in which a business can secure immediate cash is to sell part or all of its accounts receivables to a third party. Suppose a retailer does so. Who is liable for defects in a credit customer's product? Against whom does a customer press complaints regarding a credit sale, the retailer or the third party? Prior to passage of the Holder in Due Course Act, the customer had no rights against the third party—the owner of the contract. Today, however, the third party assumes the retailer's responsibility for credit contracts and is liable to customers for product defects and complaints. Thus, consumers are protected despite any special arrangements that exist between retailers and third parties (holders in due course).

The Electronic Fund Transfer Act

This act provides EFT users with the right to written receipts, bank statements that show all EFT transactions, and enforceable procedures for the handling of errors.

NEW TERMS

bank credit card	cycle billing
bank debit card	descriptive billing
company card	installment credit
conditional sales contract	open charge account
country club billing	revolving charge account
credit bureau	store credit card
credit card	travel/entertainment credit card

CHAPTER HIGHLIGHTS

1. To a retailer the advantages of offering credit are increased sales and customer loyalty, more evenly spread out sales, and less difficulty in making sales.
2. To a customer the advantages of buying on credit include the ease of returning merchandise, the fact that it is not necessary to carry substantial amounts of cash, the ability to satisfy immediate shopping needs, and the availability of records for personal budgeting and income tax purposes.
3. Credit plans offered by merchants include open charge accounts, revolving charge accounts, installment credit, and credit cards.
4. Credit card fraud is a major problem for retailers. Merchants constantly seek new ways to combat the illegal use of credit cards.
5. The criteria used by retailers for granting credit include an applicant's personal qualities, ability to pay, and the applicant's wealth. The importance assigned to each criterion by individual retailers varies.

6. The techniques used by retailers to gather credit information about applicants include application forms, personal interviews, and credit bureau reports. Credit bureaus are either cooperatively owned by retailers or entrepreneurial.

7. Billing procedures used by retailers include descriptive billing, cycle billing, and country club billing.

8. Collection techniques employed by retailers include letters, telephone calls, telegrams, personal collectors, collection agencies, and lawsuits.

9. The most important federal credit laws are the Truth-in-Lending Act, the Fair Credit Reporting Act, the Equal Credit Opportunity Act, the Fair Credit and Charge Card Disclosure Act, the Fair Debt Collection Practices Act, the Fair Credit Billing Act, the Holder in Due Course Act, and the Electronic Fund Transfer Act.

REVIEW QUESTIONS

1. Why might a policy of selling on credit enable a store to increase its sales?

2. What options for payment does a revolving charge account customer have upon receiving a monthly statement?

3. What is the difference between a bank credit card and a bank debit card?

4. At least in its initial stages, why is it important for a store's collection techniques to be nonthreatening?

5. From the retailer's viewpoint, do the benefits of extending credit outweigh the risks? Explain.

6. How does the Truth-in-Lending Act differ from the Equal Credit Opportunity Act?

7. Why are more stores accepting a variety of credit cards, not just their proprietary cards?

DISCUSSION QUESTIONS

1. In your opinion, what is the main advantage to a consumer of buying on credit? Explain.

2. Why might it be important for a consumer to carry both a bank credit card and a travel/entertainment card?

3. Do you think that credit card use is feasible in the fast-food business?

4. As a consumer, how do you feel about the Fair Credit Reporting Act? Would you feel differently if you were a retailer? Why?

CASE 1

Who Gets the Credit?

Robert Costa, the credit manager of Dubree's, a large department store, has been in charge of credit operations for 20 years. He was responsible for the overall design of the current credit system, including criteria for granting credit, the construction of the credit application form, and collection procedures. From the moment he took charge, Costa instituted a no-nonsense approach to securing new credit customers and dealing with delinquent accounts. He views his department as the store's protector, not as something to be used for promotional or sales activities. By and large, the owners of Dubree's have been satisfied with their credit operations, and they have commended Costa for his work on numerous occasions.

Lately, however, one of the store's vice-presidents has criticized the loose ties between credit operations and merchandising activities. He points out that a store's credit function is an adjunct to sales, not an end in itself, and that many of Dubree's customers view its credit department as controlling the merchandising departments. The vice-president is also critical of the stern image conveyed by the credit department, unlike the more friendly approach taken by buyers and sales personnel. Finally, he feels that a store's credit operations should enhance sales in particular departments on a flexible basis, as dictated by the store manager.

Assume that you, an outside consultant, have been asked by Dubree's owners to evaluate the role of the store's credit operations. You have been given the authority to interview *all* personnel and to review forms, reports, and the like.

a. What questions would you ask the vice-president? Costa?
b. How do you feel about the points the vice-president has raised? Explain.
c. Do you see a way of reconciling the two points of view? Explain.

CASE 2

Customers for Credit*

Competition for the consumer's credit dollar is becoming ever more fierce. And full-line, traditional department stores, many of them already saturated in their markets, are looking for new ways to reach new, or newly desirable customers.

*This article was written by Jules Abend.

For instance, they have yielded to third party cards, but have turned around and are trying to capture those customers—bought with someone else's money—by intensive, instant credit conversion programs.

Now, they are faced with banks' increasing interest in the youth market, once their province almost entirely. And some are seeing forays by financial institutions, attempting to take credit outside by offering to relieve the pressure on receivables.

Philosophically, these stores, most of whose business has come from house card customers, have dealt with credit as a very necessary, if not profitable service. But more and more the merchants are asking the credit men to put a return on investment measure against it. That means streamlining operations and devising economical, on-target promotional schemes.

In order to cope with the external and internal influences, and to grow the customer base, these executives are embarking on a variety of programs.

At the top of their lists are new efforts to attract students, both upper classmen and graduate students, at colleges and universities, as well as the emerging, important and disparate group known as working women.

Some are even offering credit to those who haven't yet reached their majority, high school students.

"The younger the better, and the better educated are best," are the watchwords today from stores attempting to replenish and expand credit business lost through attrition and an aging population.

As far as college students are concerned, "once burned, twice shy," doesn't apply for the major merchants who got nothing but trouble from them in the late '60s and early '70s, when the idea was to harass the establishment.

A senior credit man remembers the period and his company's early efforts: "It didn't take too much of that to make one realize it was time to get out of that business—in a big hurry!

"And we did. We dropped out and did not solicit in the college area for quite a long period. As we saw the climate changing, we went back into it and are very successful."

Over the last decade—and particularly the last few years—the college population has evolved into a class of "solid citizens," with significant disposable income, and is being wooed strenuously, the man notes.

It's easier to pull the college student—in many instances with the help of specialist vendors such as College Credit Card Corp.—than it is to find the working woman.

That is, to find the working woman specifically, without using an expensive scattergun promotion approach in the hope of hitting your target. Demographically, this excellent resource is hidden, unless and until she walks into the store and asks for credit.

The senior retail credit people who put STORES in the picture are: Mike Zoroya, The May Department Stores Co.; Earl Russell, ZCMI; John Gleason,

Wanamaker's; Sharon Brown, Zale's; Sherman Barto, Boscov's; R. W. Holloway, Sears; Jim Beam, D. H. Holmes, and Jim Dirlam, Dayton's.

Others who shared their experiences are: C. H. Hines, credit manager, Gulf Oil Products Co.; Steven W. Butterman, senior vp, marketing, Main-Street; Meredith Naples, vp, College Credit Card Corp., and Herb Ott, GECC.

The executives are of a mind when it comes to the college crowd: Steer clear of freshmen and sophomores—as Gleason of Wanamaker's puts it, "I was a sophomore once, and I wouldn't have trusted me"—but the more mature students should be worked.

The reason for pushing credit to this market, roughly ages 19–24, is summed up by Gleason, with: "The student population is only about 6% for us. But it is growing. And as those people move toward the emerging 30s group, you have to get them now, or you might not get them later."

Picking up on that, Brown says that specialty chains like Zale's have additional motives for attempting to focus on students and young people, pointing out that "while department stores may be saturated, we're not.

"Not everybody is interested in jewelry. So we have to find the people who are. And many of the people who are interested don't qualify. So we have to find those quality people who do. We have to go to groups such as students because it is more likely those people haven't bought yet."

She says, "Once you do get them, they stay with you forever."

Beam of Holmes attests to that.

Beam likes to talk about the loyalty factor where young folk are concerned. He tells about the Holmes sales clerk, a teacher working during Christmas, who asked, "Are you the same Mr. Beam who handled credit at Goudchaux?"

When told that he was, the man behind the counter responded, "You opened my first account there when I was going to college, and I still have it, and it's still active even though the store is 70 miles away, because I feel loyal to it for having given me my first chance at obtaining credit."

Beam is convinced that, when a young person is issued a card, that customer stays with you. He emphasizes: "We are in the Gulf area, yet we have active accounts in all 50 states. I can only attribute that to the fact most of those people lived here and went to college here once. So get 'em young, and you have a customer for life."

How you "get 'em" varies. Most retail companies have internal programs. Many are using vendors, and more are going to specialists. Holmes, for example, just signed with College Credit Card Corp., which regularly canvasses more than 600 campuses, and lists among its clients Sears, Saks, Hudson's, Gulf, Bamberger's, and Hahnes.

"CCCC," says Naples, "solicits quality applications from juniors, seniors and grad students, and works with the credit grantor to develop a special form."

Its college accounts can be acquired from $2.95 to $4.50 for retailers because students usually don't need a credit bureau report. It is estimated that more than 80% of the nearly 400,000 credit card applications the company collects annually from college students are approved.

Traditionally, major department stores have been the first stop along the credit road for young people, so the lack of a prior credit history isn't a stumbling block.

Anyway, the stores are quite capable of protecting themselves, particularly when they are issuing to freshmen. Dirlam is typical when he says, "We start them with a $100 limit, while the older ones begin with a ceiling of $200."

Barto of Boscov's, which has had a general youth program for 10 years, but is just now taking a hard look at the college market, adds, "We have the on-line technology today to control the debt and let them build a track record, getting increases as they go along."

Holloway of Sears believes it is "the front-end work" that really determines whether a store is extending credit to a potential long-term, loyal customer, or a write-off.

As he sees it, these are hard judgment calls to make, but after all is said and done, the credit seeker must have the money to make the payment "next month," not in the future, when he may or may not be affluent.

Holloway continues: "Some companies may short-cut that front-end work, but you are really not doing the young adult a favor by opening an account if he is going to wind up with a derogatory credit file, and when he tries to buy his first house, he gets busted.

"You can't substitute on the question of 'are there sufficient funds?' There are hazards in the 25-and-under group. And over-obligation is probably the biggest one."

Some agree that issuing credit to the 19–25 category is riskier than to older age segments. Others say that is just not so.

Russell of ZCMI, for example, finds, in tracking young adults over the last three years, the bad debts amounted to less than $1,000. Hines of Gulf reports "our rate of loss on this group is much higher initially—you still have some carry-over of that theory of 'big business, who cares?' With the young people, however, once it stabilizes, the write-offs drop down to normal or even below normal." Normal for Gulf "is probably less than 1%."

Both Zoroya of May and Brown see more risk. Brown says: "You do have greater skips. That happens more frequently with the student market. And it's not necessarily that they're being 'crooks,' it's simply a matter of their mobility. The money may be collected eventually. But it's more difficult."

Zoroya finds "the bad debt expense on the upper classmen accounts some-what higher than average. But we still think they're worthwhile to go after."

If college freshmen and sophomores are dangerous, then it would seem foolhardy to even consider high schoolers as credit applicants. Not so, says Dirlam. Dayton's issues cards to these children.

Dirlam explains: "We don't aggressively advertise it because we're concerned that some parents will be upset. But through word-of-mouth, we let this group know accounts are available to them if they have a verifiable job.

"And we do ask for parental consent. But we do not ask for a co-signature. The limit is $100. We open about 15,000 of these accounts a year. And the losses are very comparable to our regular accounts, which run about six to seven tenths of one percent."

One can't argue with the loss rate. However, Holloway of Sears worries about the backlash from parents, and amplifies: "I recall a situation in which a store that offered credit to an underage person without a parent as co-signer called the family when the account became past due, and the response was, 'You reject me and you take my kid who has a paper route, so it's all your problem.' "

Still, if the strategy is to get young people who will become solid accounts over a 40-year span, Dayton's approach certainly strives for that.

And ZCMI has created a "Club Plan" for the younger high school girl. Russell explains: "Our locality, more than other areas, is family-oriented. And the interest in marriage might be more entrenched in these younger girls than elsewhere.

"So we say to them, 'why don't you select merchandise on our Club Plan—it's for china and silver—and start to pay it out?' We have done some advertising and have been quite successful with the program, which is non-interest-bearing over two years—although we may shorten the payout period."

Going from preparing a trousseau to entering the workplace can be one short step. Working women are desirable. Stores want to extend credit to them.

And, although more tools, such as GECC's "Profile Plus," are available to find customers based on credit application data and demographic/lifestyle information, stores are generally still in the dark when it comes to narrowing in on women in the workforce.

There is no question in the minds of the credit men, however, that they should be doing more. Zoroya typifies the frustration they face, with: "We would like to do a better job in opening these accounts. But they're hard to find, especially the single women. If we can find them in the store, we will extend credit. And we have done things like finding apartment buildings that house business women. But it's very difficult."

Supporting that, Dirlam says, "The working women are impossible to iden-tify, as far as going out and soliciting accounts from them. You have to identify them in the store, in the areas in which they tend to shop.

"We are concentrating our efforts in-store, and making sure our sales consul-tants, in all the markets where those people might be, become credit promotion arms. Nobody in Minneapolis-St. Paul publishes a directory of such women.

"And even if you found a demographic list that has men and women and ran it against the credit bureau many times, you don't get a lot of women," Brown points out, "because either they don't have enough credit, or it is in their husbands' name."

But both Gleason and Barto say, while agreeing working women are an important market, that often stores aren't realizing they're getting this business, even if it's in a passive way.

Gleason amplifies: "One of the things people miss is that, much of the time, the working woman comes to us. If you look through all the mail-in applications, quite often they are single, working women. They are married working women also."

And Barto adds, "Most of the applications completed in department stores are by women, working or not."

However, it is understandable why retailers want to accelerate their credit efforts to both the college and working women's markets. Competition.

Stores have always been more interested in, and took more risk with, people who didn't have a credit history. Now, banks are beginning to go after that business more so than in the past.

Beam reports on a credit card convention he attended, which included banks and oil companies: "A vice president from the Rocky Mountain National Bank was talking, and he said: 'The time for banks not to become actively involved in soliciting the young adult and the student is over.

'No longer can they let retailers take that person and give him credit experience, because too many retailers are getting into the banking arena.' "

In Bean's opinion, "There is going to be a hard battle for this business in the next 10 years."

And Russell is seeing a higher number of young people applying for credit at ZCMI who already have bank cards. In fact, the store has seen a 20% increase in third party card sales in a year. They now account for nearly 12% of the business.

That's the sort of thing moving more retail credit executives in the direction of instant credit conversion plans. Those, that is, who believe in proprietary credit and have the support of their top management.

The May Co. was one of the first to push instant credit, and Zoroya says: "We are extremely loyal to our own card. We know 80% of our business comes from house card customers."

"We take third party cards in only three of our companies. And we have found, in those three, our own credit sales go down dramatically. So what happens is we are really transferring our customers to a third party, and we lose contact with them. We prefer the other route and push our own card."

What about pushing what looks like a store's own card, but is really bank or financial institution credit? Private label credit is not new.

Nor should it be so easily maligned, avers one credit executive from a large eastern store, who emphasizes: "Citicorp and GECC have something to offer to a retailer at a particular point in the marketplace.

"Depending on how that merchant wants to run his business, it could be a very good thing for him to build that kind of relationship, because those institutions can bring more sophisticated control and marketing techniques than if he tried to build his own receivables and spent a whole bunch of money building an exotic, computer-based system to support them."

That credit man had middle-tier companies in mind. A Citicorp vice president admits: "Many of the larger stores are so good at what they do that we're aiming for the medium-sized retailer."

But wait a minute. Federated just went outside and contracted Citicorp to handle its private label credit for the new, promotional department store in Chicago, Main Street.

Credit men urge industry observers not to reach any hasty conclusions as a result of the action. For one thing, the new store is still being shaped, and some consider it to fit the middle-tier profile.

For another, as Ott of GECC puts it, "management probably said, 'let someone else worry about the receivables in this case.' "

MainStreet's marketing VP, Butterman, agrees that, "In-house you have the issue of receivables; going outside you don't have to deal with that. And the public doesn't care."

However, despite the general reaction that Federated's move is not indicative of corporate policy or inclination, Butterman makes a provocative statement with: " . . . With any division, what you do, if you're part of a larger corporation, is certainly potentially applicable in other divisions. This is something new, and if it turns out, it will be looked at in a broader context. But remember we're a company (MainStreet) with practically no history."

a. What are your views about college students as credit risks?
b. The article above refers to the loyalty factor of young people in their choice of retailers. Do you feel that retailers should rely on that factor? Why?
c. Jim Dirlam of Dayton's indicates that working women are impossible to identify as potential credit card customers, using conventional outside sources. If this is so, what techniques might retailers use in their stores to solicit credit accounts from this consumer segment?

REFERENCES

ABEND, J. "Store Cards Still Strong." *Stores* (January 1991), pp. 169–174.

"Credit Card Fraud: Old Scams Still Working." *Stores* (April 1989), p. 27.

"Home Depot Finds Least Cost for Leased Lines." *Chain Store Age Executive*, **65** (September 1989), pp. 74–77.

ROBINS, G. "Credit Authorization." *Stores* (September 1990), pp. 14–20.

"Steps to Protect Against Credit Card Fraud." *Chain Store Age Executive*, **65** (July 1989), p. 88.

Part 6

Making Decisions

The last part of this book deals with the nature and scope of retail decision making. Chapter 19 is concerned with the place of research in the field of retailing. After distinguishing among the retail information system, marketing research, and retailing research, the chapter explains the research process and identifies the sources of primary and secondary data. We note the advantages and disadvantages of several research methods and identify some groups that are involved in retailing research. As an afterword, we speculate on retailing in the future.

Chapter 20 is devoted to the details and problems of going into a retail business. We identify the personal characteristics of successful retailers and stress the importance of technical skills, knowledge, and interest in ownership. After listing sources of investment funds for prospective retailers, we explain the roles of lawyers and accountants in the establishment of a new business. We note the cautions one should consider before going into business.

In discussing franchises we indicate sources of information for potential franchisees. After listing the major provisions of franchise agreements, we analyze the costs of franchise ownership and explain the purposes of franchise disclosure statements. Our treatment of franchising ends with the rights of franchisees and a list of major franchise categories.

Chapter 19

Research for Retailers

After completing this chapter, you should be able to:

- Distinguish among the terms *retail information system, marketing research,* and *retailing research.*
- Describe the major areas in which retailers use marketing research techniques.
- Explain the research process.
- Identify the sources of primary and secondary data.
- List the advantages and disadvantages of the following data collection methods: survey, observation, and experimentation.
- Identify groups involved in retailing research.
- Identify expected changes in the market, downtown revival, store development and operation, personnel and employment, and merchandising and promotion.

Practically all types of retailers have been faced with escalating costs, accelerating inflation, and a changing business environment. The challenge to remain profitable appears to be greater than ever before, with some of the nation's great retailers no longer in business. One of the oldest and largest variety chains, W. T. Grant, is gone. So is Korvette's, once considered the most innovative discounter in the country. Food Fair, once among the largest supermarket chains, has also disappeared as a result of bankruptcy; so has B. Altman, one of the most venerated department stores in the country, which closed its doors in 1990.

Merchants need answers to their questions about handling customers, meeting competition, and making a profit. At one time retailers relied on intuition and "gut" feelings to answer these questions, but today the risks are too high to trust in "hunches." Consequently, retailers use the tools of retailing information systems and market research to provide information for decision making.

RETAIL INFORMATION SYSTEMS

As indicated in Chapter 2, the use of computers and electronic data processing has made possible the development of the retail information system (RIS). This ongoing system of data collection is designed to process and retain information so that it is available to management immediately for decision making.

Types of input

The major element of an RIS is a central **data bank** that stores information. Through the use of terminals such as computerized cash registers, data are entered into the data bank and retrieved as needed. The information placed in a typical retail data bank includes records of sales, inventory, purchasing, consumer data, accounts payable, accounts receivable, personnel, and other items.

To implement this system, the retailer places all required files and records in the data bank. This becomes the core of information, which is reviewed, updated, or changed when necessary. Updating, which refers to additions, deletions, or changes in the data bank, is important if the information is to be useful. New information is obtained from such sources as sales, inventory, and personnel records.

Data are made available to managers through terminals placed in various stations, departments, and offices. These terminals are connected to the data bank and allow information to be displayed on video screens. As a result, management has access to information throughout the day without waiting for reports to be printed. However, a variety of printed reports are available as needed (Figure 19-1).

An **EIS** is an **electronic information system** specifically designed for and tailored to the needs of a company's chief executives. Although interest in EIS is growing, very few retailers have implemented it. There are software packages

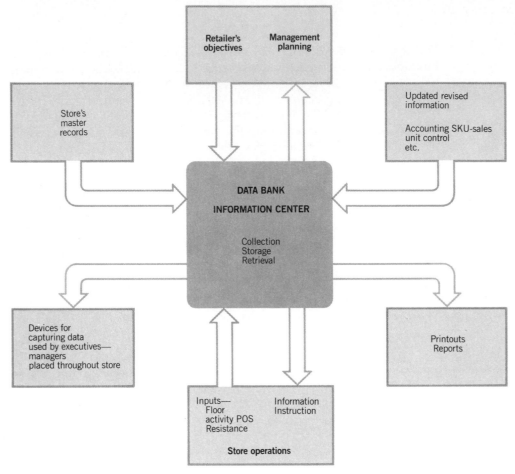

Figure 19-1   A retail information system.

available, but the main problem with implementation is executive reluctance to adopt EIS.

Advantages of RIS

Advantages and disadvantages of RIS

Among the advantages of RIS are the following.

- Information is collected continuously.
- Data are available at all times.
- Specific information can be utilized when and where it is needed most.
- As problems arise, management has an opportunity to make decisions early.
- Research can take place continuously.
- The retailer's objectives provide basic guidelines as to what information is needed and collected.

Disadvantages of RIS

An RIS does have some disadvantages. These include the following.

- It is costly.
- It is difficult to develop without using specialists.
- Large quantities of data can create complex decision-making problems.

Retailing information systems are helpful in planning for efficiency and for controlling day-to-day activities. Nevertheless, frequently problems and questions arise that require in-depth research studies to uncover the real causes of concern. In such cases the tools of marketing research in retailing are needed.

MARKETING RESEARCH

Marketing research involves the investigation and systematic gathering, recording, and analysis of data that are pertinent to a specific marketing problem. Marketing research studies institutions like wholesalers and retailers and the activities involved in moving goods and services to the consumer. These activities include the buying and selling of goods as well as advertising, packaging, and transporting them to the various markets. Manufacturers generally conduct major research studies about products, consumers, and competition. Wholesalers usually investigate markets and the costs of distributing goods. To a lesser degree, wholesalers conduct important research in the areas of display and sales incentives.

RETAILING RESEARCH

Retailing research applies the techniques of marketing research to the investigation of problems related to retail activities. Such problems include merchandise selection, customer behavior, store location, pricing policies, and promotional costs.

The Benefits of Retailing Research

Computers and point-of-sale transactions

The benefits of research techniques, once limited to large retailers, are now available to smaller merchants. As mentioned in the preceding section, the computer and other electronic machines used by retailers have paved the way for collecting valuable information in many areas. For example, in point-of-sale (POS) transactions stores are equipped with specially designed cash registers that do much more than merely ring up sales (Figure 19-2). For each customer, the salesperson records such information as product number, product description,

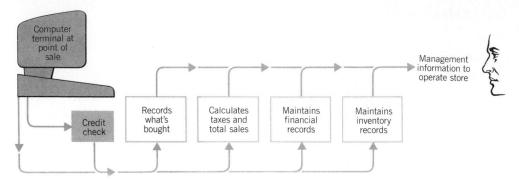

Figure 19-2   A POS computer tie-in generates management information.
Reproduced by permission of the J.C. Penney Company.

unit price, number of units sold, amount of cash tendered, and department number. In stores that grant credit, the customer's charge account number is also recorded. Besides producing a customer sales receipt, the register transfers the sales information electronically to a remote computer containing a data bank. In turn, the computer

- Records sales by product.
- Keeps a record of how much inventory is still on hand.
- Signals reorder points to maintain sufficient stock.
- Indicates how quickly each product is being sold.
- Lists sales by department and salesperson.
- Maintains records of customer charge accounts.

This information becomes available to management within hours and enables store executives to make timely decisions. Periodically—daily, weekly, monthly, semiannually—the computer prints reports about strong- and weak-selling items, the volume of returns by customers, the performance of each store, and comparisons with sales in previous periods. In some cases computers produce purchase orders based on preset reorder points. Information generated by computers regarding the purchasing habits and lifestyles of customers helps retailers determine customers' merchandise and service needs.

A commitment to research is fairly general today among large retailers. Recent projects include the Price Club's testing of a new home furniture and furnishings approach and Target's development of a "customer friendly" super-store. In the case of the Price Club, it closed its home furnishings store in San Juan Capistrano, California, in October 1990 because the approach proved unsuccessful.

Through a shared-time arrangement, small retailers that cannot afford data processing equipment can also benefit from a computer's capabilities. Through computer service companies, these retailers can become involved in research activities that would otherwise be closed to them.

Walter K. Levy, a retail marketing consultant, believes that research will become more routine, focusing on

- Identifying emerging trends.
- Latent demand that is not being satisfied.
- Undermarketed ideas and undermerchandised areas.
- Competitors' weaknesses.
- Consumers' moods and changes in their lifestyles and attitudes.[1]

The Scope of Retailing Research

**Research covers
a wide range
of areas**

The major areas of retailing research are consumers, store location and layout, advertising and promotion, merchandise selection and pricing, personnel, and competition.

Consumers

Retailers are concerned about improving their stores and offerings in order to attract more customers. Studies on how to win increased patronage and how to satisfy customers are a constant challenge to merchants. In fact, consumer motivation and behavior have probably received the greatest attention from researchers in retailing.

Broadly speaking, consumer research involves an analysis of how people live, as well as the study of demographic and psychographic information. As discussed in Chapter 3, demographic studies are concerned with such characteristics as age, sex, income, and education. On the other hand, psychographic data involve personality traits, habits, perceptions, attitudes, motivations, and values. The study of this kind of information helps merchants develop customer profiles and match the store's image and total offerings with the customers they are trying to attract. For example, surveys conducted by Safeway were instrumental in the food chain's resolve to restructure the firm's small stores into super/combo units. The research dealt with the types of stores customers expected as well as the range of products they preferred.

A good example of the importance of paying attention to demographics and lifestyles is the changing patronage of many restaurants. Eating establishments like Dalt's, TGI Friday's, Houlihan's, and Bennigan's now cater to families as well as to their former adult niche. Surprisingly, they have accomplished their goal of attracting the former and not alienating the latter.

Another example is the Pamida discount chain, selling both soft and hard goods, that has operated successfully for years in 12 midwestern states. Concen-

---

[1] "Retailing in the 21st Century," *Inside Retailing,* Special Report (November 20, 1989), p. 2.

trating exclusively in small towns, the company has had little competition until recently. However, Wal-Mart, the giant discount chain, whose stores have been located in areas with substantial populations, has begun to invade Pamida territory, reasoning that it can compete successfully even in regions with small populations and varying demographics.

Store Location and Layout

Selecting the right site is a critical decision that entails the investigation of population growth, shopping habits, traffic patterns, parking needs, competition, and cost of property. Retailers use a variety of research techniques to determine store location. For example, they study the pattern of competitive stores in a trading area to determine the viability of a new outlet. They also study the economic stability of a trading area to measure the short-and long-term chances of success.

In order to determine the most effective store layout, in-store customer traffic patterns are studied. Retailers constantly look for new ways to increase the productivity of space as well as its convenience to customers.

Advertising and Promotion

To create more effective advertising and promotion procedures, merchants study their experiences with media, types of ads, special promotions, and advertising costs.

Research provides answers to specific questions

Research can assist in answering such questions as: Should we engage in promotional or institutional advertising? Which special event was most successful? Which medium is best suited to the store's customers?

Merchants measure the effectiveness of an ad campaign by store traffic, immediate sales response, returned coupons, and the like. Sales data are also used in evaluating in-store display locations.

Merchandise Selection and Pricing

Merchandise research involves studying the buying, selling, and pricing of goods. Specifically, it is concerned with the collection and interpretation of data on markups, markdowns, profits, and sales turnover. This information is relatively easy for retailers to gather, since data processing provides internal statistics quickly.

Personnel

Personnel research is concerned with the finding, hiring, training, compensation, and evaluation of employees. Some of the important personnel areas that require ongoing evaluation are the effectiveness of training and testing, employee turnover, compensation relative to productivity, and incentive programs.

Many retailers use consulting firms to "shop" their employees and rate their salespeople. Others use sales volume as a basis for evaluation. In any case, information regarding the effectiveness of employees is important for making wise personnel decisions.

Competition

Market share studies help retailers recognize their relative positions in terms of the total market. They provide comparative information regarding the competition. Virtually all retail analysts agree that the 1990s will witness intense competition generally, with the battleground drawn particularly between department and specialty stores. Many discounters, too, will have to struggle to maintain their market niche.

RETAIL STRATEGY
A Study of Mall Shoppers

Lerner, a longtime women's wear specialty chain, had a long history of urban area profit-making years. It made its mark with consumers by offering attractive merchandise at affordable prices.

As shopping malls sprang up in the 1960s, Lerner located stores in them. Clinging to its traditional approach, it found that trendier retailers were cutting into its market share.

To meet the competitive threat, Lerner conducted a two-year study of mall consumers in order to update its merchandise strategy. The findings convinced the chain that a new merchandise approach was required, simple and logical: to sell outfits rather than single items. The switch in strategy has already proved effective for Lerner.*

*Lerner was purchased by the Limited in 1985, and the latter was largely responsible for the new strategy.

THE INFORMAL APPROACH TO RESEARCH

Retailers often use informal measures to gather information or analyze a situation. When they hesitate to spend money on research because of limited funds, or are ignorant of the benefits of research, decision errors are likely. Merchants who do not utilize research rely on intuition or use less sophisticated methods of doing business. Still others merely imitate the competition.

Cases in which research was lacking

In today's market it is increasingly difficult to make good business decisions without appropriate information. A case in point involves a retail office furniture dealer whose store was located in a business district. Over time the trading area changed from one composed of office buildings and factories to a predominantly residential community. In an attempt to sell to this new market, the retailer changed his merchandise offering to a largely household furniture line. He invested a great deal of money in home furnishings and stocked very traditional furniture. Unfortunately, the new line sold poorly and the retailer lost a major part of his investment.

Had the merchant investigated the situation in some depth, he could have learned more about the residents and their lifestyles. He would have found that this group consisted largely of young singles and marrieds and that they furnished their homes with modern, nontraditional items.

In another case a merchant selected a location for a toy shop on the basis of the size of the store, its low rent, and the sparse competition in the immediate area. The shop was stocked with the newest merchandise and was arranged attractively for self-service. The opening was timed to take advantage of the Christmas season. The merchant decided to use the store window and some local posters as a means of attracting customers.

The retailer's strategy proved unsuccessful for several reasons: first, failure to recognize that a large percentage of the trading area population was middle-aged or older; second, lack of awareness that the young marrieds did a great deal of shopping outside the area; and third, ignorance of the fact that older people are less informed about toys than consumers in other age groups and generally need greater assistance. Overall, the merchant was unaware that **outshoppers** (people shopping outside their area) generally consult media sources for information.

These cases indicate that *some* research was required to minimize risks. Research may be as simple as determining whether customers like a certain gift wrap or as complicated as selecting a store location. The procedures and tools for conducting research are similar even though the problems or types of stores differ.

THE RESEARCH PROCESS

The research process consists of five basic steps:

1. Identifying and defining the problem
2. Collecting the data: secondary and/or primary
3. Compiling and tabulating the data
4. Analyzing and interpreting the findings
5. Preparing the final report

Identifying and Defining the Problem

It is important that the retailer develop a clear statement of the problem so that the research can be organized for the collection of the necessary information. Defining the problem correctly yields useful information for a solution. For example, a manager of a department store chain noticed a significant increase in the number of refunds compared to the past year. He became even more concerned after reading a report issued by a retail trade association stressing the rising trend in refund abuse and fraud.

Though there are several facets to the problem of refunds, the need to reduce refund transactions is clear. The question is, How can this be accomplished? The answer leads to the second step of the research process: collecting the data.

Collecting the Data

Secondary and primary data   **Secondary data** are data that are already available; that is, information that was collected previously for other projects, such as the U.S. Census Reports. Secondary data are obtained from company records, libraries, the U.S. Government Printing Office, schools, private research firms, organizations, trade publications, and other sources. The main advantage of collecting secondary data is the *savings of time and money.*

The disadvantages are as follows.

- The information may be outdated.
- The data may be derived from unreliable sources.
- The information may be unsuitable for the project.

If secondary data provide sufficient information for problem solving, then it is unnecessary to collect additional data. Primary data are collected only if secondary data will not solve the problem at hand.

Primary data are collected firsthand for the particular problem under study. There are three basic data collection methods.

- Survey
- Observation
- Experimentation

Survey

Surveys involve the questioning of people. This is the most widely used of the three methods. It may be accomplished by means of mail, telephone, or personal interviews. Surveys are often used to reveal customer attitudes, opinions, and shopping habits. The following illustrations demonstrate the use of the survey method.

In assessing the effectiveness of a merchandising program, the retailer could research the repeat purchase pattern (use-up rate) of a particular product. It would be necessary to study how many times the customer returns to the marketplace to rebuy.

The merchant could use several techniques for collecting the necessary information. A questionnaire could be developed for use in mail, telephone, or personal interviews (Figure 19-3). *Mail* is most suitable when the study involves a large group or one that is widely dispersed geographically. Though it is relatively inexpensive, the rate of return is low and returns require considerable time. *Telephone* interviews are effective for short questionnaires. This method is fast and relatively inexpensive, and allows for some flexibility in questioning. The disad-

STUDENT QUESTIONNAIRE

       Mr.

Name: Mrs. _____

       Miss

College or University _____

Home City & State _____ Reside at School: At School ( )

                                                        At Home ( )

1a AGE   **b** SCHOOL YEAR   **c** MARITAL STATUS

   (Circle One)   (Circle One)   (Check One)

   1 17   1   **1** Single   ( )

   2 18   2   **2** Engaged   ( )

   3 19   3   **3** Married   ( )

   4 20   4

   5 21+

   Employment while at School:

1 None ( )   **2** Part Time ( )   **3** Full Time ( )

2   When at school, where do you buy most of your toiletries and/or cosmetics?

    1 Campus Book Store ( )   **2** Other Store ( )

3   When at home, where do you buy most of your toiletries and/or cosmetics?

    1 Drugstore   ( )   **3** Supermarket   ( )

    2 Department Store ( )   **4** Discount store ( )   **5** Other (SPECIFY) _____

3b What kind of eye makeup do you use?

    1 Mascara   ( )   **3** Eye Liner ( )

    2 Eye Shadow ( )   **4** Other   ( )   **5** None ( )

3c What brand of Cold Cream do you use? _____

4a Please list on the chart below the product and brand of samples you have obtained recently and indicate the following:

4b How or where did you receive the sample: (CHECK BELOW)

4c Degree of usage. (CHECK BELOW)

Figure 19-3 Example of a research questionnaire for students regarding their preferences, opinions, and purchasing decisions about product categories.

4d Which brands of regular size (i.e., nonsample) have you purchased since obtaining the sample pack? (RECORD BELOW)

4a Product & Brand of Sample Received	4b How or Where Sample Received		4c Usage			4d Brands Purchased Since Receiving Sample
	Campus Bookstore	Other	Have Used	Now Using	Haven't Used	
_____	( )	( )	( )	( )	( )	_____
_____	( )	( )	( )	( )	( )	_____
_____	( )	( )	( )	( )	( )	_____
_____	( )	( )	( )	( )	( )	_____
_____	( )	( )	( )	( )	( )	_____
_____	( )	( )	( )	( )	( )	_____
_____	( )	( )	( )	( )	( )	_____
_____	( )	( )	( )	( )	( )	_____
_____	( )	( )	( )	( )	( )	_____

5a How often do you use a Hand Care product?

	In Winter		In Summer	
	Hand Lotion	Hand Cream	Hand Lotion	Hand Cream
1 Occasionally—not every day	( )	( )	( )	( )
2 Every day, one or twice	( )	( )	( )	( )
3 Every day, three times or more	( )	( )	( )	( )
4 Do Not Use	( )	( )	( )	( )

5b What type of container do you prefer, for a Hand Care product?

Hand Lotion		**Hand Cream**	
1 Glass Bottle	( )	**1** Glass Jar	( )
2 Plastic Bottle	( )	**2** Plastic Tube	( )
3 Aerosol Can	( )	**3** Aerosol Can	( )
4 No preference	( )	**4** No preference	( )

5c Please rank (1, 2, 3, 4) in order of importance to you the following qualities of a hand care product: ("1" for most important, "2" for next most important, etc.)

	Hand Lotion	**Hand Cream**
Spreads easily, absorbs quickly	( )	( )
Doesn't leave hands feeling sticky or oily	( )	( )
Pleasant, distinctive fragrance	( )	( )
Creamy consistency, not too thick or thin	( )	( )

Figure 19-3 (Continued)

vantages include unlisted telephone numbers, households without phones, and the difficulty of reaching people who refuse to answer questions by phone. *Personal* interviews are most suitable for long questionnaires. This is the most flexible technique because it provides an opportunity for the interviewer to elicit lengthy responses. The disadvantages are possible interviewer bias (distortion of facts), the difficulty of recruiting trained interviewers, and expense.

A recent addition to the interview technique is the "push-button questionnaire," an automatic machine that is as easy to use as a calculator. One such machine, known as Tellus, embodies a new concept for monitoring and measuring customer opinions. It is less expensive than other questionnaire procedures and provides immediate responses. It takes little time to use, requiring only 30 seconds for the completion of a set of 11 questions. Tellus gathers customer input on the spot and avoids interviewer-interviewee confrontations. Some companies feel, in fact, that customers regard this type of survey as a sincere attempt by management to solve problems.

A very interesting survey underway at the time of this writing involves the body shapes of women 55 and older. Conducted by the The Institute for Standards Research, the information gathered should be of importance to manufacturers, retailers, and consumers of apparel and related merchandise.

Another survey, this one conducted in 1990 by Impact Resources MART/ USA, showed that Sears, Roebuck was still the nation's favorite store for full-line shopping. Behind Sears came J. C. Penney and K mart.[2] Although retailers pay close attention to this type of survey data, they are cautious about its use because of the volatility of retailing.

A good example of a recent survey that dealt with customer service was conducted by Omni Tel Survey. Specific areas covered included checkout waiting time, merchandise availability, ease of locating merchandise, and product availability.

Observation

Some problems can be solved simply through **observation.** For example, a retailer that is looking for a new location for a branch store might conduct a traffic study to learn how much automobile or pedestrian traffic passes a proposed site. Or a store buyer might determine the types of rainwear that customers use by conducting a fashion count. The "counter" uses a form to record the styles, shapes, or colors worn by customers or pedestrians. The advantages of the observation method are that observations are relatively simple to implement, that they do not require cooperation from the people being studied, and that observers do not have to be experienced. It should be noted that observation can also utilize mechanical means, such as mirrors, or films. A disadvantage is that the attitudes of the people being observed cannot be determined.

---

[2] By 1991, however, there were indications that Wal-Mart had surged ahead of Sears and K mart.

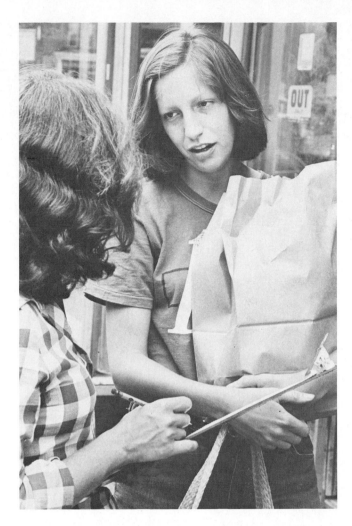

Personal interviews are useful for compiling important information about consumers. Esaias Baitel/Photo Researchers.

Experimentation

A researcher can also set up an **experiment** utilizing a control factor. For example, a retailer might be interested in learning whether assembled toys sell more than those in knockdown (KD) condition. She might want to investigate the effect on sales if several large toys are sold assembled rather than boxed. The merchant might then advertise a special promotion for assembled toys at a slightly higher price than toys to be assembled by the purchaser. The control factor would be the use of the same product in assembled and unassembled forms. The variables would be the price and service. If sales of assembled toys proved to be greater in spite of the charge, the retailer might assume that her customers are willing to pay more for convenience.

As the South Street Seaport scene in New York City shows, valuable information about pedestrian traffic can be obtained through observation. *Courtesy:* Port Authority of N.Y. & N.J.

Experiments can make use of surveys or observation. The methods used depend on the type of data needed.

Another type of experiment is the computer-based simulation. A model is created to represent all the factors a retailer would face in a real situation. It is similar to a computer game that involves actions and reactions to different inputs. In this situation the retailer can act as both consumer and merchant. This method can be very helpful in decision making because it is possible to determine cause and effect without the customer's participation and without the risks involved in actual situations. However, it is a very expensive and sophisticated method that requires tremendous expertise. Consequently, it is used infrequently by retailers.

Sampling

In conducting primary research, it is important to gather data from a sample of the population. A **sample** is a representative group of the entire population being studied. The researcher telephones, interviews, or surveys the sample to secure answers to specific questions. When composed correctly, samples provide valid information, are less costly, consume less time, and are easier to work with than the entire population.

For example, a merchant considers opening a clothing shop for men up to

5 feet 8 inches tall. The prospective owner feels that short men are neglected by stores because of limited merchandise selection and lack of true-fitting clothes. In fact, many people in this group ordinarily shop in boys' departments. The would-be retailer devises a questionnaire to determine the feasibility of opening the store.

Obviously, it would be very expensive and difficult to survey the 500,000 males in the trading area, especially since the merchant has been told by statisticians that approximately 150,000 of them would probably represent the target market. If the retailer's sample is limited to a small part of the 150,000, say, 1,000, he will probably secure sufficiently valid answers to avoid surveying the entire 150,000.

Many researchers have devised techniques that enable them to work with small samples. For example, Information Resources, a research company, has found a way to monitor the grocery purchases of a representative sample of 4,000 households; it measures how these consumers react to various marketing strategies, such as coupons, free samples, TV commercials, newspaper ads, point-of-purchase displays, and price changes. Known as Behaviorscan, the system contains 2,000 households in two test markets. An identification card is presented at the grocery store each time a member of one of these households makes a purchase. The card alerts the point-of-sale terminal to send an item-by-item accounting of the customer's purchases to a data bank in Chicago. The universal product code is read by a scanner so that researchers can pinpoint a family's purchases by price, brand, and size. This information is then correlated with the promotional stimuli to which the family was exposed.

Compiling and Tabulating the Data

Percentages are useful for comparative purposes

In this stage the data are collected, organized, and processed for analysis. Data are collected and counted manually or with data processing equipment. During this step the information is counted systematically, enabling the researcher to develop *percentages* to be used in arriving at meaningful conclusions.

For example, in a recent study a merchant noticed that out of a total of 200 shoppers in the store's cosmetics department, 38 men shopped by themselves. Stated as a figure, the number 38 is not particularly useful. When the number is stated as a percent (19 percent), however, it is more useful for comparative purposes. Continuing the example, if during the same period in the previous year the comparable finding was 14 percent, the retailer might have concluded that the 5 percent increase warranted further investigation.

Analyzing and Interpreting the Findings

This step involves studying the research findings and translating them into summary information for the final report. Interpretation is very important because it results in recommendations that usually influence decisions.

The following are examples of findings from retailing research studies.

- Store loyalty was found to be closely related to consumers' style of shopping.

- A survey of leading practitioners and observers of food retailing revealed a consistently held opinion that supermarket management would find it profitable to give direct attention to the elderly.
- A study of teenagers' responses to retailing stimuli indicated that the mass media play an important role in the formation of young people's attitudes and knowledge.
- Selecting the most effective advertising medium is vital in getting the most from a store's ad dollars. According to one survey, stores reported that an average of 74 percent of all ready-to-wear and accessories ads are placed in newspapers. Radio and television rank second, capturing an average of 17 percent, and direct mail and catalog advertising are third, with 9 percent.

Preparation of the Final Report

Reporting the results of the research project is the last step. The report may be presented in print (Figure 19-4) or given orally. In either case, the report should bring the data and analyses into permanent form so that they are always available for reference. Effective reports often stimulate action and result in important management decisions.

When a retailer implements the recommendations of the final report, it is not uncommon for him or her to undertake an evaluation to study the results.

CONDUCTING RETAILING RESEARCH

In order to carry out retailing research, some firms hire research directors to conduct inhouse studies using internal staff. Others employ consultants or commercial research companies. Sometimes merchants assign sales or office personnel to undertake simple studies based on internal records. Such research includes things like fashion counts or sales analyses. When the problems to be researched are complex, the retailer may choose to hire a commercial research agency.

Large retailing organizations have special departments devoted to research. They generally employ small staffs trained in the development and conduct of research studies. They prepare questionnaires, conduct interviews, and develop surveys. They deal with such matters as customer information, the effectiveness of advertising and promotion, customer attitudes regarding services, and employee morale. They collect information for specific problems and maintain appropriate records. The research department provides up-to-date information to management, including studies and reports from trade associations, professional groups, and government agencies. Retailers who do not have their own research departments or trained employees may need to consult with private research organizations. These firms specialize in the conduct of research and the sale of information to clients such as retailers and wholesalers. Some of the better-known ones and their specialties are included in the following list.

THE TEST RESULTS

COMBINED RESULTS

Burgoyne's overall test results—end-cap displays and shelf locations combined—show that Monarch Promotional Labels moved 44% more items than Monarch's own "regular" 1110 labels. And, they moved 58% more merchandise than no item pricing.

When contrasted with no item pricing on end-cap displays, promotional lables moved 53% more merchandise; 42% more than the regular size label. And contrasted with no item pricing on shelf locations, promotional labels moved 74% more merchandise; 50% more than the regular size label.

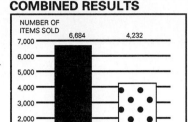

CHART #1
PROMOTIONAL LABELS MOVED **58%** MORE TOTAL MERCHANDISE THAN NO ITEM PRICING!

CHART #2
PROMOTIONAL LABELS MOVED **44%** MORE TOTAL MERCHANDISE THAN REGULAR PRICING!

END-CAP DISPLAY vs SHELF

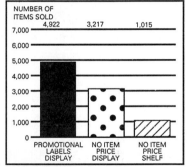

CHART #3
REGULAR LABELS MOVED **10%** MORE MERCHANDISE THAN NO ITEM PRICING!

CHART #4
PROMOTIONAL LABELS ON DISPLAY ITEMS MOVED **5** TIMES AS MUCH AS NO-PRICE SHELF ITEMS . . . NON-PRICED DISPLAY ITEMS MOVED **3** TIMES AS MUCH AS NO-PRICE SHELF ITEMS!

Figure 19-4 Example of how research results are presented. Reproduced by permission of Monarch Marking Systems, Inc.

Private research organizations

- A. C. Nielsen specializes in studies dealing with shelf turnover; it prepares retail indexes on products sold in food and drugstores. It conducts observations on shelf distribution, prices, displays, and the like.
- Market Research Corporation of America studies consumer purchasing habits through the use of consumer panels.
- Audits and Surveys specializes in the conduct of store audits of merchandise, using field people to do the physical counts.
- Dun & Bradstreet specializes in providing credit information to clients.

Simple studies can be based on internal records of fast and slow moving fashions.
Courtesy: International Business Machines.

Other groups are also involved in retailing research.

- Research consultants are outside experts who provide research expertise in areas of interest to retailers. For example, fashion consultants are available to aid the small retailer with purchasing problems; accounting experts are called upon to improve the fiscal health of some businesses; individuals who specialize in site research are involved when new locations are considered.
- Trade associations publish a great deal of information, conduct studies, and make the findings available to their members. The National Retail Federation is the largest of the retail professional groups, most of which conduct research, hold seminars, and provide current data to their members.
- Consumer panels provide services for the study of consumer purchasing habits. They are composed of nationwide households that regularly report their purchases of selected foods, household items, and clothing by logging them in diaries. These diaries are summarized in reports that help manufacturers and retailers plan more efficiently for new products, better packaging, and so forth (Figure 19-5).
- Graduate schools often participate with businesses in joint research efforts. They provide academic expertise and personnel that can be used in conducting market research.

AFTERWORD—RETAILING IN THE FUTURE

Retailing must respond to all kinds of social and economic changes in order to meet the needs of the consumer. Retail institutions have adapted to changes in demographics, lifestyles, and the environment. Therefore, it is no surprise that merchants seek organizations and individuals to conduct retailing research in order to gain insight into future retailing practices. Following are a number of factors that will probably affect the retail environment in the 1990s.

LIKE NO OTHER STORE IN THE WORLD

The Brothers Bloomingdale

Of all the successful department store chains in this country, probably none is better known or more exciting than Bloomingdale's. Its slogan, "Like No Other Store in the World," is familiar to shoppers, tourists, and international travelers.

The store was started in New York City in 1872 as Bloomingdale's Great East Side Bazaar. Its owners, Joseph B. and Lyman G. Bloomingdale, decided to sell ready-to-wear clothing, small personal items, and textiles. Concentrating heavily on advertising, they offered low prices and attractive merchandise assortments. This strategic combination proved an immediate success, and the brothers spent the next 15 years in frenzied expansion.

One of Bloomingdale's early innovations was the escalator, now found in virtually all multistoried retail establishments. The two merchants also stressed customer service and custom-made clothing. But perhaps their most insightful decision involved the heavy use of advertising to popularize the name "Bloomingdale's." Despite the store's location in a nonretailing section of the city, the cleverness and persistence of its ads drew people from widely separated areas.

Though it had started as a soft goods business, by the late 1890s Bloomingdale's had been transformed into a department store. Despite an occasional attempt to appeal to wealthier consumers, the store's basic customers at that time were drawn from middle- and low-income groups.

Bloomingdale's today is under the ownership of Federated Stores. It has also become a major trend setter among retailing giants, known by millions as "Bloomie's." To a large extent, these and other events were foreshadowed by the brother merchants whose tenure with the store ended in the early 1900s.

The Market

Changes in population and age groups are important to retailers because as people move into different age categories, their buying power, wants, and needs change.

The maturing of America

- Since the older population is growing, the group of people age 65 and over will continue to increase in importance because of their size and affluence. Retailers that cater to this group will have increased opportunities, since it will represent approximately 20 percent of the population by the year 2000.
- A significant portion of this group will continue to move to the Sunbelt area. For these areas in particular, therefore, the shift in population will call for changes in retail strategy.
- Young middle-agers (35–44) will be the fastest-growing market, with high incomes to spend.
- The very young market (14–17) will decrease in numbers, together with the 18–24-year-old group, while the 25–34-year-olds will represent the largest group of adults.

Income

- Modest economic growth will enhance living standards substantially. The

Figure 19-5 Example of a diary page used by consumer panels.

DATE BOUGHT	BRAND	PRODUCT DETAILS	QUANTITY	WEIGHT (SIZE)	PRICE PAID	SPECIAL? COUPON? ¢ OFF? DESCRIBE	WHERE BOUGHT

MARGARINE (OLEOMARGARINE) ☐ None

Product details sub-columns: Do the words below appear in larger print on the label? Check as many as appear — Corn Oil, Soft, Whipped, Diet, Unsalted, No (✓) | Check HOW PACKAGED — Four (4) Sticks, Six (6) Sticks, Two ½ lb Tub(s)/Cup(s), 1 lb. Tub, 1 lb. Solid, Squeeze Bottle or Tube, Other | How many pkgs or items of each kind | Of each can, jar, pkg, bottle, item (lbs oz pts qts etc.) | Don't include taxes — For each, Total if more than one | Describe if a special price, coupon, sale, cents off label or other offer | Name of store or delivery company

| 8/4 | (Brand) Sweet Corn | ✓ ✓ [Corn Oil, Soft] ... ✓ [1 lb. Solid] | 2 | 1 lb. | .47 .94 | | Mills |

BUTTER ☐ None

Sub-columns: Does Label say "Unsalted"? (✓) Yes / No | Check HOW PACKAGED — Four (4) Sticks, Six (6) Sticks, Other

| 8/4 | (Brand) Bossert's Farm | ✓ [No] ✓ [Four (4) Sticks] | 1 | 1 lb. | .89 | | Mills |

JAM, JELLY, PRESERVES, MARMALADE, FRUIT BUTTER, ETC. ☐ None

Sub-columns: Write KIND (Jam, Jelly, Preserves, Marmalade, Fruit Butter, Conserves, etc.) | Copy FLAVOR FROM LABEL (Strawberry, Grape, Black Raspberry, Mint Apple, Orange, etc.) | Is it Low Calorie or Dietetic? (✓) Yes / No

8/4	(Brand) Fruit Fresh	Jelly	Grape	✓ [No]	1	18oz	.49		Mills
8/4	Fruit Fresh	Jelly	Cherry	✓ [No]	1	18oz	.49		Mills
8/4	Pantry Delight		Strawberry	✓ [No]	1	24oz	.79		Mills

MARSHMALLOWS ☒ None

Sub-columns: Check SIZE — Miniatures, Regular | KIND — White (✓), Other—Describe Color or Flavor

| | (Brand) | | | | | | |

CARAMELS ☐ None

Sub-columns: WHAT IS IT CALLED ON LABEL? (Vanilla, Chocolate, Mixed, etc.) | Check HOW PACKAGED — Plastic or Cellophane Bag, Paper Bag, Box, Can, Other | (Do Not Include Toffee)

| 8/4 | (B. nd) Cherry Delite | Mixed | ✓ [Plastic or Cellophane Bag] | 1 | 10oz | .25 | 5¢ OFF | Mills |

most explosive growth of all will be in high-income groups: The number of families with incomes over $50,000 will more than double. Catering to these well-to-do consumers should prove lucrative.

Birthrate
- The increased number of women of childbearing age indicates an increased birthrate in the 1990s.

Education
- The higher overall level of education should add to the sophistication of consumers and their purchase decisions.

Working wives
- Increases in the number of working women will swell this group to over 46 percent of the labor force by 2000. It is expected that 57 percent of all women will be employed at that time.

- Nontraditional lifestyles will become more common. These include one-person domiciles, unmarried couples living together, one-spouse house-holds, and female-headed households.

Downtown Revival/Restorations

Although the outlook for downtown retailing is improving, the record is spotty. Many centers in both urban and suburban areas continue to resist a revival. However, recent examples of successful downtown operations include Woodward & Lothrop in Washington, D.C., and Macy's, 34th Street in New York City. Examples of other retail restorations that have changed the wharves into recreational/shopping complexes are Faneuil Hall Market Place in Boston, Harborplace in Baltimore, restored South Street Seaport in Manhattan, and the Harbor Plaza in San Diego.

An interesting viewpoint about downtown and strip center shopping was stated by Steven B. Greenberg, president of a real estate site-selection business:[3]

> *There is a wonderful future for specialty retailing in strip centers and good downtowns. American shoppers want a store that is well focused. The day of the housewife having all day to stroll down the mall is passé. She now has to do her shopping in a quick and efficient manner.*
>
> *A shopper who wants shoes will go to a strip mall that has three or four stores that carry the size she wants. For pots and pans, a shopper will go to the store that has the best selection. Nobody has the time to shop at a mall for three hours. The store must be convenient, highly inventoried, and well focused. It must stay within its boundaries. It must not be everything to everybody.*

Store Development and Operation

Shopping center changes
- Changes in shopping centers and malls are expected. Although the rate of construction is expected to decline, new space will be added through the upgrading and modernization of existing centers. Many centers will become

---

[3] S. Viuker, "What Makes Certain Stores Prosper and Others Falter: An Interview with Steven B. Greenberg (president of the Greenberg Group, a real estate site-selection business), *The New York Times* (September 16, 1990), Long Island Section, p. 2.

discount or off-price shopping complexes. Shopping centers will continue to house such retail outlets as state lottery booths, newspaper kiosks (magazines), and exotic food centers. An interesting innovation in shopping centers is the largest enclosed shopping mall in the Southeast. Located in Birmingham, Alabama, the Riverhouse Galleria sits under a glass dome. So striking is it that some observers call it the "city of glass."

Although often thought of as horizontal structures, shopping malls are built vertically, too. The latter are found in urban centers and include such projects as Market Place East in Philadelphia, A&S Plaza in New York City, and the conversion of Chicago's Merchandise Mart to a store/office center complex.

Productivity

- The concentration on increased productivity and cost relationships will dictate the allocation of space in stores. Areas and merchandise that do not yield sufficient profits will be eliminated. For example, service areas in department stores, such as snack bars, restaurants, theaters, and travel agencies, will be studied as to their profitability and power in attracting customers. The allocation of space in supermarkets will also undergo change as service areas such as rest rooms, luncheonettes, or snack bars are added.

- Sales per square foot of space will increase in importance as a measurement tool.

Expansion

- High interest rates plus increased land and construction costs will affect retailers' expansion plans. Consequently, some retailers will remodel rather than build new structures, while others will diversify into other types of opportunities.

- Retailers will place great emphasis on control as a means of improving profitability. Stores will rely on greater use of electronic devices to curb store theft, as well as on electronic funds systems to reduce the number of bad checks and the amount of credit card abuse.

- The increased use of self-service areas, store renovations, space reallocations, and operational efficiency is expected to reduce costs and increase sales per square foot.

- To help reduce costs, more retailers will adopt energy management systems to monitor power usage and power shedding (the reduction of power use).

- In addition, later openings and greater emphasis on afternoon, evening, and week-end shopping to accommodate working people will continue.

- The dental clinics established in retail stores will increase in importance and will probably extend to other professionals.

- We will witness a continuation of the business consolidation trend, with big companies getting bigger.

- It will probably become more difficult to classify retail institutions as new categories develop. For example, we may see such groups as diversified general merchandisers and general merchandise convenience stores.

- New stores will continue to open.

- Competition will become more intense.

- There will be an increase in the number of stores with scanning equipment at checkout counters, enabling them to generate computerized recorders. This process saves on labor costs, avoids out-of-stock situations, and reduces backroom stock-keeping.
- The disastrous experiences of the nonretailing businessman Robert Campeau (Allied Stores and Federated Stores) will lay more stress on the importance of retailing executives in retail operations.
- We are witnessing an attempt by retailers to reduce their debts. Many retail insolvencies and bankruptcies, for example, Campeau and Hooker, in the late 1980s were due to excessive liabilities.

Personnel and Employment

- Staffing will still remain a problem for retailers as young businesspeople become more demanding and seek faster advancement, increases, and recognition. In fact, many are unwilling to accept company-imposed hardships such as transfers to other locations. (A recent study showed that one out of ten employees declines transfers.)
- The continuing popularity of the four-day workweek will create problems of employee scheduling.
- A more scientific approach to recruitment, selection, and training will become a must as retailers face high turnover rates.
- Incentive programs to reward motivated store personnel are increasing. For example, worthy K mart salesclerks receive K-Notes that are redeemable for K mart gift certificates.

Merchandising and Promotion

- Preselling of merchandise via advertising will increase as self-service merchandising expands.
- The number of items carried by department stores will decrease as the specialty concept within department stores increases. Successful retailers will be those who differentiate themselves from their competition. Current examples are the Price Club, Toys "Я" Us, Wal-Mart, and The Limited.
- Private labels will increase in both department and specialty stores, in order to strengthen store identity and decrease dependence on designer labels.
- Store buyers will be able to view potential merchandise via video computer hook-ups. As the regional buying trend continues to grow, the use of computer terminals and TV for buying will increase.
- As noted earlier, regional apparel markets will attract increasing numbers of buyers from all over the country. These markets have become vital trade centers because they draw many designers and manufacturers to show their merchandise. Buyers can examine a variety of offerings at these marts, with the major ones located in Dallas, Atlanta, Miami, and Los Angeles.

- We can expect to witness an emphasis on wants, rather than needs, in consumers' shopping psyches. This change will influence merchandise mixes as premium products become more desirable.
- Consumers will opt for more one-stop shopping outlets, with a consequent increase in the number of hyperstores.
- Retailers will continue to key in on changing consumer trends.
- Many small stores will move to minicomputers to control all phases of their merchandise programs.
- As the number of working women increases, preselected shopping is expected to become more popular through the use of catalogs, phone orders, and mail orders.
- The price-conscious consumer will build discounters' sales volume of general merchandise as the credibility of off-price retailing increases.
- Electronic funds transfer will become more widespread.
- Consumers looking for service will find many more retailers willing to provide conveniences and help simplify their shopping experiences.
- Nonstore retailing will increase in importance as the in-home shopper accepts the concept of interactive television. Shoppers will view products in their homes and order by telephone or directly via a two-way system.
- As our population ages, retirement is viewed as a time for "new beginnings" in alternative ways of living. This has important implications for the spending patterns of older Americans.
- A study conducted in 1988 by Langer Associates, Inc., found that even though women under the age of 40 are the most fashionable clothes buyers, those between the ages of 40 and 54 spend more on apparel.
- As people seek more and more leisure time, department stores may enter a renaissance period brought on by a revival of the one-stop shopping approach.
- A survey conducted in 1989 for *Self* magazine resulted in a categorized profile of American women aged 18 to 49. The seven categories were searchers, traditionalists, strivers, copiers, undecideds, dreamers, and day-to-dayers. Astute retailers benefit from such profiles in their development of a market niche.

NEW TERMS

data bank

electronic informa-
   tion system (EIS)

experimentation

marketing research

observation

outshopper   sample (in a research study)
personnel research   secondary data
primary data   survey
retailing research

CHAPTER HIGHLIGHTS

1. The retail information system processes and retains information for quick decision making by management.

2. In an RIS, managers have access to data through terminals placed in store stations, departments, and offices.

3. Marketing research is the gathering, recording, and analysis of data related to a specific marketing problem.

4. Retailing research utilizes marketing research techniques to analyze retail activities.

5. Retailing research focuses on the following areas: consumers, store location and layout, advertising and promotion, merchandise selection and pricing, personnel, and competition.

6. Though research in retailing may be simple or complex, the procedures and tools used are similar in either case.

7. The research process consists of identification and definition of the problem, collection of secondary and/or primary data, compilation and tabulation of the data, analysis and interpretation of the findings, and preparation of the final report.

8. Primary data may be secured through surveys, observation, and experimentation.

9. The development of percentages from tabulated data is valuable for comparative purposes.

10. The interpretation of research findings results in recommendations that usually influence decisions.

11. Retailing research is conducted by store research departments, outside consultants, commercial research companies, and sales or office personnel.

12. Changes in retailing are expected in the following areas: market, downtown revival, store development and operation, personnel and employment, and merchandising and promotion.

REVIEW QUESTIONS

1. What type of information is usually placed in a retail data bank?
2. In conducting major research studies, with what areas are manufacturers generally concerned?
3. What kinds of information does a computer produce from point-of-sales transactions? How is this information helpful to retailers?
4. How do secondary data differ from primary data? When should each type of data be used?
5. What are the three basic methods used to secure primary data? How do they differ?
6. What is the last step in the research process? Why is it of great importance to retailers?
7. What are the functions of store research staffs?

DISCUSSION QUESTIONS

1. How can the retailer use consumer research information?
2. What are some of the retailing changes you expect to see in the 1990s?
3. How can research be used in forecasting changes for retailing in the 1990s?

CASE 1

Research on the Do-It-Yourselfer

A retail home center customer is a consumer who performs his or her own home repair and remodeling jobs instead of hiring a professional contractor. The number of such consumers has risen significantly in the last 15 years, primarily because of the high cost of contractor services. This trend appears nationwide and shows no signs of abating.

The Homebuilding Mart, a 12-store chain specializing in home-building products, wants to capitalize on the increased interest in home repair by attracting additional customers. The executives at Homebuilding Mart also want to determine *why* people are switching to do-it-yourself practices. In this way they can plan their advertising, sales promotion, and merchandise strategies to increase customer patronage.

With the aid of outside consultants, the firm designed and conducted a research study to learn the nature and demographics of retail home center customers in two major trading areas. The study included the following features of home center customers.

- Their approximate number in relation to the total population of the trading area
- Their ages
- Their educational backgrounds
- Their income levels

The study revealed the following data.

Number of Home Center Customers in Trading Area Population

Trading area no. 1   60,000
Trading area no. 2   45,000

Home Center Customer Ages

	Trading Area No. 1	*Trading Area No. 2*
Over 70	6%	8%
50–69	18	21
30–49	46	43
20–29	26	26
Below 20	4	2

Home Center Customer Educational Backgrounds

	Trading Area No. 1	*Trading Area No. 2*
College degree	47%	51%
High School diploma	31	36
Less than high school	22	13

Home Center Customer Income Levels

	Trading Area No. 1	*Trading Area No. 2*
$50,000 or more	6%	10%
$40,000–49,999	12	16
$30,000–39,999	18	18
$20,000–29,999	29	27
$10,000–19,999	18	16
Below $10,000	17	13

a. Are there differences between the customer populations of the two trading areas that might affect Homebuilding Mart's plans? If so, what are the differences?

b. Unfortunately, the study did not address itself to why customers are increasingly resorting to self-repair practices. What additional research techniques would you use to secure the necessary data?

c. With regard to the demographic data, how might the company determine the most effective means for communicating with the potential market?

CASE 2

Coca-Cola Creates a Shelf-Space Dilemma for Retailers

In April 1985, the Coca-Cola Company announced that in the following month it would introduce a new product, New Coke, with a sweeter and smoother taste than the company's original cola product. The company also announced that New Coke would completely supplant the old Coca-Cola. The original version was simply to be taken off the market and the 99-year-old formula for Coca-Cola was to be locked away permanently in a bank vault.

The announcement made headlines in the press and prompted numerous articles in news weeklies and trade journals reporting the reasons for and weighing the effects of the change. Coca-Cola officials were reported to consider the change to be the company's most significant development and its surest move.

But that was only the beginning of the story. No sooner had the announcement been made than Coca-Cola began hearing from outraged customers. To some extent, that was to be anticipated. But the furor did not die down. For three straight months, Coca-Cola headquarters received 1,500 phone calls a day in protest and mail bags full of angry letters. Old Coke groups formed all over the country, demanding the return of the original drink, some even threatening class-action suits to make the secret formula public. Bottlers and distributors often felt the protests more directly, in face-to-face confrontations with irate consumers.

Three months after introducing New Coke as *the* Coke, Coca-Cola again made national news. In fact, the Coca-Cola story was the lead item on both the ABC and NBC network evening news, and CBS featured it a bit later in the show. The story made the front page of major newspapers coast to coast, such as *The Washington Post*, *The Chicago Sun Times*, *USA Today*, and *The New York Times*, which not only ran the story on the front page, but ran it above the fold on the top half of the page.

On July 10, in one of the swiftest and most stunning reversals in the history of

American business, Coca-Cola bowed to public demand and announced it would return the original Coca-Cola to grocery shelves, fountains, and vending machines to satisfy the many thousands of vociferous old Coke customers. The company announced that the original drink, now called Coca-Cola Classic, would be available along with New Coke—one for those loyal to the old flavor, the other for those who wanted a lighter taste.

What had happened to provoke this astonishing series of events?

Coca-Cola, the best-known and largest-selling soft drink in the world, had lost ground to its major competitor, Pepsi, over a ten-year period. In 1972, Coca-Cola's market share was almost 25 percent; by 1984, it had slipped to 21.7 percent. At the same time, Pepsi's market share had risen to 18.8 percent by 1984. Each percentage point slip meant $200 million in lost sales. Moreover, Pepsi had gained sales in supermarkets, which account for 45 percent of all soda sales, and had overtaken Coca-Cola in that sector in the latter part of 1984. Even though Coca-Cola outsold Pepsi 2 to 1 worldwide, it was clear to Coke executives that Pepsi had made real inroads through its aggressive marketing and advertising campaigns against Coca-Cola in what came to be called "The Cola Wars." From 1980 on, officials at Coca-Cola became increasingly concerned about declining sales and the public's seeming preference for a sweeter, slightly less fizzy soft drink. In the course of developing Diet Coke, the company had also developed a lighter, sweeter formula that ultimately became New Coke, and decided to test it. But, because marketing a new taste in colas, and particularly one that would bear the name *Coke*, is a risky business, Coca-Cola mounted an exhaustive and wide-reaching market research program, the most intensive in company history and one that cost over $4 million.

For over two-and-a-half years, almost 200,000 consumers participated in blind taste tests that included three or more new Coke formulas, the original Coca-Cola, and Pepsi. Market research results seemed to indicate clearly that New Coke would be a winner. In unmarked testing, 55 percent preferred it to the original Coke and a similar percentage chose it over Pepsi. In tests where "old" Coke and New Coke were identified, 61 percent of participants chose the new version. After the results were analyzed, Coca-Cola made the decision to launch New Coke and abandon its original cola drink entirely.

After introducing the New Coke product, the company watched sales results carefully. After two months, sales for the new product were below company expectations, even as the outcry from old Coke drinkers continued to intensify. Ongoing research showed a resurgence of interest in—and even a preference for—the old product.

At the end of three months, Coca-Cola decided to reinstate the old Coca-Cola, a decision prompted mainly by the "passion" for the original product, according to company officials. They subsequently admitted that they had not understood how much Coca-Cola was viewed as part of Americana.

Thus Coca-Cola was left with two separate but equal products, Coca-Cola

Classic and New Coke, which could prove troublesome for the company. On the positive side, the company could satisfy both old customers and those who prefer a new taste and they can offer a close alternative to Pepsi. On the other hand, Coca-Cola added another product to stock on already crowded supermarket shelves and might be creating confusion for customers confronted by so many Coca-Cola products.

The effect on supermarket and grocery store managers has been increased pressure as more cola products mean increased demand to stock them and the competition for both shelf and display space becomes ever more intense.

In the aftermath of Coca-Cola's decisions, some market researchers have faulted the company's research program, pointing out that participants in the test were not told that a vote for New Coke meant the end of the original Coke. Others say that reported research results did not hold up overall in the testing. And with the advantage of hindsight, social historians and psychologists have concluded that the American consumer viewed Coca-Cola as much more than simply a soft drink; it was instead part of the heritage, one of the few timeless and unchanging symbols of America and not one that could be taken away.

The company believed its research indicated the consumer wanted a lighter beverage, more like Pepsi. It also believed that because they possessed the secret formula for Coca-Cola, they owned the product and could therefore modify it to suit changing tastes. The bottlers also seemed to agree that America was ready for a change and that that change was New Coke.

But what Coca-Cola did not recognize and what market research did not reveal was perhaps stated most succinctly by a bottler from Alabama: "What Coca-Cola didn't realize was that the old Coke was the property of the American public. The company thought they owned it. But the consumers knew they owned it."

a. What effect did the competition between Pepsi and Coca-Cola have on food store managers? On small food store competitors?
b. In addition to the shelf and display space problems created for retailers by the Coca-Cola decision, how else do you think retailers were affected?
c. How might Coca-Cola have benefited from the inclusion of retailers in the research process?

REFERENCES

"Department Stores Still Have a Future." *Inside Retailing* (April 23, 1990), p. 2.

FEINBERG, S. "Profile of American Women Today." *Women's Wear Daily* (September 12, 1989), p. 14.

HELLIWELL, J. "Benetton Weaves Information Systems into Unique Distribution Scheme." *PC Week* (November 10, 1987), pp. C1, C4, C58.

"No Stopping Wal-Mart; It Just Keeps Rolling On" and "Downtown Malls, a Gold Mine for Retailers?" *Inside Retailing* (January 1, 1990), p. 3.

"The Retail Battle Stage (1987–1990)." *Inside Retailing*, Special Report (May 25, 1987), pp. 1–2.

Chapter 20

Entrepreneurship and Franchising

After completing this chapter, you should be able to:

- Identify the personal characteristics that contribute to the success of retail ownership.
- Explain the importance of knowledge, technical skills, and interest in ownership of a retail business.
- Evaluate the sources of investment funds available to prospective retailers.
- Explain the roles of lawyers and accountants in the establishment of a retail business.
- Identify factors that one should investigate before purchasing or buying into an established business.
- Identify and explain sources of information about franchises.
- List the major provisions of franchise agreements and franchise disclosure statements.
- Identify major franchise categories.
- Explain the effects of acquisitions, mergers, and leveraged buyouts on franchising.
- Identify trends in franchising.

While most of this book has been devoted to a description and analysis of the practices of large retailers, we have occasionally referred to small retail operations. We have identified the functions that are common to both, as well as the differences between them. Emphasis has been placed on the need for all merchants to adhere to sound retailing principles if they are to be successful.

In this chapter we examine the concerns and problems of going into a retail business. We discuss the similarities as well as the differences between starting a new business and buying an established one. We also explore the opportunities and cautions in purchasing a franchise, and study the special problems of retailing a service. Appendix A at the end of this chapter contains a checklist for starting a retail business.

GOING INTO BUSINESS: RETAILING VERSUS OTHER FIELDS

Many opportunities for retail ownership

In probably no other field are there as many opportunities to own one's own business as there are in retailing. An examination of any trading area will demonstrate why this is so. For example, stores in a neighborhood shopping district usually range from convenience outlets to specialty shops; strip centers feature a variety of retail outlets, from auto stores to supermarkets; regional shopping centers contain numerous stores, large and small, that cater to customers' diversified needs. Additional opportunities for ownership exist in central shopping districts, secondary shopping areas, community shopping centers, and highway outlets. Needless to say, one may also own a nonstore retail business.

An indication of the growing importance that colleges place on training students for individual proprietorship was the joint entrepreneurship conference conducted by the presidents of Hampshire College and Babson College in 1987. Both institutions stress initiative and encourage students who demonstrate self-owned business aspirations. The results of this approach are promising, with about 20 percent of the schools' graduates becoming entrepreneurs.

SHOULD YOU GO INTO A RETAIL BUSINESS?

Anyone who contemplates ownership of a retail business should possess the personal characteristics, knowledge, skills, interest, and financial means for success. There is little doubt that failure usually results from the lack of one or more of these requisites.

Personal Characteristics

We have all met a variety of retail owners, ranging from the proprietors of a mom-and-pop store to the owner-manager of a specialty or small department store. Thinking about them, are you able to list the personal characteristics that distinguished the successful ones from the unsuccessful ones? Can you identify particular behavior patterns among them that captured your patronage loyalty? Let's examine some traits that appear to be necessary for success.

Ability to Make Decisions

Retailers are required to make decisions about many matters: merchandise, money, customers, personnel, and so forth. In many instances decisions must be made quickly, as with an irate customer who is dissatisfied with a store's service. At other times decisions may require careful research, for example, when deciding whether to make additional capital investments in the business. An effective retailer takes timely and decisive action even in unpleasant circumstances, while an ineffective one hesitates or procrastinates.

Ability to Organize

Whether considering inventory levels, sales campaigns, or some other business need, one must be able to organize work for smooth operations. One must be patient, pay attention to details, appreciate the need for planning, and recognize the danger of haphazard preparation.

Willingness to Accept Responsibility

Responsibility is burdensome— but rewarding

An effective retailer likes to be in charge of things and is the type of person who takes responsibility for his or her actions. While this retailer recognizes the burdens of authority, he or she shows little or no reluctance in accepting them. In fact, part of the pleasure such a person feels in assuming responsibility is the ultimate excitement of achievement in addition to the potential profits.

Ability to Lead

Retailers who employ others must be able to motivate them to perform well. This calls for the type of leadership that causes workers to feel a commitment to their jobs. Through example and understanding, owners must get employees to go along willingly with store policies and procedures.

Capacity for Hard Work and Long Hours

Almost all retail owners acknowledge the need to work hard and maintain long hours. The very nature of retailing—its concern with planning, stocking goods, selling, and so on—makes constant attention to details a necessity. The individual who contemplates owning a retail outlet, therefore, must be willing to commit much time and effort to the venture. At the risk of losing his or her capital investment, the new owner must be prepared for physical and mental stress as well as the inevitable emergencies. Early retailers like Simon Lazarus, Morris Rich, and John Bullock built successful stores through hard work and a time commitment.

Ability to Get Along with People

Poise, sureness, and tact are needed when dealing with people

In general, business owners must be able to relate well to other people. For retailers, this is a major requirement. Whether dealing with customers, employees, or vendors, the proprietor of a retail business should have the ability to act with poise, sureness, and tact. To a large extent these attributes require a liking for people and a desire to please them. On the other hand, the owner must be firmly committed to basic business principles and store policies. Weak application of established procedures inevitably cuts into earnings.

In concluding our discussion of personal characteristics that are helpful to a retail owner, it should be noted that few people are strong in all the categories. What is important is a blend of these traits that is sufficient to make the owner effective. In addition, awareness of the value of these characteristics improves the owner's chances of success.

Knowledge, Technical Skills, and Interest in Retailing

To the uninitiated, managing a small retail business appears simple. "After all," they reason, "it's all a matter of selling something to a customer. There doesn't seem to be much more to it." Having read earlier chapters of this book and discussed a variety of retail topics, you realize that such an assessment is incorrect. The myriad activities that retailing comprises call for a variety of technical and management skills as well as an interest in retailing itself. The extent of these needs is often surprising to new retail owners.

Knowledge

The operation of a retail outlet requires the owner to possess technical information about the products or services it sells. In order to offer salable merchandise or services, the owner must understand the needs of the target population. For example, stores located in college or senior citizen communities must cater to the requirements of those vastly different populations.

Retailing requires different levels of expertise

Some retail endeavors require a different level of expertise than others. For example, product knowledge is probably more important in a hardware store, where customers often ask technical questions, than in a convenience store. In the case of service retailers, the type and quantity of information needed by the owner of a travel agency are more complex than that needed by the proprietor of a laundry store. Whatever the type of business, however, a thorough knowledge of the commodities carried or services offered is important.

Certain retail businesses call for technical skills. *Courtesy:* 3M Corporation.

Retailers also need an understanding of correct selling techniques, with an appreciation of the likes and dislikes of their target populations. Where appropriate, the owner should know how to display merchandise attractively and how to promote both product and store image effectively. In addition, proprietors should be acquainted with personnel management techniques, recordkeeping procedures, and inventory control.

RETAIL STRATEGY

Want to Go into Business? Here's Some Advice

Paul B. Brown and Geoffrey N. Smith, co-authors of the book, *Sweat Equity,* offer the following advice to would-be entrepreneurs:

1. Avoid businesses that are in danger of oversaturation, for example, computer stores.
2. Originality isn't always necessary. In fact, improving on a well-established retail type of business is often the way to go.
3. Concentrate your research on filling a need in retailing, that is, niche retailing.
4. Start a business cautiously with adequate capital. Don't expect to get rich overnight.

Technical Skills

In some retail businesses owners must possess specific skills. Such businesses include service establishments like haircutters, dry cleaners, and repair shops. They also include merchandise-service operations like jewelry stores, photography outlets, and gas stations. Merchants who possess the requisite skills are able to satisfy customer needs as well as evaluate and help their employees.

Interest in Retailing

Since there is a wide variety of retail businesses among which to choose, a new owner should consider personal interests in making a selection. For example, someone who likes fashion items may enjoy operating a women's-wear specialty shop. An individual who takes pleasure in repairing mechanical items may use those skills in a repair service business.

Nevertheless, a person who is contemplating retail ownership should ask questions like the following:

- Is the field in which I'm interested overcrowded?
- Do I have the necessary experience to do well?
- Do I need formal training?
- Should I secure advice from people in the field before making a decision?

Honest and reliable answers to these questions may accomplish one of the following.

- Fortify one's determination to go into business
- Cause one to do more investigating before starting a business
- Help one decide not to become an owner

ECONOMIC ASPECTS OF GOING INTO BUSINESS

In previous chapters it was pointed out that a major reason for business failures is inadequate investment of capital. Not only must the new owner be concerned with this problem; he or she must also have a reliable source of funds on which to draw.

While it is true that many service businesses can be started with little money, virtually all merchandise outlets require at least modest funds. Few new owners can secure beginning inventories on **consignment,** that is, paying only for items that are sold. Most must secure credit to finance some of their initial purchases.

In addition to outlays for merchandise, plans must provide for the payment of store equipment and fixtures such as counters, shelves, lighting, cash registers, and office machines. If a store requires decorating, money must be available for carpeting, floor tiles, wall coverings, and the like. Supplies like bags, twine, register tapes, and postage are also needed. The extent to which any of these things is needed depends, of course, on the size and the character of the store.

Having your own money is the easiest way to finance the start of a retail store. This is because you need not depend on anyone else for financing and the required funds may be used at your own discretion. Care must be taken, of course, to leave a reserve for business needs as well as for personal use. Suppose, however, that the prospective retailer lacks the necessary funds. Are there other sources, personal and otherwise, that can be tapped? The answer is that there are, though securing the money usually takes considerable effort.

Borrowing from Personal Sources

Some people are fortunate enough to have relatives or friends who are both willing and able to lend them money. Successful retail businesses have been developed from such borrowing, and prospective owners may want to investigate this avenue. Two very successful retailers, Isaac Merritt Singer, who started The Singer Company, and Rowland Hussey Macy, founder of R. H. Macy & Company, did exactly that!

Having a limited partner

In some cases a relative or friend may want to invest in a retail business without the burden of active ownership. The investor becomes a limited partner, contributing funds but little or no time to the business. In return for making the investment, the limited partner shares in both the profits and losses of the business. The advantages to a new retailer of taking on a limited partner are the immediate infusion of cash as well as the partner's limited role in running the business. In return, of course, the active owner must share the profits.

Insurance policies as a source of funds

Some life insurance policies can serve as a source of funds. For example, if a certain type of policy has been in effect a few years, the insured party can use it to secure money by either cashing it in or borrowing against it. Borrowing against the cash value of the policy provides funds while the insurance protection remains in force. Insurance companies, of course, charge interest for the privilege of borrowing from the cash value.

Borrowing from Business Sources

Additional sources of funds for starting a new business include manufacturers, vendors, banks, the U.S. Small Business Administration, and venture capital operators.

Manufacturers and Vendors. If prospective owners can demonstrate creditworthiness through past experience or the possession of sufficient assets, it is possible that equipment and fixture manufacturers will sell their products on credit to them. This holds true for vendors of merchandise and supplies as well. However, anyone who is starting a retail business should have no illusions about the ease of securing credit without a "track record." Manufacturers and wholesalers are loath to extend credit to beginning merchants for fear of nonpayment.

Banks. Banks, of course, are the main source for business borrowing. However, securing a bank loan to start a retail business can be as frustrating as tapping friends and relatives. Why is this so?

Banks are conservative institutions and avoid risks like the plague. They are particularly averse to lending money to untested businesses. Their reasoning is as follows: Why expend funds on new ventures when low-risk investments to long-established, reliable businesses are possible?

Despite their reluctance to make small loans to new enterprises, banks may do so under the following conditions.

Before agreeing to new business loans, banks set specific conditions of performance

- The proposed venture is based on sound business practices.
- The new business shows strong promise of success.
- The new owner demonstrates a capacity for conducting a successful retail business.
- The new owner presents a credible plan for repaying the loan.

In terms of time for repayment of loans, banks accept both short- and long-term notes. **Short-term loans** are for less than a year; **long-term loans** run for a year

Banks sometimes lend funds to promising retailers. Sybil Shelton/Monkmeyer.

or more. In order to secure a loan—especially a long-term loan—a borrower often has to supply collateral. This requires the borrower to give the bank some security for the bank's protection, such as shares of stock, bonds, or other valuables. When the loan is repaid, the bank returns the collateral.

Capitalizing on former Prime Minister Margaret Thatcher's call for self-help and free enterprise, many small businesses developed in Great Britain during the last decade. Since her ascension to power in 1979, the number of self-employed people there has grown by 59 percent. This phenomenon has been accompanied by changing public attitudes toward entrepreneurship, as well as a more positive reception by banks to small retailers.

Small Business Administration.   If someone who wants to start a business has exhausted the possibilities of a loan from private or business sources without success, it may be possible to secure a loan from (or with the participation of) the **Small Business Administration,** (SBA), an agency of the federal government. While SBA loans are not easy to secure, certain categories of applicants have more opportunities than others.

The SBA Loan Guarantee Plan and Economic Opportunity Loan Program

Under the **SBA's Loan Guarantee Plan,** a successful borrower receives a bank loan which is guaranteed up to 90 percent by the SBA. While there are federal restrictions regarding principal, interest rate, and time, the bank specifies the conditions of the loan.

The **SBA's Economic Opportunity Loan Program** is designed for economically disadvantaged entrepreneurs. While the law contains guidelines regarding "disadvantaged" status, it requires applicants to put up part of the capital, as in the Loan Guarantee Plan.

In order to secure an SBA loan, an applicant must complete elaborate forms containing projected operating and personal financial statements. The new merchant is required to estimate the first year's sales, expenses, and net income.

In addition to supporting loans, the SBA provides counseling for prospective owners. It has trained personnel who help businesspeople analyze their plans in realistic terms. It also sponsors seminars on topics that are of specific interest to owners of small businesses.

Minority Business Development Agency This federal agency (MBDA) provides management, marketing, and technical assistance to minority populations. It also maintains an information clearinghouse about minority business development.

Venture Capital Operators.   A **venture capital operator** is an individual or corporation that invests money in someone else's business. For a substantial share of the profits—sometimes even more than half—the venture operator provides sufficient funds to get a business started. Long negotiations usually precede an agreement, after which the new retailer is in legal or de facto partnership with the venture operator.

PROFESSIONAL HELP WHEN GOING INTO BUSINESS: LAWYERS AND ACCOUNTANTS

Some people start a retail business without seeking professional advice, but those who recognize the pitfalls of doing so seek guidance and direction from lawyers and/or accountants. These experts can save a new owner much time and trouble.

Lawyers are valuable in helping the retailer conform to local, state, and federal laws. They identify zoning codes (regulations that specify local restrictions on certain business operations), indicate license requirements where applicable, prepare partnership contracts when two or more entrepreneurs are involved, and file the necessary documents when the business is organized as a corporation. In addition, lawyers suggest appropriate insurance coverage and offer general advice on how to avoid legal problems.

A lawyer's role in a small retail business

A word of caution is in order regarding a lawyer's role in a small business enterprise. Since lawyers are usually not entrepreneurs, their knowledge of business practices may be limited. While the retailer should consider their opinions, they should question them closely on both the legal and business sides of an issue. Only then should the owner make a decision, weighing the lawyer's judgments as one element of the business mix.

Accountants help new owners of retail businesses by developing systems for the maintenance of their financial records. In this capacity, they suggest tests and measurements by which the success of the business may be determined. While after their initial input lawyers are usually called upon only when needed, accountants serve retailers on a regular periodic basis: monthly, quarterly, and so on.

Among an accountant's specific contributions are the following.

The Small Business Administration provides help to retailers and would-be retailers.

- Preparation of payroll, sales, and income tax reports
- Preparation of income statements and balance sheets, followed by analysis and recommendations
- Development of billing procedures
- Design of procedures for the control of accounts receivable and accounts payable
- Development of forms and procedures for the control of inventory
- Analysis of cash flow, followed by recommendations

Like lawyers, accountants may not be good merchants. Consequently, the new owner should accept only those judgments of the accountant that seem logical and sensible in light of the financial or retail problems under consideration.

BUYING AN ESTABLISHED BUSINESS

Instead of starting a new business, a prospective merchant may decide to purchase or buy into an existing one. In this case several aspects of the enterprise should be considered.

Reasons for Sale of an Established Business

Though it is not always possible, the buyer must try to determine why the merchant wants to sell the business. Since the seller is trying to get the highest possible price for the enterprise, the buyer must be wary of the seller's explanations. Common reasons advanced by sellers include health, change of family location, and age. However, behind these avowed reasons may lurk some damaging aspects of the business itself. These may include the following.

Negative aspects of an established business

- A deteriorating neighborhood
- A changing trading area population
- An impending steep increase in rent or expiration of a lease
- Poor management
- Mounting debts
- Falling profits or steady losses

As you can imagine, this list can be extended considerably. In order to determine the truth, the prospective merchant should talk to other local retailers, bank officials, and local chambers of commerce.

Examining Business Records

A prospective owner should examine the financial records of the seller's business, including ledgers, financial statements (especially income statements), income tax reports, sales tax reports, and insurance policies. If possible, the examination should be done with the help of an accountant.

Checking Inventory, Supplies, and Equipment

When purchasing a merchandise business, a thorough evaluation should be made of the seller's inventory. This includes stock on shelves, in stockrooms, in warehouses, and on order. In addition, all types of retail outlets should be checked for office, store, and maintenance supplies.

Miscellaneous Items to Consider

In addition to those mentioned earlier, the number of specific items to investigate depends on the nature and complexity of the business. Among the more common ones are the following.

- The level of employee salaries and benefits.
- The operational status of the equipment.
- The condition of the furniture and fixtures.
- The existence of lawsuits or liens against the business.
- The present discount policy, if any, of the business.
- If the store is rented, the terms and duration of the existing lease.
- The amount attributed to goodwill in the purchase price. **Goodwill** is an intangible asset of a business that is derived from the reputation of its owner, products, or services. The specific monetary value of goodwill, when claimed, is always a debatable item between buyer and seller.
- The types of insurance that should be carried (see Appendix B of this chapter).
- Legal aspects that may require attention (see Appendix C of this chapter).

BUYING INTO A BUSINESS

Virtually all of the concerns connected with purchasing an existing business apply to buying *into* a business. The buyer becomes a partner, assuming rights and obligations under the partnership contract. Since the new partner is responsible for the debts of the partnership, he or she must examine the reliability and trustworthiness of the other partners with great care.

FRANCHISING

Franchisors provide instruction and guidance to franchisees

As you learned in Chapter 4, franchising is a relatively recent addition to retailing. It was pointed out that a basic reason for the popularity of this form of ownership is the instruction and guidance provided by franchisors to franchisees. Though it is not without risks, a franchise does give a franchisee some protection against inexperience and adversity.

Now we examine franchising in greater depth, with emphasis on this form of ownership as a way of getting started in retailing.

Investigating a Franchise

All of the cautions about going into a retail business as an independent pertain equally well to purchasing a franchise. In fact, there are additional factors to consider because of the significant relationship between franchisor and franchisee.

Sources of Franchise Information

Because so much interest in franchising has been generated during the last 30 years, a good deal of helpful literature about the field is available. Anyone who is interested in purchasing a franchise should read these publications for both general and specific information. Among the better-known ones are the following.

Bond, Robert E. *The Source Book of Franchise Opportunities.* Homewood, IL: Dow Jones-Irwin, 1985.

Foster, Dennis L. *The Complete Franchise Book.* Rocklin, CA: Prima Publishing and Communications, 1988.

Franchising as a form of ownership is a way of getting started in retailing. (left) Van Bucher; (right) *Courtesy:* 7-Eleven Corporation, Southland Corporation.

Foster, Dennis L. *The Rating Guide to Franchises.* New York: Facts on File Publications, 1988.

U.S. Department of Commerce. *Franchising in the Economy.* Washington, D.C.; U.S. Government Printing Office, 1987.

Small, Anne, and Robert S. Levy. *A Woman's Guide to Her Own Franchised Business.* Babylon, NY: Pilot Books, 1986.

The *Franchise Opportunities Handbook* lists data about major American franchisors

Additional publications or help may be secured from the U.S. Department of Commerce, the Small Business Administration, and the International Franchise Association. The Superintendent of Documents, U.S. Government Printing Office, publishes the *Franchise Opportunities Handbook,* which lists the major American franchisors together with important aspects of their operations.

Visiting or Calling Franchisees

One of the best ways to learn about a particular franchise is to visit a franchise location or telephone its owner. A visit provides an opportunity to see how the business operates and ask specific questions, while a call sometimes yields valuable information. Whether you are calling or visiting, it is essential to make an appointment beforehand.

Questions to ask a franchisee

The questions that one asks during a visit or call should deal with the following areas.

- The profitability of the franchise (this is a delicate topic, and reliable answers may not be forthcoming)
- The honesty and reliability of the franchisor
- The aid and services provided by the franchisor
- The extent of the franchisor's involvement in the selection of a franchise location
- The amount of competition from other outlets within the franchise
- The amount of time the franchisee spends in the business
- The conditions under which the franchise may be sold

Advice from Relatives, Friends, Professionals, and Businesspeople

While the final decision on whether to invest in a franchise rests with the prospective franchisee, valuable advice can sometimes be secured from others. A person's immediate family, for example, may have insight into his or her ability to handle the problems of a franchise. Relatives and friends may supply helpful perspectives on business ownership. Professionals such as lawyers, accountants, and chamber of commerce officials can offer technical guidance. Businesspeople, whether they are experienced in franchising or not, can offer advice on location, inventory control, employee relations, cash flow, and so forth. The aspiring franchisee must sift the significant information and opinions from the unimportant or damaging suggestions to arrive at a sensible decision.

Franchise Advertisements, Meetings, and Shows

Some franchisors solicit potential franchisees through newspaper and magazine advertisements. Before considering a respondent as a serious prospect, however, the franchisor may require a written indication of ability and willingness to finance an outlet.

Franchise meetings are held periodically in various parts of the country at which participants receive information and literature about franchising. After listening to a speaker, the audience usually asks basic questions such as

- What are a franchisee's rights and obligations?
- What kind of training does the franchisor provide?
- Does the franchisor help the franchisee with financing?
- What share of advertising costs do franchisees bear?
- How much help does the franchisor provide in the selection of a location?
- Is the franchisor available when things go wrong?

In addition to meetings, some private organizations sponsor business shows at which different franchisors maintain exhibit booths. This arrangement gives attendees an opportunity to investigate a variety of franchise businesses and to speak personally with franchise representatives.

Franchise Agreements

A thorough investigation of a possible franchise affiliation should provide solid evidence for a decision. If the decision is affirmative, the future franchisee must be approved by the franchisor. In the case of established and successful franchises, acceptance comes after two or more interviews during which specific matters of concern to both parties are discussed. A would-be franchisee is well advised to be accompanied by an attorney on these occasions.

In addition to the interviews, the franchisor will require some indication of the franchisee's financial capabilities. While some franchises may be purchased for as little as $1,000, most cost more and really desirable ones sell for amounts in five or six figures. Consequently, anyone who is contemplating owning a franchise must have some ready cash and a reliable source for additional borrowing. As indicated earlier, some franchisors offer financing help.

When an agreement has been reached by the franchisor and the prospective franchisee, the two sign a contract called a **franchise agreement** or a **license agreement** (Appendix D). Most franchise contracts contain the following major sections.

Major features of franchise agreements

- Identification of the parties. The franchisor is sometimes called the company or distributor; the franchisee is known as the owner or franchisee.
- The purpose and duration of the agreement.
- Obligations of both parties.
- Location of the franchise.
- Startup and renewal fees; additional payments to the franchisor.
- Sale or transfer of the franchise.
- Operating standards.
- Purchasing of inventory, supplies, equipment, and so forth from the franchisor and others.
- The locale for setting disputes between the franchisor and the franchisee.
- Accounting and recordkeeping provisions.
- Insurance requirements.

In addition to these features, some franchise contracts include such items as protected franchise territories, advertising rights and obligations, termination features, and rules of employee conduct.

Franchise Employees

Like any retail business with multiple employees, the success of a franchise depends greatly on the dedication and efficiency of its staff. In order to stimulate employee motivation, management-oriented franchisees often develop a personnel manual that addresses such topics as job titles, rates of pay, benefits, insurance, and training. A copy of the table of contents of a Burger King restaurant manual is contained in Appendix E.

Costs of a Franchise

One of the major causes of retail business failures is insufficient capital. Often new retailers see their investments disappear as a result of poor or unrealistic financial planning. This is true of franchises as much as it is of independently owned businesses. If there is an advantage to franchising, it is the willingness of some franchisors—but far from all—to help franchisees during times of financial stress.

In addition to paying a franchise fee and (usually) a percentage of gross receipts to the franchisor, the franchisee must be prepared to absorb the following initial costs.

Initial costs of starting a franchised outlet

- Beginning inventory
- Rent
- Design and construction of store interior and exterior, if required
- Store and office supplies

The cost of a franchise ranges from low to very high figures. Burger King is a high-cost franchise. *Courtesy:* Burger King Corporation.

- Fixtures, furniture, and equipment
- Payroll
- Accounting and legal fees
- Grand opening promotions
- Miscellaneous and emergency

Take a good look at the last item in this list. It is the least specific of the costs, yet it can cause panic and grief if it is not provided for sufficiently. For example, unexpected incidents and price rises during construction and preparation can cause a run on available funds. Unanticipated legal problems may cost additional money. Although no surefire contingency fund can be planned, some provision should be made for emergencies. On the basis of their experience, most franchisors can provide guidance in this area.

Franchise Disclosure Statements

In the early days of franchising, many investors were seriously damaged by ignorance of the risks of franchising and unrealistic expectations regarding its rewards. After numerous legal confrontations between franchisors and franchisees, as well as political pressure exerted by irate franchisees, the Federal Trade Commission (FTC) issued a trade regulation requiring franchisors to supply prospective franchisees with **franchise disclosure statements.** Also known as offering circulars or prospectuses, these statements contain information about the franchisor's business experience and key personnel; franchise fees; territorial protection for franchisees; and many other items of importance to franchisees. The statements enable readers to judge the value of particular franchises and to assess them. Appendix F contains a more complete list of the types of information required in disclosure statements.

Evaluating a franchise disclosure statement

Having secured a copy of a disclosure statement, a franchise should evaluate it in two ways.

1. By matching it against disclosure statements issued by other companies to estimate its *apparent* value.
2. By interviewing other franchisees in the same franchise to estimate its *actual* value.

A word of caution is in order here. Questions to be addressed to other franchisees should be prepared in advance so that all important areas are covered. Furthermore, the franchisees interviewed should have owned their franchises for various periods so that they represent both short- and long-term experiences.

Potential franchisees should also beware of the increasing number of fraudulent operators posing as legitimate franchisors. *Investor Alert*, a newsletter published jointly by the North American Securities Administrators Association and the Council of Better Business Bureaus, points out that thousands of individuals lose upward of one-half billion dollars annually in franchise and business opportunity frauds.

Lawyers and the Legal Rights of Franchisees

Since franchise agreements contain items of legal import to franchisees, it is essential that the latter retain lawyers for their protection. One look at the legal terminology of a franchise contract is enough to convince the reader of this need (see Appendix D). In addition, attorneys are needed to clarify vague clauses in the contract. For example, a contract term reading, "The franchisee will take such steps as are necessary to increase service capabilities" is certainly in need of review. What does "such steps" mean? Who determines the adequacy of the steps? A lawyer can be of great service to the prospective franchisee in this and similar instances.

As in the case of going into business as an independent retailer, starting a franchise operation involves the probable study of pertinent government regulations and the filing of business documents: local, state, and federal forms; local zoning and building codes; permissible labeling; business agreements; and so forth. A lawyer is helpful in analyzing the documents.

Though the contents of disclosure statements are regulated by law, their authenticity must be reviewed by the franchisee. While the FTC has procedures for the redress of franchisee grievances arising out of disclosure statements, it is usually advisable for a franchisee to retain a lawyer. While the franchisee may be knowledgeable about business, it is the lawyer who knows the law.

Another important FTC regulation gives franchisees vital legal rights. Basically, they refer to periods for examining disclosure statements and franchise agreements, the right to receive substantiation of earnings claims made by franchisors, the right to receive refunds from franchisors under certain conditions, and the right to rely on items listed in disclosure statements. Figure 20-1 contains a synopsis of these rights.

Strengthening a Franchise

In an effort to revitalize the franchise, the new executives at Burger King decided in 1989 to encourage its franchisees to modernize facilities, offer better service, reduce overhead, and adopt more effective personnel policies. After years

---

1. The right to receive a disclosure statement at your first personal meeting with a representative of the franchisor to discuss the purchase of a franchise; but in no event less than ten business days before you sign a franchise or related agreement, or pay any money in connection with the purchase of a franchise.

2. The right to receive documentation stating the basis and assumptions for any earnings claims that are made at the time the claims are made; but in no event less than ten business days before you sign a franchise or related agreement, or pay any money in connection with the purchase of a franchise. If an earnings claim is made in advertising, you have the right to receive the required documentation at your first personal meeting with a representative of the franchisor.

3. The right to receive sample copies of the franchisor's standard franchise and related agreements at the same time as you receive the disclosure statement, and the right to receive the final agreements you are to sign at least five business days before you sign them.

4. The right to receive any refunds promised by the franchisor, subject to any conditions or limitations on that right which have been disclosed by the franchisor.

5. The right not to be misled by oral or written representations made by the franchisor or its representatives that are inconsistent with the disclosures made in the disclosure statement.

Figure 20-1   Legal rights of franchises. *Source:* U.S. Department of Commerce, Bureau of Industrial Economics and Minority Business Development, Franchise Opportunities Handbook, (Washington, D.C., July 1985,) pp. xxvii–xxviii.

of neglect, and with franchisees disillusioned by the franchisor's indifference to their needs, the company seemed finally to recognize that its position as the country's number two fast-food chain was jeopardized.

An example of how hard work, helpful service, and attention to details often result in success is the experience of Bev and George Karmanos, franchisees of an American Speedy quick-print store in Tallahassee, Florida. Their enlightened human relations approach to customers pays big dividends, as evidenced by their having outpaced similar franchisees' sales by a whopping 344 percent! The husband-wife entrepreneurs attribute their phenomenal progress to commonsense care of both personnel and customers.

Selecting a Franchise Field

With franchising claiming an increasingly larger share of the retail market, more and more pioneer entrepreneurs are settling on this mode of business operation. After all, they reason, there must be great opportunities in a field that accounts for some $400 billion in annual sales and represents some 35 percent of all retail sales.

Franchise categories and sample franchisors

As the aspiring retailer contemplates ownership of a franchise, he or she has a wide selection from which to choose. Recognizing the limitations posed by one's personal and financial abilities, the range of fields is still considerable. A list prepared by the U.S. Department of Commerce includes the following franchise categories.

Franchise Category	Sample Franchisors
Automotive products/services	AAMCO Transmissions, Inc.
	B. F. Goodrich Co.
Auto trailers/rentals	Budget Rent A Car Corp.
	Hertz System, Inc.
Beauty salons/supplies	Command Performance
	Roffler Industries, Inc.
Business aids/services	H&R Block, Inc.
	General Business Services, Inc.
Clothing, shoes	Mode O'Day Co.
	Pauline's Sportswear, Inc.
Construction, remodeling—materials/ services	Davis Caves, Inc.
	General Energy Devices, Inc.
Educational products/services	Barbizon Schools of Modeling
	Image Improvement, Inc.
Employment services	Acme Personnel Service
	Management Recruiters International, Inc.

Foods—grocery/specialty stores	The Southland Corp.
	Tiffany's Bakeries, Inc.
Foods—ice cream, yogurt, candy, popcorn, beverages	Baskin-Robbins, Inc.
	Mister Softee, Inc.
Foods—restaurants, drive-ins, carry-outs	Burger King Corp.
	McDonald's Corp.
General-merchandising stores	Ben Franklin
	Coast to Coast Stores
Maintenance, cleaning, sanitation—services/supplies	Roto Rooter Corp.
	Servpro Industries, Inc.
Motels, hotels	Holiday Inns, Inc.
	Ramada Inns, Inc.
Real estate	Century 21 Real Estate Corp.
	Gallery of Homes, Inc.
Soft drinks, water—bottling	Cott Corp.
	Double-Cola Co.
Tools, hardware	Mac Tools, Inc.
	Snap-On Tools Corp.
Video	Blockbuster Video
	West Coast Video

Additional categories include campgrounds, cosmetics, foods, lawn and garden supplies, pet shops, and printing. As you can see, someone who is truly interested in starting a franchise should have little difficulty finding an available field. Once a choice has been made, the next step is investigation of a specific franchise.

Relatively new entrants into the franchise field are companies selling leg wear (socks, pantyhose, etc.). Capitalizing on the sometimes dizzying changes in fashion, these franchisors have established specialty stores with names like Sox Appeal and Sock Appeal.

FRANCHISE ACQUISITIONS, MERGERS, AND LEVERAGED BUYOUTS

In Chapter 4, you were introduced to the topic of acquisitions, mergers, and leveraged buyouts. The consequences to retailers of these actions were examined, particularly with reference to Robert Campeau's acquisition of Federated Department Stores and Allied Stores.

Not surprisingly, the retail franchise industry has not been immune to the buyout phenomenon. For example, the Blockbuster Entertainment Corporation acquired the Major Video Corporation in 1988, the Southland Corporation (7-Eleven franchisor) went private in 1987 in a leveraged buyout, and Better Homes and Gardens, a real estate brokerage franchisor, acquired one of its competitors, First Carskadon, Inc., in 1987.

In most cases, franchisee reactions to franchisor acquisition, merger, and leveraged buyout activities have included anger, hostility, and fear. Concerned with possible decreases in advertising and other financial support, franchisees have turned increasingly to litigation as a way to thwart their franchisors' intentions. In order to strengthen their ranks, franchisees have formed organizations of similar store units. Their efforts have been largely successful in wringing concessions from the franchisors.

In a more friendly vein, Dunkin Donuts, Inc., agreed in 1989 to be acquired by a British firm, the franchisor of the Baskin-Robbins ice cream chain. Dunkin Donuts, with 1,600 outlets in the United States and 250 in foreign countries, met with little resistance from its franchisees.

In a move that made it the country's third largest fast-food franchise chain, Hardee's acquired the Roy Roger chain from the Marriott Corporation in 1989. Hardee's also owns the Sandy's and Burger Chef chains.

Hardee's uses a point-of-sale computer system that is the envy of the fast-food restaurant business. Sales are analyzed at its headquarters in Rocky Mount, North Carolina, within 15 minutes of their taking place. As a result, the chain can tell its franchisees how well each food item is selling. Franchisees can then make inventory (menu) decisions quickly and intelligently.

Trends and Outlook for Franchising[1]

Many franchisors are currently involved in testing a new form of franchising comprised of different products under the same roof. In other words, a franchisor would sell products and/or services within the unit of another franchisor. Most of these involved in this new trend are currently in food-related services. This new trend is known as a combination franchise or a franchise within a franchise.

An increasing trend is the movement of new and small companies into the franchise system of distribution. In 1985, the net gain of companies converting to franchising jumped dramatically to almost 8 percent, the highest percentage increase for the last five years. A total of 273 firms turned to franchising in 1985, and this growing trend is expected to continue for the next few years.

---

[1] U.S. Department of Commerce, *Franchising in the Economy, 1985–87* (Washington, D.C.: U.S. Government Printing Office, January 1987).

Several other trends are currently affecting the franchising sector. Expansion through acquisition is on the upswing with the absorption of many recently formed franchisors by others within the same field. Growing numbers of franchisors are seeking multiunit franchisees who have the financial muscle to bring additional vitality into the system. Interest in improved franchisor-franchisee relationships is on the rise resulting in growing numbers of advisory councils formed by franchisees.

Franchising trends in the renewals and terminations of franchisee-owned units in business format franchising has basically remained unchanged for the nine-year period ending in 1985, and all indications are that this trend will persist for the next few years. In 1985, 91 percent of all franchisee-owned units were renewed, with the nine-year average also standing at 91 percent. Of the nonrenewals in 1985, 30 percent was attributed to franchisors, 34 percent to franchisees, and 36 to mutual agreement. For the nine-year period ending in 1985, 28 percent of nonrenewals was attributed to franchisors, 41 to franchisees, and 31 percent to mutual agreement. Of units terminated in 1985, 36 percent were ended by franchisors, 58 percent by franchisees, and 6 percent by mutual agreement. For the nine-year period ending in 1985, 40 percent of the units were terminated by franchisors, 51 percent by franchisees, and 9 percent by mutual agreement.

The diminishing number of younger people and the rapidly expanding "mature" population, along with an increase in the number of two-earner families continue to foster the growth of the service sector in franchising in such areas as maid services, repair and home remodeling, carpet cleaning, household furnishings, and various other maintenance and cleaning services.

All services related to various types of business aids are growing strongly and should continue. This can be attributed to the large numbers of both small and large companies going outside of their own organizations to fulfill many service functions previously performed internally. This is demonstrated, for example, by the rapid rise of franchising services in accounting, collection services, mail processing, advertising services, message taking, package wrapping and shipping, business consulting, security, business record keeping, tax preparation, personnel services, and others.

With the closing of about 106,000 gasoline service stations since 1972, franchises that specialize in automotive repairs and service are increasing in numbers in many areas of the huge automotive aftermarket. Franchised growth will be in specialized automotive centers providing service in tune-up, quick lube, muffler, transmission, brake, painting, tires, electric repairs, and general car care. This trend will expand throughout this decade.

Other areas in franchising that are expected to advance rapidly for the remainder of the 1980s are weight control centers, hair salons, temporary help services, printing and copying services, medical centers, and clothing stores.

PRACTITIONER'S CORNER

What follows is the summary of an interview with Henry Hintermeister, president of Coastal Group Management Corporation, franchisee of multiple Burger King restaurants.*

1. Franchisor-franchisee relationships
   a. The franchisor has no control over what the franchisee pays employees or what prices he charges.
   b. A franchisee's "clout" with the franchisor depends on the number of outlets owned and the franchisee's commitment to the business.
   c. A franchisee can purchase food supplies from any source.
2. Business practice considerations
   a. Fifty percent of Coastal's business is drive-through selling.
   b. Attempting to sell different products in different parts of the country or world presents a confusing image.

*Interviewed by the authors.

    c. Nutrition is a major concern today in the fast-food business.

    d. There is an increasing emphasis on cholesterol-free foods and low-calorie salad dressings.

    e. Coastal's Burger King restaurants distribute Gold Cards to senior citizens for free coffee, etcetera.

3. Financial considerations

    a. Coastal has remodeled its stores over the last few years at an average cost of $250,000 each.

    b. As a percentage of sales, fast-food costs today are lower than in the past.

4. Personnel

    a. Coastal does its own training and has few employment problems.

    b. Pay rates depend on supply and demand.

    c. Pay rates are not the most important concern of employees. Peer concerns and how the individual is treated are more important.

    d. Treating employees well is critical to good management.

    e. Coastal's fringe benefits for employees include profit sharing, medical treatment, and vacations. Vacation time is calculated on the number of hours an employee has worked.

    f. Coastal stresses the concept of "the hidden paycheck," that is, earnings plus benefits.

    g. Cash problems involving employees in fast-food operations are largely drug related.

    h. Mr. Hintermeister believes there is a good employee potential in society. Success with employees depends on how they are motivated and treated.

    i. Coastal publishes a house organ for employees and others.

    j. Due to its enlightened personnel policies, Coastal has a low manager turnover rate.

    k. When remodeling a store, employee considerations are as important as customer considerations.

    l. A store manager's success depends on his or her understanding of human relations.

    m. When an employee shows potential, he or she is awarded additional responsibilities and commensurate pay.

5. Competition

    a. Monthly price comparisons of competitors and other Burger King outlets are noted. When appropriate, price changes are made.

    b. McDonald's is the pacemaker in fast-food innovations.

    c. Drive-through fast-food outlets are impacting seriously on Burger King and McDonald's restaurants.

    d. Price wars in the fast-food business are usually started by franchisors who distribute coupons to the public.

    e. Grand Metropolitan, the Burger King franchisor, avoids discounting because customers come to expect constant sales.

      f. McDonald's has succeeded in developing a more focused public image than Burger King.

6. Goals
    a. Short range: To stop the recent loss of sales.
    b. Long range: To become more focused.

7. Trends
    a. Since 1983, fast-food sales capacity has exceeded demand. The microwave oven is the fast-food business's biggest competitor.
    b. Mr. Hintermeister sees an approaching bloodbath in the fast-food restaurant business. Wendy's will become a regional competitor, while Hardee's, Sizzler, and Ponderosa are strong.
    c. The verdict is not yet in on the success of food courts.
    d. Unrelated companies have entered the fast-food restaurant business. These include Woolworth, Greyhound Bus, and Heinz Foods (in Puerto Rico)—all of which own Burger King outlets.

NEW TERMS

consignment	short-term loan
franchise agreement	Small Business Administration (SBA)
franchise disclosure statement	SBA Economic Opportunity Loan
goodwill	Program
license agreement	SBA Loan Guarantee Plan
long-term loan	venture capital operator
Minority Business Development	
Agency (MBDA)	

CHAPTER HIGHLIGHTS

1. Retail owners should be good decision makers and should possess organizational ability and willingness to accept responsibility. Ability to lead, capacity for hard work and long hours, and ability to get along with people are important attributes of retail owners. Ownership of a retail business calls for the possession of knowledge, technical skills (in some instances), and an interest in retailing.

2. Sources of funds to start a retail business include the owner's personal resources,

      loans from friends or relatives, credit provided by manufacturers and vendors, loans from banks and the SBA, and venture capital operators.

3. In certain cases new retailers can secure loans from the Small Business Administration, a federal agency that administers a Loan Guarantee Plan and an Economic Opportunity Loan Program.

4. A venture capital operator invests money in someone else's business and becomes a partner in the business.

5. A new owner of a retail business should seek the help of lawyers and accountants in the formation of the business.

6. When considering the purchase of an established retail business, a buyer should talk with other local retailers, bank officials, and local chambers of commerce—in addition to the seller—before making a decision. The same concerns hold true for buying *into* an established business.

7. Information about franchising may be obtained from books and publications of the U.S. Department of Commerce, the U.S. Small Business Administration, and the International Franchise Association.

8. Visiting or calling franchises may provide valuable information about particular franchises. Relatives, friends, certain professionals, and businesspeople can sometimes be of help to someone who is investigating a franchise. Anyone who is interested in franchising can learn about the field and about specific franchises through newspaper and magazine advertisements, regional franchise meetings, and business shows.

9. Franchise agreements contain the terms of the contract between a franchisor and a franchisee.

10. The initial costs of owning a franchise include the franchise fee; beginning inventory; rent, design, and construction of store interior and exterior; supplies; furniture; equipment; payroll; accounting and legal fees; promotions; and miscellaneous.

11. A franchise disclosure statement contains information about a franchisor's experience, key personnel, and franchise fee; territorial protection for franchisees; and training programs. A Federal Trade Commission regulation gives franchisees certain legal rights regarding periods for examining disclosure statements and franchise agreements, franchisor earnings claims, refunds from franchisors, and the truthfulness of disclosure statements.

12. Although franchisees are protected to some extent by regulations of the Federal Trade Commission, they should retain an attorney to deal with legal problems.

13. The U.S. Department of Commerce publishes a list of franchise categories that is valuable for the would-be franchisee.

14. Like other retail areas, franchising has been affected by acquisitions, mergers, and leveraged buyouts.

15. Trends in franchising include combination franchising, the movement of new and small companies into the franchise system of distribution, expansion through acquisitions, an increase in service franchising, and an increase in automotive centers.

REVIEW QUESTIONS

1. Why is it important for retail owners to balance their ability to get along with people with a strong commitment to basic business principles and store policies?
2. What conditions must usually be present for banks to agree to make a small-business loan to a new enterprise?
3. In what ways is the Small Business Administration helpful to new retailers?
4. Why should someone who is seeking to buy an existing retail outlet be skeptical about the reasons advanced by the owner for wanting to sell?
5. On what grounds might a franchisor find a franchisee applicant unacceptable?
6. Why is it important to set up a reasonable contingency fund as part of the initial cost of starting a franchise?
7. Why is it essential for a prospective franchisee to evaluate a franchise disclosure statement before deciding to purchase a franchise?
8. Why has the service sector in franchising fared so well in recent years?

DISCUSSION QUESTIONS

1. Cite some examples of retail businesses to demonstrate the different levels of expertise required to operate them.
2. In what ways can an accountant be of help to an owner of a new retail business? Are there any conditions that should be placed on the advice of such an expert? Why?
3. If you were developing a checklist to evaluate a franchise opportunity, what questions would you ask?
4. Do you think that the trend toward acquisitions in the franchising field is beneficial to franchisees? Why?

CASE 1

Franchise Pluses and Minuses

The rising franchise fees and start-up costs for product franchises like Burger King, Big T Family Restaurant Systems, and Hardee's Food Systems have caused increasing numbers of aspiring retail owners to purchase franchise service outlets instead.

Iris Glar, who seeks to change her working status from personnel manager to entrepreneur, is torn between product and service franchise ownership. Though she has accumulated enough funds to consider the purchase of a well-established fast-food franchise that promises immediate and lucrative returns, she realizes that her background is more suited to a service-type business such as a personnel agency.

After detailed research and soul searching, Glar committed the following facts and thoughts to paper.

Franchise name	Eat-'Em-Hot Emporium, Inc.	Efficiency Personnel, Inc.
Description of operation	24-hour fast-food restaurant specializing in hamburgers. Indoor and outdoor seating. Capacity 40 to 125 people. Food, equipment, layout, and procedures are standardized.	Supplies clerical, secretarial, bookkeeping, computer, and word-processing personnel to business firms, Full- and part-timers. Qualified applicants only.
Number of franchisees	260 in 18 states of the West and Southwest.	40 in 23 states of the Northeast and Midwest.
Length of time in business	Since 1974.	Since 1962.
Funds needed	Total capital needed: $120,000. Includes franchise fee of $40,000, remainder for construction and equipment. $70,000 cash required, must be able to finance the rest.	Total capital needed: $40,000. Includes franchise fee of $15,000, remainder for start-up expenses and office furnishings. $10,000 cash required, franchisor helps finance the rest.
Training provided	Complete operational training. Two- Week course at no cost except for living expenses. Update training periodically at franchisee's expense.	One-week orientation at company headquarters. Two-week training at franchisee's office prior to opening.
Managerial assistance	Start-up and continuing supervision and help. Unannounced visits to check on operations.	Complete service to ensure smooth start and continuing efficient service. Help with office procedures, public relations, forms, staffing, ideas.

Glar's personal considerations are as follows.

- She enjoys mild weather, is uncomfortable in cold areas.
- She wants to make a lot of money as quickly as possible.
- She is concerned that she knows little about the fast-food business.
- She enjoys working with people, especially helping them.
- She is not certain that she can secure a bank loan for investment in the franchise.
- She learns quickly, but has difficulty with mechanical and arithmetic matters.
- She loves to work with ideas, is creative.

a. What are the major items that should help Glar make a decision?
b. Which franchise appears more promising, considering her background and aspirations? Why?
c. What advice would you offer her? Explain.

CASE 2

Banana Republic

Entrepreneur is derived from a French verb meaning to undertake and can be defined as one who sets up and runs a business and assumes the risks of that business.

Retailing history is filled with entrepreneurs who perceived a need for goods and services and an opportunity to provide them, who believed in their own abilities to prosper, and who took the risks inherent in setting up the enterprise. Some of these enterprises, of course, failed. Others, like Rowland H. Macy, Richard Sears, and Aaron Montgomery Ward, achieved spectacular success.

The small businesses started by entrepreneurs were and continue to be the backbone of retailing and of business in general.

According to research conducted by the Massachusetts Institute of Technology, the majority of new jobs created in the United States in recent years has been generated by small businesses, not by *Fortune* 1000 companies.

Banana Republic is one such enterprise. The company was started in 1978 in Mill Valley, California, a small suburb north of San Francisco, by a husband and wife team, Mel and Patricia Gwilliam Ziegler.

Neither of the Zieglers possessed a background in retailing: He had been a journalist and she was an illustrator. Nonetheless, they had an idea for a retailing enterprise that would sell "no-nonsense" travel and safari clothing in natural fibers.

The initial stock at the store consisted of $1,500 worth of Army surplus garments that they purchased in Europe.

At first, the Zieglers were unsure that their concept would attract a substantial customer base, though they did believe their merchandise might appeal to a small limited clientele.

But the Zieglers also decided to take advantage of the growing popularity of catalog selling. They issued a catalog that over the next several years attracted a wider and wider group of customers who found Banana Republic's merchandise comfortable, practical, versatile, and affordable. The venture prospered.

Through its catalogs, Banana Republic was able to expand the merchandise offered. Patricia Ziegler designed many of the new items based on the military garments of various countries. Often the Zieglers traced the original manufacturers and asked them to recreate the clothes for the Banana Republic label.

The distinctive catalogs themselves also contributed to the company's success. The copy is well written and interesting, with descriptions and comments by well-known contemporary writers. No photographs are used; instead, clothes like gurkha shorts and safari jackets are sketched against backgrounds that suggest their exotic and faraway origins.

Five years after establishing Banana Republic, the Zieglers sold the company to The Gap, Inc., a $535 million retailing organization. The Zieglers remained with the company and retained a good measure of control and autonomy.

Since the purchase, however, there have been some changes. The company has greatly increased the number of its stores and expanded its operations. And although the original owners think of Banana Republic as primarily a catalog business, expansion has shifted sales emphasis strongly in the direction of store business.

a. What problems do you think could confront entrepreneurs like the Zieglers when they are bought by a larger retailing organization?

b. What adjustments, if any, do you think a successful entrepreneur needs to make in such a situation?

c. What advantages does an entrepreneur gain by selling to a larger organization? Are there disadvantages? Explain.

d. Since it was founded, Banana Republic has successfully offered a line of practical "travel and safari" clothing. Do you think such clothing is a fad or does it have enduring popularity? Explain.

REFERENCES

Franchise Opportunities: A Business of Your Own. New York: Sterling, 1989.

FRIEDLANDER, M. P., AND G. GURNEY. *Handbook of Successful Franchising.* Blue Ridge Summit, PA: TAB Books, 1989.

HALL, P., AND R. DIXON. *Franchising.* Aulander, NC: Pitman, 1988.

HICKS, T. G. *Franchise Riches Success Kit.* Rockville Centre, NY: International Wealth Success, 1990.

REDDEN, T. *Franchise Buyers' Handbook.* Glenview, IL: Scott, Foresman, 1989.

APPENDIX A

Checklist for Starting a Retail Business

I Selecting a Retail Business
   A Store
   B Nonstore
   C Buying an established business
   D Starting a new business
   E Franchise
   F Location: shopping center, in town, etc.
   G Zoning laws

II Personal Considerations
   A Interests
   B Experience
   C Capabilities
   D Knowledge

III Capital Requirements
   A Starting capital
   B Working capital
   C Contingency capital
   D Banks and loans
   E Small Business Administration

IV Type of Business Organization
   A Sole proprietorship
   B Partnership
   C Corporation
   D Tax advantages and disadvantages
   E Services of an attorney

V Recordkeeping Requirements
  A Management needs
  B Inventory control
  C Tax considerations
  D Payroll system
  E Financial statements
  F Budgeting
  G Forecasting
  H Filing business documents with the government
  I Services of an accountant

VI Office Requirements
  A Furniture
  B Equipment
  C Supplies
  D Filing system
  E Personnel

VII Exterior and Interior Considerations
  A Store façade
  B Window design
  C Parking
  D Lighting
  E Displays
  F Showcases and other furniture
  G Storage
  H Receiving, marking, distribution of merchandise
  I Traffic flow

VIII Insurance Coverage
  A Selecting an insurance company
  B Services of an insurance broker
  C Types of insurance
    1 Liability
    2 Plate glass
    3 Fire
    4 Water damage
    5 Workers' compensation
    6 Life
    7 Other
  D Cost of insurance coverage versus ability to pay premiums

IX Credit Policies
  A Cash, credit, or both
  B Type(s) of credit
  C Checking customers for creditworthiness
  D Billing procedures
  E Delinquent account procedures
  F Knowledge of credit laws

X Personnel (Sales)
  A Assessing personnel needs
  B Sources of personnel
  C Hiring
  D Training
  E Compensation scales and plans
  F Employee benefits
  G Grievance policies
  H Unions

XI Selling Considerations
  A Types of selling
  B Advertising
  C Sales promotions
  D Incentive plans for salespeople

XII Dealing with Shrinkage
  A Prevention of shoplifting
  B Prevention of employee theft and pilferage
  C Control of stock
  D Protecting cash

XIII Management Concerns
  A Organization chart
  B Decision making
  C Delegating authority
  D Basic management principles

APPENDIX B

Retailers and Insurance Coverage

Although retailers can protect against certain business losses by purchasing insurance, the types of insurance carried depend on the nature of the business and the cost of the insurance (premiums). The list that follows contains the more common types of insurance coverage available to retailers.

I Employee Insurance
  A Unemployment insurance—Insurance payments to employees who are laid off and cannot find other employment.
  B Workers' compensation insurance—Insurance payments for medical expenses and salaries to employees who are injured while working.
  C Disability insurance—Insurance payments to employees who become sick or who are injured away from their employment.
  D Employee bonding—Compensation to employers for thefts of money by employees. Employees included in this type of insurance are those responsible for large amounts of money.

II Crime Insurance

A Robbery insurance—Compensation to business owners for the loss of money and property caused by the threat of violence in or away from the place of business.

B Burglary insurance—Compensation to business owners for the loss of money and property caused by the forced entry of a burglar.

C Theft insurance—Compensation to business owners for the loss of money and property caused by a crime that is considered neither robbery nor burglary.

III Property Insurance

A Plate-glass insurance—Compensation to business owners for the breakage of windows.

B Fire insurance—Compensation to business owners for damage or loss caused by fire, smoke, or lightning. Additional cause for reimbursement may include windstorms, explosions, hail, and riots.

C Business interruption insurance—Compensation to business owners for expenses that are paid during the stoppage of business caused by fire or some other misfortune.

D Goods-in-transit insurance—Compensation to business owners for the damage, theft, or loss of goods that are in shipment.

IV Liability Insurance

A General liability insurance—Protection against in-store injuries sustained by customers.

B Product liability insurance—Protection against legal action by customers who claim injury from a product purchased from the retailer.

V Vehicle Insurance

Also called automobile insurance, this type of insurance protects retailers against claims caused by injury to drivers and passengers in the retailer's vehicles. This insurance also compensates retailers for damage to their vehicles, and provides for medical payments to drivers and passengers who are injured in the retailer's vehicles.

APPENDIX C

Retailers and the Law

All retailers, especially newcomers to the field, should become acquainted with federal, state, and local laws and regulations that affect them. The more common ones are listed below. Note: Several laws not listed below are treated in other chapters of this book. (e.g., zoning, consumer laws).

I Federal Laws

A Fair Labor Standards Act (1938)

Also known as the federal Wage and Hour Law and amended since 1938, this act regulates minimum wages to be paid to employees. It also provides for the compensation of overtime hours worked.

B Civil Rights Act (1964) and Age Discrimination and Employment Act (1967)

These laws help insure equal employment opportunities and prohibit retailers and others from discriminating against employees and consumers because of race, age, sex, religion, and national origin.

C Occupational Safety and Health Act (1970)

This law protects employees by setting safety and health standards on the job.

II State Laws

A Sales tax—Retailers are required by the state to collect taxes from customers based on the value of merchandise purchased. The retailer remits the taxes to the state. Each state that imposes a sales tax sets its own tax rate.

B Business license—Certain retailers may not operate without permission from the state. Permission is given in the form of a license. Typical retail establishments requiring a license include restaurants, liquor stores, dry cleaners, and theaters.

III Local Laws

A Taxes—Included are those on sales, real estate, store inventories, and income.

B Building—Most localities regulate the size and placement of signs on buildings, enforce fire code rules, and provide for the health and safety of employees and customers.

C Hours—Some cities and counties regulate the hours when stores may be open. There has been a loosening of this restriction during the last decade.

APPENDIX D

Contents of a Burger King Franchise Agreement

Introduction
I Franchise Grant: Term and Location
II Franchise Fee
III Franchise Representations
IV Standards and Uniformity of Operation
A M.O.D. Manual
B Building and Premises
C Signs
D Equipment

E Vending Machines, etc.
F Menu and Service
G Hours of Operation
H Uniforms
I Advertising and Promotional Materials
J Right of Entry and Inspection
K Interference with Employment Relations of Others
V Services Available to Franchise
VI Restaurant Site
VII Training
VIII Royalty and Advertising Contribution
A Royalty
B Advertising, Sales Promotion, and Public Relations
C Gross Sales
D Late Charge
E Payment
IX Accounting Procedures: Right of Audit
A Accounting
B Annual Financial Statements
C Audits
D Release of Financial Information
X Limitations of Franchise
A Trademarks, Trade Names, Service Marks, and Trade Secrets
B Independent Contractor
XI Unfair Competition
XII Insurance: Indemnification
XIII Taxes
XIV Assignment: Conditions and Limitations
XV Right of First Refusal
XVI Option to Obtain Successor Franchise Agreement
XVII Default and Effect of Termination
A Default
B Effect of Termination
XVIII Restrictive Covenant
XIX Miscellaneous: General Conditions
A Interpretation
B Non-Waiver
C Governing Law, Forum, and Compliance
D Severability
E Notices
F Liability of Multiple Franchisees
G Modification
H Binding Effect

I Survival
J Attorney's Fees
K Entire Agreement

APPENDIX E

Contents of a Burger King Restaurant Manual

I QUALIFICATIONS FOR ADVANCEMENT
OPERATIONS JOB TITLES
A Customer Service Expert Requirements
B Service Leader Requirements
C Food Production Leader Requirements

COASTAL'S MANAGEMENT COURSE OUTLINE

D Hourly Manager Requirements
E Assistant Manager Requirements
F Assistant Manager Restaurant Operations Requirements
G Executive AMRO Requirements
H General Manager Requirements
I Training Manager Requirements
J District Supervisor Requirements
K Director of Operations Requirements
II CUSTOMER FOCUS
A Customer Complaints
B Complimentary Cards
C Senior Citizen Policy
D Birthday Parties
E Newspapers
III CREW PERSONNEL
A Work Week
B Vacation
C Paid Holidays
D Uniforms
E Meals
F Hiring of 14 and 15 Year Olds
G Employee-of-the-Month
H Rap Sessions
I Suggestions
J Movement of Personnel
K Grievance Procedure
IV CREW EVALUATION AND RATES OF PAY
A Crew Performance Evaluation
B Rates of Pay

V MANAGEMENT PERSONNEL
    A Hidden Paycheck
    B Work Week
    C Holidays
    D Vacations
    E Meals
    F Travel Allowance
    G Rap Sessions
    H Suggestions
    I Military Leave
    J Jury Duty
    K Exit Interview
    L Grievance Procedure
    M Movement of Personnel
VI MANAGEMENT RATES OF PAY
VII ASSISTANT MANAGERS AND ASSISTANT MANAGER RESTAURANT OPERATIONS PERFORMANCE EVALUATION
VIII GENERAL MANAGER, TRAINING MANAGER, AND SUPERVISORS PERFORMANCE EVALUATION
IX MONTHLY POINTS
X BONUSES
    A Quarterly
    B Monthly
    C General Managers Double Bonus
XI SECURITY POLICY
    A Cash and Banking Procedures
    B General Security
    C Store Safes
    D Locks
XII FOOD SERVICE
    A Competitor Coupons
    B Breakfast Hours
    C Prepacked Salads
    D Lending and Borrowing
    E Product Problems
    F Butter and Condiments Policy
    G Hot Chocolate
    H Danish
XIII MANAGERS' RESPONSIBILITIES
    A Scheduling
    B Preventative Maintenance
    C Ordering
    D Ending Inventories
    E Local Store Marketing

F Quality, Service, and Cleanliness
G Repair and Maintenance Invoices (R&M)
H Budget Profits
I In-Store Management Meetings

XIV INSURANCE
A Robbery
B Employee or Customer Injury
C Property Damage
D Fire
E Power Failure

XV STORE EQUIPMENT AND MAINTENANCE
A Summer Preparations
B Winter Preparations
C Snow Removal
D Sprinkler Systems
E Landscaping
F Exterminating
G Hood Cleaning
H Window cleaning
I Registers

XVI PAPERWORK
A Regular Weekly Paperwork
B Monthly Paperwork
C Store Hours Form
D Employee Files
E FDR
F Petty Cash and Safe Reimbursement

XVII OUTSIDE INFORMATION
A Labor Department
B Health Department
C Newspaper Reporters
D Unemployment and Disability Forms
E Request for Phone Information

APPENDIX F

Information Required in Franchise Disclosure Statements*

1. Information identifying the franchisor and its affiliates and describing their business experience.

*U.S. Department of Commerce, Bureau of Industrial Economics and Minority Business Development, *Franchise Opportunities Handbook* (Washington, D.C. U.S. Government Printing Office, July 1985,) pp. xxv–xxvi.

2. Information identifying and describing the business experience of each of the franchisor's officers, directors, and management personnel responsible for franchise services, training, and other aspects of the franchise program.

3. A description of the lawsuits in which the franchisor and its officers, directors, and management personnel have been involved.

4. Information about any previous bankruptcies in which the franchisor and its officers, directors, and management personnel have been involved.

5. Information about the initial franchise fee and other initial payments that are required to obtain the franchise.

6. A description of the continuing payments franchisees are required to make after the franchise opens.

7. Information about any restrictions on the quality of goods and services used in the franchise and where they may be purchased, including restrictions requiring purchases from the franchisor or its affiliates.

8. A description of any assistance available from the franchisor or its affiliates in financing the purchase of the franchise.

9. A description of restrictions on the goods or services franchisees are permitted to sell.

10. A description of any restrictions on the customers with whom franchisees may deal.

11. A description of any territorial protection that will be granted to the franchisee.

12. A description of the conditions under which the franchise may be repurchased or refused renewal by the franchisor, transferred to a third party by the franchisee, and terminated or modified by either party.

13. A description of the training programs provided to franchisees.

14. A description of the involvement of any celebrities or public figures in the franchise.

15. A description of any assistance in selecting a site for the franchise that will be provided by the franchisor.

16. Statistical information about the present number of franchises; the number of franchises projected for the future; and the number of franchises terminated, the number the franchisor has decided not to renew, and the number repurchased in the past.

17. The financial statements of the franchisors.

18. A description of the extent to which franchisees must personally participate in the operation of the franchise.

19. A complete statement of the basis for any earnings claims made to the franchisee, including the percentage of existing franchises that have actually achieved the results that are claimed.

20. A list of the names and addresses of other franchisees.

Glossary*

Abandoned Goods Unclaimed merchandise at post offices, customs offices, shippers' storehouses, and the like; sometimes sold in sealed shipping cartons. (5)

Advance Dating The practice in which a merchant arranges to have the credit date based on a date later than the invoice date. (10)

Advertising Any paid form of nonpersonal presentation and promotion of ideas, goods, or services by an identified sponsor. (15)

Advertising Budget A means of determining and controlling advertising expense and dividing it among departments, merchandise lines, and services. (15)

Advertising Plan A strategy for advertising that reflects the store's objectives, the budget, and the types of media to be used. (15)

Anticipation An extra discount for retailers when bills are paid before the expiration of the cash discount period. (10)

Apparent Self How others see an individual. (3)

Application Form A form completed by a prospective employee to provide important data regarding education, work experience, and references. (6)

Area Display A display set up for special merchandising needs, such as model rooms or seasonally used sports equipment. (14)

Armchair Shopping (In-Home Shopping) Purchasing done at home through the use of computers, brochures, and catalogs. (1)

Assets Things of monetary value that are owned by a business (i.e., land, buildings, stock, and cash). (1)

Assistant Buyer An individual who assists the buyer by performing assigned duties in areas with less responsibility. (1)

Assistant Department Manager An individual who assists the department manager by performing assigned duties in areas with less responsibility. (1)

Associate Buyer A person who assists the main store buyer with re-orders and follow-up orders. (9)

Associated Resident Buying Office (Cooperative Resident Buying Office) A buying office that is owned and managed by a group of stores. (9)

*Numbers in parentheses indicate chapters where a fuller discussion may be found.

Assortment Display A display that shows a complete line of merchandise in depth, including colors, sizes, styles, and prices. (14)

Assortment Plan A strategy that aims to achieve merchandise balance, composed of lines of goods that are suited to the demands of customers. (10)

Automated Price Lookup System (PLU) A computer system that provides salespeople with instant price information. (2)

Automated Teller Machine (ATM) Equipment that enables an individual to conduct banking transactions on his or her own. (2)

Automatic Price Reduction Policy A pricing policy by which prices of unsold merchandise are reduced on an automatic basis. (11)

Average Collection Period The relationship of year-end receivables to an average day's sales; the approximate time it has taken to collect a store's debts. (17)

Average Turnover Days A figure that is arrived at by dividing the number of days in the accounting period by the turnover rate. (17)

Backup Stock Merchandise that a vendor will reserve without any obligation on the store's part to purchase it. (10)

Bait-and-Switch Advertising The practice of luring a customer into a store with the intention of selling something other than the merchandise advertised. (2)

Balance Sheet A statement of the financial position of a business at a particular time. (17)

Bank Credit Card A type of credit card with which a customer charges merchandise, the retailer pays the bank a percentage of the purchase price, and the bank collects from the customer. (18)

Bank Debit Card A card used by a customer to deduct the cost of purchases from the customer's bank account balance. (18)

Bantam Store (Convenience Store) A small neighborhood store carrying inexpensive, easy-to-sell merchandise that is consumed daily or frequently. (5)

Bar Code (Universal Product Code UPC) A system in which sensitized lines on product labels serve as symbols for numbers that can be "read" by a scanner and indicate the manufacturer, type of product, weight, and size. (2)

Bargain Store (Barn Store) An outlet that specializes in selling factory seconds, distressed and salvage goods, closeouts, manufacturers' overruns, and abandoned goods at low prices. (5)

Barn Store (Bargain Store) An outlet that specializes in selling factory seconds, distressed and salvage goods, closeouts, manufacturers' overruns, and abandoned goods at low prices. (5)

Barter To trade by exchanging one commodity for another. (1)

Bill of Lading A receipt from a transporter giving title to goods being shipped. (12)

Bin A receptacle used to hold incoming merchandise. (12)

Biogenic Motive One that is related to physical needs, such as the need for food, sex, drink, or comfort. (3)

Blind Ad   A type of advertisement that does not identify the store and provides only a post office box number as an address. (6)

Blind Checking (Indirect Checking)   A type of merchandise checking that requires a thorough check; instead of invoices, special forms are used. (12)

Blue-Collar Worker   An individual who works in a factory or trade, or as a laborer. (3)

Boutique Pattern   A layout arrangement that creates a small specialty shop within an area of the selling floor. (8)

Box Store (Warehouse Store)   A cross between a limited-assortment store and a supermarket; stocks several thousand items, including nonfood products, limited lines of perishables, and meat; customers mark and bag their own items. (5)

Branch Store   A scaled-down version of an established store operating at a separate location. (5)

Breadth (Width)   The number of product classifications that a merchant stocks. (10)

Broad and Shallow Plan   An approach to retailing in which the merchant carries a few items in many styles in a product class. (10)

"Brood Hen and Chick"   A system of organization in which the main store operates the branch by performing functions both for itself and for the branch. (6)

Bulk Checking   A form of direct checking of incoming cartons, but not contents; used when bulk units are received. (12)

Buyer   An individual who is responsible for the purchasing and selling of merchandise in one or several departments. (1)

Buyer's Commitment System   A system that provides a buyer with facts so that the buyer can respond immediately to the store's merchandise needs. (9)

Buying Club (Warehouse Club)   A no-frills store offering sizable discounts to member groups. (2)

Buying Motive   An emotional, rational, biogenic, or psychogenic motive that causes consumers to act or buy. (3)

Cafeteria Plan (Flex-Benefits)   Employees select a combination of fringe benefits from a list of offerings. (6)

Canvassing   A method of soliciting orders for goods by calling on people in a certain area. (5)

"Cargo Prices"   Another term for low prices. (15)

Carrier   Transporter. (12)

Cash Budget   An estimate of cash receipts and payments for a given period. (17)

Cash Discount   A reduction of purchase price offered in return for prompt payment. (10)

Catalog Retailing   A nonstore retailing method whereby selling is done through catalogs. (5)

Catalog Showroom   A store where merchandise samples are displayed and consumers place orders from a catalog. (5)

Catchall Display   A large container that holds large quantities of one kind of merchandise. (14)

Caveat Venditor   "Let the seller beware." (2)

Centralized Buying A system in which the buyers make all the decisions regarding selection, quantities, and distribution of merchandise to all the stores in a retailing concern. (9)

Centralized Distribution Plan A plan in which buyers make all the purchasing decisions but individual store managers have control over depth of stock. (9)

Central Shopping District (Downtown Shopping District) A large collection of department stores and specialty shops located in the central or downtown area of a city. (7)

Centralization An arrangement in which the major store functions are controlled through a home or regional office. (6)

Chain Store One of a group of centrally owned retail stores that carry merchandise of the same type. (1)

Channel of Distribution The path a product takes to reach the consumer. (1)

Checkout Counter Display A display located close to the cashier and featuring "impulse items" like candy, gum, or cigarettes. (14)

Civil Recovery A law that permits retailers, without the requirement of criminal prosecution, to collect money from shoplifters. (12)

Classic A style that remains in fashion for a long time. (2)

Closed Display A display in which valuable items are protected behind glass and are handled by a salesperson. (14)

Closeout Discontinued merchandise of stores that have closed or gone into bankruptcy. (5)

Close-out Store A retail store that offers an attractive mixture of brand names, lower prices, and, for the most part, first-quality goods. (5)

Combination Advertising An approach that combines the advertisement of a specific item with an attempt to build a favorable image of the store. (15)

Combination Plan A compromise between narrow and deep, and broad and shallow, breadth-and-depth plans. (10)

Combination Store (Combostore) A store that offers one-stop shopping with a full line of food products, substantial quantities of nonfood items, and some services. (5)

Combostore (Combination Store) A store that offers one-stop shopping with a full line of food products, substantial quantities of nonfood items, and some services. (5)

Commissionaire A foreign resident buying office. (9)

Community Shopping Center A shopping center whose largest tenant is either a scaled-down department store or a specialty store; smaller than a regional shopping center. (7)

Company Card A card issued by a large company for use in purchasing its products or services. (18)

Comparison Shopper An individual who checks competitors' prices, assortments, and services. (11)

Conditional Sales Contract An arrangement under which the retailer maintains title to the merchandise and may repossess it if the buyer fails to make a payment. (18)

Consignment An arrangement under which the retailer must pay only for items that are sold. (20)

Consignment Buying An arrangement in which the vendor permits the retailer to pay only for goods that are sold. (10)

Constant Dollars Income calculated by reference to a base year (real income). (3)

Consultive Selling A method of selling in which the salesperson consults with consumers to determine products and services that fulfill their needs. (5)

Consumer Behavior The process whereby consumers decide whether, what, where, when, and how to buy goods and services. (3)

Consumer Cooperative Association A type of retail business in which consumers own shares, decide store policy, and share profits. (4)

Consumer Movement The demand by consumers for the establishment of economic fair play through laws protecting the public against unfair trade practices. (2)

Consumerism The activities of individuals and organizations that are involved in safe-guarding the buyer in the marketplace. (2)

Control Department The department that is responsible for protecting the store's finances. (1)

Convenience Goods Items that consumers buy to meet immediate and pressing needs. (5)

Convenience Store (Bantam Store) A small neighborhood store carrying inexpensive, easy-to-sell merchandise that is consumed daily or frequently. (5)

Conveyor Mechanism A mechanism that carries goods from receiving areas to stockrooms or selling spaces. (12)

Cooperative Advertising An arrangement whereby retailers share the costs of advertising with manufacturers, suppliers, or other merchants. (15)

Cooperative Chain A group of independent retailers organized to combine orders so as to secure volume discounts for the purpose of competing with large retailers. (4)

Cooperative Resident Buying Office (Associated Resident Buying Office) A buying office that is owned and managed by a group of stores. (9)

Corporate Resident Buying Office A division of a parent company that buys and distributes merchandise for all of its stores. (9)

Corporation A form of business ownership that is chartered by the state and recognized as a business entity separate from its owners; ownership is represented by shares of stock. (4)

Counter Display A special arrangement of merchandise at a store counter. (14)

Country Club Billing A time- and work-saving system in which the retailer mails sales slips and a simple statement listing the balance owed by the customer at the end of the period. (18)

Coupon A form of promotion that allows a specific reduction in the price of an item. (16)

CPM (Cost per Thousand) A formula that is commonly used to assess a medium's impact on a desired audience. (15)

Creative Selling Selling that involves the use of selling techniques to help solve customers' problems. (13)

Credit Bureau An organization that gathers personal information about shoppers from stores, employers, banks, and the like, and develops summary reports for use by stores that request them. (18)

Credit Card A plastic or metal card bearing the owner's name and identification number, used for the purpose of charging a purchase to the customer's account. (18)

Current Ratio The relationship of a company's current assets to its current liabilities. (17)

Cut-Case Display A display in which packing boxes are cut and folded to create the display unit. (14)

Cycle Billing A method used by stores to stagger their customer statements throughout the month instead of billing all customers at once. (18)

Data Bank A storage unit for information such as sales records, inventory, purchasing, consumer data, accounts payable, accounts receivable, and personnel. (19)

Date of Invoice (DOI) Credit terms in which the credit period starts on the invoice date. (10)

Dating The period allowed by vendors to buyers for the payment of bills. (10)

Debt-to-Equity Ratio The relationship between a company's liabilities and net worth. (17)

Decentralization An arrangement under which store functions such as selling and sales promotion are decided by the individual store. (6)

Decentralized Buying Equipping a chain's divisions with their own buying staffs. (9)

Delivery Receipt A form supplied by a carrier and used by a receiving clerk to indicate that delivery has been made. (12)

Demographics The breakdown of the population into statistical categories such as age, education, sex, occupations, income, households, and marital status. (3)

Department Manager An individual who supervises a merchandise department and is responsible for service and merchandise activities. (1)

Department Store A large retail institution that offers a variety of carefully selected merchandise organized into specific departments. (1)

Depth The number of styles or brands within a product classification. (10)

Descriptive Billing A system whereby a computer printout of a customer's account identifies transactions by date, department, description of transaction, price charged, payments, and credits. (18)

Direct Checking A method of comparing numbers and markings on incoming items directly against the manufacturer's invoice. (12)

Direct Mail The medium that retailers use to send catalogs and brochures to customers. (15)

Direct Premium An item that is given to a customer free with a purchase, at the time of purchase. (16)

Discharged Dismissed from the company ("fired"). (6)

Discount Department Store A store that sells well-known brands below the suggested retail price, offers wide variety and one-stop shopping, but lacks personal service. (5)

Discount Store A retailing institution that offers a wide variety of merchandise at low prices with few customer services. (1)

Discretionary Income Money that a person or household has available to spend or save freely after payments for fixed commitments have been deducted. (3)

Display A nonpersonal approach to the selling process through the use of windows, signs, and fixtures. (14)

Display Stand An attractive, permanent, self-service display that comes in various sizes, occupies little space, and stores a great deal of merchandise. (14)

Disposable Income The amount of money a person has to spend after taxes have been deducted. (3)

Distressed Goods Items that have been damaged or soiled in shipping or handling. (5)

Dividend The distributed profits of a corporation. (17)

DOI (Date of Invoice) A system in which the credit period starts on the invoice date. (10)

Dollar Control A system for gathering information about inventory

using the retail dollar value of merchandise. (17)

Door-to-Door Selling Selling in which the salesperson contacts customers and demonstrates merchandise by going from door to door. (5)

Downtown Shopping District (Central Shopping District) A large collection of department stores and specialty shops located in the central or downtown area of a city. (7)

Drawing Account A compensation arrangement that allows salespeople to take or "draw" a set amount each payday regardless of their sales. (6)

Dual Distribution An arrangement in which a manufacturer has its own retail outlets, and vice versa. (9)

Dump Display A display in which merchandise is heaped in a pile. (14)

Electronic Article Surveillance (EAS) The use of electronic devices to control shoplifting. (12)

Electronic Data Integration (EDI) (Quick Response) An inventory delivery system in which retailers, manufacturers, and mills work together as partners. (17)

Electronic Data Interchange (EDI) A system that enables retailers to integrate their purchasing activities within their stores and with vendors. (2)

Electronic Data Processing (EDP) The use of computers to amass large quantities of information, process the data at electronic speeds, and turn out reports quickly. (2)

Electronic Funds Transfer (EFT) A

system for making deposits and withdrawals electronically, thereby eliminating most of the paper work involved in sales and banking transactions. (2)

Electronic Information System (EIS) A computerized information system designed for a company's chief executives. (19)

Electronic Point-of-Sales (EPOS), Point-of-Sales (POS) A specially designed cash register system that is connected electronically to a computer. (2)

Electronic Retailing A method of selling using two-way cable television communications, videophones, and personal computers. (5)

Electronic Spreadsheet A computer-generated record that is updated automatically by the computer. (2)

Emotional Motive A motive that is not based on logical thinking, such as love or vanity. (3)

End-Aisle Display A display in which merchandise is placed in a vacant area at the end of an aisle in a supermarket or variety store. (14)

End of Month (EOM) Credit terms in which the discount period starts at the end of the month in which the invoice is dated. (10)

Engel's Laws Economic "laws" that show that as household income increases, there are decided shifts in the manner in which that income is spent. (3)

Ensemble Display A display in which the item to be promoted is combined with related merchandise for a total effect. (14)

Equal Store An organizational approach in which buying is done through a central or regional office and the branches are responsible for sales and promotion. (6)

Expense Budget An estimate of expenses over a specified period based on past experience and future plans. (17)

Experimentation A method of gathering information in which a researcher sets up an experiment whereby one or more factors are controlled in the situation being studied. (19)

Extra Dating An extension of the cash discount period. (10)

Factory Outlet A retail establishment, owned and operated by a manufacturer, selling the manufacturer's merchandise of irregulars, discounted lines, closeouts, odd lots, etc. (2)

Factory Seconds Imperfect merchandise with manufacturing flaws. (5)

Fad A fashion that is adopted and discarded within a short period. (2)

Family Life Cycle A tool used to examine and understand the consumer. (3)

Fashion The prevailing manner in which people live, dress, work, and play at a given time and place. (2)

Fashion Cycle The movement of a style through the phases of introduction, acceptance, and peak of popularity to eventual decline. (2)

Fashion Goods Items that are popular at a particular time. (5)

Fashion Trend The direction in which different styles move according to consumer demand. (2)

First in, First out (FIFO) A method

of accounting for ending inventory in which merchandise purchased first is assumed to be sold completely before any subsequently purchased items are sold. (17)

Flea Market A retail outlet composed of a collection of independent retailers selling different lines of goods, old and new, at bargain prices. (5)

Flex-Benefits (Cafeteria Plan) Employees select a combination of fringe benefits from a list of offerings. (6)

Flexible Pricing (Variable-Price Policy) A method of selling that enables customers to bargain with retailers. (11)

Flex-Place Employees select the retail outlet in which they prefer working. (6)

Flex-Time Employees select their working hours. (6)

FOB ("Free on Board") Destination A system in which the seller pays transportation costs to the buyer's location and retains title to the goods while they are in transit. (10)

FOB ("Free on Board") Shipping Point A system in which the seller delivers the merchandise to the starting point of shipment; the buyer pays transportation costs and has title from that point on. (10)

Formal Communication The use of employee handbooks, manuals, house organs, bulletins, and meetings to keep employees informed. (6)

Forward Stock Merchandise that is stored in drawers, bins, or racks in or close to a selling area. (12)

Franchise The exclusive right to perform a service or sell a product. (4)

Franchise Agreement (License Agreement) A contract signed by a franchisor and a prospective franchisee. (20)

Franchise Disclosure Statement A document that contains information about a franchisor's experience, key personnel, and franchise fee, and other items of importance to franchisees. (20)

Franchisee A company or individual that receives a franchise. (4)

Franchisor (Licensor) A manufacturer, wholesaler, or service company that gives a franchise to another company or individual. (4)

Free-flow Pattern A layout arrangement that allows the shopper more room to move about and browse. (8)

Freestanding Store A retail outlet that stands by itself. (7)

Full-Service Wholesaler A merchandise resource that provides many services to retailers, including storage, credit, and market information. (9)

General Merchandise An assortment of products in several unrelated merchandise lines. (5)

General Store A retail outlet that maintains a limited but varied stock of merchandise; the first authentic American retailing institution. (1)

Goodwill An intangible asset of a business that is derived from the reputation of its owner, products, or services. (20)

Grapevine An unofficial communication network. (6)

Grid Pattern A layout arrangement

that routes traffic in a straight, rectangular fashion. (8)

Gross Margin   Profit before deducting operating expenses. (17)

Guaranteed Sales   An agreement by the vendor to take back merchandise that the retailer cannot sell. (10)

Hard Goods   Merchandise such as cameras, jewelry, furniture, and appliances. (1)

Highway Outlet   A store located on a main road, apart from other businesses, that offers easy access and convenient parking. (7)

Honesty Test   A paper-and-pencil test designed to detect undesirable job applicants. (6)

Horizontal Price Fixing   A conspiracy by retailers, wholesalers, or manufacturers to fix prices in such a way as to stifle competition. (11)

Human Resource Department (Personnel Department)   The department that is responsible for employee selection, training, advancement, and welfare. (1)

Hypermarket   An extremely large self-service retail outlet in a warehouse setting. (1)

Ideal Self   What an individual would like to be. (3)

Impact Fee   Costs imposed on shopping center developers by communities. (7)

Importer   A wholesaler that brings goods from foreign markets for resale to retailers. (9)

Impression Management   A store's attempts to present a distinct image that distinguishes it from its competition. (8)

Impulse Goods   Consumer products generally purchased without prior planning. (5)

Income Statement   A summary of the income and expenses of a business over a specific period. (17)

Incoming Trend   Styles that are just becoming popular. (2)

Independent Resident Buying Office   A buying office that charges fees based on the types of services performed and the volume of merchandise purchased. (9)

Independently Owned Store   A retailing institution that is controlled by its own individual management. (4)

Indirect Checking (Blind Checking)   A type of merchandise checking that requires a thorough check; instead of invoices, special forms are used. (12)

Informal Communication   Verbal communication through vertical and horizontal channels. (6)

In-Home Retailing   The selling of goods and services in people's homes. (5)

In-Home Shopping (Armchair Shopping)   Purchasing that is done at home through the use of computers, brochures, and catalogs. (1)

Initial Markup (Original Markup)   The first markup on an item. (11)

Installment Credit   Credit that is extended in the sale of high-ticket items. The buyer is required to sign a contract, make a down payment, and make periodic payments (including principal and interest) until the invoice price has been paid. (18)

Institutional Advertising   Attempts to sell the entire concept of the store and its image rather than a particular type of merchandise. (15)

Institutional Display An attempt to build goodwill by permitting charities, schools, or the arts to become the central theme of a store display. (14)

Interactive Kiosk A booth that displays products and information on a video screen. (14)

Interior Display An arrangement of merchandise within a store whose purpose is to create product awareness and stimulate sales. (14)

Internship Program A method of testing future employees through on-the-job evaluation. (6)

Invoice A bill for merchandise that usually specifies the time of shipment and terms of payment. (12)

Item Pricing A state law requiring stores to put a price on each piece of merchandise. (11)

Job Analysis A detailed study of the duties and abilities needed to perform a job efficiently. (6)

Job Description A written description of a job based on information from a job analysis. (6)

Job Rotation A system in which employees are moved from one area to another so that they can view the total business operation prior to permanent assignment. (6)

Job Specification The type of person and qualifications needed to fill a job description. (6)

Job Transfer The assignment of an experienced worker to another job within the store or to a branch store. (6)

Joint Venture A partnership or co-operative agreement for a specific purpose. (1)

Keystone Markup A markup that is double the cost of the merchandise. (11)

Kiosk A freestanding booth that displays specialized product lines. (14)

Last in, First out (LIFO) A method of accounting for ending inventory in which merchandise purchased last is assumed to be sold completely before any earlier-purchased items are sold. (17)

Layaway Plan A system in which the customer gives the store a deposit on merchandise, which is held until a later date. (8)

Layoff The temporary or permanent termination of an employee because of an economic slowdown or problems within the firm. (6)

Leader Pricing Pricing in which a retailer sells one or more products at lower than usual prices in order to attract shoppers. (11)

Learning Any change in an individual's response or behavior resulting from practice or experience. (3)

Leased Department Rented space in a retail establishment. (4)

Liabilities The debts or obligations of a business. (17)

License Agreement (Franchise Agreement) A contract signed by a franchisor and a prospective franchisee. (20)

Licensor (Franchisor) A manufacturer, wholesaler, or service company that gives a franchise to another company or individual. (4)

Lie Detector (Polygraph Instrument) A device used to indicate whether answers to questions are lies or the truth. (6)

Lifestyle   The unique way in which a particular group sets itself apart from others. (3)

Limited-Function Wholesaler   A merchandise resource for retailers that offers few services and low prices. (9)

Limited-Item Store   A store that carries fewer than 1,000 products, with few perishables and a limited number of brands. (5)

Limited-Line Merchandise   Goods within a particular classification. (5)

Limited-Line Store (Specialty Store)   A retail store that features a full line of a particular type of merchandise. (1)

Line-and-Staff Organization Chart   A chart that combines the lines of delegated authority with specialists (staff) who provide expertise in certain areas. (6)

Line Organization Chart   A chart that shows each worker's position with relation to his or her immediate superior or supervisor. (6)

Line Position   A position that is characterized by direct authority and responsibility. (6)

Listing Plan (Price List Agreement)   A plan that gives store managers responsibility for selecting merchandise from lists and catalogs supplied by the central buyer. (9)

Loading Dock (Receiving Dock, Loading Platform)   A large area that can accommodate trucks or other vehicles for the unloading of merchandise. (12)

Loading Platform (Loading Dock, Receiving Dock)   A large area that accommodates trucks or other vehicles for the loading or unloading of merchandise. (12)

Long-Term Loan   Credit terms that require repayment in a year or more. (20)

Loss Leader   Merchandise that is sold by a retailer at or below cost. (11)

Low-Margin (Low-Profit) Operator   A retailer that offers a minimum of service and low prices. (2)

Mail Order House   A retail institution that sells through the mail. (1)

Mail Order Retailing   The sale of goods and services to customers through the mail. (5)

Maintained Markup   The final markup on an item based on the actual selling price. (11)

Mall (Regional Shopping Center)   A combination of many small specialty shops and two or more major stores, usually in an enclosed mall, designed to service a large geographic area. (7)

Manufacturer   A firm that makes products that people buy. (1)

Mapping   The process of determining the locations of departments and merchandise within a store. (8)

Markdown   A reduction in selling price. (11)

Market Segmentation   The process of dividing the total market into smaller sections based on a shared characteristic. (3)

Marketing Research   The investigation and systematic gathering, recording, and analysis of data that are pertinent to a specific marketing problem. (19)

Marking The recording of a retail price on an item of merchandise. (12)

Markup The difference between selling price and cost. (11)

Maslow's Hierarchy of Needs A theory to explain why consumers are motivated to satisfy their needs and desires. (3)

Mass Merchandiser A retailer, usually a discounter, that sells a wide variety of goods and generates a large sales volume. (1)

Mazur Plan A plan that divides all retail store activities into four major areas: merchandising, publicity, store management, and control. (6)

Merchandise Budget Estimates of the factors that affect merchandise activities. (17)

Merchandise Display An interior display that creates product awareness and stimulates impulse buying. (14)

Merchandising The buying and selling of goods. (1)

Merchandising Department The department that is responsible for buying and selling all goods and keeping merchandise records. (2)

Middleman (Wholesaler) An individual or firm that purchases merchandise for resale to retailers. (1)

Minimum Price Law (Unfair Trade Practices Law) A law that requires retailers to charge a minimum price for goods based on the cost of the merchandise plus a percentage for overhead. (11)

Minority Business Development Agency (MBDA) A federal agency that provides management, marketing, and technical assistance to minorities. (20)

Misses Merchandise Line Clothing for mature women. (11)

Mobile A display that hangs from the ceiling and moves, thereby attracting attention. (14)

Motivation The force that causes people to behave the way they do. (3)

Movable Table (Portable Table) A table used to wheel incoming goods from the checking room to the marking room and then to the stockroom or selling floor. (12)

Multiple-Price Policy A policy in which the retailer sells two or more items of the same merchandise at a unit price that is lower than the unit price if only one item is bought. (11)

Narrow and Deep Plan An approach to retailing in which only a few selections are offered, but they are stocked in depth. (10)

Neighborhood Shopping Center (Strip Center, String Street) A small group of stores located alongside each other in a residential area. (7)

Neighborhood Shopping District An area that contains a selection of convenience stores (e.g., a variety store, a bakery, a hardware store, a drugstore, a grocery, and a laundromat), as well as an occasional specialty store. (7)

Net Worth (Owner's Equity) The difference between the assets of a business and its liabilities. (17)

No-Frills Operator A retailer whose facilities are minimal and whose prices are low. (2)

Nonmarking A policy in which prices are not marked on merchandise. (12)

Objective-and-Task Method A budget technique that relates the advertising budget to the sales objectives for the coming year. (15)

Observation A method of gathering information that consists of observing and recording consumer behavior in a particular situation. (19)

Odd Price A price just below an even dollar or cents amount. (11)

Off-Price Retailing The sale of name brands at discounted prices targeted to the price-conscious consumer. (2)

On-the-Job Training Training in which a new employee is assigned to a more experienced person until he or she has learned the job. (6)

On-the-Shelf Display A device that utilizes shelf space as a basis for displaying merchandise. (14)

One-Price Policy A policy in which all customers pay the same price for the same product. (1)

One-Stop Shopping The opportunity to purchase a variety of goods and services in one retail establishment. (1)

Open Ad An advertisement that supplies all the information about a job as well as the name, address, and telephone number of the employer. (6)

Open Charge Account An account in which, up to a specified limit, a customer may charge purchases to the account and pay for them at a later date. (18)

Open Display A display in which merchandise is shown on tables, carts, and baskets designed for easy access and handling by the customer. (14)

Open-to-Buy (OTB) The difference between planned purchases and stock already ordered; the dollar amount of merchandise that a buyer can order for a particular period. (10)

Operations That part of store management that maintains the store's physical plant and directs sales-supporting activities and customer services. (1)

Operations Department The department that is responsible for maintaining the store's physical plant and receiving and protecting merchandise. (2)

Opinion Leader A member of a group who exerts influence on consumer decision making. (3)

Optical Character Recognition—Font A (OCR-A) A classification system used in universal vendor marking. (12)

Order Taking A routine form of selling in which a store clerk fills a request, accepts payment, and wraps items. (13)

Organization Chart A diagram that clearly indicates the lines of authority and responsibility in an organization. (6)

Orientation Training New-employee instruction covering such topics as the history of the firm, procedures and policies, rules and regulations, promotions, and fringe benefits. (6)

Original Markup (Initial Markup) The first markup on an item. (11)

Outgoing Trend Styles that are experiencing reduced consumer demand. (2)

Outshopper A person who is shopping outside his or her usual shopping area. (19)

Overhead Business expenses such

as rent, salaries, and advertising. (11)

Overrun   A quantity of custom-made articles in excess of retailers' orders. (5)

Owner's Equity (Net Worth)   The difference between the assets of a business and its liabilities. (17)

Ownership Group   A parent organization that owns a group of stores. (4)

Partnership   A form of business ownership in which two or more people invest time and money in the business. (4)

Party Plan   A direct-sales method of retailing in which a salesperson enlists the aid of one consumer in selling to others. (5)

Patronage Motive   The reason a consumer chooses one place to shop rather than another. (3)

Peddler   A person who hawks or sells goods. (1)

Percentage-of-Sales Method   The most commonly used method of preparing an advertising budget, basing it on a percentage of a sales figure such as past sales, anticipated sales, or a combination of past and anticipated sales. (15)

Perception   A personal interpretation of information. (3)

Performance Appraisal   A personnel tool that measures employee performance and the effectiveness of training. (6)

Periodic Inventory   A method of finding the value of merchandise at a particular time only by taking a physical count of the stock. (17)

Perpetual Inventory   A method for knowing the value of an inventory at any given time. (17)

Personal Income   All the moneys an individual receives from wages, salaries, investments, interest, and dividends. (3)

Personal Selling   A form of selling in which face-to-face methods are used to help customers with their buying problems. (13)

Personal Shopper   A store employee who selects merchandise for a customer prior to the customer's store visit. (8)

Personality   The sum of attributes that causes an individual to behave in a distinctive manner. (3)

Personnel Department (Human Resource Department)   The department that is responsible for employee selection, training, advancement, and welfare. (1)

Personnel Research   Studies concerned with the finding, hiring, training, compensation, and evaluation of employees. (19)

Planogramming   An inventory control method that enables a retailer to maintain shelf inventory for maximum efficiency. (17)

PM (Push Money, Spiff)   A premium, prize, or extra commission offered to salespeople as an incentive to increase sales of a particular type of merchandise. (6)

Point-of-Purchase (POP) Display   Devices or structures sponsored by vendors that are used in, on, or adjacent to a point of sale. (14)

Point-of-Sales (POS); Electronic Point-of-Sales (EPOS)   A specially designed cash register system that is connected electronically to a computer. (2)

Polygraph Instrument (Lie Detector)   A device used to indicate whether answers to questions are lies or the truth. (6)

Portable Table (Movable Table) A table used to wheel incoming goods from the checking room to the marking room and then to the stockroom or selling floor. (12)

Postdating An extension of the cash discount period for an additional month when the invoice is dated on or after the twenty-fifth of the month and end-of-month terms are given. (10)

Power Center A shopping center containing multiple anchor stores and category leaders. (7)

Premarking (Source Marking) A policy in which the vendor marks the goods before delivery to the store according to the merchant's specifications. (10)

Premium An article of merchandise that is given to a shopper free or at a reduced price as an incentive to buy a particular product. (16)

Preretailing A policy in which buyers are required to list retail prices on purchase orders. (12)

Press Release A formal statement prepared by a firm for submission to the media for publication. (16)

Price Lining Carrying several lines of a given product, each with a different price. (11)

Price List Agreement (Listing Plan) A plan that gives store managers responsibility for selecting merchandise from lists and catalogs supplied by the central buyer. (9)

Price War Action engaged in by retailers to underprice competitors. (11)

Primary Data Information collected for the particular problem under study. (19)

Private Label (Store Brand) Merchandise that is sold only in the retailer's own store. (9)

Private Resident Buying Office (Store-Owned Resident Buying Office) A buying office that is owned by the firm it serves. (9)

Profit Sharing A plan that gives employees an opportunity to share in the profits of the firm. (6)

Promotion Moving an employee to another position that carries greater responsibility and an increase in salary. (6)

Promotion Calendar A calendar used by stores to pinpoint special events, local and national events, holiday promotions, advertising, and so forth. (16)

Promotional Advertising Routine advertising that attempts to sell specific items or services by bringing customers into a store. (15)

Promotional Display An attempt to sell merchandise directly and dramatically. (14)

Psychogenic Motive A motive that stems from psychological needs such as the need for satisfaction, protection, or enhancement of the ego. (3)

Psychographics A method that measures trends in consumer lifestyles and behavior patterns. (3)

Public Relations A continuing program designed to encourage positive public attitudes toward the firm. (16)

Publicity Free space and time given by newspapers, magazines, radio, and TV for newsworthy events. (16)

Purchase Order A form that specifies the kind of goods ordered, their price, the date, shipping instructions, and terms. (12)

Purchase Privilege Offer A promotion offered on a limited-continuity basis and designed to build traffic over a longer period. (16)

Push Money (PM, Spiff) A premium, prize, or extra commission offered to salespeople as an incentive to increase sales of a particular type of merchandise. (6)

Quantity Discount A discount based on the volume of purchases. (10)

Quick Ratio The relationship of a company's quick assets (current assets less inventory and supplies) to its current liabilities. (17)

Quick Response (Electronic Data Integration, EDI) An inventory delivery system in which retailers, manufacturers, and mills work together as partners. (17)

Rack Jobber A wholesaler that is allowed by a retail store to install, stock, and replenish selected items on display racks. (5)

Rail Interview An initial screening that takes place before a prospective employee is asked to fill out an application form. (6)

Rational Motive A motive that involves judgment and logical thinking; examples are security and durability. (3)

Real Income In measuring an individual's purchasing power, the figure that determines the actual number of dollars available. (3)

Real Self What the consumer is as a person; his or her physical, mental, and emotional characteristics. (3)

Receipt of Goods (ROG) The cash discount period begins with the receipt of the merchandise. (10)

Receiving Book A record of pertinent information about incoming goods. (12)

Receiving Dock (Loading Dock, Loading Platform) A large area that can accommodate trucks or other vehicles for the unloading of merchandise. (12)

Reference Group A group that is influential in shaping the attitudes, opinions, and lifestyle that an individual chooses. (3)

Referral Premium A gift that is awarded to customers who send in the names of potential new customers. (16)

Regional Shopping Center (Mall) A combination of many small specialty shops and two or more major stores, usually in an enclosed mall, designed to service a large geographic area. (7)

Related-Merchandise Display An arrangement of products with matching items (e.g., cheese and crackers), usually found in supermarkets and drugstores. (14)

Remarking Showing a markdown by crossing out the old price and writing or stamping in the new one. (12)

Reserve Stock Merchandise that is stored in a central stockroom or in a stockroom adjoining a department. (12)

Resident Buying Office A service organization that helps retailers buy merchandise on a fee basis. (9)

Retail Life Cycle A way of viewing changes in the retail environment. (2)

Retail Merchandise Management System (RMM) A system that tracks the performance of merchandise, reordering "hot" items and identifying the "cold" ones, enabling store buyers to make timely decisions. (9)

Retail Method A method for estimating the cost of the ending inventory on the basis of a ratio of the cost of the goods available for sale to the retail price of the goods available for sale. (17)

Retailer An individual or firm that sells goods and services directly to the ultimate consumer. (1)

Retailing The selling of goods and services to the ultimate consumer. (1)

Retailing Information System (RIS) An ongoing computer-based process for collecting both internal and external data. (2)

Retailing Research Research that applies the techniques of marketing research to the investigation of problems related to retailing. (19)

Return on Investment (ROI) The relationship of a corporation's net income to stockholders' equity. (17)

Revolving Charge Account An account that enables a customer to charge purchases up to a specific amount; the customer has a specific period within which to make full payment without an interest (finance) charge. (18)

ROG (Receipt of Goods) Credit terms in which the cash discount period begins when goods are received by the buyer. (10)

Route Selling A method of door-to-door selling used by retailers that sell frequently purchased convenience items. (5)

Salary Supplement Money or prizes offered to salespeople as an incentive to increase sales of a particular type of merchandise. (6)

Sales Forecasting Estimating future sales volume on the basis of current sales figures and information from manufacturers, wholesalers, accountants, economists, and bankers. (2)

Sales per Square Foot of Selling Space Net sales divided by the square feet of selling space. (17)

Sales Promotion Methods used by a merchant to generate sales, attract customers to the store, build customer loyalty, and promote goodwill. (1)

Salvage Goods Goods that have been damaged in transit or storage. (5)

Sample (in a research study) A representative group of the entire population studied. (19)

Sample (offered as a premium) A trial size of a product that is provided by the manufacturer as an inducement to shoppers to try new items. (16)

SBA Economic Opportunity Loan Program A program designed to counsel economically disadvantaged entrepreneurs and assist them in obtaining low-interest financing. (20)

SBA Loan Guarantee Plan A program that enables a qualified businessperson to receive a bank loan guaranteed up to 90 percent by the Small Business Administration. (20)

Scrambled Merchandising Increasing the types of goods that have traditionally been carried by a store. (5)

Seasonal Discount   A trade discount given to retailers willing to order, receive, and pay for goods during the "off season." (10)

Seasonal Merchandise   Products that are in demand at a certain time of the year. (5)

Secondary Data   Information that is already available, having been collected previously for other projects. (19)

Secondary Shopping Area   An area that is smaller than a central shopping district and serves a specific part of a city. (7)

Self-concept Theory   Involves an individual's perception of himself or herself. (3)

Self-image   How the consumer views himself or herself. (3)

Self-liquidator Premium   An item of merchandise sold (usually at cost) to a shopper after he or she has bought a product or tried a new service. (16)

Semiautomatic Stock Control System   A system that replenishes the stocks of non-seasonal merchandise in stores quickly and almost automatically. (9)

Semiblind Checking (Semi-Indirect Checking)   A type of merchandise checking in which checkers use invoices whose quantities are omitted. (12)

Semi-Indirect Checking (Semiblind Checking)   A type of merchandise checking in which checkers use invoices on which quantities are omitted. (12)

Separate-Unit Concept   An organization structure for branch stores that treats the branch as a separate store. Under this arrangement the branch has a great deal of autonomy, including the responsibility for its own buying and selling functions. (6)

Shopper's Report   A method of evaluating a salesperson's performance by means of observation and written reports. (6)

Shopping Goods   Products that consumers buy after spending time and effort to evaluate them. (5)

Short-Term Loan   Credit terms that require repayment in less than a year. (20)

Shrinkage   Merchandise losses due to shoplifting, internal theft, damage, and the like. (12)

Single-Price Policy   A policy in which the retailer sells all the merchandise in the store at one price. (11)

Small Business Administration (SBA)   An agency of the federal government that provides small businesses with advice and assistance in obtaining low-interest financing, and offers numerous other services. (20)

Social Class   A homogeneous division within a society in which a family or individual can be classified for comparative purposes. (3)

Soft Goods   Merchandise such as apparel, linen, and bedding. (1)

Sole Proprietorship   A business owned by one person, who invests time and money in it. (4)

Source Marking (Premarking)   A policy in which the vendor marks the goods before delivery to the store according to the merchant's specifications. (10)

Special-Event Display An approach to display that is used by department stores and mass merchandisers for thematic storewide promotions. (14)

Specialty Goods Particular brands for which a consumer shops. (5)

Specialty Shopping Area A group of limited-line stores that sell similar merchandise. (7)

Specialty Store (Limited-Line Store) A retail store that features a full line of a particular type of merchandise. (1)

Specification Buying A system in which buyers develop product specifications for their purchases rather than selecting from what is available in the market. (9)

Spiff (PM, Push Money) A premium, prize, or extra commission offered to salespeople as an incentive to increase sales of a particular type of merchandise. (6)

Split Run A method that magazine publishers use to divide their national circulation into smaller sections at a lower cost to advertisers. (15)

Spot Checking A method of merchandise checking in which only one or a few cartons of a shipment are checked at random against the invoice or purchase order. (12)

Staff Position A position that is advisory or serves a support function to line employees. (6)

Staple Goods Products that are constantly in demand and infrequently influenced by fashion changes. (5)

Stationary Table A table in the receiving area on which goods are laid out, counted, and ticketed. (12)

Step Theory (AIDA) A view of retailing in which a customer's decision to buy or not to buy follows a pattern of steps: attention, interest, desire, action. (13)

Stockholders' Equity The net worth of a corporation. (17)

Stockkeeping Unit (SKU) One item of inventory that has distinct characteristics. (9)

Stock Option A plan that allows employees to purchase company stock at prices below the stock's market value. (6)

Stock Turnover A measure for determining how quickly merchandise has been sold. (10)

Store Brand (Private Label) Merchandise that is sold only in the retailer's own store. (2,9)

Store Credit Card A card issued by a department store or large specialty shop for use in its establishment. (18)

Store-Owned Resident Buying Office (Private Resident Buying Office) A buying office that is owned by the firm it serves. (9)

Street Vendor A retailer that sells merchandise in the street rather than in a store or in people's homes. (5)

String Street (Strip Center, Neighborhood Shopping Center) A small group of stores located alongside each other in a residential area. (7)

Strip Center (Neighborhood Shopping Center, String Street) A small group of stores located alongside each other in a residential area. (7)

Stuffers An advertising piece that accompanies a billing statement. (15)

Style A distinct feature or concept that makes a product different from others within the same classification. (2)

Substitute Selling Selling in which the salesperson offers the customer an alternative item when the store does not carry the specific brand asked for. (13)

Suggestion Selling Selling in which after a sale has been made, the salesperson suggests additional items that are related to the original purchase. (13)

Supermarket A self-service, cash-and-carry store that offers a wide variety of food and nonfood products in large quantities. (1)

Superstore A store that offers one-stop shopping with a full line of food and nonfood products; it carries a greater proportion of food products than combination stores; some services. (5)

Survey A method of obtaining information directly from individuals by using mail, telephone, and personal interviews. (19)

Syndicator A retailer that sells goods and services in conjunction with credit card companies. (5)

Target Market A defined group of consumers whom the retailer tries to satisfy. (3)

Tearsheet An actual copy of an advertisement. (15)

Telephone Selling Selling in which customers use the telephone to order goods and services from retail stores and mail order houses. (5)

Theme Display A display designed with an idea as a selling theme to stimulate the interest of consumers. (14)

TO (Turnover) Selling in which the salesperson turns the customer over to someone in authority or with particular expertise when it appears that the sale will not be closed. (13)

Trade Discount A reduction in list price given by vendors to volume purchasers. (10)

Trading Area A geographic area from which a store draws the bulk of its customers. (7)

Trading Post A place where trade may be carried on, by barter or cash, usually in a sparsely populated area. (1)

Trading Stamps Stamps that are given to shoppers who spend a specified dollar amount; they are accumulated and traded for a variety of merchandise items. (16)

Trading Up Selling in which the salesperson persuades the customer to buy a more expensive item or a larger quantity than originally intended. (11)

Travel/Entertainment Credit Card A card that can be used to charge purchases at motels, airlines, restaurants, and the like up to a predetermined limit; now accepted by some stores. (18)

Trending Service A series of information bulletins on current fashion trends issued by a resident buying office. (9)

Trickle-Across Theory The theory

that each social class has opinion leaders who can influence others to accept a new style; thus, the style moves horizontally. (2)

Trickle-Down Theory The theory that styles are introduced by the upper class and passed down to the masses in a vertical flow. (2)

Trickle-Up Theory The theory that fashion innovation may start at the bottom of a price range and flow upward to higher prices. (2)

Trunk Show A vendor presents his (her) merchandise to store personnel and/or customers in the store. (16)

Twig A small department store branch that stocks only one kind of merchandise or several similar lines. (5)

Unit Control A system for gathering information about inventory by recording the stock in terms of units of merchandise. (17)

Unit-of-Sales Method A method of preparing an advertising budget on the basis of the unit (number) of sales rather than dollar amounts, with a fixed sum set aside for each unit expected to be sold. (15)

Unit Pricing Labeling merchandise with unit prices as well as total prices. (11)

Universal Product Code (UPC) (Bar Code) A system in which sensitized lines on product labels serve as symbols for numbers that can be "read" by a scanner and indicate the manufacturer, type of product, weight, and size. (2)

Universal Vendor Marking (UVM) The premarking of merchandise by manufacturers in language that can

be read by people and machines. (12)

Variable-Price Policy (Flexible Pricing) A method of selling that enables customers to bargain with retailers. (11)

Variety Store A retailing institution that sells a wide assortment of novelty items at low prices. (1)

Vending Machine A piece of automated equipment that dispenses a wide variety of goods and services. (5)

Venture Capital Operator An individual or corporation that invests money in someone else's business. (20)

Vestibule Training Training in which a store uses its own classrooms to train employees prior to assignment. (6)

Voluntary Chain A group of independent retailers that sells a wholesaler's products and uses the wholesaler's name. (4)

Warehouse Club (Buying Club) A no-frills store offering sizable discounts to member groups. (2)

Warehouse Outlet A no-frills retail store that specializes in a particular line of nonfood merchandise, such as furniture, toys, or sporting goods. (5)

Warehouse Store (Box Store) A cross between a limited-assortment store and a supermarket; stocks several thousand items, including nonfood products, limited lines of perishables, and meat; customers mark and bag their own items. (2)

Warehouse-Style Home Center A very large store that undersells home-building merchandise to "do-it-yourselfers" and contractors. (2)

Warranty A written guarantee of a manufacturer's or retailer's responsibility. (2)

Wheel of Retailing A theory to explain the institutional changes that take place when innovators enter the retail arena. (2)

White-Collar Worker An individual who earns a living as a professional, in an office, or in a service occupation. (3)

Wholesaler (Middleman) An individual or firm that purchases merchandise for resale to retailers. (1)

Width (Breadth) The number of product classifications that a merchant stocks. (10)

Window Display The use of store windows to attract customers by showing the quality of merchandise handled, price lines, and store image. (14)

Zoning Code (Zoning Law) Regulations restricting the type of building that may take place in a community. (7)

Zoning Law (Zoning Code) Regulations restricting the type of building that may take place in a community. (7)

INDEX